MOTOCOURSE™

THE WORLD'S LEADING GRAND PRIX & SUPERBIKE ANNUAL

icon
PUBLISHING LIMITED

CONTENTS

MOTOCOURSE 2012–2013
is published by:
Icon Publishing Limited
Regent Lodge
4 Hanley Road
Malvern
Worcestershire
WR14 4PQ
United Kingdom

Tel: +44 (0)1684 564511

Email: info@motocourse.com
Website: www.motocourse.com

Printed in the United Kingdom by
Butler Tanner and Dennis Ltd
Caxton Road, Frome
Somerset BA11 1NF

ISBN: 978-1905334-78-0

DISTRIBUTORS
Gardners Books
1 Whittle Drive, Eastbourne,
East Sussex BN23 6QH
Tel: +44 (0)1323 521555
email: sales@gardners.com

Chaters Wholesale Ltd
25/26 Murrell Green Business Park,
Hook, Hampshire RG27 9GR
Telephone: +44 (0) 1256 765 443
Fax: +44 (0)1256 769 900
email: books@chaters.co.uk

NORTH AMERICA
Quayside Distribution Services
400 First Avenue North, Suite 300
Minneapolis, MN 55401 USA
Telephone: 612 344 8100
Fax: 612 344 8691

Dust jacket: Yamaha's Jorge Lorenzo,
who won six races on his way to the
2012 MotoGP World Championship.

Title page: The veteran Max Biaggi
took the Superbike World Championship on his Aprilia.

Photos: Gold & Goose

publisher
STEVE SMALL
steve.small@iconpublishinglimited.com

commercial director
BRYN WILLIAMS
bryn.williams@iconpublishinglimited.com

editor
MICHAEL SCOTT

text editor
IAN PENBERTHY

results and statistics
PETER McLAREN

chief photographers
GOLD & GOOSE
David Goldman
Gareth Harford
Patrik Lundin
Brian Nelson
David 'Chippy' Wood.

www.goldandgoose.com

tel +44 (0)208 444 2448

MotoGP and circuit illustrations
ADRIAN DEAN
f1artwork@blueyonder.co.uk

Acknowledgements

The Editor and staff of *MOTOCOURSE* wish to thank the following for their assistance in compiling the 2012–13
edition: Henny Ray Abrams, Majo Botella, Peter Clifford, Federica de Zottis, Rhys Edwards, William Favero,
Aldo Gandolfo, Nick Harris, Chris Jonnum, Milena Koerner, Isabelle Lariviere, Gavin Matheson, Dennis Noy-
es, Elisa Pavan, David Pato, Hervé Poncharal, Gemma Rodes, Ignacio Sagnier, Paolo Scalera, Elisa Tam-
burro, Mike Trimby, Frine Vellila, Mike Webb and Günther Wiesinger, as well as the riders and technicians who
helped with inside information for this book. A special thanks to Marlboro, Repsol and Honda hospitality staff
for fine food, and numerous colleagues and friends for their always well-intended, but seldom heeded advice.

Photographs published in *MOTOCOURSE 2012–2013* have been contributed by:
Chief photographers: Gold & Goose.
Other photographs contributed by: AMA Pro Series, Gavan Caldwell, Clive Challinor Motorsport Photography,
David Collister/www.photoctycles.com, Mark Walters.

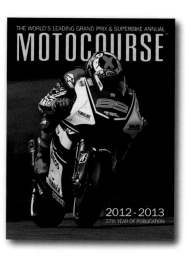

THE WORLD'S LEADING GRAND PRIX & SUPERBIKE ANNUAL

2012 - 2013
37th YEAR OF PUBLICATION

MOTOCOURSE
www.motocourse.com

FOREWORD by JORGE LORENZO

FROM the start, I knew 2012 would be special: more power, more speed and more competition. It would be necessary not only to win races on the days when everything was right, but also to take the maximum possible every time, even when maybe some other rider or other bike would be more competitive on that day.

This was my aim, but we started on the right foot with a win at Qatar.

From then on, it was total concentration and focus on perfection. Not only from me, but also from Yamaha and from my crew.

I think we all did a great job. The bike was faultlessly reliable; the team decisions were clear and almost always worked for the best.

When I secured the title in Australia, it not only wiped out the bad memories of my crash there in 2011, it also sealed the reward. Finally, we'd won six races and finished second in the all but two of the others.

My only non-finishes of the year were when somebody else knocked me down, and I high-sided out of the last race trying to lap a back-marker.

The other guys didn't make it easy. Casey was always powerful, though he missed three races. Dani really earned everybody's respect with his run at the end of the year. He certainly kept our focus sharp. The strength of his challenge made the title all the more worthwhile.

Racing is a team effort, and there are a lot of people to thank: from Yamaha's designers and engineers to the suppliers of brakes and so on, to the guys in the pit, and especially my crew chief, Ramon Forcada. We all work well together and we all share the success.

Now I will take the time to enjoy my second world title, and settle into my new house in Barcelona.

Until the next time. I'll be back, and I'll be aiming for the top once again.

DARKNESS BEFORE LIGHT?

Above: In troubled times and turbulent weather, MotoGP continued its schizophrenic evolution.

Right: Spaniards Lorenzo and Pedrosa provided an engrossing battle.

Centre right: HRC's Nakamoto was the manufacturers' immovable force.

Above centre right: Marc Marquez: primed for stardom.

Above far right: Christmas came early for Rossi, back on his beloved M1 Yamaha.

Bottom right: Casey Stoner's early retirement at just 27 robbed racing of a spectacular talent.

Photos: Gold & Goose

IS motorcycle racing ever not at the crossroads? For a sport dedicated to going round in circles as quickly as possible, the metaphor seems ill-suited, yet it was truer in 2012 than ever.

Then Dorna's take-over of World Superbikes changed all the road signs. Now the Spanish company has complete control. We can expect both MotoGP and SBK to be slowed down and dumbed down. Sport – or the sporting show – holds sway over the adventures of technology. The battle is over, at least for the moment.

It makes the 2012 season all the sweeter. Bigger more powerful MotoGP bikes made for a better show (especially in mid-field) at the same time as raising speeds and favouring the brave. The same cream rose to the top.

Lorenzo was the creamiest: close to perfection; Pedrosa boosted his reputation with an unprecedented late season charge. The all-Spanish rivalry will gain more intensity next year when Marquez arrives... at his first test, he was barely a second slower than Pedrosa.

But for Casey Stoner, the present and future changes to racing were just too retrograde. He quit.

Others will take his place. Cal Crutchlow took a giant step; Andrea Dovizioso underlined his quality in depth.

CRT bikes arrived, and were largely instantly forgettable. New technical rules introduced right at year's end means the production-powered ponies will also be officially forgotten after one more year.

Moto3 also turned up, and the size of the grids and quality of the new racing made the four-stroke 250 class an instant hit.

Valentino Rossi and Ducati were the counterpoint – a bad marriage came to an unhappy end, a disheartened Valentino resigned and one-time technical guru Filippo Preziosi was dropped. The iconic Italian firm's new German owners Audi were making themselves felt.

Next year Rossi's back on a Yamaha, back alongside uneasy bedfellow Lorenzo, asking himself the question: "Can I still cut it up front?" The answer should be fascinating; as importantly MotoGP has at least one more year with the most marketable star in its history. His eventual departure removes a world-wide icon of popularity, threatening the value of TV rights and crowd appeal. But in a time of international crisis, the financial fears were not only for the future.

In MotoGP, several Moto2 and 3 teams struggled financially: it has become almost the norm to have to pay for your ride. Instability was reflected in almost 50 rider changes, less than 20 through injury.

Similar problems face SBK, where grids shrank and where a thrilling title climax coincided with news of the Dorna take-over. All awaited the consequences: most likely to be a move away from factory involvement with much more restricted bikes run by importer or dealer teams.

The racing was good though, almost everywhere, in spite of shocking weather that cancelled the Isle of Man Senior TT. A fine BSB battle overturned fears that banning traction control would be lethal; there was a good year on the roads. But in the USA the dumbed-down AMA series was still trying to regain strength. Racing at the crossroads indeed.

Tell you what – why not let's have a race, from the crossroads round that far hill and back again.

FIM WORLD CHAMPIONSHIP 2012

TOP TEN RIDERS

THE EDITOR'S CHOICE

Photographs by Gold & Goose

1 CASEY STONER

A MISTAKE at Indianapolis cost Casey Stoner the chance of a valedictory title. His rival Lorenzo made no mistakes until the title was won. But the Australian brought at least one extra ingredient to back the claim that he was without equal in his final season. Excitement. The sight of him wringing a MotoGP bike's neck will be sorely missed. At most corners of most tracks, there was no one faster.

In a world where racing is everything, it was not easy to understand his decision to quit while still so clearly at the height of his powers.

The reasons he gave were many, mainly concerned with how the hand of commercial greed increasingly takes away the wilder elements of racing: the side that doesn't care about the cost and only wants to keep going faster.

"It's not the sport I fell in love with," he opined. "Disappointed" was the word he used most all year.

The way he rode in 2012, once he was on the bike, he never let it show.

2 JORGE LORENZO

JORGE LORENZO spoke the words himself. "I think we made an almost perfect season," he said in Australia, after securing his second title.

Over 11 years of GP racing, the Mallorcan has carefully and deliberately crafted and polished his natural talent, he seems to have it completely under control. Fast laps come with metronomic consistency; considered race tactics likewise. He could fight when he had to, could accept second place when he had to. He never finished lower than that all year. By the same token, he didn't finish any higher in the last five. But by then, he didn't need to.

There was a flash of the old Lorenzo, the hot-shoe who had arrived in MotoGP in 2008, in the last race at Valencia, when an ill-judged passing move on a lapped rider triggered a crash as spectacular as any of the several he had had in that year.

He certainly deserved the title, and he will go into 2013 as the justifiable favourite. He is a very complete championship animal.

3 DANI PEDROSA

THERE was a time, at the mid-point of the year, when it seemed that Dani Pedrosa's too-fitful star was finally on the wane. Top backing for six years had brought only 15 wins to the once-dominant 125 and 250 rider. His repertoire went little further than lightning starts and occasional runaway victories; if anyone caught up, almost invariably they would ride straight past. And he was injury prone.

Pedrosa was in serious danger of losing his Honda ride.

Could this be the spark that ignited the blue touch-paper?

In the latter half of the season, Dani dominated. He racked up seven wins in the season, more than double his previous average. More importantly, he proved at Brno that he was ready to fight hard, when he beat up Lorenzo in the last corners, and in Malaysia that he could win in the wet.

The absence of the injured Stoner was a factor; likewise that Lorenzo was in a position to be defensive. Yet Dani's speed and new-found aggression remain highly impressive. He kept his ride.

4 MARC MARQUEZ

FOR a rider to rise so far above the rest in a class of such technical equality as Moto2 speaks volumes. Marc Marquez did so consistently, in 2011 as well as in 2012.

His high points were wins from the back: at Motegi because he missed his gear at the start, at Valencia because he was being punished with a back-of-the-grid start. There were seven other wins in the year; he only finished off the rostrum once.

The 19-year-old Catalunyan has two faces: mild-mannered, courteous and considered face to face, a merciless fighter on the bike. It got him into trouble several times over the year, and makes him a very feared competitor.

As Pedrosa had ex-racer Puig to guide him step by step, Marquez has ex-125 champion Emilio Alzamora, a valuable influence.

Rossi-like, he took one year to learn and one to win in 125 and then Moto2 (though he almost won that in 2011). He takes Stoner's factory Honda in MotoGP in 2013, and in his first test was barely a second off team-mate Pedrosa.

5 ANDREA DOVIZIOSO

THE experienced Andrea Dovizioso was easily best of the rest in MotoGP. Sidelined by Honda, Dovi had a point to prove, and a target in sight – to beat Ben Spies and earn a factory Yamaha ride for 2013. Beating Spies was the easy part.

Dovi was not only consistent, the only rider to finish every race, he was also fast, with six podiums, although never better than third. He was entertaining as well, in several ultra-close battles with team-mate Crutchlow – it took him a few races before he got the upper hand.

The Yamaha, he explained, was completely different from the Honda, relying on corner speed rather than acceleration; he had to re-think his technique.

Dovi is measured and analytical: "It is my character." But there was no way he could anticipate Rossi's shock return to Yamaha, which deprived him of a saddle.

His final option was Ducati and the dollars. Dovi will require all his powers of analysis with the Italian team.

6 CAL CRUTCHLOW

AFTER a patchy first season in MotoGP, it all came together in the second for the rider from Coventry. Former World Supersport champion, Cal Crutchlow now had track knowledge, while the torquier and faster new-generation 1000cc bikes suited his hard-charging style.

He was compared directly with team-mate Dovizioso, frequently very directly, when they were in close company. That Dovi eventually outranked him was understandable, given 12 years of GP experience.

Crutchlow is strong all round and a fast qualifier, seven times on the front row, starting at the first round in Qatar. He also made the rostrum twice.

His strongest suit is utter determination, never shown more strongly than at his home race at Silverstone, after crashing and breaking his ankle during free practice. He argued his way past the doctors and pushed through from the back of the grid to take an epic sixth.

His arrival at the practice and race press conferences injected a welcome strain of scampish humour. We can hope to hear more or it in 2013.

7 STEFAN BRADL

IF there seemed to have been an element of luck to Stefan Bradl's Moto2 championship after Marquez missed the last races, any doubts about the depth of his talent didn't last long in MotoGP.

Bradl gelled almost from the first and was frequently in fast company near the front. His weak point was a lack of experience in preserving tyre life, but even so he was in the top ten, often well up in it, at every race he finished, all but four. His best was fourth at Mugello, where he missed the rostrum (to Dovi) by less than half a tenth.

Bradl carries a heavy burden as Germany's best hope for long-delayed national success in the top class. The last German to win in the 500 class was privateer Edmund Czihak on a 351 Yamaha at the Nürburgring in a boycotted race with just four finishers.

Son of a racing father, Stefan is mature and intelligent, qualities that should take him further when combined with his obvious talent.

8 POL ESPARGARO

IT hurts to be number two, and it's hard when you're up against a potential racing giant like Marquez, but the cheerful younger Espargaro carried the burden in good part and with good courage.

He was certainly fast: eight times on pole, including at the last four races in a row. But he only managed four wins to Marquez's nine, the younger rider always there to thwart him.

Remarkably, they retained friendly relations, a tribute to Pol's essential good nature.

The margins were usually small. Espargaro's win in Australia, by contrast, was by 16.8 seconds, more than double the previous Moto2 record, set in the wet.

Espargaro switched from his FTR of 2011 to a Kalex, which he preferred, and joined the team run by former double champion Sito Pons, a valuable ally. Elder brother Aleix was frequently in his pit, and vice versa.

Espargaro will start the 2013 season as favourite – a just reward for his unfailing efforts. As he said, "I made Marc work for it every weekend.

9 ALVARO BAUTISTA

ALVARO BAUTISTA was more steadfast than really fast, but he made a good fist of the tricky switch from Suzuki to Honda, where he had the additional disadvantage of being the only rider on Showa suspension, the Japanese manufacturer having been out of the top class for more than a year.

That left him with a lot to learn, and with no previous reference to give him a starting point. Together with his highly professional team, he moved steadily forward, and if his first-ever pole position at Silverstone had more to do with changing weather conditions than anything else, two rostrums were backed by ten more top-six finishes, and he had done enough for fifth overall.

The former 125 champion has had a challenging three years in MotoGP, the first two with Suzuki, and has taken some flak during that time. Nor did he gain kudos when a rare headstrong move at Assen caused him to knock Lorenzo down and out.

He remained conspicuously cheerful throughout and improved steadily all season. Could there be more to come?

10 SANDRO CORTESE

RIDERS who burst on to the scene and start winning immediately tend to take most of the attention in racing. Sandro Cortese is different. He was in his seventh season on a 125 when he won his first GP at Brno in 2011. A second followed, and a barrier had been breached.

He won five more in 2012 in the new Moto3 class, in some of the closest racing ever seen. As importantly, he was only off the rostrum twice all year, never out of the points, and he finished every race.

Raised in Germany by Italian parents, Cortese happily admits to sharing the strengths of each national stereotype: "For the first 18 laps, I think like a German, planning my race and looking after the tyres. For the last two laps, like an Italian. I have my elbows, and I show them."

Such worthy success in the smaller classes sometimes, but not always, indicates a great future. At 22, Cortese will move up to Moto2 in 2013. We shall see then what happens next to this late developer.

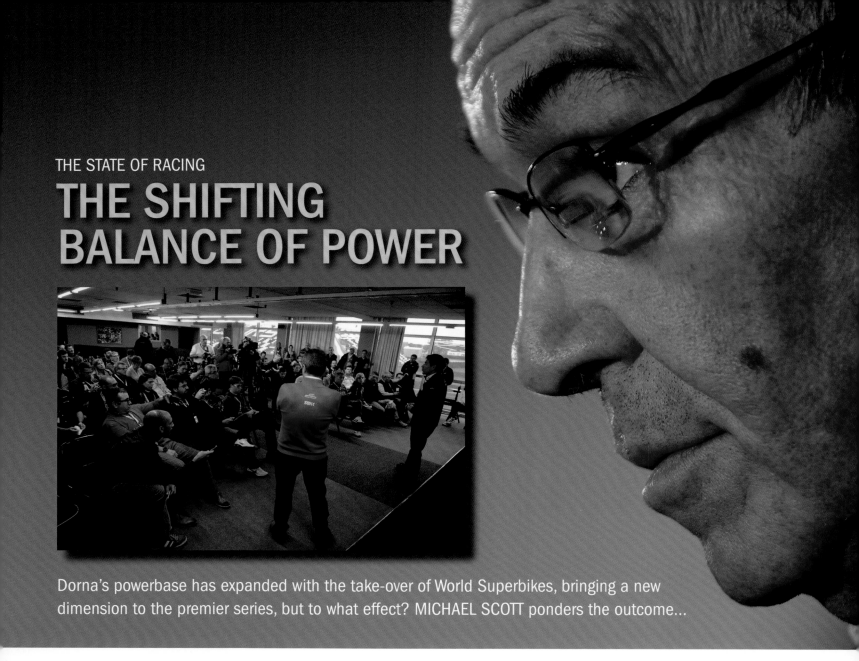

THE SHIFTING BALANCE OF POWER

Dorna's powerbase has expanded with the take-over of World Superbikes, bringing a new dimension to the premier series, but to what effect? MICHAEL SCOTT ponders the outcome...

Above: The Grand Poobah of racing – Dorna's Carmello Ezpeleta.

Inset above: Paulo Flammini a muted press conference after the shock announcement.

Centre right: WSBK director Paulo Ciabatti was an early departure, returning to Ducati.

Bottom right: New Race Director Mike Webb had an eventful first year.

Photos: Gold & Goose

BY far the most important thing to happen in grand prix racing since the Dorna take-over of 1992 was the Dorna take-over of 2012.

It came after a period of growing argument between the series promoters and the factory entrants, of interminable procrastination in defining all-important new rules for MotoGP, and of increasingly acrimonious sniping between MotoGP and World Superbikes.

Now, out of the blue on 2nd October, came the announcement from Bridgepoint, the private equity firm that owns both Dorna and thus MotoGP, and InFront Sports & Media, thence also World Superbikes. Dorna would take over Superbikes, with CEO Carmelo Ezpeleta in charge of both series. Lord of all he surveyed and the Grand Poobah to boot.

It seemed to settle everything, and in retrospect seemed to have been coming for a long time. It certainly shifted the balance of power.

Until that moment, MotoGP and SBK had essentially been in competition for the same, currently shrinking market, and in a simmering row over the status of production-based (SBK) racing and prototype (MotoGP). This had begun when Moto2 adopted production engines, and had intensified since the introduction of line-blurring CRT bikes, new to MotoGP in 2012. At the same time, looser engine-life and electronic rules meant that the Superbikes kept getting faster even while MotoGP bikes were being slowed down. Aprilia's ART bike for the CRT class used a power-down version of the achingly similar Superbike, to extend engine life.

The manufacturers – or at least Honda, the one that matters most – had been using the rivalry to play one off against the other in their own argument with Dorna.

The dispute was about the very future of racing and went back more than five years, with a single central theme: sustaining grid numbers in the top class and thereafter working on making the racing closer.

There had been problems of dwindling entries before, but they had started to become acute with the introduction of four-stroke MotoGP bikes in 2002. Compared with the two-stroke predecessors, material costs more than doubled. And then came the burgeoning of electronics – an inevitable consequence when fuel injection replaced the carburettors that two-strokes preferred. Electronics are not expensive in themselves, but the brainpower needed to understand and develop them is. For success, a manufacturer needed as many boffins as it could afford, both in the pit and at racing HQ – the sky the limit.

In 2006, the last year of the first-generation 990 MotoGP bikes, regular grid numbers dropped below 20. In 2010, there were just 17. Dorna's contract is to provide a minimum of 15 starters. In Australia in 2011, injuries in practice meant only 14 riders lined up. This was not the least in history – the final round in 1961, the Argentine GP, attracted only one foreign entry (Briton Frank Perris) to swell the grid to six starters. But as a rule that year, more than 30 bikes lined up for each race. (The highest numbers were always at the Isle of Man TT, with a peak of 97 in 1969 – but that special event and its Ulster counterpart aside, the West German GP of 1972 saw 54 starters).

Aprilia, Kawasaki and, at the end of last season, Suzuki decided that the game was not worth the candle (although Suzuki promise to be back in 2014). The trend was deeply worrying: as costs continued to rise, the premier class was in the process of disappearing up its own fundament.

Dorna's Ezpeleta first made entreaties to the factories to

supply affordable equipment to private teams more than five years ago. A request to lease engines fell on deaf ears, and meeting after meeting over the years brought no solution as sponsorship income and grid numbers shrank while costs continued to spiral.

CRT was Ezpeleta's urgent response: prototype chassis with tuned production engines, with 24 versus 21 litres of fuel, and 12 rather than the six engines of the factory bikes (the notion of a claiming rule that gave the Claiming Rule Teams the designation had become irrelevant long before the bikes arrived). In their first year, the bikes were underwhelming, but nine of them added to 12 factory/satellite bikes did return grid numbers to more than 20.

But CRT was only the start, as well as giving Ezpeleta a fall-back position should the factories decide to depart. He was demanding technical regulation changes that would cut costs and performance, bringing the factory riders to within closer reach of the privateers: the main instrument was the introduction of a control ECU and a proposed rev limit.

The leader of the opposition was HRC executive vice-president Shuhei Nakamoto, a constant presence at the racetrack overseeing the company's most important racing venture since it had pulled its cars and Nakamoto himself out of F1. His holy grail was free electronics, considered a vital and valuable research area. In the face of the loss of this possibility, he was unequivocal – he would switch Honda's effort to SBK, where electronics remained free.

Dorna had gained control of MotoGP in 1992, after a complex series of events involving Bernie Ecclestone (who came, and went). Bridgepoint took over Dorna from CVC Capital Partners in 2006, when CVC was obliged to sell by the Monopolies Commission after it also acquired F1.

World Superbikes, founded in 1987, had fallen under the control of Italy's Flammini group, and Paolo Flammini was still in charge in 2012, by which time ownership of the rights had, after several twists and turns, also fallen into the hands of Bridgepoint, when they acquired InFront in September, 2011. This purchase was centred on international football rights; SBK happened to come along with the package via subsidiary company InFront Motor Sports.

The structure of Bridgepoint meant that the two series occupied different parts of the company, with different sets of investors. But with both series struggling in difficult economic times, it was obvious that rationalisation was the only commercially sensible course.

When it happened, it left Superbike's long-term management in a state of limbo yet to be fully resolved (although SBK director Paolo Ciabatti promptly resigned to return to Ducati), and Ezpeleta with the whip hand.

Honda's threat to leave became absurd. Ezpeleta's counter-threat, to impose a rev limit and control electronics or to switch to all CRT bikes, gained weight accordingly.

He had originally demanded that new technical regulations be finalised in May, 2012, for imposition in 2013. Instead the factories had managed to keep putting things off; soon Ezpeleta's target became 2014. It had seemed this process might drag on forever, but now it was crunch time.

The GP Commission did reach a decision at the final race of the year – admittedly only a provisional one. It relies on the factories making affordable alternative bikes or engines available to privateers. Honda had already been talking about a million-euro production-racer version of its RC213V, Yamaha pondering either leasing or selling M1 motors. Contractual commitment is required by the first race of 2013, or Ezpeleta will impose his alternative (CRT) solution.

The new landscape retained a two-tier (factory/privateer) structure while consigning the CRT concept to history.

There had been compromise on both sides. There will be a control ECU, but with the possibility of some electronic freedom for Honda and no further mention of a rev limit.

The ECU and other data-logging hardware will be provided by Dorna. A voluntary control ECU from Magneti Marelli for 2013 – an option welcomed by several CRT teams – will

clearly be the prototype.

Factory teams (maximum four per manufacturer) will use their own electronic software, but at a cost. The maximum fuel capacity drops from 21 to 20 litres, the engine allocation from six to five (nine for a factory in its first season – a sanction not only for the supposedly returning Suzuki, but also for anticipated newcomers). Furthermore, mid-season engine development is banned: engines are 'frozen' – all five must be sealed at the first race.

Other entries must employ the software provided, but are permitted double the number of engines (12), and as importantly the same 24 litres of fuel currently enjoyed by the CRT entrants.

The changes are to be welcomed, especially when you consider the alternatives. At least some of the prototype nature of MotoGP is preserved, while the overwhelming dominance of the factories is cut back and independent entries encouraged. Of course, it remains to be seen whether the factories oblige with worthwhile alternatives.

The level of current technology and parlous economic conditions combine to rule out any return to the glory days of the 1970s, when anyone could buy a Suzuki RG500 and, with a bit of fettling, have a serious chance of being genuinely competitive.

Footnote: Barely three weeks after Bridgepoint's first announcement came a second, which meshed neatly with the rationalisation of the business – they had sold 39 per cent of their stake in Dorna to the Canada Pension Plan Investment Board for a reported 400 million euros. The nature of the new part-owners was hailed by some as an indication of long-term faith in the business.

BUMPY RIDE FOR NEW DIRECTOR

There was a change at the top in the control tower, when former technical director Mike Webb took over as race director from the retired long-serving Paul Butler.

Webb did not get an altogether smooth ride: along with a number of new rules – some of them significant and introduced on the hoof – he was faced with the first serious opposition (it might even be called rebellion) by FIM officials.

It concerned – as did so many things – that marvellous racer Marc Marquez, not yet 20 and already hogging the limelight. He lived up to his *MOTOCOURSE* nickname: Marquez the Merciless.

His transgressions are documented race by race: Qatar – pushed Luthi wide while battling for the lead; Catalunya – cut across Espargaro, knocking him off; Valencia – did the same to Corsi, in free practice, forsooth. With the shadow of his crash into Wilairot in Australia the previous year, his reputation erred on the wrong side of hard riding.

The one that counted was in Catalunya. Race Direction – a committee comprising Webb, Claude Danis (FIM), Franco Uncini (riders' representative) and Javier Alonso – penalised him directly by one minute, dropping him from third out of the points. That seemed fair, since Espargaro had suffered a zero score. The punishment took into account that he had been warned after Qatar and (said Webb) at least one other over-aggressive move in the Catalunyan race. The published citation, however, mentioned only the Espargaro crash.

Upon this point hinged the subsequent debacle. The FIM stewards judged only on that incident and viewed it differently. For the first time since the race direction system had been instituted in 1999, they overturned the decision.

Never mind what petty personal rivalries may have been involved, never mind the drawn-out process of protest and legal procedure that followed. It made no difference. One thing was clear: that the oft-criticised and apparently often whimsical process of disciplining dangerous riders case by case needed serious attention.

Webb was nonplussed by the FIM's action, likening it to second-guessing a football referee after the game was over.

Above: Anthony West fell foul of anti-doping laws intended to catch much more serious transgressions.

Top: The MotoGP season was beset by wet weather. It did give a chance to see top riders, such as Nicky Hayden, show their extraordinary skills.

Photos: Gold & Goose

One immediate response would be to tighten up the wording of future citations. He defended the case-by-case approach, however, and the need for flexibility in applying punishments.

It was Marquez again, with his ill-timed attack on Corsi, who brought matters to a head and elicited a significant statement from Dorna's Alonso. During the season, they had been working on a system that borrowed from football and other sports, where penalties could be accumulated from one event to the next. It's less like a yellow/red card system than accumulating points on your driving licence. If it brings more coherence to the system, it should at least avoid embarrassing aberrations like the one that occurred at Catalunya.

The year generally ran smoothly and safely in spite of some challenging weather conditions: red flags were particularly prompt, and a standard of organisation and marshalling has been achieved that made another system failure stand out. It was at Misano, where Abraham stalled on the line and, once again, the procedure was promptly aborted. The problem came later when the grid was invaded, and when riders took off their helmets, contrary to regulations.

In the case of an aborted start, only three mechanics and a brolly-holder per rider are allowed on the grid, rather than the hordes that appeared at Misano. Was it the sinners at fault, or the officials? It seemed none was familiar with the rules, and the subsequent delay of more than ten minutes, and the consequent disaster to Dani Pedrosa, reflected badly on everyone.

WEIGHTY MATTERS

Rule changes came through the season, starting with one applied in November, 2011, when the MotoGP class was hit with the addition of an extra 4kg minimum weight. This was in addition to the 3kg already added to the 800's minimum of 150kg.

The timing was critical: by then, manufacturers were well advanced with construction of 2012's bikes, designed and tested to a minimum of 153kg. It drew an angry response from the factories, which was mollified somewhat by an easing of testing restrictions – this was effectively free at a nominated test track, limited only by the allocation of tyres.

For 2013, the minimum weight will be 160kg.

There was mild amusement at Ezpeleta's about-face on the rookie rule, introduced in 2009 and banning new riders from joining factory teams. Honda wanted it rescinded to clear the way for Marquez (that name again) to join their top

squad. Ezpeleta was implacably against it. Until he changed his mind abruptly, announcing at Silverstone that the rule would be rescinded forthwith.

Bearing in mind that he was involved in a dispute with Honda over much more important matters, Marquez for once was a pawn in the game.

The other significant change came at the last race of the year, to take effect directly for 2013: the change in Moto2 minimum weight rules from machine only to machine plus rider. This had been sought loudly by the likes of Scott Redding, tired of being regularly out-accelerated by featherweight rivals like Marquez. The old minimum machine weight of 140kg is replaced with a bike/rider minimum of 215kg.

PUNISHMENT BEFITTING THE CRIME

Anthony West became the first person in the MotoGP era to fall foul of doping regulations, after a sample taken at the French GP tested positive for the drug methylhexaneamine. That the offence was considered inadvertent and of a minor nature was reflected in the mild punishment – doping can result in a life ban. That it all came to a head at the same time as the Lance Armstrong doping scandal was unfortunate. So was the fact that it happened at all.

Methylhexaneamine, originally formulated as a nasal decongestant, is very low on the list of stimulants and a fairly common ingredient not only in over-the-counter medication (including sinus treatment), but also in freely-available energy supplements. It is so common that it is not always listed among the ingredients. West had inadvertently taken it in one of these, he told the FIM court, which obviously sympathised, handing out only retrospective disqualification from Le Mans and an immediate 30-day ban, ruling the long-serving and GP-winning Australian rider out of the last round at Valencia.

Rules are rules, and the FIM follows World Anti-Doping Authority (WADA) lists. This particular drug seems to occupy a particularly grey area, which needs looking at.

West was not the first athlete to fall foul of the inclusion of this substance in the World Anti-Doping Authority (WADA) list, followed to the letter by the FIM. One controversial case in South Africa is still under consideration on appeal: the winner of 2012's gruelling 89km Comrades Marathon, Ludwick Mamabolo, is still protesting his innocence.

Race director Webb said, "I don't know if this is seriously a substance we need to be worried about, or if we need to be more picky rather than just taking the whole WADA list."

Too late, alas, for the perennially luckless West.

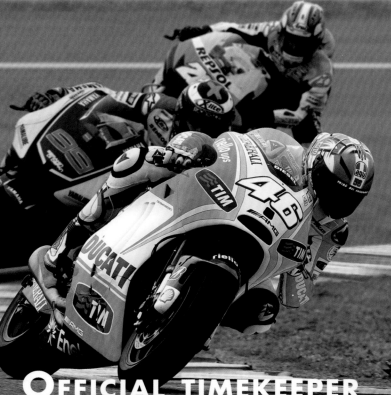

UNFINISHED LEGEND

MICHAEL SCOTT reviews the career of double MotoGP champion CASEY STONER

Above: Stoner Style: sliding the 1000cc Honda at Catalunya.
Photo: Gold & Goose

Right, top to bottom: Aged 14, Stoner had already left home to win in Britain; developing his style in the 2001 British 125 series; first GP – a baleful Stoner on the Donington 125 grid (he was 17th).
Photos: Clive Challinor Motorsport Photography

Bottom right: The big time – second place in MotoGP in Turkey in 2006.

Far right: So close: Melandri beat him by two-tenths at Istanbul; Honda 990 was his favourite MotoGP bike.
Photos: Gold & Goose

WHO will most miss Casey Stoner? The fans? He often had a troubled relationship with them, especially those who tried to get too close. His rivals? They'd be delighted, to a man – Casey always made it much harder to get a good result. The sport? Yes and no: it is in the nature of things that riders come and go. Sometimes even voluntarily.

History will miss him. The number of truly great riders who have quit grand prix racing at the peak of their talent can be counted on one hand. All of them left a big hole. Casey Stoner joins the likes of John Surtees and Gary Hocking. The ranks of the unfinished legends.

The Australian icon – his stature up there with Mick Doohan's – never cared much about history either. Fiercely independent, marvellously outspoken, disputatious to a fault, the only thing he ever did really seem to hold dear (personal matters apart) was discovering the outer limits of a racing motorcycle. He never wasted much track time doing anything else – you seldom saw Casey on a slow lap. Unless, of course, it was to shake a fist at a lesser rider who had got in his way.

Casey's own history has been well documented by *MOTOCOURSE*. He started racing when he was four, and pretty much straight away was winning everything on the dirt-tracks – 41 national titles, the first aged six. Five classes a day, 37 races a weekend – once he took 32 wins. This was on minibikes, then bigger dirt bikes, on the loose. But Doohan was his hero, road-racing his goal. At 14, he was old enough to join the Australian junior road-racing series, but he found himself turned away, he explained. Whatever the reason, he wasn't for hanging around and wasting his talent. His father,

Colin, another forthright man, felt the same. He could see that Casey was meant for bigger things.

The Stoners sold up what they had back in Kurri-Kurri, where Colin farmed beef, and took to the road. It was a tough time for the family, hard years living in caravans and motorhomes. The repayment was British Aprilia Cup victory at his first attempt at road-racing. He made his mark also in Spain, where he was spotted by Pedrosa's *eminence grise* Alberto Puig, who knew a good thing when he saw it. He was a strong influence in pushing Casey to GPs as soon as he was old enough, to start a chequered, but always highly noticeable world championship career. Already then, at the time of his second ever GP as a Telefonica MoviStar wild-card in Australia in 2001 (he finished 12th, first time out at Phillip Island), he was dubbed a teenage sensation.

Between 2002 and 2005, he switched to and fro between 125 and 250 classes. His first win came in year three, back on a 125 Aprilia at Valencia, where his career would end so prematurely eight years later. He rode for KTM the next year, giving the Austrian factory its first win; but 2005 was when he truly arrived, challenging defending champion Dani Pedrosa on an LCR Aprilia. Casey took five races, but lacked consistency (the phrase 'crash happy' was not ill-suited).

There was no question of his talent. He was the natural choice when team owner Lucio Cecchinello (himself fairly recently retired) moved up to join the MotoGP class with a satellite Honda.

Casey was a natural, his impact immediate. On the results and rather often also against the barrier. While Hayden went on to win the last 990 crown, Casey shared the record number of recorded crashes with Randy de Puniet: 17. But

he'd also taken pole at only the second race, and had come within two-tenths of winning in Istanbul. The V5 Honda, he says now, was special: "Almost to this day, it's probably the best bike I've ridden. One of the most raw, especially of the MotoGP bikes." The crashes? "I was probably trying to keep up with tyres that weren't special enough."

By the end of the season, Colin was back in the paddock, looking for a factory contract. Yamaha was dithering, but Ducati firm. He signed. It was the start of a purple patch for both rider and machine. It's funny in retrospect that Stoner was some way down Ducati's short list: Hopkins, Hayden and Melandri had already declined the slot alongside incumbent Capirossi. Number-four choice would overshadow his experienced team-mate from the start.

Casey, now showing a growing maturity that soon outstripped his 21 years, was newly wed to willowy first-generation Australian Adriana and inseparable. Career-wise, he was where he needed to be. With factory-level support, there were no more dodgy Michelin tyre questions: he was on Bridgestones and had the pick. No question about the level of equipment. And in the first year of the 800 generation, Ducati had stolen an electronic march on the Japanese, combining strong power with accurate use of the restricted fuel.

In Casey, the Italians found a rider who could make the most of the bike's strong points, and make up for any gaps with his own talent and determination. Time and again, he handed Rossi a drubbing, taking ten wins and an assured championship.

He wouldn't repeat the feat on the Ducati. The next year he won six times, but Yamaha had closed up and Rossi was on fire, winning nine races. His strength was thrown into focus by new team-mate Melandri, 250 champion and MotoGP race winner. Melandri and the Desmosedici were poles apart. He was a dismal 17th overall. At the time, it was regarded as an aberration – something particular in the Italian's style that didn't suit the bike. In retrospect, given Rossi's only slightly better experience over the last two years, this was the first clear indication that in Casey's case, the rider was much better than the bike, rather than the other way around.

In 2009, Casey suffered a wrist injury and endured a controversial episode that still causes resentment: stricken with a mysterious debilitating ailment, he won two of the first five races, but results suffered as his condition worsened, until he took unilateral leave of absence; the paddock was stunned and quick to condemn. His dedication and even his mental strength were questioned. Unfairly, as it transpired, when the condition was eventually diagnosed as lactose intolerance. He came back fighting at the end: second, and then two wins. He'd probably have won the last round in Valencia as well, had he not crashed out on the warm-up lap.

His last year at Ducati saw the switch from steel trellis to the subsequently notorious carbon chassis. Rossi was keen to get rid of it; to Casey it was an improvement. "I think too many people looked at the speed of those bikes and thought, 'They're so fast, they've got to be easy to race.' But every other rider that's got on them, they want a more manageable engine, a more manageable bike. The Ducatis were pretty maniac, to be honest. Very, very difficult and tricky to set up, but very, very rewarding when you do get it right. Of course, the carbon was better; otherwise we would have stuck with the trellis frame. For me, there were too many negatives with the trellis that we were never able to solve and fix. Steel is too difficult to get the correct flex. With carbon, we got the stiffness that we wanted, and it improved the bike all round," he said.

Stoner suffered from front-end problems that caused a number of crashes, almost always while leading or going for the lead. When he stayed on, he was nine times on the rostrum with three wins.

He didn't let on then, but late that year explained that he had pretty much decided to quit: "I almost just finished my Ducati contract and said goodbye." But there was an interesting new prospect to turn his thoughts from retirement. Honda had yet to win a championship in the 800cc category, and there was just one more year to do it. They targeted Stoner, and he was intrigued enough to sign up "to see how it went."

It went rather well. The bike was good; he was once again dominant, by an impressive margin. Ten wins, never off the rostrum, finished every race except the one at Jerez, where he was knocked down by Rossi. He was champion by almost 100 points.

Ah, Rossi. Funny it should be him. But inevitable that the thrusting new kid should have come up against the reigning superstar head to head. And deeply satisfying to Casey the way it all worked out.

For it had been Rossi who had taken over Casey's Ducati,

confidently predicting that once they'd sorted out all Casey's setting mistakes, he'd also be able to win on it. After all, why not? Everyone knew he was better than Casey.

Stoner admits that Rossi is the rider he most enjoys beating, "not for any other reason but that he is the one who has always tried to bash me down and belittle me, and tried a lot of different things to play games and all the rest of it. He's been doing this a lot longer than me, and I was still able to beat him. So he can play all the games he wants, but I know it hurts him when I beat him. And I've beaten him a heck of a lot more than he's beaten me."

The bad blood goes back a way, to the US GP of 2008. A brutish pass on the dirt at the Corkscrew had left Stoner saying, "I've lost some respect". Sympathy went Rossi's way, however: winner takes all.

Now, however, the pendulum started to swing the other way. And kept right on swinging.

Stoner was unable to take revenge on the track: Rossi was never close enough as he struggled with the Desmosedici. A bike on which Casey could win races.

The signal moment came at Jerez in 2011. It was wet, Rossi more than ready to take advantage of the conditions. Too eagerly, he put an early pass on Stoner into the first corner. Lost it. Crashed. Right into the Honda. Partisan marshals helped Valentino get going again while Stoner fumed, unable to restart (thereafter the slipper clutch was revised to make a bump-start possible).

Afterwards, followed by TV cameras, Valentino went to Stoner's pit to apologise, cautiously keeping his helmet on. Stoner's reply was unforgettable. "What happened?" he asked. "Did your ambition outweigh your talent?"

Stoner, opinionated and articulate, was never at a loss for a snappy comment. Sometimes he would get carried away: people are still puzzling over exactly what he meant when, while talking to the press later that afternoon, he slammed Race Direction for favouritism and failing to sanction Valentino. "It's time they got some Christians on the committee," he opined.

Most of the time, he was right on the button. At his last race at Valencia, riders met an all-new track surface. Asked how it was, they politely brushed aside a lack of grip and praised its smoothness. Only Casey dissented. "The new surface sucks," he said bluntly. By the end of the weekend, most of the other riders were in agreement.

Every time Rossi had another bad race, it was yet more proof of how much he, crew chief Jerry Burgess and, to be fair, most other people had underestimated Stoner's achievements on the red bike. "I think they had a lot more expectations of what that bike was, and maybe less respect for what I was doing than they should have," he told MOTO-COURSE in 2011. "When they got on it, they realised that maybe I'm a little better than they thought I was; maybe I used less electronics than they thought I did."

His sympathies are firmly with the Italian company, and when at his last race news broke that race-department chief Filippo Preziosi was to be relieved of his duties, Stoner's was the lone voice firmly sticking up for the beleaguered engineer. He's the sort of guy you want on your side, because he'll stay there.

Unless he decides to do the other thing. He stunned the paddock when he announced his retirement at Le Mans, but his reasons were clear and numerous. Control tyres and fuel limits were making the bikes slower instead of faster. The off-track demands from sponsors were becoming more onerous, while the chances to go riding were dwindling, thanks to testing bans and teams frowning on too-risky motocross training. "We don't get to have a lot of fun in motorsport. You go out there and race, which is great, but you don't get the time to enjoy the bikes."

Commercialism had turned the paddock from a friendlier place into something more like a soulless New Town, dominated by sealed-off hospitality suites. The new ban on riders in the smaller classes bringing motorhomes to the paddock

particularly stuck in his craw: when he'd arrived in 2002, impecunious, but hungry for success, he'd lived in the back of a van with good friend Chaz Davies. "If I hadn't have been able to do that, I wouldn't be where I am today," he said.

He declined to add the birth of his first child (Alessandra arrived on Rossi's birthday!) to his litany of reasons, though he admitted, "Allie certainly made the decision easier, but it had been coming for a long time."

Perhaps the biggest reason was beyond anybody's control. Stoner was in the wrong era. "I was born too late," he laughingly admitted when pressed. Not just because of the changing paddock ambience, either. "I would have liked to have ridden in 500s. I feel that I am in one of the toughest eras around, which is kind of good because if you win, you know you've really won. But it's also very easy not to win. As a challenge goes, this is the best era to race in, along with the late 1980s and early 1990s. But I would like to race 500s more than MotoGP."

The Indy crash wrecked his chances of going out with another championship; his signal sixth successive win at Phillip Island made up for it. Retiring or not, he was still at the top of his game.

Fiercely logical, he never wavered from the decision. Even an offer of ten million euros from Honda, their biggest ever, couldn't tempt him. Some (Mick Doohan for one) predict a change of heart. More likely is a move to the rough-and-tumble Australian V8 Supercars series.

MotoGP will have to get on without him. It happens. Even the fastest riders come and go. This one, just a bit early. He leaves behind the memory of a broad, but dangerous smile, a hang-it-out riding style that recalls wilder days in racing. And a big gap at the top of the timing screens, where it would almost invariably take no more than a couple of laps before he was setting the pace again.

Above: A family affair: Stoner with father Colin, Adriana and mother Bronwyn in 2010.

Top left: "The Ducatis were a bit maniac." No one could master them like Casey. This is his 2007 title winner.

Top right: A dangerous smile – the world champion at Valencia in 2007.

Top centre right: No one faster. On the limit at Phillip Island, 2011.

Right: The family with whom Casey wants to spend more time: Adriana holds the infant Allie.

Photos: Gold & Goose

THE NUMBER'S UP

New rules, new numbers and a brave new world. In 2012, 81mm was set as the maximum bore size for the biggest and the smallest classes. Why that number? And what did it mean to each? NEIL SPALDING explains...

Above: The Hondas were always fast, but it took the 2013 version of the RC213V to allow them to become the undisputed masters, unfortunately a little late to grab the title.

Photo: Gold & Goose

THE 2012 season effectively saw the introduction of two new classes: Moto3 – all new with 250cc four-stroke singles replacing 125cc two-strokes; and the new version of MotoGP – up from 800 to 1000cc four-strokes. These classes have more in common than their start date. The major point of commonality is the 81mm maximum bore.

This is a new restriction for MotoGP regulations, and it is important that the size is the same. MotoGP must be four-cylinder. That means it is four times a Moto3 cylinder. Or is it? The requirements for each were very different.

GENESIS OF THE RULE

From the arrival of the four-strokes until Dorna changed their policy during 2011, the manufacturers' association (MSMA) wrote the technical rules. The policy in MotoGP was a reset every five years, to stimulate development and refresh the grid.

The 2008 financial crisis brought a new element: the money for complete re-engineering was not available, so the regulations for 2012 took that into account. It was decided that keeping the current 800cc cylinder heads would be more economical. The methodology was simple: freeze the bore sizes at their current sizes.

The first proposal was a maximum bore of 80mm. A small protest came from Ducati: 81mm would be better, for that was their current bore size. So it was that the

bore size of the last of the 800cc Ducatis was adopted for the new 1000cc MotoGP.

Ducati engines have always been more over-square than their rivals. The 990 had a bore/stroke ratio of 2.02: a massive 86mm bore and a short stroke of 48.6mm. This allowed piston acceleration and speed to remain at reasonable levels while the revs were ramped up for more power. It is clear from this negotiation that the 800 was from the same mould.

The rules for the Moto3 class were being negotiated at the same time; the logic of having a small class that used one MotoGP cylinder was compelling, hence an 81mm maximum bore for the new, rev-limited 250cc four-stroke singles. And that's where it all starts to become interesting.

POWER CORRUPTS

When you are after power, pumping the maximum possible amount of combustible material is an advantage. A bigger bore allows a shorter stroke, in turn permitting higher rpm before critical stress limits are reached on the piston and rings. In a motorcycle environment, however, the biggest possible bore is far from a perfect cure, for it brings significant down-sides as well.

Applying classic unlimited F1 technology to a 1000cc engine could easily yield 300bhp and 20,000rpm. But there are limits on just how much power a bike can use. Tearing down the long straight at Mugello, a bike will be starting to lift at the front as air pressure builds. The centre of pressure of a bike is higher than the centre of gravity – both far higher than a car because of the need to lean to corner. The bike is upright, so the tyre contact patch isn't at its largest; and with current designs making nearly 260 crankshaft horsepower, the bike will be about to spin its rear wheel, or wheelie, or both as it crests the hill before the first corner.

The larger the bore, the more difficult it is to design a clean burning combustion chamber, while higher revs mean a shorter time for a full burn. A crowned piston is required, protruding into the chamber, and the valve lift and duration needed for high rpm mean that the valve pockets cut into the crown have to be larger. The higher the rpm, and the wider the bore, the earlier the ignition has to fire to achieve a complete burn of the fuel charge, and uneven combustion-chamber shape makes it all the more difficult.

Low-rpm operation is also affected: the resulting wide, flat and uneven combustion chamber needs very good fuel atomisation to promote a stable flame front; any deficiency will help cause misfires and an irregular throttle response.

High crankshaft inertia can help smooth the engine's reactions, but again the shorter the stroke, the less inertia in the crank.

The 21-litre fuel restriction was kept. In the latter days of the 800s, it seemed that combustion-chamber and ECU software technology had caught up with the restriction. Running out of fuel was no longer a concern. With 1000cc, 21 litres is a real limiting factor once again. We saw both Tech 3 Yamahas run out of fuel on the cooling-down lap at Brno, and Crutchlow lost a possible podium in Japan, yet the Yamahas were not as powerful as the super-economical Hondas up the famous 'god's own dyno' that is Brno's hill.

With the new 81mm rule, MotoGP engines would be rev-restricted by the laws of physics.

Essentially, Honda and Yamaha built stroked versions of their 800s, with additional modifications to improve reliability, as this was the first major engine design revamp since the limited engine number regulations were introduced.

MotoGP retained open electronics, so extreme engines could still have the worst effects of their behaviour massaged away by the programmers. Over in Moto3, an rpm limit of 14,000 was mandated, and a fairly restrictive control ECU was also required. This meant that engines didn't need to be built to cope with the highest rpm possible and some thought could be given to other aspects of engine performance, like mid-range and smooth torque curves.

MOTOGP: SIZE MATTERS

Were Ducati campaigning an under-size '1000'? The company denied it, but their rivals couldn't understand how else the new engine – now rolled back 28 degrees with a revised sump and oil pick-up – could rev like it did.

One look at the rev-counter sparked confusion: the limit appeared to be set around 17,800rpm. Yamaha and Honda engineers, sharing the confusion, were recording and analysing the sound of the Ducati on the straights, and they had it revving at nearly 18,000rpm. Several other groups monitoring the revs of different bikes had similar reports.

The reason for the confusion was simple.

The 81mm bore predicates a 48.5mm stroke to displace 1000cc. The Ducati's level of revs meant that piston speeds and acceleration were higher than most would have considered wise.

Ducati have always sought higher revs in MotoGP, at least partly to maximise valve-seat seal with their spring-less desmodromic valve system. The new 1000 engines were clearly going to make a lot more power and torque, however, and the 800s already had too much power everywhere except in the top two gears. If the new formula would result in excess power needing to be kept in check by sophisticated electric throttle systems, why bother making it in the first place?

A smaller engine that revs higher quite often can have a wider usable power band, and its lighter, smaller-diameter crankshaft allows better manoeuvrability. The downside is less torque, but it wasn't looking easy to use that torque anyway.

Most engineers are resigned to a mean 27m/sec as maximum practical piston speed. In an engine with dimensions of 81x48.5mm, that equates to 16,700rpm. With that red line, and aiming for peak power a little slower at 26m/sec, the engine would be making 251bhp (187Kw) at 16,100.

A stroke of 45mm would give 27m/sec at 18,000rpm; and a speed of 26m/sec theoretically would also yield 251bhp at 17,330rpm – the same as a full-size 1000 at the same piston speed, the only sacrifice being in basically unusable torque.

With that 45mm stroke, the capacity would be 925cc. Perhaps Ducati were trying to repeat their 'commando raid' of 2007 by having an engine that was easily capable of higher revs than the limited fuel supply would initially suggest was possible.

With a wider spread of usable rpm, it is likely that the bike will be able to do similar lap times with fewer gear changes, and with the advantage in agility of a slightly smaller crankshaft.

Ducati were unimpressed by allegations of their engine being undersize, and in an official briefing, design chief Filippo Preziosi maintained that the bike was a full 1000. If so, the reliability achieved was very impressive given the strain the very high piston speeds and high g levels would have been placing on the engine.

Below: The new rules kept the old 21-litre fuel limit to slow things down.

Bottom: A new dash on the Ducati gave us much greater insight into the engine's settings as it was warmed up.
Photos: Gold & Goose

MOTO3: SAME BORE, NOT THE SAME DIFFERENCE

THE 81mm bore limit is in place in the Moto3 category, too. Moto3 was intended as a sea change, to switch motorcycle racing's basic starter class from small, two-stroke 125cc singles to small four-stroke 250cc singles.

Specifications were tight, with a control ECU and a 14,000rpm rev limit, as well as price restrictions on engines (eight per season), and their spare parts and tuning kits; suppliers had to be prepared to furnish a minimum of 15 riders if required.

The cost cap was in response to the financial situation. Final 125 lease deals were capped at 100,000 euros a year for the top-of-the-line GP bikes. Honda's new NRS250 was for sale, race-ready, at only 20,000 euros plus taxes. That was a basic racer, not ready to win at GP level. However, the start point was close enough to make a grand prix bike with limited modifications.

While the basic (13,500rpm) bike can serve national series and GP beginners, tuning kits are available to take full advantage of Moto3's extra 500rpm. In accordance with the rules, the kits have to be available to all – in Honda's case, Moto2 engine suppliers Geo Technology provide GP support. The maximum price of each Moto3 engine is 12,000 euros. Compared with the sum of the individual parts, that makes each engine a very cost effective proposition.

The Honda is a complete package. The engine shares its 78mm bore with their 250cc moto-crosser, but little else comes from that source. The road-racer uses a reversed-head, rear-sloping 250cc single. The high-downdraft inlet port breathes through an airbox behind the steering head, drawing from a duct just above the radiator. The exhaust pipe routing may seem unnecessarily tortuous, but it allows the right primary length to be built into a pipe that puts the bulky standard silencer into the undertray and out of the air stream.

Standard power is a claimed 47.6bhp (35.5kW) at 13,000rpm, implying a bmep of 13.1 bar. With some tuning, an increase in peak rpm should result in 53.5+bhp (40+kW), assuming 13,800rpm and an improved 14-bar bmep.

The engine is nearly 9kg heavier than the 125cc single it replaces – inevitable given the four-stroke's additional mass of camshafts, valves, springs and oil pumps. Honda's weight management, however, has resulted in only a 0.5 per cent increase in front weight distribution. This is important because the class runs on control Dunlop tyres, their construction being based on the previous generation of 125 tyres. They work best on bikes with a similar weight distribution; Honda's creative packaging has solved that dilemma very neatly.

But it is the other stuff that is interesting. The bore and stroke are 78 x 52.2mm, with an 'as delivered' compression ratio of at least 12:1. Included valve angle is a flat 21.5 degrees, with titanium valves – a generous 32.5mm inlet and 26mm exhaust. Honda chose not to go to maximum bore size because they found it much easier to find a flat torque curve with the smaller bore.

There is clear use of ideas developed on the old MotoGP RC211V 990cc V5, the 'semi-dry' sump being one of them. There is a scavenge pump, but no separate tank, simply a sealed tank cast at the lowest part of the engine. There is also a reed valve located just outboard of the bottom edge of the cylinder liner, venting into the cam-chain tunnel area to reduce crankcase pressure.

The gearbox employs the same size gears as the RS125, and indeed that engine's race gearbox can be employed, but with the gears set at a reduced mileage due to the increased torque. The supplied gears have a higher material specification to allow them to survive in 250 use.

The 125 engine, however, was a two-stroke and thus the gearbox had its own oil supply. Most current four-strokes use the engine oil for this purpose. There is a down-side – oil degradation and wear, but the packaging advantage outweighs this. In this case, the gearbox

Above: KTM built a very fine engine with a conventional layout. A quick retune for more mid-range saw it fastest overall.

Top: Suter's Moto3 chassis for the Honda NSF engine turned up just as the season started, but it worked very well.

Photos: Gold & Goose

retains the separate oil supply. It means that a lighter oil can be used, along with existing gearbox parts.

The throttle system is also simple – a single 'under-butterfly' injector is used for better rider feel as standard. A single overhead injector would provide higher peak power, but that wasn't the aim on the standard bike. Bikes tuned for GP use have two injectors, one over the throttle body, and the control ECU allows their use to be controlled. The throttle body also has an intake air control valve, a needle valve that bleeds air to the intake port to reduce engine braking and prevent destabilising rear-wheel hop. This is not adjustable as standard, but both a higher-grade ECU from Honda and the Dell'Orto control ECU allow this setting to be adjusted by gear, rpm and throttle position.

The 15-degree rearward tilt of the cylinder brings together several mass centralisation and packaging strategies. The airbox – all five litres of it – fits easily between the back of the radiator and the cylinder. The balance shaft then fits under the higher front edge of the cylinder liner as close as possible to the crank. The decision to tilt the heavy cylinder head rearwards means that the crankshaft can be placed much further forward than with the two-stroke 125s, leaving room for the gearbox and a rear suspension swing-arm that is almost the same as that of the old 125.

At KTM, they went the opposite way, opting to follow the 'biggest is best' route. With an 81mm bore combined with a stroke of 48.5mm, they have a capacity of 249.9cc in an entirely conventional layout. KTM consciously decided to make an aggressive engine; the logic was that the bottom-end power of a Moto3 engine wouldn't really matter, so initially they went for the best peak power. The target was to make more than the old 125s (about 50bhp) and that means peak is between 13,000 and 13,500rpm. Balancing the engine was also very important: a gear-driven shaft sits on the front of the crankcases. The target was to keep the overall level of vibration similar to one of their old 125cc two-strokes.

Honda took a patent on the reverse cylinder head idea, and although the arrangement has been around for years, KTM haven't seen fit to challenge them. Their head is an all-new, double-overhead-cam unit with four valves placed radially. The inward tilt is quite small at two degrees off vertical, in an attempt to maximise swirl and tumble to take the incoming mixture closer to the spark plug. Despite their thought that top-end power would be more important, KTM spent a lot of time after the first races of the season developing a new engine tune with more mid-range, and it wasn't until that engine was in use that they became truly competitive.

To achieve the correct weight distribution with a conventional-layout engine, KTM had to move their engine a long way forward in the chassis, to the point where the front-exit exhaust effectively splits the radiator in two.

KTM fielded four bikes with their own steel-tube frames, while four were run with aluminium beam chassis from Kalex. The steel-tube option is unusual in any MotoGP class, where aluminium beam frames are the norm.

Below left: Dunlop became the control tyre supplier for Moto3. They offered a close variant of their very successful 125 GP tyre.

Below: Penned by ex-Ferrari engine designer Mauro Forghieri, the Mahindra engine suffered reliability problems.

Bottom: KTM's tubular-framed Moto3 challenger. This is the later, stiffer version. It was good enough to bring Sandro Cortese the title.

Photos: Gold & Goose

2012 MOTOGP
BIKE BY BIKE

DUCATI DESMOSEDICI GP12

Above: Ducati's electronics were inside the front cowling: an experiment moving them to the centre was abandoned.

Top right: Rossi had a new, more flexible carbon swing-arm at San Marino. It gave better grip at full lean.

Opposite: Rossi's Ducati unclothed. Note the external flywheel, introduced after Mugello to allow fine-tuning of throttle response.

Photos: Gold & Goose

DUCATI responded to their disastrous 2011 season by bringing new aluminium beam-frame chassis to post-Valencia tests for all their riders. Just eight week later they had another new bike, more compact and looking more purposeful. There was a 'new' V4 engine, with cylinders that sat in the chassis as a 'V' rather than as an 'L'. Rossi and Burgess sounded upbeat initially: there was something here to work on, but lap times didn't improve as the test went on. Different set-ups were tested exhaustively, but no new parts were forthcoming for the tests, and little changed until the test that followed the Catalunya race.

There Ducati had an engine with an 'adjustable' external flywheel that allowed them to test different levels of crankshaft inertia. It made some difference to throttle response, but was not a great success.

Rossi had argued that the bike didn't accelerate as fast as the opposition, and that throttle response was far too 'harsh'. For the Catalunya and Aragon tests, a new engine tune with more bottom end was tried, but the ECU cut the power back to where it always had been. An aluminium swing-arm, which had been successful at a private Mugello test, was also tried, but after suffering issues with chatter it was put away, never to be seen again.

Parallel projects that didn't require a 'new' engine to be taken from the allocation also followed. By Misano, revised throttle bodies with a secondary injector had been introduced. These retained the overhead injectors, so valuable for good fuel atomisation and top-end power, but added injectors under the butterflies to allow low-rpm running that didn't result in puddles of fuel sitting on top of nearly closed butterflies. Rossi scored a second place at Misano with this set-up and a new frame, his best result so far.

The new frame had its headstock moved back 10mm, and the swing-arm pivot brought forward 10mm, the swing-arm being lengthened to suit. The modifications at the rear would have reduced the bike's reaction to chain pull, slightly calming the rear. The headstock position mod, however, allowed substantially more static weight to be put on the front, or for the front forks to be raked out, or a bit of both. The result was more front grip and less rear, just what Rossi wanted. Having finally found a 'direction', something only possible if you attempt something different, Ducati took the modification further, using a chassis that would allow even more weight to be placed on the front. At Sepang, several other frames with different flexibility were also tried.

While there was some significant progress towards the end of the year, Rossi had already decided to depart. His tenure at Ducati has to be regarded as a saga of lost opportunities. Ducati were too slow to react initially and then too tied up in trying to understand the physics of the changes they were making to bring alternative chassis to the circuit. As a result, they lost the services of the finest test rider the world has ever known, and the racing world lost the benefit of a truly competitive Ducati.

HONDA RC213V

HONDA'S first 1000, tested at Brno in August, 2011, was very narrow, the chassis beams closer together with engine air intakes ducted down the outside of the beams, then over the top into the airbox. The result was that the engine was also very narrow, and the beams had been lowered so that the air ducts did not obstruct the rider's arms. By the time the bike got to race, the chassis had been changed so that it was almost identical to that seen on the last of the 800s, with beams much wider and higher, the air intakes ducted through the side of the beam.

To be narrow enough to fit into the original Brno test design, however, it is highly likely that the Honda engine had been re-engineered. Unfortunately, Honda was very successful in keeping the engine out of sight. It remained a V4 and was believed, by everyone except Ducati, to still be in the 72–76-degree range (the Italians suspected it was closer to 90 degrees). The Honda had a relocated water pump, which appeared to be in the middle of the Vee. The easiest way to have made the engine narrower would have been to move the cam drive system up the centreline of the Vee, in a similar manner to Ilmor with their aborted 800 MotoGP project.

All four of the Hondas used the 'seamless-shift' gearboxes of the 2011 works bikes. These were deemed so secret that the private teams had to take on a dedicated HRC technician, the only person allowed to work on the gearbox. It was removed and stored in the official HRC truck between meetings.

The original 2012 design was competitive on the 'old' Bridgestone front tyres, but both Stoner and Pedrosa were scathing of the new softer version (as were all of the Honda management) introduced after the start of the year, and compulsory from Silverstone in June. After the race at Mugello, the 2013 version of the RC213V was rolled out early. This bike had a revised, more usable engine tune and a chassis with revised rigidities. Both Repsol riders liked the engine, but only Pedrosa wanted the new chassis.

Stoner had serious chatter issues all year. This affected the bike only under hard acceleration; it wasn't the conventional 'off throttle, neutral load' type of chatter we normally hear about and that says a lot about his riding style. Honda zeroed in on the chain drive as the most likely culprit, and several different cush-drive assemblies were tried before the Australian was injured at Indianapolis. No cure was ever really found however.

YAMAHA YZR MI

YAMAHA finished the last season of the 800 era second, but their bike was the most successful when you take into account the whole five years. With Lorenzo champion in 2010, Yamaha brought very few modifications for 2011; they duly lost to a resurgent Honda, desperate to win at least one 800 championship.

Yamaha, however, hadn't stopped working; they had merely decided to concentrate on their 2012 bike. From the outside, it looked quite similar to the last of the 800s, with small alterations here and there; but it wasn't long before some quite startling changes became apparent. The bike began to grow longer immediately; very soon it was normal to see the rear axle at the limit of its rearward adjustment. New swing-arms followed, maybe 15mm longer, but the axle didn't move much more. The Yamahas were very long indeed at that point. It seemed to calm the bike on acceleration and didn't put too much pressure on the new softer-carcase Bridgestones.

Yamaha addressed their long-term weak point, lack of ultimate speed, with some delicate aerodynamics. They started the year with fairings that looked very similar to the 800's. At Catalunya, however, the fairings sprouted small plates that sat over half of the surface area of all the major water and oil radiator exhaust ducts. Initial thinking was that the plates were there to improve top speed by keeping the airflow attached to the sides of the fairings. The plates were not smoothed into the surface of the fairing; rather they sat proud of the surface and seemed designed to create turbulence over the remaining duct. Yamaha claimed the modification was for top speed; Honda later experimented with similar fairings and said it was for cooling.

Certainly, if the turbulence over the exhaust port reduced the air pressure behind the radiator and improved the airflow through it, that would have improved both cooling and top speed, reducing the drag suffered as the air pushed its way through the radiator.

The new engine from Yamaha was based heavily on the previous-generation 800, but with major changes to aid reliability. A much bigger sump and a separate oil supply for the gearbox met the lubrication needs of the engine in a far better manner. Unlike Honda and Ducati, Yamaha's gearbox design seems to have remained as a fairly conventional 'sliding dog ring' design, but Yamaha had given a lot of attention to programming the quick-shift system in an attempt to minimise power loss as the box was shifted from gear to gear.

Yamaha maintained a programme of engine development through the year, desperate to maintain their early lead over Honda. The evidence was seen in ever-lengthening secondary pipes; also noticeable was the speed at which the Tech3 customer bikes received equivalent kit to the works team, usually on the next engine change. The same was true of the swing-arm changes, with the usual clear Yamaha differentiation as to who was where in the pecking order. Lorenzo would receive and test stuff; Spies would have equivalent kit almost immediately, then Dovizioso and last (but certainly not least) Crutchlow.

Above: Lorenzo's Yamaha showed clear development links with its 800cc forebear. Note the dimpling in the alloy beam surface, an indication of its thinness; also how strongly the front engine mount is braced to help withstand braking forces.

Opposite: Yamaha's customer team was right up to speed with the latest mechanical parts, but they didn't seem so fast with electronic upgrades. Crutchlow ran out of fuel while fighting for a podium in Japan.

Photos: Gold & Goose

CLAIMING RULE TEAMS – CRT

THE idea that road engines could be competitive with prototypes must seem obvious if you simply compare the lap times for World Superbike and MotoGP. The trouble is that it isn't a fair comparison; the tyres are different, which is important, and the MotoGP bikes have fuel limits that keep performance down. So, maybe we could remove all tuning restrictions and allow more fuel? Again, not quite a fair comparison: CRT engines should be 'claimable' for 20,000 euros, and you can only have 12 a year, although with a more generous 24-litre fuel allowance compared to 21 for the prototypes. Add this lot up and the only real solution is detuned World Superbike engines.

Dorna restricted the number of pure prototypes to four from each factory. The main reason was that they were subsidising the typical three-million-euro annual lease price of each bike. As an alternative, teams that took the Spanish shilling were invited to build their own bikes, or buy a pair of Aprilias for 1.2 million euros.

If you wanted to build your own bike, FTR, Suter and Inmotec were up to the challenge: Suter used the BMW superbike engine; FTR made chassis for the Honda CB1000RR and the Kawasaki ZX-10. It took a while for everyone to realise that the Bridgestones, designed as they are for 260bhp full works prototypes, weren't going to work very well on 225bhp superbikes. The soft variant was always selected, and an even softer version would have helped. In addition, chassis flex took a while for people to work out. The real problem, however, was the absence of good electronic throttle systems.

With Bosch cutting their teeth in two-wheeled competition on the Suter BMW, and Cosworth bringing their Ten Kate system from World Superbike, there were bound to be a few problems. Avintia-Blusens, unfancied before the season, seemed to have got it right by mid-year. They had a bike that handled well and a throttle system that didn't upset the riders: two small things that mattered a lot.

Aprilia entered the fray building ART bikes, essentially RSV1000 superbike racers, with mildly detuned engines and a 'prototype' chassis that copied the geometry of the superbike and, as far as we could tell, the stiffness of the original, too. This meant that the bikes were much too stiff in the lateral plane for the notoriously fickle Bridgestones.

Aprilia brought their superbike electronics, too: by far the best throttle system in CRT. The Dorna-supported teams that bought these bikes put well on the way to 4.8 million euros into Aprilia's superbike racing war chest. One wonders if they could have been as competitive there without such a bonus. Could that mean that Dorna not only now runs World Superbike, but also won the championship in 2012?

Above, clockwise from top left: Avintia Blusens used FTR chassis, but tried this carbon special from Inmotec as well; Edwards's Suter BMW – Bosch software wasn't a success and new parts were slow to arrive; Pirro's FTR chassis with Ten Kate-tuned Honda Fireblade – several chassis were tried, but there were a number of unexplained chain failures; Petrucci's IODA, a tubular-steel-framed Aprilia – quite successful given the virtually untuned engine.

Left: By mid-season, Aspar's top-level ARTs had a stiffer swing-arm and a new engine spec with gear-driven cams and a red line raised to 15,500rpm.

Photos: Gold & Goose

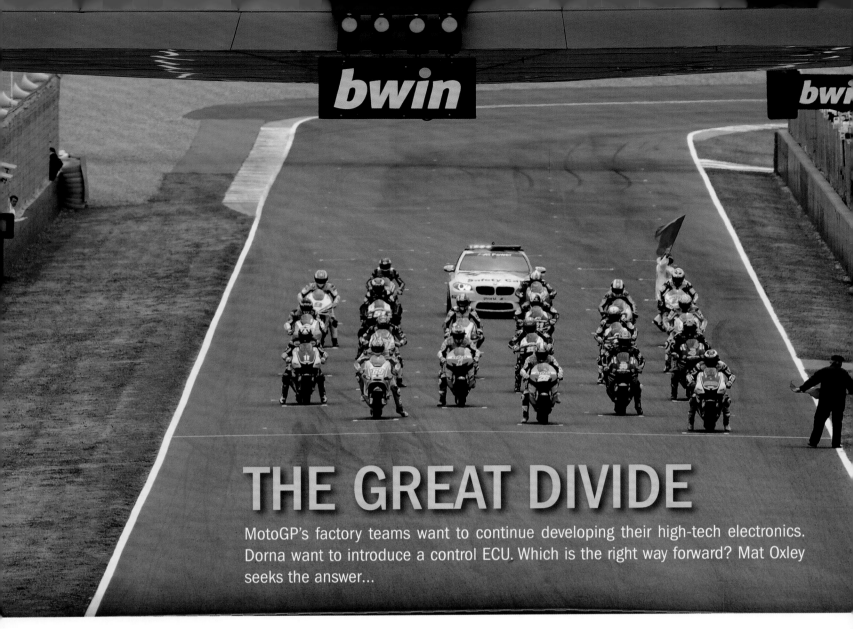

THE GREAT DIVIDE

MotoGP's factory teams want to continue developing their high-tech electronics. Dorna want to introduce a control ECU. Which is the right way forward? Mat Oxley seeks the answer...

Above: Jerez, and the 2012 Spanish GP is about to start. There are 21 bikes on the grid, only 12 of them prototypes. CRT made up numbers at the back.

Opposite: The protagonists of power: Yamaha's Masahiko Nakajima (*top*) and Honda's Shuhei Nakamoto want to retain the factories' technological grip on MotoGP.

Photos: Gold & Goose

IT is motorsport's clash of ideologies, the fundamental divide between those who believe that racing is about technology and those who believe it belongs to show business. This isn't a clash that's unique to MotoGP, it's a war that's being waged in every major racing series, on two wheels and four.

On the one side are the earnest engineers poring over their laptops. On the other are the businessmen, sealing deals with TV executives and corporate CEOs.

Or, as Tech 3 team owner and IRTA president Hervé Poncharal puts it, "We need to understand that GP racing's time as an engineering laboratory isn't over, but that role is less important than it was before. We are a sport, but sport can only live if there is a show, so this is show business."

In recent years, MotoGP engineers have had to give way to the showmen, conceding ground on many fronts. But it seems as though some of them are ready to halt their retreat, to draw a line in the sand. The issue at stake is electronics development.

Dorna intend to curb electronics R&D because they believe MotoGP's high-end electronics technology to be an excessive expense at a time of economic woe. They believe that introducing a control ECU will reduce costs and shrink the gap between the richer teams occupying the front of the grid and the poorer outfits at the back. Dorna say they don't want to ban traction control and other rider aids, even though many fans would like them to do just that. However, a control ECU would allow them to reduce or get rid of traction control altogether if they wanted to do so at some point in the future.

"Engine management R&D is a huge cost," asserted MotoGP director of technology Corrado Cecchinelli, formerly an engineer with Ducati. "It's also an area in which the smaller teams have no chance to compete. So a control

ECU would reduce costs and level performance. We know that we need to keep some scope for electronics work in MotoGP, because this is the way to keep the manufacturers in the game.

"For me, the idea about getting rid of traction control is a non-issue. I like to see the bikes sliding, but the bigger issue is making the racing closer, with more equal performance between all the bikes. We cannot go back, so what we want to do is put a roof on the current electronics technology, so there are no new areas in which to spend money."

In fact, there are some people in the pit lane who believe that MotoGP has to go back to go forward. They would like a complete ban on high-tech electronics by reverting to carburettors and throttle cables. "Give control back to the rider," say the Luddites. "Then the factories would have to design rider-friendly motorcycles and rider-friendly tyres."

Valentino Rossi is one of many riders who believe that high-tech electronics aren't a good thing because he enjoys wrestling with his machine as much as the fans enjoy watching him wrestle his machine.

"For sure, electronic systems in general are very bad for motorsport," he said. "Is very good for safety, but very bad for the sport. I tried my first system with Honda at the end of 2002 because we made the first season of MotoGP without traction control. What they had then is one per cent of what we have now, but when I tried the first time I went back into the pits and I say, 'F*ck, noooo.' I mean with this system everybody can ride the bike."

Although most riders agree with Rossi, they baulk at the idea of a total ban on traction control.

"The bikes are producing so much horsepower that riding without traction control could be catastrophic; there'd be savage high-sides," said double MotoGP champion Casey Stoner. "But I think there should be a limit to electronics:

a control ECU that determined how much traction control everyone could have would be fantastic."

Despite factory opposition, Dorna are already pushing ahead with their control ECU plan. From 2013, all teams will be able to use a state-of-the-art Magneti Marelli control ECU for free, although only CRT teams are expected to take up the option, as part of the plan to get them closer to the prototypes. If the kit is as good as Dorna say it is, it will certainly do just that, because some CRT teams are currently using very basic electronics, lacking lean-angle software and so on.

"A control ECU would be good for us," explained Ricard Jove, team manager of the Blusens Avintia CRT outfit, which ran FTR Kawasakis in 2012. "You only have to look at Formula One: they use the same tyres, the same electronics and very similar engines. This is the way forward; all teams should have the same chance."

Once the CRT black box has been fully developed, Dorna plan to impose it upon the entire grid. This ECU will be nothing like the Moto2 control ECU, which allows engineers to do nothing more than adjust fuelling and ignition. Instead it will be more like the system used in Formula One cars over the past five years, so it will allow engineers to load their own engine maps, but it won't allow them to introduce their own algorithms. Engineers will have to work within the set strategies written into the control ECU, so they won't be able to invent anything new. The ECU will also include an rpm limit (once again to reduce costs and equalise performance across the grid) and be open to scrutiny by Dorna's technical control staff.

It will come as no surprise that the factories hate the idea of such restrictions. They argue that although times are hard, we live in a digital age, so it makes no sense to prevent development of high-tech electronics that may create all kinds of improvement within the motorcycling industry. Honda are so adamant that HRC vice-president Shuhei Nakamoto had threatened to switch Honda's factory team to World Superbikes if Dorna went ahead with their control ECU plan.

"At the moment, Honda only have a factory team in MotoGP, while we have a 'dealer team' in World Superbike," said Nakamoto at Brno in August. "But if we have a single ECU here in MotoGP, then Honda's interest will change to World Superbike. Ciao Carmelo! Dorna can make the decision, but we must continue spending on electronics development. This is very important to Honda."

Nakamoto's threat followed an earlier announcement from World Superbike promoter Paolo Flammini, who made it clear that he was entirely happy to have "advanced engine control electronics" in SBK. Flammini was obviously hoping to take advantage of MotoGP's discomfiture by tempting the factories to defect, even if it made no sense for motorcycling's prototype series to control electronics while its production-based championship ran an open house.

Nakamoto's threat lost its sting in October, however, when Bridgepoint announced that Dorna will run SBK as well as MotoGP. Since Dorna will decide the technical regulations for both championships, Honda and any other factories immediately lost all room for manoeuvre. Nevertheless, they don't want to give up without a fight.

"The factories have said from day one they don't want a control ECU, because the main reason they are here is to develop electronics," said MotoGP race director Mike Webb. "It's their research; they want to do it to gain knowledge. But, as Carmelo often says, we are in show business and if there isn't a show to sell, then we are all out of business. If the manufacturers say we don't want to change anything, then it will come to hard negotiations. It may happen that Dorna will have to say, 'These are the rules and you can play or not.'"

Nakamoto insisted that he was making a stand to protect all manner of electronics development work, not just rider-aid R&D.

"Don't forget, electronics isn't only traction control," he said. "The most important information we get from our work in MotoGP isn't about traction control and wheelie control, it is about engine driveability and fuel consumption. Everything we have learned from running MotoGP bikes with 21 litres of fuel is useful to us. Already in Asia we have some smaller-capacity models using systems we learned from MotoGP, which is why Honda machine fuel consumption is better than our rivals."

"Not so many road bikes have traction control at the moment, just like not so many cars had traction control 15 years ago. If someone can guarantee that road bikes will not use traction control in the future, then maybe we would be happy to stop electronics R&D."

Inevitably, more and more road bikes will use traction control, but does that technology need to be developed in MotoGP? BMW's recently launched S1000R HP4 has fantastically sophisticated electronics. The machine features semi-active suspension that adjusts damping every 11 milliseconds depending on lean angle, speed, damper speed, throttle position and other parameters. But this technology wasn't even developed in bike racing – it was adapted from a BMW 7-series road car ECU.

It should also be remembered that the most important electronic rider aid – life-saving ABS technology – was developed without any racing input.

Nakamoto's other argument insists that restrictions on electronics in MotoGP wouldn't save Honda any money.

"We would have to continue development, either in another racing category or, if World Superbike also went to a single ECU, then we would have to continue work at our R&D centres, with test riders and engineers working at our test tracks instead. So a control ECU would make no difference to our budget. It is a nonsense for prototype machines."

Yamaha's MotoGP project leader, Masahiko Nakajima, largely agrees, although his stance in respect of Dorna is less aggressive.

"A control ECU is a problem for us," Nakajima explained. "We learn many new electronics strategies from MotoGP, so this know-how and data is very useful for production R&D. Racing is our laboratory, where we can work on new ideas for production.

"If we cannot do trial-and-error R&D in MotoGP, then it becomes very difficult for me to explain to Yamaha board members why we should still spend so much money in MotoGP. On the other hand, MotoGP is becoming very expensive, so although we do not wish to make a cap on electronics technology, maybe we can work on a compromise. Maybe if everyone has the same hardware and operating system, with the software capped, then maybe we could agree to this."

IS THERE A BETTER WAY?

The subject of control electronics in MotoGP is so divisive that perhaps it might be better to explore alternative ways of reducing costs and creating closer, more exciting racing.

Some people in the MotoGP paddock look to World Superbike for inspiration. SBK switched to a control tyre before MotoGP, employing Pirelli slicks. These tyres have less grip than the Bridgestones employed in MotoGP. Bridgestone make very stiff tyres, which only really suit the faster riders, thus stretching the gap between the front and the back of the pack.

Former SBK champion and 2013 Ducati MotoGP rider Ben Spies believes that friendlier tyres would help MotoGP in several ways.

"MotoGP is a prototype class, so you want to see the bikes developing, so my opinion on making better racing isn't control ECUs, changing bore and stroke, all that stuff," he said. "If you want closer racing, like World Superbike,

Above: Race engineer Pat Symonds opposed F1's common ECU, but the experience changed his views.
Photo: Peter J. Fox

Top: Casey Stoner is the most fearless user of electronics.
Photo: Gold & Goose

Top right: Motec M170 ECU on the Ducati Panigale.
Photo: Clive Challinor

Above right: "High-side city didn't happen." BSB chief Stuart Higgs successfully introduced a control ECU in the important national championship.
Photo: Gold & Goose

Right: Careful with that twist-grip. Triple champion Shakey Byrne leads Josh Brookes and Tommy Hill in the close, traction-control-free 2012 BSB championship.
Photo: Clive Challinor

just make the Bridgestone tyres with 20 per cent less grip and performance. Then it's much easier for all the riders to get to a certain lap time. The best will still win, but you're going to see closer racing in a much cheaper way than changing the electronics and so on. That's my two cents. It's such an easy thing to do to make the racing cheaper, to make the fights better for TV and to make it safer."

Jonathan Rea's Ten Kate Honda crew chief, Chris Pike, agreed. "To me, the tyre is always the determining factor of how fast you can go, so Dorna should be able to control it there," said Pike. "That way, you can keep the essence of MotoGP, so the big teams still have the freedom to spend lots of money on development, but they won't get too far ahead because the tyre is the determining factor. Development of the Bridgestones has been pushed by the fastest riders in the world, but most other riders struggle to bridge the gap with those tyres.

"You can do whatever you want with tyres. Look at Formula One: they've engineered some interesting racing by designing a tyre that degrades, and the top guys still win. You can have the fastest engine and the best electronics out there, but those black rubber things will only deliver so much performance."

No matter how Dorna decide to slow down MotoGP's fastest – with reduced electronics or slower tyres – another problem will arise: the pace will fall into the realms of World Superbike. That's why Dorna will also rewrite the SBK rules, to maintain a reasonable gap between the prototype and production categories.

FORMULA ONE'S CONTROL ECU EXPERIENCE

The concept of a control ECU is far from uncharted territory in motorsport. All major car racing championships – from Formula One to NASCAR – have featured control ECUs for several years.

Most Formula One teams were horrified by Max Mosley's intention to ban free electronics in the world's biggest motorsport championship. F1 finally succumbed to a control ECU in 2008, not so much to reduce costs, but as a means of fully exorcising traction control. Anti-spin control had already been banned, but rumours were rife in the pit lane that some teams were still using the technology.

Renowned F1 engineer Pat Symonds was one of the many boffins who believed that curbing electronics R&D was the wrong thing to do. Symonds has spent most of his career with the Benetton and Renault F1 teams – he was Michael Schumacher's race engineer when the German won his first F1 titles – and now works for the Marussia squad.

"I was very much against the adoption of a common ECU," said Symonds. "At Renault F1, we had a lot of know-how and a lot of legacy from all our work on electronics, so we were quite reluctant to change.

"Max's feeling was that if F1 had a standard ECU with a standard set of software – albeit software that you could calibrate yourself without altering the fundamental way it worked – then it would be impossible to have traction control. Max was quite correct: the common ECU stopped everyone arguing about who was using traction control and we all got on with the racing. It also contributed to a significant reduction in costs.

"At the time of introduction, it wasn't a cost saver, because at Renault we had a lot of Magneti Marelli ECUs that were scrap and then we had to buy a lot of very expensive McLaren Electronics ECUs. But once we had accepted that capital cost, we stopped spending so much money developing control strategies in certain areas. Perhaps the control ECU was a little dumbed down compared to what we'd been used to, but overall it's not a bad thing."

Symonds reckons the restrictions allowed Renault F1 to halve its electronics personnel, contributing to significant ongoing cost savings.

"At first, there was a massive workload. Every single aspect of the system was different. Our people had to look at all the control structures within the single ECU to understand how they related to the control structures they were used to and then change the way they did things.

"For example, take the task of mapping a differential. You don't just populate a big table with numbers, you have a lot of tools that assist you in doing that, whether it be a graphics interface so you can see exactly how your diff lock is working, or even a system that can superimpose a virtual differential on to your data traces. But once the initial work had been done, the workload was significantly reduced. At Renault, we went from ten people to five.

"With the McLaren ECU, you can't change the strategies; you have to operate with the algorithms they give you, so you can't write your own algorithm that says if the rear

wheel is travelling faster than the front wheel, then lift off the throttle. That's how they managed to get rid of things like traction control, so all of that was good."

A common argument from those opposing a similar direction in MotoGP suggests that it will be impossible to create a common ECU that works with a variety of engine configurations, from inline fours with pneumatic valves to V4s with desmodromic valves. Symonds doesn't agree.

"It's a slightly more complex mapping job if you've got significantly different engines, but I don't see why it should be a real problem. For example, we've had the same ECU in F1 for five years now, so next year we'll have a new ECU, the TAG 320. In 2013, it will drive normally-aspirated 2.4-litre V8s, then in 2014 F1 switches to turbo V6s, but the ECU will be the same. So long as you have enough hooks in your algorithms, I don't see it as being a problem. If you've got pneumatic valves, then there needs to be a strategy in there that monitors air-valve pressure. If you've got desmo valves, you just wouldn't use that part of the software.

"And even with a control ECU, some things come along that are better than before. At Renault, we could never have our cars sitting on the grid or idling at the end of pit lane for a long while, and we always wondered how the Mercedes [run by McLaren] seemed to be untroubled by this. Then when we got the control ECU, we discovered that they just cut down to four cylinders on idle. So you do learn things along the way."

Symonds believes that useful R&D can still be done on the racetrack, but he is unconvinced by the factories' argument that they need to be able to develop electronics in MotoGP so they can build better road bikes.

"The motor and motorcycle industries are working a lot harder to get efficient engines, which has always been our goal in racing. While we use a lot of fuel in racing, we produce a hell of a lot of power with it, so the specific fuel consumption of racing engines has always been extremely impressive. But in engineering, we are moving more and more into virtual worlds, so a lot of stuff is done by simulation. It's no longer necessary to go out there on Sunday and race something new to prove that it's good.

HRC's Nakamoto understands Symonds' point on development, but says it's wrong. "F1 and MotoGP are completely different," he said. "Most F1 teams don't make production machines, so they don't need development platforms."

Symonds may be a highly decorated F1 engineer, but during the last few years his position on the technology-versus-showbiz argument has shifted.

"As an engineer who has had a lot of fun playing with technology, I've always liked the engineering side of racing," he said. "But I'm also very aware that it's the people watching, not the clever engineering, that pays the bills. In F1, we've been trying for years to figure out the right balance. People want to see great racing, but it's also important to the spectators that we are operating on technical frontiers, or at least there needs to be a *belief* that we are operating on technical frontiers.

"Ultimately, what pays us is good racing, because that's what gets the people coming in through the gates, the TV companies paying more for the rights and new sponsors coming on board. That's what really counts, I'm afraid, so in my advancing years I'm moving a little more towards putting on a good show, so long as we've got some toys to play with."

However, Symonds isn't sure that Dorna's current practice of slowing the prototypes to give the CRT machines a better chance is a good way forward. "That doesn't make sense. It's the communist principle to make everyone equally bad. Our way of life is to try to get everyone to strive for the best."

BSB'S CONTROL ECU EXPERIENCE

Motorcycle racing has been slow to follow in F1's tyre marks and curb electronics technology. The world's first champion-ship to adopt a single ECU and ban rider aids was the British Superbike Championship, which took the step at the start of 2012.

BSB differs from MotoGP. It's a national championship with a relatively low income that runs significantly less powerful street bikes, so the series promoters had few qualms about switching off high-tech electronics, including the all-important traction control.

"Before the season started, there were a few people going on about how BSB was going to be high-side city," admitted BSB director Stuart Higgs, "but the prophecies of doom haven't come to pass."

Higgs's reasons for introducing a control ECU were slightly different to Dorna's. Like Dorna, he wanted to reduce costs, but unlike Dorna he definitely wanted to get rid of rider aids.

BSB's Motec M170 black box certainly reduces costs – it retails at £3,000 and its spec is fixed for five years. The M170 doesn't feature traction/wheelie/launch control, but it does permit teams to play with basic engine management settings like fuelling, ignition and engine braking. The box provides two engine maps so that riders can choose a softer map for the wet. The M170 also features 250Mb of memory for data logging, with inputs for wheel-speed sensors and suspension potentiometers, so teams can work on chassis set-up as before. The unit also includes an rpm limit, set at 750rpm above the red line of each model.

The system's inaugural season was a success, with most riders quite happy to be riding without traction control and other rider aids.

"To be honest, it's probably safer now because too many riders were starting to rely too much on electronics," explained triple BSB champion Shakey Byrne. "That's great until the electronics don't work and then you're going to have a massive crash. Now you have it all in your right hand. I think the new rules are pretty cool."

Byrne admitted that he did have his doubts about losing the security of traction control: "When we went pre-season testing at Aragon, I remember going through Turns Two and Three thinking, 'Effin' hell, if this thing lets go here it's going to be massive,' because it's pretty much full throttle, knee on the floor, which is a recipe for a ginormous high-side. But I never had one."

The loss of traction control has certainly forced riders to use the throttle more conservatively. "Sure, there's corners where you're a bit more careful than you used to be," Byrne added. "Like the exit of Clearways [at Brands Hatch], where you come over the top of the crest. Before you'd be hard on the throttle, with the traction control going da-da-da-da-da-da. Now it's like, whooooaaaa!" Byrne mimed the act of gently modulating the throttle, searching for grip, while looking slightly worried.

"But even with traction control, you never just get to mid-corner and pin the throttle. The trickiest system I've used was the Magneti Marelli kit when I was with Ducati. You open the throttle a bit until you feel you're against the traction control, which feels like being in a berm on a motocross bike, then you pin it, lift the bike, the electronics open up and you drive off the turn.

"But it's good fun riding without electronics. I remember riding without any electronics when I was coming through in 2000 and 2001, and having a whole load of fun, and I'm having a load of fun this year."

The introduction of the Motec ECU wasn't the only big change for BSB during 2012. The engine rules were also changed, with engine tuning largely banned. Peak power is down by about ten per cent, compensated by better driveability, which reduces the risk of high-sides and thus softens the impact of the traction-control ban.

Dorna have made moves in a similar direction. The recently introduced minimum-bore-width regulations and the forthcoming restriction on rpm both encourage more rider-friendly engines.

But how slow can you go and still be fast enough?

TECHNICAL ESSAY
FUTURE INDICATIVE

MotoGP is increasingly beset with rules designed to improve the racing, with more to come. KEVIN CAMERON examines the technical aspects of the alternative future, and concludes that well-intentioned rules can never replace a good crew chief...

PEOPLE discuss MotoGP as if its problems had an obvious answer. Bernie Ecclestone, the F1 chief, has said that Dorna CEO Carmelo Ezpeleta must either run Honda out of the series or show them who's boss. Kenny Roberts has said the factories are ruining racing by the unattainable excellence of their prototype machines. The discussion is troubling because in almost every case, the critics act as though some easy answer is staring the sport in the face, but no one in authority has the sense to implement it.

Yet the alternatives are so numerous. Which of them is the obvious right answer? In the case of US AMA road racing, taken over by NASCAR affiliate DMG in 2009, it was assumed by many that everything would fall into place by applying the never-fail Bill France/NASCAR remedy – automatic success follows booting the factories out plus adoption of rules to deliver close racin'.

Evidently there was more to Big Bill's method than met the eye. After half the factories and most of the spectators had left, DMG CEO Roger Edmondson said, "I underestimated the importance of the factories to the series."

Let's now turn to the alternatives themselves, which group themselves into a sort of 'decision tree'.

The first question is, can the series be fixed 'on the fly', by fine-tuning the regulations, or must the series be restarted on a new basis? When the Second World War ended, Formula One continued the 1500cc supercharged formula. Because supercharging was technology intensive and costly, only Alfa Romeo could win races. BRM in Britain built a fabulously complex V16 around wartime supercharger technology, but couldn't make their car run for long enough to do anything. Race promoters, seeing crowds bored by promenading Alfas, switched top billing to Formula Two – a much more accessible two-litre unsupercharged class. Lots of F2 entries showed up and gave the word 'racing' back its meaning.

The FIA could have hung on to its formula, banning this and that in an effort to fine-tune it into success, but they saw which way the river was running, dumped supercharging and attracted more competitors. Here came Ferrari, Mercedes, Maserati,

Lancia and even a British car – the Manx-Norton-based four-cylinder Vanwall – competing and winning exciting races. The new formula was seen as within reach.

If MotoGP were to be restarted on a fresh basis, what might that be? The obvious example of a more accessible series, not dominated by one or one-and-a-half technological giants, is the production-based World Superbike, with its six brands in contention, and five winners in 2012. This example is complicated by the fact that corporate restructuring has lately put World Supers under Dorna management, but ignore that for a moment.

Here's the problem. Four-stroke prototype grand prix racing is too rich for this industry, since only Honda can actually afford to participate fully. Yamaha keep up appearances and Ducati are unable to do even that. Aprilia, Suzuki, KR Racing and Kawasaki came and went, and a few project engines were offered at F1 prices, but there were no takers (remember the Swissauto 500 two-stroke V4, which made 20hp more than anything on the grid, but once in a chassis was the slowest thing on the track?). This suggests that eventually the class must fall back to what every manufacturer already has – 1000cc production engines.

This is the CRT model. In SBK, such engines have provided good racing, especially when tech inspector Steve Whitelock implemented the policy of 'giving them what they need'. This has meant allowing only change that restores rather than destroys competition.

The marketplace pushes production engines toward equality, and the 'what they need' policy allows older designs to compete with more recent ones. The example is Honda's CBR1000RR, which two years ago had hit an uncompetitive dead end. But allowing the Ten Kate team to give it throttle-by-wire put it back in the running.

Now for the other choices. Ezpeleta has said that the future of MotoGP will follow either the Moto2 or the Moto3 model.

In Moto3, approved racing engines, available for sale to all (including any modifications), power prototype chassis. At present, there are two competitive engines: KTM and Honda. In applying this to MotoGP, Honda and Yamaha have somewhat complicated the picture – Honda plan to offer *for sale* (this is very different from lease bikes, which must be given back at the end of the season) a 'production racer', a reduced-cost version of their prototype RC213V. Yamaha have said they would *lease* engines – but Ezpeleta wants an end to leasing. Without resale, it is expensive, but it has provided prototype performance very close to that of factory bikes (as in the hands

of Dovizioso and Crutchlow).

The Moto2 model is a contingency plan in case Honda will not accept what HRC's Shuhei Nakamoto has called "crazy regulations". In this case, engines that have already been priced from Ducati would become the spec powerplant of MotoGP for a radical manufacturer-free future. Since they would not have to compete except with each other, such engines could be conservatively tuned for long service life. Whether their power bands were easy or difficult, it would be the same for all users.

Now we come to the present. An informal poll of Spanish MotoGP viewers asked the question, "Do you watch MotoGP (a) for the show, or (b) for the technology?" As you would expect, the result was 16 to 1 in favour of the show. This is backed up by the popularity of Moto2, which is said currently to have a larger audience than MotoGP. If you need more, Valentino Rossi adds his voice, saying, "MotoGP is boring."

At present, there are 12 factory prototypes and lease bikes – fewer than the 15 starters required by contract. So-called 'CRT' bikes brought the grid up to more than 20: production-based engines powering artisan chassis, from builders like Suter and FTR, who currently supply Moto2. Aprilia created a grey area by entering its ART as a CRT. This is really a production racer, a professionally engineered package of engine and chassis, with a baseline set-up like that of a prototype or lease bike. Some ARTs have non-production gear-driven cams, edging it closer to prototype status.

The 'genuine' CRTs have proved slow, unexciting and unreliable, with as many as half of them failing to finish. Even so, Ezpeleta once said, "In two years, CRTs will be the only machines in MotoGP." With the new possibility of factory production racers, it appeared CRTs might just have been one of Ezpeleta's 'motivational devices'.

The problem for most CRT teams has been that they lack what Moto2 has shown to be essential: MotoGP crew chiefs. Bolting a Superbike engine into a chassis, then adding brakes, wheels and suspension from usual sources does not produce a raceable motorcycle. It looks like a motorcycle, but it goes like a home project.

On the other hand, we have seen Moto2 develop into a post-graduate course in tyre management – at least for the front-runners. A hot-wrist kid can get to the front, but as his tyres fade from the punishment doled out by an amateur chassis set-up, he goes backward into obscurity. He rides harder to hold position, but this just kills the tyres more quickly. As the race winds down, the men on bikes with 20-lap set-ups from

Above: Marc Marquez listens intently to Santi Hernandez. The Moto2 champion moves up to the Repsol Honda MotoGP Team in 2013 and takes his crew chief with him.

Left: Dorna chief Carmelo Ezpeleta holds the steering wheel for motorcycle racing, but will he choose the right road?

Right: The aquisition of a fly-by-wire throttle gave Ten Kate's Honda CBR1000RR a new lease of life.

Photos: Gold & Goose

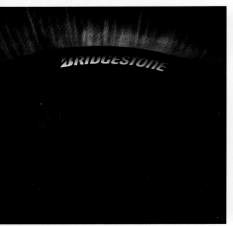

Above: Tyre warmers changed the nature of racing by giving riders less to do and fewer opportunities to exploit different skills.

Above centre: Colin Edwards and chassis builder Eskil Suter: it took most of the season to get to grips with the complexities of their BMW-powered CRT bike.

Above far right: Honda's stock CBR600 engine, successfully employed in Moto2.

Photos: Gold & Goose

real crew chiefs slash through traffic with assurance. Their tyres come good when everyone else's have faded.

Will information diffuse from faster teams to slower, levelling this inequality?

History suggests not. US AMA racing in 1977 was essentially a spec class for TZ750 Yamahas, a class in which everyone had more power than he could use, making it very much rider vs rider. The bikes had been on sale since 1974, so it was a mature class with many riders. Yet in any race, it was factory bikes 1-2, followed by experienced privateers. Then came the parade of slow riders on slow bikes. The conclusion? Nobody goes fast unless he and his crew know what they are doing.

I saw the same early in 2012 at DMG's (formerly AMA's) Atlanta national. The paddock gleamed with professionally painted 45-foot transporters. Just as in the days of TZ750s, paint and uniforms didn't make bikes faster. Just as the majority of TZ750s had been, most of the new big-truck teams were slow. Going fast requires knowledge.

It's easy to think that if factory bikes are out front in a near-stock class, it must be because costly electronics and software are putting them there. Yet the dominant DMG rider, Josh Hayes, is known for his limited use of electronics. And top MotoGP riders are currently using less and less traction control. With the torque smoothing achieved by throttle-by-wire, top riders find manual control's wider choices enable them to go faster. Electronics are retained as a safety net against big mistakes.

Yet pressure to ban or restrict technology continues.

Just as more rules are unlikely to make an inexperienced crew chief effective, so rev limits, spec ECUs and spec software may not make production-based engines the equal of engines designed for racing.

For example, where production engines have little vents above their main bearings, intended to reduce losses from the back-and-forth pumping of crankcase air, race engines have:

1. For in-line engines, a crankcase evacuation pump, which greatly reduces pumping loss by reducing the density of crankcase air to a low value.

2. For V-engines, crank chambers that are sealed off from each other, which means that each crankpin pair of pistons just move the crankcase air to and fro beneath them with little compression or expansion (effectively none in a 90-degree example), minimising loss.

Production engines must be strictly cost-accounted to hit price-point. This means that when Superbike engines reach the vicinity of 15,000rpm, their oil systems, bearings, and structure are near their limit. Some margin of durability is necessary to compensate for predictable owner abuse, but economic limits are strict. Production engines have low-production-cost die-cast cases, which are vulnerable to cracking. Race engine

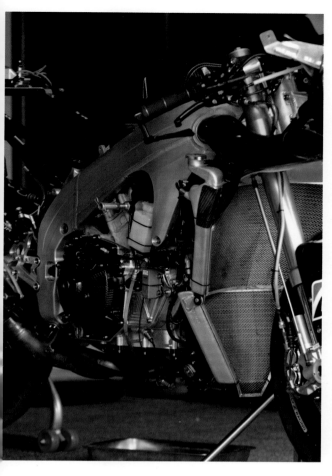

within reach. Another result of no-variables racing is that at the flag, the race becomes a procession in order of rider lap time. What passes for surprise in such controlled racing is the fading of early leaders on poor chassis set-ups. That may have to be good enough.

Dani Pedrosa once commented on the changes that resulted from spec tyres, the use of tyre warmers and faster-warming rubber. Together, he noted, they eliminated much of the old push-and-shove – the variability we used to see in the early laps, as riders employed their own strategies for tyre warm-up and for managing their fading tyres in the final laps. These tyre strategies were the source of a lot of passing.

Erratic cold tyre performance in early laps has caused many crashes since slicks were introduced in 1974, which is why tyre warmers were introduced in 1987. Yet we hear insistent calls to put the excitement back into racing. Can clever rules separate excitement from injury?

Racing's admired Masters of the Game – Ecclestone for F1 and the France family for NASCAR – are all billionaires. If racing so desperately needs to be made cheaper, how does it afford such expensive management?

No one in power wants to share power, but at present Honda and Dorna are deadlocked, neither sure they can get what they want without the presence of the other. Maybe no basic decision will be made. Maybe MotoGP will muddle on as it is – an endless struggle between what racing used to be and what businessmen insist it must become.

Far left: The 2012 championship winning Aprilia RSV4 Superbike was based on a production model. The ART CRT bike, in turn, was a production racer based on the Superbike.

Left: Aprilia's World Superbike coffers were supplemented by the sale of CRT machines.

Below: Moto3 was successful, relying mainly on over-the-counter production racing engines. Is this the way forward for MotoGP?

Photos: Gold & Goose

cases may be milled from solid (Yamaha M1) or sand-cast (Ducati, Honda). Billet or sand-cast cases can be heat treated to increase strength, but die-castings usually cannot be.

Race engines benefit from intensive combustion chamber development, the goal of which is to combine torque-boosting high compression ratio with fast, efficient combustion. Private team skills include mainly changing engines, wheels and brake pads, but do not include research.

Other goals of race engine development are friction reduction and improved sealing. Japanese engine development in recent years is said to have gained more from friction research than from traditional tuning methods. Piston-ring sealing is invisible, difficult to achieve, but essential.

The main-bearing bores of production engines are difficult to keep round, but unless they are, the small clearances necessary to allow the use of friction-saving low-viscosity oils cannot be employed. Cooling adequate for production engines in road use may not prevent chronic valve seat distortion and leakage in racing service.

The crankcase flexure of production in-line engines is well known from such symptoms as case bolt breakage, frettage between castings and chronic gasket leakage. Honda adopted V4 architecture in the 1980s as a result.

It is assumed that pneumatic valve springs are useful only to reach extreme rpm, but as Honda's Nakamoto has said in the past, pneumatics are useful also at lower rpm – in making valve trains follow the radical cam shapes that best combine high power and wide torque range. This allows a pneumatic-spring engine to breathe more deeply than a metal-spring engine – even at 'only' 15,500.

Now let's consider the Moto3 model – approved production racers, or approved engines in artisan chassis. For the first case, there are the Aprilia ARTs, the Honda MotoGP production racer said to be coming in 2014 and possibly the prototype Suzuki MotoGP bike seen earlier in 2012. This could work, but only if enough makers participate. If they don't, one maker will likely prevail, as Yamaha did in F750, leading to the abandonment of that class. The use of artisan chassis compels each team to do the intensive engineering required to achieve a handling baseline – something that Colin Edwards's CRT team were unable to accomplish in 16 races.

It is fashionable for rules to 'homogenise' racing by taking more and more variables off the table. This is postulated to cut costs, and attract more and smaller teams who see success

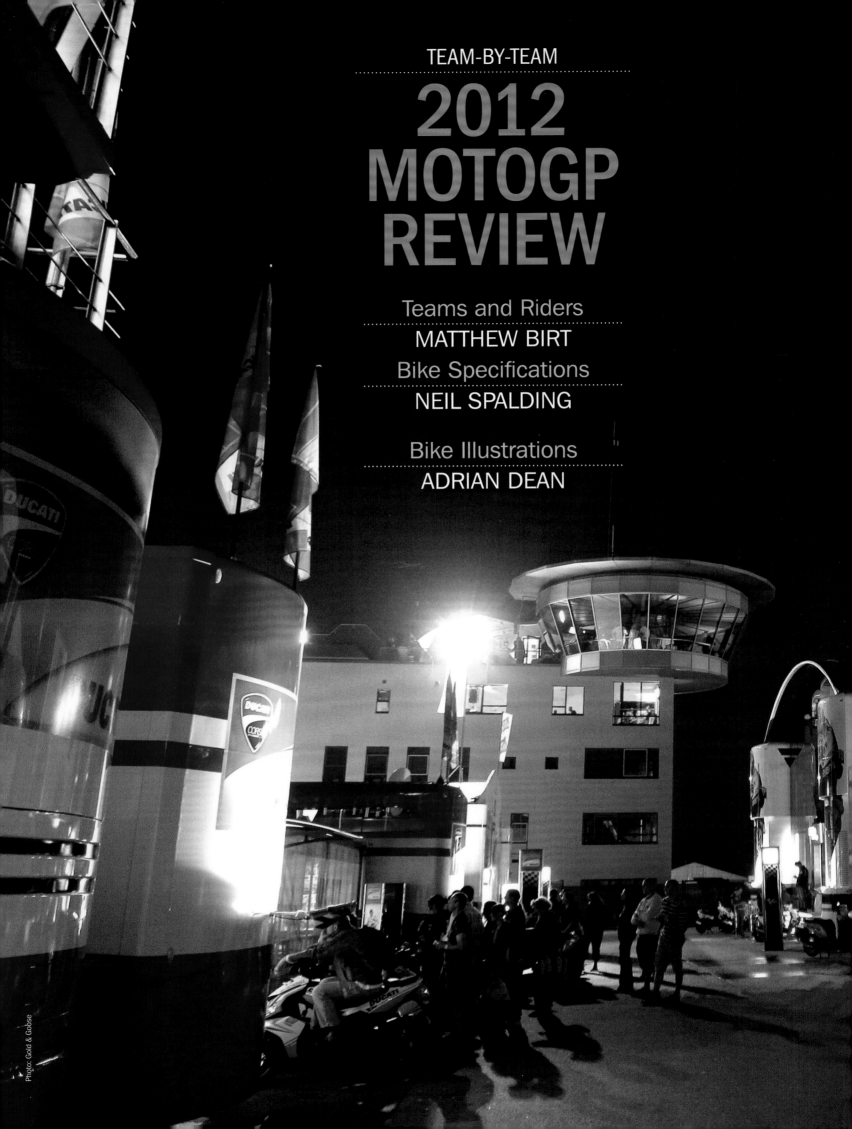

TEAM-BY-TEAM

2012 MOTOGP REVIEW

Teams and Riders
MATTHEW BIRT

Bike Specifications
NEIL SPALDING

Bike Illustrations
ADRIAN DEAN

REPSOL HONDA TEAM

TEAM STAFF

Shuhei NAKAMOTO: HRC Executive Vice-President
Shinichi KOKUBU: Technical Director
Hideki IWANO: Director, Assistant to Team Principal
Livio SUPPO: HRC Communications and Marketing
Director
Roger VAN DER BORGHT: Co-ordinator
Tetsuhiro KUWATA: Electronics Engineer
Toshio ISHIKURA: Electronics Engineer
Katsura SHIBASAKI: Spare Parts Control
Rhys EDWARDS: Communication & Marketing Manager

DANI PEDROSA PIT CREW

Mike LEITNER: Chief Engineer
Alberto PUIG: Advisor
Christophe LEONCE: Chief Mechanic
Mechanics
Mark BARNETT: Engine Technician
Emanuel BUCHNER, Masashi OGO, John EYRE
Jose Manuel ALLENDE: Data Analyst
Ramon AURIN: Data Engineer
Takeo YOKOYAMA: HRC Engineer

CASEY STONER PIT CREW

Cristian GABARRINI: Chief Engineer
Bruno LEONI: Chief Mechanic
Mechanics
Roberto CLERICI, Andrea BRUNETTI, Lorenzo GAGNI
Filippo BRUNETTI
Carlo LUZZI: Electronics Engineer
Giulio NAVA: Data Analyst
Norihisa MATSUURO: Technical Staff

DANI PEDROSA
Born: 29 September, 1985 – Sabadell, Spain
GP Starts: 194 (116 MotoGP, 32 250cc, 46 125cc)
GP Wins: 45 (22 MotoGP, 15 250cc, 8 125cc)
World Championships: 3 (2 250cc, 1 125cc)

CASEY STONER
Born: 16 October, 1985 – Southport, Australia
GP Starts: 176 (115 MotoGP, 31 250cc, 30 125cc)
GP Wins: 45 (38 MotoGP, 5 250cc, 2 125cc)
World Championships: 2 MotoGP

AFTER they had dominated the final 800cc world championship in 2011, the smart money was on Repsol Honda to repeat the feat in the first 1000cc campaign. In Casey Stoner and Dani Pedrosa, it boasted arguably the fastest and most feared duo on the grid, HRC having reverted to a two-rider effort after releasing Andrea Dovizioso at the end of 2011.

The team was backed by Repsol once again, and the success of 2011, which was Honda's first world championship triumph since 2006, saw the senior management remain in place.

Shuhei Nakamoto continued in his role as HRC Executive Vice-President, while responsibility for the Japanese factory's new 1000cc prototype RC213V fell to Shinichi Kokubu.

Kokubu saw his steed win 12 races, but it was a tough season, as he and his engineering group were thrown a curve ball by new softer-compound front and rear Bridgestone tyres that left Stoner and Pedrosa battling a chronic chatter issue for most of the season. The problem became so severe that HRC dramatically advanced its 2013 RC213V project, a brand-new bike being ridden by Pedrosa from the Laguna Seca race onwards.

HONDA RC212V

Sponsors and Technical Suppliers: Repsol • One HEART • Gas • AON • Bridgestone • NGK Spark Plugs • Puma • RK Chains • Shindengen • Snap-on • Termignoni • Yutaka

Engine: 1000cc, 76-degree V4, 360-degree crank (tbc), PVRS. *Power:* More than 260ps

Ancillaries: HRC electronics, ride-by-wire throttle and fuel injection system with torducter; NGK sparking plugs

Lubrication: Repsol *Fuel:* 21 litres

Transmission: Gear primary drive, multi-plate dry slipper clutch, six-speed seamless-shift cassette-style gearbox; RK chain

Suspension: Front, Öhlins TRSP25 48mm 'Through Rod' forks • Rear, TRSP44 gas shock with linkage

Wheels: Front, 16.5in Marchesini • Rear, 16.5in Marchesini *Tyres:* Bridgestone

Brakes: Front, Brembo carbon-carbon 320mm • Rear, Yutaka steel 218mm

JONATHAN REA
Born: 2 February, 1987 – Larne, Northern Ireland
GP Starts: 2 MotoGP

Livio Suppo, a key element in tempting Casey Stoner away from Ducati at the end of 2010, also continued in his role as communications and marketing director.

Stoner continued to work with the crew that had followed him from Ducati, with Cristian Gabbarini chief engineer. Carlo Luzzi and Giulio Nava took responsibility for electronics and data respectively, while Bruno Leoni, Roberto Clerici, Andrea Brunetti, Lorenzo Gagni and Filippo Brunetti continued as the pit crew.

Stoner's charge to ten victories and the final 800cc title in his first year with Honda meant he started the year as a hot favourite to retain the crown. The season began well with wins at Jerez and Estoril before he stunned the paddock at Le Mans with a bombshell announcement. He had deflected speculation about imminent retirement at Jerez and Estoril, and when he arrived at the pre-event press conference in Le Mans, only those in his inner circle were aware of the gravity of the news he was about to break.

He announced that 2012 would be his last season. He had fallen out of love with racing and wanted to spend more time at home in Australia with his young family; his new daughter, Alessandra, had been born ahead of the first race.

That threw HRC's future plans into turmoil. Nakamoto and Suppo had been negotiating a new contract with Stoner, which would have made him the highest-paid employee in Honda history. Figures bandied around suggested £500,000 a race.

Honda's dream line-up for 2013 was supposed to retain Stoner and promote Spanish starlet Marc Marquez from the Moto2 class. Patience with Pedrosa's continued failure to deliver a world title appeared finally to have snapped, and Stoner's retirement decision saw management launch a raid on Yamaha for Jorge Lorenzo.

Honda were willing to cut Pedrosa adrift, and he did briefly talk with Yamaha, but after Lorenzo rebuffed Honda's approach, Pedrosa's new two-year deal was confirmed on the eve of the Italian Grand Prix in mid-July. Marquez's move was announced at the same time and, after much deliberation, it was confirmed that he would work with the majority of Stoner's crew.

But desperate to give Marquez the best possible chance to adapt quickly, HRC allowed him to bring crew chief Santi Hernandez and one mechanic from his Moto2 squad. Gabbarini would be retained to work above Hernandez in an advisory capacity, while Gagni was the only one of Stoner's crew to make way.

Stoner's hopes of bowing out of MotoGP as world champion ended in cruel and painful fashion in Indianapolis with a vicious high-side in qualifying that seriously damaged ligaments in his right ankle. Somehow he rode to a heroic fourth just 24 hours later and intended to race on, only to be told on his arrival in Brno that the injury was so serious he needed im-

mediate surgery to prevent potentially life-changing damage.

He missed three races, returning at Motegi with a low-key fifth. Then he took third in treacherous conditions at Sepang, before marking his farewell appearance in Australia with a commanding win, a record sixth in a row at Phillip Island.

The last act from arguably the fastest and one of the most outspoken riders in history saw him bow out with a final farewell rostrum in Valencia.

Honda drafted in British rider Jonathan Rea for Misano and Aragon, giving the team the chance to assess his future MotoGP potential. He finished a respectable eighth at Misano and seventh at Aragon, but despite HRC recommending him for the Gresini Honda ride, the door to MotoGP remained shut.

Pedrosa enjoyed his best ever season in MotoGP, but significantly the title eluded him once again.

His crew chief remained Mike Leitner, while Alberto Puig was listed as an advisor. The Spaniard's influence though continued in all aspects of Pedrosa's life, including contract negotiations, and he was a constant presence in technical debriefs.

Pedrosa's crew also remained largely the same, with Jose Manuel Allende the electronics engineer and Christophe Leonce, Emanuel Buchner, Masahi Ogo, Mark Barnett and John Eyre as mechanics. The only addition was Ramon Aurin as data engineer, whose expertise was retained by Honda after he had been Dovizioso's crew chief.

He didn't win until the eighth round in Germany, but that provided a launch pad to the most devastating spell in his premier-class career. He took five wins in six races, but a start-line fiasco in Misano seriously undermined his title challenge when he was taken out on lap one, having been relegated from pole to the back of the grid.

He started the penultimate race in Australia trailing Lorenzo by 23 points, but his valiant second-half surge ended when he crashed out of the lead on the second lap, though his final tally of seven victories was still a personal best.

Above: HRC's Shuhei Nakamoto called the shots.

Top: Out on their own, race winner Pedrosa leads Stoner at the German GP.

Above far left: Casey Stoner, faster than ever, could not be persuaded to stay.

Above left: Livio Suppo.

Left: Cristian Gabarrini, Stoner's crew chief.

Below left: Technical director Shinichi Kokubu.

Below: Alberto Puig was 'advisor' to Pedrosa's team.
Photos: Gold & Goose

YAMAHA TEAM

TEAM STAFF

Kouichi TSUJI: MotoGP Group Leader

Lin JARVIS: Managing Director, Yamaha Motor Racing

Massimo MEREGALLI: Team Director

Wilco ZEELENBERG: Team Manager

William FAVERO: Communications Manager

Matteo VITELLO: Race Events Co-ordinator

Gavin MATHESON: Press Officer

Mark CANELLA:Team Co-ordinator

Takhiro SUZUKI: Parts Co-ordinator

JORGE LORENZO PIT CREW

Ramon FORCADA: Crew Chief

Mechanics

Walter CRIPPA, Javier ULLATE, Valentino NEGRI

Juan Llansa HERNANDEZ

Takashi MORIYAMA: Yamaha Engineer

Davide MARELLI: Data Engineer

BEN SPIES PIT CREW

Tom HOUSEWORTH: Crew Chief

Mechanics

Gregory WOOD, Jurij PELLEGRINI, Ian GILPIN

Olivier BOUTRON

Hiroya ATSUMI: Yamaha Engineer

Erkki SIUKOLA: Data Engineer

JORGE LORENZO

Born: 4 May, 1987 – Palma de Mallorca, Spain

GP Starts: 175 (81 MotoGP, 48 250cc, 46 125cc)

GP Wins: 45 (24 MotoGP, 17 250cc, 4 125cc)

World Championships: 3 (1 MotoGP, 2 250cc)

BEN SPIES

Born: 11 July, 1984 – Memphis, Tennessee, USA

GP Starts: 53 MotoGP

MotoGP Wins: 1

World Championships: 1 World Superbike

YAMAHA'S Milan-based factory MotoGP squad re-established itself as the powerhouse of the four-stroke MotoGP era. Since MotoGP went exclusively four-stroke in 2003, Yamaha had prevailed five times – twice with 990s and three years in a row in the 800cc era between 2008 and 2010, when the Japanese factory boasted an enviable line-up of Valentino Rossi and Jorge Lorenzo.

The 2012 season proved what Yamaha had believed all along – that success wasn't dependant on the magic of Rossi.

Senior management remained unchanged, with Masahiko Nakajima continuing as General Manager Motorsports Division Yamaha Motor Company. Shigeto Kitagawa also continued in the role of President Yamaha Motor Racing.

Both were infrequent visitors to the paddock, and the public face of Yamaha's hierarchy remained the long-serving Lin Jarvis, under the title of Managing Director Yamaha Motor Racing. But his long-running quest to find a title sponsor to replace Fiat continued and, as in 2011, Yamaha's factory team raced in corporate colours.

Technical responsibility fell once again to MotoGP Group Leader Kouichi Tsuji.

Massimo Meregalli continued as team director,

YAMAHA M1

Sponsors and Technical Suppliers: Eneos • Semakin Di Depan • Yamalube • Pizzoli • BM Group • Iveco • Akrapovic • Beta • Alpinestars • Exedy • NGK Spark Plugs • DID • 2D • Magnetti Marelli • BMC • MFR • Bridgestone

Engine: 1000cc, across-the-frame in-line 4; reverse-rotating cross-plane crankshaft, DOHC, 4 valves per cylinder, Pneumatic Valve Return System
    Power: Around 250bhp at approx 16,000rpm

Ancillaries: Magneti Marelli electronics, NGK sparking plugs, full electronic ride-by-wire   *Lubrication:* Yamalube   *Fuel:* 21 litres

Transmission: Gear primary drive, multi-plate dry slipper clutch, six-speed constant-mesh floating-dog-ring cassette-style gearbox; DID chain

Suspension: Front, Öhlins TRSP25 48mm 'Through Rod' forks • Rear, Öhlins TRSP44 shock with linkage

Wheels: Front, 16.5in Marchesini • Rear, 16.5in Marchesini   *Tyres:* Bridgestone

Brakes: Front, Brembo carbon-carbon 320mm • Rear, Yamaha steel

KATSUYUKI NAGASUGA

Born: 9 August, 1981 – Shizuoka, Japan

GP Starts: 5 (2 MotoGP, 3 250cc)

also operating as team manager to Ben Spies, the Texan in his second year in the official factory team.

Reporting to Meregalli was team manager Wilco Zeelenberg, but in truth he operated almost exclusively with Lorenzo.

Lorenzo's crew remained unchanged and he continued a successful relationship with experienced crew chief Ramon Forcada, who had worked with Lorenzo since he moved to Yamaha in 2008.

Davide Marelli, Javier Ullate, Walter Crippa, Valentino Negri and Juan Llansa Hernandez all stayed in an unchanged crew line-up. Together they formed a powerful group, and Lorenzo put on an exhibition of consistency and speed seldom witnessed in any era. Five wins in the opening nine races, including three on the bounce in Le Mans, Catalunya and Silverstone, put the Spaniard in the pound seats at the mid-point of the season.

He would only win once again, however – in Misano to punish Dani Pedrosa's catastrophic early exit to the maximum. But fundamental to his success was his unrivalled consistency. In the 17 races he finished, never was he lower than second and had it not been for a barmy braking move by Bautista at Assen and his single error at Valencia, Lorenzo's season would have been near on perfection.

His consistency piled pressure on his rivals, who knew they could ill afford to make a mistake. When it got to the stage where Pedrosa was in 'win-it or bin-it' mode to prolong the title race, one mistake would hand Lorenzo the crown.

Lorenzo's unbridled joy was in stark contrast to the thoroughly miserable season experienced by Spies. The 2009 World Superbike champion was again working with long-term crew chief Tom Houseworth. Erkki Suikola, Gregory Wood, Jurij Pellegrini, Ian Gilpin and Olivier Boutron were all kept on as well. A combination of wretched luck and Spies's own error-riddled riding saw the season in which many expected that he wouldd be a serious challenger turn into an unmitigated disaster.

It wasn't until round six at Silverstone that he broke into the top six. A badly chunked Bridgestone rear tyre ended his podium hopes in Assen, however, and food poisoning left him languishing outside of the top ten in Mugello.

That wasn't the worst of it, though. A broken subframe spoiled Qatar, a swing-arm link failed in Laguna Seca and then his YZR-M1 suffered a terminal and spectacular engine blow-up in Indianapolis.

A conservative fifth as he tried to rebuild his shattered morale in Aragon would be his last finish as a factory Yamaha rider. Overheating front brake discs in Japan caused an early crash and when he tumbled out again in a storm-lashed Sepang race, he suffered serious ligament damage in his right shoulder that would rule him out for up to three months.

Japanese test rider rider Katsuyuki Nakasuga replaced him at Valencia for an impressive second.

Yamaha didn't only hog the on-track headlines.

At the start of the season, it would have seemed preposterous to contemplate Rossi ever returning. Yamaha's intention was to retain Lorenzo and Spies, with absolute priority given to Lorenzo's contract renewal once it became apparent that 2012 would be Stoner's last and an inevitable rival bid would be launched by HRC.

Lorenzo penned a new two-year deal with Yamaha that was announced in the build-up to the British Grand Prix, and at that stage he had no inkling of the bombshell that would follow.

First, he took the drastic action of ending his relationship with manager Marcos Hirsch amid speculation that he had not been informed about a lucrative counter-offer to join Repsol Honda.

Would Lorenzo also have been so keen to sign had he known that Rossi was emerging as a shock candidate to return?

Despite his early-season woes, Yamaha was still willing to throw Spies a lifeline, and it wasn't until Mugello that Lorenzo was informed of the possibility of Rossi's return. Spies pre-empted the formal announcement when he declared ahead of the Laguna Seca race that he would relinquish his YZR-M1 berth, citing "a litany of reasons" that he didn't divulge.

The return of the prodigal son was confirmed during

the August summer sojourn, while Spies publicly stated in Indianapolis that if he would be racing in 2013, it would be in World Superbikes and not MotoGP. He signed a pre-contract to partner Marco Melandri in a factory-backed BMW World Superbike squad and subsequently was linked with Gresini Honda.

Then the American had a sudden and dramatic change of heart, choosing the least likely option when he signed to partner Iannone in Ducati's satellite squad. Houseworth and Gilpin were expected to move with him.

MONSTER YAMAHA TECH 3

TEAM STAFF

Hervé PONCHARAL: Team Manager

Gérard VALLEE: Team Co-ordinator

Laurence LASSERRE: Team Assistant

Eric REBMANN: Parts Manager

Benjamin BOUVIER: Fuel/Tyres

Milena KOERNER: Press and Communications

ANDREA DOVIZIOSO PIT CREW

Guy COULON: Crew Chief

Mechanics

Laurent DUCLOYER, Jerôme PONCHARAL

Josian RUSTIQUE

Andrew GRIFFITH: Telemetry

Youichi NAKAMAYA: Yamaha Motor Company Engineer

CAL CRUTCHLOW PIT CREW

Daniele ROMAGNOLI: Crew Chief

Mechanics

Steve BLACKBURN, Julien LAJUNIE, Sebastien LETORT

Nicolas GOYON: Telemetry

Masahiko IWATA: Yamaha Motor Company Engineer

ANDREA DOVIZIOSO
Born: 23 March, 1986 – Forli, Italy
GP Starts: 186 (88 MotoGP, 49 250cc, 49 125cc)
GP Wins: 10 (1 MotoGP, 4 250cc, 5 125cc)
World Championships: 1 125cc

CAL CRUTCHLOW
Born: 29 October, 1985 – Coventry, England
GP Starts: 34 MotoGP,
World Championships: 1 World Superbike

THE French-based Monster Yamaha Tech 3 Yamaha squad entered its second decade in MotoGP with confidence and optimism sky high. Highly-respected team boss Hervé Poncharal declared his 2012 line-up of Andrea Dovizioso and Cal Crutchlow as the strongest in the team's distinguished history.

Not even his wildest dreams could he have predicted such a successful campaign, which saw Tech 3 shatter its podium record in MotoGP.

A vital element of success came with Italian Dovizioso. Surplus to requirements at Repsol Honda, he brought a wealth of experience to fill the void left by Colin Edwards, released after a four-year spell.

Initially, Dovizioso had flirted with the idea of taking his own crew chief into the Tech 3 operation, Tom O'Kane (ex-Team Roberts and Suzuki) being a prime candidate. However, he started winter testing under the stewardship of Tech 3 co-owner and technical mastermind Guy Coulon. The Frenchman had originally planned to concentrate on the team's Moto2 project, while also undertaking a potential future chassis venture for a CRT machine.

Dovizioso quickly came to realise that Coulon's wealth of Yamaha experience would be invaluable, and eventually he opted to inherit all of Edwards's technical staff, which included telemetry specialist

YAMAHA M1 YZR

Sponsors and Technical Suppliers: DeWalt • Facom • Motul • Leo Vince • Bridgestone • Capit Performance • Caffitaly • Rancilio • LightTech • Rochet • Antonio Lupi
Stanley • Smeg • Roc de Calon • Rudy Project

Engine: 1000cc, across-the-frame in-line 4; reverse-rotating cross-plane crankshaft, DOHC, 4 valves per cylinder, Pneumatic Valve Return System
  Power: Around 250bhp at approx 16,000rpm

Ancillaries: Magneti Marelli electronics, NGK sparking plugs, full electronic ride-by-wire *Lubrication:* Yamalube *Fuel:* 21 litres

Transmission: Gear primary drive, multi-plate dry slipper clutch, six-speed constant-mesh floating-dog-ring cassette-style gearbox; DID chain

Suspension: Front, Öhlins TTxTR25 48mm forks • Rear, Öhlins TRSP44 shock with linkage

Wheels: Front, 16.5in Marchesini • Rear, 16.5in Marchesini *Tyres:* Bridgestone • *Brakes:* Front, Brembo carbon-carbon 320mm • Rear, Yamaha steel

Andrew Griffith, Laurent Ducloyer, Jerômé Poncharal and Josian Rustique.

The Italian would become the most successful rider in Tech 3 history in a season of trademark consistency. He finished all 18 races and was only outside of the top five on four occasions. His first podium was at round five, followed by a mid-season purple patch with successive third places in Assen, Sachsenring and Mugello. He was on the podium twice more and started from the front row three times.

Dovi was by head and shoulders the best non-factory rider in 2012, but his tenure at Yamaha would be brief. Having shunned a factory-backed RC213V at LCR Honda, he made it abundantly clear he meant to impress Yamaha sufficiently to get his factory rider status restored in 2013.

He kept his side of the bargain and was only beaten once all season, by factory rider Spies at the British Grand Prix, where he crashed, but remounted. He was trumped by an old ace in the pack, however, when Yamaha announced they had re-signed Valentino Rossi. Somewhat bitter and intent on obtaining factory support, Dovisioso became the latest high-profile rider to stake his reputation on taming Ducati's fearsome Desmosedici.

Dovizioso was the higher ranked Tech 3 rider with the most podium finishes, but it would be foolish to underestimate the value Crutchlow gave to Tech 3. The switch to the more forgiving 1000cc prototypes and the introduction of softer-compound Bridgestone tyres galvanised the Brit, who completed a remarkable turn-around in his fortune. Even he admitted that his rookie campaign in 2011 had fallen somewhat short, yet he built on the confidence gained with an inspired performance in winter testing to emerge as a regular podium threat.

Continuity was crucial. Crutchlow's crew remained unchanged from 2011. Lorenzo's former factory Yamaha boss, Daniele Romagnoli, was crew chief, heading a close-knit crew that included Steve Blackburn, Julien Lajunie, Sebastien Letort and telemetry engineer Nicolas Goyon.

Crutchlow and Dovizioso battling closely in a respectful inter-team tussle was a frequent sight in 2012. In eight races, they finished consecutively, with Crutchlow one of the year's outstanding exponents of the flat-out qualifying lap.

Seven times he was on the front row, but it wasn't until Brno that he became the first British rider in 12 years to finish on a premier-class podium.

The final part of the season was punctuated with flashes of brilliance, bad luck and costly blunders. He fell out of podium contention in Misano and Malaysia's monsoon, but redeemed himself with a brilliant third in Australia. Luck conspired against him in Japan, where his YZR-M1 ran out of fuel on the last lap while dicing with Bautista for third.

He had put his home fans through the mill again after his British Grand Prix was marred by injury. He had broken and dislocated his left ankle in a heavy crash in final practice, but had bounced back from 20th on the grid after missing qualifying to claim a heroic sixth.

Crutchlow's rise to prominence made him a wanted man for 2013. Ducati dominated the early scrabble for his signature, but dithered when it came to the crunch, leaving him to showcase his fondness for speaking his mind. He branded Ducati "liars" as the Bologna factory's interest switched to Andrea Dovizioso, and penned a new one-year deal with Tech 3 at Brno.

Crutchlow will be one half of an all-British Tech 3 line-up in 2013, compatriot Bradley Smith being promoted from the Tech 3 Moto2 squad as part of a multi-year agreement initially signed in September, 2011. Ever since, Smith has been the subject of a malicious whispering campaign about whether his performances merited such a prized seat in MotoGP. He will work with Coulon and all of Dovizioso's pit staff.

Above: Crutchlow with crew chief Romagnoli and the gang.

Above left: Andrea Dovizioso kept his side of the bargain, and finished every race.

Left: Team principal Hervé Poncharal.

Left: Guy Coulon changed plans to stay with Dovi.

Below: Crutchlow's gritty sixth at Silverstone was one of many strong rides in his second season.

Photos: Gold & Goose

DUCATI MARLBORO TEAM

TEAM STAFF

Filippo PREZIOSI: Ducati General & Technical Director
Alessandro CICOGNANI: MotoGP Project Director
Vittoriano GUARESCHI: Team Manager
Fabiano STERLACCHINI: Track Technical Co-ordinator
Massimo BARTOLINI: Track Performance Advisor
Francesco RAPISARDA: Communications Director
Federica DE ZOTTIS: Press Manager
Chris JONNUM: Press Officer
Amedeo COSTA: Team Co-ordinator
Paola BRAIATO: Administration, Logistics & Hospitality
Mauro GRASSILLI: Sponsor Account
Alfredo DENTE: Team Physiotherapist
Davide BARALDINI: Warehouse and Components

VALENTINO ROSSI PIT CREW

Jeremy BURGESS: Crew Chief
Matteo FLAMIGNI: Track Engineer
Mechanics
Alex BRIGGS, Bernard ANSIU, Brent STEVENS,
Gary COLEMAN, Mark ELDER
Gabriele CONTI: Electronics Engineer
Roberto BRIVIO: Crew Co-ordinator

NICKY HAYDEN PIT CREW

Juan MARTINEZ: Crew Chief
Roberto BONAZZI: Track Engineer
Davide MANFREDI: Chief Mechanic
Mechanics
Massimo MIRANO, Pedro Calvet CARALT,
Lorenzo CANESTRARI, Luca ROMANO
Jose Manuel CASEAUX: Electronics Engineer
Emanuele MAZZINI: Crew Co-ordinator

VALENTINO ROSSI
Born: 16 February, 1979 – Urbino, Italy
GP Starts: 276 (216 MotoGP/500cc, 30 250cc, 30 125cc)
GP Wins: 105 (79 MotoGP/500cc, 14 250cc, 12 125cc)
World Championships: 9 (6 MotoGP, 1 500cc, 1 250cc, 1 125cc)

NICKY HAYDEN
Born: 30 July, 1981 – Owensboro, Kentucky, USA
GP Starts: 167 MotoGP
GP Wins: 3 MotoGP
World Championships: 1 MotoGP

THE last time a new capacity limit was introduced in the premier class in 2007, Ducati blitzed its Japanese opposition to dominate the inaugural 800cc world championship. A repeat of that feat was never remotely close, however, as the Bologna factory toiled through another success-starved campaign. A season of major disappointment, frustration and upheaval culminated in the end of a dream marriage of two Italian icons, as Valentino Rossi decided to switch back to Yamaha.

Ducati's factory team was in its tenth season, in the striking livery of title sponsors Marlboro. The world-renowned Phillip Morris brand was no longer allowed to have its named emblazoned on the Desmosedici bodywork, though.

Filippo Preziosi remained the figurehead as general and technical director, while Gabriele del Torchio remained as CEO and Claudio Domenicali as general manager. At the end of the season, however, Preziosi was relieved of his position.

Senior management appearances were few and far between, with MotoGP project director Alessandro Cicognani and team manager Vittoriano Guareschi charged with the on-site running of the squad.

Fabiano Sterlacchini, no stranger to the Ducati set-up after a long history with the satellite Pramac

DUCATI Desmosedici GP12

Sponsors and Technical Suppliers: Philip Morris (Marlboro) • TIM (Telecom Italia) • Generali Insurance • Enel • Riello • Shell Advance • Bridgestone • Diesel • Acer
Bosch • Guabello • Inver • Lampo • Puma • Sandisk • Capit • CM Composit • DID Chain • Fiamm Batteries • Magneti Marelli
NGK Spark Plugs • SKF Bearings • Termignoni Exhausts • Mechanix

Engine: 1000cc, 90-degree V4; irregular-fire crank, DOHC, 4 valves per cylinder, Desmodromic valve gear, variable-length inlet tracts
   Power: Around 255bhp, revs up to 17,800rpm

Ancillaries: Magneti Marelli electronics, NGK sparking plugs, full electronic ride-by-wire *Lubrication:* Shell Advance *Fuel:* 21 litres

Transmission: Cassette Xtrac seamless-shift gearbox

Suspension: Front, Öhlins TRSP25 48mm 'Through Rod' forks • Rear, Öhlins TRSP44 shock with linkage

Wheels: Front, 16.5in Marchesini • Rear, 16.5in Marchesini *Tyres:* Bridgestone *Brakes:* Front, Brembo carbon-carbon 320mm • Rear, steel 200mm

squad, took up a new role of track technical co-ordinator, and a new position of track performance advisor was filled by Massimo Bartolini. There was certainly no lack of personnel and no lack of experience, but Ducati's 2012 season will be instantly forgettable, despite the promise of future investment and influence from German car giant Audi.

The multi-million-pound acquisition of Ducati Motor Holding by Audi AG was completed in July, and despite speculation of a major management reshuffle, del Torchio and Domenicali were both appointed to a new board of directors, which included Audi CEO Rupert Stadler and senior figures Horst Glaser and Axel Strotbek.

Audi's involvement, though, failed to sway Rossi into prolonging his agony, in spite of personal track visits by Audi bosses Wolfgang Durheimer and Stadler to Mugello and the Sachsenring. Audi also offered Rossi the pick of a drive in its extensive four-wheeled motorsport portfolio when he retired, but he was more curious to know whether he still had the talent and speed to fight with the younger generation in MotoGP.

Less of a surprise was the fact that Rossi's long-serving and loyal technical crew, who had moved from Honda to Yamaha and then to Ducati, were heading back to old pastures, too. They were led by hugely experienced Aussie Jerry Burgess. Matteo Flamigni was Rossi's track engineer, while Gabriele Conti was the electronics engineer again, the lone survivor of a mass exodus when Stoner departed.

Alex Briggs, Bernard Ansiau, Brent Stephens, Gary Coleman and Mark Elder were Rossi's mechanics and Roberto Brivio the crew co-ordinator. All but Conti, Elder and Brivio would go to Yamaha.

Rossi and his crew's reputation took another battering in 2012 as he struggled to just two podium finishes He made only three other visits to the top six and admitted that his biggest frustration had been that understeer and power delivery issues, which had handicapped him at the start of his tenure, were still the limiting problems when he left.

New parts simply weren't delivered quickly enough in the eyes of Rossi, and there was a surprise revelation in the middle of the season when it became apparent that Preziosi had sought the assistance of Yamaha's retired engineering guru and figurehead, Masao Furusawa. The much-lauded Japanese engineer had politely declined a permanent or consultancy role.

Three podiums in 35 races for a rider of Rossi's calibre highlighted Ducati's hard times. It was no less of a struggle on the opposite side of the garage for the popular Nicky Hayden. For the first time in his MotoGP career, the American didn't claim a single podium finish in 2012, with a best of fourth at rain-soaked Sepang.

Hayden's crew was led once again by Juan Martinez, and his track engineer was Roberto Bonazzi. Jose Manuel Caseaux was the electronics engineer, while Davide Manfredi, Massimo Mirano, Pedro Calvet Caralt, Lorenzo Canestrari and Luca Romano were his mechanics.

Earlier, Hayden's future at Ducati had been uncertain. The Bologna factory had made no secret of its desire to retain Rossi and negotiated at length with British rider Cal Crutchlow before turning to the experience of Andrea Dovizioso when it became obvious that Rossi was abandoning ship, but Hayden's new one-year extension had already been confirmed at that stage.

The second half of his season was injury ravaged. He was ruled out of his home race in Indianapolis after a sickening qualifying high-side that broke bones in his right hand. He missed the race at Brno and then took a reluctant role in one of the season's most horrifying crashes in Aragon, where he somersaulted a trackside advertising barrier that he'd slammed into head-on at over 40mph.

Above: Ducati Corse CEO Claudio Domenicali and team manager Vito Guareschi.

Top left: Rossi took advantage of poor weather at Le Mans for the first of two rostrums.

Left: Project director Alessandro Cicognani.

Centre left: Engineering mastermind Filippo Preziosi, relieved of his duties at the end of the season after two downbeat years.

Left: Hayden's crew chief Juan Martinez.

Below left: Jerry Burgess, Rossi's long-serving crew chief.

Below: No podium in a tough year for loyal and dedicated Nicky Hayden.
Photos: Gold & Goose

HONDA LCR

TEAM STAFF

Lucio CECCHINELLO: Team Owner and Manager
Martine FELLONI: Administration and Legal
Elisa PAVAN: Press Officer

STEFAN BRADL PIT CREW

Christophe BOURGIGNON: Chief Engineer
Mechanics
Joan CASAS, Xavier CASANOVAS
Chris RICHARDSON
Brian HARDEN: Telemetry
Makoto NAGAYAMA/Yuki KIKUCHI: HRC engineer
Ugo GELMI: Tyres
Masao AZUMA: Bridgestone Technician
Paul TREVATHAN: Öhlins Technician

STEFAN BRADL

Born: 29 November, 1989 – Augsberg, Germany

GP Starts: 105 (18 MotoGP, 33 Moto2, 54 125cc)

GP Wins: 7 (5 Moto2, 2 125cc)

World Championships: 1 Moto2

NO team enjoyed such a dramatic transformation in fortunes as Lucio Cecchinello's highly respected satellite Honda operation in 2012. Following a year riddled with dire results and tension with Toni Elias, LCR rose like a phoenix with reigning Moto2 world champion Stefan Bradl.

He had only been signed after impressing in an audition on an 800cc RC212V at the post-Valencia test, yet in only his fourth race in a rain-lashed French round at Le Mans, he showed his potential by taking fifth. The season highlight was undoubtedly a stunning fight for the podium at Mugello, where he missed third by less than 0.1 second to circuit specialist Dovizioso.

Bradl frequently slugged it out with much more experienced combatants and only once did he finish outside the top six in the last ten races. There was never any danger of Italian team boss Cecchinello not exercising an option to retain the German for 2013.

Bradl was the catalyst, but he had unwavering support from Cecchinello, and one of the most loyal and underrated pit crews in the paddock. Christophe Bourguignon remained as crew chief, while data technician Brian Harden was a key element in the rider's seamless transition from Moto2.

Bradl's success also rewarded the loyalty of Cecchinello's sponsors, who had been persuaded to stay despite the negative headlines and minimum exposure of 2011.

Cecchinello, in his seventh season as a team owner in MotoGP, continued his sponsorship rotation policy throughout the season, with numerous brands, including Playboy, Linear, Givi , Elf and Red Bull, taking over the title sponsorship in their key markets.

LUCIO CHECCHINELLO

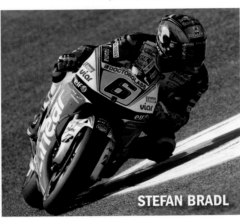

STEFAN BRADL

Photos: Gold & Goose

HONDA RCV212V

Sponsors and Technical Suppliers: Playboy • Eurobet • Givi • TS Vision • Elettronica Discount • Dinamica • Elf • VIAR

Engine: 1000cc, 76-degree V4; 360-degree crank (tbc), PVRS *Power:* More than 260ps

Ancillaries: HRC electronics, ride-by-wire throttle and fuel injection system, Denso sparking plugs *Fuel:* 21 litres

Transmission: Gear primary drive, multi-plate dry slipper clutch, six-speed seamless-shift constant-mesh cassette-style gearbox, RK chain

Suspension: Front, Öhlins TRSP25 48mm forks • Rear, Öhlins TRSP44 shock with linkage

Wheels: Front, 16.5in Marchesini • Rear, 16.5in Marchesini *Tyres:* Bridgestone

Brakes: Front, Nissin carbon-carbon 320mm • Rear, HRC steel 218mm

SAN CARLO HONDA GRESINI

TEAM STAFF

Fausto GRESINI: Team Manager
Carlo MERLINI: Sales and Marketing Manager
Ivo TAMBURINI: Marketing
Aldo GANDOLFO: Press and Media Relations
Fulvia CASTELLI: Logistics
Fabrizio CECCHINI: Team Co-ordinator

ALVARO BAUTISTA PIT CREW

Antonio JIMINEZ: Chief Mechanic
Mechanics
Ryoichi MORI, Alberto PRESUTTI
Renzo PINI (assistant)
Elvio DEGANELLO: Telemetry

ALVARO BAUTISTA

Born: 21 November, 1984 – Talavera de La Reina, Spain

GP Starts: 166 (50 MotoGP, 49 250cc, 67 125cc)

GP Wins: 16 (8 250cc, 8 125cc)

World Championships: 1 125cc

FAUSTO GRESINI

FAUSTO GRESINI'S 15th year in MotoGP was an emotional roller coaster as the Italian squad tried to come to terms with the tragic loss of rising star Marco Simoncelli in the penultimate race of 2011. It cast a dark cloud over the team for the entire season..

As a mark of respect, Alvaro Bautista's Honda RC213V and Michele Pirro's CRT bike ran an all-black livery until the Italian round in Mugello, where they reverted to the traditional all white.

Bautista took the ride after Suzuki's late decision to withdraw and had the unenviable task of plugging the huge void. He worked with experienced crew chief Antonio Jimenez, Simoncelli's crew chief Aligi Degenallo moving to lead Max Biaggi to his second World Superbike crown with Aprilia.

Telemetry engineer Elvio Degenallo and mechanic Renzo Pini were the only two members of Simoncelli's crew to work with Bautista; the rest moved to the new CRT project.

The consistency Bautista found so hard at Suzuki arrived in 2012, and the Spaniard failed to finish in only one race when he was the prime instigator in a controversial first-turn incident at Assen, crashing into Lorenzo.

Other than that indiscretion, Bautista claimed 12 top-six finishes with a notable career-first MotoGP pole and hard ride to fourth at Silverstone.

One major obstacle was Gresini's decision to accept a bundle of cash in return for running Showa suspension. That put Bautista out on a limb, with the rest of the grid on proven Öhlins suspension. Bautista had no reference or data to fall back on, and frequently he and Jimenez would be scratching around for a set-up on race day.

So it was to Bautista's credit that he didn't finish outside of the top six in the final eight races. The first of two rostrums was at Misano, with jubilant and emotional scenes at the circuit renamed in honour of Simoncelli.

He was third again in Japan just 24 hours after Gresini and San Carlo had confirmed him as its 2013 rider. Gresini had spoken to Ben Spies, Jonathan Rea and Scott Redding, but none appealed to San Carlo, and in the case of Rea and Redding they were required to bring substantial investment of their own.

HONDA RCV212V

Sponsors and Technical Suppliers: San Carlo • Agos Ducato • Barracuda • Berner • Castrol • Go & Fun • Neatshot • Nissin • PBR • Prink • SAG • Showa • Termignoni

Engine: 1000cc, 76-degree V4; 360-degree crank (tbc), PVRS *Power:* More than 260ps

Ancillaries: HRC electronics, ride-by-wire throttle and fuel injection system, NGK sparking plugs *Lubrication:* Castrol *Fuel:* 21 litres

Transmission: Gear primary drive, multi-plate dry slipper clutch, six-speed seamless-shift constant-mesh cassette-style gearbox, RK chain

Suspension: Front, Showa twin-tube 48mm forks • Rear, Showa twin-tube gas shock with linkage

Wheels: Front, 16in Marchesini • Rear, 16.5in Marchesini *Tyres:* Bridgestone

Brakes: Front, Nissin carbon-carbon 320mm • Rear, HRC steel 218mm

PRAMAC RACING TEAM

TEAM STAFF

Paolo CAMPINOTI: Team Principal
Francesco GUIDOTTI: Team Manager
Felix RODRIGUEZ: Team Coordinator
Carlo PERNAT: Head of Communication
Nicoletta SALVADOR: Press Officer
Maurizio CASARIL: Spare Parts

HECTOR BARBERA PIT CREW

Marco RIGAMONTI: Track Engineer
Michael PERUGINI: Chief Mechanic
Mechanics
Christian AIELLO, Francesco GALINDO
Pedro RIVERA
Edward CIFERRI (tyres and fuel)
Thomas PAGANO: Data Engineer

HECTOR BARBERA
Born: 2 November, 1986 – Dos Aguas, Spain
GP Starts: 171 (49 MotoGP, 75 250cc, 47 125cc)
GP Wins: 10 (4 250cc, 6 125cc)

TONI ELIAS
Born: 26 March, 1983 – Manresa, Spain
GP Starts: 212 (99 MotoGP, 30 Moto2, 48 250cc, 35 125cc)
GP Wins: 17 (1 MotoGP, 7 Moto2,17 250cc, 2 125cc)
World Championships: 1 Moto2

THE fortunes of this Italian squad continued to fluctuate more than the Dow Jones in 2012. With Pramac, the Italian generator and solar-power firm, teetering on the brink of bankruptcy in May, there was real concern that the team wouldn't see out the season. By mid-September, however, it was announced that Ben Spies and Andrea Iannone would spearhead a mouthwatering new line-up with the assurance of full factory support from Ducati. Rumours were also rife at season's end that American basketball legend Michael Jordan would be involved in a new sponsorship agreement.

For 2012, Paolo Campinoti remained team principal, with team manager Francesco Guidotti and co-ordinator Felix Rodriguez charged with the day-to-day running of the squad.

Campinoti had reluctantly reduced his involvement to one rider, Spaniard Hector Barbera having been signed for his third Ducati season after two years with the high-profile Aspar outfit.

Michele Perugini was a survivor of the cuts, as was Ducati track engineer Marco Rigamonti. The remainder of the crew was a combination of those who'd worked with de Puniet and the now retired Loris Capirossi in 2011.

The abiding memory of Barbera's season was his rash move at Misano that wiped out Pedrosa. It had been Barbera's comeback after a three-race absence, initially caused by a double break to his left leg during a training accident ahead of Laguna. He had attempted a brave return at Indianapolis 27 days later, but a vicious high-side in first practice fractured three vertebrae.

Barbera's place at Brno was taken by former Pramac rider Toni Elias, whose career was in freefall after he had parted company with the Aspar Moto2 squad. He claimed 11th at Indianapolis and Brno.

The factory support promised for 2013 was lacking in 2012. Barbera was forced to toil on a machine that the factory squad had skipped months in advance. In the opening nine races, though, he only finished outside the top ten once.

DUCATI Desmosedici GP11

Sponsors and Technical Suppliers: Pramac • Ducati • ENI • Bridgestone • IVECO • Temporary Agency • Lavorint • ABEA • FAAM • Valmy • Riello • SC Project • AION Ferrise • Ticino.com

Engine: 1000cc, 90-degree L4; 360-degree crank, DOHC, 4 valves per cylinder, Desmodromic valve gear, variable-length inlet tracts
        Power: Around 225bhp, revs up to 17,800rpm

Ancillaries: Magneti Marelli electronics, NGK sparking plugs, full electronic ride-by-wire *Lubrication:* Shell *Fuel:* 21 litres

Transmission: Xtrac seamless-shift cassette gearbox

Suspension: Front, Öhlins TRSP25 48mm forks • Rear, Öhlins TRSP44 shock with linkage

Wheels: Front, 16.5in Marchesini • Rear, 16.5in Marchesini *Tyres:* Bridgestone *Brakes:* Front, Brembo carbon-carbon 320mm • Rear, steel 200mm

CARDION AB DUCATI

TEAM STAFF

Karel ABRAHAM Sr: Team Manager

Jiri SMETANA: Communications

KAREL ABRAHAM PIT CREW

Christian PUPULIN: Track Engineer

Dario MASSARIN: Telemetry

Lindo SPARRAGLIA: Logistics

Marco GRANA: Chief Mechanic

Mechanics

Yannis MAIGRET, Martin HAVLICEK, Martin NESVADBA

Pietro BERTI (Tyres and Transport)

KAREL ABRAHAM
Born: 2 January, 1990 – Brno, Czech Republic
GP Starts: 123 (30 MotoGP, 14 Moto2, 48 250cc, 31 125cc)
GP Wins: 1 (Moto2)

FRANCO BATTAINI
Born: 22 July, 1972 – Brescia, Italy
GP Starts: 144 (17 MotoGP, 127 250cc)

A BEST result of seventh, a four-race mid-season absence through injury and a lowly 14th place in the final classification made 2012 an instantly forgettable second MotoGP season for the Czech Cardion AB squad.

Karel Abraham, son of team owner Karel senior, had silenced plenty of critics in 2011 with an accomplished rookie campaign on Ducati's temperamental Desmosedici. Confidence quickly ebbed away, however, after zero points in the opening four races. It wasn't until round ten at Laguna that Abraham finished inside the top ten.

That was followed by eighth at Indianapolis: the two American races triggered a spell of five further top-ten finishes. His only DNF thereafter was in Misano, where he inadvertently took a starring role in an aborted start, Pedrosa's first-lap exit and one of the defining moments of the season.

Abraham's team remained unchanged, with Marco Grana extending his long-term association into a seventh consecutive campaign as crew chief.

Ducati, too, were keen for continuity to help Abraham's progress. Christian Pupulin remained as the factory-appointed track engineer and Dario Massarin operated under the title of telemetry specialist again.

It was the hardware and not the human support, though, that ended Cardion AB's brief association with Ducati. Self-made multi-millionaire Karel senior didn't feel the huge investment for very little technical support from Borgo Panigale represented good business. Abraham rode the entire year on a Desmosedici spec that Valentino Rossi had dismissed as a no-hoper at the end of 2011.

Abraham senior decided to invest the wealth generated from AB Cardion, a hugely successful Czech medical supplies enterprise, into a new project for 2013. Abraham will switch to Aprilia, to ride an ART for the new season.

When a nasty hand injury in post-race testing at Catalunya sidelined Abraham for four races, veteran Ducati test rider Franco Battaini filled the breach in Germany, taking 16th position.

DUCATI Desmosedici GP11

Sponsors and Technical Suppliers: Cardion AB Moto Racing • Brno Circuit • KAPE • ABR Invest • Ducati • Arai • Bridgestone • PSI Racing • IFL • ENI • Boxeur des Rues • Motorex • Forma

Engine: 1000cc, 90-degree L4; 360-degree crank, DOHC, 4 valves per cylinder, Desmodromic valve gear, variable-length inlet tracts
      Power: Around 255bhp, revs up to 17,800rpm

Ancillaries: Magneti Marelli electronics, NGK sparking plugs, full electronic ride-by-wire *Fuel:* 21 litres

Transmission: Xtrac seamless-shift cassette-style gearbox

Suspension: Front, Öhlins TRSP25 48mm forks • Rear, Öhlins TRSP44 shock with linkage

Wheels: Front, 16.5in Marchesini • Rear, 16.5in Marchesini *Tyres:* Bridgestone *Brakes:* Front, Brembo carbon-carbon 320mm • Rear, steel 200mm

CRT TEAMS AND RIDERS

ALEIX ESPARGARO

POWER ELECTRONICS ASPAR

REVERED Spaniard Jorge 'Aspar' Martinez was a leading torch bearer for the new CRT category, with Aleix Espargaro and veteran Frenchman Randy de Puniet dominant in the second-tier series.

Aspar, who had built a successful racing empire since his retirement in 1997, had not intended to join CRT in 2012. He had already agreed to expand his relationship with Ducati to a two-rider effort when the Spanish banking crisis worsened and Mapfre couldn't commit the additional funding.

With no bikes and no title sponsor, Martinez began the process of rebuilding from scratch, with sporting director Gino Borsoi once again playing a pivotal role.

Fresh investment came from Power Electronics, a global concern. Then the team struck a deal to lead development of the new Aprilia ART machine. As a result, the Aspar Team once again appeared one of the slickest, most professional and well-financed outfits on the grid.

In the right hands, like de Puniet and Espargaro, the ART could occasionally trouble the slower prototypes.

Frenchman de Puniet was looking for redemption after a shocking season at Pramac Ducati. Hopes that a dazzling ride on Suzuki's GSV-R 800 in Valencia testing could convince the Japanese factory to reverse the decision to depart quickly vanished, leaving de Puniet as pre-season CRT favourite.

He was working under crew chief Andrea Orlandi, but more often than not the gulf in performance between the prototypes and the best CRT machinery was huge. He was only inside the top ten in three races with a season best of eighth in Assen and Brno.

Star CRT performer was the ever-smiling Espargaro, who claimed six top-ten finishes with a best of eighth in a storm-lashed Sepang race.

The Spaniard worked under crew chief Mauro Noccioli and was the highest ranked CRT rider in the final classification, with only two DNFs to blot his copybook.

RANDY DE PUNIET

Born: 14 February, 1981 – Maisons Laffitte, France

GP Starts: 234 (121 MotoGP, 80 250cc, 33 125cc)

GP Wins: 4 (4 250cc)

ALEIX ESPARGARO

Born: 30 July, 1989 – Granollers, Spain

GP Starts: 124 (40 MotoGP, 17 Moto2, 44 250cc, 23 125cc)

RANDY DE PUNIET

AVINTIA BLUSENS

A MAINSTAY of the smaller classes, the Spanish BQR Racing Team took advantage of the new CRT class to add MotoGP to its portfolio.

Led by team manager Raul Romero, the squad quickly seized on its new prime paddock slot to attain maximum exposure for its backers with an outlandish, oversized hospitality that dwarfed its counterparts.

Sponsor Avintia is a leading construction company that appears to be bucking the downward economic trend; Blusens a leading pioneer in multimedia entertainment. They put their faith in a brand-new project, based on a tuned Kawasaki ZX-10R motor in a British FTR frame, and in rookie riders Ivan Silva and Yonny Hernandez.

Silva had previous experience with rides for D'Antin Ducati in 2006 and '07, his full-time chance the result of winning the Spanish Stock Extreme championship.

Former BSB champion Gregorio Lavilla headed Silva's crew, but the going was tough. Only four points-scoring finishes in 12 races saw the team demote him to testing duties. David Salom, a World Supersport podium finisher having an undistinguished year in SBK, took over. He was 15th at Misano, but after failing to finish at Aragon, he was dropped after just two races and Silva returned.

Silva was frequently outpaced by hard riding Colombian Hernandez, up from the BQR Moto2 squad. He established himself as a regular top-15 finisher in the second half of the season, with a best of ninth at Indy starting a run of five successive points-scoring finishes. That came to an abrupt and painful end in Japan, however, where he dislocated his left collarbone and missed the final three races.

His place at Valencia went to final 250cc champion Hiroshi Aoyama, confirmed as one of the BQR riders for 2013. Claudio Corti had a wild-card ride at Valencia. With both Silva and Hernandez released, the second ride went to ousted Pramac Ducati rider Hector Barbera.

IVAN SILVA
Born: 12 June, 1982 – Barcelona, Spain
GP Starts: 24 (20 MotoGP, 4 250cc)

YONNY HERNANDEZ
Born: 25 July, 1988 – Medellin, Colombia
GP Starts: 46 (15 MotoGP, 31 Moto2)

DAVID SALOM
Born: 16 October, 1984 – Palma de Mallorca, Spain
GP Starts: 2 (2 MotoGP)

HIROSHI AOYAMA
Born: 25 October, 1981 – Chiba, Japan
GP Starts: 134 (30 MotoGP, 104 250cc)
GP Wins: 9 250cc
World Championships: 1 250cc

CLAUDIO CORTI
Born: 25 June, 1987 – Como, Italy
GP Starts: 47 (1 MotoGP, 46 Moto2)

SAN CARLO GRESINI

MORE than half of the crew manning Fausto Gresini's new CRT venture with Michele Pirro had expected 2012 to be a very different proposition. Ivo Brandi, Marco Rosa Gastaldo and Federico Vicino had been members of rising star Marco Simoncelli's crew before the Italian's untimely death.

With the team's talisman gone, they were shifted to the new MotoGP project, combining British firm FTR's chassis expertise with Dutch tuning know-how from Honda specialists Ten Kate, who developed a production-derived CBR1000RR motor.

Gresini had been forced to enter the more affordable CRT category to keep a two-rider programme going, having lacked the budget to continue leasing two Honda prototypes.

Initially, he intended to use an Aprilia RSV4 motor in a Moriwaki or FTR chassis, but HRC vetoed that plan and insisted on the Fireblade engine.

The project was late coming together, and Pirro, with long-serving Gresini employee Diego Gubellini as crew chief, started the season with hardly any noteworthy testing mileage under his belt.

He had just scored a best-so-far ninth in Assen when a disastrous run of four successive non-finishes halted his impressive progress.

Pirro and the FTR-Honda continued to improve, and he scored points in the final seven races including another top-ten finish in the squad's home race at Misano. His final flourish was a fine fifth in the wet at Valencia, the best result of the year for any CRT machine.

By the end of the season, there had been no clarification on whether Gresini's CRT entry would remain, but Pirro's fling in MotoGP had been brief.

Keen to find a faster rider to help development of their GP13 Desmosedici project, Ducati signed Pirro as official test rider, with the promise of two or three wild-card appearances in 2013.

MICHELE PIRRO
Born: 5 July 1, 1986 – San Giovanni, Rotondo, Italy
GP Starts: 65 (18 MotoGP, 18 Moto2, 29 125cc)
GP Wins: 1 (1 Moto2)

FAUSTO GRESINI

MICHELE PIRRO

PAUL BIRD MOTORSPORT

BRITISH multi-millionaire businessman Paul Bird has been a prominent and controversial figure in the World and British Superbike championships in the past, but 2012 was his first full-time foray into MotoGP.

Bird leased one Aprilia ART machine for James Ellison, while he also ran a two-man Kawasaki effort in BSB that culminated in a third title for Shane Byrne.

Bird's ethos was simple. As much of his squad as possible had to be British. Phil Borley was the track engineer, while Mick Shanley operated as crew chief. Shanley had some MotoGP experience, having previously worked with the Shell Advance Honda 250 squad, as did Ellison, having raced for WCM and Tech 3 Yamaha. The Cumbrian rider had to cope with uncertainty surrounding his future almost from the first.

He failed to score in the first three races, testing Bird's patience to the extent that he threatened to replace him with Byrne for the Le Mans race. Byrne's reluctance to risk compromising his British Superbike assault kept Ellison on board, and that faith in him saw him claim 11th in a rain-lashed French Grand Prix.

As his confidence grew, Ellison established himself as a frequent top-15 finisher, but Bird still had to resist pressure from Dorna to replace him from Misano onwards. Bird persevered again and the reward was a hard-earned ninth in monsoon conditions at Sepang, which equalled Ellison's best ever result.

Bird's intention for 2013 was always to expand to a two-rider effort, with one ART and a second rider on a British chassis, designed by Barry Ward of GPMS, who previously had collaborated with Team Roberts. Bird nominated Byrne, Sam Lowes and Tommy Hill as candidates, but with Dorna investing heavily in the CRT teams, they were exerting pressure for him to field Colombian Yonny Hernandez.

PAUL BIRD

JAMES ELLISON
Born: 19 September, 1980 – Kendal, Great Britain
GP Starts: 57 (57 MotoGP)

JAMES ELLISON

Photos: Gold & Goose

NGM MOBILE FORWARD RACING

COLIN Edwards was the CRT poster boy, the highest-profile rider to throw his weight behind Dorna's grid-boosting scheme. His Suter-BMW was the most extensively tested CRT ahead of 2012, but the legwork was exposed when a rider of the Texan's calibre hopped on board. From that moment, he took relish in demonstrating his talent as MotoGP's most recognised rent-a-quote.

He slammed chassis designer Eskil Suter, bemoaned the lack of support from BMW and often publicly referred to his bike as a "piece of s**t".

When Edwards lined up alongside team owner Giovanni Cuzari and MD Marco Curioni for his signing press conference at Misano in 2011, his vision had been very different. He wanted Yamaha superbike motors in a chassis built by his former Tech 3 crew chief, Guy Coulon. What he got was a super-rigid Suter frame, a BMW S1000RR that turned a motorcycle into a 200mph rodeo bull, and Bosch electronics that were so rudimentary and unpredictable that he thought he had stepped back a decade to when he first rode Aprilia's wild 990cc RS3 Cube.

There was no shortage of MotoGP experience in the garage. Electronics engineers Manfred 'Tex' Geissler had been with Suzuki's factory squad, while data engineer Bernard Martignac and mechanics Florian Ferracci and Guglielmo Andreini had all seen top-class service in various MotoGP teams.

Crew chief Kornelis Veldeman departed quickly, however, and was replaced by team director Sergio Verbana.

The boost of an encouraging 12th in Qatar quickly fizzled out, and more momentum was lost at Estoril, where Edwards broke his left collarbone. Chris Vermeulen replaced him at Le Mans.

Later, Edwards was constantly linked with changing machinery. He tested Aprilia's ART, FTR-Honda and FTR-Kawasaki, but stayed on the Suter-BMW. It wasn't clear which bike he would be riding in 2013.

COLIN EDWARDS
Born: 27 February, 1974 – Houston, Texas, USA
GP Starts: 168 (168 MotoGP)
World Championships: 2 World Superbike

CHRIS VERMEULEN
Born: 19 June, 1982 – Brisbane, Australia
GP Starts: 73 (73 MotoGP)
GP Wins: 1

COLIN EDWARDS

SPEED MASTER

WHEN the Speed Master squad was established at the end of 2010, it had a distinct family feel to it, the primary intention being to capture the Moto2 crown for cavalier, but highly-rated Italian Andrea Iannone. His father, Regalino, was team manager with co-owner Silvio Vercilli, and both remained in those roles when the team opted for an ambitious MotoGP venture with an Aprilia ART. Also involved in an external support role was Valentino Rossi's ever-present paddock sidekick, Alessio 'Uccio' Salucci.

Right from the word go, the switch appeared to leave Speed Master bogged down in a financial mire. A wheel hadn't even been turned in anger when Aussie Anthony West's MotoGP lifeline was cruelly cut because he couldn't finance the deal out of his own pocket.

Then Italian Mattia Pasini stepped in to fill the vacancy, but before mid-season, rumours began to circulate that his time on the ART machine was running out as fast as the money.

At one stage, it looked like the operation would fold and Pasini switch to Forward Racing, his two ART bikes shared with Colin Edwards, who wanted to ride anything but his Suter-BMW.

Tommaso Raponi was the crew chief, and the role of data recorder went to Renato Penacchio, who had worked previously with Suzuki and HRC.

Pasini's stay of execution finally ran out after he'd finished 16th in Aragon. Prior to his premature departure, he had been a prolific crasher and only scored points in four races.

Pasini's seat went to seasoned campaigner Roberto Rolfo, who had endured a miserable return to Moto2 and parted company with his Technomag-CIP squad after failing to score a single point in 11 races. His MotoGP return – for the first time since 2005 – didn't yield any significant improvement.

MATTIA PASINI
Born: 13 August, 1985 – Rimini, Italy
GP Starts: 136 (14 MotoGP, 26 Moto2, 32 250cc, 64 125cc)

ROBERTO ROLFO
Born: 23 March, 1980 – Torino, Italy
GP Starts: 151 (21 MotoGP, 28 Moto2, 102 125cc)
GP Wins: 4 (1 Moto2, 3 125cc)

MATTIA PASINI

ROBERTO ROLFO

Photos: Gold & Goose

CAME IODA RACING PROJECT

NOBODY embraced the CRT philosophy more than the new Came Ioda project. The Aprilia ART machine was effectively factory supported, but the Italian squad opted to run its own chassis and tuned standard Aprilia RSV4 1000cc motor, more in the spirit of the CRT concept.

The driving force was hugely experienced Giampiero Sacchi, one of racing's most renowned talent spotters, who has nurtured a who's who of Italian stardom. Max Biaggi, Valentino Rossi and the late Marco Simoncelli all owed much to Sacchi for their success.

The latest home-grown talent to be given a big GP opportunity was Danilo Petrucci, previously a Ducati test rider and runner-up in the 2011 FIM Superstock 1000 Cup.

The step was immense, yet Petrucci acquitted himself with distinction, helped by Sacchi's skill at assembling a vastly experienced backroom crew. Giovanni Sandi was a familiar face in the paddock and most recently had worked with Biaggi in Aprilia's World Superbike squad.

Petrucci had the unenviable task of developing a completely new chassis while handcuffed by an embarrassing lack of engine performance. At fast tracks like Qatar, Mugello and Catalunya, the difference in top speed was a morale-sapping 30mph, yet Petrucci sealed a creditable 11th in Assen.

It was a momentous challenge, but for 12 races Ioda persevered, Petrucci only three times in the points. With one eye on the future, Sacchi opted for a shift in strategy from Misano onwards, the team switching to the Suter-BMW machine that had been lambasted by Edwards.

It improved Petrucci's prospects, however, and he was able to score points in four of the final six races, claiming a best of eighth at the last round at Valencia. Ioda Racing will continue with the Suter-BMW project for the 2013 season, with Petrucci remaining – at one stage, he had been linked with a switch to Ducati's new 'Junior Team'.

DANILO PETRUCCI
Born: 24 October, 1990 – Terni, Italy
GP Starts: 18 (18 MotoGP)

DANILO PETRUCCI

GIAMPIERO SACCHI

2012 TEAMS AND RIDERS

By PETER McLAREN

MARC MARQUEZ

THOMAS LUTHI

RATHAPARK WILAIROT

MARC MARQUEZ departed for MotoGP as the most successful rider in Moto2's short history, the Spanish teenager raising the bar for both season and class wins as he blazed his way to the 2012 title.

Main technical regulations remained stable for the third year of Moto2: prototype chassis designs powered by identical 600cc four-stroke Honda engines, Dunlop as exclusive tyre supplier and a minimum machine weight of 140kg.

Grid numbers were trimmed from a lofty 38 to a more manageable 32, with inaugural 2010 champion Toni Elias heading the 'new' entries after an ill-fated return to MotoGP.

Arriving from the opposite direction to head up the rookies list were Nico Terol and Johann Zarco, first and second respectively in the final season of the 125cc World Championship, with Takaaki Nakagami also progressing to the intermediate grand prix class.

The most prominent newcomer from outside the paddock was Gino Rea, a race winner in the 2011 World Supersport championship. Alexander Lundh, Marco Colandrea, Angel Rodriguez, woman racer Elena Rosell and, bizarrely, Anthony West (riding in his third Moto2 season) completed those eligible for Rookie of the Year honours.

Reigning Moto2 champion Stefan Bradl had graduated to MotoGP. Michele Pirro, Mattia Pasini and Yonny Hernandez had followed the German, but Bradl and Pirro were the only riders from 2011's Moto2 top ten to leave. Those staying put, alongside title runner-up Marquez, included race winners Andrea Iannone, Alex de Angelis and Thomas Luthi.

In terms of nationality, the 2012 intake comprised ten riders from Spain, four each from Italy and Switzerland, three from Great Britain, two each from France and Japan, plus one each from Finland, Australia, Belgium, Germany, San Marino, Sweden and Thailand.

The eight constructors present at the start of 2011 – Suter, Kalex, FTR, Motobi, Tech 3, Moriwaki, Pons Kalex and MZ-RE Honda – all lined up for year three, although the (purely nominal) distinction between Pons Kalex and Kalex was removed. Swelling the chassis ranks was a return by Speed Up, after missing 2011, while AJR made its full season debut.

Suter and Kalex had won all but two of 2011's races, and the title-winning Kalex gained the most new customers over the winter.

Chassis choice began with nine Kalex, eight Suter, four each FTR and Moriwaki, two apiece for Tech 3 and Speed Up, plus one each for Motobi, AJR and MZ. Fewer than half of these manufacturers were still supplying the same number of machines by the end of the season, some teams playing musical chairs in pursuit of performance.

Heaviest hit was Moriwaki, which won the inaugural Moto2 title with Elias, but lost all four of its entries in the space of ten rounds. The MZ badge also disappeared long before Valencia.

Suter and Speed Up gained in numbers from the in-season reshuffle, with Bimota back from round four and a second Motobi arriving when Eric Granado was old enough to race.

All the wins and indeed all the rostrums went to Suter, Kalex, Speed Up and FTR, Suter claiming the constructors' championship for a perfect third year in a row. Seven different manufacturers had celebrated a 2011 rostrum.

Of the riders, Marquez stood head and shoulders above the rest with nine victories – including two stunning rides from the back of the field – followed by four wins for nearest rival Pol Espargaro, two for Iannone and one each for Luthi and de Angelis.

Five different winners continued a decreasing trend from six in 2011 and nine in 2010. It was a similar story with podiums – 17 riders in 2010, 16 in 2011 and 13 in 2012. But the racing at the front was closer than ever, with nine of the 17 races won by less than a second, compared with six in 2011 and seven in 2010. The average 2012 Moto2 race was won by 2.3 seconds, significantly closer than both Moto3 (5.1 seconds) and MotoGP (7.0 seconds).

The closest Moto2 win was just 0.061 second, achieved by Marquez at Qatar and Brno. The widest was 16.811 seconds by Espargaro at Phillip Island, the biggest yet in Moto2. New race lap records were set at 11 events, with four of the other six being wet.

SUTER

Marc Marquez's CatalunyaCaixa Repsol squad was one of five teams continuing with Suter for the start of 2012, alongside Interwetten-Paddock (Thomas Luthi), Mapfre Aspar (Toni Elias, Nicolas Terol), NGM Mobile Forward Racing (Alex de Angelis, Yuki Takahashi) and Technomag-CIP (Dominique Aegerter, Roberto Rolfo).

A ninth Suter joined the grid at round two, when Julian Simon's Avintia Blusens team made the switch from FTR, before the Swiss manufacturer reached a peak of 11 entries when Federal Oil/Thai Honda PTT Gresini (Gino Rea, Ratthapark Wilairot) moved from Moriwaki at round four.

The final change to the 'permanent' Suter line-up occurred when Forward Racing – a partner of Suter in MotoGP – went against the tide by changing its Moto2 team to FTR from round six, Silverstone.

Spaniard Marquez (19), 2010 125cc world champion, was starting his fifth grand prix season, but had missed much of winter testing due to double vision problems caused by a practice accident at Sepang in the previous October, for which he underwent surgery in January.

It didn't hold him back. A seven-time winner during his debut Moto2 campaign, Marquez began the new season with a perfect 25 points under the floodlights at Losail, squeezing an angry Luthi off track at the start of the final lap, then slipstreaming past Iannone in the dash to the flag.

The straight-line performance of Marquez's machine caused envy among his rivals throughout the season. But while the acceleration was certainly impressive, he only set the highest top speed at two of the 17 events.

After leading the championship for the first three rounds, including a further victory at Estoril, he came down to earth with a bump when he crashed out of the wet French Grand Prix. The following Catalunya round will be remembered for a controversial Marquez-Espargaro clash in the closing stages. Marquez initially received a one-minute penalty from Race Direction, but the decision was overturned by the FIM stewards, whose ruling was upheld on appeal.

Thus Marquez remained third and returned to the head of the table, with the same result next time at Silverstone. He ruled the title chase thereafter, despite suffering a second crash and DNF at a wet Sepang, being confirmed as champion just one week later at Phillip Island.

The Valencia finale saw both sides of Marquez the racer. An unnecessary practice incident with Simone Corsi saw him penalised with last place on the grid, but he still delivered a brilliant victory in his final Moto2 ride. He set a best lap 0.6 second faster than any other rider in the wet race, having already achieved a similar back-to-front feat in the dry Japanese round, when he left his bike in neutral for the start.

Marquez finished the year with nine wins, 14 podiums, seven poles, five fastest laps and a title advantage of 56 points over Espargaro.

Luthi, riding in his third season of Moto2, put his Qatar disappointment behind him by producing his best podium form since his title-winning 2005 125cc season, claiming consecutive rostrums at Jerez, Estoril, Le Mans and Catalunya. The 25-year-old's French win was only his second in the intermediate class, where he has raced since 2007, although it was a runner-up finish next time out in Catalunya that briefly made him the only rider other than Marquez or Espargaro to lead the standings.

The second half of the season was less successful for the Swiss rider, although he added two more podiums – at Mugello and Brno – on his way to fourth overall, equalling his ranking during the inaugural 2010 championship.

Marquez and Luthi were joined in the top ten by one other Suter rider, Aegerter in eighth.

Swiss 21-year-old Aegerter had claimed his first rostrum in the 2011 Valencia finale, and again provided a reliable pair of hands for the Technomag-CIP team, scoring in all but one round with a best result of fifth. By contrast, Italian veteran Rolfo – a Moto2 winner with Suter in 2010 – had failed to score a point by the time he left the team following round 11. Later he was pushed up to 15th place at Le Mans, following West's disqualification.

After departing Moto2, Rolfo appeared in MotoGP with Speed Master, at the expense of Mattia Pasini.

Former 125cc race winner Tomoyoshi Koyama – without a full-time grand prix ride since 2010 – was drafted in to take Rolfo's place, but the 29-year-old Japanese didn't claim a point from six starts.

Mapfre Aspar had an all-new, all-Spanish and all-champion line-up in the form of reigning 125cc title holder Terol and former Moto2 king Elias. But the results didn't live up to the theory, and after finishing no higher than seventh in the opening nine events, Elias departed Jorge Martinez's team on amicable terms.

The 29-year-old former MotoGP race winner then made some stand-in appearances for the injured Hector Barbera at Pramac Ducati in the premier class, before making an end-of-season Moto2 comeback with Italtrans (Kalex).

Jordi Torres, who had raced for Aspar during the second half of the 2011 season, was recalled in place of Elias from Indianapolis onwards. The 24-year-old Spaniard – who had helped the Avintia MotoGP team with winter testing, then made a one-off Tech 3 appearance at Catalunya alongside Spanish championship duties – made good use of his local knowledge to claim eighth at Aragon and sixth at Valencia.

Terol found the transition to four-stroke taxing, but progressed from an occasional scorer in the first half of the season to a regular in the second. The 23-year-old saved his best for last by qualifying fourth at Valencia, then riding to a first Moto2 podium in the wet race, almost doubling his points score.

At Gresini, 22-year-old Englishman Rea was rumoured to be under threat by a possible return by Elias. The speculation turned out to be false, but the pressure was certainly mounting when the change to Suter didn't bring the desired results. Despite frequent struggles in the dry, Rea's speed in the wet provided a reminder of his raw talent. He and Gresini finally received some reward with third place at Sepang, from 22nd on the grid, in a race Rea was leading when it was halted due to worsening rain.

The 2012 season was the first Moto2 campaign in which Gresini failed to win a race, Rea's better-funded Thai team-mate, 23-year-old Wilairot, only managing points on two occasions, during his sixth GP season. Rea finished the season 21st in the standings, six places ahead of Wilairot.

Julian Simon – 125cc champion in 2009, Moto2 runner-up in 2010, then injured for much of 2011 – had severed his Aspar ties for a fresh start at Avintia. The 24-year-old Spaniard wasted no time in seeking a Suter return after a single point on his FTR debut at Qatar, and was confident chassis familiarity would breed success. Instead the season proved a hard slog, and he managed only single-digit race points prior to a podium at Indianapolis (round ten). Simon returned to the rostrum with a bittersweet second place at the Valencia finale, where a first Moto2 win was snatched away by Marquez. Simon was 13th overall.

During his six rides with Suter, de Angelis scored a best placing of sixth, with team-mate Takahashi outside the points.

Suter took the constructors' title with a 55-point margin over Kalex.

KALEX

After carrying Stefan Bradl to the 2011 crown, the Kalex was unsurprisingly in demand for 2012.

Kalex continued its partnerships with Kiefer Racing (Max Neukirchner), GP Team Switzerland (Randy Krummenacher) and Pons HP 40 (Pol Espargaro, Esteve Rabat, Axel Pons), while attracting Marc VDS (Scott Redding, Mika Kallio) and Italtrans (Claudio Corti, Takaaki Nakagami) from Suter.

The Pons team had taken just a single podium in each previous Moto2 season, but the signing of Espargaro proved inspired. The 20-year-old Spaniard had taken two rostrums during a 2011 debut with Speed Up FTR, and won his second race for Pons in front of their home fans at Jerez.

Marquez's mistake at Le Mans put Espargaro at the head of the championship, reviving their 2010 title battle in the 125cc class. However two DNFs either side of victory at Silverstone, starting with the Catalunya clash, put Espargaro on the back foot and he couldn't pull Marquez back within reach.

Nevertheless, it was a breakthrough season for Espargaro, who added further wins at Aragon and Phillip Island on his way to second place in the world championship, which was a massive improvement over 13th in his rookie season.

Countryman Rabat also moved to Pons after spending his debut Moto2 year on an FTR at Blusens STX. Although unable to match Espargaro, the 22-year-old repeated his single podium and climbed three places to seventh overall.

Twenty-year-old Axel Pons, son of team owner Sito, remained free of injuries to complete a full season for the first time since 2009, taking a GP best of ninth place at Motegi.

At Marc VDS, Redding – with the team since the formation of Moto2 – had dropped from eighth with two podiums in the inaugural season to 15th without a rostrum in 2011. The former British 125cc winner was refreshed by the move to Kalex and a contender during winter testing, but he had to wait until the wet Le Mans race for his first rostrum. Three more podiums followed

Photos: Gold & Goose

SCOTT REDDING

POL ESPARGARO

AXEL PONS

CLAUDIO CORTI

ANTHONY WEST

TAKAAKI NAKAGAMI

ESTEVE RABAT

ANDREA IANNONE

BRADLEY SMITH

MIKA KALLIO

on the way to a best yet fifth in the world championship, but it wasn't all smiles.

At 184cm tall and 74kg, Redding regularly struggled for straight-line performance against lighter rivals. "For me, it's stopped being about who's the best rider in Moto2, because physical size seems to be more important than skill," said the 19-year-old.

Despite Redding's troubles, Kalex machines set the highest top speed at 14 events in the hands of Espargaro (5), Kallio (3), Rabat (3), Krummenacher (2) and Nakagami (1).

Kallio (58kg) also set the maximum speed of the year with 294.3km/h (182.9mph) at Phillip Island, where team-mate Redding was 11.3km/h slower. Redding will get his wish of a combined rider and bike weight limit for 2013.

Former MotoGP rider Kallio, at Marc VDS for a second season, was the only rider to claim points in the first 12 rounds, including a second in Germany. But the Finn failed to score in three of the last five events, ending his chances of challenging Redding for fifth position. Redding, linked with several MotoGP teams after a promising debut test for Ducati in August, will remain in Moto2 alongside Kallio in 2013.

The fifth Kalex rider to conquer the podium was Corti, courtesy of second place in the wet of Le Mans, but that wasn't enough to stop the Italian from being dropped in favour of Elias for the final four rounds.

Elias performed competitively on his Kalex debut at Motegi, until he crashed out of fifth place. The Span-

iard scored in his other three starts, including a ninth at Valencia.

After his Italtrans exit, Corti took a top-ten finish in the final round of the World Superbike championship for Pedercini Kawasaki, then made a surprise MotoGP debut on an Avintia Inmotec-Kawasaki at Valencia.

Team-mate and class rookie Nakagami rode the full season, the highlight being fifth at Jerez on the way to 15th overall.

Bradl's former Kiefer team swapped one German for another in the form of Max Neukirchner, but there would be no continuation of their 2011 success. World Superbike race winner Neukirchner, who had spent his debut grand prix season with MZ, battled lingering left-hand fractures after a qualifying crash at Qatar, then called it a season after suffering right-hand breaks at Brno. He took his only points of the year with eighth at Le Mans.

Drafted in to replace Neukirchner was former 125cc world champion Mike di Meglio. The Frenchman began a nomadic season with S/Master Speed Up, left after Assen and reappeared with MZ at Mugello, then switched to the Kiefer seat from Misano. The 24-year-old's best result remained a seventh place, with Speed Up, in Qatar.

Twenty-two-year-old Swiss Krummenacher scored five times, including an eighth at Catalunya, prior to injury at Brno. Rookie countryman Jesko Raffin took over from Aragon, before Krummenacher returned for the last two events, taking a ninth at Phillip Island.

Speed Up

The Speed Up name returned to Moto2 in 2012, recreating its race-winning partnership with Italian star Andrea Iannone.

Speed Up began the year supporting Speed Master's Iannone and Mike di Meglio, then increased its presence to four bikes when QMMF switched Anthony West and later Elena Rosell from Moriwaki.

Iannone – winner of three races with Speed Up in 2010, and again with Suter in 2011 – was listed initially with an FTR chassis, before the team's Speed Up decision in early March.

Following his narrow defeat by Marquez in Qatar, Iannone was made to wait until round five, Catalunya, for his first victory of the year. A further rostrum at Assen put him back up to second in the standings and later he claimed what would be a final Moto2 win, on home ground at Mugello. But the 2013 Ducati MotoGP rider lacked the podium consistency needed for a title challenge and once again was left third in the standings, this time by just three points over Luthi.

After funding issues prompted di Meglio's S/Master exit, Italian Alessandro Andreozzi – a wild-card for the Andreozzi Reparto Corse FTR squad at Silverstone – took over from round eight (Sachsenring). The rookie didn't score in 11 starts.

After struggling for success with Moriwaki, West and QMMF made the shift to Speed Up just before the summer break, at Mugello. It was the latest in a long line of

SIMONE CORSI

JOHANN ZARCO

XAVIER SIMEON

changes for the rider, a winner in both 250cc and WSS, who had spent the previous Moto2 seasons with MZ.

The 31-year-old Australian planned a 2012 MotoGP return with Speed Master, but lost the chance due to a lack of sponsorship. Then he was in contention for a Swan Yamaha BSB ride, only for that to pass him by as well. Next he looked set for an alternative BSB seat at Supersonic BMW, before finally snatching a last-minute grand prix place at the expense of countryman Damian Cudlin at QMMF.

As was the experience of many mid-season chassis changers, West's results were slow to improve after the switch to Speed Up. His season finally exploded into life with second place and a debut Moto2 podium at Sepang – his first in grands prix since 2005 – which he backed up with a dry second place in front of his home fans the next week in Australia.

Then came the news that he would miss the Valencia finale, after being handed a one-month ban by the FIM following an anti-doping test carried out at Le Mans in May.

The FIM also disqualified him from seventh at the French GP – his only points on the Moriwaki. West was 16th in the final standings. Indonesian rookie Rafid Topan Sucipto took his place for Valencia.

Having made her first two grand prix starts with Aspar, Rossell signed with QMMF for the full 2012 campaign, receiving the Speed Up chassis from Brno onwards. The closest the 25-year-old Spaniard got to a point was 20th at Sepang.

Speed Up relied on Iannone for its constructors' championship points in all but three races, when West scored higher.

FTR

FTR's Losail line-up consisted of Came IodaRacing Project (Simone Corsi), SAG (Marco Colandrea), Desguaces La Torre SAG (Angel Rodriguez) and Blusens Avintia (Julian Simon). FTR numbers were halved by round four, however, following Blusens' switch to Suter and Desguaces's to Bimota, but returned to their original level with the addition of Forward Racing (from Suter) at Assen.

Forward's de Angelis took FTR's first podium of the year at Sachsenring and its only other rostrum with victory in the shortened Sepang monsoon. The 28-year-old San Marino rider, who arrived at Forward from JiR, thus continued his trend of one win in each Moto2 season, despite missing the last two races following a hand injury in Australia.

Mattia Pasini, who began the year in MotoGP, stood in for de Angelis at Valencia.

Whilst 12th overall for de Angelis was a long way off his fourth place in 2011's championship, team-mate and fellow Moto2 winner Takahashi endured a greater decline, from 11th to 30th after scoring just two points.

With de Angelis injured, the top FTR rider in the final classification was 24-year-old Italian veteran Corsi. He claimed five top-six finishes and a pole at Aragon, but also a disproportionate eight non-scores on his way to 11th overall.

SAG's 17-year-old rookie Colandrea didn't score in his first grand prix season, which saw him replaced by local riders at Motegi (Kohta Nozane) and Valencia (Roman Ramos).

Rodriguez was expecting his first full season since 2006, but lasted just six rounds and didn't finish higher than 20th on either the FTR or Bimota.

Creating a bigger impact was 18-year-old wild-card Hafizh Syahrin. Riding an FTR for the local Petronas Raceline Malaysia team, he scythed from 27th on the grid to lead his home Sepang event in the wet. Syahrin finished fourth, an improvement of 16 places relative to his only previous GP appearance.

Corsi and de Angelis divided top FTR honours between them in all but one of the 17 rounds.

Tech 3

Bradley Smith and Xavier Simeon formed Tech 3's reduced 2012 line-up, with Smith eager to build on his three rookie-season podiums for the French team/constructer. But it would prove a frustrating year for the 21-year-old Englishman. He was ahead of his team-mate in all but one grand prix, where he suffered a technical failure, but found his Mistral lacking top speed and struggling to match the mid-race performance of the front-runners.

Smith finished fourth – within 0.128 second of the rostrum and one second from victory – at Mugello, and scored points in all but three events. However, a tough final round at Valencia saw the 2013 MotoGP rider slip from seventh to ninth in the championship.

Belgian Simeon (22) scored on six occasions during his second Tech 3 season, including an eighth in Germany. Torres took 16th while replacing an injured Simeon at Catalunya.

Motobi

The Motobi project, combining Japanese chassis spe-

cialists TSR and the JiR team, expanded back to a two-rider, all-rookie line-up for most of 2012. French 125cc title runner-up Johann Zarco had been signed to replace de Angelis, with Brazilian Eric Granado joining the team from Silverstone, once he had reached 16.

Zarco (21) comfortably won the Rookie of the Year title with tenth in the championship. The highlight of the Frenchman's season was a fourth place in Portugal, but he had been closing on race winner Luthi before crashing out of his wet home round.

Granado didn't break the top 20 during 11 races.

AJR

Spanish manufacturer AJR made its Moto2 debut in partnership with the Arguinano Racing Team, running a single entry for Ricard Cardus.

Nephew of former 250 title contender Carlo, Ricky had made 25 previous grand prix starts but never run a full season. Again, he didn't quite go the distance, missing Brno, Misano and Aragon due to injury. South African Steven Odendaal took his place for two races.

Cardus (23) scored points on six occasions, with a best of 13th.

Moriwaki

Moriwaki, which took Elias to the inaugural Moto2 title and won the final race of 2011 with Michele Pirro, began the season with two teams.

Gresini (Gino Rea, Ratthapark Wilairot) and QMMF (Anthony West, Elena Rosell) were both continuing customers, with a wild-card entry also provided for QMMF's Nasser Hasan Al Malki in Qatar.

But all the Moriwakis had gone by round ten, as Gresini and then QMMF sought alternatives.

Moriwaki collected ten points before it was forced off the grid, then lost all but one of them – a 15th for Rea at Jerez – due to West's Le Mans disqualification. Moriwaki plans to return in partnership with a new team headed by Tady Okada in 2013.

MZ-RE Honda/Bimota/IAMT

Non-scoring appearances were made by MZ-RE Honda, Bimota and IAMT.

MZ had been present since the first season of Moto2, albeit switching to badged FTR machinery during 2011. The 2012 season began with a single entry for Swede Alexander Lundh, running an updated version of predecessor West's 2011-spec FTR.

The 25-year-old rookie competed in seven rounds, but didn't return after injury at Assen. Eighteen-year-old Markus Reiterberger took over for his home Sachsenring event, before Mike di Meglio rode for MZ at Mugello, Indianapolis and Brno, the last event MZ attended.

Bimota, which had raced the full 2010 season, but skipped 2011, made a late start to 2012, debuting with Desguaces La Torre SAG in place of FTR at round four (Le Mans).

Damian Cudlin, spurned by QMMF just before the start of the season, took over riding duties from Angel Rodriguez at Assen and Sachsenring, with Italian Massimo Roccoli at the helm for Mugello.

Some stability arrived when ex-Mahindra Moto3 rider Marcel Schrotter was given the seat from Indianapolis onwards, but points proved unobtainable for the German teenager.

The IAMT finished 24th as a wild-card entry for German Kevin Wahr, run by Kiefer Racing at Sachsenring.

2012 TEAMS AND RIDERS

By PETER McLAREN

THE last surviving classic class of 125cc made way for Moto3 in 2012, a series some would hail as a template for post-financial crisis grand prix racing. Sandro Cortese was its first champion in a season of seven different race winners.

While MotoGP struggles with high costs and stale racing, and Moto2's single engine supply seems a little contrived for a grand prix class, Moto3 offered a compromise, featuring 250cc, four-stroke, single-cylinder motorcycles with a control ECU and rev limit of 14,000rpm. Dunlop signed-up as the official tyre supplier, and the class had a combined minimum weight for rider and bike of 148kg.

Crucially, chassis and some elements of engine design remained open, though significant efforts were made to control engine costs, clearing the way for both independent and mainstream manufacturers.

Each engine manufacturer had to be prepared to supply eight riders, for a maximum engine price of 12,000 euros. Eight engines per rider were allowed during the season. Costs of parts, rebuilds and upgrades were also controlled.

Nico Terol and Johann Zarco – first and second in the final 125cc championship – had moved up to Moto2, but seven of the remaining 125cc top ten joined the transition to Moto3.

Maverick Vinales and Cortese, third and fourth in the last two-stroke standings, headed the list, with Hector Faubel and Jonas Folger also previous grand prix winners. Efren Vasquez, Luis Salom, Alberto Moncayo and Adrian Martin had prior podium pedigree, too.

Fittingly, 11 of the 33 entries were rookies: Romano Fenati, Jack Miller, Toni Finsterbusch, Ivan Moreno, Niccolo Antonelli, Isaac Vinales, Brad Binder, Alex Rins, Kenta Fujii, Arthur Sissis and Alan Techer.

Spain was the most represented nation with nine riders, followed by Italy (five), Germany (four), France (three), and Australia and Great Britain (two). Portugal, Malaysia, Finland, Czech Republic, Japan, The Netherlands, South Africa and Switzerland each had a single full-time rider.

The season concluded with Cortese and Maverick Vinales with five victories apiece, Salom and Briton Danny Kent two, and one apiece for Fenati, Louis Rossi and Folger. Fenati, Salom, Rossi and Kent were all first-time winners.

Fourteen different riders took a podium, more than in any other 2012 class and greater than the ten seen in the last year of 125.

In 125's last year, only Piaggio's Aprilia/Derbi brands had finished on the rostrum. Piaggio didn't participate in Moto3, but Honda and KTM built machinery for the new class, the Austrian firm supporting an official team as well. The engines were also favoured by chassis specialists, most already competing in Moto2. Independent constructors Ioda and Oral went in at the deep end with complete motorcycles, with Mahindra making the cross-over from 125 using Oral power.

The year began with 11 constructors: FTR Honda (seven entries), Honda, (five), KTM (five), Kalex KTM (four), Suter Honda (two), TSR Honda (two), Ioda (two), Mahindra (two), Oral (two), FGR Honda (one) and MZ-RE Honda (one). Changes during the season saw some Honda entries migrate to the FTR chassis, while MZ and Oral dropped away and KRP Honda arrived.

By the close of the year, three different motorcycles had won races, two more had taken a podium and 11 had scored points.

Moto3 had much to live up to in terms of close racing – and it delivered: 11 of the 17 races were won by less than one second, compared to six in the last year of 125. The closest victory was by 0.020 second – Vinales over Fenati at Mugello, where the top three were covered by 0.071 second. Depth was demonstrated at Assen, where the top 15 were within 12.533 seconds: in the entire history of 125s from 1949 to 2011, only two races had been closer.

One area where 125 remained superior was lap times. Moto3's best was usually 1–2 seconds adrift of the two-stroke race records, but got to within 0.268 second at Indianapolis.

KTM

KTM fielded five full-time entries, led by Sandro Cortese, Danny Kent and Arthur Sissis at the factory Red Bull KTM Ajo team. The others were Zulfahmi Khairuddin at the sister AirAsia-Sic-Ajo outfit and Niklas Ajo at TT Motion Events Racing.

Cortese (22) arrived at Aki Ajo's squad as a double grand prix winner with Racing Team Germany Aprilia in the final season of the 125cc class, his seventh year of world championship competition. The German with Italian parents claimed Moto3's first ever pole in Qatar, but was made to wait until round three at Estoril for his and KTM's debut Moto3 victory, a result that also put him on top of the championship for the first time.

Vinales regained the title initiative at round six, but Cortese continued to clock podiums in all but one round and burst back to the top of the standings with a damp home victory in the eighth round at Sachsenring.

Cortese kept control thereafter, being the only rider to score points in every event – despite a last-lap crash in Motegi, where he missed his first title opportunity – and secured the inaugural Moto3 crown in style with a final-turn victory in Malaysia.

The championship decided, Cortese set his sights on most season wins, trailing Vinales 5–4 heading into the penultimate Phillip Island round. Cortese duly won in Australia, marking his first back-to-back GP wins, but saw a sixth victory slip away at the last turn of the Valencia finale when team-mate Kent proved braver on the brakes.

Cortese, who will move to Moto2 for 2013, was Ajo's third world champion after Mike di Meglio (2008) and Marc Marquez (2010) in the 125cc class.

Kent (18) began his second full GP season, and second at Ajo, having finished 11th in the 125cc championship on Aprilia RSW machinery. The 18-year-old Briton made a slower start than Cortese, and was next in line for developments, but kick-started his season with a debut front row and podium at Assen.

Two further front rows followed, but Kent didn't grace the podium again until his debut victory from pole in Japan, an achievement slightly marred by Cortese's sour post-race behaviour, for which he later apologised.

Having gathered 42 points from the opening eight rounds, Kent concluded the year with 101 points from the last eight – highlighted by the pair of victories – lifting him to fourth in the standings.

Sixteen-year-old Sissis earned his place in grand prix through performances in the Red Bull Rookies Cup. The Australian was a regular points scorer in the second half of the season, taking his first podium in a thrilling fight to the line at his home Phillip Island race. Sissis was 12th in the standings.

Khairuddin made history in his third grand prix season by becoming the first Malaysian to take a grand prix pole position and podium, achieving both landmarks in front of adoring home fans at Sepang. The 20-year-old repeated the podium feat with a last-turn pass at Valencia, helping him rise from 18th on an Ajo Aprilia in 2011 to seventh best in Moto3. Khairuddin was also the top speed king, setting the highest mark at ten events, including a season best 238.4km/h (148.1mph) at Phillip Island.

Finn Niklas Ajo (17), son of Aki, served race bans at Estoril and Indianapolis after an altercation with marshals and a fellow rider respectively. In between, Ajo claimed an eighth place, from fifth on the grid, at Assen, but only improved on his rookie championship ranking by two places, for 19th. Spanish veteran Joan Olive stepped in when Ajo was absent, but didn't break the top 15.

Cortese was the top-scoring KTM rider in all but three of the 17 rounds, as KTM won the inaugural constructors' title by 40 points over FTR Honda. The Austrian marque won five of the final six races and dominated the top-speed charts throughout the year, setting the peak figure at all but three events

FTR HONDA

The FTR Honda was the most popular Moto3 machine, starting the season with seven entries: Blusens Avintia (Maverick Vinales), Racing Team Germany (Louis Rossi), Redox-Ongetta-Centro Seta (Jakub Kornfeil, Isaac Vinales), Andalucia JHK Laglisse (Ivan Moreno) and

DANNY KENT

ARTHUR SISSIS

MAVERICK VINALES

ROMANO FENATI

JAKUB KORNFEIL

IVAN MORENO

ADRIAN MARTIN

NIKLAS AJO

ZULFAHMI KHAIRUDDIN

NICCOLO ANTONELLI

EFREN VAZQUEZ

Team Italia FMI (Romano Fenati, Alessandro Tonucci) – the national federation-backed team switched from Ioda during pre-season testing.

Spurred on by the performances of Vinales and Fenati in Qatar, three more FTR Hondas then joined the grid from round two, when San Carlo Gresini Moto3 (Niccolo Antonelli) and JHK T-Shirt Laglisse (Efren Vazquez, Adrian Martin) changed from the standard NSF250R chassis.

A four-time winner – including at the last two events – during his rookie 2011 grand prix season on a Paris Hilton backed Blusens Aprilia, Vinales entered the new championship as favourite and topped the final pre-season test.

The 17-year-old overcame the surprise challenge of Fenati to win the Qatar season opener, but Losail also highlighted KTM's speed advantage, with the nine Austrian-powered bikes leading the maximum-speed list.

More power was to become a frequent request from Vinales, who trailed Cortese by 12 points following his first DNF in the wet at Le Mans (round four). The Spaniard got back into his stride by becoming Moto3's first double winner at the following Catalan round, the first of three wins in a row that catapulted him back to the top of the standings.

A roller-coaster season continued with a poor weekend at round eight in Germany, where Vinales finished outside the points on a damp track, then a close victory at Mugello. Vinales won five of the opening nine races, yet was still nine points behind the consistent Cortese.

The title tipping point arguably came on the last lap at Indianapolis, where Vinales fell while fighting for vic-

tory, allowing Cortese to move 29 points clear. When Vinales missed the podium at the next two rounds, the championship became little more than a distant dream. Then he lost second place after a soul destroying mechanical fault on the warm-up lap at Aragon (round 14).

A runner-up finish in Japan ended a four-round rostrum drought for Vinales, who also returned to second in the standings above Luis Salom. But then he shocked the paddock by 'quitting' the Avintia team – for whom he had recently signed a new two-year contract – at Sepang.

An apologetic Vinales returned in Australia, just one week after his Malaysian meltdown, having decided to see out the season and try to regain second in the standings. But he crashed out Down Under and then could only manage eighth in the Valencia rain, which lost him the runner-up spot to Salom.

Fenati arrived in grand prix racing having won the 2011 European 125cc championship and finished as runner-up, to Antonelli, in the Italian series. Third at the conclusion of pre-season testing put the 16-year-old firmly on the radar for Qatar, although a sixth-place in qualifying didn't suggest a victory challenge. However, he led the very first Moto3 race lap and, having been passed by Vinales, made his intentions clear by retaking the lead.

Vinales finally got the better of Fenati, but the young Italian was undoubtedly the star of the night. He won at only his second attempt, by a colossal 36 seconds, at a damp Jerez. The rank rookie was leading the world championship.

Fenati was hailed as Italy's next motorcycling great, but the weight of expectation perhaps became a little too much and he crashed out of the next two events. He wasn't seen on the podium again until a second place at his home Mugello race (round eight).

A first front-row start and third rostrum followed at the next Italian round at Misano, but Fenati only scored twice from the last five events and dropped to sixth in the standings, losing top rookie honours to Rins.

Despite a season of 125cc grands prix under his belt, 18-year-old team-mate Tonucci scored in only half of the events, the overwhelming highlight being a debut podium at Motegi.

Louis Rossi was the third FTR Honda rider to win a race in 2012. The 22-year-old Frenchman claimed a dream 15th-to-first win in front of his home fans in the Le Mans rain, his first rostrum in 49 GP starts. But it would be his only podium of the year and eventually he slipped outside the title top ten.

None of the other FTR Honda riders graced the podium, although Gresini's 16-year-old rookie, Antonelli, came frustratingly close with a pair of fourth places. Antonelli, who was declared unfit to race at Phillip Island after a big practice crash, finished in 14th place in the championship.

Tenth place in the standings for Vazquez made him the highest-ranked rider without a rostrum. Kornfeil took a peak race finish of sixth, Moreno ninth, with Isaac Vinales (cousin of Maverick) and Martin topping out at tenth.

Ex-Aspar rider Alberto Moncayo replaced Moreno from Indianapolis, but didn't threaten a repeat of his

LUIS SALOM

MIGUEL OLIVEIRA

BRAD BINDER

ALEX MARQUEZ

JONAS FOLGER

KENTA FUJII

TONI FINSTERBUSCH

MIROSLAV POPOV

ALEX RINS

MARCEL SCHROTTER

DANNY WEBB

early-season podium. In a late twist, Faubel took former team-mate Moncayo's Laglisse ride for the Valencia finale, finishing fifth.

FTR Honda won seven of the opening nine races, but the victory celebrations ended abruptly at Mugello.

Kalex KTM

While the KTM featured a tubular-steel frame, as on the manufacturer's motocross bikes, exclusive chassis partner Kalex opted for the now conventional aluminium twin-spar design, as used for its title-winning Moto2 chassis.

Signing up for the 'satellite' KTMs were the RW Racing GP (Luis Salom, Brad Binder) and Mapfre Aspar (Hector Faubel, Alberto Moncayo) teams.

Twenty-year-old Salom, who had taken his first two grand prix podiums with RW in 2011, soon emerged above the other Kalex riders. The Spaniard followed up a fourth at Losail with podiums at Jerez and Estoril, then Silverstone and Germany.

A clever last lap at Indianapolis was rewarded with a first grand prix victory, and marked the start of a blistering period of form that produced two wins and two seconds from four rounds.

The Aragon win also put Salom above Vinales for second in the championship, but Salom took the shine off his growing reputation with a reckless last-lap lunge at Motegi. Salom and race leader Jonas Folger both crashed out in the incident, earning the former a grid penalty for Sepang. Salom fought Vinales for second overall over the last two rounds, securing the runner-up spot by seven points.

Salom's 16-year-old South African team-mate, Binder, riding in his first grand prix season, scored on

four occasions, including a stand-out performance that took him to within one corner of a rostrum at the wet Valencia finale.

Starting with high expectations after winning the final 125cc title, then seeing the success of Salom with the same machinery, Aspar replaced both its riders during the season.

Moncayo, who had taken the team's only podium with a wet second place at Le Mans, was first to go. The 20-year-old Spaniard got the chop during the summer break and was replaced by Folger.

The German had scored points just once in eight Moto3 races for IodaRacing, but Martinez clearly believed in the 18-year-old, who had taken a single 125cc race win in 2011. He immediately repaid Aspar with a podium on his Indianapolis debut, then a runaway victory at the following Brno round.

Further podiums at Aragon and Malaysia book-ended the Salom-Motegi clash and Folger finished his fourth grand prix year with pole at Valencia, only to suffer bike problems on the warm-up lap of the race. Folger was ninth in the championship.

Faubel was the most experienced and decorated rider to sign-up for Moto3. The 28-year-old remained with Aspar for his twelfth season of grand prix, with eight wins and 25 125cc podiums under his belt.

That success didn't translate to the four-stroke, however, and he was unable to break into the top six during the first 11 races. Aspar picked 16-year-old German rookie Luca Amato to take Faubel's place for the last six events, but the CEV front-runner could do no better than 20th.

German Philipp Oettl, fourth in the Red Bull Rookies Cup, made his grand prix debut as a wild-card at Valencia, claiming 11th.

SUTER HONDA

Like FTR, Suter also had a presence in all three grand prix classes, backing the Estrella Galicia team (Miguel Oliveira, Alex Rins) from round one. Suter Honda numbers subsequently doubled when Ambrogio Next Racing (Giulian Pedone, Simone Grotzkyj) switched from Oral at round four.

Despite missing some pre-season tests after dislocating his shoulder on a dirt bike, grand prix rookie and reigning Spanish CEV champion Rins snatched a home pole for round two at Jerez. However, an off-track moment in the race cost him a podium, which the 16-year-old later achieved at the wet French round, before heading for surgery to repair a finger injured in a Saturday fall.

The Spaniard didn't repeat his rostrum, but numerous top-six finishes cleared the way for a highly creditable fifth overall and Rookie of the Year title by five points from Fenati.

Portuguese team-mate Oliveira had raced in 11 125cc grands prix, but got off to a bad start in Moto3 with three non-scores from the opening four rounds. A debut podium at Catalunya followed, but the 17-year-old had only made sporadic top-six appearances until he battled Cortese for victory on his way to a career-best second in Australia. Oliveira finished the season in eighth.

Alex Marquez, younger brother of Marc and narrowly beaten to the 2011 CEV crown by Rins, made wild-card appearances for Estrella at Jerez, Estoril and Catalunya (best finish sixth), before joining Ambrogio from Indianapolis onwards.

The 16-year-old – who continued his CEV commitments, winning the Moto3 title – replaced experienced

Italian Simone Grotzkyj, who had taken just one point in eight races. Marquez scored in four rides for Ambrogio, but didn't beat his earlier wild-card result, falling while fighting for victory in Valencia.

Qatar aside, team-mate Pedone raced the full season, his second in grand prix, claiming all but one of his points with a tenth place at Le Mans.

Honda

With Gresini and Laglisse switching to the FTR chassis, Caretta Technology (Jack Miller, Alexis Masbou) was the only team to spend the full season with the complete NSF250R.

Masbou (24), a semi-permanent GP rider since 2005, hit a rich vein of form just before mid-season, including second at the Sachsenring. However the Frenchman broke his femur in a testing accident and was sidelined from Brno onwards.

Having raced in the final six 125GPs for Caretta, 17-year-old Miller signed to race the full 2012 season. The lively Australian missed three races due to injury, but took points on three occasions, the best of which by far was fourth in Germany.

Manuel Tatasciore took Miller's place at Estoril, with fellow Italian Michael Ruben Rinaldi subbing at Brno. Rinaldi then rode alongside Miller as a replacement for Masbou at Misano, before John McPhee took over – albeit on a KRP Honda – from Aragon.

Cresto Guide MZ Racing began the year running 18-year-old German Toni Finsterbusch on a standard Honda, but with plans to build its own chassis by mid-season. The title of the team's machinery changed in each of the opening three events, from MZ-RE Honda, to MZ FTR before settling as Honda. MZ. They skipped several rounds and Finsterbusch switched to Racing Team Germany from Misano.

Honda was the machine of choice for wild-cards in 2012, the best result being an eighth place for Luca Gruenwald at his home German event.

TSR HONDA

TSR, which builds the Motobi Moto2 chassis, supplied Honda-powered motorcycles to the Technomag-CIP-TSR team.

Frenchman Alan Techer was most successful of the all-rookie line-up, netting points at five of the first eight rounds, but he was scoreless thereafter and missed the Brno race following a heavy fall. Japanese rider Kenta Fujii didn't claim a point.

FGR HONDA

Czech manufacturer FGR ran its own Honda-powered racer, starting the year with Jasper Iwema. The 22-year-old Dutchman, riding in his fourth GP season, scored just once, in the wet at Le Mans, before splitting from the team after Aragon (round 14).

Spanish teenager Josep Rodriguez, who had made earlier appearances on an FTR Honda at Jerez and Misano, was hired in his place and took a point in the Valencia finale.

Ioda

Independent constructor Ioda's round-one roll-call consisted of IodaRacing Project (Jonas Folger) and Ioda Team Italia (Luigi Morciano).

After missing Jerez, a sick Folger was replaced by Italian teenager Armando Pontone for Estoril. Folger then returned to claim Ioda's only points of the season with 11th in the French rain.

When Folger switched to Aspar after nine rounds, grand prix rookie Pontone was brought back in.

Ioda, like Oral, was hit hard by the engine reliability regulations. Morciano was the first Moto3 rider to face a pit-lane start for exceeding the eight-engine limit, by round eight (Sachsenring).

Further engine penalties for Morciano followed at Indianapolis and Brno. Ioda Team Italia then skipped the late-summer rounds, only returning for Valencia. Pontone suffered engine penalties at Brno and Sepang.

Mahindra

Indian company Mahindra (Danny Webb, Marcel Schrotter) entered its own motorcycle, featuring a tubular-steel frame, but the team's Oral engines proved a constant handicap.

Mahindra, like Ioda, spent much of the season at the tail end of the top speed charts, with 19-year-old Schrotter jumping ship after his home German round (later joining SAG in Moto2).

Webb soldiered on, missing Indianapolis and Brno through injury, receiving an engine penalty at Sepang, and then withdrawing on the opening day in Australia due to a lack of spare engine parts.

The 21-year-old Englishman concluded his sixth grand prix season with a pit-lane start, followed by a broken chain, at Valencia, which left him without a 2012 point. All four of Mahindra's points came from Schrotter in the wet Le Mans race.

Schrotter was replaced by 27-year-old Riccardo Moretti, running second in the Italian 125 championship on a two-stroke Mahindra. The Italian sustained neck and shoulder injuries at Brno, which forced him to skip Misano and Aragon, where he was replaced by Miroslav Popov.

Czech teenager Popov (17) had impressed as a replacement for Webb at his home event, running inside the top three before falling on the drying track. He returned for the final round, following another injury sustained by Moretti.

Mahindra will form an engine and chassis partnership with Suter for 2013, when Vazquez and Oliveira will join the team.

KRP HONDA

KRP Honda completed a partial season, starting with wild-card appearances for John McPhee at Catalunya, Silverstone and Brno under the Racing Steps Foundation KRP banner. The 17-year-old Scot then joined Caretta Technology for the last five rounds, taking his KRP Honda with him, but he wasn't able to add to his single point for 15th place at Brno in spite of some impressive runs.

Fellow Briton Fraser Rogers had a one-off KRP ride alongside McPhee at Silverstone.

Oral

Ambrogio Next Racing (Simone Grotzkyj, Giulian Pedone) ran complete Oral motorcycles for the first three rounds prior to a Suter Honda switch, which left Mahindra as the only Oral-powered team.

Pedone, competing in his second GP season, claimed Oral's only point with 15th at Jerez.

MOTOGP · MOTO2 · MOTO3

GRANDS PRIX 2012

Reports by MICHAEL SCOTT

Statistics compiled by PETER McLAREN

FÉDÉRATION INTERNATIONALE DE MOTOCYCLISME

AIRASIA AUSTRALIAN GRAND PRIX
Phillip Island 2012

AIRASIA AUSTRALIAN GRAND PRIX

AirAsia

Photo: Gold & Goose

Inset, right: Let battle commence. Lorenzo and Stoner shake hands at the MotoGP rider photo-call.

Inset, centre top: Silva's FTR Kawasaki – no blow-ups this time.

Inset, centre bottom: Mattia Pasini was another CRT hopeful to bolster the grid.

Main photo: Lorenzo leads away from Stoner and fast-starter Pedrosa.

Photos: Gold & Goose

FIM WORLD CHAMPIONSHIP · ROUND 1

QATAR GRAND PRIX

LOSAIL CIRCUIT

TESTING – twice at Sepang and once at Jerez – had belonged to Stoner, fastest everywhere in spite of missing the first day with a recurring back problem (it seized painfully when he was stretching prior to his first run). But the Yamahas had run him close, two out of three times ridden by Lorenzo; and Stoner's final top time in Spain had come only at the last minute. "I wanted to be cheeky," he said, adding that any more testing would be a waste of time – it just didn't take that long to find out what you needed to know. But Lorenzo showed a quiet confidence as he asserted that Yamaha had closed the gap on Honda, while cynics observed that Casey was yet to run a race simulation.

This was important because, among all the other changes, the Bridgestones had been revised significantly. Acceding to rider requests for faster warm-up following a string of (usually injurious) cold-tyre high-sides, the new safety generation had a softer construction. These, to the delight of ex-Superbike rider Crutchlow, emulated the Pirellis used in that series, as well as the similar trend in F1. They gripped brilliantly from cold and gave a handful of laps with the same response. Then they dropped off, quite quickly at first. Where in 2011 fastest laps often as not came late in the race, now riders would be dealing with the loss of grip instead. Tyre conservation would become a tactical consideration, and riders accustomed to dealing with late-race slithering would be favoured.

Or would they? This was just one question to be answered at the ninth Qatar GP, the fifth under floodlights. Since 2011, they'd finally found a way to fit a GP weekend into the rather narrow window between sunset and dew point, so once again the meeting started on Thursday; while both smaller classes ran so-called race warm-up on the previous day, giving plenty of time to cool down again. Spots of rain on race-day morning were an uncomfortable reminder of the race postponement in 2009. It wouldn't take another such desert deluge to have the same result, the track having been declared unsafe at night in the wet due to reflections.

Because of this artificiality, along with an ever-ready dusting of desert sand, Qatar is not considered an indicator. Only three times in the past eight years had the race winner become champion (Stoner twice, with four wins to Rossi's three). However, there were few real surprises, and some of those were self-generating – like the continuation

of Rossi's nightmare; an increasingly troubled weekend for double-faller Spies ("I tested my airbag twice; good to know it works well."), and an unexpected CRT turn-around for old fox Colin Edwards.

Perhaps the most significant was another unsettling sign of erratic physical strength from Stoner, stricken by arm-pump. It didn't stop him leading most of the race or hitting the rostrum, but at the end "I felt like a back-marker, getting in everybody's way."

The Ducati story was more complicated than ever. A complete rethink of the bike – aluminium twin-beam chassis, engine canted backwards – had seemed promising in early tests, but ever since then Rossi had been going in fits and starts, finding a direction, then losing it again. Vexingly, Hayden didn't seem to suffer the same problems, or as badly – a reflection perhaps of his dirt-track background, making him more adaptable and able to ride around problems. He qualified fifth, Rossi 12th – at the back of the prototypes. In the race, they were sixth and tenth.

For Valentino, it was still all about understeer, and an inability to get the bike to respond to modifications as he required and expected. After the race, for the first time, his criticism of Ducati became more specific, leading to an immediate flurry of rumours that this marriage, which had seemed made in heaven, had seriously hit the rocks.

The Yamahas all looked strong – Crutchlow fast in all tests, Dovizioso fastest Yamaha at Sepang Two. The Hondas likewise, Pedrosa for once without any residual injury; Bradl was already impressing in his MotoGP debut, and Bautista was picking up speed.

And the CRT bikes? Here was much variety – even among the four Aprilia ART models that dominated the nine-strong entry (the fifth Ioda Aprilia had a production engine, tuned by the team, who had also constructed the Ducati-like steel trellis tubular chassis). In testing, de Puniet had been considerably the fastest – at Jerez, he could stay with the lesser prototypes, but not pass them. "I will have to try to push them into a mistake," he threatened.

The rest of the B-team generation languished some way back. Both FTR Kawasakis had even blown up at the first tests (blamed on unexpected oil surge with the carbon brakes), but clearly had moved forward. Pirro's FTR Honda

Above: CRT pioneer Randy de Puniet and fiancé Lauren Vickers.

Top left: Stoner led, but was already in trouble with arm-pump.

Top right: New aluminium chassis, new year, same old story for the troubled Ducati dream team.

Above centre right: Rossi's impish grin was gone after the race; talks of divorce began directly.

Right: Moto2 champion Bradl made an impressive start, battling with Hayden, Bautista and Barbera.

Photos: Gold & Goose

was barely beyond shakedown, having missed all but the final test and completed, according to the rider, only 500km. Edwards, on the sole Suter BMW, also struggled in tests, with electronics in their infancy. A surge of progress meant that he emerged from nowhere as the strongest of them all – but still 58 seconds adrift at race end.

The move to 1000cc hiked top speeds as expected: Barbera was fastest in 2011 and 2012, with 330.2 and 342.3km/h respectively. By contrast, the CRT bikes ranged from much slower to worryingly so. Edwards clocked 319.5; Petrucci's Ioda was slowest at 301.1. Rather unexpectedly, lap times did not reflect the top-speed increase, for which the new tyres took the blame: Lorenzo's pole was half a second slower than Stoner's in 2011.

Moto2 was the only class where the regulations had barely changed. Nor had the desperation of the racing. Marquez was the obvious favourite, but persistent double-vision problems in 2011 had required surgery in January and he was late to the tests, and supposedly still recovering after five months out of the saddle. This made his victory all the more impressive, but it was controversial – his crucial last-lap pass on Luthi earned him a figurative yellow card from new race director Mike Webb; while Luthi got the same after giving his rival a vengeful punch as he passed on the slow-down lap.

The other novelty of course was Moto3: same or similar cast of characters (minus 2011 title rivals Zarco and Terol), but the bikes all new. They made a good first impression in every respect except noise. The more charitable described their passing as like a squadron of First World War fighters; but rider Danny Webb had another phrase: "like a lawn-mower with a hole in the exhaust". The racing was excellent, however, and if lap times were a couple of seconds slower none of the riders seemed to mind.

MOTOGP RACE – 22 laps

Stoner was fastest out of the box, but by the end Lorenzo had claimed the first 1000cc pole, and by two whole tenths. The Yamaha threat looked increasingly real as Crutchlow took to the front row for the first time, after consistently fast laps.

Spies led row two, after crashing twice – the second time (in the last free practice) dragged by his bike, his left hand worryingly, if only briefly, trapped by the right clip-on. At first the mandatory new brake protector was blamed, but exhaustive study of replays showed that it had already snapped off per design.

Hayden was top Ducati, ahead of Dovizioso. Rossi was last prototype on the grid.

Pedrosa led row three, but not for long, vaulting off the line to push inside Stoner and follow Lorenzo into the first corner. Spies was fourth, but clearly fighting to keep the pace and

soon dropping back fast. Later it turned out that his seat unit had a hidden crack from his practice crash: "It was like a bike with no rear damper," he said.

Thus the front five were settled: Lorenzo, Pedrosa and Stoner already better than a second clear, and then the two satellite Yamahas. All that remained to be established was the final order. That took some doing.

There was a sense of inevitability as Stoner took second off his team-mate into the first corner at the start of lap three. By lap's end, he was ahead of Lorenzo as well, and by half-distance he had stretched his lead to better than two seconds. But the way he told it, it was bound to be temporary. His right arm had tightened even before he took the lead, and the pump had worsened rapidly. Having had trouble braking and even holding on, he spoke of switching style from aggressive to smooth to hold his pace. But it couldn't last and, with five laps to go, both his rivals were on his back wheel.

Lorenzo wasted no time, passed him easily and carried on reeling off near-perfect laps. Later Pedrosa said, "He was smarter than me passing when he did," for he took two more laps before his first-corner move, and by then it was too late for him to attack the Yamaha, as he had previously been doing vigorously. He was less than a second behind; the fading Stoner was another two away.

The battle for fourth was no less absorbing. Dovi led for lap after lap – but it was by inches, and neither rider was making errors. Crutchlow finally pounced with five laps to go and held on all the way to shade his team-mate – much more experienced, but a Yamaha newbie – by a well-earned three-tenths.

Behind these, and losing ground impressively slowly, came rookie Bradl. He was alone for more than half the race, and on lap ten all but four seconds clear of the pursuit. Then experience started to tell.

Hayden led a trio, by inches from Bautista and the feisty Barbera. By lap 14, they were on the rookie, but they were so involved with one another that it took five more laps before anyone got in front. It was Barbera first, and at the start of the last lap all of them, Hayden leading – until in familiar style Barbera outbraked himself into the first corner, rejoining out of touch. Hayden just held off Bautista's final lunge to the line; Bradl was a fine eighth.

Barbera was two seconds down, Rossi the same distance behind him. He had been close to this gang in the early stages, but on lap five he fell foul of Barbera's kamikaze tactics and was forced off on to the paved run-off, losing touch and unable to do much about it.

The next question was whether the fading Spies would fall into the clutches of Edwards – and for a while that looked possible. Edwards had seen off de Puniet when the French-

Right: Colin Edwards was happily surprised to be first CRT winner. The Suter BMW rider's results went downhill from then on.

Below: Night rider. Lorenzo signals his delight at taking first blood.

Photos: Gold & Goose

man ran wide early on, and was lapping sometimes a second faster than his factory-mounted compatriot, but was still 1.2 adrift at the line.

The rest of the CRT gang were well spread by the end: de Puniet getting back ahead of a surprisingly strong and steadfast Hernandez; then came Espargaro, Silva, Pasini and finally Ellison, survivor of an early run-off. Petrucci and Pirro both pitted, as did prototype rider Abraham, with brake trouble.

MOTO2 RACE – 20 laps

Third time out, and no change in Moto2. Good news for fans of sustained close racing, played out by a quality cast of former world champions and GP winners.

This was an extraordinary comeback for Marquez, five months off a bike. Neither his ability nor his tactics had changed: his win ended up with an official reprimand. Marquez the Merciless was back.

Pole went to testing leader Luthi, calm and confident. Marquez was second, Iannone third. Pol Espargaro led row two. These four, along with seventh qualifier Rabat, would play a leading role in a thrilling race with a dramatic final lap.

Luthi led into the first corner from Marquez and Espargaro, Rabat fourth. By the end of the lap, Espargaro was second and pushing hard, likewise Iannone in third, now past Rabat.

Most of the shuffling came through over-ambitious braking at the end of the long straight for the wide right-hander with its tempting paved run-off. It began as they started lap two: Luthi was pushed wide by eager Espargaro and dropped to fourth. He settled to let the race develop, as Espargaro led from laps two to six.

He had Marquez and Iannone behind him, the Italian challenging frequently and furiously, leading on lap seven. He held it for two more laps, but only because Marquez let him, sitting up on the straight – it was obvious that the lighter rider had more speed. On lap ten, he didn't sit up, blew past and led for the first time at half-distance.

Espargaro, Rabat, Luthi and a thrusting Corsi were right there; close behind, di Meglio was fending off Redding, who eventually had got ahead of compatriot Smith, leaving him to fight off de Angelis. Moto2 at its best.

Up front, Espargaro led again as Marquez ran wide at the first corner, dropping to fourth and then fifth as Iannone (who had earlier done the same) got by.

Espargaro narrowly got the better of Rabat as they battled up front, then Luthi moved ahead on lap 15. He attempted

to escape, but Marquez and Iannone followed. Luthi was feeling Marquez's breath down the straight. In a sprint to the line, he would come off worse.

They started the last lap almost side by side, but this time Marquez stayed tucked in. At the braking zone, Luthi's front wheel was still alongside as Marquez swung firmly left. The Swiss rider was pushed on to the painted kerb, ran wide and then off, seething with rage.

Marquez was not clear, Iannone pushing ahead. But he played the speed card again, creeping past on the long run to the line to win by inches.

Espargaro was a close third, two-tenths ahead of Rabat; Luthi fourth.

Redding prevailed over di Meglio; a little further back Smith was ninth, relieved of pressure when de Angelis crashed out, amazingly the only faller. Kallio and Krummenacher were close, class rookie Zarco impressively just behind, while returned former champion Elias headed the next group.

Marquez was warned, but not punished, for his move, which cast a long shadow.

MOTO3 RACE – 18 laps

All change, except the name at the top. Vinales had won the last two 125 races, changed bikes and made it three in a row. The favourite didn't have it all his own way. His rival was 2012's rookie sensation elect, Italian Romano Fenati, 16.

With both riding FTR Hondas for different teams, the issue was in doubt until after halfway. Fenati led away; Vinales finished the first lap fourth. He was at once up to second and closing a gap of more than 1.5 seconds to lead for the first time on lap six. But he couldn't shake off the new boy, and Fenati would lead again before Vinales swooped past for the last time on the 12th. From there, he drew away as Fenati's lap times stretched.

The track first-timer was well over ten seconds clear of a fierce pack, still seven-strong with two laps remaining. A battle of barging, drafting and tactics finally resolved in favour of pole qualifier Cortese, two-tenths ahead of Salom, Oliveira and Khairuddin.

Another impressive rookie, Arthur Sissis, played a strong role and threatened for the rostrum, before running wide and finishing at the back of the group.

Kent and Rossi were less than two seconds down, rookie Rins heading the next group to complete a top ten in which Hondas in various chassis had taken six places, including the top two. It was a slow start for the smattering of independents, with Webb 18th on the Mahindra, his team-mate Schrotter and both Iodas failing to finish; Grotzkyj's Oral was 22nd. But it was an encouragingly close race for the new class, only a little slower (some 2.5km/h) than the departed two-strokes.

Above: Marquez outdragged Iannone for the Moto2 win.

Left: Team-mates at war: Crutchlow and Dovizioso raced inches apart, and the Englishman won out.

Below left: Looking thoughtful, sensational 16-year-old rookie Romano Fenati.

Below: Fenati shadows eventual Moto3 winner Vinales.

Photos: Gold & Goose

FIM WORLD CHAMPIONSHIP

ROUND 1

5-8 APRIL, 2012

COMMERCIALBANK
GRAND PRIX OF QATAR

motoGP · TISSOT SWISS WATCHES SINCE 1853
OFFICIAL TIMEKEEPER

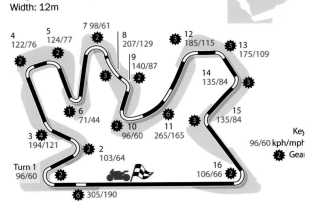

LOSAIL INTERNATIONAL CIRCUIT
22 laps
Length: 5.380 km. / 3,343 miles
Width: 12m

Turn 1 96/60

Key 96/60 kph/mph · Gear

Photos: Gold & Goose

MotoGP	RACE DISTANCE: 22 laps, 73.545 miles/118.360km · RACE WEATHER: Dry (air 24°C, humidity 53%, track 23°C)

Pos.	Rider	Nat.	No.	Entrant	Machine	Tyres	Race tyre choice	Laps	Time & speed
1	**Jorge Lorenzo**	SPA	99	Yamaha Factory Racing	Yamaha YZR-M1	B	F: Extra-hard/R: Hard	22	42m 44.214s 103.253mph/ 166.170km/h
2	**Dani Pedrosa**	SPA	26	Repsol Honda Team	Honda RC213V	B	F: Extra-hard/R: Hard	22	42m 45.066s
3	**Casey Stoner**	AUS	1	Repsol Honda Team	Honda RC213V	B	F: Extra-hard/R: Hard	22	42m 47.122s
4	**Cal Crutchlow**	GBR	35	Monster Yamaha Tech 3	Yamaha YZR-M1	B	F: Extra-hard/R: Hard	22	43m 01.328s
5	**Andrea Dovizioso**	ITA	4	Monster Yamaha Tech 3	Yamaha YZR-M1	B	F: Extra-hard/R: Hard	22	43m 01.634s
6	**Nicky Hayden**	USA	69	Ducati Team	Ducati Desmosedici GP12	B	F: Extra-hard/R: Hard	22	43m 12.627s
7	**Alvaro Bautista**	SPA	19	San Carlo Honda Gresini	Honda RC213V	B	F: Extra-hard/R: Hard	22	43m 12.660s
8	**Stefan Bradl**	GER	6	LCR Honda MotoGP	Honda RC213V	B	F: Extra-hard/R: Hard	22	43m 13.678s
9	**Hector Barbera**	SPA	8	Pramac Racing Team	Ducati Desmosedici GP12	B	F: Extra-hard/R: Hard	22	43m 15.598s
10	**Valentino Rossi**	ITA	46	Ducati Team	Ducati Desmosedici GP12	B	F: Extra-hard/R: Hard	22	43m 17.879s
11	**Ben Spies**	USA	11	Yamaha Factory Racing	Yamaha YZR-M1	B	F: Extra-hard/R: Hard	22	43m 41.121s
12	**Colin Edwards**	USA	5	NGM Mobile Forward Racing	Suter BMW S1000RR	B	F: Extra-hard/R: Hard	22	43m 42.302s
13	**Randy de Puniet**	FRA	14	Power Electronics Aspar	ART Aprilia RSV4	B	F: Extra-hard/R: Hard	22	43m 54.864s
14	**Yonny Hernandez**	COL	68	Avintia Blusens	BQR FTR Kawasaki	B	F: Extra-hard/R: Hard	22	44m 00.157s
15	**Aleix Espargaro**	SPA	41	Power Electronics Aspar	ART Aprilia RSV4	B	F: Extra-hard/R: Hard	22	44m 10.947s
16	Ivan Silva	SPA	22	Avintia Blusens	BQR FTR Kawasaki	B	F: Extra-hard/R: Hard	22	44m 27.541s
17	Mattia Pasini	ITA	54	Speed Master	ART Aprilia RSV4	B	F: Extra-hard/R: Medium	22	44m 31.633s
18	James Ellison	GBR	77	Paul Bird Motorsport	ART Aprilia RSV4	B	F: Extra-hard/R: Medium	22	44m 36.096s
	Danilo Petrucci	ITA	9	Came Ioda Racing Project	Ioda Aprilia RSV4	B	F: Extra-hard/R: Medium	15	DNF-mechanical
	Karel Abraham	CZE	17	Cardion AB Motoracing	Ducati Desmosedici GP12	B	F: Extra Hard/R: Hard	7	DNF-brakes
	Michele Pirro	ITA	51	San Carlo Honda Gresini	FTR Honda CBR1000RR	B	F: Medium/R: Hard	15	rear tyre

Fastest race laps

1	Stoner	1m 55.541s
2	Crutchlow	1m 55.984s
3	Pedrosa	1m 56.001s
4	Lorenzo	1m 56.067s
5	Dovizioso	1m 56.208s
6	Bradl	1m 56.466s
7	Barbera	1m 56.639s
8	Bautista	1m 56.796s
9	Hayden	1m 56.881s
10	Spies	1m 56.958s
11	Abraham	1m 57.051s
12	Rossi	1m 57.144s
13	Edwards	1m 58.153s
14	De Puniet	1m 58.363s
15	Hernandez	1m 58.996s
16	Espargaro	1m 59.191s
17	Pirro	1m 59.543s
18	Silva	1m 59.956s
19	Pasini	1m 59.983s
20	Petrucci	2m 00.142s
21	Ellison	2m 00.246s

Qualifying
Weather: Dry Air Temp: 26°
Humidity: 31% Track Temp: 27°

1	Lorenzo	1m 54.634s
2	Stoner	1m 54.855s
3	Crutchlow	1m 55.022s
4	Spies	1m 55.512s
5	Hayden	1m 55.637s
6	Dovizioso	1m 55.858s
7	Pedrosa	1m 55.905s
8	Barbera	1m 55.983s
9	Bradl	1m 56.063s
10	Abraham	1m 56.198s
11	Bautista	1m 56.521s
12	Rossi	1m 56.813s
13	Edwards	1m 57.644s
14	De Puniet	1m 58.266s
15	Espargaro	1m 58.520s
16	Hernandez	1m 58.795s
17	Pirro	1m 59.085s
18	Pasini	1m 59.195s
19	Petrucci	1m 59.664s
20	Silva	2m 00.493s
21	Ellison	2m 00.757s

Fastest lap: Casey Stoner, on lap 4, 1m 55.541s, 104.159mph/167.628km/h.

Lap record: Casey Stoner, AUS (Ducati), 1m 55.153s, 104.510mph/168.193km/h (2008).

Event best maximum speed: Hector Barbera, 212.7mph/342.3km/h (race).

Grid order	1	2	3	4	5	6	7	8	9	10	11	12	13	14	15	16	17	18	19	20	21	22	
99 LORENZO	99	99	1	1	1	1	1	1	1	1	1	1	1	1	1	1	1	1	99	99	99	99	1
1 STONER	26	26	99	99	99	99	99	99	99	99	99	99	99	99	99	99	99	99	1	1	26	26	2
35 CRUTCHLOW	1	1	26	26	26	26	26	26	26	26	26	26	26	26	26	26	26	26	26	26	1	1	3
11 SPIES	4	4	4	4	4	4	4	4	4	4	4	4	4	4	4	4	35	35	35	35	35	35	4
69 HAYDEN	35	35	35	35	35	35	35	35	35	35	35	35	35	35	35	35	4	4	4	4	4	4	5
4 DOVISIOSO	11	6	6	6	6	6	6	6	6	6	6	6	6	6	6	6	6	6	8	8	69	69	6
26 PEDROSA	6	11	11	11	19	19	19	19	69	69	69	69	69	69	69	69	8	8	6	6	8	19	7
8 BARBERA	69	69	69	69	69	69	69	69	19	19	19	19	19	19	19	8	19	69	69	19	6		8
6 BRADL	19	19	19	19	11	11	11	11	8	8	8	8	8	8	8	19	69	19	19	6	8		9
17 ABRAHAM	8	46	46	46	8	8	8	8	11	46	46	46	46	46	46	46	46	46	46	46	46	46	10
19 BAUTISTA	46	17	8	8	17	46	46	46	46	11	11	11	11	11	11	11	11	11	11	11	11	11	11
46 ROSSI	17	8	17	17	46	5	5	5	5	5	5	5	5	5	5	5	5	5	5	5	5	5	12
5 EDWARDS	68	68	5	5	5	68	68	68	68	14	14	14	14	14	14	14	14	14	14	14	14	14	13
14 DE PUNIET	51	41	68	14	68	14	14	14	14	68	68	68	68	68	68	68	68	68	68	68	68	68	14
41 ESPARGARO	41	5	14	68	41	41	41	41	41	41	41	41	41	41	41	41	41	41	41	41	41	41	15
68 HERNANDEZ	5	14	41	41	14	54	54	54	54	22	22	22	22	22	22	22	22	22	22	22	22	22	
51 PIRRO	14	54	54	54	54	9	9	9	22	54	54	54	54	54	54	54	54	54	54	54	54	54	
54 PASINI	54	9	9	9	9	22	22	22	9	9	9	9	9	77	77	77	77	77	77	77	77	77	
9 PETRUCCI	9	22	22	22	22	51	77	77	77	77	77	77	77	77	9								
22 SILVA	22	77	77	77	51	77	17	51	51	51	51	51	51	51	51								
77 ELLISON	77	51	51	51	77	17	51																

9 Pit stop   51 Lapped rider

Championship Points

1	Lorenzo	25
2	Pedrosa	20
3	Stoner	16
4	Crutchlow	13
5	Dovizioso	11
6	Hayden	10
7	Bautista	9
8	Bradl	8
9	Barbera	7
10	Rossi	6
11	Spies	5
12	Edwards	4
13	De Puniet	3
14	Hernandez	2
15	Espargaro	1

Constructor Points

1	Yamaha	25
2	Honda	20
3	Ducati	10
4	Suter	4
5	ART	3
6	BQR-FTR	2

Moto2

RACE DISTANCE: 20 laps, 66.860 miles/107.600km · RACE WEATHER: Dry (air 25°C, humidity 55%, track 24°C)

Pos.	Rider	Nat.	No.	Entrant	Machine	Laps	Time & Speed
1	**Marc Marquez**	SPA	93	Team CatalunyaCaixa Repsol	Suter	20	40m 34.225s 98.879mph/ 159.130km/h
2	**Andrea Iannone**	ITA	29	Speed Master	Speed Up	20	40m 34.286s
3	**Pol Espargaro**	SPA	40	Pons 40 HP Tuenti	Kalex	20	40m 35.637s
4	**Esteve Rabat**	SPA	80	Pons 40 HP Tuenti	Kalex	20	40m 35.864s
5	**Thomas Luthi**	SWI	12	Interwetten-Paddock	Suter	20	40m 38.206s
6	**Scott Redding**	GBR	45	Marc VDS Racing Team	Kalex	20	40m 40.993s
7	**Mike di Meglio**	FRA	63	S/Master Speed Up	Speed Up	20	40m 41.019s
8	**Simone Corsi**	ITA	3	Came IodaRacing Project	FTR	20	40m 41.211s
9	**Bradley Smith**	GBR	38	Tech 3 Racing	Tech 3	20	40m 45.053s
10	**Mika Kallio**	FIN	36	Marc VDS Racing Team	Kalex	20	40m 45.604s
11	**Randy Krummenacher**	SWI	34	GP Team Switzerland	Kalex	20	40m 46.975s
12	**Johann Zarco**	FRA	5	JIR Moto2	Motobi	20	40m 48.346s
13	**Toni Elias**	SPA	24	Mapfre Aspar Team	Suter	20	40m 51.859s
14	**Takaaki Nakagami**	JPN	30	Italtrans Racing Team	Kalex	20	40m 52.100s
15	**Julian Simon**	SPA	60	Blusens Avintia	FTR	20	40m 52.119s
16	Claudio Corti	ITA	71	Italtrans Racing Team	Kalex	20	40m 53.239s
17	Xavier Simeon	BEL	19	Tech 3 Racing	Tech 3	20	40m 53.339s
18	Dominique Aegerter	SWI	77	Technomag-CIP	Suter	20	41m 03.027s
19	Yuki Takahashi	JPN	72	NGM Mobile Forward Racing	Suter	20	41m 10.823s
20	Angel Rodriguez	SPA	47	Desguaces La Torre SAG	FTR	20	41m 10.963s
21	Ratthapark Wilairot	THA	14	Thai Honda Gresini Moto2	Moriwaki	20	41m 11.372s
22	Axel Pons	SPA	49	Pons 40 HP Tuenti	Kalex	20	41m 11.668s
23	Nicolas Terol	SPA	18	Mapfre Aspar Team	Suter	20	41m 13.748s
24	Ricard Cardus	SPA	88	Arguiñano Racing Team	AJR	20	41m 19.485s
25	Anthony West	AUS	95	QMMF Racing Team	Moriwaki	20	41m 28.011s
26	Gino Rea	GBR	8	Federal Oil Gresini Moto2	Moriwaki	20	41m 28.233s
27	Marco Colandrea	SWI	10	SAG Team	FTR	20	41m 53.279s
28	Alexander Lundh	SWE	7	Cresto Guide MZ Racing	MZ FTR	20	41m 53.296s
29	Elena Rosell	SPA	82	QMMF Racing Team	Moriwaki	20	42m 09.375s
30	Max Neukirchner	GER	76	Kiefer Racing	Kalex	19	40m 47.986s
	Alex de Angelis	RSM	15	NGM Mobile Forward Racing	Suter	18	DNF
	Nasser Hasan Al Malki	QAT	96	QMMF Racing Team	Moriwaki	10	DNF
	Roberto Rolfo	ITA	44	Technomag-CIP	Suter	3	DNF

Fastest lap: Marc Marquez, on lap 15, 2m 0.645s, 99.753mph/160.537km/h (record).
Previous lap record: Alex de Angelis, RSM (Motobi), 2m 1.003s, 98.458mph/160.062km/h (2011).
Event best maximum speed: Randy Krummenacher, 177.1mph/285.0km/h (race).

Qualifying: Dry — Air: 28° Humidity: 29% Track: 28°

	Rider	Time		Rider	Time
1	Luthi	2m 00.187s	18	Simeon	2m 01.718s
2	Marquez	2m 00.259s	19	Zarco	2m 01.910s
3	Iannone	2m 00.296s	20	Rolfo	2m 02.018s
4	Espargaro	2m 00.597s	21	Krummenacher	2m 02.097s
5	Di Meglio	2m 00.625s	22	Rodriguez	2m 02.142s
6	Neukirchner	2m 00.658s	23	Cardus	2m 02.500s
7	Rabat	2m 00.793s	24	Pons	2m 02.535s
8	Corti	2m 00.874s	25	Takahashi	2m 02.637s
9	Nakagami	2m 00.898s	26	Terol	2m 02.811s
10	Corsi	2m 00.986s	27	Rea	2m 02.934s
11	Simon	2m 00.992s	28	Wilairot	2m 03.031s
12	Smith	2m 01.015s	29	West	2m 03.621s
13	Redding	2m 01.031s	30	Lundh	2m 04.130s
14	Kallio	2m 01.111s	31	Colandrea	2m 04.424s
15	De Angelis	2m 01.181s	32	Rosell	2m 05.183s
16	Aegerter	2m 01.374s	33	Al Malki	2m 05.591s
17	Elias	2m 01.618s			

Fastest race laps

	Rider	Time		Rider	Time
1	Marquez	2m 00.645s	18	Simeon	2m 01.717s
2	Luthi	2m 00.803s	19	Elias	2m 01.734s
3	Iannone	2m 00.824s	20	Aegerter	2m 01.971s
4	Rabat	2m 00.979s	21	Terol	2m 02.504s
5	Redding	2m 01.160s	22	Cardus	2m 02.559s
6	Espargaro	2m 01.170s	23	Pons	2m 02.601s
7	Corti	2m 01.176s	24	Wilairot	2m 02.669s
8	De Angelis	2m 01.248s	25	Takahashi	2m 02.734s
9	Smith	2m 01.329s	26	Rodriguez	2m 02.790s
10	Di Meglio	2m 01.416s	27	Rea	2m 03.139s
11	Corti	2m 01.428s	28	West	2m 03.204s
12	Krummenacher	2m 01.445s	29	Rolfo	2m 04.220s
13	Simon	2m 01.589s	30	Lundh	2m 04.496s
14	Zarco	2m 01.594s	31	Colandrea	2m 04.636s
15	Kallio	2m 01.619s	32	Rosell	2m 04.850s
16	Nakagami	2m 01.640s	33	Al Malki	2m 06.191s
17	Neukirchner	2m 01.640s			

Championship Points

	Rider	Pts
1	Marquez	25
2	Iannone	20
3	Espargaro	16
4	Rabat	13
5	Luthi	11
6	Redding	10
7	Di Meglio	9
8	Corsi	8
9	Smith	7
10	Kallio	6
11	Krummenacher	5
12	Zarco	4
13	Elias	3
14	Nakagami	2
15	Simon	1

Constructor Points

		Pts
1	Suter	25
2	Speed Up	20
3	Kalex	16
4	FTR	8
5	Tech 3	7
6	Motobi	4

Moto3

RACE DISTANCE: 18 laps, 60.174 miles/96.840km · RACE WEATHER: Dry (air 25°C, humidity 55%, track 28°C)

Pos.	Rider	Nat.	No.	Entrant	Machine	Laps	Time & Speed
1	**Maverick Viñales**	SPA	25	Blusens Avintia	FTR Honda	18	38m 40.995s 93.332mph/ 150.204km/h
2	**Romano Fenati**	ITA	5	Team Italia FMI	FTR Honda	18	38m 45.296s
3	**Sandro Cortese**	GER	11	Red Bull KTM Ajo	KTM	18	38m 59.008s
4	**Luis Salom**	SPA	39	RW Racing GP	Kalex KTM	18	38m 59.195s
5	**Miguel Oliveira**	POR	44	Estrella Galicia 0,0	Suter Honda	18	38m 59.740s
6	**Zulfahmi Khairuddin**	MAL	63	AirAsia-Sic-Ajo	KTM	18	39m 00.047s
7	**Arthur Sissis**	AUS	61	Red Bull KTM Ajo	KTM	18	39m 00.461s
8	**Danny Kent**	GBR	52	Red Bull KTM Ajo	KTM	18	39m 02.093s
9	**Louis Rossi**	FRA	96	Racing Team Germany	FTR Honda	18	39m 02.148s
10	**Alex Rins**	SPA	42	Estrella Galicia 0,0	Suter Honda	18	39m 09.728s
11	**Alan Techer**	FRA	89	Technomag-CIP-TSR	TSR Honda	18	39m 10.770s
12	**Hector Faubel**	SPA	55	Bankia Aspar Team	Kalex KTM	18	39m 10.808s
13	**Niklas Ajo**	FIN	31	TT Motion Events Racing	KTM	18	39m 16.935s
14	**Alberto Moncayo**	SPA	23	Bankia Aspar Team	Kalex KTM	18	39m 16.978s
15	**Jakub Kornfeil**	CZE	84	Redox-Ongetta-Centro Seta	FTR Honda	18	39m 19.636s
16	Efren Vazquez	SPA	7	JHK T-Shirt Laglisse	Honda	18	39m 21.214s
17	Niccolò Antonelli	ITA	27	San Carlo Gresini Moto3	Honda	18	39m 31.624s
18	Danny Webb	GBR	99	Mahindra Racing	Mahindra	18	39m 35.746s
19	Ivan Moreno	SPA	21	Andalucia JHK Laglisse	FTR Honda	18	39m 35.984s
20	Adrian Martin	SPA	26	JHK T-Shirt Laglisse	Honda	18	39m 46.178s
21	Kenta Fujii	JPN	51	Technomag-CIP-TSR	TSR Honda	18	40m 02.234s
22	Simone Grotzkyj	ITA	15	Ambrogio Next Racing	Oral	18	40m 16.786s
23	Toni Finsterbusch	GER	9	Cresto Guide MZ Racing	MZ-RE Honda	18	40m 22.286s
24	Jasper Iwema	NED	53	Moto FGR	FGR Honda	18	40m 35.288s
25	Jack Miller	AUS	8	Caretta Technology	Honda	17	39m 13.062s
	Jonas Folger	GER	94	IodaRacing Project	Ioda	11	DNF
	Luigi Morciano	ITA	3	Ioda Team Italia	Ioda	7	DNF
	Brad Binder	RSA	41	RW Racing GP	Kalex KTM	6	DNF
	Marcel Schrotter	GER	77	Mahindra Racing	Mahindra	5	DNF
	Alexis Masbou	FRA	10	Caretta Technology	Honda	0	DNF
	Alessandro Tonucci	ITA	19	Team Italia FMI	FTR Honda	0	DNF
	Isaac Viñales	SPA	32	Ongetta-Centro Seta	FTR Honda	0	DNF

Fastest lap: Maverick Viñales, on lap 3, 2m 7.276s, 94.556mph/152.173km/h (record).
Previous lap record: New category.
Event best maximum speed: Zulfahmi Khairuddin, 142.7mph/229.7km/h (race).

Qualifying: Dry — Air: 29° Humidity: 25% Track: 30°

	Rider	Time		Rider	Time
1	Cortese	2m 08.188s	17	Iwema	2m 09.876s
2	M. Viñales	2m 08.204s	18	Techer	2m 09.991s
3	Rossi	2m 08.303s	19	Kornfeil	2m 10.142s
4	Salom	2m 08.566s	20	Antonelli	2m 10.150s
5	Ajo	2m 08.734s	21	Vazquez	2m 10.577s
6	Fenati	2m 08.799s	22	Moreno	2m 10.760s
7	Khairuddin	2m 08.847s	23	Schrotter	2m 11.055s
8	Oliveira	2m 08.926s	24	Martin	2m 11.264s
9	Sissis	2m 09.001s	25	Webb	2m 11.317s
10	Masbou	2m 09.107s	26	Miller	2m 11.461s
11	Tonucci	2m 09.119s	27	I. Viñales	2m 11.651s
12	Kent	2m 09.126s	28	Fujii	2m 12.845s
13	Rins	2m 09.139s	29	Grotzkyj	2m 12.960s
14	Moncayo	2m 09.370s	30	Morciano	2m 13.024s
15	Binder	2m 09.560s	31	Finsterbusch	2m 13.254s
16	Faubel	2m 09.869s	32	Folger	2m 13.695s

Fastest race laps

	Rider	Time		Rider	Time
1	M. Viñales	2m 07.276s	16	Techer	2m 09.352s
2	Fenati	2m 07.855s	17	Vazquez	2m 09.476s
3	Oliveira	2m 08.178s	18	Ajo	2m 09.503s
4	Salom	2m 08.280s	19	Moreno	2m 09.829s
5	Cortese	2m 08.446s	20	Schrotter	2m 09.961s
6	Kent	2m 08.459s	21	Webb	2m 10.025s
7	Khairuddin	2m 08.543s	22	Martin	2m 10.045s
8	Rins	2m 08.770s	23	Miller	2m 10.182s
9	Rossi	2m 08.912s	24	Iwema	2m 11.385s
10	Sissis	2m 08.924s	25	Grotzkyj	2m 12.191s
11	Binder	2m 09.041s	26	Fujii	2m 12.322s
12	Antonelli	2m 09.070s	27	Folger	2m 12.754s
13	Moncayo	2m 09.173s	28	Finsterbusch	2m 12.762s
14	Kornfeil	2m 09.186s	29	Morciano	2m 12.896s
15	Faubel	2m 09.326s			

Championship Points

	Rider	Pts
1	M. Viñales	25
2	Fenati	20
3	Cortese	16
4	Salom	13
5	Oliveira	11
6	Khairuddin	10
7	Sissis	9
8	Kent	8
9	Rossi	7
10	Rins	6
11	Techer	5
12	Faubel	4
13	Ajo	3
14	Moncayo	2
15	Kornfeil	1

Constructor Points

		Pts
1	FTR Honda	25
2	KTM	16
3	Kalex KTM	13
4	Suter Honda	11
5	TSR Honda	5

SPANISH GRAND PRIX
JEREZ CIRCUIT

Main photo: End of lap two, and Stoner has forced through to first from Lorenzo and Hayden. Arm-pump notwithstanding, he would stay there.

Inset, left: The weather was seasonable, and unpleasant.

Inset, below: Stoner was unstoppable.

Photos: Gold & Goose

Above: Youth versus experience, Honda versus Ducati – and Bradl pipped Hayden for seventh by inches.

Top right: Lorenzo surveys looming skies before the start.

Above right: Hervé Poncharal had another race worrying about the tooth-and-nail battle between his riders. There would be many more.

Above far right: Marquez Mk2 – younger brother Alex made his GP debut at Jerez.

Right: Barbera heads the midfield pack from Rossi, Spies, Abraham and de Puniet.

Photos: Gold & Goose

JEREZ, late to be confirmed on the calendar, opened the European season again in typical seasonal weather. Unsettled. Practice and, to an extent, qualifying were interrupted by squalls and blusters. Race day started worse, in front of a relatively small crowd claimed at 103,728. It was raining for morning warm-up, soggy for a crash-happy Moto3 race, and then the dry Moto2 race was red-flagged when a shower hit close enough to the end to rule out a restart.

The main race was dry, but with damp patches, making tyre choice as well as the actual riding a vexatious gamble.

Particularly so with a third choice available for the front – a new softer-construction tyre that Bridgestone had essayed at Jerez tests to almost universal approval – to the extent that they decided to offer it as soon as possible. Given production in Japan and a preference for shipping by sea rather than sending tyres air freight, the rubber for upcoming races had already been produced, so it was not until round six at Silverstone that the tyre was available in significant quantities. In the meantime, they would ship in small numbers, two per rider per weekend, and the tyre rules were temporarily tweaked to increase the allocation accordingly.

The dissenters were both Repsol Honda riders, who found that the softer carcase not only squirmed more under braking to spoil corner-entry stability, but also worsened their already troublesome chatter. Their complaints would continue, but to little effect, leading Pedrosa to describe the change in plans as "unfair to Honda".

After a three-week break, the rainy start was so dispiriting that hardly anyone went out in the MotoGP class on the Friday morning, leaving Ivan Silva to post fastest time. His CRT Kawasaki had something new to show: an Inmotec half-carbon chassis replaced the usual FTR, which would continue to appear fitfully as the season wore on, but was not yet used for racing.

Conditions left everyone short of set-up time: often a formula that yields a good race, with riders tentative in the early laps, and nobody's technical edge as acute as usual. Wet patches mixed things further, and the second 1000cc race was even better than the first.

The rain did allow the factory Ducati riders to have some fun, playing up near and sometimes at the top of the lists in free practice, and adding another layer to the Ducati puzzle: why should a bike so troublesome improve so much in the rain? This would prove to be the case again in the future, with no explanation now or then. They'd puzzled for a long time, said Nicky. "With the carbon, we used to think it was because our bike was too stiff; then in the wet they were all too stiff." With the chassis change, perhaps it was "because our bike gets heat into the tyres more" – a drawback in the dry, but helpful in the rain.

Hayden would end up on the front row, but the dry race brought out the worst in the red bikes, especially for Rossi, who qualified last of the factory bikes and even behind de Puniet's CRT machine. He explained how the bike didn't respond to changes as he required. His confusion was so great that on race day he abandoned his own direction altogether to follow Hayden's settings. He discovered that rather than his preferred short and tall bike, giving plenty of front-to-rear weight transfer, "this bike needs to be low and long and more flat." Although not at this race, the new direction would bring some cheer, though Rossi was at pains to point out that he was not copying his team-mate. "They are settings from Ducati," he said; while Hayden just gave a slow smile and said, "It shows my crew chief has been working in a good direction."

With the chatter in the dry, Stoner was concerned that the muscle problems that had spoiled his Qatar race would resurface. Typically mysterious, he explained that he had been treating the arm "with our own methods that I prefer not to disclose"; but the greater boon was the wet. "It puts less force on your arms," he said.

Second race in, and Crutchlow was already being taken seriously: as he quipped when he joined luminaries Stoner and co at the pre-event conference, "It's good to be here. Last year I had to pay to get in." The quickening of international media interest was reflected by the worldwide circulation of the story of his mouse: one had moved into his motorhome, in situ since Jerez tests, and was proving difficult to dislodge. "He's so clever," said Crutchlow, after the rodent had cunningly removed the bait from a number of different

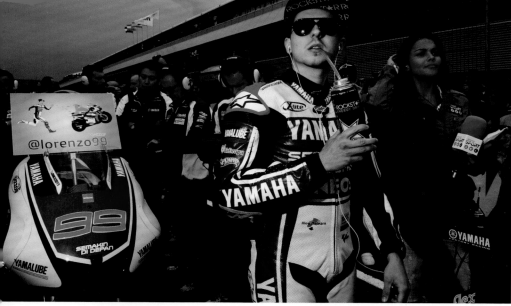

traps without triggering any, and he moved out to sleep in a hotel. More to the point was his progress on track. He was proving not only capable of fast laps on the re-shod 1000s, but of stringing them together all race long. Once again he had a better race than team-mate Dovi. With your team-mate always the first person you want to beat, things were hotting up in the Tech 3 pit, and they would get hotter.

Interesting times in Moto3 showed that the tide of youth was in no way receding.

Firstly there was an amazing victory for Italian teen Romano Fenati, who took the title lead in only his second GP. In the Italian Federation-backed team, run by former champion Roberto Locatelli, he was rawer than most rookies, in that he had never raced at Jerez before. Where most had served apprenticeships in the prestigious Spanish national series, the CEV, and several others also on the GP trail with the Red Bull Rookies cup, he was straight from winning his own national championship, a more local affair that meant he had never raced outside Italy.

Then there was the debut of Marquez's younger brother, Alex, who had reached the minimum age of 16 four days before practice began. Riding a Suter Honda at a familiar track, he qualified 13th and raced to 12th, prompting his brother to say, "It's time to open the gas. He is coming." He was following the footsteps of Lorenzo, who had made his GP debut at Jerez in 2002 after missing the first day of practice because he was too young. On Saturday, his birthday, he turned 15, then the minimum age.

Finally, rider Niklas Ajo was disqualified from the next race, the Portuguese GP, after a shoving match with marshals, who were preventing him from restarting the race after crashing, ended with one being pushed to the ground.

MOTOGP RACE – 27 laps

Pole seemed to belong to Pedrosa – until Lorenzo shaded him by just over a tenth at the last gasp. Their surprising companion was Hayden, his first front row in more than a year. He was hoping for a wet race.

Row two saw Crutchlow fourth after a crash, Stoner at a very unfavourite track, then Spies; Dovizioso led the third from Bautista (another to fall) and Bradl. De Puniet's CRT bike headed the fourth, Rossi behind him, leading row five.

The race started under lowering skies and with lingering damp patches. All chose the harder rear, and most the new-spec harder front; exceptions were both Honda and Yamaha factory riders, plus Hayden, Dovizioso, Abraham and Silva. "If I'd had the hard front, I think I would have won," Lorenzo said later.

Pedrosa led away from Lorenzo, Crutchlow, Hayden and Dovizioso. But it was a bruising scramble, and by the end of the lap it was Dovi second and Stoner poised to take fourth from Crutchlow. The Honda rider hadn't gone out in wet warm-up, so an overnight setting change was untested: "a lucky dip", as he smiled later.

Stoner was up to second by the end of lap two and took the lead at Dry Sack hairpin. Lorenzo and a charging Hayden also got past Pedrosa by the end of that lap, and Pedrosa immediately lost another place to Dovi, who had recovered quickly after being punted out wide at Dry Sack by Lorenzo. Onlookers took the Spaniard's wave for an apology, but it was a reprimand. "We both ride for Yamaha, but if he had the pace, he should attack later, not ride crazy and try and win the race in the first two laps," Lorenzo said.

Stoner and Lorenzo immediately started to pull clear as Hayden held on to third for the next three laps. The gap was 2.6 seconds by the time Pedrosa got back to third on lap seven, and it continued to grow, to more than four seconds at half-distance.

As the 20-lap mark approached, Lorenzo started pushing harder, and while Stoner wasn't able to stop him from getting on his tail, he couldn't find a way past.

By now the Australian was suffering worsening arm-pump

and several times ran wide. But he wouldn't give way. Obviously it would go to the wire – and so it did.

Lorenzo was half a second behind as they started the last lap. But Stoner proved impregnable, and by the time they reached the flag, Lorenzo had decided that a safe second would have to do. It was Stoner's first win at the circuit.

Pedrosa had closed steadily at the end, fighting front-end slides at the same time as fending off a fast and persistent Crutchlow. The Briton was still looking for a way past as they crossed the line. "Trouble is, he never makes any mistakes," he said.

Dovi had been with them until almost half-distance, when he started to drop away. He was more than 15 seconds adrift at the end, but safe from Bautista behind.

Hayden had run short of grip after lap seven, losing place after place until at half-distance he was behind Bautista and under pressure from Bradl. The rookie was ahead from lap 13, Hayden in front again as they started the last lap – but Bradl used his exit grip to reverse the positions at the flag.

Some way back, Rossi had been battling with Barbera, Spies and Abraham. The last-named slipped off on lap 20, remounting for last place; at the same time, Spies lost touch, his handling problems becoming worse after missing the settings.

Barbera was ahead of Rossi on lap 21. Only three laps from the end was the multi-champion able to get back in front, to lead narrowly over the line.

De Puniet had been running a couple of seconds adrift, but retired with two laps to go with a fuel pump failure. This left team-mate Espargaro top CRT bike, six seconds ahead of Petrucci's well-ridden Aprilia.

The under-class was still not yet making a race of it: Pasini took the last point, almost 15 seconds down, but comfortably clear of Silva's FTR Kawasaki. Edwards was another eight seconds away, last rider not to be lapped, with the remounted Abraham last.

Ellison and Pirro joined de Puniet on the retirement list, the Briton suffering tooth-loosening chatter; Hernandez had trouble on the start line, started from the pit lane and completed one slow lap before retiring.

Above: CRT makes its European debut – Aleix Espargaro heads Ellison.

Above right: Crutchlow's strong second season continued as he beat team-mate Dovi once again.

Right: Moto2 mayhem as usual, with winner Espargaro and Marquez (93) heading the pack.

Below: Cortese heads Salom and newcomer Rins in the fight for Moto3's final podium slot.

Below right: The amazing Fenati scored his maiden GP victory in only his second race, at a track he'd not seen before.

Photos: Gold & Goose

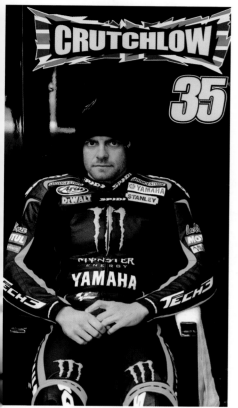

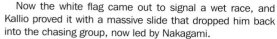

MOTO2 RACE – 17 laps

Marquez took pole by less than a tenth from Nakagami and Espargaro; Luthi led row two from Kallio and Corti. Class rookie Zarco had been strong in the wet, but ended up tenth in dry qualifying; his 125 victor Terol was 28th. Australian Anthony West had frequently topped the time sheets in the wet, but in the dry he could manage no better than 29th on his ill-favoured Moriwaki.

The race started dry, with a familiar brawl into the first corner, Espargaro pushing Marquez wide. Luthi was in front, and he stayed there all lap long, and for the next six ahead of a barging and shuffling pack.

Espargaro was in the mix, along with Marquez, Corti and team-mate Nakagami, di Meglio and Redding, di Meglio forcing ahead briefly on the third lap. Krummenacher was close and soon to join them, setting fastest lap on the seventh as he moved through to fourth. He slipped off soon afterwards, remounting to rejoin at the back.

Redding was charging and took over up front on lap eight, holding on for the next five laps at a track where his size and weight told against him less than elsewhere.

With the race approaching half-distance, the front pack was four strong, with Marquez, Luthi and Espargaro all up close to the Briton. A second behind, Kallio had taken over the chase, closing up to make it five.

It was still anybody's guess – except that as usual Marquez seemed strongest, and certainly fastest, on the straight.

On lap 14, Luthi regained the lead and tried to break away; he was almost half a second clear as they crossed the line, Marquez second.

Now the white flag came out to signal a wet race, and Kallio proved it with a massive slide that dropped him back into the chasing group, now led by Nakagami.

The rain was light and lap times hardly dropped, but it was clear that the race might be stopped. The only question was when. This intensified the battle, and Marquez took to the front as Redding lost touch.

Espargaro made his move at the Dry Sack hairpin to lead lap 17 from Marquez and Luthi, and though the younger rider seized the lead firmly into the first corner, it was a few yards too late. He led as they finished lap 18, and as they crossed the line (completing two-thirds race distance) the red flags came out.

Results were taken from the previous lap, so it was a joyful Espargaro who won, Marquez second and Luthi third.

Nakagami had broken away from his gang and was closing on Redding, half a second off at the flag. He was followed in short order by Corti, Kallio, Aegerter, Elias and Zarco, with Smith another second away in 11th, fending off de Angelis.

Both di Meglio and Neukirchner joined a surprisingly short crash list.

MOTO3 RACE – 23 laps

Wet qualifying yielded a surprise pole for yet another hot teenage rookie, Spaniard Alex Rins, from Cortese and Oliveira. Earlier in the session, Australian rookies Miller and Sissis had been fastest; they ended up sixth and eighth.

Race conditions were foul, patchy showers leading to wildly changing fortunes and many crashes. Of 34 starters, 20 crashed, with several remounting to make 17 finishers. Miller was unluckiest, breaking his collarbone in a first-lap pile-up with Grotzkyj and Kent. Schrotter also fell right by the pit entrance, pushing in for repairs and rejoining.

The brave dashed away only for most to fall. Except for Fenati. Vinales was an early victim, dropping from sixth on lap two to 28th next time around.

Kornfeil led first, crashing after two laps. Rins was with him, and almost four seconds clear at the end of lap seven before he dropped to second after a spectacular save.

Now Rossi led for a lap, falling directly after Rins and Fenati had pushed past. Rins lasted four more laps before falling, but lost only 15 seconds. Fenati, however, was pulling clear remorselessly.

In pursuit, Salom, Cortese and Rins battled to the flag, Masbou losing touch for fifth.

Vinales stormed back through to sixth, past Moncayo, Antonelli, Faubel and Khairuddin, all spaced out to complete the top ten, the last riders not to be lapped. Webb had tagged on to Vinales as he came through, but stopped abruptly with a broken con-rod.

Other notable crashers included Vazquez, Ajo, Binder, Oliveira, Sissis and Martin. Young Alex Marquez also fell, but remounted and kept his head for a good 12th.

ROUND **2**

27–29 APRIL, 2012

GRAN PREMIO
bwin
DE ESPAÑA

motoGP | **TISSOT** SWISS WATCHES SINCE 1853
OFFICIAL TIMEKEEPER

CIRCUITO DE JEREZ

27 laps
Length: 4.423 km. / 2.748 miles
Width: 11m

Expo '92 90/56
Alex Criville 160/99
Peluqui 115/72
271/168
Ferrari 180/112
131/81
Michelin 78/48
Jorge Martinez Aspar
Turn 4 166/103
Angel Nieto 99/62
Turn 7 170/106
Ducados 72/45
Sito Pons 130/81
Dry Sack 72/45
275/171

Key
96/60 kph/mph
Gear

Photos: Gold & Goose

MotoGP | RACE DISTANCE: 27 laps, 74.205 miles/119.421km · RACE WEATHER: Dry (air 14°C, humidity 78%, track 15°C)

Pos.	Rider	Nat.	No.	Entrant	Machine	Tyres	Race tyre choice	Laps	Time & speed
1	**Casey Stoner**	AUS	1	Repsol Honda Team	Honda RC213V	B	F: Medium/R: Soft	27	45m 33.897s 97.712mph/ 157.253km/h
2	Jorge Lorenzo	SPA	99	Yamaha Factory Racing	Yamaha YZR-M1	B	F: Medium/R: Soft	27	45m 34.844s
3	Dani Pedrosa	SPA	26	Repsol Honda Team	Honda RC213V	B	F: Medium/R: Soft	27	45m 35.960s
4	Cal Crutchlow	GBR	35	Monster Yamaha Tech 3	Yamaha YZR-M1	B	F: Hard/R: Soft	27	45m 36.362s
5	Andrea Dovizioso	ITA	4	Monster Yamaha Tech 3	Yamaha YZR-M1	B	F: Medium/R: Soft	27	45m 51.997s
6	Alvaro Bautista	SPA	19	San Carlo Honda Gresini	Honda RC213V	B	F: Hard/R: Soft	27	45m 55.292s
7	Stefan Bradl	GER	6	LCR Honda MotoGP	Honda RC213V	B	F: Hard/R: Soft	27	46m 02.534s
8	Nicky Hayden	USA	69	Ducati Team	Ducati Desmosedici GP12	B	F: Medium/R: Soft	27	46m 02.766s
9	Valentino Rossi	ITA	46	Ducati Team	Ducati Desmosedici GP12	B	F: Hard/R: Soft	27	46m 08.749s
10	Hector Barbera	SPA	8	Pramac Racing Team	Ducati Desmosedici GP12	B	F: Hard/R: Soft	27	46m 09.000s
11	Ben Spies	USA	11	Yamaha Factory Racing	Yamaha YZR-M1	B	F: Hard/R: Soft	27	46m 11.938s
12	Aleix Espargaro	SPA	41	Power Electronics Aspar	ART Aprilia RSV4	B	F: Hard/R: Soft	27	46m 46.625s
13	Danilo Petrucci	ITA	9	Came Ioda Racing Project	Ioda Aprilia RSV4	B	F: Hard/R: Soft	27	46m 52.566s
14	Mattia Pasini	ITA	54	Speed Master	ART Aprilia RSV4	B	F: Hard/R: Soft	27	47m 03.039s
15	Ivan Silva	SPA	22	Avintia Blusens	BQR FTR Kawasaki	B	F: Medium/R: Soft	27	47m 06.375s
16	Colin Edwards	USA	5	NGM Mobile Forward Racing	Suter BMW S1000RR	B	F: Hard/R: Soft	27	47m 14.474s
17	Karel Abraham	CZE	17	Cardion AB Motoracing	Ducati Desmosedici GP12	B	F: Medium/R: Soft	26	45m 49.303s
	Randy de Puniet	FRA	14	Power Electronics Aspar	ART-Aprilia RSV4	B	F: Hard/R: Soft	25	DNF-fuel pump
	James Ellison	GBR	77	Paul Bird Motorsport	ART-Aprilia RSV4	B	F: Hard/R: Soft	24	DNF-handling
	Michele Pirro	ITA	51	San Carlo Honda Gresini	FTR-Honda CBR1000RR	B	F: Hard/R: Soft	18	DNF-electronics
	Yonny Hernandez	COL	68	Avintia Blusens	BQR-FTR Kawasaki	B	F: Hard/R: Soft	0	DNF-electronics

Fastest lap: Cal Crutchlow, on lap 15, 1m 40.019s, 98.920mph/159.197km/h.

Lap record: Dani Pedrosa, SPA (Honda), 1m 39.731s, 99.206mph/159.657km/h (2010).

Event best maximum speed: Stefan Bradl, 179.6mph/289.0km/h (race).

Qualifying

Weather: Dry
Air Temp: 16° Humidity: 62%
Track Temp: 21°

1	Lorenzo	1m 39.532s
2	Pedrosa	1m 39.667s
3	Hayden	1m 40.563s
4	Crutchlow	1m 40.570s
5	Stoner	1m 40.577s
6	Spies	1m 41.090s
7	Dovizioso	1m 41.180s
8	Bautista	1m 41.447s
9	Bradl	1m 41.550s
10	De Puniet	1m 41.700s
11	Abraham	1m 41.724s
12	Barbera	1m 41.871s
13	Rossi	1m 42.961s
14	Espargaro	1m 43.135s
15	Pirro	1m 43.363s
16	Pasini	1m 44.308s
17	Hernandez	1m 44.467s
18	Petrucci	1m 44.645s
19	Silva	1m 44.717s
20	Ellison	1m 45.724s
21	Edwards	1m 46.200s

Fastest race laps

1	Crutchlow	1m 40.019s
2	Pedrosa	1m 40.062s
3	Stoner	1m 40.151s
4	Lorenzo	1m 40.350s
5	Dovizioso	1m 40.548s
6	Bautista	1m 41.009s
7	Barbera	1m 41.047s
8	Rossi	1m 41.062s
9	Bradl	1m 41.195s
10	Hayden	1m 41.363s
11	Spies	1m 41.521s
12	Abraham	1m 41.569s
13	De Puniet	1m 41.996s
14	Espargaro	1m 42.742s
15	Ellison	1m 42.975s
16	Petrucci	1m 42.989s
17	Edwards	1m 43.034s
18	Pirro	1m 43.143s
19	Silva	1m 43.300s
20	Pasini	1m 43.419s

Championship Points

1	Lorenzo	45
2	Stoner	41
3	Pedrosa	36
4	Crutchlow	26
5	Dovizioso	22
6	Bautista	19
7	Hayden	18
8	Bradl	17
9	Rossi	13
10	Barbera	13
11	Spies	10
12	Espargaro	5
13	Edwards	3
14	Petrucci	3
15	De Puniet	3
16	Pasini	2
17	Hernandez	2
18	Silva	1

Constructor Points

1	Honda	45
2	Yamaha	45
3	Ducati	18
4	ART	7
5	Suter	4
6	Ioda	3
7	BQR-FTR	2
8	BQR	1

Grid order

Grid order	1	2	3	4	5	6	7	8	9	10	11	12	13	14	15	16	17	18	19	20	21	22	23	24	25	26	27	
99 LORENZO	26	26	1	1	1	1	1	1	1	1	1	1	1	1	1	1	1	1	1	1	1	1	1	1	1	1	1	1
26 PEDROSA	4	1	99	99	99	99	99	99	99	99	99	99	99	99	99	99	99	99	99	99	99	99	99	99	99	99	99	2
69 HAYDEN	99	99	69	69	69	69	26	26	26	26	26	26	26	26	26	26	26	26	26	26	26	26	26	26	26	26	26	3
35 CRUTCHLOW	35	69	26	4	4	4	69	35	35	35	35	35	35	35	35	35	35	35	35	35	35	35	35	35	35	35	35	4
1 STONER	1	4	4	26	26	26	4	4	4	4	4	4	4	4	4	4	4	4	4	4	4	4	4	4	4	4	4	5
11 SPIES	69	35	35	35	35	35	35	69	69	69	19	19	19	19	19	19	19	19	19	19	19	19	19	19	19	19	19	6
4 DOVISIOSO	11	6	6	6	6	6	6	6	19	19	69	69	6	6	6	6	6	6	6	6	6	6	6	69	6		7
19 BAUTISTA	19	19	19	19	19	19	19	6	6	69	69	69	69	69	69	69	69	69	69	69	69	69	69	6	69		8
6 BRADL	6	11	11	11	8	8	8	46	46	46	46	46	46	46	46	46	8	8	8	8	8	46	46	46			9
14 DE PUNIET	46	46	46	8	11	11	46	46	46	8	8	8	8	8	8	8	46	46	46	46	46						10
17 ABRAHAM	8	8	8	46	46	46	11	17	11	11	11	11	11	11	11	11	11	11	11	11	11	11	11					11
8 BARBERA	14	17	17	17	17	17	11	11	17	17	17	17	17	17	17	14	14	14	14	14	14	41	41					12
46 ROSSI	17	14	14	14	14	14	14	14	14	14	14	14	14	14	14	41	41	41	41	41	9	9	9					13
41 ESPARGARO	41	77	77	77	77	77	41	41	41	41	41	41	41	41	41	77	77	77	77	9	9	54	54					14
51 PIRRO	77	41	41	41	41	41	77	77	51	51	51	77	77	77	9	9	9	9	77	54	22	22						15
54 PASINI	51	51	51	51	51	51	51	51	77	77	77	51	51	77	77	51	9	54	54	54	54	22	5	5				
68 HERNANDEZ	9	54	54	9	9	9	9	9	9	9	9	9	9	54	22	22	22	22	22	5	17							
9 PETRUCCI	54	9	9	54	54	54	54	54	54	54	54	54	54	9	5	5	5	5	5	17								
22 SILVA	22	22	22	22	22	22	22	22	22	22	22	22	22	5	17	17	17	17	17									
77 ELLISON	5	5	5	5	5	5	5	5	5	5	5	5	5															
5 EDWARDS																												

51 Pit stop **17** Lapped rider

Moto2

RACE DISTANCE: 17 laps, 46.722 miles/75.191km · RACE WEATHER: Dry (air 14°C, humidity 73%, track 15°C)

Pos. Rider	Nat.	No.	Entrant	Machine	Laps	Time & Speed
1 Pol Espargaro	SPA	40	Pons 40 HP Tuenti	Kalex	17	30m 12.879s 92.779mph/ 149.313km/h
2 Marc Marquez	SPA	93	Team CatalunyaCaixa Repsol	Suter	17	30m 13.120s
3 Thomas Luthi	SWI	12	Interwetten-Paddock	Suter	17	30m 13.362s
4 Scott Redding	GBR	45	Marc VDS Racing Team	Kalex	17	30m 17.293s
5 Takaaki Nakagami	JPN	30	Italtrans Racing Team	Kalex	17	30m 17.716s
6 Claudio Corti	ITA	71	Italtrans Racing Team	Kalex	17	30m 18.760s
7 Mika Kallio	FIN	36	Marc VDS Racing Team	Kalex	17	30m 19.028s
8 Dominique Aegerter	SWI	77	Technomag-CIP	Suter	17	30m 19.976s
9 Toni Elias	SPA	24	Mapfre Aspar Team	Suter	17	30m 20.745s
10 Johann Zarco	FRA	5	JIR Moto2	Motobi	17	30m 21.559s
11 Bradley Smith	GBR	38	Tech 3 Racing	Tech 3	17	30m 22.261s
12 Alex de Angelis	RSM	15	NGM Mobile Forward Racing	Suter	17	30m 22.647s
13 Xavier Simeon	BEL	19	Tech 3 Racing	Tech 3	17	30m 23.312s
14 Andrea Iannone	ITA	29	Speed Master	Speed Up	17	30m 44.245s
15 Gino Rea	GBR	8	Federal Oil Gresini Moto2	Moriwaki	17	30m 44.383s
16 Anthony West	AUS	95	QMMF Racing Team	Moriwaki	17	30m 47.051s
17 Simone Corsi	ITA	3	Came IodaRacing Project	FTR	17	30m 47.329s
18 Axel Pons	SPA	49	Pons 40 HP Tuenti	Kalex	17	30m 49.289s
19 Ricard Cardus	SPA	88	Arguiñano Racing Team	AJR	17	30m 49.682s
20 Angel Rodriguez	SPA	47	Desguaces La Torre SAG	FTR	17	30m 50.328s
21 Yuki Takahashi	JPN	72	NGM Mobile Forward Racing	Suter	17	30m 52.344s
22 Randy Krummenacher	SWI	4	GP Team Switzerland	Kalex	17	30m 58.661s
23 Julian Simon	SPA	60	Blusens Avintia	Suter	17	30m 59.042s
24 Alexander Lundh	SWE	7	Cresto Guide MZ Racing	MZ-RE Honda	17	30m 59.130s
25 Roberto Rolfo	ITA	44	Technomag-CIP	Suter	17	31m 12.472s
26 Ratthapark Wilairot	THA	14	Thai Honda Gresini Moto2	Moriwaki	17	31m 12.866s
27 Nicolas Terol	SPA	18	Mapfre Aspar Team	Suter	17	31m 13.889s
28 Esteve Rabat	SPA	80	Pons 40 HP Tuenti	Kalex	16	30m 15.969s
Max Neukirchner	GER	76	Kiefer Racing	Kalex	12	DNF
Mike di Meglio	FRA	63	S/Master Speed Up	Speed Up	8	DNF
Marco Colandrea	SWI	10	SAG Team	FTR	6	DNF
Elena Rosell	SPA	82	QMMF Racing Team	Moriwaki	4	DNF

Fastest lap: Randy Krummenacher, on lap 7, 1m 44.905s, 94.314mph/151.783km/h.
Lap record: Toni Elias, SPA (Moriwaki), 1m 44.710s, 94.489mph/152.065km/h (2010).
Event best maximum speed: Mika Kallio, 154.1mph/248.0km/h (race).

Qualifying: Dry
Air: 17° Humidity: 57% Track: 21°

1	Marquez	1m 43.005s
2	Nakagami	1m 43.085s
3	Espargaro	1m 43.273s
4	Luthi	1m 43.310s
5	Kallio	1m 43.367s
6	Corti	1m 43.396s
7	Rabat	1m 43.651s
8	Di Meglio	1m 43.778s
9	Krummenacher	1m 43.858s
10	Zarco	1m 43.959s
11	De Angelis	1m 44.052s
12	Redding	1m 44.144s
13	Iannone	1m 44.204s
14	Neukirchner	1m 44.212s
15	Aegerter	1m 44.223s
16	Elias	1m 44.254s
17	Simeon	1m 44.308s
18	Corsi	1m 44.354s
19	Smith	1m 44.406s
20	Cardus	1m 44.532s
21	Rolfo	1m 44.640s
22	Takahashi	1m 44.719s
23	Rea	1m 45.095s
24	Rodriguez	1m 45.309s
25	Simon	1m 45.538s
26	Pons	1m 45.607s
27	Lundh	1m 45.834s
28	Terol	1m 45.961s
29	West	1m 46.117s
30	Wilairot	1m 46.211s
31	Rosell	1m 47.284s
32	Colandrea	1m 47.304s

Fastest race laps

1	Krummenacher	1m 44.905s
2	Zarco	1m 45.022s
3	Nakagami	1m 45.114s
4	Smith	1m 45.150s
5	Espargaro	1m 45.180s
6	Kallio	1m 45.219s
7	Marquez	1m 45.287s
8	Redding	1m 45.436s
9	Elias	1m 45.473s
10	Aegerter	1m 45.475s
11	Luthi	1m 45.476s
12	Corti	1m 45.476s
13	De Angelis	1m 45.654s
14	Iannone	1m 45.716s
15	Di Meglio	1m 45.759s
16	Simeon	1m 45.788s
17	Rabat	1m 45.984s
18	Neukirchner	1m 46.338s
19	Corsi	1m 46.379s
20	West	1m 46.499s
21	Rea	1m 46.512s
22	Pons	1m 46.541s
23	Rodriguez	1m 46.545s
24	Takahashi	1m 46.739s
25	Simon	1m 46.773s
26	Cardus	1m 47.001s
27	Lundh	1m 47.299s
28	Rolfo	1m 47.373s
29	Wilairot	1m 47.557s
30	Terol	1m 47.650s
31	Rosell	1m 49.923s
32	Colandrea	1m 49.928s

Championship Points

1	Marquez	45
2	Espargaro	41
3	Luthi	27
4	Redding	23
5	Iannone	22
6	Kallio	15
7	Rabat	13
8	Nakagami	13
9	Smith	13
10	Corti	10
11	Elias	10
12	Zarco	10
13	Di Meglio	9
14	Aegerter	8
15	Corsi	8
16	Krummenacher	5
17	De Angelis	4
18	Simeon	3
19	Rea	1
20	Simon	1

Constructor Points

1	Suter	45
2	Kalex	41
3	Speed Up	22
4	Tech 3	12
5	Motobi	10
6	FTR	8
7	Moriwaki	1

Moto3

RACE DISTANCE: 23 laps, 63.211 miles/101.729km · RACE WEATHER: Dry (air 14°C, humidity 72%, track 14°C)

Pos. Rider	Nat.	No.	Entrant	Machine	Laps	Time & Speed
1 Romano Fenati	ITA	5	Team Italia FMI	FTR Honda	23	43m 50.885s 86.495mph/ 139.201km/h
2 Luis Salom	SPA	39	RW Racing GP	Kalex KTM	23	44m 27.024s
3 Sandro Cortese	GER	11	Red Bull KTM Ajo	KTM	23	44m 27.780s
4 Alex Rins	SPA	42	Estrella Galicia 0,0	Suter Honda	23	44m 27.946s
5 Alexis Masbou	FRA	10	Caretta Technology	Honda	23	44m 39.921s
6 Maverick Viñales	SPA	25	Blusens Avintia	FTR Honda	23	44m 46.742s
7 Alberto Moncayo	SPA	23	Bankia Aspar Team	Kalex KTM	23	44m 48.390s
8 Niccolò Antonelli	ITA	27	San Carlo Gresini Moto3	FTR Honda	23	44m 54.568s
9 Hector Faubel	SPA	55	Bankia Aspar Team	Kalex KTM	23	45m 06.236s
10 Zulfahmi Khairuddin	MAL	63	AirAsia-Sic-Ajo	KTM	23	45m 26.535s
11 Alessandro Tonucci	ITA	19	Team Italia FMI	FTR Honda	22	43m 55.642s
12 Alex Marquez	SPA	12	Estrella Galicia 0,0	Suter Honda	22	43m 57.315s
13 Ivan Moreno	SPA	21	Andalucia JHK Laglisse	FTR Honda	22	44m 04.458s
14 Alan Techer	FRA	89	Technomag-CIP-TSR	TSR Honda	22	44m 33.818s
15 Giulian Pedone	SWI	12	Ambrogio Next Racing	Oral	22	44m 34.172s
16 Marcel Schrotter	GER	77	Mahindra Racing	Mahindra	22	45m 12.115s
17 Jasper Iwema	NED	53	Moto FGR	FGR Honda	22	45m 18.768s
Adrian Martin	SPA	26	JHK T-Shirt Laglisse	FTR Honda	15	DNF
Kenta Fujii	JPN	51	Technomag-CIP-TSR	TSR Honda	15	DNF
Danny Webb	GBR	99	Mahindra Racing	Mahindra	14	DNF
Louis Rossi	FRA	96	Racing Team Germany	FTR Honda	9	DNF
Isaac Viñales	SPA	32	Ongetta-Centro Seta	FTR Honda	6	DNF
Josep Rodriguez	SPA	28	Wild Wolf BST	FTR Honda	4	DNF
Miguel Oliveira	POR	44	Estrella Galicia 0,0	Suter Honda	3	DNF
Arthur Sissis	AUS	61	Red Bull KTM Ajo	KTM	3	DNF
Jakub Kornfeil	CZE	84	Redox-Ongetta-Centro Seta	FTR Honda	2	DNF
Brad Binder	RSA	41	RW Racing GP	Kalex KTM	2	DNF
Efren Vazquez	SPA	7	JHK T-Shirt Laglisse	FTR Honda	2	DNF
Niklas Ajo	FIN	31	TT Motion Events Racing	KTM	2	DNF
Toni Finsterbusch	GER	9	Cresto Guide MZ Racing	MZ FTR	2	DNF
Luigi Morciano	ITA	3	Ioda Team Italia	Ioda	2	DNF
Jack Miller	AUS	8	Caretta Technology	Honda	0	DNF
Danny Kent	GBR	52	Red Bull KTM Ajo	KTM	0	DNF
Simone Grotzkyj	ITA	15	Ambrogio Next Racing	Oral	0	DNF

Fastest lap: Romano Fenati, on lap 21, 1m 52.774s, 87.733mph/141.192km/h (record).
Previous lap record: New category.
Event best maximum speed: Zulfahmi Khairuddin, 129.7mph/208.7km/h (race).

Qualifying: Wet
Air: 15° Humidity: 73% Track: 15°

1	Rins	1m 57.507s
2	Cortese	1m 57.519s
3	Oliveira	1m 57.975s
4	Masbou	1m 58.301s
5	Kornbou	1m 58.438s
6	Miller	1m 58.793s
7	I. Viñales	1m 58.911s
8	Sissis	1m 59.023s
9	M. Viñales	1m 59.101s
10	Fenati	1m 59.155s
11	Vazquez	1m 59.198s
12	Rossi	1m 59.450s
13	Marquez	1m 59.500s
14	Martin	1m 59.729s
15	Kent	1m 59.859s
16	Faubel	1m 59.925s
17	Antonelli	2m 00.009s
18	Rodriguez	2m 00.312s
19	Salom	2m 00.391s
20	Moncayo	2m 01.153s
21	Webb	2m 01.191s
22	Fujii	2m 01.281s
23	Moreno	2m 01.319s
24	Tonucci	2m 01.364s
25	Schrotter	2m 01.450s
26	Binder	2m 01.477s
27	Ajo	2m 01.702s
28	Khairuddin	2m 01.752s
29	Iwema	2m 02.499s
30	Finsterbusch	2m 02.737s
31	Grotzkyj	2m 03.041s
32	Morciano	2m 03.055s
33	Pedone	2m 03.123s

Outside 107%

	Techer	No Time

Fastest race laps

1	Fenati	1m 52.774s
2	Salom	1m 53.389s
3	Rins	1m 53.519s
4	Cortese	1m 53.533s
5	Rossi	1m 53.821s
6	Masbou	1m 54.439s
7	Moncayo	1m 54.723s
8	M. Viñales	1m 54.835s
9	Oliveira	1m 55.040s
10	Antonelli	1m 55.174s
11	Martin	1m 55.194s
12	Faubel	1m 55.243s
13	Fujii	1m 55.629s
14	I. Viñales	1m 55.773s
15	Marquez	1m 55.965s
16	Schrotter	1m 56.032s
17	Webb	1m 56.068s
18	Kornfeil	1m 56.298s
19	Sissis	1m 56.422s
20	Iwema	1m 56.607s
21	Khairuddin	1m 56.785s
22	Binder	1m 57.035s
23	Tonucci	1m 57.506s
24	Vazquez	1m 57.590s
25	Moreno	1m 57.696s
26	Ajo	1m 58.384s
27	Rodriguez	1m 58.686s
28	Techer	1m 58.696s
29	Pedone	1m 59.357s
30	Finsterbusch	1m 59.377s
31	Morciano	2m 00.544s

Championship Points

1	Fenati	45
2	M. Viñales	35
3	Salom	33
4	Cortese	32
5	Rins	19
6	Khairuddin	16
7	Masbou	11
8	Oliveira	11
9	Moncayo	11
10	Faubel	11
11	Sissis	9
12	Antonelli	8
13	Kent	8
14	Rossi	7
15	Techer	7
16	Tonucci	7
17	Marquez	4
18	Moreno	3
19	Ajo	3
20	Pedone	1
21	Kornfeil	1

Constructor Points

1	FTR Honda	50
2	Kalex KTM	33
3	KTM	32
4	Suter Honda	24
5	Honda	11
6	TSR Honda	7
7	Oral	1

FIM WORLD CHAMPIONSHIP · ROUND 3

PORTUGUESE GRAND PRIX

ESTORIL CIRCUIT

Above: Lorenzo closed down on Stoner, but once again had to settle for second.

Main photo: Pedrosa loses the lead in the first corner with the first of several big slides.

Photos: Gold & Goose

Above: Dovizioso bought his own Brembos, which had a longer and stiffer calliper, ...

Top right: ... and beat team-mate Crutchlow for the first time.

Top: Bautista was still learning his new Honda and Showa suspension.

Centre right: Pedrosa in pensive mood – he was very much the third man.

Right: Over-enthusiasm made for a third poor race for Ben Spies, left to dispute eighth with Bradl.

Photos: Gold & Goose

ITH even shakier finances than across the border, Estoril had been confirmed on the calendar only in mid-February, six weeks later than Jerez, and it was common cause that this would be the last hurrah. Ticket prices matched national economic problems with the desire to entertain as big a crowd as possible. The cheapest was two euros for race-day standing room. The response was a good race-day crowd of 48,951.

The potential loss of an interesting circuit at a moodily attractive venue was widely mourned. Built in 1972 inland from the coastal port and resorts of Cascais and Estoril, it's typical of its era, full of variety and character, from a first-gear uphill chicane to an epic last corner taken at increasing speed and debouching on to a long downhill straight. A breath of fresh air compared with the latter-day sterility of tracks like Valencia, Qatar and Motegi.

"It is very complex and very narrow... I like it," said three-times winner Lorenzo, who claimed his first premier-class victory here. Stoner concurred: "It's a complete circuit – you have everything: on-camber, off-camber, slow turns, fast sweepers, up- and downhill. There are a lot of opportunities for passing, also a lot of opportunities for making mistakes."

The weekend started with a masterpiece of double-speak by Stoner at the pre-event press conference, and ended with an object lesson in the role of electronics in MotoGP from Nicky Hayden.

Stoner's moment was a response to Spanish magazine *Solomoto*, which had headlined a 'Stoner to quit' story that turned out prescient. Stoner was adamant in denial. "I've said many times that my career's not going to go on for long, but there is nothing in my mind about retirement right now," he said; then he turned to the reporter responsible to say, "Don't believe everything you read. Don't believe everything you produce."

He might have added, "And don't believe me either." Likewise Carmelo Ezpeleta, who told Spanish pressmen emphatically that the Rookie Rule (introduced in 2008 and banning MotoGP rookies from factory teams) would definitely not be changed. It would take him longer than Casey's fortnight for a complete about-face.

The Hayden affair was purely technical, and rather amusing, though not for the rider. His bike got lost. Blame was later put on an under-track cable for the top-speed timing beams on the back straight. For some reason, Nicky's Ducati thought this was the start-finish line.

This left the poor bike in a terrible muddle. GPS is banned, and the electronics rely for location on the start-finish beam. Electronics are programmed corner by corner from there on. Hayden first noticed a shortage of power on the main straight. When his dashboard recorder clicked up his first lap time on the back straight, "I realised straight away what was wrong. When I was in Turn One, the bike thought I was in Turn Nine. With the amount of electronics we have now, it was impossible to ride. The main problem was engine braking. I'd been using quite a lot on some downhill corner entries. Now where I needed it, I didn't have it. It was quite dangerous at the last turn: I'd open the throttle and the weight would change, then all of a sudden I'd lose power and almost lose the front."

Parts of the track had been resurfaced, in spite of its uncertain future, leading to an unusual problem on the classic final power-on parabola. Even a full day after it had stopped raining, seepage left a wet patch, difficult to see because of the dark surface colour. "I asked for a cone to be put there, to mark the start of it," said Ben Spies. This was done, while Crutchlow only half jokingly suggested, "They need about ten cones; there are that many wet patches."

Sure enough, on the Atlantic seaboard, the rain did come. Friday morning was wet, but thereafter the threat of far more held off until Sunday night. By Monday morning, the track was flooding, and the first post-race tests of the season were called off, to be run later in June at Aragon instead. A minor blow to all except Ducati: they had important tests of a new softer-delivery engine scheduled. This programme was delayed by several weeks.

The surface was not to blame for an ugly crash in qualifying, with mercifully relatively minor consequences. Edwards was cruising back to the pits, doing his best to stay off line through the snaking approach to the last corner; de Puniet was coming up fast behind and was taken by surprise by how slowly the BMW was travelling. The resultant swerve took his front wheel away and his sliding bike skittled the Texan.

Edwards lay worryingly prone, but escaped with a broken left collarbone, repaired on race day by busy Barcelona surgeon Xavier Mir, who had performed the same service for the American just under a year before.

The cloud over Spies lifted, then came down again. In practice, a major and counter-intuitive setting change showed him that "1000s respond differently from 800s. Usually I like a lot of weight on the front to make the bike turn, but in fact we've taken weight off the front. That's how feelings are sometimes – the opposite of what you think. It would never have worked for me on the 800." He qualified on the second row after losing time in traffic, but his upbeat mood turned to over-enthusiasm for another poor race.

A controversy was soon to start over an acquisition at the satellite Yamaha team. Dovizioso had bought himself a brake calliper set from Brembo, the same longer and stiffer unit used by the factory bikes. No one noticed at first; by the next race, it would be different.

Lorenzo celebrated his 25th birthday on the first day of practice, marking exactly one decade since his GP debut at Jerez the day he turned 15. He and Stoner tweeted to and fro: "Happy Birthday." "Thanks mate, I felt old on track today." "Be careful not to break your hip."

The long straight again showed the vast difference in speed between factory and CRT bikes: more than 40km/h from Barbera at 335.9 to Petrucci's sluggish team-developed Aprilia, 294.8. The Italian was riding this slug conspicuously well, but finding the experience daunting. "I imagined the road would be uphill," Petrucci told the pre-event Press conference, "but not a wall."

MOTOGP RACE – 28 laps

Stoner took his second pole of the year with a blazing lap with three minutes to go, in a session restarted after the de Puniet/Edwards contretemps. In a flurry of late action, Pedrosa nosed into second, displacing Crutchlow on the best Yamaha, his second front row of the season. Lorenzo, searching for balance, was fourth, from Spies and Bautista. A disappointed Dovizioso led row three from top Duke Barbera, then Rossi, ahead of team-mate Hayden for the first time in the season.

Pedrosa led into the first corner as usual, but narrowly, and Stoner was in front on the way out, Lorenzo also ahead of his compatriot by the end of the lap. Pedrosa would explain that "I couldn't get the tyres warm … I had some big slides and lost about a second."

These positions would not change, but the lap chart doesn't tell the whole story. Stoner galloped away for the first three laps by 1.25 seconds. Now Lorenzo picked up the pace, and by lap ten he was within half a second, two laps later right on his tail and looking like he would soon be past.

Stoner was troubled by chatter and arm-pump, "just holding on and trying lots of different ECU maps." When he did smooth it out, the arm loosened up somewhat, confirming that the two were related. And all the while he didn't give Lorenzo a chance, riding on the edge and drifting over the painted kerbs. With three laps to go, the Spaniard, smooth and pin-sharp, gave up the unequal task. "I am happy to be second in the last two races. Casey had something more … more energy," he said.

Pedrosa held a watching brief and likewise nothing changed. He dropped away a little earlier than Lorenzo and was two seconds adrift of the Yamaha at the end.

Spies suffered another setback. He was fourth on lap one, then at the end of the back straight he made the first of a series of errors that he blamed on himself, running wide and off the edge of the track to drop behind the Yamahas of Crutchlow and Dovizioso.

This left the satellite pair scrapping hard again, and on lap five Dovizioso found his way past. Once again, the positions did not change to the end, in spite of several attempts by the

Englishman that intensified in the closing stages, until he too ran wide with two laps to go. The brakes, he said later, made a difference: "I nearly hit him so many times."

Spies had more trouble to come: another slip on lap three saw him drop behind Bautista, who had passed Rossi the lap before. The three were together for a couple of laps, then Spies lost two more spots, to Rossi and Bradl, the German riding in steadfast style once again.

Barbera had been at the back of this group, but by lap six he started to lose ground, even as Rossi gained a little breathing space at the front.

Spies was in front of Bradl again by lap 14, but they stayed together, and on lap 22 the American almost high-sided, losing the second he had gained to fall behind again. It took him until three laps from the end before he could reverse the position.

Hayden was in trouble from the start, behind Barbera by lap three and from there on alone and clearly battling. As the race wore on, Abraham was closing threateningly, only 1.5 seconds away when he crashed out on lap 23.

Behind Hayden, the CRT bikes were at play in at last a livelier race. Hernandez led the group for the first three laps, giving way to Espargaro's ART and a lap or two later to the Spaniard's team-mate, Randy de Puniet, suffering badly after his practice crash with Edwards.

Then Hernandez came under attack from Pasini, until his assailant crashed out. Soon afterwards, the Colombian followed suit.

De Puniet got ahead of Espargaro on lap 23, but couldn't stay there more than another lap; the Spaniard was two seconds ahead in 12th at the finish.

The crashes gave 14th and two points to the distant Pirro, while Petrucci took the last one on his near-standard Aprilia, one lap down on the leaders.

Still with dire chatter problems, Ellison pitted with ten laps left; Silva had done so five laps earlier.

A second win in a row gave Stoner a one-point lead over Lorenzo. Three races in and nobody was running away yet.

MOTO2 RACE – 26 laps
. . . .

Marquez took a second successive pole from Luthi, with Redding alongside, his first front row of the season, and glad to be there. "With the first corner here at the end of the long straight, it'll be carnage," he predicted.

Impressive rookie Zarco led row two from Espargaro and Iannone; Simon the third from Elias and de Angelis.

There were a few able to try to prevent Marquez from taking a second win of the season, but they were doomed to failure in another dramatic race of skill, tactics and force.

He led into the first corner, but by the end of lap two Luthi had pushed past, and he held on until lap 19. But it was never by much.

By half-distance, there were still four in the leading group, Espargaro second and Zarco at the back. The latter had a slip next time around and lost touch to fall away slowly, although still safe in fourth.

On lap 20, Marquez and Espargaro both passed Luthi, who also lost touch slightly. But a dramatic last lap almost handed second back to the Swiss rider.

Espargaro attacked into the first corner. Marquez imme-

Above: Former champion Emilio Alzamora, mentor to Marquez.

Above left: Michael Bartholemy, manager of Redding's Marc VDS team.

Top: Marquez achieves near-horizontal lean angles as he strives to escape from Espargaro and Luthi.

Photos: Gold & Goose

diately regained the place. Ditto at the next corner. And at the third.

Marquez resisted at the end of the back straight, then it was decided at the tight uphill chicane. Espargaro went inside, braking ultra-late – only to lose it, almost crashing as he ran wide.

Marquez won by almost two seconds. Espargaro scrambled back just ahead of Luthi, and held him off over the line by less than a tenth.

Zarco by now was another seven seconds away.

Iannone had been with the leaders in the early stages after battling past Redding, off the pace from the beginning. On lap 11, the Italian had a major moment under braking at the end of the back straight, saving disaster, but running off to rejoin behind Redding and Elias.

It took him two laps to get back past them, pulling clear to close down a five-second gap on Zarco to 1.2 seconds.

Behind him, a big group caught and swallowed Redding and Elias, now in the thick of an entertaining free-for-all. Redding dropped back quickly in the brawl, to the ultimate displeasure of being consigned to 11th by compatriot Smith. Both had been promoted when Rabat and Corsi crashed out of the group ahead. This was led over the line by de Angelis, from Elias, Simon and Kallio, all across the line within four-tenths of a second.

Aegerter led a similar mob over the line for 12th, from Simeon, Corti, Cardus and Terol, all five within a second and Terol missing the points by two-tenths.

Takahashi, Pons and di Meglio also crashed out; runner-up Espargaro – now nine points adrift overall – had the consolation of setting a new record on the eighth lap.

MOTO3 RACE – 23 laps

Cortese took his second pole by an impressive three-tenths, from the Hondas of Vinales and Oliveira.

Unusually the last race of the day, it was not as close as normal, with three pairs up front, each in a private battle.

That for the lead comprised Cortese and Vinales, clear by half-distance and all over one another. Vinales led most over the line, but the KTM was clearly faster down the straight. He passed there several times, only to lose the lead through the twists. Other times he would sit up and hang back.

The battle, a good one, was for the last lap, the riders jockeying to and fro, Cortese in front as they approached the final corner, Vinales poised to pounce. But a group of back-markers was already there.

Cortese went inside, Vinales outside, and they ran together to the line, where Cortese was just six-hundredths ahead.

Oliveira, second on lap two, might have made a difference, but slowed and cruised to the pits, slumped in despair. Salom and Vazquez were with the leaders early on, but it was Khairuddin who made up the second pair as Vazquez lost touch. Salom escaped by a second only in the last laps.

Vazquez's new partner was rookie Antonelli, and they were almost joined at the end by Rins and Kent, who had escaped from a gang of nine.

There were six covered by less than two seconds at the end – Masbou, Kornfeil, Binder, Faubel, Sissis and Moncayo. A second away wild-card Alex Marquez took the last point.

Above: Vinales and Cortese raced side by side, and finished the same way.

Top: Veteran Vazquez (7) and rookie Antonelli battled to the flag.

Above left: Marquez saw off Espargaro for his second win of the year.
Photos: Gold & Goose

FIM WORLD CHAMPIONSHIP

ROUND 3

GRANDE PREMIO
DE PORTUGAL CIRCUITO ESTORIL

4–6 MAY, 2012

OFFICIAL TIMEKEEPER — motoGP / TISSOT SWISS WATCHES SINCE 1853

CIRCUITO DO ESTORIL

28 laps
Length: 4.182 km / 2.598 miles
Width: 14m

Key
96/60 kph/mph
Gear

Turn 8 145/90 · Variante 58/36 · Esses 105/65 · Orelha 87/54 · Turn 3 74/46 · Turn 2 131/81 · VIP 81/50 · Recta da Meta 250/155 · Turn 1 76/47 · 312/194 · Parabolica Interior 95/59 · Parabolica 210/130

Photos: Gold & Goose

MotoGP	RACE DISTANCE: 28 laps, 72.760 miles/117.096km · RACE WEATHER: Dry (air 17°C, humidity 59%, track 35°C)

Pos.	Rider	Nat.	No.	Entrant	Machine	Tyres	Race tyre choice	Laps	Time & speed
1	Casey Stoner	AUS	1	Repsol Honda Team	Honda RC213V	B	F: Medium/R: Medium	28	45m 37.513s 95.684mph/ 153.988km/h
2	Jorge Lorenzo	SPA	99	Yamaha Factory Racing	Yamaha YZR-M1	B	F: Medium/R: Medium	28	45m 38.934s
3	Dani Pedrosa	SPA	26	Repsol Honda Team	Honda RC213V	B	F: Medium/R: Medium	28	45m 41.134s
4	Andrea Dovizioso	ITA	4	Monster Yamaha Tech 3	Yamaha YZR-M1	B	F: Medium/R: Medium	28	45m 51.359s
5	Cal Crutchlow	GBR	35	Monster Yamaha Tech 3	Yamaha YZR-M1	B	F: Medium/R: Medium	28	45m 54.203s
6	Alvaro Bautista	SPA	19	San Carlo Honda Gresini	Honda RC213V	B	F: Medium/R: Medium	28	45m 59.397s
7	Valentino Rossi	ITA	46	Ducati Team	Ducati Desmosedici GP12	B	F: Medium/R: Medium	28	46m 04.310s
8	Ben Spies	USA	11	Yamaha Factory Racing	Yamaha YZR-M1	B	F: Medium/R: Medium	28	46m 10.775s
9	Stefan Bradl	GER	6	LCR Honda MotoGP	Honda RC213V	B	F: Medium/R: Medium	28	46m 13.380s
10	Hector Barbera	SPA	8	Pramac Racing Team	Ducati Desmosedici GP12	B	F: Medium/R: Medium	28	46m 30.876s
11	Nicky Hayden	USA	69	Ducati Team	Ducati Desmosedici GP12	B	F: Medium/R: Medium	28	46m 40.143s
12	Aleix Espargaro	SPA	41	Power Electronics Aspar	ART Aprilia RSV4	B	F: Medium/R: Medium	28	46m 58.249s
13	Randy de Puniet	FRA	14	Power Electronics Aspar	ART Aprilia RSV4	B	F: Medium/R: Medium	28	47m 00.996s
14	Michele Pirro	ITA	51	San Carlo Honda Gresini	FTR Honda CBR1000RR	B	F: Medium/R: Medium	28	47m 15.418s
15	Danilo Petrucci	ITA	9	Came Ioda Racing Project	Ioda Aprilia RSV4	B	F: Medium/R: Medium	27	46m 01.358s
	Karel Abraham	CZE	17	Cardion AB Motoracing	Ducati Desmosedici GP12	B	F: Medium/R: Medium	23	DNF-crash
	James Ellison	GBR	77	Paul Bird Motorsport	ART Aprilia RSV4	B	F: Medium/R: Medium	18	DNF-handling
	Yonny Hernandez	COL	68	Avintia Blusens	BQR FTR Kawasaki	B	F: Medium/R: Medium	16	DNF-crash
	Mattia Pasini	ITA	54	Speed Master	ART Aprilia RSV4	B	F: Medium/R: Medium	11	DNF-crash
	Ivan Silva	SPA	22	Avintia Blusens	BQR FTR Kawasaki	B	F: Medium/R: Medium	11	DNF-mechanical
	Colin Edwards	USA	5	NGM Mobile Forward Racing	Suter BMW S1000RR	B	F: –/R: –	0	DNS-injured

Fastest lap: Jorge Lorenzo, on lap 3, 1m 36.909s, 96.532mph/155.353km/h (record).

Previous lap record: Dani Pedrosa, SPA (Honda), 1m 36.937s, 99.505mph/155.309km/h (2009).

Event best maximum speed: Hector Barbera, 208.7mph/335.9km/h (qualifying practice).

Qualifying

Weather: Dry
Air Temp: 19° Humidity: 56%
Track Temp: 25°

1	Stoner	1m 37.188s
2	Pedrosa	1m 37.201s
3	Crutchlow	1m 37.289s
4	Lorenzo	1m 37.466s
5	Spies	1m 37.723s
6	Bautista	1m 37.917s
7	Dovizioso	1m 37.943s
8	Barbera	1m 38.006s
9	Rossi	1m 38.059s
10	Hayden	1m 38.253s
11	Bradl	1m 38.265s
12	Espargaro	1m 39.353s
13	Abraham	1m 39.398s
14	De Puniet	1m 39.586s
15	Hernandez	1m 40.029s
16	Pirro	1m 40.225s
17	Pasini	1m 40.387s
18	Edwards	1m 40.964s
19	Ellison	1m 41.394s
20	Petrucci	1m 41.486s
21	Silva	1m 41.490s

Fastest race laps

1	Lorenzo	1m 36.909s
2	Stoner	1m 37.09s
3	Pedrosa	1m 37.178s
4	Crutchlow	1m 37.461s
5	Dovizioso	1m 37.513s
6	Bautista	1m 37.846s
7	Spies	1m 38.077s
8	Rossi	1m 38.146s
9	Barbera	1m 38.162s
10	Bradl	1m 38.207s
11	Hayden	1m 38.834s
12	Abraham	1m 38.853s
13	De Puniet	1m 39.569s
14	Espargaro	1m 39.838s
15	Pasini	1m 40.170s
16	Hernandez	1m 40.214s
17	Pirro	1m 40.454s
18	Petrucci	1m 41.072s
19	Ellison	1m 41.309s
20	Silva	1m 42.396s

Championship Points

1	Stoner	66
2	Lorenzo	65
3	Pedrosa	52
4	Crutchlow	37
5	Dovizioso	35
6	Bautista	29
7	Bradl	24
8	Hayden	23
9	Rossi	22
10	Barbera	19
11	Spies	18
12	Espargaro	9
13	De Puniet	6
14	Edwards	4
15	Petrucci	4
16	Pirro	2
17	Pasini	2
18	Hernandez	2
19	Silva	1

Constructor Points

1	Honda	70
2	Yamaha	65
3	Ducati	27
4	ART	11
5	Suter	4
6	Ioda	4
7	FTR	2
8	BQR-FTR	2
9	BQR	1

Grid order	1	2	3	4	5	6	7	8	9	10	11	12	13	14	15	16	17	18	19	20	21	22	23	24	25	26	27	28	
1 STONER	1	1	1	1	1	1	1	1	1	1	1	1	1	1	1	1	1	1	1	1	1	1	1	1	1	1	1	1	1
26 PEDROSA	99	99	99	99	99	99	99	99	99	99	99	99	99	99	99	99	99	99	99	99	99	99	99	99	99	99	99	99	2
35 CRUTCHLOW	26	26	26	26	26	26	26	26	26	26	26	26	26	26	26	26	26	26	26	26	26	26	26	26	26	26	26	26	3
99 LORENZO	11	35	35	35	4	4	4	4	4	4	4	4	4	4	4	4	4	4	4	4	4	4	4	4	4	4	4	4	4
11 SPIES	35	4	4	4	35	35	35	35	35	35	35	35	35	35	35	35	35	35	35	35	35	35	35	35	35	35	35	35	5
19 BAUTISTA	4	11	19	19	19	19	19	19	19	19	19	19	19	19	19	19	19	19	19	19	19	19	19	19	19	19	19	19	6
4 DOVIZIOSO	19	46	11	11	11	46	46	46	46	46	46	46	46	46	46	46	46	46	46	46	46	46	46	46	46	46	46	46	7
8 BARBERA	46	19	46	46	46	6	6	6	6	6	6	6	11	11	11	11	11	11	11	11	6	6	6	6	11	11	11	11	8
46 ROSSI	6	6	6	6	11	11	11	11	11	11	11	11	6	6	6	6	6	6	6	6	11	11	11	11	6	6	6	6	9
69 HAYDEN	69	8	8	8	8	8	8	8	8	8	8	8	8	8	8	8	8	8	8	8	8	8	8	8	8	8	8	8	10
6 BRADL	8	69	69	69	69	69	69	69	69	69	69	69	69	69	69	69	69	69	69	69	69	69	69	69	69	69	69	69	11
41 ESPARGARO	17	17	17	17	17	17	17	17	17	17	17	17	17	17	17	17	17	17	17	14	14	41	41	41	41	41		12
17 ABRAHAM	41	68	68	41	41	41	41	41	41	41	41	41	41	41	41	41	41	41	41	41	41	14	14	14	14	14		13
14 DE PUNIET	68	41	41	14	68	68	14	14	14	14	14	14	14	14	14	14	14	14	51	51	51	51	51	51	51	51		14
68 HERNANDEZ	77	14	14	68	14	14	68	68	68	68	54	68	68	68	68	68	51	51	51	51	51	9	9	9	9	9		15
51 PIRRO	14	54	54	54	54	54	54	54	54	54	68	51	51	51	51	9	9	9	9	9	9					17		
54 PASINI	54	77	77	51	51	51	51	51	51	51	51	9	9	9	9	9	77	77										
77 ELLISON	9	51	51	77	77	9	9	9	9	9	9	77	77	77	77	77												
9 PETRUCCI	51	9	9	9	9	77	77	77	77	77	77																	
22 SILVA	22	22	22	22	22	22	22	22	22	22	22																	

22 Pit stop   9 Lapped rider

Moto2

RACE DISTANCE: 26 laps, 67.563 miles/108.732km · RACE WEATHER: Dry (air 17°C, humidity 62%, track 32°C)

Pos.	Rider	Nat.	No.	Entrant	Machine	Laps	Time & Speed
1	**Marc Marquez**	SPA	93	Team CatalunyaCaixa Repsol	Suter	26	44m 04.086s / 91.988mph/ / 148.041km/h
2	**Pol Espargaro**	SPA	40	Pons 40 HP Tuenti	Kalex	26	44m 06.073s
3	**Thomas Luthi**	SWI	12	Interwetten-Paddock	Suter	26	44m 06.157s
4	**Johann Zarco**	FRA	5	JIR Moto2	Motobi	26	44m 13.313s
5	**Andrea Iannone**	ITA	29	Speed Master	Speed Up	26	44m 14.567s
6	**Alex de Angelis**	RSM	15	NGM Mobile Forward Racing	Suter	26	44m 25.266s
7	**Toni Elias**	SPA	24	Mapfre Aspar Team	Suter	26	44m 25.480s
8	**Julian Simon**	SPA	60	Blusens Avintia	Suter	26	44m 25.590s
9	**Mika Kallio**	FIN	36	Marc VDS Racing Team	Kalex	26	44m 25.667s
10	**Bradley Smith**	GBR	38	Tech 3 Racing	Tech 3	26	44m 28.186s
11	**Scott Redding**	GBR	45	Marc VDS Racing Team	Kalex	26	44m 31.334s
12	**Dominique Aegerter**	SWI	77	Technomag-CIP	Suter	26	44m 34.173s
13	**Xavier Simeon**	BEL	19	Tech 3 Racing	Tech 3	26	44m 34.218s
14	**Claudio Corti**	ITA	71	Italtrans Racing Team	Kalex	26	44m 34.343s
15	**Ricard Cardus**	SPA	88	Arguinano Racing Team	AJR	26	44m 34.965s
16	Nicolas Terol	SPA	18	Mapfre Aspar Team	Suter	26	44m 35.183s
17	Anthony West	AUS	95	QMMF Racing Team	Moriwaki	26	44m 47.185s
18	Takaaki Nakagami	JPN	30	Italtrans Racing Team	Kalex	26	44m 51.368s
19	Randy Krummenacher	SWI	4	GP Team Switzerland	Kalex	26	44m 51.485s
20	Max Neukirchner	GER	76	Kiefer Racing	Kalex	26	44m 52.229s
21	Roberto Rolfo	ITA	44	Technomag-CIP	Suter	26	44m 57.649s
22	Angel Rodriguez	SPA	47	Desguaces La Torre SAG	FTR	26	44m 58.616s
23	Ratthapark Wilairot	THA	14	Thai Honda PTT Gresini Moto2	Moriwaki	26	44m 59.752s
24	Esteve Rabat	SPA	80	Pons 40 HP Tuenti	Kalex	26	45m 28.975s
25	Alexander Lundh	SWE	7	Cresto Guide MZ Racing	MZ-RE Honda	26	45m 36.553s
26	Elena Rosell	SPA	82	QMMF Racing Team	Moriwaki	26	45m 44.834s
27	Marco Colandrea	SWI	10	SAG Team	FTR	26	44m 45.500s
28	Gino Rea	GBR	8	Federal Oil Gresini Moto2	Moriwaki	25	44m 59.731s
	Mike di Meglio	FRA	63	S/Master Speed Up	Speed Up	20	DNF
	Simone Corsi	ITA	3	Came IodaRacing Project	FTR	19	DNF
	Axel Pons	SPA	49	Pons 40 HP Tuenti	Kalex	11	DNF
	Yuki Takahashi	JPN	72	NGM Mobile Forward Racing	Suter	5	DNF

Qualifying: Dry — Air: 20° Humidity: 52% Track: 27°

				Fastest race laps			Championship Points		
1	Marquez	1m 40.934s		1	Espargaro	1m 40.921s	1	Marquez	70
2	Luthi	1m 41.054s		2	Marquez	1m 40.926s	2	Espargaro	61
3	Redding	1m 41.278s		3	Zarco	1m 41.128s	3	Luthi	43
4	Zarco	1m 41.311s		4	Luthi	1m 41.135s	4	Iannone	33
5	Espargaro	1m 41.424s		5	Iannone	1m 41.136s	5	Redding	28
6	Iannone	1m 41.461s		6	Rabat	1m 41.493s	6	Zarco	23
7	Simon	1m 41.469s		7	Redding	1m 41.601s	7	Kallio	22
8	Elias	1m 41.504s		8	Kallio	1m 41.624s	8	Elias	19
9	De Angelis	1m 41.536s		9	Elias	1m 41.626s	9	Smith	18
10	Aegerter	1m 41.539s		10	Simon	1m 41.626s	10	De Angelis	14
11	Nakagami	1m 41.636s		11	De Angelis	1m 41.637s	11	Rabat	13
12	Cardus	1m 41.671s		12	Corti	1m 41.674s	12	Nakagami	13
13	Smith	1m 41.733s		13	Smith	1m 41.811s	13	Corti	12
14	Di Meglio	1m 41.815s		14	Terol	1m 41.824s	14	Aegerter	12
15	Terol	1m 41.841s		15	Di Meglio	1m 41.848s	15	Di Meglio	9
16	Rabat	1m 41.954s		16	Corti	1m 41.864s	16	Simon	9
17	Kallio	1m 41.990s		17	Cardus	1m 41.879s	17	Corsi	8
18	Corsi	1m 42.130s		18	Simeon	1m 42.018s	18	Simeon	6
19	Krummenacher	1m 42.138s		19	Aegerter	1m 42.113s	19	Krummenacher	5
20	Takahashi	1m 42.319s		20	Nakagami	1m 42.148s	20	Cardus	1
21	Corti	1m 42.359s		21	West	1m 42.312s	21	Rea	1
22	Simeon	1m 42.377s		22	Krummenacher	1m 42.357s			
23	Pons	1m 42.527s		23	Rea	1m 42.442s	**Constructor Points**		
24	Rolfo	1m 42.947s		24	Takahashi	1m 42.456s	1	Suter	70
25	Rea	1m 43.032s		25	Rolfo	1m 42.570s	2	Kalex	61
26	West	1m 43.134s		26	Pons	1m 42.708s	3	Speed Up	33
27	Neukirchner	1m 43.205s		27	Neukirchner	1m 42.779s	4	Motobi	23
28	Wilairot	1m 43.450s		28	Rodriguez	1m 42.782s	5	Tech 3	18
29	Lundh	1m 44.105s		29	Wilairot	1m 42.966s	6	FTR	8
30	Rodriguez	1m 44.253s		30	Lundh	1m 43.786s	7	AJR	1
31	Rosell	1m 45.154s		31	Rosell	1m 44.508s	8	Moriwaki	1
32	Colandrea	1m 45.845s		32	Colandrea	1m 45.093s			

Fastest lap: Pol Espargaro, on lap 8, 1m 40.921s, 92.695mph/149.178km/h (record).
Previous lap record: Andrea Iannone, ITA (Suter), 1m 42.026s, 91.691mph/147.562km/h (2011).
Event best maximum speed: Pol Espargaro, 177.1mph/285.0km/h (race).

Moto3

RACE DISTANCE: 23 laps, 59.767 miles/96.186km · RACE WEATHER: Dry (air 17°C, humidity 62%, track 34°C)

Pos.	Rider	Nat.	No.	Entrant	Machine	Laps	Time & Speed
1	**Sandro Cortese**	GER	11	Red Bull KTM Ajo	KTM	23	41m 34.536s / 86.253mph/ / 138.811km/h
2	**Maverick Vinales**	SPA	25	Blusens Avintia	FTR Honda	23	41m 34.591s
3	**Luis Salom**	SPA	39	RW Racing GP	Kalex KTM	23	41m 45.574s
4	**Zulfahmi Khairuddin**	MAL	63	AirAsia-Sic-Ajo	KTM	23	41m 46.731s
5	**Efren Vazquez**	SPA	7	JHK T-Shirt Laglisse	FTR Honda	23	41m 55.470s
6	**Niccolo Antonelli**	ITA	27	San Carlo Gresini Moto3	FTR Honda	23	41m 55.512s
7	**Alex Rins**	SPA	42	Estrella Galicia 0,0	Suter Honda	23	41m 56.328s
8	**Danny Kent**	GBR	52	Red Bull KTM Ajo	KTM	23	41m 56.424s
9	**Alexis Masbou**	FRA	10	Caretta Technology	Honda	23	41m 57.582s
10	**Jakub Kornfeil**	CZE	84	Redox-Ongetta-Centro Seta	FTR Honda	23	41m 57.846s
11	**Brad Binder**	RSA	41	RW Racing GP	Kalex KTM	23	41m 57.915s
12	**Hector Faubel**	SPA	55	Bankia Aspar Team	Kalex KTM	23	41m 58.299s
13	**Arthur Sissis**	AUS	61	Red Bull KTM Ajo	KTM	23	41m 58.844s
14	**Alberto Moncayo**	SPA	23	Bankia Aspar Team	Kalex KTM	23	41m 59.551s
15	**Alex Marquez**	SPA	12	Estrella Galicia 0,0	Suter Honda	23	42m 00.986s
16	Joan Olive	SPA	6	TT Motion Events Racing	KTM	23	42m 07.177s
17	Alan Techer	FRA	89	Technomag-CIP-TSR	TSR Honda	23	42m 07.279s
18	Alessandro Tonucci	ITA	19	Team Italia FMI	FTR Honda	23	42m 11.047s
19	Marcel Schrotter	GER	77	Mahindra Racing	Mahindra	23	42m 28.063s
20	Ivan Moreno	SPA	21	Andalucia JHK Laglisse	FTR Honda	23	42m 38.550s
21	Toni Finsterbusch	GER	9	Cresto Guide MZ Racing	Honda	23	42m 38.600s
22	Manuel Tatasciore	ITA	73	Caretta Technology	Honda	23	42m 38.607s
23	Kenta Fujii	JPN	51	Technomag-CIP-TSR	TSR Honda	23	43m 05.436s
24	Luigi Morciano	ITA	3	Ioda Team Italia	Ioda	22	41m 34.893s
25	Kevin Hanus	GER	86	Thomas Sabo GP Team	Honda	22	41m 35.114s
	Armando Pontone	ITA	80	IodaRacing Project	Ioda	NA	Finished in pits
	Giulian Pedone	SWI	30	Ambrogio Next Racing	Oral	NA	Finished in pits
	Jasper Iwema	NED	53	Moto FGR	FGR Honda	15	DNF
	Louis Rossi	FRA	96	Racing Team Germany	FTR Honda	14	DNF
	Romano Fenati	ITA	5	Team Italia FMI	FTR Honda	14	DNF
	Isaac Vinales	SPA	32	Ongetta-Centro Seta	FTR Honda	13	DNF
	Danny Webb	GBR	99	Mahindra Racing	Mahindra	8	DNF
	Adrian Martin	SPA	26	JHK T-Shirt Laglisse	FTR Honda	6	DNF
	Miguel Oliveira	POR	44	Estrella Galicia 0,0	Suter Honda	3	DNF

Qualifying: Dry — Air: 18° Humidity: 54% Track: 19°

				Fastest race laps			Championship Points		
1	Cortese	1m 47.145s		1	Cortese	1m 47.354s	1	Cortese	57
2	M. Vinales	1m 47.460s		2	M. Vinales	1m 47.549s	2	M. Vinales	55
3	Oliveira	1m 47.916s		3	Fenati	1m 47.556s	3	Salom	49
4	Kent	1m 47.950s		4	Khairuddin	1m 47.777s	4	Fenati	45
5	Khairuddin	1m 48.083s		5	Antonelli	1m 47.831s	5	Khairuddin	29
6	Fenati	1m 48.191s		6	Kent	1m 47.854s	6	Rins	28
7	Salom	1m 48.238s		7	Masbou	1m 47.932s	7	Masbou	18
8	Vazquez	1m 48.299s		8	Salom	1m 48.000s	8	Antonelli	18
9	Faubel	1m 48.349s		9	Kornfeil	1m 48.058s	9	Kent	16
10	Masbou	1m 48.476s		10	Sissis	1m 48.110s	10	Faubel	15
11	Kornfeil	1m 48.478s		11	Rins	1m 48.307s	11	Moncayo	13
12	Antonelli	1m 48.696s		12	Vazquez	1m 48.322s	12	Sissis	12
13	Martin	1m 48.871s		13	Rossi	1m 48.349s	13	Vazquez	11
14	Binder	1m 48.900s		14	Binder	1m 48.350s	14	Oliveira	11
15	Rossi	1m 48.927s		15	Marquez	1m 48.415s	15	Rossi	7
16	Sissis	1m 49.013s		16	Moncayo	1m 48.434s	16	Kornfeil	7
17	Moncayo	1m 49.154s		17	Techer	1m 48.585s	17	Techer	7
18	Webb	1m 49.326s		18	Faubel	1m 48.594s	18	Binder	5
19	Marquez	1m 49.374s		19	Tonucci	1m 48.872s	19	Tonucci	5
20	Techer	1m 49.377s		20	Olive	1m 49.017s	20	Marquez	5
21	Tonucci	1m 49.397s		21	Oliveira	1m 49.122s	21	Moreno	3
22	Rins	1m 49.447s		22	Webb	1m 49.397s	22	Ajo	3
23	Schrotter	1m 49.752s		23	Iwema	1m 49.540s	23	Pedone	1
24	Olive	1m 49.880s		24	Schrotter	1m 49.660s			
25	Tatasciore	1m 50.117s		25	Tatasciore	1m 49.811s	**Constructor Points**		
26	Moreno	1m 50.176s		26	Moreno	1m 49.814s	1	FTR Honda	70
27	I. Vinales	1m 50.220s		27	Finsterbusch	1m 50.080s	2	KTM	57
28	Iwema	1m 51.193s		28	Martin	1m 50.277s	3	Kalex KTM	49
29	Pedone	1m 51.288s		29	I. Vinales	1m 50.347s	4	Suter Honda	33
30	Finsterbusch	1m 51.583s		30	Fujii	1m 51.601s	5	Honda	18
31	Hanus	1m 52.275s		31	Morciano	1m 51.685s	6	TSR Honda	7
32	Morciano	1m 52.630s		32	Hanus	1m 51.967s	7	Oral	1
33	Fujii	1m 52.820s		33	Pedone	1m 52.011s			
34	Pontone	1m 53.408s		34	Pontone	1m 52.013s			

Outside 107%
Grotzkyj — No Time

Fastest lap: Sandro Cortese, on lap 18, 1m 47.354s, 87.140mph/140.238km/h (record).
Previous lap record: New category.
Event best maximum speed: Joan Olive, 142.4mph/229.1km/h (race).

FRENCH GRAND PRIX

LE MANS CIRCUIT

Above: The Doctor is back in the house. Rossi claimed his first podium of the year, between Lorenzo and Stoner.

Main photo: Lorenzo was untouchable in streaming wet conditions.

Photos: Gold & Goose

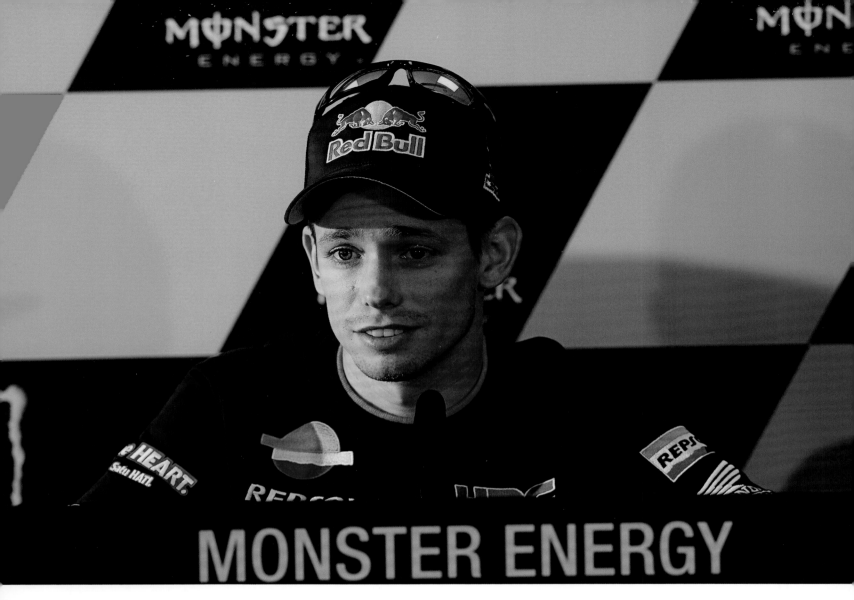

Above: Stoner remained mainly dry-eyed as he dropped his bombshell.

Top right: Randy de Puniet had a double-crash nightmare at home.

Above centre right: A scary moment for Hayden. He remained on board for sixth.

Above right: Former Le Mans winner Vermeulen took over injured Edwards's CRT bike.

Right: James Ellison shone in the tricky conditions – first CRT home.
Photos: Gold & Goose

THE regular pre-event Press conference is generally a lacklustre affair. Nothing has happened so far, the stories have yet to emerge and develop, the real news is filed at the far end of the weekend. Instead you get platitudes and promises. Many people (invited riders included) only attend out of politeness.

The Press conference at Le Mans, however, was not one to miss. Stoner chose the occasion to unleash staggering news. Never mind that two weeks before he'd denied it. Now he would tell the truth. He was quitting.

"It's not the championship I fell in love with, it's not the championship I always wanted to race in," he said. As for his statement a fortnight before that, "there are no thoughts of retirement"? Well, he insisted, he hadn't been lying; he'd only decided in the intervening time. But the thoughts had been there. "This has come after a long time of thinking and talking with my family and my wife."

Stoner backed it up with a litany of heart-felt complaint about what was wrong with grand prix racing – a list that touched a chord with many older listeners. Complaints ranged from flexible and increasingly restrictive rules that downgraded the prototypes and the introduction of slow-coach CRT bikes to criticism of the commercialism that had so filled the paddock with hospitality units and suchlike that there was no room for the riders any more. Motorhomes are being eased out for Moto2 and Moto3 riders; when impecunious young Stoner started, he had shared the back of a van with fellow rookie Chaz Davies (now also a world champion). "If I hadn't been able to do that, I wouldn't be where I am now," he said.

Stoner kept his emotions in check: the first high-level retirement *MOTOCOURSE* can remember with no tears. His companions at the table failed to hide their astonishment. And when the Australian launched into riders who prolong their careers well past their peak, did Rossi flinch? "Every rider here is the same … would say when they lose the passion they will retire," said Casey. "But I think for many riders this is not the truth. I've seen there is always something holding them here … whether it is the money or the fame, or other aspects."

Reaction in the paddock ranged from disbelief to bemused admiration. People respected his courage and conviction, but were baffled that anyone with such rampant talent could bear to stop using it, and give away the top seat at the top table of the top racing series. Stoner had been racing for more than 20 of his 26 years, and had been away from home in Europe since he was 14. Furthermore (though he was at pains to say this was not a reason), he had just become a father, a life-changing experience for most. Even past champions like Roberts, Rainey and Schwantz at first said they could understand.

But as the news sank in, a feeling of resentment began to grow. Racing is a love affair for everyone involved: there's little logic in it. Having a giant of this love object pointing out the flaws was reminiscent of somebody describing the faults in your wife. He may be right, but... Which is more or less what Dorna chief Ezpeleta said, telling interviewers, "You cannot please everyone … it is not necessary that everyone is satisfied." Dorna had given considerable financial support during Casey's career. "We have helped him become who he is, and he has helped us." The cost-cutting rule changes were made necessary by prevailing circumstances. "You cannot ignore the world financial situation," he said.

Rossi promptly calmed fears that he might follow suit, given the daunting and still fruitless task of trying to return the Ducati to the race-winning form it had achieved when Casey had ridden it. Questioned, his reply was emphatic. "No. I never think to stop. Every rider has a different character and motivation … or reason for racing. I like a lot the racing life, the weekend of the GP. To stop at the top is the dream of every sportsman. But for me, the price is too high," he said.

High prices were a talking point over at the Tech 3 team. Dovizioso's purchase of his own brakes had become known since the last race, although the rider was still denying it.

The story triggered embarrassment for team boss Hervé Poncharal, caught between the strictures of his Yamaha contract to use equipment as supplied and the desires of his well-heeled new rider, who had dug into his pocket to the tune of tens of thousands of euros and gone shopping. Poncharal was accused of profiteering from his rider, while second rider Crutchlow was voluble on the matter. He would not pay for the brakes and would live without them if he had to. "Why should a rider buy his own equipment? Out of principle, I won't be buying anything. I'm racing in MotoGP, not club racing." As it turned out, he had the brakes for the next race – and it was expected that he would have to pay for them.

Chris Vermeulen made a brief MotoGP return at the track where he had won his and Suzuki's only victory in the past dozen years. Rain helped, but he would need more than that in a single outing on the absent Edwards's Suter BMW. He'd deliberately avoided talking to Colin. "I wanted to come with an open mind, to give them some information," he explained, but his comments echoed the Texan's: "It's reasonably quick, but very aggressive. The electronic system is very new and undeveloped, and at this stage it doesn't help the bike. It's very raw."

Down in Moto3, there was a blow to the hopes of those trying to avoid the Honda-KTM axis of power. There are two alternative engines: the Ioda used by that team and the Italian Oral. This had been dropped before the start of the year by the national federation Team Italia, fielding Fenati and Tonucci, in favour of Honda-powered FTRs. Now a second team, Ambroglio Next, also dumped Oral in favour of Suter Hondas for riders Grotzkyj and Pedone. This left only Mahindra using Oral, and commercially unable to change. Unreliability and a lack of top-end power were costing Indian-entered riders Webb and Schrotter dear.

MOTOGP RACE – 28 laps

Free practice was dry and cool; qualifying started properly wet, gradually drying. It meant an anxious wait in the pits for Dovi, who ran out of petrol with five minutes to go. He stayed in third, his first Yamaha front row, with the factory Hondas alongside, Pedrosa heading Stoner. Lorenzo led row two with Spies on the far end; Crutchlow split the factory pair.

Rossi headed row three, his best of the year. Importantly, by some quirky paradox, his new all-aluminium Ducati's faults were not amplified in the wet, but diminished, particularly corner-exit grip. He was amused to be hoping for rain. "Any time you want it to be wet, you are in sh*t," he joked.

His wishes came true. The track was wet and drying only slowly as they lined up.

Stoner had kept the pack waiting by running two sighting laps. The Hondas had problems getting heat into their tyres, and it would show over the early laps.

It was spitting and the track fully wet. The race was spoiled early on for some: a suspected patch of oil or coolant lurked unseen on the right-hand side of the track some 100 yards from the start line. Dovizioso slid on it; Spies behind him suffered a much worse slide that threw him out of the saddle so that he smashed his helmet on the screen. Hayden narrowly maintained control, but lost several places. Hapless de Puniet actually crashed, a home-GP nightmare. He vaulted the pit rail as his bike was wheeled back, getting going over a lap behind.

Pedrosa led Stoner and Lorenzo up the hill. The Yamaha's tyres were gripping, and Lorenzo made short work of the cautious Honda pair to lead them by eight-tenths first time across the line.

Pedrosa was still second, but Stoner took over directly, and on lap three Rossi was also past him as the Spaniard

Above: Scott Redding took his first podium of the season with a strong third place.

Top: After Thursday's veiled insults, Rossi had the satisfaction of beating Stoner.

Top right: Luthi made good his escape while others stumbled and fell.

Top far right: Louis Rossi rode the storm for a surprise home win to please the sodden crowd.

Above right: Claudio Corti was another survivor. It earned him second place in Moto2.

Right: Vinales falls from grace; Rossi manages to dodge the wreckage to inherit the lead.

Photos: Gold & Goose

lost place after place. But Rossi was having visor fogging problems, and though he closed on Stoner again, he lost touch on lap ten.

It took Stoner a couple more laps to become confident with the grip, and now he started to work on Lorenzo, "though it was a long shot". By lap 13, he'd closed a gap of almost five seconds to 2.7, and he managed to hold it there for two more laps. Then he was slipping away again.

Rossi's vision problems had dropped him four seconds back into the hands of Dovi and Crutchlow, once again circulating inches apart. They were fiercely engaged, both Yamahas ahead of the Ducati at half-distance. Then as Rossi moved past again, Crutchlow slipped off on lap 19, losing only three places as he scrambled back. Down on speed, he said, "I was having to make it up in the corners. Sooner or later, it was bound to happen."

Rossi shook off Dovi over the next four laps, before the Italian copied his team-mate, also losing three places and rejoining ahead of the Englishman.

Rossi was now 3.6 seconds off Stoner, but gaining speed and confidence. It took him five laps and then they were engaged, just like the good old days. Rossi attacked at the chicane, but was slow on the exit, letting Stoner by again. Next lap, he made it stick. They shook hands warmly up the hill after the flag. So much for old riders only in it for the money.

Pedrosa was steady, solid, but undistinguished. He'd succumbed to the satellite Yamahas early on and dropped back into the hands of Bradl, having a remarkable ride. The Tech 3 twins' mishaps promoted Dani to a lucky fourth.

The German rookie harried the factory bike, losing touch with a slide only after half-distance. Hayden, meantime, had been among the CRT bikes after his start-line mishap, but now was on the charge. Bradl was equal to his last-lap attack, however, claiming an impressive fifth by four-tenths.

Dovi, Crutchlow, Barbera and Bautista completed the top ten. Behind them, Ellison was top CRT bike, taking 11th in the final laps from Pasini, the last riders not to be lapped.

Espargaro held off Pirro; Hernandez trailed in behind, then a distant Spies. After yet more misfortune, he wondered if somebody had a voodoo doll somewhere. The start-line seat-flick had dislodged his visor and water had leaked inside. Unsighted, he suffered a near crash on the first lap, and after five pitted for a change of helmet.

Vermeulen was another lap down in his one-weekend ride, ahead of remounted faller Silva. Petrucci had led the CRT

gang, but crashed out with four laps to go; de Puniet crashed a second time; Abraham also fell, but he got back on, only to retire.

MOTO2 RACE – 26 laps

Moto2 qualifying started dry, but spitting and ended wet. Marquez used his soft tyre early to set a time that kept him on top in spite of a crash on the following lap. Luthi and Espargaro joined him on the front row; Redding – fastest on day one – led the second from Iannone and Kallio. French class rookie Zarco was on row three.

The race started streaming, and while (rather unexpectedly) there was only one faller as they funnelled through the tight first chicane – Corsi – Takahashi, di Meglio and Krummenacher had followed suit by the end of the lap. It set the tone for a race of many tumbles.

Espargaro was a second clear at the end of lap one, the pursuit piling up behind Redding, and he stayed narrowly ahead of a frantic shuffle, rookie Gino Rea prominent in the front pack until he was knocked flying by Zarco into the fast first corner.

By lap three, Luthi was heading the chase, and on lap eight he pounced on Espargaro and was immediately a second clear. Espargaro ran wide trying to make amends, dropping to the back of a group that now was eight strong. Smith had left the party, lying fourth after running third when he ran off on lap nine, rejoining 14th for a strong recovery ride.

Two laps later came a major upset. Marquez had been playing his usual waiting game in the front pack early on, and had moved through to fourth by lap ten when he slid off.

Luthi made good his escape, building a cushion of better than three seconds by half-distance. It was now that the only threat came, as Zarco emerged from the dwindling pack. He shook off Corti and was closing fast, to within a second on lap 20. Luthi regained a couple of tenths next time around, and then Zarco paid the price for over-enthusiasm, sliding into the gravel.

In the end, Luthi was more than six seconds ahead of Corti, with Redding hanging on to third after seeing off a last-laps challenge from Iannone.

West had finished the first lap 19th, but in conditions that bring out the best in him was moving steadily forward. He was up to fifth by lap 22 and hanging on grimly as a small group closed up.

By the end, Kallio came through to head a furious quintet that became a trio through the often crucial last right-hander. Smith and Simon crashed out together, leaving Espargaro and West to follow the Finn.

It was close enough to the line for Smith to take tenth behind Neukirchner and Wilairot; Simon's engine was dead and he pushed across the line for 13th.

De Angelis crashed out early, near the top of the ever-growing list of falls. In addition to those mentioned, Rodriguez, Cardus, Nakagami and Rosell also crashed, as did the remounted di Meglio for a second time.

With Marquez out, Espargaro assumed the title lead by a single point.

MOTO3 RACE – 24 laps

Vinales snatched pole from Vazquez, while Oliveira was third for an all-Honda front row; there were two more (Kornfeil and Masbou) on the second before Cortese's KTM. He'd crashed early on and had got back out only at the end, the rain getting worse.

It was a sodden, manic race with six different leaders, five of whom crashed out. Vazquez fell on the warm-up lap and was unable to rejoin. Conditions got worse in the second half, spilt oil making the track even more treacherous.

Khairuddin led for two heady laps, but dropped away to crash out later, well out of the top ten.

Next up was veteran Faubel, Salom nosing ahead briefly. Faubel was at the head of a pack of seven at half-distance when he became the first falling leader. Third-placed Kornfeil slipped off at almost the same time. Oliveira took over for three laps, then he fell.

Now it was the turn of Vinales, and it seemed that he might repeat his win of 2011 – until he too succumbed in the last corners.

Rossi was the last survivor, now more than 22 seconds clear with eight laps to go. The tension was high at home, but he kept cool to win by 27 seconds from Moncayo and Rins, who prevailed in a last-lap battle with charging Italian rookie Antonelli. Fellow-rookie Sissis held on for an impressive fifth.

Cortese had come through from 11th to a distant second when he fell at the last corners, but he kept the engine running to remount for sixth.

Fenati was an early faller; there were only 15 finishers.

ROUND 4

MONSTER ENERGY
GRAND PRIX DE FRANCE

TISSOT SWISS WATCHES SINCE 1853

OFFICIAL TIMEKEEPER

Photos: Gold & Goose

LE MANS – BUGATTI
28 laps
Length: 4.185 km / 2.600 miles
Width: 13m

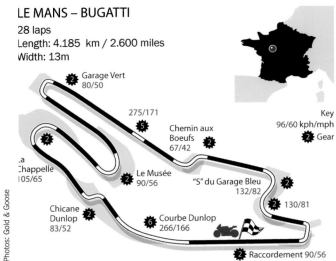

Garage Vert 80/50
275/171
Chemin aux Boeufs 67/42
La Chappelle 105/65
Le Musée 90/56
"S" du Garage Bleu 132/82
130/81
Chicane Dunlop 83/52
Courbe Dunlop 266/166
Raccordement 90/56

Key
96/60 kph/mph
Gear

MotoGP — RACE DISTANCE: 28 laps, 72.812 miles/117.180km · RACE WEATHER: Wet (air 13°C, humidity 96%, track 19°C)

Pos.	Rider	Nat.	No.	Entrant	Machine	Tyres	Race tyre choice	Laps	Time & speed
1	**Jorge Lorenzo**	SPA	99	Yamaha Factory Racing	Yamaha YZR-M1	B	F: Soft Wet/R: Soft Wet	28	49m 39.743s 87.968mph/ 141.571km/h
2	**Valentino Rossi**	ITA	46	Ducati Team	Ducati Desmosedici GP12	B	F: Soft Wet/R: Soft Wet	28	49m 49.648s
3	**Casey Stoner**	AUS	1	Repsol Honda Team	Honda RC213V	B	F: Soft Wet/R: Soft Wet	28	49m 51.041s
4	**Dani Pedrosa**	SPA	26	Repsol Honda Team	Honda RC213V	B	F: Soft Wet/R: Soft Wet	28	50m 09.104s
5	**Stefan Bradl**	GER	6	LCR Honda MotoGP	Honda RC213V	B	F: Soft Wet/R: Soft Wet	28	50m 12.220s
6	**Nicky Hayden**	USA	69	Ducati Team	Ducati Desmosedici GP12	B	F: Soft Wet/R: Soft Wet	28	50m 12.585s
7	**Andrea Dovizioso**	ITA	4	Monster Yamaha Tech 3	Yamaha YZR-M1	B	F: Soft Wet/R: Soft Wet	28	50m 39.502s
8	**Cal Crutchlow**	GBR	35	Monster Yamaha Tech 3	Yamaha YZR-M1	B	F: Soft Wet/R: Soft Wet	28	50m 44.895s
9	**Hector Barbera**	SPA	8	Pramac Racing Team	Ducati Desmosedici GP12	B	F: Soft Wet/R: Soft Wet	28	50m 47.589s
10	**Alvaro Bautista**	SPA	19	San Carlo Honda Gresini	Honda RC213V	B	F: Soft Wet/R: Soft Wet	28	50m 52.936s
11	**James Ellison**	GBR	77	Paul Bird Motorsport	ART Aprilia RSV4	B	F: Soft Wet/R: Soft Wet	28	51m 06.406s
12	**Mattia Pasini**	ITA	54	Speed Master	ART Aprilia RSV4	B	F: Soft Wet/R: Soft Wet	28	51m 07.376s
13	**Aleix Espargaro**	SPA	41	Power Electronics Aspar	ART Aprilia RSV4	B	F: Soft Wet/R: Soft Wet	27	49m 55.456s
14	**Michele Pirro**	ITA	51	San Carlo Honda Gresini	FTR Honda CBR1000RR	B	F: Soft Wet/R: Soft Wet	27	50m 03.709s
15	**Yonny Hernandez**	COL	68	Avintia Blusens	BQR FTR Kawasaki	B	F: Soft Wet/R: Soft Wet	27	50m 13.248s
16	Ben Spies	USA	11	Yamaha Factory Racing	Yamaha YZR-M1	B	F: Soft Wet/R: Soft Wet	27	50m 55.642s
17	Chris Vermeulen	AUS	7	NGM Mobile Forward Racing	Suter BMW S1000RR	B	F: Soft Wet/R: Soft Wet	26	49m 42.348s
18	Ivan Silva	SPA	22	Avintia Blusens	BQR FTR Kawasaki	B	F: Hard Wet/R: Soft Wet	26	51m 28.427s
	Danilo Petrucci	ITA	9	Came Ioda Racing Project	Ioda Aprilia RSV4	B	F: Soft Wet/R: Soft Wet	24	DNF-crash
	Randy de Puniet	FRA	14	Power Electronics Aspar	ART Aprilia RSV4	B	F: Soft Wet/R: Soft Wet	22	DNF-crash
	Karel Abraham	CZE	17	Cardion AB Motoracing	Ducati Desmosedici GP12	B	F: Soft Wet/R: Soft Wet	11	DNF-retired

Fastest lap: Valentino Rossi, on lap 21, 1m 44.614s, 89.487mph/144.015km/h.
Lap record: Dani Pedrosa, SPA (Honda), 1m 33.617s, 99.999mph/160.932km/h (2011).
Event best maximum speed: Hector Barbera, 192.1mph/309.2km/h (free practice 2).

Qualifying
Weather: Wet
Air Temp: 16° Humidity: 67%
Track Temp: 19°

1	Pedrosa	1m 33.638s
2	Stoner	1m 33.941s
3	Dovizioso	1m 33.976s
4	Lorenzo	1m 34.104s
5	Crutchlow	1m 34.178s
6	Spies	1m 34.669s
7	Rossi	1m 34.907s
8	Bautista	1m 34.922s
9	Barbera	1m 34.950s
10	Abraham	1m 35.250s
11	Hayden	1m 35.291s
12	De Puniet	1m 35.694s
13	Bradl	1m 35.862s
14	Pirro	1m 36.646s
15	Hernandez	1m 37.202s
16	Ellison	1m 37.666s
17	Espargaro	1m 37.760s
18	Petrucci	1m 37.767s
19	Silva	1m 38.198s
20	Pasini	1m 38.511s
21	Vermeulen	1m 38.658s

Fastest race laps
1	Rossi	1m 44.614s
2	Dovizioso	1m 44.919s
3	Lorenzo	1m 44.947s
4	Stoner	1m 45.122s
5	Crutchlow	1m 45.362s
6	Hayden	1m 45.607s
7	Pedrosa	1m 45.693s
8	Barbera	1m 46.185s
9	Spies	1m 46.254s
10	Bradl	1m 46.307s
11	Ellison	1m 46.599s
12	Bautista	1m 47.070s
13	Pasini	1m 47.378s
14	Petrucci	1m 47.586s
15	Vermeulen	1m 47.799s
16	Espargaro	1m 48.712s
17	Pirro	1m 48.880s
18	De Puniet	1m 48.953s
19	Hernandez	1m 49.513s
20	Silva	1m 50.041s
21	Abraham	1m 50.272s

Championship Points
1	Lorenzo	90
2	Stoner	82
3	Pedrosa	65
4	Crutchlow	45
5	Dovizioso	44
6	Rossi	42
7	Bradl	35
8	Bautista	35
9	Hayden	33
10	Barbera	26
11	Spies	18
12	Espargaro	12
13	Pasini	6
14	De Puniet	6
15	Ellison	5
16	Edwards	4
17	Petrucci	4
18	Pirro	4
19	Hernandez	3
20	Silva	1

Constructor Points
1	Yamaha	90
2	Honda	86
3	Ducati	47
4	ART	16
5	Suter	4
6	Ioda	4
7	FTR	4
8	BQR-FTR	2
9	BQR	2

Grid order

		1	2	3	4	5	6	7	8	9	10	11	12	13	14	15	16	17	18	19	20	21	22	23	24	25	26	27	28	
26	PEDROSA	99	99	99	99	99	99	99	99	99	99	99	99	99	99	99	99	99	99	99	99	99	99	99	99	99	99	99	99	1
1	STONER	26	1	1	1	1	1	1	1	1	1	1	1	1	1	1	1	1	1	1	1	1	1	1	1	1	1	1	46	2
4	DOVIZIOSO	1	26	46	46	46	46	46	46	46	46	46	46	4	4	4	4	4	46	46	46	46	46	46	46	46	46	1	3
99	LORENZO	46	46	26	4	4	4	4	4	4	35	35	35	35	35	46	46	46	46	4	4	4	4	4	26	26	26	26	4
35	CRUTCHLOW	4	4	4	35	35	35	35	35	35	4	4	4	46	46	35	35	35	35	26	26	26	26	26	6	6	6	6	5
11	SPIES	35	35	35	26	26	26	26	26	26	26	26	26	26	26	26	26	26	26	6	6	6	6	6	69	69	69	69	6
46	ROSSI	6	6	6	6	6	6	6	6	6	6	6	6	6	6	6	6	6	6	69	69	69	69	69	4	4	4	4	7
19	BAUTISTA	19	19	19	19	19	69	69	69	69	69	69	69	69	69	69	69	69	35	35	35	35	35	35	35	35	35	8
8	BARBERA	17	69	69	69	69	19	19	19	19	19	19	8	8	8	8	8	8	8	19	8	8	8	8	8	8	9
17	ABRAHAM	51	17	8	8	8	8	8	8	8	8	8	19	19	19	19	19	19	19	8	19	19	19	19	19	19	10
69	HAYDEN	69	8	17	17	9	9	9	9	9	9	9	9	9	9	9	9	9	9	9	9	9	54	77	77	77	11
14	DE PUNIET	41	51	54	9	17	54	54	54	54	54	54	54	54	54	54	54	54	54	54	54	54	77	54	54	54	12
6	BRADL	8	54	9	54	54	17	17	17	77	77	77	77	77	77	77	77	77	77	77	77	77	41	41	41	13
51	PIRRO	54	9	51	11	11	11	77	77	17	17	41	41	41	41	41	41	41	41	41	41	41	51	51	51	14
68	HERNANDEZ	9	41	11	51	77	77	51	51	41	41	51	51	51	51	51	51	51	51	51	68	68	68	15
77	ELLISON	77	77	41	77	51	51	41	41	51	51	17	68	68	68	68	68	68	68	68	68	11	11	11
41	ESPARGARO	68	11	77	41	41	41	68	68	68	68	68	14	14	11	11	11	11	11	11	7	7
9	PETRUCCI	11	68	68	68	68	68	11	7	7	7	7	11	11	14	14	14	14	14	14	22	22
22	SILVA	22	7	7	7	7	7	7	11	14	14	14	7	7	7	7	7	7	7	7	22	22
54	PASINI	7	14	14	14	14	14	14	14	11	11	11	22	22	22	22	22	22	22	22
7	VERMEULEN	14	22	22	22	22	22	22	22	22	22	22								

11 Pit stop 22 Lapped rider

Moto2

RACE DISTANCE: 26 laps, 67.611 miles/108.810km · RACE WEATHER: Wet (air 13°C, humidity 96%, track 14°C)

Pos. Rider	Nat.	No.	Entrant	Machine	Laps	Time & Speed
1 Thomas Luthi	SWI	12	Interwetten-Paddock	Suter	26	50m 02.816s / 81.057mph / 130.449km/h
2 Claudio Corti	ITA	71	Italtrans Racing Team	Kalex	26	50m 09.170s
3 Scott Redding	GBR	45	Marc VDS Racing Team	Kalex	26	50m 14.978s
4 Andrea Iannone	ITA	29	Speed Master	Speed Up	26	50m 19.154s
5 Mika Kallio	FIN	36	Marc VDS Racing Team	Kalex	26	50m 22.094s
6 Pol Espargaro	SPA	40	Pons 40 HP Tuenti	Kalex	26	50m 23.690s
7 Anthony West	AUS	95	QMMF Racing Team	Moriwaki	26	50m 24.521s
8 Max Neukirchner	GER	76	Kiefer Racing	Kalex	26	50m 30.933s
9 Ratthapark Wilairot	THA	14	Thai Honda PTT Gresini Moto2	Suter	26	50m 41.133s
10 Bradley Smith	GBR	38	Tech 3 Racing	Tech 3	26	50m 43.756s
11 Esteve Rabat	SPA	80	Pons 40 HP Tuenti	Kalex	26	50m 46.893s
12 Toni Elias	SPA	24	Mapfre Aspar Team	Suter	26	51m 02.399s
13 Julian Simon	SPA	60	Blusens Avintia	Suter	26	51m 04.601s
14 Nicolas Terol	SPA	18	Mapfre Aspar Team	Suter	26	51m 06.246s
15 Dominique Aegerter	SWI	77	Technomag-CIP	Suter	26	51m 13.157s
16 Roberto Rolfo	ITA	44	Technomag-CIP	Suter	26	51m 24.961s
17 Axel Pons	SPA	49	Pons 40 HP Tuenti	Kalex	26	51m 49.810s
18 Yuki Takahashi	JPN	72	NGM Mobile Forward Racing	Suter	25	50m 39.902s
19 Marco Colandrea	SWI	10	SAG Team	FTR	25	52m 05.435s
Johann Zarco	FRA	5	JIR Moto2	Motobi	21	DNF
Elena Rosell	SPA	82	QMMF Racing Team	Moriwaki	18	DNF
Takaaki Nakagami	JPN	30	Italtrans Racing Team	Kalex	17	DNF
Mike di Meglio	FRA	63	S/Master Speed Up	Speed Up	16	DNF
Ricard Cardus	SPA	88	Arguinano Racing Team	AJR	13	DNF
Marc Marquez	SPA	93	Team CatalunyaCaixa Repsol	Suter	11	DNF
Gino Rea	GBR	8	Federal Oil Gresini Moto2	Suter	7	DNF
Alexander Lundh	SWE	7	Cresto Guide MZ Racing	MZ-RE Honda	7	DNF
Alex de Angelis	RSM	15	NGM Mobile Forward Racing	Suter	3	DNF
Angel Rodriguez	SPA	47	Desguaces La Torre SAG	Bimota	2	DNF
Simone Corsi	ITA	3	Came IodaRacing Project	FTR	2	DNF
Randy Krummenacher	SWI	4	GP Team Switzerland	Kalex	1	DNF

Fastest lap: Claudio Corti, on lap 21, 1m 53.855s, 82.224mph/132.326km/h.
Lap record: Marc Marquez, SPA (Suter), 1m 38.533s, 95.010mph/152.903km/h (2011).
Event best maximum speed: Nicolas Terol, 161.4mph/259.8km/h (free practice 1).

Qualifying: Wet
Air: 16° Humidity: 67% Track: 19°

1	Marquez	1m 37.710s
2	Luthi	1m 37.739s
3	Espargaro	1m 38.190s
4	Redding	1m 38.369s
5	Iannone	1m 38.399s
6	Kallio	1m 38.574s
7	De Angelis	1m 38.662s
8	Zarco	1m 38.752s
9	Corti	1m 38.795s
10	Elias	1m 38.826s
11	Simon	1m 38.827s
12	Aegerter	1m 38.880s
13	Krummenacher	1m 38.880s
14	Corsi	1m 38.961s
15	Cardus	1m 39.061s
16	Pons	1m 39.105s
17	Terol	1m 39.229s
18	Rabat	1m 39.258s
19	Smith	1m 39.301s
20	Takahashi	1m 39.315s
21	Simeon	1m 39.353s
22	Rolfo	1m 39.414s
23	Di Meglio	1m 39.520s
24	Rea	1m 39.796s
25	Nakagami	1m 39.797s
26	Lundh	1m 39.924s
27	Neukirchner	1m 40.120s
28	West	1m 40.573s
29	Wilairot	1m 40.784s
30	Rodriguez	1m 41.443s
31	Rosell	1m 41.634s
32	Colandrea	1m 42.182s

Fastest race laps

1	Corti	1m 53.855s
2	Zarco	1m 53.929s
3	Luthi	1m 54.027s
4	Iannone	1m 54.146s
5	Redding	1m 54.375s
6	Simon	1m 54.588s
7	Cardus	1m 54.600s
8	West	1m 54.737s
9	Kallio	1m 54.756s
10	Wilairot	1m 54.781s
11	Smith	1m 54.791s
12	Neukirchner	1m 54.888s
13	Marquez	1m 54.929s
14	Espargaro	1m 54.933s
15	Nakagami	1m 54.987s
16	Elias	1m 55.235s
17	Terol	1m 55.690s
18	Rea	1m 55.730s
19	Rabat	1m 55.743s
20	Pons	1m 56.068s
21	Di Meglio	1m 56.280s
22	Aegerter	1m 56.308s
23	De Angelis	1m 56.848s
24	Rolfo	1m 56.872s
25	Takahashi	1m 58.104s
26	Rosell	1m 58.722s
27	Rodriguez	2m 01.614s
28	Colandrea	2m 01.994s
29	Lundh	2m 02.430s

Championship Points

1	Espargaro	71
2	Marquez	70
3	Luthi	68
4	Iannone	46
5	Redding	44
6	Kallio	33
7	Corti	32
8	Smith	24
9	Zarco	23
10	Elias	23
11	Rabat	18
12	De Angelis	14
13	Nakagami	13
14	Aegerter	13
15	Simon	12
16	West	9
17	Di Meglio	9
18	Neukirchner	8
19	Corsi	8
20	Wilairot	7
21	Simeon	6
22	Krummenacher	5
23	Terol	2
24	Cardus	1
25	Rea	1

Constructor Points

1	Suter	95
2	Kalex	81
3	Speed Up	46
4	Tech 3	24
5	Motobi	23
6	Moriwaki	10
7	FTR	8
8	AJR	1

Moto3

RACE DISTANCE: 24 laps, 62.411 miles/100.440km · RACE WEATHER: Wet (air 15°C, humidity 75%, track 11°C)

Pos. Rider	Nat.	No.	Entrant	Machine	Laps	Time & Speed
1 Louis Rossi	FRA	96	Racing Team Germany	FTR Honda	24	49m 12.390s / 76.100mph / 122.471km/h
2 Alberto Moncayo	SPA	23	Bankia Aspar Team	Kalex KTM	24	49m 39.738s
3 Alex Rins	SPA	42	Estrella Galicia 0,0	Suter Honda	24	49m 41.289s
4 Niccolo Antonelli	ITA	27	San Carlo Gresini Moto3	FTR Honda	24	49m 45.585s
5 Arthur Sissis	AUS	61	Red Bull KTM Ajo	KTM	24	49m 49.379s
6 Sandro Cortese	GER	11	Red Bull KTM Ajo	KTM	24	49m 57.702s
7 Jasper Iwema	NED	53	Moto FGR	FGR Honda	24	50m 11.035s
8 Alan Techer	FRA	89	Technomag-CIP-TSR	TSR Honda	24	50m 17.412s
9 Ivan Moreno	SPA	21	Andalucia JHK Laglisse	Honda	24	50m 21.584s
10 Giulian Pedone	SWI	30	Ambrogio Next Racing	Suter Honda	24	50m 58.141s
11 Jonas Folger	GER	94	IodaRacing Project	Ioda	23	49m 46.804s
12 Marcel Schrotter	GER	77	Mahindra Racing	Mahindra	23	50m 10.213s
13 Kevin Hanus	GER	86	Thomas Sabo GP Team	Honda	23	50m 40.631s
14 Alessandro Tonucci	ITA	19	Team Italia FMI	Honda	22	50m 24.017s
15 Niklas Ajo	FIN	31	TT Motion Events Racing	KTM	20	49m 56.694s
Zulfahmi Khairuddin	MAL	63	AirAsia-Sic-Ajo	KTM	17	DNF
Maverick Vinales	SPA	25	Blusens Avintia	FTR Honda	16	DNF
Miguel Oliveira	POR	44	Estrella Galicia 0,0	Suter Honda	15	DNF
Luis Salom	SPA	39	RW Racing GP	Kalex KTM	13	DNF
Hector Faubel	SPA	55	Bankia Aspar Team	Kalex KTM	12	DNF
Jakub Kornfeil	CZE	84	Redox-Ongetta-Centro Seta	FTR Honda	12	DNF
Isaac Vinales	SPA	32	Ongetta-Centro Seta	FTR Honda	12	DNF
Adrian Martin	SPA	26	JHK T-Shirt Laglisse	FTR Honda	8	DNF
Jack Miller	AUS	8	Caretta Technology	Honda	8	DNF
Simone Grotzkyj	ITA	15	Ambrogio Next Racing	Suter Honda	7	DNF
Danny Webb	GBR	99	Mahindra Racing	Mahindra	7	DNF
Danny Kent	GBR	52	Red Bull KTM Ajo	KTM	5	DNF
Romano Fenati	ITA	5	Team Italia FMI	FTR Honda	2	DNF
Alexis Masbou	FRA	10	Caretta Technology	Honda	1	DNF
Kenta Fujii	JPN	51	Technomag-CIP-TSR	TSR Honda	1	DNF
Brad Binder	RSA	41	RW Racing GP	Kalex KTM	0	DNF
Luigi Morciano	ITA	3	Ioda Team Italia	Ioda	0	DNF
Efren Vazquez	SPA	7	JHK T-Shirt Laglisse	FTR Honda	0	DNS

Fastest lap: Jakub Kornfeil, on lap 6, 2m 1.056s, 77.332mph/124.454km/h (record).
Lap record: New category.
Event best maximum speed: Maverick Vinales, 133.2mph/214.4km/h (free practice 2).

Qualifying: Wet
Air: 13° Humidity: 83% Track: 15°

1	M. Vinales	1m 55.865s
2	Vazquez	1m 56.847s
3	Oliveira	1m 57.114s
4	Kornfeil	1m 57.392s
5	Masbou	1m 57.673s
6	Cortese	1m 57.801s
7	Moncayo	1m 57.846s
8	Faubel	1m 57.899s
9	Salom	1m 58.000s
10	Khairuddin	1m 58.133s
11	Folger	1m 58.304s
12	Martin	1m 58.315s
13	Ajo	1m 58.563s
14	Sissis	1m 58.570s
15	Rossi	1m 58.576s
16	Binder	1m 58.590s
17	Kent	1m 58.673s
18	Techer	1m 58.679s
19	Pedone	1m 58.932s
20	I. Vinales	1m 58.938s
21	Fenati	1m 58.978s
22	Miller	1m 59.233s
23	Tonucci	1m 59.251s
24	Grotzkyj	1m 59.335s
25	Iwema	1m 59.539s
26	Rins	1m 59.888s
27	Antonelli	2m 00.129s
28	Fujii	2m 00.903s
29	Moreno	2m 02.379s
30	Finsterbusch	2m 03.240s
31	Hanus	2m 03.626s

Outside 107%

	Webb	2m 04.144s
	Schrotter	2m 05.206s
	Morciano	2m 05.565s

Fastest race laps

1	Kornfeil	2m 01.056s
2	Salom	2m 01.062s
3	M. Vinales	2m 01.068s
4	Oliveira	2m 01.232s
5	Faubel	2m 01.357s
6	Rossi	2m 01.477s
7	Kent	2m 01.849s
8	Grotzkyj	2m 01.994s
9	Cortese	2m 01.995s
10	Antonelli	2m 02.170s
11	Khairuddin	2m 02.507s
12	Sissis	2m 02.561s
13	Moncayo	2m 02.584s
14	Rins	2m 02.617s
15	Miller	2m 03.041s
16	Techer	2m 03.202s
17	Iwema	2m 03.287s
18	Martin	2m 03.876s
19	I. Vinales	2m 03.940s
20	Moreno	2m 04.090s
21	Tonucci	2m 04.209s
22	Ajo	2m 04.593s
23	Pedone	2m 05.285s
24	Fenati	2m 05.624s
25	Webb	2m 06.130s
26	Folger	2m 06.648s
27	Schrotter	2m 07.609s
28	Hanus	2m 09.887s

Championship Points

1	Cortese	67
2	M. Vinales	55
3	Salom	49
4	Fenati	45
5	Rins	44
6	Moncayo	33
7	Rossi	32
8	Antonelli	31
9	Khairuddin	29
10	Sissis	23
11	Masbou	18
12	Kent	16
13	Techer	15
14	Faubel	15
15	Vazquez	11
16	Oliveira	11
17	Moreno	10
18	Iwema	9
19	Pedone	7
20	Kornfeil	7
21	Tonucci	7
22	Folger	5
23	Binder	5
24	Marquez	5
25	Schrotter	4
26	Ajo	4
27	Hanus	3

Constructor Points

1	FTR Honda	95
2	Kalex KTM	69
3	KTM	68
4	Suter Honda	49
5	Honda	21
6	TSR Honda	15
7	FGR Honda	9
8	Ioda	5
9	Mahindra	4
10	Oral	1

Insets, left and far left: Lorenzo and his fans. Both sides were well rewarded at his home race.

Inset, right: The colour is yellow, but it's for Maverick Vinales, not Rossi.

Main photo: Punishing the Bridgestones. Lorenzo was a comfortable winner from Pedrosa and Dovizioso.

Photos: Gold & Goose

CATALUNYA GRAND PRIX

CATALUNYA CIRCUIT

Above: Every race another win: Bridge-stone's Hiroshi Yamada.

Top: One goes down, one carries on. Luckless Espargaro falls in the controversial incident with Marquez.

Above right: Count-down to clutch time for Barbera.

Above far right: Aleix Espargaro won the best-yet CRT battle.

Top right: Overruled, and underwhelmed: Race Director Mike Webb.

Right: Eyes front: Rostrum-bound Dovi ignores distractions to get in the zone.

Far right: Elbows down: Stoner style. Enough to fend off Crutchlow.

Photos: Gold & Goose

SUNNY Spain didn't quite lay on a blue-sky weekend, with race-morning warm-up sodden. It did provide exciting racing in all three classes and left plenty to talk about. In one case, for many weeks afterwards...

It was the last race on the 'old' Bridgestone front tyre, so disliked by the factory Honda pair. They (or more correctly their Hondas) didn't much like the new-for-2012 rear either, and Stoner and Pedrosa would be the only fast men to choose the harder tyre option, and they suffered for it. In one of those paradoxes that confirms the complexities of motorcycle dynamics, the lower grip meant more wheelspin, especially on the punishingly long set of right-handers, the harder tyres becoming hotter than the soft. As a result, Dani missed out on a win and Stoner finished off the rostrum for the first time in 19 races.

The more lasting controversy came in Moto2, demonstrating potentially damaging cracks in the structure of racing management and throwing the result of the race into doubt for weeks to come.

Like most of the Moto2 action, it involved Marquez, but soon passed out of his hands.

The race had been a four-way battle: Iannone, Luthi, Marquez, Espargaro. With three laps to go, Marquez almost crashed at the apex of the corner after the back straight. A miracle save sent him wide, and he lost only a little speed before swooping back to the inside to resume the fast line.

Espargaro had seen his chance and dived inside the bucking Suter. When their trajectories crossed, he was still a little behind. Down he went, while Marquez wobbled again, but recovered to hang on to a rostrum third.

The title favourite, now nicknamed Marquez the Merciless in some quarters, had form. At Qatar, he'd been warned, but not penalised for a race-winning bad move on Luthi; earlier in this race, he'd done something similar to Iannone at the end of the main straight, said Race Director Mike Webb. And now this. "With any other rider, it would have been a warning," said Webb. But taking the accumulation of opprobrium into account, Race Direction sanctioned him with a 60-second penalty, dropping him to 23rd and crucially out of the points. With both participants non-scoring, this left him fourth overall, one point behind Espargaro.

Then it got messy. Marquez's team chief, Emilio Alzamora,

promptly protested, and the FIM stewards upheld his protest. Marquez was back in third.

This sensational reversal was unprecedented in modern racing: Race Direction (Webb, riders' safety rep Franco Uncini, the FIM's Claude Danis and Dorna's Javier Alonso) had never had a decision overturned. And the argument would go on: Espargaro's team owner, Sito Pons (like Alzamora another ex-world champion), appealed the stewards' decision and when, four weeks later, the FIM's Disciplinary Committee backed the stewards, he continued to make threatening noises about taking it to the independent Court of Arbitration for Sport, until stepping back in August.

The muddle stemmed from the wording of the sanction. Race Direction named only the single incident with Espargaro and said nothing about a warning or any earlier clash. This left the stewards with an admittedly 50-50 situation to judge, and they voted accordingly. The train of events suggested it is time for a more formal 'yellow card' system in place of the clearly woolly current verbal warning.

Elsewhere, the general this-and-that of a GP weekend proceeded much as normal.

The GP Commission met to discuss future technical rules, but the meeting concluded without reaching any conclusion. The MSMA's blocking tactics prevailed. Dorna chief Ezpeleta's original deadline for a firm decision had passed the day before; his threat of "all CRT bikes" receded in the same way. "There's a lot of card playing going on at the moment," vouchsafed observer Webb.

Over at Tech 3, Crutchlow's bikes were now fitted with the latest Brembos, to match those of team-mate Dovi. "I've got the brakes, but I am not allowed to say so," said the Englishman.

Stoner resumed his criticism of racing and the way it was developing. Taxed by *MOTOCOURSE* that his views were understandable, but somewhat old-fashioned, he happily agreed: "I should have been born 20 years earlier. It's disappointing the paddock's turned out this way. You could have a good battle on the track, then all talk to each other afterwards, instead of living in a bubble." Then he sprang to racing's defence: "It's disappointing people say the racing was better back then. If you look at the records, there were plenty of times they weren't as close as today."

Above: The battle for sixth: Bautista, Rossi, Bradl.

Top right: Spanish Eyes. Alex Marquez (left) and Maverick Vinales.

Above right: A subdued Marc Marquez eventually retained his contentious third place.

Right: Moto2 maulers: eventual winner Iannone battles with Marquez, Luthi and Espargaro.

Below right: Chasing Vinales: Oliveira leads Cortese (11), Faubel, Alex Marquez (12), Masbou and Salom in the quest for second in Moto3.

Photos: Gold & Goose

Ducati were fresh from three days of largely fruitless testing, bringing revised electronics that improved the power delivery and an aluminium swing-arm that Hayden had liked, but which had promoted chatter. He didn't use it, and Rossi only briefly.

Hayden came up with another rather worrying problem during the race: his right hand went to sleep. The last time that had happened, he said, had been at Laguna Seca in 2010, and he had faced corrective surgery at year's end as a result.

Stefan Bradl continued to make a good impression after his top five at Le Mans, and was fresh back from a foray to the USA, where he'd run a track day on a CBR1000 to learn his way around Laguna, where he would be a circuit first-timer. He had surprised everybody so far with his speed, including himself, and was working on sustaining it all race long. Once again, here this weakness would drop him from sixth in the early stages.

Ben Spies's nightmare continued after a blazing start, with an over-impetuous attack on Pedrosa that ended in a sprawl in the gravel. He remounted for a furious ride and managed not to be last of the factory bikes.

For the first time, there was a lively CRT battle behind them, between the ARTs of Espargaro and de Puniet and Michele Pirro's FTR Honda. The rest were miles behind, but at least they were doing more than just filling the spaces behind the fast guys.

MOTOGP RACE – 25 laps

Two days of fiery heat made practice and qualifying something of an ordeal. Stoner took his 40th career pole, by 0.146 second from Lorenzo. Crutchlow was third, his third time on the front row in five races, by just four-thousandths from Spies. Pedrosa had hit traffic and ended up fourth; Dovi completed row two. Hayden led the third, with Rossi at the far end.

Stoner started well, but Pedrosa weaved through into the lead, followed into the first corner by Spies and Lorenzo. Stoner would lose another place by lap's end to Dovizioso, then fall behind Crutchlow as well on the next lap, when he ran wide at the end of the back straight.

If Pedrosa up front was having similar trouble getting his hard tyres to work right, then Spies thought he could capitalise. "I was getting held up in the corners," he said. On lap

three, he led briefly after diving inside at the right-hand Turn Four over the hill, but his line carried him wide and out to the edge of the track, and he was down. Although soon back on board, he had gone from first to last.

This promoted Lorenzo to second. The order was unchanged in the top five for the next three laps, but as they started the seventh Lorenzo pushed past Pedrosa at Turn One, while Stoner did the same to Crutchlow.

Stoner could keep the Englishman behind him, but he couldn't stay with the leaders, and the front three pulled clear, the gap up to two seconds by lap ten. Next time around, Dovi was a second adrift and soon to drop further with a near crash.

Now Pedrosa took to the front again, the two Spaniards drawing away rapidly for a close and exciting battle. Only when Lorenzo got ahead again on lap 20 did it become clear that he had a slightly better pace. "It was a very complicated race," he said. "I had to be patient. When I saw that Dani was slowing a bit, I decided to wait for a mistake, and when I saw him go wide, I took my opportunity."

It was not the tyres, said Dani, "more to do with bike character. There was a lot of spinning with hard and soft, but with the soft, the bike was pumping." He added, "After he passed me, I could hardly keep the bike straight."

Four seconds behind, Dovi had his hands full with Stoner and Crutchlow, although by the end the Englishman had dropped away with a shortage of rear grip. The other two battled to the flag, Stoner pushing and probing, but unable to find a way by. He'd expected more of the harder tyre later in the race, "but it just didn't come in," he said. "Today was a worse result, but not that much worse … if it was a 12-round championship, I might be worried."

Bradl held sixth for the first five laps as behind him Bautista made his way past Rossi, fell behind him again, then passed him for good. Then one by one the pair passed the German and drew clear – and it looked as though Hayden might do the same until he started to lose ground after ten laps, battling his hand problem.

Rossi pushed Bautista until lap 20, but was obliged to accept a safe seventh; Bradl and Hayden were alone behind him. Likewise Barbera, until Spies arrived at speed with two laps left to push him out of the top ten.

Abraham had a lonely race, ahead of the first real CRT brawl. Espargaro was in front for most of the distance, until team-mate de Puniet passed him on lap 16, only to

run wide, forfeiting the place again and then losing out to Pirro as well.

Ellison and Edwards had been close, the Briton losing touch only in the final stages. Edwards, in his first race since his Estoril misadventure, was battling pain as well as his unruly Suter BMW and finally succumbed, slowing and pitting on the last lap.

Pasini regained 17th from Hernandez on the last lap after another good CRT fight; Petrucci did the same to Silva. All finishers were on the same lap as the leader, if only just.

Lorenzo was the first to win three races in 2012 and stretched his points lead over Stoner to a handy 20, with Pedrosa another ten away.

MOTO2 RACE – 23 laps

Marquez claimed pole by almost two-tenths from Espargaro and Luthi, with Iannone leading row two from Corsi and Aegerter; he led away into the first corner.

By the end of the lap, however, Iannone and fast-starting Aegerter had pushed past, with Elias also on the scene.

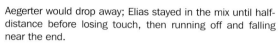

Aegerter would drop away; Elias stayed in the mix until half-distance before losing touch, then running off and falling near the end.

Iannone would lead over the line every lap but three. Marquez was another leader, on laps eight and 17, as was Luthi on the penultimate lap, but there was plenty of to and fro elsewhere on the track, in a typically close Moto2 battle. Espargaro was with the trio almost all the way in a threatening fourth.

The crucial crash came just after Luthi had seized second from Marquez under braking at the end of the back straight. Marquez tried to hang on through the left, but almost crashed before diving back across to the left, as Espargaro got there. While the latter writhed in the gravel clutching his foot, Marquez lost a second he would not regain.

That left the leaders jousting to the end, Luthi's final attacking lunge failing by less than a tenth.

It was the flashy, but erratic Italian's first win in seven races. Second at Qatar served him well enough for joint third overall at this stage, but 14th place at Jerez was an all too typical lapse.

More than ten seconds behind, Rabat had managed to get away from the next group, leaving Corsi a couple of seconds adrift and only narrowly holding off Nakagami, who had picked his way through after finishing the first lap 13th.

Seventh to eleventh were covered by less than a second, Aegerter fending off Krummenacher and team-mates Kallio and Redding. The Englishman had taken fifth off Elias on lap nine, but was already two seconds adrift; as usual, his size meant he was having to ride too hard in the corners, punishing his tyres and slowing him later in the race.

Rookie Zarco was 11th, five seconds away; his 125 conqueror, Terol, was ten seconds back in 15th. An off-form Smith managed to stay six-tenths clear of Corti to take 12th.

Elias had landed with this group until he crashed out on lap 17.

Rea and the luckless Simon (still not back to speed after his crash here in 2011) crashed out together at the first corner, di Meglio later on the first lap. Remarkably there were no other crashes, though Rolfo retired after executing a ride-through penalty for a jumped start.

MOTO3 RACE – 22 laps

Rossi led away; Khairuddin took over briefly on lap three. Vinales led for the first time on lap four.

Rossi and Vazquez stayed with him and gained a little gap as Khairuddin had a moment and dropped to tenth, behind a growling gaggle. Then wild-card Alex Marquez pulled them together as he came through to second, setting fastest lap, then dropping behind Cortese as the pack closed up. Faubel and Oliveira were in it; Khairuddin was coming back, accompanied by Rins and Masbou.

They fought over second, regained by Rossi on lap nine, then Marquez again. But Vinales had his head down and pulled clear impressively: a gap of one second on lap 11 was more than doubled next time around and up to 4.9 seconds on the following lap. He was better than ten seconds clear on lap 19 and only then responded to his team's frantic 'slow down' signals. He still won by more than seven seconds.

Vazquez would lead the pursuit again before dropping away and eventually crashing out on the same lap as Rins.

Amazingly, there were no other fallers. Cortese and Oliveira completed the rostrum, then Rossi, Masbou, Marquez, Faubel, Khairuddin and Fenati, catching up in the closing stages, second to ninth in less than a second; Salom (Kalex KTM) was a fighting tenth.

FIM WORLD CHAMPIONSHIP

ROUND
5
1-3 JUNE, 2012

GRAN PREMI
APEROL
DE CATALUNYA

OFFICIAL TIMEKEEPER
TISSOT — SWISS WATCHES SINCE 1853

Photos: Gold & Goose

CIRCUIT DE CATALUNYA

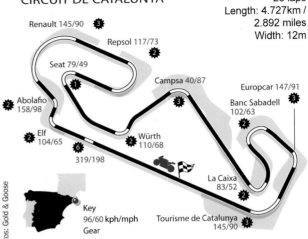

25 laps
Length: 4.727km /
2.892 miles
Width: 12m

Renault 145/90
Repsol 117/73
Seat 79/49
Campsa 40/87
Europcar 147/91
Abolafio 158/98
Banc Sabadell 102/63
Elf 104/65
Würth 110/68
319/198
La Caixa 83/52
Tourisme de Catalunya 145/90

Key
96/60 kph/mph
Gear

MotoGP RACE DISTANCE: 25 laps, 73.431 miles/118.175km · RACE WEATHER: Dry (air 27°C, humidity 49%, track 40°C)

Pos.	Rider	Nat.	No.	Entrant	Machine	Tyres	Race tyre choice	Laps	Time & speed
1	**Jorge Lorenzo**	SPA	99	Yamaha Factory Racing	Yamaha YZR-M1	B	F: Hard/R: Medium	25	43m 07.681s 102.157mph/ 164.405km/h
2	**Dani Pedrosa**	SPA	26	Repsol Honda Team	Honda RC213V	B	F: Hard/R: Hard	25	43m 12.684s
3	**Andrea Dovizioso**	ITA	4	Monster Yamaha Tech 3	Yamaha YZR-M1	B	F: Hard/R: Medium	25	43m 17.042s
4	**Casey Stoner**	AUS	1	Repsol Honda Team	Honda RC213V	B	F: Hard/R: Hard	25	43m 17.225s
5	**Cal Crutchlow**	GBR	35	Monster Yamaha Tech 3	Yamaha YZR-M1	B	F: Hard/R: Medium	25	43m 20.187s
6	**Alvaro Bautista**	SPA	19	San Carlo Honda Gresini	Honda RC213V	B	F: Hard/R: Medium	25	43m 21.629s
7	**Valentino Rossi**	ITA	46	Ducati Team	Ducati Desmosedici GP12	B	F: Hard/R: Medium	25	43m 25.236s
8	**Stefan Bradl**	GER	6	LCR Honda MotoGP	Honda RC213V	B	F: Hard/R: Medium	25	43m 31.159s
9	**Nicky Hayden**	USA	69	Ducati Team	Ducati Desmosedici GP12	B	F: Hard/R: Medium	25	43m 38.091s
10	**Ben Spies**	USA	11	Yamaha Factory Racing	Yamaha YZR-M1	B	F: Hard/R: Medium	25	43m 40.578s
11	**Hector Barbera**	SPA	8	Pramac Racing Team	Ducati Desmosedici GP12	B	F: Hard/R: Medium	25	43m 43.825s
12	**Karel Abraham**	CZE	17	Cardion AB Motoracing	Ducati Desmosedici GP12	B	F: Hard/R: Medium	25	44m 03.910s
13	**Aleix Espargaro**	SPA	41	Power Electronics Aspar	ART Aprilia RSV4	B	F: Hard/R: Medium	25	44m 15.735s
14	**Michele Pirro**	ITA	51	San Carlo Honda Gresini	FTR Honda CBR1000RR	B	F: Hard/R: Medium	25	44m 16.456s
15	**Randy de Puniet**	FRA	14	Power Electronics Aspar	ART Aprilia RSV4	B	F: Hard/R: Hard	25	44m 18.164s
16	James Ellison	GBR	77	Paul Bird Motorsport	ART Aprilia RSV4	B	F: Hard/R: Medium	25	44m 20.771s
17	Mattia Pasini	ITA	54	Speed Master	ART Aprilia RSV4	B	F: Hard/R: Medium	25	44m 28.584s
18	Yonny Hernandez	COL	68	Avintia Blusens	BQR FTR Kawasaki	B	F: Hard/R: Medium	25	44m 28.916s
19	Danilo Petrucci	ITA	9	Came Ioda Racing Project	Ioda Aprilia RSV4	B	F: Hard/R: Medium	25	44m 48.888s
20	Ivan Silva	SPA	22	Avintia Blusens	BQR FTR Kawasaki	B	F: Hard/R: Medium	25	44m 49.569s
	Colin Edwards	USA	5	NGM Mobile Forward Racing	Suter BMW S1000RR	B	F: Hard/R: Medium	24	Finished in pits

Fastest lap: Jorge Lorenzo, on lap 3, 1m 42.642s, 103.018mph/165.791km/h.
Lap record: Dani Pedrosa, SPA (Honda), 1m 42.358s, 103.304mph/166.251km/h (2008).
Event best maximum speed: Valentino Rossi, 210.1mph/338.2km/h (qualifying practice).

Qualifying
Weather: Dry
Air Temp: 31° Humidity: 38%
Track Temp: 52°

1	Stoner	1m 41.295s
2	Lorenzo	1m 41.441s
3	Crutchlow	1m 41.548s
4	Spies	1m 41.552s
5	Pedrosa	1m 41.656s
6	Dovizioso	1m 41.687s
7	Hayden	1m 42.029s
8	Bradl	1m 42.065s
9	Rossi	1m 42.175s
10	Bautista	1m 42.356s
11	Barbera	1m 42.375s
12	Abraham	1m 43.266s
13	De Puniet	1m 43.500s
14	Edwards	1m 44.024s
15	Espargaro	1m 44.041s
16	Pirro	1m 44.356s
17	Ellison	1m 44.763s
18	Pasini	1m 44.764s
19	Hernandez	1m 44.833s
20	Petrucci	1m 45.730s
21	Silva	1m 45.962s

Fastest race laps

1	Lorenzo	1m 42.642s
2	Pedrosa	1m 42.667s
3	Crutchlow	1m 42.770s
4	Dovizioso	1m 42.808s
5	Stoner	1m 42.816s
6	Bautista	1m 42.852s
7	Spies	1m 43.037s
8	Bradl	1m 43.048s
9	Rossi	1m 43.198s
10	Hayden	1m 43.215s
11	Barbera	1m 43.704s
12	Abraham	1m 44.528s
13	Hernandez	1m 45.092s
14	Ellison	1m 45.241s
15	De Puniet	1m 45.269s
16	Espargaro	1m 45.287s
17	Pasini	1m 45.408s
18	Edwards	1m 45.427s
19	Pirro	1m 45.471s
20	Silva	1m 45.998s
21	Petrucci	1m 46.450s

Championship Points

1	Lorenzo	115
2	Stoner	95
3	Pedrosa	85
4	Dovizioso	60
5	Crutchlow	56
6	Rossi	51
7	Bautista	45
8	Bradl	43
9	Hayden	40
10	Barbera	31
11	Spies	24
12	Espargaro	15
13	De Puniet	7
14	Pasini	6
15	Pirro	6
16	Ellison	5
17	Abraham	4
18	Edwards	4
19	Petrucci	4
20	Hernandez	3
21	Silva	1

Constructor Points

1	Yamaha	115
2	Honda	106
3	Ducati	56
4	ART	19
5	FTR	6
6	Suter	4
7	Ioda	4
8	BQR-FTR	2
9	BQR	2

Grid order / lap chart

Grid order	1	2	3	4	5	6	7	8	9	10	11	12	13	14	15	16	17	18	19	20	21	22	23	24	25
1 STONER	26	26	26	26	26	26	99	99	99	99	99	26	26	26	26	26	26	26	26	99	99	99	99	99	99
99 LORENZO	11	11	99	99	99	99	26	26	26	26	26	99	99	99	99	99	99	99	99	26	26	26	26	26	26
35 CRUTCHLOW	99	99	4	4	4	4	4	4	4	4	4	4	4	4	4	4	4	4	4	4	4	4	4	4	4
11 SPIES	4	4	35	35	35	35	1	1	1	1	1	1	1	1	1	1	1	1	1	1	1	1	1	1	1
26 PEDROSA	1	35	1	1	1	1	35	35	35	35	35	35	35	35	35	35	35	35	35	35	35	35	35	35	35
4 DOVIZIOSO	35	1	6	6	6	19	19	19	19	19	19	19	19	19	19	19	19	19	19	19	19	19	19	19	19
69 HAYDEN	6	6	46	19	19	6	6	46	46	46	46	46	46	46	46	46	46	46	46	46	46	46	46	46	46
6 BRADL	69	19	19	46	46	46	46	6	6	6	6	6	6	6	6	6	6	6	6	6	6	6	6	6	6
46 ROSSI	46	46	69	69	69	69	69	69	69	69	69	69	69	69	69	69	69	69	69	69	69	69	69	69	69
19 BAUTISTA	19	69	8	8	8	8	8	8	8	8	8	8	8	8	8	8	8	8	8	8	8	11	11		
8 BARBERA	8	8	17	17	17	17	17	17	17	17	11	11	11	11	11	11	11	11	11	11	11	8	8		
17 ABRAHAM	17	17	41	41	41	41	41	41	41	11	11	11	17	17	17	17	17	17	17	17	17	17	17		
14 DE PUNIET	41	41	77	68	77	77	11	11	41	41	41	41	41	14	41	41	41	41	41	41	41	41	41		
5 EDWARDS	51	14	68	77	14	14	77	77	14	14	14	14	14	41	14	14	14	14	51	51	51	51	51		
41 ESPARGARO	14	77	14	14	51	51	11	14	77	77	77	77	51	51	51	51	14	14	14	14	14	14	14		
51 PIRRO	77	68	51	51	5	5	51	51	51	51	51	51	77	77	77	77	5	77	77	77	77	77	77		
77 ELLISON	68	51	5	5	54	54	54	54	54	54	54	54	54	54	54	54	54	54	54	54	68	68	54		
54 PASINI	5	5	54	54	68	68	11	54	54	54	68	54	68	68	68	68	68	54	54	54	54	54	68		
68 HERNANDEZ	9	54	9	22	22	11	68	68	68	68	68	54	54	68	68	54	68	68	68	9	22	22	9		
9 PETRUCCI	54	9	22	9	11	22	22	22	22	22	9	22	22	22	9	22	22	22	22	9	9	9	22		
22 SILVA	22	22	11	11	9	9	9	9	9	9	9	9	9	9	22	9	9	9	5	5	5	5			

5 Pit stop   5 Lapped rider

Moto2

RACE DISTANCE: 23 laps, 67.556 miles/108.721km · RACE WEATHER: Dry (air 26°C, humidity 47%, track 40°C)

Pos.	Rider	Nat.	No.	Entrant	Machine	Laps	Time & Speed
1	**Andrea Iannone**	ITA	29	Speed Master	Speed Up	23	41m 16.852s 98.190mph/ 158.021km/h
2	**Thomas Luthi**	SWI	12	Interwetten-Paddock	Suter	23	41m 16.935s
3	**Marc Marquez**	SPA	93	Team CatalunyaCaixa Repsol	Suter	23	41m 17.989s
4	**Esteve Rabat**	SPA	80	Pons 40 HP Tuenti	Kalex	23	41m 29.368s
5	**Simone Corsi**	ITA	3	Came IodaRacing Project	FTR	23	41m 31.078s
6	**Takaaki Nakagami**	JPN	30	Italtrans Racing Team	Kalex	23	41m 31.924s
7	**Dominique Aegerter**	SWI	77	Technomag-CIP	Suter	23	41m 33.107s
8	**Randy Krummenacher**	SWI	4	GP Team Switzerland	Kalex	23	41m 33.206s
9	**Mika Kallio**	FIN	36	Marc VDS Racing Team	Kalex	23	41m 33.458s
10	**Scott Redding**	GBR	45	Marc VDS Racing Team	Kalex	23	41m 33.645s
11	**Johann Zarco**	FRA	5	JIR Moto2	Motobi	23	41m 34.150s
12	**Bradley Smith**	GBR	38	Tech 3 Racing	Tech 3	23	41m 39.094s
13	**Claudio Corti**	ITA	71	Italtrans Racing Team	Kalex	23	41m 40.615s
14	**Alex de Angelis**	RSM	15	NGM Mobile Forward Racing	Suter	23	41m 40.921s
15	**Nicolas Terol**	SPA	18	Mapfre Aspar Team	Suter	23	41m 43.891s
16	Jordi Torres	SPA	81	Tech 3 Racing	Tech 3	23	41m 49.010s
17	Max Neukirchner	GER	76	Kiefer Racing	Kalex	23	41m 51.241s
18	Ratthapark Wilairot	THA	14	Thai Honda PTT Gresini Moto2	Suter	23	41m 52.239s
19	Ricard Cardus	SPA	88	Arguinano Racing Team	AJR	23	41m 52.353s
20	Angel Rodriguez	SPA	47	Desguaces La Torre SAG	Bimota	23	41m 52.475s
21	Yuki Takahashi	JPN	72	NGM Mobile Forward Racing	Suter	23	41m 52.655s
22	Axel Pons	SPA	49	Pons 40 HP Tuenti	Kalex	23	41m 53.755s
23	Anthony West	AUS	95	QMMF Racing Team	Moriwaki	23	42m 09.488s
24	Alexander Lundh	SWE	7	Cresto Guide MZ Racing	MZ-RE Honda	23	42m 33.161s
25	Marco Colandrea	SWI	10	SAG Team	FTR	23	42m 35.425s
26	Elena Rosell	SPA	82	QMMF Racing Team	Moriwaki	23	42m 52.403s
	Pol Espargaro	SPA	40	Pons 40 HP Tuenti	Kalex	20	DNF
	Roberto Rolfo	ITA	44	Technomag-CIP	Suter	20	DNF
	Toni Elias	SPA	24	Mapfre Aspar Team	Suter	19	DNF
	Julian Simon	SPA	60	Blusens Avintia	Suter	0	DNF
	Gino Rea	GBR	8	Federal Oil Gresini Moto2	Suter	0	DNF
	Mike di Meglio	FRA	63	S/Master Speed Up	Speed Up	0	DNF

Fastest lap: Thomas Luthi, on lap 3, 1m 46.631s, 99.164mph/159.589km/h (record).
Previous lap record: Andrea Iannone, ITA (Speed Up), 1m 47.543s, 98.323mph/158.236km/h (2010).
Event best maximum speed: Mika Kallio, 177.9mph/286.3km/h (race).

Qualifying: Dry
Air: 31° **Humidity:** 34% **Track:** 54°

1	Marquez	1m 46.187s
2	Espargaro	1m 46.382s
3	Luthi	1m 46.430s
4	Iannone	1m 46.477s
5	Corsi	1m 46.816s
6	Aegerter	1m 46.844s
7	Redding	1m 46.866s
8	Elias	1m 47.107s
9	Rabat	1m 47.107s
10	De Angelis	1m 47.115s
11	Torres	1m 47.239s
12	Nakagami	1m 47.275s
13	Smith	1m 47.423s
14	Zarco	1m 47.427s
15	Terol	1m 47.468s
16	Corti	1m 47.583s
17	Simon	1m 47.631s
18	Rolfo	1m 47.646s
19	Kallio	1m 47.654s
20	Krummenacher	1m 47.753s
21	Rodriguez	1m 47.841s
22	Takahashi	1m 47.843s
23	Rea	1m 48.041s
24	Di Meglio	1m 48.060s
25	Cardus	1m 48.074s
26	Neukirchner	1m 48.090s
27	Wilairot	1m 48.096s
28	Pons	1m 48.453s
29	West	1m 48.751s
30	Lundh	1m 49.081s
31	Colandrea	1m 49.740s
32	Rosell	1m 50.478s

Fastest race laps

1	Luthi	1m 46.631s
2	Elias	1m 46.831s
3	Marquez	1m 46.848s
4	Redding	1m 46.954s
5	Rabat	1m 47.019s
6	Iannone	1m 47.044s
7	Zarco	1m 47.112s
8	Espargaro	1m 47.125s
9	Kallio	1m 47.150s
10	Aegerter	1m 47.221s
11	De Angelis	1m 47.319s
12	Corsi	1m 47.343s
13	Nakagami	1m 47.380s
14	Krummenacher	1m 47.489s
15	Smith	1m 47.650s
16	Wilairot	1m 47.675s
17	Torres	1m 47.809s
18	Terol	1m 47.865s
19	Corti	1m 47.888s
20	Cardus	1m 47.889s
21	Neukirchner	1m 48.016s
22	Takahashi	1m 48.078s
23	Rolfo	1m 48.156s
24	Pons	1m 48.366s
25	Rodriguez	1m 48.485s
26	West	1m 48.596s
27	Colandrea	1m 49.680s
28	Lundh	1m 49.743s
29	Rosell	1m 50.758s

Championship Points

1	Luthi	88
2	Marquez	86
3	Espargaro	71
4	Iannone	71
5	Redding	50
6	Kallio	40
7	Corti	35
8	Rabat	31
9	Zarco	28
10	Smith	28
11	Nakagami	23
12	Elias	23
13	Aegerter	22
14	Corsi	19
15	De Angelis	16
16	Krummenacher	13
17	Simon	12
18	West	9
19	Di Meglio	9
20	Neukirchner	8
21	Wilairot	7
22	Simeon	6
23	Terol	3
24	Cardus	1
25	Rea	1

Constructor Points

1	Suter	115
2	Kalex	94
3	Speed Up	71
4	Motobi	28
5	Tech 3	28
6	FTR	19
7	Moriwaki	10
8	AJR	1

Moto3

RACE DISTANCE: 22 laps, 64.619 miles/103.994km · RACE WEATHER: Dry (air 26°C, humidity 47%, track 33°C)

Pos.	Rider	Nat.	No.	Entrant	Machine	Laps	Time & Speed
1	**Maverick Vinales**	SPA	25	Blusens Avintia	FTR Honda	22	41m 50.965s 92.645mph/ 149.097km/h
2	**Sandro Cortese**	GER	11	Red Bull KTM Ajo	KTM	22	41m 58.717s
3	**Miguel Oliveira**	POR	44	Estrella Galicia 0,0	Suter Honda	22	41m 58.818s
4	**Louis Rossi**	FRA	96	Racing Team Germany	FTR Honda	22	41m 58.972s
5	**Alexis Masbou**	FRA	10	Caretta Technology	Honda	22	41m 59.040s
6	**Alex Marquez**	SPA	12	Estrella Galicia 0,0	Suter Honda	22	41m 59.232s
7	**Hector Faubel**	SPA	55	Bankia Aspar Team	Kalex KTM	22	41m 59.320s
8	**Zulfahmi Khairuddin**	MAL	63	AirAsia-Sic-Ajo	KTM	22	41m 59.445s
9	**Romano Fenati**	ITA	5	Team Italia FMI	FTR Honda	22	41m 59.565s
10	**Luis Salom**	SPA	39	RW Racing GP	Kalex KTM	22	42m 06.988s
11	**Jakub Kornfeil**	CZE	84	Redox-Ongetta-Centro Seta	FTR Honda	22	42m 07.092s
12	**Niccolo Antonelli**	ITA	27	San Carlo Gresini Moto3	FTR Honda	22	42m 07.187s
13	**Alan Techer**	FRA	89	Technomag-CIP-TSR	TSR Honda	22	42m 07.757s
14	**Alberto Moncayo**	SPA	23	Bankia Aspar Team	Kalex KTM	22	42m 21.097s
15	**Jack Miller**	AUS	8	Caretta Technology	Honda	22	42m 21.097s
16	Jasper Iwema	NED	53	Moto FGR	FGR Honda	22	42m 21.269s
17	Adrian Martin	SPA	26	JHK T-Shirt Laglisse	FTR Honda	22	42m 21.628s
18	Ivan Moreno	SPA	21	Andalucia JHK Laglisse	FTR Honda	22	42m 21.935s
19	John McPhee	GBR	17	Racing Steps Foundation KRP	KRP Honda	22	42m 22.007s
20	Danny Kent	GBR	52	Red Bull KTM Ajo	KTM	22	42m 34.703s
21	Niklas Ajo	FIN	31	TT Motion Events Racing	KTM	22	42m 34.730s
22	Arthur Sissis	AUS	61	Red Bull KTM Ajo	KTM	22	42m 35.084s
23	Simone Grotzkyj	ITA	15	Ambrogio Next Racing	Suter Honda	22	42m 52.972s
24	Isaac Vinales	SPA	32	Ongetta-Centro Seta	FTR Honda	22	43m 02.285s
25	Kenta Fujii	JPN	51	Technomag-CIP-TSR	TSR Honda	22	43m 10.025s
26	Luigi Morciano	ITA	3	Ioda Team Italia	Ioda	22	43m 10.279s
27	Giulian Pedone	SWI	30	Ambrogio Next Racing	Suter Honda	22	43m 10.296s
28	Alessandro Tonucci	ITA	19	Team Italia FMI	FTR Honda	21	41m 54.614s
	Danny Webb	GBR	99	Mahindra Racing	Mahindra	16	DNF
	Marcel Schrotter	GER	77	Mahindra Racing	Mahindra	16	DNF
	Alex Rins	SPA	42	Estrella Galicia 0,0	Suter Honda	15	DNF
	Efren Vazquez	SPA	7	JHK T-Shirt Laglisse	FTR Honda	15	DNF
	Brad Binder	RSA	41	RW Racing GP	Kalex KTM	6	DNF
	Jonas Folger	GER	94	IodaRacing Project	Ioda	4	DNF

Fastest lap: Alex Marquez, on lap 9, 1m 52.583s, 93.921mph/151.152km/h (record).
Previous lap record: New category.
Event best maximum speed: Danny Kent, 145.2mph/233.6km/h (warm up).

Qualifying: Dry
Air: 29° **Humidity:** 42% **Track:** 49°

1	M. Vinales	1m 52.160s
2	Khairuddin	1m 52.428s
3	Rossi	1m 52.603s
4	Cortese	1m 52.629s
5	Oliveira	1m 52.757s
6	Salom	1m 52.833s
7	Masbou	1m 52.950s
8	Vazquez	1m 52.951s
9	Faubel	1m 53.033s
10	Antonelli	1m 53.131s
11	Marquez	1m 53.140s
12	Kornfeil	1m 53.145s
13	Fenati	1m 53.207s
14	Kent	1m 53.346s
15	McPhee	1m 53.402s
16	Rins	1m 53.478s
17	Moncayo	1m 53.516s
18	Tonucci	1m 53.634s
19	Sissis	1m 53.663s
20	Miller	1m 53.717s
21	Techer	1m 53.972s
22	Binder	1m 54.004s
23	Moreno	1m 54.059s
24	Ajo	1m 54.112s
25	Iwema	1m 54.281s
26	Grotzkyj	1m 54.528s
27	I. Vinales	1m 54.657s
28	Martin	1m 54.697s
29	Folger	1m 54.776s
30	Schrotter	1m 54.829s
31	Webb	1m 55.168s
32	Pedone	1m 55.695s
33	Fujii	1m 55.805s
34	Morciano	1m 56.178s

Fastest race laps

1	Marquez	1m 52.583s
2	Cortese	1m 52.697s
3	Oliveira	1m 52.783s
4	Antonelli	1m 52.897s
5	Faubel	1m 52.956s
6	M. Vinales	1m 52.994s
7	Khairuddin	1m 52.999s
8	Rossi	1m 53.123s
9	Vazquez	1m 53.146s
10	Rins	1m 53.225s
11	Kornfeil	1m 53.326s
12	Masbou	1m 53.346s
13	Fenati	1m 53.396s
14	Tonucci	1m 53.421s
15	Salom	1m 53.432s
16	Moncayo	1m 53.762s
17	Moreno	1m 53.805s
18	Miller	1m 53.809s
19	Techer	1m 53.838s
20	McPhee	1m 53.860s
21	Martin	1m 53.864s
22	Binder	1m 53.888s
23	Iwema	1m 54.204s
24	Ajo	1m 54.620s
25	Grotzkyj	1m 54.766s
26	Kent	1m 54.785s
27	Webb	1m 54.791s
28	Sissis	1m 54.807s
29	Schrotter	1m 54.913s
30	I. Vinales	1m 55.170s
31	Fujii	1m 55.967s
32	Morciano	1m 56.263s
33	Pedone	1m 56.357s
34	Folger	1m 56.636s

Championship Points

1	Cortese	87
2	M. Vinales	80
3	Salom	55
4	Fenati	52
5	Rossi	45
6	Rins	44
7	Khairuddin	37
8	Moncayo	35
9	Antonelli	35
10	Masbou	29
11	Oliveira	27
12	Faubel	24
13	Sissis	23
14	Techer	18
15	Kent	16
16	Marquez	15
17	Kornfeil	12
18	Vazquez	11
19	Moreno	10
20	Iwema	9
21	Pedone	7
22	Tonucci	7
23	Folger	5
24	Binder	5
25	Schrotter	4
26	Ajo	4
27	Hanus	3
28	Miller	1

Constructor Points

1	FTR Honda	120
2	KTM	88
3	Kalex KTM	78
4	Suter Honda	65
5	Honda	32
6	TSR Honda	18
7	FGR Honda	9
8	Ioda	5
9	Mahindra	4
10	Oral	1

BRITISH GRAND PRIX

SILVERSTONE CIRCUIT

Left: Bulldog on a bike. Fresh fractures notwithstanding, Crutchlow forced through from the back of the grid to sixth.

Main photo: It's Spies, from Stoner, Bautista, Lorenzo, Pedrosa and Co. The futuristic pit complex is a dramatic backdrop as the field round Farm for the first time.

Photos: Gold & Goose

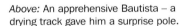

Above: An apprehensive Bautista – a drying track gave him a surprise pole.

Top: Bulldog on the move: Crutchlow has passed Bradl and is hunting down Hayden on his brave surge from the back to sixth.

Above right: Ago turned 70; Yamaha gave him a scooter. And full honours.

Above far right: Rossi slides off in qualifying. Hayden would follow suit.

Top right: Guess whose motorhome – Cal Crutchlow was in no mood for disturbance.

Top centre right: Yonny Hernandez with mentor Gregorio Lavilla.

Right: Still close in the early stages, Pirro heads Ellison, de Puniet and the CRT pack.

Photos: Gold & Goose

I F there is a rule that it must be rainy at Silverstone, it was broken in 2012, in spite of dire predictions and even flood warnings during a spell named 'the European monsoon'. There was plenty of rain and mud, but race day was dry for 66,230 fans.

They had a far greater reward. At last, after so many years, the British GP provided a British hero, at a historic and still grand venue.

Crutchlow's performance was flawed, but magnificent. The flaw came on Saturday morning, a repeat of 2011, although this time it was a low-sider, at speed. He fractured bones in his left ankle, and it looked as though he would miss his home GP for a second year running.

The bulldog spirit thought otherwise. Crutchlow returned from hospital and told the track doctors that he had no fractures. They'd said he couldn't race if any were found. His lie was in vain: surgeons at nearby Oxford had already sent a full report. But his determination was bigger than that.

Crutchlow persuaded the doctors that he was fit to start only after a series of gruelling tests, including running back and forth across the medical centre, and left-leg toe and heel lifts that were, he said, "effing painful". Having missed qualifying, he started from the back of the grid.

What a charge. He scythed through the CRT ranks, then quickly dispatched Barbera, Rossi and Bradl, before closing a gap of more than five seconds on Hayden and passing him on the final lap to take sixth, only 15 seconds behind the leader.

"I race motorcycles for a living, and there were people watching, so I didn't want to ride around like a knobber," he explained.

The other major excitement of the weekend was on paper – Lorenzo's signature, to be precise, to stay with Yamaha for the next two years. He spoke warmly about loyalty and his liking for the bike, but he'd been talking to Honda and only a significant increase in his fee had sealed the deal. He was the first big name to sign, leaving major questions unanswered, with Rossi at the centre. He sang from the company song sheet: "For now, I am only thinking how to be competitive with Ducati. My first objective is to continue down this road, also in the years to come."

Progress on that road remained disappointingly slow, however, in spite of two full days of group tests: the first on Monday after the Catalunyan round, and one two days later at Aragon, which took the place of washed-out Estoril. The *Ducatisti* had already tried and adopted the softer electronics package and were left to retest the chatter-inducing aluminium swing-arm (it still induced chatter); in Rossi's case, there were also set-up changes, which revealed the best was that used for the race the day before. The pair had a purple patch in wet first free practice – Rossi first, Hayden second. In the dry, they suffered carbon-copy crashes within minutes of one another, the front tucking under braking for the last left-right corner set, losing grip over a crest. They ended up with Hayden seventh on the grid, Rossi tenth.

Honda had been fastest at every test since the second day of pre-season gallops in February. This time, the bragging rights went to Lorenzo at both circuits, while the Repsol

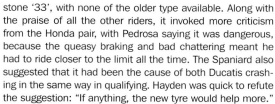

riders, with little to test and none of the dreaded new front Bridgestones available, didn't bother to go to Aragon. Dovi was fastest at Catalunya; Lorenzo at Aragon. But Yamaha had little new: the tests were more valuable for Bautista, who had kept setting changes to a minimum as he adapted to the Honda, but had planned to try a significant forward weight shift at Estoril. Now at last he could do so, and though he said it was only the first step, the pronouncement came from his first pole position.

Yamaha celebrated an important anniversary with a well-attended party: Agostini's 70th birthday. Ago did most of his winning with MV Agusta, but after switching to Yamaha in 1974, he won the company's first 500cc title the following year, ensuring a special place. Old rivals Jim Redman and John Cooper were in attendance, along with one of Ago's GP bikes. The suave old master, still the most decorated rider in history, was in good form and at a loss to explain Stoner's retirement at the height of his powers, except in terms of a love affair gone stale.

"When I decided to stop, I thought every day for two months, and when I decided I cried for three days – because I love motorcycles. Maybe he doesn't love motorcycles any more. If you love motorcycles like we do, like Valentino does, then we prefer to race. With Casey… it's like your wife: if you don't love her any more, then you must stop."

This was the first race with the new front tyre, the Bridge-

stone '33', with none of the older type available. Along with the praise of all the other riders, it invoked more criticism from the Honda pair, with Pedrosa saying it was dangerous, because the queasy braking and bad chattering meant he had to ride closer to the limit all the time. The Spaniard also suggested that it had been the cause of both Ducatis crashing in the same way in qualifying. Hayden was quick to refute the suggestion: "If anything, the new tyre would help more."

The annual Riders for Health jamboree on the Thursday braved bad weather and again broke the record for the amount raised, thanks to the Government, which had pledged to match donations pound for pound. This added £65,000 to the £254,989 total. The balance came from the auction and gate receipts, beating 2011's total by £60,000. MotoGP's official charity provides transport (mainly motorcycles) for healthcare work in rural Africa.

MOTOGP RACE – 20 laps

Bautista's first pole came through good timing. He set it ten minutes before the end, just as the drizzle set in. Anyone waiting for the end had left it too late. Spies was alongside at a track he admitted he feared as well as enjoyed; Stoner was third.

Lorenzo had led early on, but now headed row two, Pedrosa next to him, then Barbera on the top Duke. Hayden led row three from Dovisioso and Bradl; Rossi was on row four, barely eight-tenths ahead of Espargaro's top CRT bike after his early crash.

Spies took a flier to lead Stoner and Bautista through the first corners, with Hayden bursting through from the third row to join in. The pace was furious, and by the end of the lap Lorenzo was already a second adrift, chased by Dovizioso, Pedrosa – for once slow away and boxed in the first corners – and Barbera. Behind, Rossi was about to be passed by rookie Bradl.

The first four held station for four laps, then Stoner pounced on Spies as the Texan ran wide. A rogue rear tyre was blistering and deforming, and he would soon lose pace and places.

At the back of the group, Hayden was attacking Bautista strongly. Then he twice ran wide on corner entry, dropping

from fourth to seventh. The early charge had "just destroyed the tyre. The bike was hard to get stopped and I started to get a lot of chatter." He too would continue to lose pace until the final indignity of surrendering sixth to Crutchlow on the final lap.

Lorenzo was now getting going, setting a new lap record on lap three, eight-tenths of a second faster than his old one – proving that on a long and fast circuit, the extra 200cc can really make a difference.

He passed Bautista and Spies in a single lap, and now was less than a second behind Stoner. Smoothly and steadily he closed up, clearly the faster. Again, he later explained, he'd waited his time while the front men were going at it, knowing it couldn't last.

Nor could Stoner's lead. Lorenzo passed him as they started the 11th lap, and while the Australian put up a strong fight through the ensuing twists, it was a hopeless quest, though highly entertaining to see the contrast in styles and corner speeds.

From there on, Lorenzo continued with his masterclass. "We have made a perfect season until now," he glowed, after winning his fourth out of six races. But Stoner didn't give up, the gap wavering between 1.5 and 2.5 seconds until the penultimate lap. He was under pressure from behind.

Dovizioso had been challenging Bautista when he slipped off on lap ten, leaving the way clear for Pedrosa to attack. He was past in one lap, number 11, and over the next two closed a gap of almost two seconds to half a second.

From there to the end, Pedrosa harried his team-mate, but Casey didn't offer him any easy chances. The Spaniard seemed set for a last-lap lunge, but instead followed him over the line by less than three-tenths. He had a vision, he explained, of two Repsol Hondas in the dirt and opted for a safe double team rostrum instead.

Bautista was fourth, less than two seconds adrift; another five and Spies came home after "a bitter-sweet day".

And then Cal Crutchlow, after a truly heroic performance, at times having to shift gears by moving his whole leg, gritting his teeth against the pain, surging ever forward. Sixth place seemed a meagre reward; more impressively, he was but 15 seconds behind the leader.

A lone Bradl followed Hayden, with a down-in-the-mouth Rossi fully 14 seconds adrift. He had passed Barbera on lap 14, which showed that his unique choice of the harder rear

tyre did eventually pay a small dividend. "Even with the other tyre, I wouldn't have won," he commented wryly.

Espargaro was less than half a second clear of de Puniet for 11th; Pirro was 12th; Ellison came through at the end to take 14th, ahead of Hernandez by three-tenths. Edwards, Petrucci and Silva were well spaced out behind, the remounted Dovi a lap adrift after pitting for running repairs.

Lorenzo's win, at the one-third point of the season, marked a milestone. He was now 25 points clear of Stoner – one full race win.

MOTO2 RACE – 18 laps

Spain took pole in all three classes, but not Marquez this time. Espargaro, limping, but still cheerful, showed an affinity with the long and complex lap, dominating free practice as well. Iannone was second, then the battling British pair. Redding had the upper hand on the front row; Smith led Marquez – a full eight-tenths down – and Corti.

The first lap was a thriller, Smith diving around the outside to take the lead at the first corner, only to find himself scrapping to and fro with Redding. Smith led over the line; Redding pushed firmly past him as they started the next lap, and the crowd enjoyed the sight of him leading for the first seven laps.

Espargaro had been in second from lap two, with Iannone, Marquez and Corsi closing up as Smith gradually lost ground. On lap eight, Pol powered into the lead down the main straight, with Iannone and Marquez following over the next two laps to consign Redding to fourth.

Marquez took second on lap 11, and shortly afterwards Iannone ran wide, letting Redding through once more. Iannone would spend the rest of the afternoon heavily engaged with Corsi for fourth, eventually winning out narrowly.

Up front, Espargaro got his head down and started to open a gap – better than a second by lap 12. "I love this fast track," he said later.

That left Marquez and Redding scrapping, with the smaller Spaniard clearly faster down the main straight. This would seem to be his trump card in the inevitable last-lap battle.

But Redding would have none of it. He pushed past earlier in the lap, lost out again as expected down the straight, but kept on harrying Marquez until the last corners, where he managed to get alongside and force the issue on the last

Above: Crutchlow earned every ounce of applause.

Top: Redding hurls his huge frame groundward as he fights to stay ahead of Marquez, Corsi (3) and Iannone. In the end, he made it.

Photos: Gold & Goose

corner set. It was a hard move – the pair touched, and for once Marquez was on the losing side. "I wanted it badly," said Redding.

Marquez had to be happy with the 16 points for third, blaming set-up difficulties all weekend that were even worse in the race.

With Iannone and Corsi fourth and fifth, Smith had managed to get back ahead of Corti before half-distance, and he stayed there to the flag. Luthi gradually closed on the pair to the finish.

Aegerter was a lone ninth. Another four seconds down, Kallio finally prevailed in a race-long battle with de Angelis; another two seconds away, former champion Elias held on ahead of Rabat, Krummenacher and Wilairot.

Zarco and Pons were the only crash casualties.

Marquez may have been thoroughly duffed up on the track by Redding, a rare opportunity, but he returned with the points lead thanks to Luthi's downbeat eighth.

MOTO3 RACE – 17 laps

The third Spanish pole-sitter, for a third race in a row, was Vinales, less than two-tenths clear of fellow FTR Honda rider Vazquez. Masbou's production Honda was next; Cortese's top KTM headed row two.

Unusually last race of the day, the new four-strokes managed to get it done before the threat of rain came to fruition. The wide track and the nature of Moto3 made for a huge pack exploiting a variety of lines, slipstreaming like mad and changing places almost constantly.

It was the slipstreaming, said Vinales, that had prevented him from making a break. He was still having to ride to the maximum at the end.

He led over the line more often than not, the only other to do so being Salom. They and Cortese had managed to get clear over the last two laps – rapidly. Salom led as they started the last; Vinales forced through with a tough block pass into the first corner. He was able to escape as Salom and Cortese tussled to the end.

The pack of seven behind lost a leading member when Rossi crashed on the last lap. This left Masbou inches ahead of Vazquez, Kent, Fenati, the again impressive Sissis and Khairuddin. They crossed the line within 1.1 seconds.

Miller, Rins, wild-card McPhee and Pedone crashed out, Miller suffering a broken collarbone.

Left: Pol Espargaro enjoys his second win of the year.

Below left: Danny Kent (52) and Efren Vazquez wheel to wheel.

Below: Luis Salom – his third Moto3 rostrum – was becoming a factor.

Bottom: Vinales, Salom (39) and Cortese – they finished in this order.
Photos: Gold & Goose

FIM WORLD CHAMPIONSHIP

ROUND 6

HERTZ
BRITISH GRAND PRIX

15–17 JUNE, 2012

motoGP · **T+ TISSOT** SWISS WATCHES SINCE 1853

OFFICIAL TIMEKEEPER

Photos: Gold & Goose

SILVERSTONE GRAND PRIX CIRCUIT
20 laps
Length: 5.902km / 3.667 miles
Width: 17m

Key
96/60 kph/mph
Gear

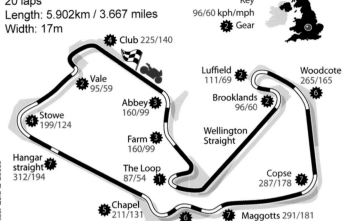

Club 225/140
Vale 95/59
Luffield 111/69
Woodcote 265/165
Abbey 160/99
Brooklands 96/60
Stowe 199/124
Farm 160/99
Wellington Straight
Hangar straight 312/194
The Loop 87/54
Copse 287/178
Chapel 211/131
Becketts 249/155
Maggotts 291/181

MotoGP — RACE DISTANCE: 20 laps, 73.322 miles/118.000km · RACE WEATHER: Dry (air 15°C, humidity 71%, track 23°C)

Pos.	Rider	Nat.	No.	Entrant	Machine	Tyres	Race tyre choice	Laps	Time & speed
1	**Jorge Lorenzo**	SPA	99	Yamaha Factory Racing	Yamaha YZR-M1	B	F: Medium/R: Med-Soft	20	41m 16.429s 106.588mph/ 171.537km/h
2	**Casey Stoner**	AUS	1	Repsol Honda Team	Honda RC213V	B	F: Soft/R: Med-Soft	20	41m 19.742s
3	**Dani Pedrosa**	SPA	26	Repsol Honda Team	Honda RC213V	B	F: Medium/R: Med-Soft	20	41m 20.028s
4	**Alvaro Bautista**	SPA	19	San Carlo Honda Gresini	Honda RC213V	B	F: Medium/R: Med-Soft	20	41m 21.625s
5	**Ben Spies**	USA	11	Yamaha Factory Racing	Yamaha YZR-M1	B	F: Medium/R: Med-Soft	20	41m 27.960s
6	**Cal Crutchlow**	GBR	35	Monster Yamaha Tech 3	Yamaha YZR-M1	B	F: Medium/R: Med-Soft	20	41m 31.541s
7	**Nicky Hayden**	USA	69	Ducati Team	Ducati Desmosedici GP12	B	F: Medium/R: Med-Soft	20	41m 31.956s
8	**Stefan Bradl**	GER	6	LCR Honda MotoGP	Honda RC213V	B	F: Medium/R: Med-Soft	20	41m 38.950s
9	**Valentino Rossi**	ITA	46	Ducati Team	Ducati Desmosedici GP12	B	F: Medium/R: Medium	20	41m 52.567s
10	**Hector Barbera**	SPA	8	Pramac Racing Team	Ducati Desmosedici GP12	B	F: Medium/R: Med-Soft	20	41m 57.757s
11	**Aleix Espargaro**	SPA	41	Power Electronics Aspar	ART Aprilia RSV4	B	F: Soft/R: Med-Soft	20	42m 19.586s
12	**Randy de Puniet**	FRA	14	Power Electronics Aspar	ART Aprilia RSV4	B	F: Soft/R: Med-Soft	20	42m 19.872s
13	**Michele Pirro**	ITA	51	San Carlo Honda Gresini	FTR Honda CBR1000RR	B	F: Medium/R: Med-Soft	20	42m 23.719s
14	**James Ellison**	GBR	77	Paul Bird Motorsport	ART Aprilia RSV4	B	F: Medium/R: Med-Soft	20	42m 31.211s
15	**Yonny Hernandez**	COL	68	Avintia Blusens	BQR FTR Kawasaki	B	F: Medium/R: Med-Soft	20	42m 31.537s
16	Colin Edwards	USA	5	NGM Mobile Forward Racing	Suter BMW S1000RR	B	F: Medium/R: Med-Soft	20	42m 46.328s
17	Danilo Petrucci	ITA	9	Came Ioda Racing Project	Ioda Aprilia RSV4	B	F: Soft/R: Med-Soft	20	42m 56.731s
18	Ivan Silva	SPA	22	Avintia Blusens	BQR FTR Kawasaki	B	F: Soft/R: Med-Soft	20	43m 08.528s
19	Andrea Dovizioso	ITA	4	Monster Yamaha Tech 3	Yamaha YZR-M1	B	F: Soft/R: Med-Soft	19	41m 51.265s
	Mattia Pasini	ITA	54	Speed Master	ART Aprilia RSV4	B	F: Soft/R: Med-Soft	14	DNF-broken seat

Fastest lap: Jorge Lorenzo, on lap 3, 2m 2.888s, 107.398mph/172.840km/h (record).
Previous lap record: Jorge Lorenzo, SPA (Yamaha), 2m 03.526s, 106.879mph/172.005km/h (2010).
Event best maximum speed: Dani Pedrosa, 200.7mph/323.0km/h (race).

Qualifying
Weather: Dry
Air Temp: 17° Humidity: 64%
Track Temp: 21°

1	Bautista	2m 03.303s
2	Spies	2m 03.409s
3	Stoner	2m 03.423s
4	Lorenzo	2m 03.763s
5	Pedrosa	2m 03.835s
6	Barbera	2m 03.876s
7	Hayden	2m 04.162s
8	Dovizioso	2m 04.304s
9	Bradl	2m 05.035s
10	Rossi	2m 05.416s
11	Espargaro	2m 06.283s
12	De Puniet	2m 06.303s
13	Hernandez	2m 06.814s
14	Pirro	2m 07.016s
15	Edwards	2m 07.376s
16	Pasini	2m 07.511s
17	Ellison	2m 08.228s
18	Petrucci	2m 08.686s
19	Silva	2m 10.092s

Outside 107%
	Crutchlow	No Time

Fastest race laps
1	Lorenzo	2m 02.888s
2	Spies	2m 02.909s
3	Dovizioso	2m 02.922s
4	Hayden	2m 02.922s
5	Stoner	2m 02.975s
6	Pedrosa	2m 02.980s
7	Bautista	2m 03.069s
8	Barbera	2m 03.291s
9	Crutchlow	2m 03.500s
10	Bradl	2m 03.907s
11	Rossi	2m 04.393s
12	De Puniet	2m 05.260s
13	Espargaro	2m 05.690s
14	Pirro	2m 05.777s
15	Pasini	2m 06.594s
16	Hernandez	2m 06.654s
17	Ellison	2m 06.678s
18	Edwards	2m 06.976s
19	Petrucci	2m 07.548s
20	Silva	2m 07.738s

Championship Points
1	Lorenzo	140
2	Stoner	115
3	Pedrosa	101
4	Crutchlow	66
5	Dovizioso	60
6	Rossi	58
7	Bautista	58
8	Bradl	51
9	Hayden	49
10	Barbera	37
11	Spies	35
12	Espargaro	20
13	De Puniet	11
14	Pirro	9
15	Ellison	7
16	Pasini	6
17	Abraham	4
18	Edwards	4
19	Petrucci	4
20	Hernandez	4
21	Silva	1

Constructor Points
1	Yamaha	140
2	Honda	126
3	Ducati	65
4	ART	24
5	FTR	9
6	Suter	4
7	Ioda	4
8	BQR	3
9	BQR-FTR	2

Grid order	1	2	3	4	5	6	7	8	9	10	11	12	13	14	15	16	17	18	19	20	
19 BAUTISTA	11	11	11	11	1	1	1	1	1	1	99	99	99	99	99	99	99	99	99	99	1
11 SPIES	1	1	1	1	11	11	99	99	99	99	1	1	1	1	1	1	1	1	1	1	2
1 STONER	19	19	19	19	19	19	19	19	19	19	26	26	26	26	26	26	26	26	26	26	3
99 LORENZO	69	69	69	69	69	99	11	11	4	26	19	19	19	19	19	19	19	19	19	19	4
26 PEDROSA	99	99	99	99	99	4	4	4	26	11	11	11	11	11	11	11	11	11	11	11	5
8 BARBERA	4	4	4	4	4	26	26	26	11	69	69	69	69	69	69	69	69	69	69	35	6
69 HAYDEN	26	26	26	26	26	69	69	69	69	6	35	35	35	35	35	35	35	35	35	69	7
4 DOVIZIOSO	8	8	8	8	8	8	6	6	6	35	6	6	6	6	6	6	6	6	6	6	8
6 BRADL	46	6	6	6	6	6	8	35	35	8	8	8	8	46	46	46	46	46	46	46	9
46 ROSSI	6	46	46	46	46	35	35	8	8	46	46	46	46	8	8	8	8	8	8	8	10
41 ESPARGARO	41	35	35	35	35	46	46	46	46	14	14	14	14	14	14	14	14	41	41		11
14 DE PUNIET	51	41	41	41	41	14	14	14	14	41	41	41	41	41	41	41	41	14	14		12
68 HERNANDEZ	35	14	14	14	14	41	41	41	41	51	51	51	51	51	51	51	51	51	51		13
51 PIRRO	14	51	51	51	51	51	51	51	51	77	77	77	77	77	77	77	77	77	77		14
5 EDWARDS	77	68	68	68	77	77	77	77	68	68	68	68	68	68	68	68	68	68	68		15
54 PASINI	68	77	77	77	68	68	77	68	68	54	54	54	54	5	5	5	5	5	5		
77 ELLISON	54	54	54	54	54	54	54	54	54	5	5	5	9	9	9	9	9	9	9		
9 PETRUCCI	5	5	5	5	5	5	5	5	9	9	9	9	54	22	22	22	22	22	22		
22 SILVA	9	9	9	9	9	9	9	9	22	22	22	22	22	4	4	4	4	4			
35 CRUTCHLOW	22	22	22	22	22	22	22	22	4	4	4	4	4								

4 Pit stop   4 Lapped rider

Moto2

RACE DISTANCE: 18 laps, 65.990 miles/106.200km · RACE WEATHER: Dry (air 15°C, humidity 69%, track 17°C)

Pos.	Rider	Nat.	No.	Entrant	Machine	Laps	Time & Speed
1	**Pol Espargaro**	SPA	40	Pons 40 HP Tuenti	Kalex	18	38m 29.792s 102.85mph/ 165.521km/h
2	**Scott Redding**	GBR	45	Marc VDS Racing Team	Kalex	18	38m 31.254s
3	**Marc Marquez**	SPA	93	Team CatalunyaCaixa Repsol	Suter	18	38m 31.313s
4	**Andrea Iannone**	ITA	29	Speed Master	Speed Up	18	38m 32.643s
5	**Simone Corsi**	ITA	3	Came IodaRacing Project	FTR	18	38m 33.595s
6	**Claudio Corti**	ITA	71	Italtrans Racing Team	Kalex	18	38m 36.901s
7	**Bradley Smith**	GBR	38	Tech 3 Racing	Tech 3	18	38m 37.419s
8	**Thomas Luthi**	SWI	12	Interwetten-Paddock	Suter	18	38m 37.461s
9	**Dominique Aegerter**	SWI	77	Technomag-CIP	Suter	18	38m 45.639s
10	**Mika Kallio**	FIN	36	Marc VDS Racing Team	Kalex	18	38m 49.971s
11	**Alex de Angelis**	RSM	15	NGM Mobile Forward Racing	Suter	18	38m 50.242s
12	**Toni Elias**	SPA	24	Mapfre Aspar Team	Suter	18	38m 52.809s
13	**Esteve Rabat**	SPA	80	Pons 40 HP Tuenti	Kalex	18	38m 52.947s
14	**Randy Krummenacher**	SWI	4	GP Team Switzerland	Kalex	18	38m 53.028s
15	**Ratthapark Wilairot**	THA	14	Thai Honda PTT Gresini Moto2	Suter	18	38m 54.299s
16	Roberto Rolfo	ITA	44	Technomag-CIP	Suter	18	38m 56.210s
17	Max Neukirchner	GER	76	Kiefer Racing	Kalex	18	38m 57.835s
18	Mike di Meglio	FRA	63	S/Master Speed Up	Speed Up	18	38m 58.157s
19	Takaaki Nakagami	JPN	30	Italtrans Racing Team	Kalex	18	38m 58.369s
20	Nicolas Terol	SPA	18	Mapfre Aspar Team	Suter	18	39m 05.892s
21	Xavier Simeon	BEL	19	Tech 3 Racing	Tech 3	18	39m 09.265s
22	Julian Simon	SPA	60	Blusens Avintia	Suter	18	39m 09.510s
23	Ricard Cardus	SPA	88	Arguinano Racing Team	AJR	18	39m 09.787s
24	Gino Rea	GBR	8	Federal Oil Gresini Moto2	Suter	18	39m 10.285s
25	Yuki Takahashi	JPN	72	NGM Mobile Forward Racing	Suter	18	39m 11.262s
26	Angel Rodriguez	SPA	47	Desguaces La Torre SAG	Bimota	18	39m 32.403s
27	Anthony West	AUS	95	QMMF Racing Team	Moriwaki	18	39m 35.116s
28	Alexander Lundh	SWE	7	Cresto Guide MZ Racing	MZ-RE Honda	18	39m 38.730s
29	Marco Colandrea	SWI	10	SAG Team	FTR	18	40m 04.787s
30	Alessandro Andreozzi	ITA	22	Andreozzi Reparto Corse	FTR	18	40m 12.567s
31	Elena Rosell	SPA	82	QMMF Racing Team	Moriwaki	18	40m 13.894s
32	Eric Granado	BRA	57	JIR Moto2	Motobi	18	40m 27.843s
	Axel Pons	SPA	49	Pons 40 HP Tuenti	Kalex	7	DNF
	Johann Zarco	FRA	5	JIR Moto2	Motobi	1	DNF

Fastest lap: Thomas Luthi, on lap 17, 2m 7.667s, 103.378mph/166.370km/h (record).
Previous lap record: Thomas Luthi, SWI (Moriwaki), 2m 09.886s, 101.646mph/163.583km/h (2010).
Event best maximum speed: Randy Krummenacher, 168mph/270.4km/h (warm up).

Qualifying: Dry
Air: 15° Humidity: 67% Track: 18°

1	Espargaro	2m 08.011s
2	Iannone	2m 08.396s
3	Redding	2m 08.616s
4	Smith	2m 08.844s
5	Marquez	2m 08.864s
6	Corti	2m 08.883s
7	Luthi	2m 09.120s
8	Zarco	2m 09.353s
9	De Angelis	2m 09.639s
10	Corsi	2m 09.776s
11	Aegerter	2m 09.801s
12	Krummenacher	2m 09.830s
13	Rolfo	2m 09.994s
14	Rea	2m 10.077s
15	Di Meglio	2m 10.080s
16	Neukirchner	2m 10.092s
17	Nakagami	2m 10.154s
18	Kallio	2m 10.202s
19	Wilairot	2m 10.276s
20	Rabat	2m 10.298s
21	Pons	2m 10.383s
22	Elias	2m 10.473s
23	Rodriguez	2m 10.921s
24	Simeon	2m 10.987s
25	Cardus	2m 11.383s
26	Simon	2m 11.654s
27	Terol	2m 11.713s
28	Takahashi	2m 11.764s
29	Lundh	2m 12.084s
30	West	2m 13.265s
31	Colandrea	2m 13.502s
32	Andreozzi	2m 14.633s
33	Granado	2m 14.803s
34	Rosell	2m 15.024s

Fastest race laps

1	Luthi	2m 07.667s
2	Redding	2m 07.669s
3	Espargaro	2m 07.690s
4	Iannone	2m 07.711s
5	Marquez	2m 07.714s
6	Corsi	2m 07.739s
7	Corti	2m 07.883s
8	Smith	2m 07.934s
9	Aegerter	2m 08.317s
10	Kallio	2m 08.387s
11	Krummenacher	2m 08.468s
12	De Angelis	2m 08.603s
13	Neukirchner	2m 08.664s
14	Elias	2m 08.751s
15	Rolfo	2m 08.816s
16	Rabat	2m 08.823s
17	Wilairot	2m 08.855s
18	Nakagami	2m 08.992s
19	Di Meglio	2m 09.079s
20	Pons	2m 09.131s
21	Simon	2m 09.216s
22	Rea	2m 09.261s
23	Terol	2m 09.286s
24	Simeon	2m 09.456s
25	Cardus	2m 09.507s
26	Takahashi	2m 09.789s
27	Rodriguez	2m 09.832s
28	Lundh	2m 10.283s
29	West	2m 10.533s
30	Colandrea	2m 12.435s
31	Rosell	2m 13.041s
32	Andreozzi	2m 13.203s
33	Granado	2m 13.508s

Championship Points

1	Marquez	102
2	Espargaro	96
3	Luthi	96
4	Iannone	84
5	Redding	70
6	Kallio	46
7	Corti	45
8	Smith	37
9	Rabat	34
10	Corsi	30
11	Aegerter	29
12	Zarco	28
13	Elias	27
14	Nakagami	23
15	De Angelis	21
16	Krummenacher	15
17	Simon	12
18	West	9
19	Di Meglio	9
20	Neukirchner	8
21	Wilairot	8
22	Simeon	6
23	Terol	3
24	Cardus	1
25	Rea	1

Constructor Points

1	Suter	131
2	Kalex	119
3	Speed Up	84
4	Tech 3	37
5	FTR	30
6	Motobi	28
7	Moriwaki	10
8	AJR	1

Moto3

RACE DISTANCE: 17 laps, 62.324 miles/100.300km · RACE WEATHER: Dry (air 18°C, humidity 48%, track 30°C)

Pos.	Rider	Nat.	No.	Entrant	Machine	Laps	Time & Speed
1	**Maverick Vinales**	SPA	25	Blusens Avintia	FTR Honda	17	38m 55.210s 96.079mph/ 154.624km/h
2	**Luis Salom**	SPA	39	RW Racing GP	Kalex KTM	17	38m 56.143s
3	**Sandro Cortese**	GER	11	Red Bull KTM Ajo	KTM	17	38m 56.233s
4	**Alexis Masbou**	FRA	10	Caretta Technology	Honda	17	39m 03.310s
5	**Efren Vazquez**	SPA	7	JHK Laglisse	FTR Honda	17	39m 03.624s
6	**Danny Kent**	GBR	52	Red Bull KTM Ajo	KTM	17	39m 03.847s
7	**Romano Fenati**	ITA	5	Team Italia FMI	FTR Honda	17	39m 04.150s
8	**Arthur Sissis**	AUS	61	Red Bull KTM Ajo	KTM	17	39m 04.256s
9	**Zulfahmi Khairuddin**	MAL	63	AirAsia-Sic-Ajo	KTM	17	39m 04.418s
10	**Miguel Oliveira**	POR	44	Estrella Galicia 0,0	Suter Honda	17	39m 10.823s
11	**Jakub Kornfeil**	CZE	84	Redox-Ongetta-Centro Seta	FTR Honda	17	39m 15.607s
12	**Hector Faubel**	SPA	55	Bankia Aspar Team	Kalex KTM	17	39m 15.769s
13	**Niccolo Antonelli**	ITA	27	San Carlo Gresini Moto3	FTR Honda	17	39m 16.579s
14	**Niklas Ajo**	FIN	31	TT Motion Events Racing	KTM	17	39m 22.736s
15	**Alberto Moncayo**	SPA	23	Bankia Aspar Team	Kalex KTM	17	39m 22.918s
16	Alessandro Tonucci	ITA	19	Team Italia FMI	FTR Honda	17	39m 23.242s
17	Brad Binder	RSA	41	RW Racing GP	Kalex KTM	17	39m 30.211s
18	Jasper Iwema	NED	53	Moto FGR	FGR Honda	17	39m 50.666s
19	Toni Finsterbusch	GER	9	Cresto Guide MZ Racing	Honda	17	39m 50.769s
20	Simone Grotzkyj	ITA	15	Ambrogio Next Racing	Suter Honda	17	39m 51.039s
21	Alan Techer	FRA	89	Technomag-CIP-TSR	TSR Honda	17	39m 51.440s
22	Ivan Moreno	SPA	21	Andalucia JHK Laglisse	FTR Honda	17	39m 51.595s
23	Isaac Vinales	SPA	32	Ongetta-Centro Seta	FTR Honda	17	40m 00.593s
24	Kenta Fujii	JPN	51	Technomag-CIP-TSR	TSR Honda	17	40m 06.493s
25	Luigi Morciano	ITA	3	Ioda Team Italia	Ioda	17	40m 13.365s
26	Marcel Schrotter	GER	77	Mahindra Racing	Mahindra	16	39m 17.152s
27	Giulian Pedone	SWI	30	Ambrogio Next Racing	Suter Honda	16	39m 53.769s
28	John McPhee	GBR	17	Racing Steps Foundation KRP	KRP Honda	15	39m 55.750s
	Louis Rossi	FRA	96	Racing Team Germany	FTR Honda	16	DNF
	Fraser Rogers	GBR	79	Racing Steps Foundation KRP	KRP Honda	14	DNF
	Danny Webb	GBR	99	Mahindra Racing	Mahindra	11	DNF
	Adrian Martin	SPA	26	JHK Laglisse	FTR Honda	8	DNF
	Jonas Folger	GER	94	IodaRacing Project	Ioda	4	DNF
	Alex Rins	SPA	42	Estrella Galicia 0,0	Suter Honda	1	DNF
	Jack Miller	AUS	8	Caretta Technology	Honda	0	DNF

Fastest lap: Sandro Cortese, on lap 11, 2m 16.055s, 97.004mph/156.113km/h (record).
Previous lap record: New category.
Event best maximum speed: Zulfahmi Khairuddin, 137mph/220.4km/h (warm up).

Qualifying: Dry
Air: 15° Humidity: 69% Track: 18°

1	M. Vinales	2m 16.187s
2	Vazquez	2m 16.385s
3	Masbou	2m 17.043s
4	Cortese	2m 17.123s
5	Kent	2m 17.337s
6	Salom	2m 17.485s
7	Rossi	2m 17.539s
8	Khairuddin	2m 17.873s
9	Fenati	2m 17.904s
10	Rins	2m 17.908s
11	Oliveira	2m 18.090s
12	Tonucci	2m 18.151s
13	Antonelli	2m 18.238s
14	Kornfeil	2m 18.422s
15	Sissis	2m 18.535s
16	Moncayo	2m 18.832s
17	Techer	2m 18.937s
18	Ajo	2m 18.978s
19	Folger	2m 19.015s
20	Martin	2m 19.033s
21	Webb	2m 19.128s
22	Iwema	2m 19.530s
23	Faubel	2m 19.707s
24	Miller	2m 19.723s
25	Grotzkyj	2m 20.041s
26	Binder	2m 20.080s
27	Finsterbusch	2m 20.240s
28	I. Vinales	2m 20.440s
29	McPhee	2m 21.063s
30	Fujii	2m 21.154s
31	Morciano	2m 21.310s
32	Pedone	2m 21.428s
33	Rogers	2m 21.687s
34	Moreno	2m 21.744s
35	Schrotter	2m 21.807s

Fastest race laps

1	Cortese	2m 16.055s
2	M. Vinales	2m 16.103s
3	Salom	2m 16.300s
4	Kent	2m 16.481s
5	Rossi	2m 16.570s
6	Masbou	2m 16.572s
7	Fenati	2m 16.618s
8	Vazquez	2m 16.671s
9	Sissis	2m 16.702s
10	Faubel	2m 16.800s
11	Khairuddin	2m 16.891s
12	Oliveira	2m 16.943s
13	Binder	2m 17.183s
14	Antonelli	2m 17.210s
15	Kornfeil	2m 17.219s
16	Moncayo	2m 17.492s
17	Ajo	2m 17.497s
18	Tonucci	2m 17.733s
19	Techer	2m 17.929s
20	McPhee	2m 18.206s
21	Martin	2m 18.434s
22	Iwema	2m 18.646s
23	Rogers	2m 18.817s
24	Finsterbusch	2m 18.921s
25	Webb	2m 19.112s
26	Moreno	2m 19.264s
27	I. Vinales	2m 19.374s
28	Grotzkyj	2m 19.431s
29	Morciano	2m 19.853s
30	Fujii	2m 20.037s
31	Folger	2m 20.692s
32	Schrotter	2m 20.935s
33	Pedone	2m 22.142s

Championship Points

1	M. Vinales	105
2	Cortese	103
3	Salom	75
4	Fenati	61
5	Rossi	45
6	Rins	44
7	Khairuddin	44
8	Masbou	42
9	Antonelli	38
10	Moncayo	36
11	Oliveira	33
12	Sissis	31
13	Faubel	28
14	Kent	26
15	Vazquez	22
16	Techer	18
17	Kornfeil	17
18	Marquez	15
19	Moreno	10
20	Iwema	9
21	Pedone	7
22	Tonucci	7
23	Ajo	6
24	Folger	5
25	Binder	5
26	Schrotter	4
27	Hanus	3
28	Miller	1

Constructor Points

1	FTR Honda	145
2	KTM	104
3	Kalex KTM	98
4	Suter Honda	71
5	Honda	45
6	TSR Honda	18
7	FGR Honda	9
8	Ioda	5
9	Mahindra	4
10	Oral	1

Above: The sparks fly as Bautista skittles the unlucky Lorenzo to earth.

Left: Cal Crutchlow (35) is forced to sit up to avoid the fallen riders.

Right: Bautista and Lorenzo slide to safety as Crutchlow, Rossi and Hayden race on.

Far right: Frustration for Lorenzo, who throws a glove at one of the marshals.

Photos: Gold & Goose

Above: Casey Stoner broke Pedrosa's resistance in the Repsol Hondas unimpeded duel for victory following Lorenzo's abrupt race departure.

Above right, clockwise from left: Colin Edwards was finding life increasingly unrewarding on the NGM bike; Hector Barbera survived this moment in front of Hayden; Randy de Puniet was the top CRT finisher; Carmen Ezpeleta and and Argentinian Minister of Tourism, Enrique Meyer, had a rather uncomfortable time in their press conference to showcase the proposed Argentine Grand Prix in 2013.

Above near right: Andrea Dovizioso took a podium for the second race in succession.

Right: Casey Stoner strengthed his championship champions, if only temporarily.

Photos: Gold & Goose

CRASHES can be decisive. Especially when they happen to the two leading men, and especially at the start of a gruelling three weekends in a row. Both Stoner and Lorenzo came down at the Dutch TT, and it changed the balance of the championship, if only temporarily.

Bad weather continued, if fitfully, though again it stayed dry for race day, when a not inconsiderable 90,248 fans gathered around the now-shrunken old track, with a single small revision this year (Ruskenhoek at the end of the back straight slightly eased), making if officially a new track. Still prey to an old Assen bugbear: micro-showers affecting only sections of the circuit.

One of these caught Stoner during Friday morning's third free practice. There had been spots of rain earlier on the lap and a mini cloudburst on the approach to the fast Ramshoek left-hander before the final chicane. It hardly showed on the track surface, and he was the first to arrive, with no chance of making the corner. Flicked violently over the bars, he landed awkwardly head down, obviously in pain. Three or four riders ran off the track behind him on the slippery surface.

It was "one of the worst crashes in my career. Usually I just hurt one part. I landed on my head, shoulder and wrist, and somehow did something to the top of my right knee, which is giving the most trouble," he said. It didn't stop him winning from pole position.

A different fate awaited Lorenzo, knocked off here in 2011 on the first lap by Simoncelli, remounting for a furious sixth. He didn't get that far this time. As they peeled into the first tight corner, Bautista came spearing up the inside way too fast, from the third row of the grid. He fell and slid out, straight into the Yamaha.

Worse was to follow. The bike landed with the throttle jammed wide, at full revs. Within seconds, as Jorge ran towards it, it expired in a cloud of white oil smoke. A brand-new engine, third of six and sealed for use the day before, was finished after less than 200km. As much as the points, the loss of a precious engine left him angry and distraught, and he roundly condemned Bautista. Race Direction agreed, though in more measured tones, and Bautista was condemned to a back-of-the-grid start for the next round.

Track temperatures were surprisingly high – approaching 40 degrees and more than double the previous year's. Bridgestone blamed this unexpected change for three highly embarrassing tyre failures. One victim, for a second race, was 2011 winner Spies, whose bid for a first rostrum of the year was foiled when his rear shed a chunk in the closing laps. Another was Rossi, who slowed radically, then pitted for a new tyre. The third was Barbera, who plodded on to the end, just able to stay ahead of the CRT gang. Bridgestone flew the offending tyres and other batch samples to Japan for a hasty investigation while discontent rumbled among the riders. In a fortnight, they would be at baking-hot and sizzlingly-fast Mugello, scene in 2004 of the most worrying of all of Bridgestone's (extremely rare) failures, when Shinya Nakano miraculously escaped injury when his tyre disintegrated at full speed as he was passing the pits..

There was another GP Commission meeting, again with no decisions (or even discussion) on major rule changes – but not devoid of significance.

At Silverstone, Dorna's Ezpeleta had announced a surprise U-turn on the so-called rookie rule, which banned first-timers from factory teams. Earlier he had insisted emphatically that the rule must stay. Now he said he would personally propose its cancellation at the Assen GP Commission meeting. And lo it was gone.

This was a bargaining chip in the battle with the manufacturers, and particularly the most powerful: Honda, who now could proceed with their plan to slot Marquez straight into the factory team.

This meant pressure for Pedrosa, although with Stoner going at least he was relieved of fear of the sack. Marquez is set to become Repsol's new favourite son, a position Dani has held unchallenged since 2006. Honda's Livio Suppo vehemently denied he was facing a fee cut (rumoured to be 50 per cent or greater), but said, "To be honest, neither of us has much choice." Dani would sign, no doubt gratefully, within a fortnight.

Other commission decisions nibbled at the edges: proposals for one-bike teams and to ban carbon brakes were laid to rest; while factory teams were limited to two riders, with

only two more in satellite teams. Gearing alternatives were reduced: 24 alternative ratios for the six gears; only four for the primary drive.

Another cost-cutting ruling caused some surprise: bore and stroke were to remain unaltered until the end of 2014. Since most already used the maximum permitted bore of 81mm, this meant little – except possibly to Ducati, widely suspected of running a shorter-stroke, higher-revving under-size engine. If so, now they were stuck with it.

Quite apart from racing, Repsol was engaged in a battle with the Argentine government after it had summarily nationalised the Spanish company's 51 per cent share of the YPF oil company – a row that reached into the highest levels of Spanish government. It made a bad atmosphere for the announcement of an Argentine GP, pencilled in for early 2013 at a still uncompleted Termas de Rio Hondo circuit in the remote interior. The Argentine minister of tourism was among a party of dignitaries there to insist that plans were on schedule, but questions unsurprisingly homed in on the controversy. Ezpeleta revealed that recently he had been asked by Repsol whether he could guarantee the safety of its personnel; in turn, he had referred to Spain's department of foreign affairs. "Last week, we received a letter from the ministry saying that at this moment we do not recommend Repsol personnel to visit Argentina," he said. He was sure, he added, that it would all be sorted out in time for the race.

Yet another defection from Suter chassis to FTR in Moto2 bore immediate fruit for NGM Mobile rider Alex de Angelis, with fifth his best of the year and more to come. This dropped the numbers of the previously most numerous chassis to nine, equalling Kalex, and brought the number of FTRs to four.

MOTOGP RACE – 26 laps

Thursday was dry, Friday sprinkly, with riders in and out of the pits. Qualifying was fully dry only for the last ten minutes, with a flurry of fast laps and a triumphal Stoner bouncing back to oust Pedrosa from pole by just over a tenth. Lorenzo was third and looked threatening, the only rider to have

reeled off quite so many strings of consistently fast laps.

Conditions mixed them up behind: best-ever Bradl headed row two from Crutchlow and Spies; then came Dovizioso, Bautista and Hayden, with Rossi leading row four.

It went well enough for the first few hundred metres, with Pedrosa outbraking Stoner into the first tight right-hander, Lorenzo next. Then Bautista suddenly appeared on the inside, going very fast and clearly about to crash.

Amazingly only Lorenzo was hit and his black Honda skittered out sideways. Crutchlow was forced on to the paved run-off, rejoining at the back.

Pedrosa carried on around the first giddy loops with Stoner and Spies in hot pursuit, then came Dovizioso from Bradl, Hayden and Rossi. Crutchlow was already pushing through the CRT gang.

Bradl slid off next time around, his first race crash, then Hayden ran across the gravel at the chicane, dropping behind Barbera. That left Rossi in fourth place, but rapidly losing ground.

Up front, Stoner shadowed Pedrosa patiently, swapping positions cleanly on lap 17 after a little slip and immediately pulling clear, as he had known he could.

"It wasn't how I had planned the race," said Stoner, a stiff and swollen right knee his worst problem. "I wanted the lead from the start, but when Dani came past he was very late on the brakes, and I decided to wait and see and try to be gentle on the tyre."

Losing ground behind at a couple of tenths each lap, Spies narrowly led Dovi. Then the Italian got in front on lap eight, but the positions were reversed four laps later after a little slip. This was Spies's chance, and he pushed hard, to gain a second's advantage in another four laps or so. He seemed set for the rostrum, until his tyre problem struck with three laps to go. "Every time I leaned to the right, the bike was shaking and trying to come around. I looked back at Andrea … I just wanted him to come past me. I thought the tyre might come apart and he'd hit me. For the last two laps, I was scared as hell."

Even so, it was only on the last lap that Dovi got ahead on the entrance to the first corner.

Rossi had pulled a train for the first eight laps, with Barbera, Hayden and Crutchlow jammed up behind him from lap three. Hayden was strong and took to the front of the group before half-distance; Crutchlow had a big moment and lost a second, but soon closed up again. On lap 12, he finally made it stick over Barbera, and three laps later was ahead of Rossi when the multi-champion slowed as his tyre chunked, pitting two laps later for a replacement.

The battle with Hayden didn't last much longer, and Crutchlow left the American going back and forth with Barbera, until the Spaniard had his own tyre disaster and fell back radically.

He was still six seconds clear of de Puniet, best CRT after a lively battle with Espargaro and Pirro, which ended when Espargaro crashed out after half-distance. Pirro finished less than three seconds adrift.

Pasini was a lone tenth; Petrucci's near-stock Aprilia won out over Silva's FTR Kawasaki. Team-mate Hernandez crashed out; Abraham withdrew before the start, losing the battle to beat his injuries

And then came Rossi, claiming 13th and three points one lap behind. In spite of a pit stop, he managed to shade Ellison by two-thousandths over the line. There were just 14 finishers.

Not among them was Colin Edwards, at a favourite circuit, where he'd been so dismayed by qualifying last, 4.6 seconds off pole, that he had tweeted a message to the fans, suggesting they fill in the blanks: "My bike is - ----- -- ----!!!" By now growing tired of the unequal struggle with surging torque and primitive Bosch electronics, he pitted to retire with 19 laps to go.

The result put Stoner and Lorenzo equal on points, but Stoner declined to exult in his rival's misfortune. "No one wants to take points because of an accident that wasn't his fault. I hope he can get his own back during the season." Eight days later, he would give it to him.

MOTO2 RACE – 24 laps

Marquez crashed twice on Saturday, the second late in qualifying, but after securing his fifth pole in six races, ousting rival Espargaro, who had dominated free practice. Iannone completed an unusually spread front row, more than eight-tenths covering the three.

Krummenacher led row two from Aegerter and Corsi; Redding and Smith shared row three with de Angelis, who had gelled immediately with his new FTR.

Moto2 also suffered a first-corner indiscretion involving a title contender when Wilairot lost it and cannoned into Luthi. Both went down; Luthi was out. Wilairot remounted at the back, only to crash out again later.

Espargaro led away from Aegerter, Iannone and Marquez. Head down, he was trying to escape when he crashed spectacularly on the second lap, slumping in despair in the gravel.

Iannone took over up front on lap four; Marquez had struggled in the early stages for rear grip and was now fourth behind Aegerter and Redding. Then the Englishman took over second, and Iannone sensed a chance to escape. By lap ten, he led by 1.7 seconds; three laps later, it was almost double that.

Iannone's runaway wins are legendary, but on lap 11 Marquez had finally managed to get ahead of Redding after several previous attacks had been firmly repulsed.

Could he hunt down Iannone? Not at first, as the Italian drew 3.3 seconds clear on lap 14. But now his pace slackened; he had punished his tyres, and soon Marquez began closing rapidly.

With four laps to go, he was on him, and they swapped two and fro several times, Iannone leading as they started the final lap. Marquez outbraked him into the first corner, and Iannone's plans to get back were thwarted when he missed a gear. He finished four-tenths behind.

Redding was left to prevail over a strong battle with Rabat,

de Angelis and Smith. Aegerter was a couple of seconds further back.

Class rookie Zarco won the next brawl, from former champion Elias and Krummenacher, They had caught Kallio on the last lap, all but Krummenacher ahead at the end of it.

Neukirchner had been part of a strong five-way battle six seconds behind, but he crashed out on the final lap. Nakagami got the best of it, passing Simeon on the last lap, with Simon and di Meglio taking the last points; Corti, Terol and Cardus were right behind. Pons crashed out, likewise Corsi and Lundh, the former lying fifth on lap ten at the time. Temporary Team Desguaces replacement rider Damian Cudlin retired. The win was a handy boost to Marquez's title hopes, with Iannone moving to second ahead of non-scorers Espargaro and Luthi.

Above: Iannone and Marquez continued their battle for supremacy in Moto2.

Top: James Ellison just fails to hold off a charging Rossi, recovering from a pit-stop to change a chunking tyre.

Above right: Danny Kent, leading the usual suspects, in the Moto3 battle.

Right: The Red Bull-KTM youngster took a well-earned first podium.

Photos: Gold & Goose

Below: Iannone and Marquez and Redding share the Moto2 podium.
Photo: Gold & Goose

MOTO3 RACE – 22 laps

Danny Kent looked like claiming a first pole, until team-mate Cortese edged ahead. Rookie Antonelli was alongside; Vinales at the far end of row two.

Assen's first race for the droning singles was a thriller from start to finish. For the first half of the race, a 20-strong front pack were swapping constantly, running into corners three abreast, and all covered by 2.5 seconds.

Kent was prominent, leading the first lap before Cortese took the next six. Then Vinales worked through to take control, albeit only by the tips of his fingers. He led every other lap except the penultimate.

That had Kent up front again, the youngster having already survived a collision with a forceful Cortese that earned comment and criticism from other riders, including Stoner, although Race Direction studied it carefully before declaring him innocent.

They scrambled through the last chicane somehow, Vinales taking a third successive win, his fourth of the year, by inches from Cortese; third eventually was awarded to a deserving Kent from Salom after a photo-finish. Rossi was just half a second behind.

There was a fine fight for sixth. Rookie Rins managed to get free at the end, followed by Masbou, Ajo, Vazquez and Oliveira to complete the top ten; Khairuddin and Fenati were inches behind.Antonelli had been impressive in the front gang until his wild riding ended in a crash; Australian Jack Miller was black-flagged for a jumped start – he was far too busy in the pack to see penalty flags.

FIM WORLD CHAMPIONSHIP

ROUND 7

IVECO
TT ASSEN

28–30 JUNE, 2012

motoGP

TISSOT SWISS WATCHES SINCE 1853

OFFICIAL TIMEKEEPER

Photos: Gold & Goose

TT ASSEN

26 laps
Length: 4.555km / 2.830 miles
Width: 13m

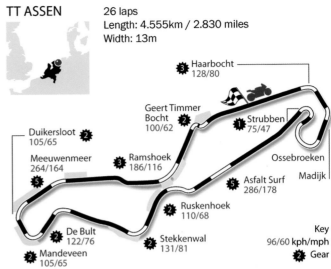

Haarbocht 128/80
Geert Timmer Bocht 100/62
Strubben 75/47
Duikersloot 105/65
Meeuwenmeer 264/164
Ramshoek 186/116
Ossebroeken
Asfalt Surf 286/178
Madijk
Ruskenhoek 110/68
De Bult 122/76
Stekkenwal 131/81
Mandeveen 105/65

Key
96/60 kph/mph
Gear

MotoGP — RACE DISTANCE: 26 laps, 73.379 miles/118.092km · RACE WEATHER: Dry (air 23°C, humidity 44%, track 37°C)

Pos.	Rider	Nat.	No.	Entrant	Machine	Tyres	Race tyre choice	Laps	Time & speed
1	**Casey Stoner**	AUS	1	Repsol Honda Team	Honda RC213V	B	F: Medium/R: Med-Soft	26	41m 19.855s 106.524mph/ 171.433km/h
2	**Dani Pedrosa**	SPA	26	Repsol Honda Team	Honda RC213V	B	F: Medium/R: Med-Soft	26	41m 24.820s
3	**Andrea Dovizioso**	ITA	4	Monster Yamaha Tech 3	Yamaha YZR-M1	B	F: Medium/R: Medium	26	41m 31.849s
4	**Ben Spies**	USA	11	Yamaha Factory Racing	Yamaha YZR-M1	B	F: Medium/R: Medium	26	41m 34.630s
5	**Cal Crutchlow**	GBR	35	Monster Yamaha Tech 3	Yamaha YZR-M1	B	F: Medium/R: Medium	26	41m 41.929s
6	**Nicky Hayden**	USA	69	Ducati Team	Ducati Desmosedici GP12	B	F: Medium/R: Med-Soft	26	41m 51.515s
7	**Hector Barbera**	SPA	8	Pramac Racing Team	Ducati Desmosedici GP12	B	F: Medium/R: Med-Soft	26	42m 18.962s
8	**Randy de Puniet**	FRA	14	Power Electronics Aspar	ART Aprilia RSV4	B	F: Medium/R: Med-Soft	26	42m 24.296s
9	**Michele Pirro**	ITA	51	San Carlo Honda Gresini	FTR Honda CBR1000RR	B	F: Medium/R: Med-Soft	26	42m 26.835s
10	**Mattia Pasini**	ITA	54	Speed Master	ART Aprilia RSV4	B	F: Medium/R: Med-Soft	26	42m 44.942s
11	**Danilo Petrucci**	ITA	9	Came Ioda Racing Project	Ioda Aprilia RSV4	B	F: Medium/R: Med-Soft	26	42m 51.958s
12	**Ivan Silva**	SPA	22	Avintia Blusens	BQR FTR Kawasaki	B	F: Medium/R: Med-Soft	26	42m 53.652s
13	**Valentino Rossi**	ITA	46	Ducati Team	Ducati Desmosedici GP12	B	F: Medium/R: Medium	25	41m 38.492s
14	**James Ellison**	GBR	77	Paul Bird Motorsport	ART Aprilia RSV4	B	F: Medium/R: Med-Soft	25	41m 38.494s
	Aleix Espargaro	SPA	41	Power Electronics Aspar	ART Aprilia RSV4	B	F: Medium/R: Med-Soft	14	DNF-crash
	Colin Edwards	USA	5	NGM Mobile Forward Racing	Suter BMW S1000RR	B	F: Medium/R: Med-Soft	7	DNF-mechanical
	Yonny Hernandez	COL	68	Avintia Blusens	BQR FTR Kawasaki	B	F: Medium/R: Med-Soft	5	DNF-crash
	Stefan Bradl	GER	6	LCR Honda MotoGP	Honda RC213V	B	F: Medium/R: Med-Soft	1	DNF-crash
	Jorge Lorenzo	SPA	99	Yamaha Factory Racing	Yamaha YZR-M1	B	F: Medium/R: Medium	0	DNF-crash
	Alvaro Bautista	SPA	19	San Carlo Honda Gresini	Honda RC213V	B	F: Medium/R: Med-Soft	0	DNF-crash
	Karel Abraham	CZE	17	Cardion AB Motoracing	Ducati Desmosedici GP12	B	F: –/R: –		DNS-injured

Fastest lap: Dani Pedrosa, on lap 15, 1m 34.548s, 107.460mph/172.940km/h.

Previous lap record: New circuit layout.

Event best maximum speed: Andrea Dovizioso, 192.3mph/309.4km/h (warm up).

Qualifying

Weather: Dry
Air Temp: 22° Humidity: 54%
Track Temp: 29°

1	Stoner	1m 33.713s
2	Pedrosa	1m 33.828s
3	Lorenzo	1m 34.001s
4	Bradl	1m 34.035s
5	Crutchlow	1m 34.486s
6	Spies	1m 34.644s
7	Dovizioso	1m 34.698s
8	Bautista	1m 34.722s
9	Hayden	1m 34.751s
10	Rossi	1m 35.057s
11	Barbera	1m 35.289s
12	De Puniet	1m 35.830s
13	Espargaro	1m 36.007s
14	Pirro	1m 36.647s
15	Pasini	1m 36.943s
16	Petrucci	1m 36.967s
17	Abraham	1m 37.110s
18	Hernandez	1m 37.191s
19	Ellison	1m 37.281s
20	Silva	1m 37.554s
21	Edwards	1m 38.305s

Fastest race laps

1	Pedrosa	1m 34.548s
2	Stoner	1m 34.693s
3	Crutchlow	1m 34.814s
4	Dovizioso	1m 34.816s
5	Spies	1m 34.828s
6	Hayden	1m 35.114s
7	Barbera	1m 35.575s
8	Rossi	1m 35.641s
9	Espargaro	1m 36.808s
10	De Puniet	1m 36.854s
11	Hernandez	1m 36.964s
12	Pirro	1m 37.117s
13	Pasini	1m 37.246s
14	Silva	1m 38.019s
15	Petrucci	1m 38.025s
16	Ellison	1m 38.200s
17	Edwards	1m 39.002s

Championship Points

1	Lorenzo	140
2	Stoner	140
3	Pedrosa	121
4	Crutchlow	77
5	Dovizioso	76
6	Rossi	61
7	Hayden	59
8	Bautista	58
9	Bradl	51
10	Spies	48
11	Barbera	46
12	Espargaro	20
13	De Puniet	19
14	Pirro	16
15	Pasini	12
16	Petrucci	9
17	Ellison	9
18	Silva	5
19	Abraham	4
20	Edwards	4
21	Hernandez	4

Constructor Points

1	Yamaha	156
2	Honda	151
3	Ducati	75
4	ART	32
5	FTR	16
6	Ioda	9
7	BQR	7
8	Suter	4
9	BQR-FTR	2

Grid order

Grid order	1	2	3	4	5	6	7	8	9	10	11	12	13	14	15	16	17	18	19	20	21	22	23	24	25	26	
1 STONER	26	26	26	26	26	26	26	26	26	26	26	26	26	26	26	26	1	1	1	1	1	1	1	1	1	1	1
26 PEDROSA	1	1	1	1	1	1	1	1	1	1	1	1	1	1	1	1	26	26	26	26	26	26	26	26	26	26	2
99 LORENZO	11	11	11	11	11	11	11	4	4	4	4	11	11	11	11	11	11	11	11	11	11	11	11	11	11	4	3
6 BRADL	4	4	4	4	4	4	4	11	11	11	11	4	4	4	4	4	4	4	4	4	4	4	4	4	11	11	4
35 CRUTCHLOW	6	46	46	46	46	46	46	46	69	69	69	69	69	69	35	35	35	35	35	35	35	35	35	35	35	35	5
11 SPIES	46	8	8	8	8	8	69	46	46	46	46	35	69	69	8	8	8	69	69	69	69	69	69	69	6		
4 DOVIZIOSO	8	69	69	69	69	69	8	8	8	8	35	35	8	8	69	69	69	8	8	8	8	8	8	7			
19 BAUTISTA	69	35	35	35	35	35	35	35	35	35	8	8	46	46	14	14	14	14	14	14	14	14	14	8			
69 HAYDEN	41	41	41	41	41	41	41	41	14	41	41	41	41	14	51	51	51	51	51	51	51	51	51	9			
46 ROSSI	51	51	51	14	14	14	14	14	14	41	14	14	14	51	46	54	54	54	54	54	54	54	54	10			
8 BARBERA	14	14	14	51	51	51	51	51	51	51	51	51	51	54	54	9	9	22	22	22	22	22	22	9	11		
14 DE PUNIET	35	54	54	54	68	54	54	54	54	54	54	54	54	22	22	22	22	9	9	9	9	9	22	12			
41 ESPARGARO	54	68	68	68	54	22	22	22	9	9	9	9	9	9	77	77	77	77	77	77	77	77	46	13			
51 PIRRO	68	77	22	22	22	9	9	9	22	22	22	22	22	77	77	46	46	46	46	46	46	46	77	14			
54 PASINI	77	9	77	9	9	77	77	77	77	77	77	77	77														
9 PETRUCCI	9	22	9	5	77	5	5																				
68 HERNANDEZ	22	5	5	77	5																						
77 ELLISON	5																										
22 SILVA																											
5 EDWARDS																											

5 Pit stop 46 Lapped rider

Moto2

RACE DISTANCE: 24 laps, 67.734 miles/109.008km · RACE WEATHER: Dry (air 22°C, humidity 51%, track 26°C)

Pos. Rider	Nat.	No.	Entrant	Machine	Laps	Time & Speed
1 **Marc Marquez**	SPA	93	Team CatalunyaCaixa Repsol	Suter	24	39m 43.170s 102.319mph/ 164.666km/h
2 **Andrea Iannone**	ITA	29	Speed Master	Speed Up	24	39m 43.575s
3 **Scott Redding**	GBR	45	Marc VDS Racing Team	Kalex	24	39m 50.501s
4 **Esteve Rabat**	SPA	80	Pons 40 HP Tuenti	Kalex	24	39m 50.800s
5 **Alex de Angelis**	RSM	15	NGM Mobile Forward Racing	FTR	24	39m 51.022s
6 **Bradley Smith**	GBR	38	Tech 3 Racing	Tech 3	24	39m 51.748s
7 **Dominique Aegerter**	SWI	77	Technomag-CIP	Suter	24	39m 53.187s
8 **Johann Zarco**	FRA	5	JIR Moto2	Motobi	24	39m 57.651s
9 **Toni Elias**	SPA	24	Mapfre Aspar Team	Suter	24	39m 57.884s
10 **Mika Kallio**	FIN	36	Marc VDS Racing Team	Kalex	24	39m 57.904s
11 **Randy Krummenacher**	SWI	4	GP Team Switzerland	Kalex	24	39m 58.114s
12 **Takaaki Nakagami**	JPN	30	Italtrans Racing Team	Kalex	24	40m 05.276s
13 **Xavier Simeon**	BEL	19	Tech 3 Racing	Tech 3	24	40m 06.238s
14 **Julian Simon**	SPA	60	Blusens Avintia	Suter	24	40m 06.702s
15 **Mike di Meglio**	FRA	63	S/Master Speed Up	Speed Up	24	40m 06.903s
16 Claudio Corti	ITA	71	Italtrans Racing Team	Kalex	24	40m 08.789s
17 Nicolas Terol	SPA	18	Mapfre Aspar Team	Suter	24	40m 09.083s
18 Ricard Cardus	SPA	88	Arguinano Racing Team	AJR	24	40m 09.144s
19 Roberto Rolfo	ITA	44	Technomag-CIP	Suter	24	40m 17.810s
20 Yuki Takahashi	JPN	72	NGM Mobile Forward Racing	FTR	24	40m 27.227s
21 Anthony West	AUS	95	QMMF Racing Team	Moriwaki	24	40m 27.909s
22 Gino Rea	GBR	8	Federal Oil Gresini Moto2	Suter	24	40m 42.954s
23 Marco Colandrea	SWI	10	SAG Team	FTR	24	40m 53.295s
24 Eric Granado	BRA	57	JIR Moto2	Motobi	24	40m 55.309s
25 Elena Rosell	SPA	82	QMMF Racing Team	Moriwaki	24	41m 16.403s
Max Neukirchner	GER	76	Kiefer Racing	Kalex	23	DNF
Alexander Lundh	SWE	7	Cresto Guide MZ Racing	MZ-RE Honda	22	DNF
Simone Corsi	ITA	3	Came IodaRacing Project	FTR	14	DNF
Damian Cudlin	AUS	50	Desguaces La Torre SAG	Bimota	14	DNF
Axel Pons	SPA	49	Pons 40 HP Tuenti	Kalex	8	DNF
Ratthapark Wilairot	THA	14	Thai Honda PTT Gresini Moto2	Suter	5	DNF
Pol Espargaro	SPA	40	Pons 40 HP Tuenti	Kalex	1	DNF
Thomas Luthi	SWI	12	Interwetten-Paddock	Suter	0	DNF

Fastest lap: Marc Marquez, on lap 17, 1m 38.391s, 103.263mph/166.185km/h.

Lap record: New circuit layout.

Event best maximum speed: Esteve Rabat, 161.6mph/260.1km/h (qualifying practice).

Qualifying: Dry
Air: 21° Humidity: 59% Track: 31°

1	Marquez	1m 37.133s
2	Espargaro	1m 37.588s
3	Iannone	1m 37.956s
4	Krummenacher	1m 38.279s
5	Aegerter	1m 38.349s
6	Corsi	1m 38.400s
7	Redding	1m 38.401s
8	Smith	1m 38.414s
9	De Angelis	1m 38.483s
10	Luthi	1m 38.488s
11	Rabat	1m 38.511s
12	Kallio	1m 38.525s
13	Wilairot	1m 38.573s
14	Nakagami	1m 38.636s
15	Cardus	1m 38.642s
16	Rolfo	1m 38.665s
17	Corti	1m 38.899s
18	Neukirchner	1m 38.950s
19	Zarco	1m 38.996s
20	Pons	1m 39.191s
21	Elias	1m 39.200s
22	Di Meglio	1m 39.207s
23	Simon	1m 39.257s
24	Simeon	1m 39.302s
25	Terol	1m 39.584s
26	Rea	1m 39.628s
27	Lundh	1m 39.941s
28	West	1m 40.333s
29	Takahashi	1m 40.675s
30	Cudlin	1m 40.746s
31	Granado	1m 40.970s
32	Colandrea	1m 41.276s
33	Rosell	1m 42.273s

Fastest race laps

1	Marquez	1m 38.391s
2	Rabat	1m 38.468s
3	Smith	1m 38.499s
4	Iannone	1m 38.527s
5	De Angelis	1m 38.652s
6	Redding	1m 38.654s
7	Aegerter	1m 38.774s
8	Elias	1m 38.806s
9	Corsi	1m 38.820s
10	Kallio	1m 38.830s
11	Krummenacher	1m 38.890s
12	Zarco	1m 39.030s
13	Nakagami	1m 39.131s
14	Corti	1m 39.165s
15	Cardus	1m 39.220s
16	Simon	1m 39.224s
17	Simeon	1m 39.275s
18	Di Meglio	1m 39.335s
19	Neukirchner	1m 39.338s
20	Terol	1m 39.451s
21	Rolfo	1m 39.718s
22	West	1m 40.111s
23	Lundh	1m 40.147s
24	Pons	1m 40.165s
25	Takahashi	1m 40.198s
26	Rea	1m 40.395s
27	Wilairot	1m 41.103s
28	Colandrea	1m 41.272s
29	Granado	1m 41.420s
30	Cudlin	1m 41.509s
31	Rosell	1m 41.776s

Championship Points

1	Marquez	127
2	Iannone	104
3	Espargaro	96
4	Luthi	96
5	Redding	86
6	Kallio	52
7	Rabat	47
8	Smith	47
9	Corti	45
10	Aegerter	38
11	Zarco	36
12	Elias	34
13	De Angelis	32
14	Corsi	30
15	Nakagami	27
16	Krummenacher	20
17	Simon	14
18	Di Meglio	10
19	West	9
20	Simeon	9
21	Neukirchner	8
22	Wilairot	8
23	Terol	3
24	Cardus	1
25	Rea	1

Constructor Points

1	Suter	156
2	Kalex	135
3	Speed Up	104
4	Tech 3	47
5	FTR	41
6	Motobi	36
7	Moriwaki	10
8	AJR	1

Moto3

RACE DISTANCE: 22 laps, 62.090 miles/99.924km · RACE WEATHER: Dry (air 21°C, humidity 61%, track 32°C)

Pos. Rider	Nat.	No.	Entrant	Machine	Laps	Time & Speed
1 **Maverick Vinales**	SPA	25	Blusens Avintia	FTR Honda	22	38m 45.432s 96.121mph/ 154.692km/h
2 **Sandro Cortese**	GER	11	Red Bull KTM Ajo	KTM	22	38m 46.263s
3 **Danny Kent**	GBR	52	Red Bull KTM Ajo	KTM	22	38m 46.274s
4 **Luis Salom**	SPA	39	RW Racing GP	Kalex KTM	22	38m 46.275s
5 **Louis Rossi**	FRA	96	Racing Team Germany	FTR Honda	22	38m 46.784s
6 **Alex Rins**	SPA	42	Estrella Galicia 0,0	Suter Honda	22	38m 50.465s
7 **Alexis Masbou**	FRA	10	Caretta Technology	Honda	22	38m 53.249s
8 **Niklas Ajo**	FIN	31	TT Motion Events Racing	KTM	22	38m 53.287s
9 **Efren Vazquez**	SPA	7	JHK Laglisse	FTR Honda	22	38m 53.469s
10 **Miguel Oliveira**	POR	44	Estrella Galicia 0,0	Suter Honda	22	38m 53.675s
11 **Zulfahmi Khairuddin**	MAL	63	AirAsia-Sic-Ajo	KTM	22	38m 53.810s
12 **Romano Fenati**	ITA	5	Team Italia FMI	FTR Honda	22	38m 53.991s
13 **Jakub Kornfeil**	CZE	84	Redox-Ongetta-Centro Seta	FTR Honda	22	38m 57.565s
14 **Toni Finsterbusch**	GER	9	Cresto Guide MZ Racing	Honda	22	38m 57.790s
15 **Hector Faubel**	SPA	55	Bankia Aspar Team	Kalex KTM	22	38m 57.965s
16 Arthur Sissis	AUS	61	Red Bull KTM Ajo	KTM	22	38m 58.086s
17 Alan Techer	FRA	89	Technomag-CIP-TSR	TSR Honda	22	38m 58.268s
18 Adrian Martin	SPA	26	JHK Laglisse	FTR Honda	22	38m 58.308s
19 Alberto Moncayo	SPA	23	Bankia Aspar Team	Kalex KTM	22	38m 58.376s
20 Brad Binder	RSA	41	RW Racing GP	Kalex KTM	22	39m 06.774s
21 Isaac Vinales	SPA	32	Ongetta-Centro Seta	FTR Honda	22	39m 06.939s
22 Alessandro Tonucci	ITA	19	Team Italia FMI	FTR Honda	22	39m 07.013s
23 Simone Grotzkyj	ITA	15	Ambrogio Next Racing	Suter Honda	22	39m 24.304s
24 Jasper Iwema	NED	53	Moto FGR	FGR Honda	22	39m 24.669s
25 Bryan Schouten	NED	22	Dutch Racing Team	Honda	22	39m 24.704s
26 Julian Miralles	SPA	40	MIR Racing	Honda	22	39m 24.809s
27 Kenta Fujii	JPN	51	Technomag-CIP-TSR	TSR Honda	22	39m 24.965s
28 Luigi Morciano	ITA	3	Ioda Team Italia	Ioda	22	39m 26.440s
29 Ivan Moreno	SPA	21	Andalucia JHK Laglisse	FTR Honda	22	39m 28.625s
Marcel Schrotter	GER	77	Mahindra Racing	Mahindra	20	DNF
Giulian Pedone	SWI	30	Ambrogio Next Racing	Suter Honda	16	DNF
Danny Webb	GBR	99	Mahindra Racing	Mahindra	14	DNF
Niccolo Antonelli	ITA	27	San Carlo Gresini Moto3	FTR Honda	3	DNF
Jonas Folger	GER	94	IodaRacing Project	Ioda	0	DNF
Jack Miller	AUS	8	Caretta Technology	Honda		DSQ

Fastest lap: Zulfahmi Khairuddin, on lap 12, 1m 44.004s, 97.690mph/157.217km/h (record).

Previous lap record: New category.

Event best maximum speed: Maverick Vinales, 131.4mph/211.4km/h (race).

Qualifying: Dry
Air: 21° Humidity: 59% Track: 28°

1	Cortese	1m 43.645s
2	Kent	1m 43.894s
3	Antonelli	1m 43.988s
4	Faubel	1m 44.074s
5	Ajo	1m 44.097s
6	M. Vinales	1m 44.178s
7	Masbou	1m 44.273s
8	Oliveira	1m 44.311s
9	Kornfeil	1m 44.329s
10	Salom	1m 44.376s
11	Moncayo	1m 44.408s
12	Rossi	1m 44.451s
13	Sissis	1m 44.533s
14	Techer	1m 44.534s
15	Tonucci	1m 44.541s
16	Rins	1m 44.542s
17	Fenati	1m 44.561s
18	Khairuddin	1m 44.750s
19	Binder	1m 44.826s
20	Webb	1m 45.174s
21	Martin	1m 45.254s
22	Miralles	1m 45.280s
23	Finsterbusch	1m 45.391s
24	Vazquez	1m 45.420s
25	Moreno	1m 45.596s
26	I. Vinales	1m 45.697s
27	Grotzkyj	1m 45.955s
28	Schouten	1m 45.981s
29	Morciano	1m 46.027s
30	Schrotter	1m 46.059s
31	Iwema	1m 46.173s
32	Pedone	1m 46.883s
33	Miller	1m 47.277s
34	Fujii	1m 47.419s

Outside 107%

	Folger	1m 51.731s

Fastest race laps

1	Khairuddin	1m 44.004s
2	Kent	1m 44.370s
3	Salom	1m 44.465s
4	Cortese	1m 44.505s
5	Rossi	1m 44.528s
6	Fenati	1m 44.563s
7	Rins	1m 44.572s
8	M. Vinales	1m 44.683s
9	Antonelli	1m 44.711s
10	Masbou	1m 44.730s
11	Sissis	1m 44.856s
12	Vazquez	1m 44.905s
13	Moncayo	1m 44.906s
14	Binder	1m 44.921s
15	Oliveira	1m 44.935s
16	Ajo	1m 44.949s
17	Finsterbusch	1m 44.963s
18	Kornfeil	1m 45.011s
19	Martin	1m 45.049s
20	Faubel	1m 45.059s
21	I. Vinales	1m 45.136s
22	Techer	1m 45.140s
23	Tonucci	1m 45.382s
24	Webb	1m 45.658s
25	Morciano	1m 45.673s
26	Schouten	1m 45.937s
27	Miralles	1m 46.005s
28	Schrotter	1m 46.225s
29	Grotzkyj	1m 46.295s
30	Fujii	1m 46.296s
31	Iwema	1m 46.375s
32	Moreno	1m 46.453s
33	Miller	1m 46.488s
34	Folger	1m 46.933s
35	Pedone	1m 47.835s

Championship Points

1	M. Vinales	130
2	Cortese	123
3	Salom	88
4	Fenati	65
5	Rossi	56
6	Rins	54
7	Masbou	51
8	Khairuddin	49
9	Kent	42
10	Oliveira	39
11	Antonelli	38
12	Moncayo	36
13	Sissis	31
14	Vazquez	29
15	Faubel	29
16	Kornfeil	20
17	Techer	18
18	Marquez	15
19	Ajo	14
20	Moreno	10
21	Iwema	9
22	Pedone	7
23	Tonucci	7
24	Folger	5
25	Binder	5
26	Schrotter	4
27	Hanus	3
28	Finsterbusch	2
29	Miller	1

Constructor Points

1	FTR Honda	170
2	KTM	124
3	Kalex KTM	111
4	Suter Honda	81
5	Honda	54
6	TSR Honda	18
7	FGR Honda	9
8	Ioda	5
9	Mahindra	4
10	Oral	1

FIM WORLD CHAMPIONSHIP · ROUND 8

GERMAN GRAND PRIX

SACHSENRING

Dani's day, after Stoner spurned
second place. His bin-it-or-win-it move
was one corner early (inset, top).
Photos: Gold & Goose

Above: Slow-speed, high-intensity corners define the major part of the Sachsenring track.

Right, from left: Veteran Franco Battaini took over injured Abraham's Ducati; Pasini was more shocked than injured after his pit-lane collision; FIM President Vito Ippolito was in attendance.

Below right: Former rider, now a TV commentor, Alex Hofmann interviews centre of attention Stefan Bradl on the grid.

Far right: Dovizioso beat Spies in the Yamaha battle for third place.

Photos: Gold & Goose

I N the still at least partially quaint former East Germany, crammed on to the flank of a steep hill, ringed by stands heaving with more than 80,000 hardy fans, racing at the pocket-handkerchief Sachsenring is reliably intense. Made the more so in 2012 by extreme weather, with rain on Saturday and Sunday so heavy that it ran in rivers across the track and threw the schedule out of kilter.

The canted countryside meant the rivers quickly ran away and the track became usable. On race day, the heaviest cloudburst of the weekend held off until the start of the Moto3 race, unusually last of the day, sending them from the grid to scurry for cover while the start was delayed by half an hour. Since the small paddock area behind the pits was reserved for MotoGP and a handful of Moto2 teams, they had to trail through a tunnel to the second paddock on the other side of the track, a good five-minute walk away.

By then, the main business of the day was out of the way, a MotoGP race where Stoner proved that while other riders may have been prepared to play the percentages, coming second just wasn't good enough for him. In a first race crash

in 23 GPs (except Jerez in 2011, when he was knocked off by Rossi), he slid off while attacking winner Pedrosa at the penultimate corner. Not part of the plan. "I wanted to leave my win-it-or-bin-it move to the last corner," he said later.

Casey had been in fighting form all weekend, especially in his firm reaction to Bridgestone's explanation of the Assen tyre failures. Investigation of the tyres and others from the batch had revealed that overheating had been the cause, rather than construction or material failure, explained Motorsport Tyre Development Manager Shinji Aoki, due in part to different riding styles and electronics, and the extra torque of the 1000s, but mainly because of track temperatures that had been more than double those of the previous year. Bridgestone's figures were 18 degrees to 40; official figures showed the same gap: 16/37 degrees. The failures had nothing to do with 2012's softer construction, he said, but to quell fears of similar problems at Mugello in a week, they had commissioned a special batch of extra-hard tyres to be supplied in addition to the usual allocation.

At least they were trying, but for Stoner it was just another

element of deterioration in grand prix racing. Pointing to a scarcity of lap records in spite of extra power, he bluntly said, "Their tyres are getting worse. They will never admit that anything's wrong, which is the biggest problem."

Lorenzo turned up pre-event on crutches, ferried to and fro in a four-by-four. In retrospect, he seemed to be making a bit much of ligament injuries sustained at Assen, for he walked to his bike the next day and rode as well as ever. He ended the weekend with his own Bridgestone beef. A matter of minutes before leaving his pit, the tyre technicians had persuaded him to change his choice of soft tyres for the hard, for fear they would not last. Reluctantly he acceded ("He is a championship rider, so he took the careful choice," explained team head Zeelenberg), but said it had cost him as much as a second a lap, with less grip and more wheel-spin. CRT bikes aside, only two riders did go soft: Bautista, looking for a way to make up for his back-of-the-grid start, and Ducati tester Franco Battaini, substituting for Abraham. Irritatingly for Lorenzo, Bautista's best lap was the 24th of 29, in a stirring ride through from the rear.

Things were cooking at Ducati, where top brass from new owners Audi, including Rupert Stadler, chairman of the Audi AG board, were on hand for preliminary meetings, most especially with Rossi, though at this stage all they could really do was exhibit impressive knowledge of the situation and show great enthusiasm. Team-mate Hayden was left on the outside somewhat, particularly since news had broken in the previous days that the company had made Cal Crutchlow what turned out to be a tentative and incomplete offer for a two-year contract.

A pit-lane collision on the first day of practice evoked disturbing memories, but fortunately resulted in no serious injuries. A mechanic from the AB Cardion team, for whom Battaini was riding while Abraham recuperated from testing hand injuries that had forced him to withdraw at Assen, was hit by Pasini. His bike then skittered almost into Rossi's pit.

In 1993, before a pit-lane speed limit was introduced, Japanese rider Nobuyuki Wakai was fatally injured and a team guest badly hurt in a pit-lane collision at Jerez.

The grumbling noise from Colin Edwards's pit was growing impossible to ignore. The rider repeated his description of the bike as "a raging bull with a headache with poison ivy up its ass" and slammed the lack of progress, especially from Suter and in the electronics, though he did say the Bosch technicians – motorcycle electronics virgins – were at least hard at work every race. The week before, his Forward Racing squad had ditched their Suter Moto2 chassis in favour of FTR, with promising results; a similar move in MotoGP would also mean a change of power unit. Edwards was non-committal, but clearly keen.

Former 125 champion Mike di Meglio had fallen foul of his Speedmaster Moto2 team after a number of crashes, and was replaced by rookie Alessandro Andreozzi.

A post-race rider change in Moto3 was in the other direction: Mahindra's Marcel Schrotter was so fed up with the lack of progress to the team's sluggish and troublesome Oral engine that he had asked to be released, to seek his racing fortune elsewhere. "I am only 19," he said. "I'm not a test or development rider."

MOTOGP RACE – 30 laps

Only the first free practice was dry; qualifying was very wet, but dried enough for five minutes of mayhem at the end. The names at the top of the list shuffled constantly: Bradl had been on top, then Spies, Bradl again, Crutchlow, Spies, Bradl, Stoner, Pedrosa, Spies and finally, with the last lap of all, Stoner, for his fourth pole of the year. Spies was alongside, then Pedrosa, who commented, "You could go half a second quicker every lap." Crutchlow, Lorenzo and Bradl made row two.

Oddly, Ducati's usual advantage in the wet didn't work –

Above: Marquez leads Kallio, Iannone, Simeon and Simon in Moto2.

Top right: Alex de Angelis took his first rostrum of the season.

Above right: Mika Kallio also returned to the Moto2 podium.

Top far right: The moment – Iannone slides out of contention.

Right: Rookie Jack Miller led Moto3 in streaming wet conditions and finished a fine fourth.

Below right: With a dry line appearing, Cortese, Masbou and Salom steamed past, podium-bound.

Photos: Gold & Goose

Hayden and Rossi were either side of Dovizioso on row three. "Our advantage is more in acceleration, but here you spend so much time on the side of the tyre," explained Nicky.

Pedrosa made his usual flying start from Stoner, Spies and Lorenzo, but on lap two, Stoner cut underneath mid-way through the series of left-handers. The two orange Hondas immediately started to open a gap: better than two seconds by the time Lorenzo passed his team-mate for third. But any hope he might have had about closing up to make a race of it was soon dispelled: he was losing almost half a second every lap.

The tension was high without him. Dani stuck with Casey, matching every move. He explained later: "Before the race, we changed almost everything on the bike, so it was easy for Casey to pass while I was getting familiar with it." Once he was, after 18 laps, he outbraked Stoner into the first corner.

They stayed locked together in splendid isolation. By lap 26, they started to lap the slower CRT bikes, but it made no difference. It would be a battle to the end.

On lap 29, Pedrosa set fastest lap. Stoner was still with him, but he said later that he'd made a little mistake and lost some yards. It took him until the plunge down the 'waterfall' back straight to get back to a challenging position.

Two corners left.

The leader went in tight and defensive, Stoner took a wider run in for a fast exit, planning to pass into the next left at the top of the hill. "I was in the perfect position, but as I released the brake and the weight came off the front, it let go." He was down and sliding across the gravel, to argue with marshals who wouldn't let him restart – although far in the gravel in a dip with the engine stopped, it would not have been easy.

Dani was alone for his first win of the season; another 15 seconds down came a disgruntled Lorenzo, cheered somewhat by regaining the title lead. He'd rapidly outpaced Spies and had been on his own for the whole race.

The American lacked edge grip on the long corners, he explained: "Every time I touched the throttle, it would slide." He found himself under severe pressure from Dovizioso and Crutchlow. Dovi passed him at the start of lap nine and

Crutchlow also at the end of it. Powerless to attack, he held a watching brief, hoping that Crutchlow (who had been ahead of Dovi for a lap earlier on) might push both of them wide, giving him a chance to get through.

It didn't happen that way: instead Crutchlow – battling to make up for a speed deficit by hard braking – missed his marker and ran into the gravel at the first corner. Nor did Spies have the exit speed he needed to pass, though he was almost alongside over the line. It was an important result for the Italian, a second successive rostrum, and in front of the man whose ride he aimed to take in 2013.

Right behind was a grisly gang, swelled to six by race end as Crutchlow tagged on the back and Bautista also caught up. Bradl led throughout, resisting sustained pressure. Hayden, Barbera and Rossi were to and fro, the American dropping to the back when an attack on Bradl at the start of lap 28 went wrong. "I was going for sixth and I got tenth instead," he said ruefully.

Rossi picked his way through as the last-lap scramble approached, but we would never know if his plan to take Bradl in the last corner would have been successful, because the yellow flags for Stoner's crash spiked his guns. Bautista and Crutchlow were also charging hard; they crossed the line Bradl, Rossi, Bautista, Crutchlow and Hayden, covered by less than 1.4 seconds.

The rest were spaced out: de Puniet, Edwards, Espargaro, Ellison, then a lap down Battaini, Petrucci and Silva. Pasini had crashed out; Pirro retired his troublesome FTR Honda after one lap.

MOTO2 RACE – 29 laps

Marquez bounced back from a fast crash on the first day and conquered difficult conditions for his sixth pole in eight races. The weather muddled the rest; Simon and first-timer Kallio completed the front row; Simeon and rookie Rea led Luthi on row two; Iannone was tenth, Espargaro, fastest in the dry, down in 17th, Redding 22nd.

His rivals spaced out behind, it was no surprise to see Marquez take off in the lead. Redding crashed out directly

after coming together with Terol in the first corner, but team-mate Kallio was on the Spaniard's back wheel, chased for a lap by Simon, before he faded.

Behind, Iannone took until lap three to get past fourth-placed Smith, and one more to pass Kallio. Now he was pushing Marquez hard, and finally outbraked him at the bottom of the waterfall to lead for the eighth time over the line.

Marquez promptly reversed the order, and they were to and fro for two more laps before Iannone slid off on the Omega curve.

De Angelis had finished the first lap 11th, behind Luthi, but soon began moving forward, and when Iannone fell was about to join the leaders to make a trio pulling clear of Smith.

They stayed close, de Angelis up to second by half-distance. Marquez had managed the pace and his tyres, and with five laps to go took advantage in his usual remarkable style, motoring away as if by right, four- or five-tenths quicker each lap than his bickering pursuers, and able to relax on the last lap and still win by two seconds.

Kallio regained second with three laps to go and narrowly clung on, equalling his best result in the class; de Angelis took his first rostrum of the year, crediting his new FTR chassis. "I can really feel the bike now," he said.

Espargaro had charged through from his 17th grid place, finishing the first lap 14th and having several narrow escapes as he gained two or three places per lap in the early stages. Corsi tagged on as he caught and passed Smith around half-distance; Espargaro left them behind, but was too far adrift to gain any more places.

Luthi had been biding his time, then with ten laps to go passed Smith followed by Corsi. By the last two laps, he was on Espargaro's back wheel, trying in vain to find a way past. They finished inches apart; behind them, Corsi got the better of Smith for sixth.

Simeon held a solid eighth for most of the race; behind him, Corti finally got clear of Aegerter, completing the top ten. Not far behind, Zarco shaded Rabat; Cardus did the same to Terol. Simon took the final point, ahead of the re-mounted Iannone, past West on the final lap.

Elias, Wilairot, new-boy Andreozzi and Krummenacher joined the crash list, the last remounting near the back.

A 43-point lead was Marquez's reward for another copy-book ride.

MOTO3 RACE – 27 laps

Cortese took pole in equally bad conditions at the last minute, after missing most of the session when his bike stopped with an electrical fault at the start. He ousted Danny Kent by almost 1.5 seconds. With Martin third, Australian rookie Jack Miller was pushed off a maiden front row; Korn-feil and fellow rookie Binder were alongside.

Vinales was in all sorts of trouble, qualified 24th.

The race got under way almost 30 minutes late, lighter rain still falling. It soon stopped, and by half-distance a dry line had developed.

Miller flourished in the rain, taking the lead from Martin on lap two, convincingly fending off all rivals until team-mate Masbou finally got by on lap 16.

Cortese had finished the first lap eighth, and lost another place or two in the spray. He gained confidence as conditions improved, however, leapfrogging a group to third on lap 16. Next time around, he had passed Masbou and Miller, Salom and Martin following on. Rossi and Binder were in the lead group, but had crashed out by the end, Martin also. The track was treacherous off the dry line, the rain tyres now badly worn.

Cortese and Masbou escaped up front to finish in that order. The win returned Cortese to the points lead. Salom was third, chased over the line by Miller, Vazquez a distant fifth. Khairuddin came through to lead the next gang, followed by Faubel, who stalled on the start line, started at the back and finished lap one 29th.

Wild-card Luca Gruenwald was next, followed by Sissis ahead of Kornfeil and Finsterbusch.

Vinales finished 17th, one of several afflicted with over-heating after taping over the radiators in the earlier cold. Fenati also had a dire weekend, finishing 24th, a lap down. Kent struggled, too, retiring from midfield.

ROUND 8

eni MOTORRAD
GRAND PRIX DEUTSCHLAND

6–8 JULY, 2012

OFFICIAL TIMEKEEPER

SACHSENRING GP CIRCUIT

30 laps
Length: 3.671 km / 3,259 miles
Width: 12m

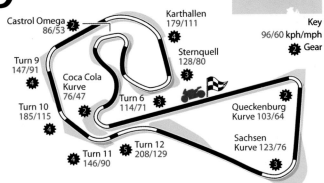

Key
96/60 kph/mph
2 Gear

Castrol Omega 86/53
Karthallen 179/111
Turn 9 147/91
Sternquell 128/80
Coca Cola Kurve 76/47
Turn 6 114/71
Turn 10 185/115
Queckenburg Kurve 103/64
Sachsen Kurve 123/76
Turn 11 146/90
Turn 12 208/129

Photos: Gold & Goose

MotoGP

RACE DISTANCE: 30 laps, 68.432 miles/110.130km · RACE WEATHER: Dry (air 26°C, humidity 47%, track 37°C)

Pos.	Rider	Nat.	No.	Entrant	Machine	Tyres	Race tyre choice	Laps	Time & speed
1	**Dani Pedrosa**	SPA	26	Repsol Honda Team	Honda RC213V	B	F: Ex-Hard/R: Hard	30	41m 28.396s 99.001mph/ 159.326km/h
2	**Jorge Lorenzo**	SPA	99	Yamaha Factory Racing	Yamaha YZR-M1	B	F: Ex-Hard/R: Hard	30	41m 43.392s
3	**Andrea Dovizioso**	ITA	4	Monster Yamaha Tech 3	Yamaha YZR-M1	B	F: Ex-Hard/R: Hard	30	41m 49.065s
4	**Ben Spies**	USA	11	Yamaha Factory Racing	Yamaha YZR-M1	B	F: Ex-Hard/R: Hard	30	41m 49.136s
5	**Stefan Bradl**	GER	6	LCR Honda MotoGP	Honda RC213V	B	F: Ex-Hard/R: Hard	30	41m 56.289s
6	**Valentino Rossi**	ITA	46	Ducati Team	Ducati Desmosedici GP12	B	F: Ex-Hard/R: Hard	30	41m 56.446s
7	**Alvaro Bautista**	SPA	19	San Carlo Honda Gresini	Honda RC213V	B	F: Ex-Hard/R: Medium	30	41m 56.642s
8	**Cal Crutchlow**	GBR	35	Monster Yamaha Tech 3	Yamaha YZR-M1	B	F: Ex-Hard/R: Hard	30	41m 56.843s
9	**Hector Barbera**	SPA	8	Pramac Racing Team	Ducati Desmosedici GP12	B	F: Ex-Hard/R: Hard	30	41m 57.449s
10	**Nicky Hayden**	USA	69	Ducati Team	Ducati Desmosedici GP12	B	F: Ex-Hard/R: Hard	30	41m 57.622s
11	**Randy de Puniet**	FRA	14	Power Electronics Aspar	ART Aprilia RSV4	B	F: Ex-Hard/R: Medium	30	42m 21.572s
12	**Colin Edwards**	USA	5	NGM Mobile Forward Racing	Suter BMW S1000RR	B	F: Ex-Hard/R: Medium	30	42m 26.600s
13	**Aleix Espargaro**	SPA	41	Power Electronics Aspar	ART Aprilia RSV4	B	F: Ex-Hard/R: Medium	30	42m 33.050s
14	**Yonny Hernandez**	COL	68	Avintia Blusens	BQR FTR Kawasaki	B	F: Ex-Hard/R: Medium	30	42m 41.939s
15	**James Ellison**	GBR	77	Paul Bird Motorsport	ART Aprilia RSV4	B	F: Ex-Hard/R: Medium	30	42m 58.714s
16	Franco Battaini	ITA	2	Cardion AB Motoracing	Ducati Desmosedici GP12	B	F: Ex-Hard/R: Medium	29	41m 35.941s
17	Danilo Petrucci	ITA	9	Came Ioda Racing Project	Ioda Aprilia RSV4	B	F: Medium/R: Medium	29	41m 43.788s
18	Ivan Silva	SPA	22	Avintia Blusens	BQR FTR Kawasaki	B	F: Ex-Hard/R: Medium	29	41m 57.963s
	Casey Stoner	AUS	1	Repsol Honda Team	Honda RC213V	B	F: Ex-Hard/R: Hard	29	DNF-crash
	Mattia Pasini	ITA	54	Speed Master	ART Aprilia RSV4	B	F: Ex-Hard/R: Medium	4	DNF-crash
	Michele Pirro	ITA	51	San Carlo Honda Gresini	FTR Honda CBR1000RR	B	F: Ex-Hard/R: Medium	3	DNF-mechanical

Fastest lap: Dani Pedrosa, on lap 30, 1m 22.304s, 99.774mph/160.570km/h.
Lap record: Dani Pedrosa, SPA (Honda), 1m 21.846s, 100.332mph/161.469km/h (2011).
Event best maximum speed: Dani Pedrosa, 182.1mph/293.0km/h (race).

Qualifying

Weather: Wet
Air Temp: 17° Humidity: 97%
Track Temp: 22°

1	Stoner	1m 31.796s
2	Spies	1m 31.989s
3	Pedrosa	1m 32.081s
4	Crutchlow	1m 32.288s
5	Lorenzo	1m 32.381s
6	Bradl	1m 32.510s
7	Hayden	1m 32.795s
8	Dovizioso	1m 33.205s
9	Rossi	1m 33.217s
10	Espargaro	1m 33.900s
11	Bautista	1m 34.088s
12	Barbera	1m 34.542s
13	Edwards	1m 34.649s
14	De Puniet	1m 34.651s
15	Pasini	1m 34.938s
16	Petrucci	1m 35.590s
17	Pirro	1m 35.595s
18	Hernandez	1m 35.962s
19	Silva	1m 36.183s
20	Ellison	1m 36.355s
21	Battaini	1m 36.438s

Fastest race laps

1	Pedrosa	1m 22.304s
2	Stoner	1m 22.510s
3	Crutchlow	1m 23.050s
4	Lorenzo	1m 23.057s
5	Spies	1m 23.086s
6	Dovizioso	1m 23.219s
7	Bautista	1m 23.228s
8	Hayden	1m 23.287s
9	Barbera	1m 23.291s
10	Rossi	1m 23.293s
11	Bradl	1m 23.416s
12	De Puniet	1m 24.069s
13	Edwards	1m 24.238s
14	Espargaro	1m 24.260s
15	Pasini	1m 24.499s
16	Hernandez	1m 24.545s
17	Ellison	1m 24.945s
18	Battaini	1m 25.300s
19	Silva	1m 25.339s
20	Petrucci	1m 25.740s
21	Pirro	1m 26.300s

Championship Points

1	Lorenzo	160
2	Pedrosa	146
3	Stoner	140
4	Dovizioso	92
5	Crutchlow	85
6	Rossi	71
7	Bautista	67
8	Hayden	65
9	Bradl	62
10	Spies	61
11	Barbera	53
12	De Puniet	24
13	Espargaro	23
14	Pirro	16
15	Pasini	12
16	Ellison	10
17	Petrucci	9
18	Edwards	8
19	Hernandez	6
20	Silva	5
21	Abraham	4

Constructor Points

1	Honda	176
2	Yamaha	176
3	Ducati	85
4	ART	37
5	FTR	16
6	Ioda	9
7	BQR	9
8	Suter	8
9	BQR-FTR	2

Grid Order	1	2	3	4	5	6	7	8	9	10	11	12	13	14	15	16	17	18	19	20	21	22	23	24	25	26	27	28	29	30	
1 STONER	26	1	1	1	1	1	1	1	1	1	1	1	1	1	1	1	1	1	26	26	26	26	26	26	26	26	26	26	26	26	1
11 SPIES	1	26	26	26	26	26	26	26	26	26	26	26	26	26	26	26	26	26	1	1	1	1	1	1	1	1	1	1	1	99	2
26 PEDROSA	11	11	11	11	99	99	99	99	99	99	99	99	99	99	99	99	99	99	99	99	99	99	99	99	99	99	99	99	4		3
35 CRUTCHLOW	99	99	99	99	11	11	11	4	4	4	4	4	4	4	4	4	4	4	4	4	4	4	4	4	4	4	4	4	11		4
99 LORENZO	4	4	4	4	4	35	4	35	35	35	35	35	35	35	35	35	35	35	35	11	11	11	11	11	11	11	11	11	6		5
6 BRADL	6	35	35	35	35	4	35	11	11	11	11	11	11	11	11	11	11	11	11	6	6	6	6	6	6	6	6	46			6
69 HAYDEN	35	6	6	6	6	6	6	6	6	6	6	6	6	6	6	6	6	6	6	6	6	6	6	69	8	46	19				7
4 DOVIZIOSO	69	69	69	69	69	69	69	69	69	69	8	8	8	8	69	69	69	69	8	8	69	8	46	19	35				8
46 ROSSI	46	8	46	46	46	46	46	8	8	69	69	69	69	69	8	8	8	46	8	69	69	46	46	19	35	8				9
41 ESPARGARO	8	46	8	8	8	8	46	46	46	46	46	46	46	46	46	46	46	8	46	46	8	69	19	35	8	69				10
8 BARBERA	41	14	14	14	14	19	19	19	19	19	19	19	19	19	19	19	19	19	19	19	35	35	69	69	14				11
5 EDWARDS	14	41	41	41	19	14	14	14	14	14	14	14	14	14	14	14	14	14	14	14	14	14	14	14	5				12
14 DE PUNIET	51	19	19	19	41	41	41	41	41	41	41	41	41	41	41	41	41	41	41	41	41	41	41	41	41				13
54 PASINI	5	51	5	5	5	5	5	5	5	5	5	5	5	5	5	5	5	5	5	5	5	5	5	5	68				14
9 PETRUCCI	19	5	68	54	68	68	68	68	68	68	68	68	68	68	68	68	68	68	68	68	68	68	68	68	77				15
51 PIRRO	9	68	54	68	77	77	77	77	77	77	77	77	77	77	77	77	77	77	77	77	77	77	77	77				
68 HERNANDEZ	68	54	77	77	2	2	2	2	2	2	2	2	2	2	2	2	2	2	2	2	2	2	2	2				
22 SILVA	54	9	2	22	22	22	22	22	22	9	9	9	9	9	22	22	22	22	22	22	22	9	9				
77 ELLISON	77	77	2	9	9	9	9	9	9	2	2	2	2	2	9	9	9	9	9	9	9	22	22				
2 BATTAINI	22	2	22	9																								
19 BAUTISTA	2	22	51																									

51 Pit stop   22 Lapped rider

Moto2

RACE DISTANCE: 29 laps, 66.151 miles/106.459km · RACE WEATHER: Dry (air 27°C, humidity 47%, track 43°C)

Pos.	Rider	Nat.	No.	Entrant	Machine	Laps	Time & Speed
1	**Marc Marquez**	SPA	93	Team CatalunyaCaixa Repsol	Suter	29	41m 32.467s 95.545mph/ 153.764km/h
2	**Mika Kallio**	FIN	36	Marc VDS Racing Team	Kalex	29	41m 34.560s
3	**Alex de Angelis**	RSM	15	NGM Mobile Forward Racing	FTR	29	41m 35.034s
4	**Pol Espargaro**	SPA	40	Pons 40 HP Tuenti	Kalex	29	41m 38.457s
5	**Thomas Luthi**	SWI	12	Interwetten-Paddock	Suter	29	41m 38.606s
6	**Simone Corsi**	ITA	3	Came IodaRacing Project	FTR	29	41m 43.518s
7	**Bradley Smith**	GBR	38	Tech 3 Racing	Tech 3	29	41m 43.876s
8	**Xavier Simeon**	BEL	19	Tech 3 Racing	Tech 3	29	41m 47.275s
9	**Claudio Corti**	ITA	71	Italtrans Racing Team	Kalex	29	41m 53.236s
10	**Dominique Aegerter**	SWI	77	Technomag-CIP	Suter	29	41m 57.608s
11	**Johann Zarco**	FRA	5	JIR Moto2	Motobi	29	41m 59.934s
12	**Esteve Rabat**	SPA	80	Pons 40 HP Tuenti	Kalex	29	41m 59.942s
13	**Ricard Cardus**	SPA	88	Arguinano Racing Team	AJR	29	42m 01.057s
14	**Nicolas Terol**	SPA	18	Mapfre Aspar Team Moto2	Suter	29	42m 01.180s
15	**Julian Simon**	SPA	60	Blusens Avintia	Suter	29	42m 05.254s
16	Andrea Iannone	ITA	29	Speed Master	Speed Up	29	42m 07.843s
17	Anthony West	AUS	95	QMMF Racing Team	Moriwaki	29	42m 08.063s
18	Gino Rea	GBR	8	Federal Oil Gresini Moto2	Suter	29	42m 10.058s
19	Max Neukirchner	GER	76	Kiefer Racing	Kalex	29	42m 18.134s
20	Takaaki Nakagami	JPN	30	Italtrans Racing Team	Kalex	29	42m 19.903s
21	Roberto Rolfo	ITA	44	Technomag-CIP	Suter	29	42m 21.808s
22	Damian Cudlin	AUS	50	Desguaces La Torre SAG	Bimota	29	42m 23.171s
23	Marco Colandrea	SWI	10	SAG Team	FTR	29	42m 45.233s
24	Kevin Wahr	GER	11	Kiefer Racing	IAMT	29	42m 46.801s
25	Randy Krummenacher	SWI	4	GP Team Switzerland	Kalex	28	41m 41.748s
26	Markus Reiterberger	GER	21	Cresto Guide MZ Racing	MZ-RE Honda	28	41m 55.018s
27	Eric Granado	BRA	57	JIR Moto2	Motobi	28	42m 22.403s
	Ratthapark Wilairot	THA	14	Thai Honda PTT Gresini Moto2	Suter	25	DNF
	Elena Rosell	SPA	82	QMMF Racing Team	Moriwaki	19	DNF
	Axel Pons	SPA	49	Pons 40 HP Tuenti	Kalex	18	DNF
	Yuki Takahashi	JPN	72	NGM Mobile Forward Racing	FTR	16	DNF
	Alessandro Andreozzi	ITA	22	S/Master Speed Up	Speed Up	6	DNF
	Toni Elias	SPA	24	Mapfre Aspar Team Moto2	Suter	5	DNF
	Scott Redding	GBR	45	Marc VDS Racing Team	Kalex	0	DNF

Fastest lap: Alex de Angelis, on lap 6, 1m 25.167s, 96.419mph/155.172km/h (record).
Previous lap record: Yonny Hernandez, COL (FTR), 1m 25.255s, 96.320mph/155.012km/h (2011).
Event best maximum speed: Esteve Rabat, 156.3mph/251.6km/h (race).

Qualifying: Wet
Air: 17° Humidity: 100% Track: 21°

1	Marquez	1m 34.503s
2	Simon	1m 34.548s
3	Kallio	1m 34.639s
4	Simeon	1m 34.686s
5	Rea	1m 34.908s
6	Luthi	1m 34.945s
7	West	1m 35.110s
8	De Angelis	1m 35.234s
9	Smith	1m 35.238s
10	Iannone	1m 35.320s
11	Takahashi	1m 35.358s
12	Cardus	1m 35.559s
13	Corsi	1m 35.702s
14	Zarco	1m 35.733s
15	Aegerter	1m 35.777s
16	Wilairot	1m 35.819s
17	Espargaro	1m 35.976s
18	Elias	1m 36.041s
19	Corti	1m 36.386s
20	Krummenacher	1m 36.407s
21	Nakagami	1m 36.461s
22	Neukirchner	1m 36.471s
23	Cudlin	1m 36.532s
24	Terol	1m 36.707s
25	Andreozzi	1m 37.072s
26	Redding	1m 37.588s
27	Rabat	1m 37.723s
28	Granado	1m 37.921s
29	Wahr	1m 38.493s
30	Reiterberger	1m 38.697s
31	Rolfo	1m 38.703s
32	Colandrea	1m 39.273s
33	Pons	1m 39.301s
34	Rosell	1m 39.716s

Fastest race laps

1	De Angelis	1m 25.167s
2	Espargaro	1m 25.319s
3	Marquez	1m 25.461s
4	Luthi	1m 25.494s
5	Corsi	1m 25.503s
6	Iannone	1m 25.551s
7	Kallio	1m 25.578s
8	Smith	1m 25.769s
9	Simeon	1m 25.820s
10	Corti	1m 25.838s
11	Aegerter	1m 26.027s
12	Krummenacher	1m 26.121s
13	Takahashi	1m 26.131s
14	Zarco	1m 26.154s
15	Rabat	1m 26.157s
16	Wilairot	1m 26.179s
17	Cardus	1m 26.273s
18	Elias	1m 26.343s
19	Terol	1m 26.403s
20	Rea	1m 26.510s
21	Simon	1m 26.517s
22	Nakagami	1m 26.623s
23	West	1m 26.632s
24	Pons	1m 26.677s
25	Neukirchner	1m 26.824s
26	Rolfo	1m 26.988s
27	Cudlin	1m 27.187s
28	Granado	1m 27.571s
29	Colandrea	1m 27.693s
30	Andreozzi	1m 27.739s
31	Wahr	1m 27.842s
32	Rosell	1m 28.085s
33	Reiterberger	1m 28.364s

Championship Points

1	Marquez	152
2	Espargaro	109
3	Luthi	107
4	Iannone	104
5	Redding	86
6	Kallio	72
7	Smith	56
8	Corti	52
9	Rabat	51
10	De Angelis	48
11	Aegerter	44
12	Zarco	41
13	Corsi	40
14	Elias	34
15	Nakagami	27
16	Krummenacher	20
17	Simeon	17
18	Simon	15
19	Di Meglio	10
20	West	9
21	Neukirchner	8
22	Wilairot	8
23	Terol	5
24	Cardus	4
25	Rea	1

Constructor Points

1	Suter	181
2	Kalex	155
3	Speed Up	104
4	FTR	57
5	Tech 3	56
6	Motobi	41
7	Moriwaki	10
8	AJR	4

Moto3

RACE DISTANCE: 27 laps, 61.588 miles/99.117km · RACE WEATHER: Wet (air 21°C, humidity 61%, track 32°C)

Pos.	Rider	Nat.	No.	Entrant	Machine	Laps	Time & Speed
1	**Sandro Cortese**	GER	11	Red Bull KTM Ajo	KTM	27	45m 36.868s 81.011mph/ 130.375km/h
2	**Alexis Masbou**	FRA	10	Caretta Technology	Honda	27	45m 37.503s
3	**Luis Salom**	SPA	39	RW Racing GP	Kalex KTM	27	45m 40.866s
4	**Jack Miller**	AUS	8	Caretta Technology	Honda	27	45m 40.919s
5	**Efren Vazquez**	SPA	7	JHK Laglisse	FTR Honda	27	45m 48.987s
6	**Zulfahmi Khairuddin**	MAL	63	AirAsia-Sic-Ajo	KTM	27	46m 02.042s
7	**Hector Faubel**	SPA	55	Mapfre Aspar Team Moto3	Kalex KTM	27	46m 02.367s
8	**Luca Gruenwald**	GER	43	Freudenberg Racing Team	Honda	27	46m 02.955s
9	**Arthur Sissis**	AUS	61	Red Bull KTM Ajo	KTM	27	46m 06.543s
10	**Jakub Kornfeil**	CZE	84	Redox-Ongetta-Centro Seta	FTR Honda	27	46m 06.759s
11	**Toni Finsterbusch**	GER	9	Cresto Guide MZ Racing	Honda	27	46m 10.046s
12	**Niccolo Antonelli**	ITA	27	San Carlo Gresini Moto3	FTR Honda	27	46m 19.726s
13	**Alan Techer**	FRA	89	Technomag-CIP-TSR	TSR Honda	27	46m 39.521s
14	**Niklas Ajo**	FIN	31	TT Motion Events Racing	KTM	27	46m 47.121s
15	**Simone Grotzkyj**	ITA	15	Ambrogio Next Racing	Suter Honda	27	46m 47.315s
16	Alessandro Tonucci	ITA	19	Team Italia FMI	FTR Honda	27	46m 47.508s
17	Maverick Vinales	SPA	25	Blusens Avintia	FTR Honda	27	46m 47.990s
18	Danny Webb	GBR	99	Mahindra Racing	Mahindra	27	46m 48.174s
19	Miguel Oliveira	POR	44	Estrella Galicia 0,0	Suter Honda	27	46m 55.746s
20	Alex Rins	SPA	42	Estrella Galicia 0,0	Suter Honda	27	46m 55.825s
21	Isaac Vinales	SPA	32	Ongetta-Centro Seta	FTR Honda	26	45m 53.006s
22	Luigi Morciano	ITA	3	Ioda Team Italia	Ioda	26	46m 11.457s
23	Kenta Fujii	JPN	51	Technomag-CIP-TSR	TSR Honda	26	46m 18.905s
24	Romano Fenati	ITA	5	Team Italia FMI	FTR Honda	26	46m 36.610s
25	Ivan Moreno	SPA	21	Andalucia JHK Laglisse	FTR Honda	26	47m 03.962s
26	Kevin Hanus	GER	86	Thomas Sabo GP Team	Honda	26	47m 04.587s
27	Giulian Pedone	SWI	30	Ambrogio Next Racing	Suter Honda	24	47m 11.903s
	Louis Rossi	FRA	96	Racing Team Germany	FTR Honda	25	DNF
	Marcel Schrotter	GER	77	Mahindra Racing	Mahindra	24	DNF
	Alberto Moncayo	SPA	23	Mapfre Aspar Team Moto3	Kalex KTM	23	DNF
	Danny Kent	GBR	52	Red Bull KTM Ajo	KTM	22	DNF
	Brad Binder	RSA	41	RW Racing GP	Kalex KTM	21	DNF
	Adrian Martin	SPA	26	JHK Laglisse	FTR Honda	20	DNF
	Jonas Folger	GER	94	IodaRacing Project	Ioda	17	DNF
	Jasper Iwema	NED	53	Moto FGR	FGR Honda	16	DNF

Fastest lap: Sandro Cortese, on lap 27, 1m 36.728s, 84.895mph/136.626km/h (record).
Previous lap record: New category.
Event best maximum speed: Alex Rins, 126.3mph/203.3km/h (free practice 2).

Qualifying: Wet
Air: 17° Humidity: 100% Track: 20°

1	Cortese	1m 42.989s
2	Kent	1m 44.474s
3	Martin	1m 44.489s
4	Miller	1m 44.532s
5	Kornfeil	1m 44.585s
6	Binder	1m 44.735s
7	Rossi	1m 44.815s
8	Folger	1m 44.893s
9	Salom	1m 44.924s
10	Masbou	1m 44.985s
11	Ajo	1m 45.150s
12	Faubel	1m 45.372s
13	Moncayo	1m 45.373s
14	Vazquez	1m 45.422s
15	Finsterbusch	1m 45.497s
16	Gruenwald	1m 45.625s
17	Iwema	1m 45.650s
18	Antonelli	1m 45.705s
19	Techer	1m 45.795s
20	Khairuddin	1m 45.939s
21	Sissis	1m 46.002s
22	Webb	1m 46.046s
23	Grotzkyj	1m 46.173s
24	M. Vinales	1m 46.602s
25	I. Vinales	1m 46.772s
26	Tonucci	1m 46.951s
27	Rins	1m 46.988s
28	Hanus	1m 47.003s
29	Pedone	1m 47.265s
30	Schrotter	1m 47.311s
31	Oliveira	1m 47.565s
32	Fujii	1m 47.854s
33	Morciano	1m 47.983s
34	Moreno	1m 49.978s
Outside 107%		
	Fenati	1m 51.012s

Fastest race laps

1	Cortese	1m 36.728s
2	Fenati	1m 36.917s
3	Masbou	1m 36.928s
4	Miller	1m 37.334s
5	Faubel	1m 37.384s
6	Gruenwald	1m 37.421s
7	Khairuddin	1m 37.498s
8	Salom	1m 37.569s
9	Sissis	1m 37.795s
10	Kornfeil	1m 37.816s
11	Vazquez	1m 37.823s
12	Rossi	1m 38.193s
13	Oliveira	1m 38.688s
14	Finsterbusch	1m 38.759s
15	Tonucci	1m 38.942s
16	Techer	1m 38.959s
17	Rins	1m 38.960s
18	Martin	1m 38.972s
19	Antonelli	1m 39.010s
20	Ajo	1m 39.203s
21	Webb	1m 39.250s
22	Schrotter	1m 39.346s
23	Grotzkyj	1m 39.385s
24	M. Vinales	1m 39.459s
25	I. Vinales	1m 39.515s
26	Moncayo	1m 40.011s
27	Binder	1m 40.027s
28	Folger	1m 40.152s
29	Morciano	1m 40.190s
30	Hanus	1m 40.416s
31	Moreno	1m 40.972s
32	Fujii	1m 41.365s
33	Kent	1m 41.751s
34	Iwema	1m 42.577s
35	Pedone	1m 48.278s

Championship Points

1	Cortese	148
2	M. Vinales	130
3	Salom	104
4	Masbou	71
5	Fenati	65
6	Khairuddin	59
7	Rossi	56
8	Rins	54
9	Kent	42
10	Antonelli	42
11	Vazquez	40
12	Oliveira	39
13	Sissis	38
14	Faubel	38
15	Moncayo	36
16	Kornfeil	26
17	Techer	21
18	Ajo	16
19	Marquez	15
20	Miller	14
21	Moreno	10
22	Iwema	9
23	Gruenwald	8
24	Pedone	7
25	Finsterbusch	7
26	Tonucci	7
27	Folger	5
28	Binder	5
29	Schrotter	4
30	Hanus	3
31	Grotzkyj	1

Constructor Points

1	FTR Honda	181
2	KTM	149
3	Kalex KTM	127
4	Suter Honda	82
5	Honda	74
6	TSR Honda	21
7	FGR Honda	9
8	Ioda	5
9	Mahindra	4
10	Oral	1

ITALIAN GRAND PRIX

MUGELLO CIRCUIT

Race number nine, win
number five: Lorenzo was
back in business.
Photo: Gold & Goose

THREE weekends on the trot meant jaded faces; sunshine and a dry track made up for it. Mugello is a favourite riders' circuit, and one year after resurfacing it was in good fettle for a fine weekend's racing, closing the first half of the season. Rather worryingly, there was a marked shrinkage in the crowd figure – 64,165, almost 20,000 down on 2011.

Was this a function of hard times, and the top price for a weekend ticket of almost 200 euros? Or Rossi doldrums, at his signature circuit with no hope of adding to his seven straight wins, amassed between 2002 and 2008.

The Ducati situation simmered – Hayden and Crutchlow still dangling. This had been the deadline for Crutchlow's decision. "It's not me holding things up," he said. Of course not. It was Rossi. It had seemed a week before that he had little option but to stay. Now came a new and powerful spin to the rumour-mill. Marlboro sponsorship chief Maurizio Arrivabene arrived for high-level meetings with Dorna's Ezpeleta and with Yamaha team chief Lin Jarvis. Was this paving the way for Rossi to return to Yamaha, with Marlboro backing? The plot continued to thicken over the coming weeks, and only the Marlboro part failed to come true.

Honda's desire to win the first 1000cc title was made plain with an announcement from vice-president Shuhei Nakamoto that 2013's prototype was being released more than half a year early. It was, he said, an all-new bike, both chassis and engine, with one for each rider arriving on Saturday in time for the third post-race tests of the season on Monday.

The engine change yielded both more power and improved throttle response for rideability; the chassis had revised stiffness in an attempt to solve persistent chatter problems. But Nakamoto admitted that they wouldn't know if this was successful until Monday. Japanese test rider Akiyoshi had not managed to induce chatter even with the old chassis, because he was not fast enough "If he was, he would be here," he joked.

Stoner liked the engine, but not the chassis. Remarkably he had only used two engines for the full first half of the season. He would take two more for the next race, both the new type; Pedrosa took the new chassis as well.

Honda's other news was the renewal of Pedrosa's contract for two years, and that Marquez had been signed up alongside him. Some considered Pedrosa lucky, since in his seventh year he had claimed just 16 in 106 starts so far, a poor rate of just 15 per cent. Marquez, by contrast, had 30 per cent, but all in the smaller classes: 21 wins in 70 starts. But the comparison is not that simple: Pedrosa's smaller-class percentage was almost as high, at 29.5.

In spite of the heat, Bridgestone's special additional supply of extra-hard tyres proved redundant, the hard performing fine. One rider dared to be different, Stoner alone using them for the race for the somewhat obtuse reason that "there is no disadvantage". They would play no direct part in a second spoiled race in succession. He was fifth when a big head

shake caused brake-pad knock off, and he missed his braking point for the Correntaio curve, at the foot of the all-red Ducati grandstand. Still too fast on the slippery outside of the track, he was well into the gravel when he regained control, losing 15 seconds and five places, only two of which he would recover.

As usual there were plenty of run-ons at the end of the very fast straight, which Pedrosa rather petulantly attributed to the squidgy new front tyre. But the problem was not confined to MotoGP, and on Saturday morning Moto2 rookie Zarco gave a fine example. He went scything in, passing three riders on the way, then lost the front while still braking at the apex; his bike promptly skittled Espargaro on the outside. His victim was stretchered off with ankle injuries, but was back the next day to claim pole. Zarco was summoned before Race Direction and – accepting that free practice was not the time or place for such a desperate lunge – took a 15-grid-place penalty on the chin.

There was a second demonstration of electronics tripping over themselves when a bike became lost. At Estoril, it had been Hayden; this time, Lorenzo. Aiming to regain pole, he had taken advantage of the opportunity for a short lap to escape traffic, pulling through the pits and rejoining on a clear track. He should have reset his electronics (GPS is not allowed); instead his bike thought it was still finishing the previous lap. On the last corners and on to the front straight, instead of getting full power, "it was slower every corner". He banged the tank angrily as he wheeled into the pit lane. (A different example occurred in the Moto3 race, when new Mahindra rider Ricardo Moretti pressed the wrong button on the start line, and instead of actuating launch control he found himself puttering along with the pit-lane speed limiter in operation.)

Valentino had his usual special Mugello helmet, this time referencing Italian singer/entertainer Gianni Morandi, with signature motto *Restiamo Uniti* (Let's stick together). "It's a message to the guys that work with me and for all the fans in a difficult moment."

There was the usual worry about speed differential between factory and CRT bikes on the long straight: best factory speed was Rossi's 346.9km/h; Edwards's BMW-powered Suter took CRT honours at a fairly respectable 327.9; Petrucci's Ioda Aprilia was again slowest by a big margin: 309.5. The Italian rider had gained respect and would be given a gallop at Ducati tests in the upcoming week, but still he couldn't really help himself from getting in Stoner's way on a fast lap in qualifying, earning a scary close pass and some harsh words. "Having these bikes out is like putting touring cars with Formula One," he said.

Half the year gone, and Lorenzo had regained momentum, opening his points lead over Pedrosa once again, while Stoner lost more ground, now almost 40 points down. "But there are still plenty more races I can win before the end of the year," the defending (and retiring) champion said.

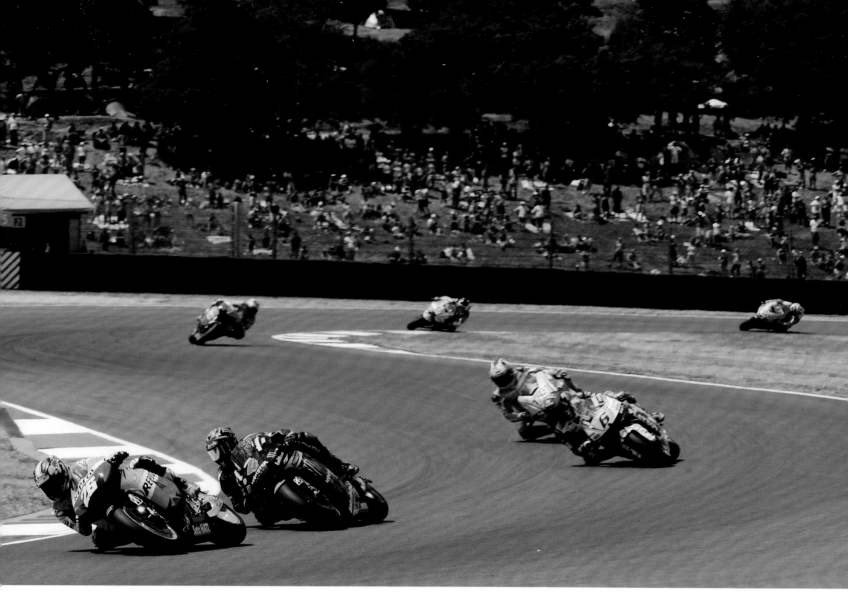

MOTOGP RACE – 23 laps

Fresh from European football success, the many Spanish paddock denizens were further cheered by the cleanest of sweeps in qualifying: not only the full MotoGP front row, but also top CRT bike (Aleix Espargaro), and pole in Moto2 (brother Pol) and Moto3 (Vinales).

Lorenzo was fastest from Friday morning until fewer than four minutes from the end of qualifying, as Pedrosa edged him by less than two-tenths. First-time front-row companion Barbera was gleeful after silencing his on-track critics, who said he only went fast by following. "I did the lap alone. Mugello is my favourite," he said.

Hayden led row two, slowed he said by traffic; from Stoner, short of edge grip, and Crutchlow, who had crashed twice. Then came Dovi, Bradl and Spies, who had also crashed; Rossi headed row four, unable to take advantage of the softer tyres.

The lap chart is simple enough for the leader. Lorenzo all the way. But it was Pedrosa who led into the first corner. "I braked very late and missed the line a little. And boom, Jorge came by." He did the same later at Casanova-Savelli, and this time Dovizioso took him by surprise.

Hayden got a good start, but was under pressure at once from Bradl. They swapped twice on the first lap, then on the third Bradl got ahead properly and they both joined the train behind the leader. But Hayden soon started losing ground, a second adrift by lap eight.

By now, Spies had started fading fast, if erratically – a quick lap, then a slow one. The explanation came later: he had been suffering from severe food poisoning, fighting waves of nausea, then recovering for a while again.

Pedrosa repassed Dovi on lap five, while Stoner had passed Barbera as well as Spies, and was closing on Hayden. He was ahead a lap later – only to run into the gravel, saving the crash, but rejoining tenth, more than five seconds

down on Bautista. Six laps later, he was on the Spaniard and passed him on to the straight, only for Bautista to outbrake him into the first corner. Stoner attacked straight back into the next chicane, but as he pushed inside at the apex Bautista came across and they collided, the Spaniard lucky not to crash. Fists were shaken after the race, but Stoner defended himself vigorously. "Nobody could call me a dangerous rider or overtaker. I'd be more worried that I'd run off and still came back past him."

Bradl was going strong, taking third off Dovi on lap ten when the Italian ran wide, and he would stay there until three laps from the end.

Lorenzo's lead had grown to better than a second on lap six, but was only two-tenths greater on lap ten. Thereafter he stretched away steadily as Pedrosa ran into tyre problems.

Pedrosa was quite alone from before half-distance. The action was gradually building up behind him as Hayden picked up speed again after hunting down the best ECU map to restore lost rear grip. He rejoined the Dovi-Bradl group with one lap to go. Dovi was in front again after tailing Bradl and confident his late braking could keep him there.

Over the second half, Rossi had been leading Crutchlow, who had closed gradually to join him, the pair catching the group as they started the last lap.

For a second race, Hayden came off worst in the ensuing brawl, after sacrificing a safe fourth or fifth in a bid for the podium. He put a strong pass on Bradl in the Turn Two/Three chicane, but it compromised his exit speed and to his surprise Bradl returned the compliment at the next corner. "It probably looked a bit aggressive on TV," said Bradl later, "but I think it was normal for the last lap." It pushed Hayden wide, and both Rossi and Crutchlow swept past.

Dovizioso's third rostrum in a row was by four-hundredths from Bradl's career-best fourth. A second behind came Rossi, Crutchlow, Hayden.

Above: Lorenzo having disappeared, Pedrosa was left to battle with Dovi, chased by Bradl, Hayden, Stoner, Barbera and Rossi.

Left: HRC's Nakamoto was in jocular mood at the announcement of an all-new bike for Casey and Dani.

Bottom row, from left: Marlboro's Maurizio Arrivabene (*right*) greets Ducati's Del Torchio amid wild rumours of a shift to Yamaha; 1981 champion Marco Lucchinelli was a welcome visitor; the point of Rossi's latest helmet creation was lost on fans outside Italy.

Photos: Gold & Goose

Above: Stoner ran off, rejoined, and finally caught and passed Barbera for a lowly eighth.

Top: Stefan Bradl held third for much of the race, but the shadowing Dovizioso took it in the end.

Photos: Gold & Goose

Stoner rapidly outdistanced Bautista and easily passed Barbera. He was almost 20 seconds off Hayden at the end.

Spies rallied in the final laps (setting fastest straight-line speed for a Yamaha) as he closed up again on de Puniet, getting ahead with two laps to go. Espargaro was next, recovering after running off on lap two and rejoining last. He took 13th off Ellison on the last lap, Pasini just a second behind for the last point.

Silva was a lap down; Pirro was black-flagged after taking a short cut back to the pits on lap one, then rejoining; Petrucci and Hernandez crashed out; Edwards had pitted his recalcitrant Suter from last after ten laps.

MOTO2 RACE – 21 laps

Marquez was on top until the battered Espargaro shaded him by less than half a tenth, grinning from ear to ear. Zarco was four-tenths down for what would have been a first front row in the class, but the penalty dropped him to 18th and promoted Iannone. De Angelis headed the revised row two from Luthi and Smith, then came Redding, Rabat and Nakagami; the first 13 within one second.

Marquez jetted away in the lead, the rest screaming in ear-tickling unison nose to tail, except when two or three abreast into the corners.

After six laps, the top ten were still covered by less than 1.3 seconds, but by then Marquez had saved one major moment and dropped to fourth, with Nakagami having deposed Luthi from the lead, Iannone third and Espargaro fifth. Redding was at the back of the gang.

The madness continued as Luthi took over again, fending off Espargaro. The pair collided on lap 14 and for once Espargaro, who came close to falling, actually came out of the encounter better. At the end of the lap, he had a little gap over Luthi and Iannone, while Marquez also lost ground with another slide. Poor set-up was his excuse for an atypically downbeat race.

Now Espargaro started to run away, better than 1.3 seconds clear two laps later while a six-strong gang piled up behind Luthi.

Iannone passed the Swiss rider and, with Espargaro's tyres starting to fade, he soon began closing up, Luthi and Smith with him. Then, at the start of the penultimate lap, Luthi missed his braking point into Turn One, and they all lost touch slightly.

Espargaro led as they began the last lap, but Iannone outbraked him into the first corner. Try as he might the Spaniard couldn't get back, crossing the line less than a tenth adrift.

Eight-tenths behind, Luthi managed to fend off Smith by a similar distance.

Marquez was almost three seconds down by then. He said he had been playing it safe and thinking of the championship, but he fought fiercely all the same to hold Redding and Nakagami at bay.

Aegerter dropped back to a lonely eighth. Two seconds away, Corti led Zarco, Kallio and Krummenacher

Neukirchner was the first of several to crash, with de Angelis, Andreozzi, Simeon, Pons, Roccoli, Rabat and finally Elias also falling victim; di Meglio tumbled as well, but remounted to finish. West, having switched chassis from Moriwaki to Speed Up, was in and out of the pits; team-mate Rosell called in and stayed there.

Marquez's off-form afternoon only slightly dented his mid-season points lead, at 163, while Iannone now equalled Espargaro on 129.

MOTO3 RACE – 20 laps

Qualifying continued the fight between the leading contenders, with Cortese on pole as the flag ended the session – until canny slipstreaming put Vinales ahead by four-tenths. Rookie Rins was alongside, Vazquez heading row two from Kent and Antonelli.

Small bikes thrive on Mugello's wide corners and slipstream-friendly straight, producing reliably huge battles. There was no difference in 2012, the lead constantly changing and a feast of overtaking in a big pack behind.

Khairuddin was first leader, for three laps, but it was so close that when Fenati came by on lap four he dropped directly to sixth.

Vinales was in the lead next time around, then Vazquez took over for one lap. Elsewhere on the track, Kent also saw the front.

Only after half-distance did the front three break away, for a battle to the final inch. Vinales led on to the last lap, Cortese moved from third to first into the first corner, but it was Fenati in front as they reached the top of the hill.

Vinales deposed him on the plunge down Casanova-Savelli and into the climbing Arrabiata set, and for the final half-lap he stayed ahead.

They were still hunting for slipstream on the long run to the line. Fenati stayed right, Vinales went left – and crossed it only inches ahead, Cortese on his back wheel. Third cut his lead over Vinales to nine points.

Rookie Antonelli led the next tight gang from Kent, Vazquez and one-lap leader Rins; Kornfeil, Khairuddin and Faubel completed the top ten.

There were amazingly few crashes; victims included Rossi, Salom and Miguel Oliveira.

Above: Fourth was a high point in Bradley Smith's difficult season.

Above left: Iannone was ecstatic after his home-race win.

Left: Bad boy Zarco overcame a grid penalty to claim a solid tenth.

Below: Moto3 by inches: Vinales went left, Fenati stayed right, the Spaniard got there first. Cortese was third.

Photos: Gold & Goose

FIM WORLD CHAMPIONSHIP

GRAN PREMIO D'ITALIA TIM

13–15 JULY, 2012

motoGP | TISSOT SWISS WATCHES SINCE 1853

OFFICIAL TIMEKEEPER

Photos: Gold & Goose

AUTODROMO INTERNAZIONALE DEL MUGELLO

23 laps
Length: 5.245 km / 3,259 miles
Width: 14m

Key
96/60 kph/mph
Gear

Scarperia 109/68
Arrabbiata 2 156/97
Palagio 106/66
Correntaio 106/66
Biondetti 1 165/103
Biondetti 2 167/104
Bucine 114/71
Savelli 117/73
San Donato 98/61
Arrabbiata 1 163/101
Cassanova 144/89
Materassi 119/74
Luco 113/70
Borgo San Lorenzo 121/75
Poggio Seco 119/74

MotoGP · RACE DISTANCE: 23 laps, 74.959 miles/120.635km · RACE WEATHER: Dry (air 25°C, humidity 43%, track 45°C)

Pos.	Rider	Nat.	No.	Entrant	Machine	Tyres	Race tyre choice	Laps	Time & speed
1	**Jorge Lorenzo**	SPA	99	Yamaha Factory Racing	Yamaha YZR-M1	B	F: Hard/R: Hard	23	41m 37.477s 108.050mph/ 173.889km/h
2	**Dani Pedrosa**	SPA	26	Repsol Honda Team	Honda RC213V	B	F: Hard/R: Hard	23	41m 42.700s
3	**Andrea Dovizioso**	ITA	4	Monster Yamaha Tech 3	Yamaha YZR-M1	B	F: Hard/R: Hard	23	41m 48.142s
4	**Stefan Bradl**	GER	6	LCR Honda MotoGP	Honda RC213V	B	F: Hard/R: Hard	23	41m 48.188s
5	**Valentino Rossi**	ITA	46	Ducati Team	Ducati Desmosedici GP12	B	F: Hard/R: Hard	23	41m 49.172s
6	**Cal Crutchlow**	GBR	35	Monster Yamaha Tech 3	Yamaha YZR-M1	B	F: Hard/R: Hard	23	41m 49.537s
7	**Nicky Hayden**	USA	69	Ducati Team	Ducati Desmosedici GP12	B	F: Hard/R: Hard	23	41m 49.712s
8	**Casey Stoner**	AUS	1	Repsol Honda Team	Honda RC213V	B	F: Hard/R: Hard	23	42m 08.094s
9	**Hector Barbera**	SPA	8	Pramac Racing Team	Ducati Desmosedici GP12	B	F: Hard/R: Hard	23	42m 09.205s
10	**Alvaro Bautista**	SPA	19	San Carlo Honda Gresini	Honda RC213V	B	F: Hard/R: Hard	23	42m 12.066s
11	**Ben Spies**	USA	11	Yamaha Factory Racing	Yamaha YZR-M1	B	F: Hard/R: Hard	23	42m 35.339s
12	**Randy de Puniet**	FRA	14	Power Electronics Aspar	ART Aprilia RSV4	B	F: Hard/R: Medium	23	42m 37.440s
13	**Aleix Espargaro**	SPA	41	Power Electronics Aspar	ART Aprilia RSV4	B	F: Hard/R: Medium	23	42m 48.677s
14	**James Ellison**	GBR	77	Paul Bird Motorsport	ART Aprilia RSV4	B	F: Hard/R: Medium	23	42m 48.935s
15	**Mattia Pasini**	ITA	54	Speed Master	ART Aprilia RSV4	B	F: Hard/R: Medium	23	42m 49.305s
16	Ivan Silva	SPA	22	Avintia Blusens	BQR FTR Kawasaki	B	F: Hard/R: Hard	22	42m 02.684s
	Colin Edwards	USA	5	NGM Mobile Forward Racing	Suter BMW S1000RR	B	F: Hard/R: Hard	10	DNF-mechanical
	Yonny Hernandez	COL	68	Avintia Blusens	BQR FTR Kawasaki	B	F: Hard/R: Hard	9	DNF-crash
	Danilo Petrucci	ITA	9	Came Ioda Racing Project	Ioda Aprilia RSV4	B	F: Hard/R: Medium	3	DNF-crash
DSQ	Michele Pirro	ITA	51	San Carlo Honda Gresini	FTR Honda CBR1000RR	B	F: Hard/R: Medium		DSQ-cut course

Fastest lap: Dani Pedrosa, on lap 10, 1m 47.705s, 108.934mph/175.312km/h (record).

Previous lap record: Jorge Lorenzo, SPA (Yamaha), 1m 48.402s, 108.233mph/174.184km/h (2011).

Event best maximum speed: Valentino Rossi, 215.6mph/346.9km/h (race).

Qualifying

Weather: Dry
Air Temp: 28° Humidity: 48%
Track Temp: 46°

1	Pedrosa	1m 47.284s
2	Lorenzo	1m 47.423s
3	Barbera	1m 47.545s
4	Hayden	1m 47.671s
5	Stoner	1m 47.689s
6	Crutchlow	1m 47.749s
7	Dovizioso	1m 47.751s
8	Bradl	1m 47.857s
9	Spies	1m 48.149s
10	Rossi	1m 48.502s
11	Bautista	1m 48.894s
12	Espargaro	1m 49.387s
13	De Puniet	1m 49.450s
14	Pirro	1m 50.263s
15	Hernandez	1m 50.610s
16	Ellison	1m 50.812s
17	Pasini	1m 50.953s
18	Silva	1m 51.242s
19	Edwards	1m 51.348s
20	Petrucci	1m 51.473s

Fastest race laps

1	Pedrosa	1m 47.705s
2	Lorenzo	1m 47.795s
3	Bradl	1m 48.121s
4	Hayden	1m 48.179s
5	Stoner	1m 48.194s
6	Dovizioso	1m 48.226s
7	Crutchlow	1m 48.405s
8	Rossi	1m 48.444s
9	Barbera	1m 48.605s
10	Bautista	1m 48.652s
11	Spies	1m 48.886s
12	De Puniet	1m 49.831s
13	Espargaro	1m 50.397s
14	Ellison	1m 50.899s
15	Hernandez	1m 50.922s
16	Pasini	1m 50.927s
17	Silva	1m 51.359s
18	Petrucci	1m 51.678s
19	Edwards	1m 52.420s

Championship Points

1	Lorenzo	185
2	Pedrosa	166
3	Stoner	148
4	Dovizioso	108
5	Crutchlow	95
6	Rossi	82
7	Bradl	75
8	Hayden	74
9	Bautista	73
10	Spies	66
11	Barbera	60
12	De Puniet	28
13	Espargaro	26
14	Pirro	16
15	Pasini	13
16	Ellison	12
17	Petrucci	9
18	Edwards	8
19	Hernandez	6
20	Silva	5
21	Abraham	4

Constructor Points

1	Yamaha	201
2	Honda	196
3	Ducati	96
4	ART	41
5	FTR	16
6	Ioda	9
7	BQR	9
8	Suter	8
9	BQR-FTR	2

Grid order	1	2	3	4	5	6	7	8	9	10	11	12	13	14	15	16	17	18	19	20	21	22	23	
26 PEDROSA	99	99	99	99	99	99	99	99	99	99	99	99	99	99	99	99	99	99	99	99	99	99	99	1
99 LORENZO	4	4	4	4	26	26	26	26	26	26	26	26	26	26	26	26	26	26	26	26	26	26	26	2
8 BARBERA	26	26	26	26	4	4	4	4	4	6	6	6	6	6	6	6	6	6	4	4	4	4	4	3
69 HAYDEN	69	69	6	6	6	6	6	6	6	4	4	4	4	4	4	4	4	4	6	6	6	6	6	4
1 STONER	6	6	69	69	69	69	69	69	1	69	69	69	69	69	69	69	69	69	69	69	69	69	46	5
35 CRUTCHLOW	8	1	1	1	1	1	1	1	69	46	46	46	46	46	46	46	46	46	46	46	46	46	35	6
4 DOVIZIOSO	11	8	8	8	8	46	46	46	46	35	35	35	35	35	35	35	35	35	35	35	35	69	69	7
6 BRADL	1	11	11	46	46	35	35	35	8	8	8	8	8	8	8	8	8	8	8	8	1	1	1	8
11 SPIES	35	35	46	35	35	8	8	8	19	19	19	19	19	19	19	1	1	1	1	8	8	8	8	9
46 ROSSI	46	46	35	11	11	19	19	19	1	1	1	1	1	1	1	19	19	19	19	19	19	19	19	10
19 BAUTISTA	19	19	19	19	19	11	11	14	14	14	14	14	14	14	14	14	14	14	14	11	11	11	11	11
41 ESPARGARO	41	14	14	14	14	14	14	11	11	11	11	11	11	11	11	11	11	11	11	14	14	14	14	12
14 DE PUNIET	54	54	54	54	54	54	54	54	54	54	54	54	54	54	54	54	54	54	77	77	41			13
51 PIRRO	14	77	77	77	77	77	77	68	77	77	77	77	77	77	77	77	77	77	54	41	77			14
68 HERNANDEZ	77	68	68	68	68	68	68	77	68	41	41	41	41	41	41	41	41	41	41	54	54			15
77 ELLISON	68	22	9	5	5	5	41	41	41	22	22	22	22	22	22	22	22	22	22	22	22			
54 PASINI	9	9	5	41	41	41	5	5	22	5														
22 SILVA	22	5	41	22	22	22	22	22	5															
5 EDWARDS	5	41	22																					
9 PETRUCCI																								

5 Pit stop   22 Lapped rider

Moto2

RACE DISTANCE: 21 laps, 68.441 miles/110.145km · RACE WEATHER: Dry (air 25°C, humidity 44%, track 43°C)

Pos.	Rider	Nat.	No.	Entrant	Machine	Laps	Time & Speed
1	**Andrea Iannone**	ITA	29	Speed Master	Speed Up	21	39m 52.523s 102.982mph/ 165.733km/h
2	**Pol Espargaro**	SPA	40	Pons 40 HP Tuenti	Kalex	21	39m 52.613s
3	**Thomas Luthi**	SWI	12	Interwetten-Paddock	Suter	21	39m 53.420s
4	**Bradley Smith**	GBR	38	Tech 3 Racing	Tech 3	21	39m 53.548s
5	**Marc Marquez**	SPA	93	Team CatalunyaCaixa Repsol	Suter	21	39m 56.319s
6	**Scott Redding**	GBR	45	Marc VDS Racing Team	Kalex	21	39m 56.434s
7	**Takaaki Nakagami**	JPN	30	Italtrans Racing Team	Kalex	21	39m 56.948s
8	**Dominique Aegerter**	SWI	77	Technomag-CIP	Suter	21	40m 03.889s
9	**Claudio Corti**	ITA	71	Italtrans Racing Team	Kalex	21	40m 05.340s
10	**Johann Zarco**	FRA	5	JIR Moto2	Motobi	21	40m 05.554s
11	**Mika Kallio**	FIN	36	Marc VDS Racing Team	Kalex	21	40m 05.652s
12	**Randy Krummenacher**	SWI	4	GP Team Switzerland	Kalex	21	40m 05.885s
13	**Nicolas Terol**	SPA	18	Mapfre Aspar Team Moto2	Suter	21	40m 07.722s
14	**Julian Simon**	SPA	60	Blusens Avintia	Suter	21	40m 09.761s
15	**Ricard Cardus**	SPA	88	Arguinano Racing Team	AJR	21	40m 29.079s
16	Ratthapark Wilairot	THA	14	Thai Honda PTT Gresini Moto2	Suter	21	40m 40.224s
17	Yuki Takahashi	JPN	72	NGM Mobile Forward Racing	FTR	21	40m 44.489s
18	Simone Corsi	ITA	3	Came IodaRacing Project	FTR	21	40m 46.492s
19	Gino Rea	GBR	8	Federal Oil Gresini Moto2	Suter	21	40m 47.177s
20	Marco Colandrea	SWI	10	SAG Team	FTR	21	41m 00.802s
21	Eric Granado	BRA	57	JIR Moto2	Motobi	21	41m 07.330s
22	Mike di Meglio	FRA	63	Cresto Guide MZ Racing	MZ-RE Honda	20	40m 16.704s
23	Anthony West	AUS	95	QMMF Racing Team	Speed Up	20	41m 40.667s
	Toni Elias	SPA	24	Mapfre Aspar Team Moto2	Suter	14	DNF
	Roberto Rolfo	ITA	44	Technomag-CIP	Suter	12	DNF
	Esteve Rabat	SPA	80	Pons 40 HP Tuenti	Kalex	10	DNF
	Massimo Roccoli	ITA	55	Desguaces La Torre SAG	Bimota	8	DNF
	Axel Pons	SPA	49	Pons 40 HP Tuenti	Kalex	7	DNF
	Xavier Simeon	BEL	19	Tech 3 Racing	Tech 3	7	DNF
	Elena Rosell	SPA	82	QMMF Racing Team	Moriwaki	6	DNF
	Alessandro Andreozzi	ITA	22	S/Master Speed Up	Speed Up	5	DNF
	Alex de Angelis	RSM	15	NGM Mobile Forward Racing	FTR	2	DNF
	Max Neukirchner	GER	76	Kiefer Racing	Kalex	1	DNF

Fastest lap: Thomas Luthi, on lap 18, 1m 52.815s, 104.000mph/167.371km/h (record).
Previous lap record: Stefan Bradl, GER (Kalex), 1m 53.362s, 103.497mph/166.563km/h (2011).
Event best maximum speed: Marc Marquez, 181.9mph/292.7km/h (race).

Qualifying: Dry
Air: 30° Humidity: 46% Track: 49°

1	Espargaro	1m 52.369s
2	Marquez	1m 52.438s
3	Zarco	1m 52.781s
4	Iannone	1m 52.835s
5	De Angelis	1m 52.883s
6	Luthi	1m 52.946s
7	Smith	1m 53.029s
8	Redding	1m 53.059s
9	Rabat	1m 53.090s
10	Nakagami	1m 53.152s
11	Terol	1m 53.258s
12	Corsi	1m 53.266s
13	Aegerter	1m 53.319s
14	Takahashi	1m 53.409s
15	Corti	1m 53.509s
16	Krummenacher	1m 53.566s
17	Di Meglio	1m 53.672s
18	Neukirchner	1m 53.683s
19	Simon	1m 53.715s
20	Cardus	1m 53.722s
21	Pons	1m 53.787s
22	Kallio	1m 53.984s
23	Elias	1m 54.038s
24	Rolfo	1m 54.164s
25	Rea	1m 54.513s
26	Simeon	1m 54.726s
27	West	1m 54.802s
28	Wilairot	1m 54.890s
29	Andreozzi	1m 55.267s
30	Colandrea	1m 55.374s
31	Roccoli	1m 55.518s
32	Granado	1m 56.337s
33	Rosell	1m 57.081s

Fastest race laps

1	Luthi	1m 52.815s
2	Iannone	1m 52.846s
3	Smith	1m 52.927s
4	Marquez	1m 53.005s
5	Espargaro	1m 53.103s
6	Corti	1m 53.139s
7	Redding	1m 53.280s
8	Nakagami	1m 53.291s
9	Zarco	1m 53.322s
10	Elias	1m 53.407s
11	Krummenacher	1m 53.454s
12	Terol	1m 53.524s
13	Kallio	1m 53.548s
14	Corsi	1m 53.569s
15	Aegerter	1m 53.591s
16	Rabat	1m 53.664s
17	Simon	1m 53.726s
18	Pons	1m 53.948s
19	Andreozzi	1m 53.985s
20	West	1m 54.269s
21	De Angelis	1m 54.277s
22	Di Meglio	1m 54.292s
23	Rea	1m 54.296s
24	Cardus	1m 54.303s
25	Wilairot	1m 54.399s
26	Simeon	1m 54.463s
27	Takahashi	1m 54.488s
28	Roccoli	1m 54.909s
29	Rolfo	1m 55.532s
30	Colandrea	1m 55.997s
31	Granado	1m 56.189s
32	Rosell	1m 58.264s

Championship Points

1	Marquez	163
2	Espargaro	129
3	Iannone	129
4	Luthi	123
5	Redding	96
6	Kallio	77
7	Smith	69
8	Corti	59
9	Aegerter	52
10	Rabat	51
11	De Angelis	48
12	Zarco	47
13	Corsi	40
14	Nakagami	36
15	Elias	34
16	Krummenacher	24
17	Simeon	17
18	Simon	17
19	Di Meglio	10
20	West	9
21	Neukirchner	8
22	Wilairot	8
23	Terol	8
24	Cardus	5
25	Rea	1

Constructor Points

1	Suter	197
2	Kalex	175
3	Speed Up	129
4	Tech 3	69
5	FTR	57
6	Motobi	47
7	Moriwaki	10
8	AJR	5

Moto3

RACE DISTANCE: 20 laps, 65.182 miles/104.900km · RACE WEATHER: Dry (air 24°C, humidity 47%, track 40°C)

Pos.	Rider	Nat.	No.	Entrant	Machine	Laps	Time & Speed
1	**Maverick Vinales**	SPA	25	Blusens Avintia	FTR Honda	20	39m 57.374s 97.880mph/ 157.522km/h
2	**Romano Fenati**	ITA	5	Team Italia FMI	FTR Honda	20	39m 57.394s
3	**Sandro Cortese**	GER	11	Red Bull KTM Ajo	KTM	20	39m 57.445s
4	**Niccolo Antonelli**	ITA	27	San Carlo Gresini Moto3	FTR Honda	20	40m 03.162s
5	**Danny Kent**	GBR	52	Red Bull KTM Ajo	KTM	20	40m 03.210s
6	**Efren Vazquez**	SPA	7	JHK Laglisse	FTR Honda	20	40m 03.234s
7	**Alex Rins**	SPA	42	Estrella Galicia 0,0	Suter Honda	20	40m 03.280s
8	**Jakub Kornfeil**	CZE	84	Redox-Ongetta-Centro Seta	FTR Honda	20	40m 15.569s
9	**Zulfahmi Khairuddin**	MAL	63	AirAsia-Sic-Ajo	KTM	20	40m 16.606s
10	**Hector Faubel**	SPA	55	Mapfre Aspar Team Moto3	Kalex KTM	20	40m 16.682s
11	**Niklas Ajo**	FIN	31	TT Motion Events Racing	KTM	20	40m 33.229s
12	**Alexis Masbou**	FRA	10	Caretta Technology	Honda	20	40m 33.246s
13	**Adrian Martin**	SPA	26	JHK Laglisse	FTR Honda	20	40m 33.549s
14	**Kevin Calia**	ITA	74	Elle 2 Ciatti	Honda	20	40m 33.569s
15	**Michael Ruben Rinaldi**	ITA	71	Racing Team Gabrielli	Honda	20	40m 33.644s
16	Alessandro Tonucci	ITA	19	Team Italia FMI	FTR Honda	20	40m 33.659s
17	Alan Techer	FRA	89	Technomag-CIP-TSR	TSR Honda	20	40m 33.820s
18	Toni Finsterbusch	GER	9	Cresto Guide MZ Racing	Honda	20	40m 34.025s
19	Isaac Vinales	SPA	32	Ongetta-Centro Seta	FTR Honda	20	40m 48.626s
20	Danny Webb	GBR	99	Mahindra Racing	Mahindra	20	40m 54.404s
21	Jack Miller	AUS	8	Caretta Technology	Honda	20	40m 54.510s
22	Simone Grotzkyj	ITA	15	Ambrogio Next Racing	Suter Honda	20	40m 54.522s
23	Giulian Pedone	SWI	30	Ambrogio Next Racing	Suter Honda	20	40m 54.525s
24	Brad Binder	RSA	41	RW Racing GP	Kalex KTM	20	41m 04.602s
25	Kenta Fujii	JPN	51	Technomag-CIP-TSR	TSR Honda	20	41m 21.053s
26	Ivan Moreno	SPA	21	Andalucia JHK Laglisse	FTR Honda	20	41m 28.715s
27	Luigi Morciano	ITA	3	Ioda Team Italia	Ioda	20	41m 53.219s
	Miguel Oliveira	POR	44	Estrella Galicia 0,0	Suter Honda	12	DNF
	Jasper Iwema	NED	53	Moto FGR	FGR Honda	8	DNF
	Jonas Folger	GER	94	IodaRacing Project	Ioda	6	DNF
	Arthur Sissis	AUS	61	Red Bull KTM Ajo	KTM	4	DNF
	Alberto Moncayo	SPA	23	Mapfre Aspar Team Moto3	Kalex KTM	3	DNF
	Luis Salom	SPA	39	RW Racing GP	Kalex KTM	3	DNF
	Louis Rossi	FRA	96	Racing Team Germany	FTR Honda	1	DNF
	Riccardo Moretti	ITA	20	Mahindra Racing	Mahindra	0	DNF

Fastest lap: Sandro Cortese, on lap 19, 1m 58.569s, 98.953mph/159.249km/h (record).
Previous lap record: New category.
Event best maximum speed: Zulfahmi Khairuddin, 146.8mph/236.2km/h (warm up).

Qualifying: Dry
Air: 28° Humidity: 50% Track: 47°

1	M. Vinales	1m 57.980s
2	Cortese	1m 58.401s
3	Rins	1m 58.821s
4	Vazquez	1m 58.840s
5	Kent	1m 59.089s
6	Antonelli	1m 59.361s
7	Khairuddin	1m 59.391s
8	Fenati	1m 59.465s
9	Salom	1m 59.473s
10	Faubel	1m 59.573s
11	Rossi	1m 59.680s
12	Moncayo	1m 59.698s
13	Kornfeil	1m 59.777s
14	Techer	1m 59.878s
15	Calia	1m 59.955s
16	Oliveira	1m 59.966s
17	Masbou	2m 00.463s
18	Binder	2m 00.774s
19	Tonucci	2m 00.784s
20	Rinaldi	2m 00.894s
21	Finsterbusch	2m 00.925s
22	Pedone	2m 00.958s
23	I. Vinales	2m 01.167s
24	Martin	2m 01.183s
25	Miller	2m 01.213s
26	Folger	2m 01.217s
27	Grotzkyj	2m 01.308s
28	Ajo	2m 01.310s
29	Sissis	2m 01.317s
30	Moreno	2m 01.319s
31	Iwema	2m 01.362s
32	Webb	2m 01.463s
33	Moretti	2m 01.780s
34	Morciano	2m 02.446s
35	Fujii	2m 04.773s

Fastest race laps

1	Cortese	1m 58.569s
2	Fenati	1m 58.642s
3	M. Vinales	1m 58.716s
4	Antonelli	1m 58.932s
5	Kent	1m 59.186s
6	Vazquez	1m 59.218s
7	Rins	1m 59.324s
8	Oliveira	1m 59.330s
9	Sissis	1m 59.522s
10	Salom	1m 59.581s
11	Khairuddin	1m 59.608s
12	Moncayo	1m 59.625s
13	Faubel	1m 59.647s
14	Kornfeil	1m 59.689s
15	Martin	1m 59.811s
16	Rinaldi	1m 59.970s
17	Masbou	2m 00.116s
18	Ajo	2m 00.140s
19	Calia	2m 00.187s
20	Finsterbusch	2m 00.236s
21	Techer	2m 00.271s
22	Tonucci	2m 00.416s
23	Grotzkyj	2m 00.839s
24	Binder	2m 00.840s
25	I. Vinales	2m 00.848s
26	Pedone	2m 01.073s
27	Miller	2m 01.156s
28	Folger	2m 01.338s
29	Webb	2m 01.340s
30	Iwema	2m 01.400s
31	Moreno	2m 02.418s
32	Fujii	2m 02.884s
33	Morciano	2m 02.947s

Championship Points

1	Cortese	164
2	M. Vinales	155
3	Salom	104
4	Fenati	85
5	Masbou	75
6	Khairuddin	66
7	Rins	63
8	Rossi	56
9	Antonelli	55
10	Kent	53
11	Vazquez	50
12	Faubel	44
13	Oliveira	39
14	Sissis	38
15	Moncayo	36
16	Kornfeil	34
17	Techer	21
18	Ajo	21
19	Marquez	15
20	Miller	14
21	Moreno	10
22	Iwema	9
23	Gruenwald	8
24	Pedone	7
25	Finsterbusch	7
26	Tonucci	7
27	Folger	5
28	Binder	5
29	Schrotter	4
30	Martin	3
31	Hanus	3
32	Calia	2
33	Rinaldi	1
34	Grotzkyj	1

Constructor Points

1	FTR Honda	206
2	KTM	165
3	Kalex KTM	133
4	Suter Honda	91
5	Honda	78
6	TSR Honda	21
7	FGR Honda	9
8	Ioda	5
9	Mahindra	4
10	Oral	1

His sights set on victory, Stoner aims at leader Lorenzo on the run to the first corner.
Photo: Gold & Goose

FIM WORLD CHAMPIONSHIP · ROUND 10

UNITED STATES GRAND PRIX

LAGUNA SECA CIRCUIT

Above: Morning sea mist delayed proceedings: the BMW M6 safety car checks the conditions.

Above right: Hayden's special US helmet evoked *Easy Rider* cool.

Above centre right: Wild-card Steve Rapp (*left*) and team owner Richard Stanboli failed to qualify their brand-new home-brewed CRT bike.

Top: Ben Spies walks away from a lucky escape. His low-rider Yamaha, collapsed at the back, mercifully failed at a slow corner.

Right: Toni Elias took over from the injured Barbera on the Pramac Duke.

Photos: Gold & Goose

NOTHING is quite normal at Laguna Seca, the dislocation of time and place just the background to a unique grand prix, at the shortest and arguably least safe track of the year, where instead of the usual three classes the meeting is shared with the national AMA series, and Motos 2 and 3 are left at home.

The atmosphere was even odder in 2012, thanks to the state of suspense surrounding Rossi, Ducati, Yamaha and all points between. Yet again, in spite of a downbeat qualifying and his silliest-yet crash in the race, Vale managed to be the centre of attention. He did so by preserving the mystery. "I will make up my mind in the next weeks," he said.

This was rather unfair to Stoner, who made a blazing return to winning form in bright Californian sunshine, in front of a good crowd of more than 52,000. His victory came with a thrilling pass on Lorenzo through the fast, blind Turn One that was a repeat of his route to victory in 2011. But the hoo-ha was a welcome relief to Yamaha – because it diverted attention from a most extraordinary mid-race misadventure for Ben Spies. Halfway through the Corkscrew and looking set for fourth, his factory Yamaha suddenly flicked sideways and folded under him, the rider half-surfing on top and lucky not to become entangled. The bike painted a broad black streak from the rear tyre as it fell, suggesting a seize, but as it was wheeled away you could see that the back suspension had

collapsed. The potential consequences at a fast corner like Turn One stretched the imagination.

A sober Spies gave a minimal explanation: "The swing-arm broke. I can't say any more," adding dutifully if rather surprisingly, "It was nobody's fault." It was certainly a catastrophic component failure; in aviation, all other aircraft of the same type would have been grounded forthwith until a satisfactory explanation was forthcoming. In the MotoGP paddock, Yamaha closed ranks and took a vow of silence, leaving us to imagine the frisson of fear other Yamaha riders might have been feeling for the safety of their own mounts. A few weeks later, at Brno, they admitted that a link had broken, but insisted that it had nothing to do with crash damage – Spies was riding with a suspected heel fracture after a heavy crash in practice.

This was all to come as the senior class assembled in the makeshift container-paddock and open pits for what felt like the end of the first half of the season, with a two-weekend break to follow, although numerically it was the start of the second half.

Behind the scenes, it was all intrigue, and all about Valentino. Ducati mounted a last-ditch attempt to keep him on board, CEO del Torchio putting in an offer rumoured at 17 million euros. "If it was only about money, I would have already decided," said Rossi at the pre-event conference.

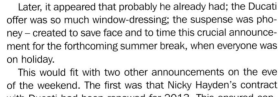

Left: Rossi played it cool amid rumours of his defection from Ducati back to Yamaha.

Below: Adriana Stoner, back on brolly duty, looks concerned before the start of the race.

Photos: Gold & Goose

Later, it appeared that probably he already had; the Ducati offer was so much window-dressing; the suspense was phoney – created to save face and to time this crucial announcement for the forthcoming summer break, when everyone was on holiday.

This would fit with two other announcements on the eve of the weekend. The first was that Nicky Hayden's contract with Ducati had been renewed for 2013. This ensured continuity for the company in the absence of Rossi, and was also a reward for his efforts so far in the season. In ten races, he'd out-qualified Valentino eight times, and he had finished in a higher position five times. He would do so again at Laguna.

The second was a surprise to all except the person who issued it: Ben Spies. Not so much the content, for Yamaha, but the timing – Ben went solo with the news that he would be leaving the team at the end of the year, sidestepping any carefully planned corporate announcement by blurting it out on social media. It was, he said, "for a litany of reasons", and declined to comment further on a flurry of speculation. This mainly centred on an expected move to the BMW Superbike team, and a potential return with the German factory when they come MotoGP racing – or was this just wishful thinking inspired by Dorna's desire to get BMW on board?

In retrospect, however, it looked less like a litany, and more like "thank you and goodbye" as Yamaha cleared the decks for the return of Rossi.

On another topic of concern, Colin Edwards had kick-started the weekend with a broadside at the failure of the CRT class, and his disillusionment with his own mount. "The formula's just not right yet. How can you compete?" he said. "It's more dangerous than anything. I'm spending more time looking behind so I don't get in anybody's way. The remarks gave little comfort to Dorna: Edwards was the highest-profile pioneer of the new sub-category, and Ezpeleta had spoken honeyed words at the launch of the team in 2011.

AMA veteran Steve Rapp was entered as a wild-card, for an effort more plucky than fruitful. His Kawasaki-powered CRT had a one-off chassis built by Richard Stanboli, owner of Attack Performance, and ready only just in time. The first free practice was its shakedown test, and while Rapp cut a full three seconds off his time from then until qualifying, he was still seven-tenths outside the 107 per cent cut, and he crossed the paddock to concentrate on his AMA Pro-Series duties, where he retired with a broken chain after six laps.

California's weather lived up to its reputation for the weekend, but even so smooth progress was still interrupted by bad conditions. Laguna's location a couple of miles inland from the cold Pacific shore often sees thick sea mist rolling in to settle among the scrub oaks in the morning, and on

Saturday it took an unusually long time to clear. The last free practice was delayed, but it was still too hazy for the factory Honda riders, who stayed in the pits, while several others only did a handful of laps.

Did this contribute to a handful of crashes? Certainly this was the case in morning warm-up, again delayed by mist, when both Bautista and Lorenzo tumbled at low speed at the last corner. Probably not on Friday afternoon, however, when Crutchlow took a fast crash on the right-hander after Rainey's; and when Bautista and Rossi had near-identical falls on Turn Three. Then Spies had a carbon-copy crash at the very same spot in qualifying, landing hard and thwarting his hopes for the front row. The blame was put on a slight bump at a crucial point, braking under lean – though in Rossi's case it was another example of the lack of front-end fidelity, which would recur on Sunday.

Crutchlow was lucky to escape with little more than a skinned thigh after his leathers split. He'd tried to match Pedrosa's speed, and it had been too much – a matter, he thought, of set-up. "When you go in the same speed as another rider, and you fall off and he doesn't, then something's obviously wrong," he said.

MOTOGP RACE – 32 laps

The first afternoon's practice saw a slew of crashes: Crutchlow at Turn Ten, plus Bautista and Rossi at Turn Three – the session red-flagged for a while because the latter's bike had deflated the air-fence. With the next morning misty, qualifying put extra emphasis on set-up and tyre selection. It didn't interfere with an all-action end.

Spies missed it after a heavy crash with 12 minutes to go, but team-mate Lorenzo seized control with a fastest ever motorcycle lap. Casey was stalking, however, and pounced with less than two minutes to go – only for Jorge to snatch it back after the flag.

Pedrosa was a quarter of a second adrift to complete the front row; Spies was still close, heading Crutchlow and Dovizioso; Hayden was on row three, and the thoroughly out-of-form Rossi one row back, barely three-tenths ahead of de Puniet on the top CRT bike.

Lorenzo got a fine start, and Pedrosa edged Stoner to third into the tight second corner. Tyre choice was interesting and ultimately vital for the winner. Most of the factory riders, and all those with serious rostrum ambitions, had gone for the harder rear tyre, except for Stoner. They feared fast drop-off in warm conditions; he decided to gamble, having had problems with the harder tyre at recent races, the down-side being "I knew I would have to be gentle. It wouldn't last if you were pushing and spinning all race."

He tailed the Spanish pair for two laps, then pounced on Pedrosa in Turn Three, to commence a long game of shadowing Lorenzo while nursing his tyres. Pedrosa was locked on close behind at first, but a big slide after one-third distance caused him to lose a second. He never recovered it and was two seconds adrift after another ten laps or so. "I tried to catch up, but I kept losing the front," he said. "I was lucky not to crash."

It was just about the two of them, and played out with maximum tension, if only one actual overtake. That came on lap 21, after Stoner had been pushing and probing closely for the previous two; it came not as a carbon copy of 2011, but as the mirror image. As before, Stoner got a stronger exit from the tight last corner, but this time he passed on the inside at Turn One, where in the previous year it had been an even bolder move around the outside.

The job was done, and although Lorenzo stayed close for the next three laps, as the end approached he dropped first one, then two and finally 3.4 seconds behind. The hard tyre had been the wrong choice. "Usually it comes better in the middle of the race, but today was the opposite," he said.

The next group was already almost a second behind from the first lap, with the gap growing steadily. The first gaggle of seven factory bikes soon broke into two groups, with Spies heading the front quartet from Dovizioso and Crutchlow (together again), and Bradl. They stayed close, order unchanged, for the first 15 laps.

Behind them, it took the first eight laps for Hayden and

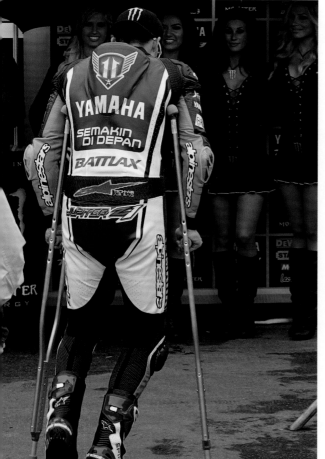

then Rossi to find a way past Bautista. Hayden had his head down and started working at once on a gap of two seconds to Bradl, and by lap 17 he was with him, even as the German lost touch with the Yamahas ahead of him.

At the same time, Spies had gathered some momentum, the gap to Dovi up to a second by half-distance and stretching. Fourth seemed safe. Until halfway through the Corkscrew on lap 21, when his bike collapsed beneath him.

This left the Tech 3 pair circulating in familiar close company, Crutchlow waiting for Dovi to make a mistake that never came. "He never put a foot wrong," said the Englishman, just two-tenths behind.

A growing distance further back, Hayden was with Bradl again, finally passing him with six laps to go in a brave move at Rainey Corner, and this time escaping to cross the line almost 1.5 seconds clear.

Rossi was circulating quite alone some way back. Then on lap 30, he found his misfortune, losing the front under braking for the Corkscrew. Crew chief Burgess blamed the crash on a lack of concentration, "because we haven't kept him motivated"; Rossi pointed to a front tyre that was hardly worn at all, showing it had never been up to temperature, a question of set-up or machine geometry.

Bautista was a distant eighth, but still well clear of top CRT finisher Espargaro. His usual adversaries, de Puniet and Pirro, tangled at Turn Two on the first lap: Pirro down and out, de Puniet running off to rejoin at the back, battling through to 11th one lap down, behind Abraham, back at last after his testing injury. Toni Elias, substituting for injured Barbera, was also involved, rejoining only to crash himself on lap two.

Three more CRTs trailed in, Hernandez and Silva straddling Edwards. Ellison crashed out; Petrucci and Pasini pitted.

Above: On top of the world and back on track after the German misadventure. But Stoner's season would soon take a nasty turn.

Left: Spies had a weekend to forget. Here he is on crutches after his practice spill.

Far left: Abraham (17) takes the Rossi line at the Corkscrew in his battle with Yonny Hernandez.

Photos: Gold & Goose

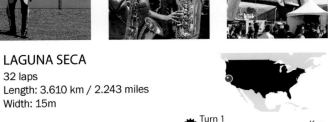

FIM WORLD CHAMPIONSHIP

ROUND 10

RED BULL
U.S.
GRAND PRIX

27–29 JULY, 2012

*moto*GP

TISSOT SWISS WATCHES SINCE 1853

OFFICIAL TIMEKEEPER

LAGUNA SECA
32 laps
Length: 3.610 km / 2.243 miles
Width: 15m

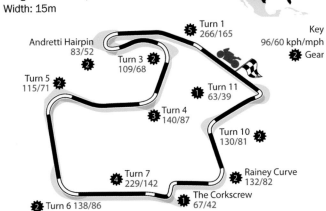

Turn 1 266/165
Andretti Hairpin 83/52
Turn 3 109/68
Turn 5 115/71
Turn 11 63/39
Turn 4 140/87
Turn 10 130/81
Turn 7 229/142
Rainey Curve 132/82
The Corkscrew 67/42
Turn 6 138/86

Key 96/60 kph/mph
Gear

Photos: Gold & Goose

MotoGP · RACE DISTANCE: 32 laps, 71.781 miles/115.520km · RACE WEATHER: Dry (air 18°C, humidity 65%, track 24°C)

Pos.	Rider	Nat.	No.	Entrant	Machine	Tyres	Race tyre choice	Laps	Time & speed
1	**Casey Stoner**	AUS	1	Repsol Honda Team	Honda RC213V	B	F: Hard/R: Soft	32	43m 45.961s 98.406mph/ 158.369km/h
2	Jorge Lorenzo	SPA	99	Yamaha Factory Racing	Yamaha YZR-M1	B	F: Hard/R: Medium	32	43m 49.390s
3	Dani Pedrosa	SPA	26	Repsol Honda Team	Honda RC213V	B	F: Hard/R: Medium	32	43m 53.594s
4	Andrea Dovizioso	ITA	4	Monster Yamaha Tech 3	Yamaha YZR-M1	B	F: Hard/R: Medium	32	44m 04.563s
5	Cal Crutchlow	GBR	35	Monster Yamaha Tech 3	Yamaha YZR-M1	B	F: Hard/R: Medium	32	44m 04.740s
6	Nicky Hayden	USA	69	Ducati Team	Ducati Desmosedici GP12	B	F: Hard/R: Soft	32	44m 12.863s
7	Stefan Bradl	GER	6	LCR Honda MotoGP	Honda RC213V	B	F: Hard/R: Soft	32	44m 14.354s
8	Alvaro Bautista	SPA	19	San Carlo Honda Gresini	Honda RC213V	B	F: Medium/R: Soft	32	44m 36.207s
9	Aleix Espargaro	SPA	41	Power Electronics Aspar	ART Aprilia RSV4	B	F: Hard/R: Soft	32	45m 04.954s
10	Karel Abraham	CZE	17	Cardion AB Motoracing	Ducati Desmosedici GP12	B	F: Hard/R: Soft	32	45m 08.037s
11	Randy de Puniet	FRA	14	Power Electronics Aspar	ART Aprilia RSV4	B	F: Hard/R: Soft	31	43m 47.392s
12	Yonny Hernandez	COL	68	Avintia Blusens	BQR FTR Kawasaki	B	F: Hard/R: Soft	31	43m 55.108s
13	Colin Edwards	USA	5	NGM Mobile Forward Racing	Suter BMW S1000RR	B	F: Hard/R: Medium	31	44m 17.426s
14	Ivan Silva	SPA	22	Avintia Blusens	BQR FTR Kawasaki	B	F: Hard/R: Soft	31	44m 20.627s
	Valentino Rossi	ITA	46	Ducati Team	Ducati Desmosedici GP12	B	F: Hard/R: Soft	29	DNF-crash
	Ben Spies	USA	11	Yamaha Factory Racing	Yamaha YZR-M1	B	F: Hard/R: Medium	21	DNF-crash
	James Ellison	GBR	77	Paul Bird Motorsport	ART Aprilia RSV4	B	F: Hard/R: Soft	19	DNF-crash
	Danilo Petrucci	ITA	9	Came Ioda Racing Project	Ioda Aprilia RSV4	B	F: Hard/R: Soft	18	DNF-handling
	Mattia Pasini	ITA	54	Speed Master	ART Aprilia RSV4	B	F: Hard/R: Soft	11	DNF-mechanical
	Toni Elias	SPA	24	Pramac Racing Team	Ducati Desmosedici GP12	B	F: Medium/R: Soft	1	DNF-crash
	Michele Pirro	ITA	51	San Carlo Honda Gresini	FTR Honda CBR1000RR	B	F: Hard/R: Soft	0	DNF-crash

Fastest lap: Dani Pedrosa, on lap 5, 1m 21.229s, 99.414mph/159.992km/h (record).

Previous lap record: Casey Stoner, AUS (Ducati), 1m 21.376s, 99.235mph/159.703km/h (2010).

Event best maximum speed: Cal Crutchlow, 166.7mph/268.3km/h (race).

Qualifying
Weather: Dry
Air Temp: 20° Humidity: 63%
Track Temp: 27°

1	Lorenzo	1m 20.554s
2	Stoner	1m 20.628s
3	Pedrosa	1m 20.906s
4	Spies	1m 21.094s
5	Crutchlow	1m 21.268s
6	Dovizioso	1m 21.539s
7	Bautista	1m 21.732s
8	Hayden	1m 21.734s
9	Bradl	1m 21.753s
10	Rossi	1m 22.544s
11	De Puniet	1m 22.886s
12	Espargaro	1m 23.075s
13	Edwards	1m 23.699s
14	Abraham	1m 23.704s
15	Hernandez	1m 23.769s
16	Pirro	1m 23.877s
17	Elias	1m 23.898s
18	Pasini	1m 24.017s
19	Petrucci	1m 24.227s
20	Silva	1m 24.560s
21	Ellison	1m 24.715s

Outside 107%
| | Rapp | 1m 26.887s |

Fastest race laps
1	Pedrosa	1m 21.229s
2	Lorenzo	1m 21.255s
3	Stoner	1m 21.282s
4	Spies	1m 21.753s
5	Bradl	1m 21.819s
6	Crutchlow	1m 21.914s
7	Dovizioso	1m 21.931s
8	Hayden	1m 21.996s
9	Rossi	1m 22.189s
10	Bautista	1m 22.391s
11	Espargaro	1m 23.514s
12	De Puniet	1m 23.640s
13	Abraham	1m 23.718s
14	Hernandez	1m 23.731s
15	Pasini	1m 24.132s
16	Ellison	1m 24.555s
17	Edwards	1m 24.587s
18	Silva	1m 24.678s
19	Petrucci	1m 25.033s

Championship Points
1	Lorenzo	205
2	Pedrosa	182
3	Stoner	173
4	Dovizioso	121
5	Crutchlow	106
6	Bradl	84
7	Hayden	84
8	Rossi	82
9	Bautista	81
10	Spies	66
11	Barbera	60
12	De Puniet	33
13	Espargaro	33
14	Pirro	16
15	Pasini	13
16	Ellison	12
17	Edwards	11
18	Abraham	10
19	Hernandez	10
20	Petrucci	9
21	Silva	7

Constructor Points
1	Honda	221
2	Yamaha	221
3	Ducati	106
4	ART	48
5	FTR	16
6	BQR	13
7	Suter	11
8	Ioda	9
9	BQR-FTR	2

Grid order

Grid order	1	2	3	4	5	6	7	8	9	10	11	12	13	14	15	16	17	18	19	20	21	22	23	24	25	26	27	28	29	30	31	32
99 LORENZO	99	99	99	99	99	99	99	99	99	99	99	99	99	99	99	99	99	99	99	99	99	1	1	1	1	1	1	1	1	1	1	1
1 STONER	26	26	1	1	1	1	1	1	1	1	1	1	1	1	1	1	1	1	1	1	1	99	99	99	99	99	99	99	99	99	99	2
26 PEDROSA	1	1	26	26	26	26	26	26	26	26	26	26	26	26	26	26	26	26	26	26	26	26	26	26	26	26	26	26	26	26	26	3
11 SPIES	11	11	11	11	11	11	11	11	11	11	11	11	11	11	11	11	11	11	11	11	11	4	4	4	4	4	4	4	4	4	4	4
35 CRUTCHLOW	4	4	4	4	4	4	4	4	4	4	4	4	4	4	4	4	4	4	4	4	4	35	35	35	35	35	35	35	35	35	35	5
4 DOVIZIOSO	35	35	35	35	35	35	35	35	35	35	35	35	35	35	35	35	35	35	35	35	35	6	6	6	6	69	69	69	69	69	69	6
19 BAUTISTA	6	6	6	6	6	6	6	6	6	6	6	6	6	6	6	6	6	6	6	6	6	69	69	69	69	6	6	6	6	6	6	7
69 HAYDEN	19	19	19	19	19	69	69	69	69	69	69	69	69	69	69	69	69	69	69	69	69	46	46	46	46	46	46	46	19	19	19	8
6 BRADL	69	69	69	69	69	46	46	46	46	46	46	46	46	46	46	46	46	46	46	46	46	19	19	19	19	19	19	19	41	41	41	9
46 ROSSI	46	46	46	46	46	19	19	19	19	19	19	19	19	19	19	19	19	19	19	19	19	41	41	41	41	41	41	41	17	17	17	10
14 DE PUNIET	41	41	41	41	41	41	41	41	41	41	41	41	41	41	41	41	41	41	41	41	41	17	17	17	17	17	17	17	14	14		11
41 ESPARGARO	68	68	68	68	68	68	68	68	68	68	68	68	68	68	68	68	17	17	68	14	14	14	14	14	14	14	68	68				12
5 EDWARDS	54	54	17	17	17	17	17	17	17	17	17	17	17	17	17	17	68	68	14	68	68	68	68	68	68	68	5	5				13
17 ABRAHAM	5	17	54	54	54	54	54	54	54	54	14	14	14	14	14	14	14	14	22	22	22	5	5	5	5	5	22	22				14
68 HERNANDEZ	17		5	77	77	77	14	14	14	14	14	54	77	77	77	77	77	77	5	5	5	22	22	22	22	22						
51 PIRRO	77	77		5	9	14	77	77	77	77	77	77	22	22	22	22	22	22	22	5	5											
24 ELIAS	22	9	9	5	5	5	5	22	22	22	22	5	5	5	5	5	5	5														
54 PASINI	9	22	22	14		9	22	22	5	5	5	9	9	9	9	9	9															
9 PETRUCCI	24	14	14	22	22		9	9	9	9	9																					
22 SILVA	14																															
77 ELLISON																																

22 Lapped rider

INDIANAPOLIS GRAND PRIX

INDIANAPOLIS CIRCUIT

Main photo: The 1000s give chase out of the first tight corner set, downtown Indianapolis a powerful backdrop.

Inset, left: Pedrosa was starting to hit top form.

Inset, centre left: Stoner's ride to fourth was quite simply heroic.

Inset, far left: Once again, Lorenzo had to settle for second to a Honda.

Photos: Gold & Goose

Above: Lorenzo swallowed his pride (or was it a wasp?) as he welcomed Rossi back to Yamaha for 2013.

Right: AMA Superbike champion Aaron Yates was in the unfamiliar role of back-marker …

Centre right: … But second wild-card entry Steve Rapp earned a championship point.

Centre far right: Spies was one of three high-profile victims of Turn 13 treachery. He emerged relatively unscathed.

Sequence, top right: The rise and fall of Nicky Hayden: the luckless local rider was out for the count, and out of the race.

Right: Stoner, in agony, still made Dovizioso work for the final podium place – his fifth so far.

Photos: Gold & Goose

THE attempts at conjunction (let's not call it marriage) between motorcycle grand prix and the USA have long been fraught with difficulty. They first tried at Daytona in the 1960s, a short-lived affair; Laguna has been more successful – re-emerging in spite of all kinds of troubles over the years, albeit now only as a single-class event.

Nobody could criticise the Indianapolis Motor Speedway's efforts nor the slick organisation, fantastic facilities and the unique atmosphere conferred by the vast surrounding banked oval. But the race was born under a bad sign – the inaugural event of 2008 hit by Hurricane Ike. The gremlins have remained.

The little-used 2.62-mile circuit had earned plenty of criticism – for bumps and a lack of grip. For 2011's race, IMS had resurfaced the track from Turns Five to Sixteen in response. But the legacy remained, and in 2012 riders once more complained from the start of bad grip all the way around the underused infield circuit, and again of inconsistency. Three different surfaces are encountered on a lap: the old from Turns One to Four, the new thereafter, and the section of the actual Brickyard oval past the pits.

Just to make things worse, torrential rain the night before the meeting cleaned off any rubber that might have helped. The passage of all three classes through practice served to lay down some grip, at least on the line; but stray off the line, for whatever reason, and you were on eggshells.

And in some very costly cases, riders were caught out even without having strayed.

It was no less expensive or painful for Moto3 riders Danny Webb, Jack Miller and Hector Faubel, all ruled out by injuries in qualifying, but incidents in MotoGP qualifying took a much higher profile. Three top riders had massive high-siders at the same corner set during qualifying – the last double lefts before the slow right-left on to the front straight.

The first was the most sensational, for all sorts of reasons: Stoner, working to keep his title challenge alive, had just completed his third lap, topping the time sheets, when his back wheel stepped out. It was much too fast to save, and he was launched high and landed hard. His bike also: the back tyre off and the wheel smashed. Stoner tried to stand, but went down again. "As soon as I stood up, I saw my foot was at a strange angle. I had a shooting pain, then I felt a crack as my ankle popped back in." He was stretchered away to be diagnosed with chipped bone, a small fracture and ligament damage. Amazingly, his foot in an over-size boot to hold his ankle rigid (unable as a result to use the rear brake), he came back next day to race. Less than a week later, he withdrew from Brno for surgery.

Next down was Spies, going for the front row, in much the same way though a little earlier on the corner. He was luckier, coming away with a bashed shoulder.

Then it was homeboy Nicky Hayden's turn, a little further around the same bend, but with equal force and violence. It left him briefly unconscious, with fractures in his right hand – out of this race and the next.

The day before, in first free practice, there had been an-

other: Barbera, essaying an early return after the leg fractures sustained motocrossing following the Italian GP. He was among a group going into the last corner, lost the rear on the entry and landed badly from the subsequent high-side. Although his pinned and plated leg survived, he sustained fractures to three dorsal vertebrae, another victim of the treacherous circuit.

There are two more years to run at Indianapolis, the MotoGP contract having been extended to 2014. With an at the time still nebulous threat from the Circuit of the Americas in Texas and Laguna signed up until the same date, it will be interesting to see if Indy gives the infield circuit the full new surface it clearly needs so badly.

Spies may have thought after crashing that his bad luck was over for the weekend. Not so. The toolbox devil was still on duty. He led the first two laps. Then, as Pedrosa powered past starting the third, he felt something wasn't right. "As soon as he passed, I started slowing a bit." Three laps later, he found out why, with a massively smoky top-end blow-up just before peeling into the first corner.

The weekend opened with the five-day-old news that Rossi was to return to Yamaha for 2013 – greeted with little surprise and (in the absence of senior Yamaha personnel) plentiful speculation. The Italian spoke of "wanting to find out if I can still be a top rider", while Lorenzo dutifully said it would "strengthen Yamaha's position", adding that he didn't mind who his team-mate was. As if.

In the absence of anything fresh, some press-men had re-run selected adverse Rossi-Ducati comments hand-picked from Stoner interviews over the previous two years. Stoner was somewhat aggrieved, owning up to the comments, but pointing out that they had been taken out of context.

Following on came the news that Ducati was close to agreement with Dovizioso. This triggered an outburst from Crutchlow, who felt he'd been led a long way up the garden path by the Italian company. He'd only had definite word days before, and it had been negative.

Steve Rapp was back on the Attack Kawasaki, qualifying this time and promoted to 15th in the race when Ellison was penalised for cutting the course. At 40, he became the oldest American ever to have scored a premier-class point. Aaron Yates (38) was a second wild-card, making his race debut on a Suzuki-powered BCL chassis for GP Tech. He too qualified, and finished last.

GP winner Jonas Folger's up-and-down progress got a boost, rescued from the troubled Ioda Moto3 team to replace Moncayo in the top-grade Aspar team. He was straight on to the rostrum.

MOTOGP RACE – 28 laps

Stoner led free practice, but eliminated himself early after laying down a qualifying time. By the end of a fraught session, five riders had gone faster, with Pedrosa snitching pole from Lorenzo by a tenth; Dovizioso completed the first row; Spies and Bradl headed the world champion on the second. Crutchlow led the third from the now absent Hayden.

Pedrosa led away, but Spies pushed past on the first lap. Dovizioso and Lorenzo were next; Stoner was a cautious seventh behind Bradl and Bautista, Crutchlow and Rossi behind.

Lorenzo made short work of Dovi and set off after the leaders, now 1.3 seconds clear. He would never make an impression on the gap.

As they started the third lap, Pedrosa powered past Spies, and over the next three the Yamaha gradually lost ground. He was 1.6 seconds behind when his engine blew. Lorenzo, a couple of tenths further back, then Dovizioso, Bradl, Stoner, Bautista and Crutchlow in a gang had a terrifying ride into a thick pall of smoke, with no idea of what was on the other side, but Spies had managed to pull off to the side of the track on Turn One without laying down oil or being hit.

His return to the pits saw a major tantrum, behind closed doors, and Spies would say he couldn't wait to leave MotoGP for somewhere where "I can enjoy racing". The departure plan lasted less than a week.

Pedrosa had missed it all and Lorenzo didn't have time to shut off, which doubled their advantage – now up to eight seconds. That settled that for first and second, Pedrosa relentlessly pulling away with one fast lap after another – a new record on lap 15, by which time Lorenzo was four seconds down. The margin of victory was a yawning ten seconds.

Third was very much under dispute. Dovi narrowly led while Bradl got past Stoner again for a couple of laps. On the ninth, Stoner was back and about to pass Dovi. Bradl, Bautista and Crutchlow were inches behind, third to seventh covered by just over one second over the line.

Then Crutchlow slipped off, on the low side. "A silly crash." And his first of the year in a race.

Above: Brave ride: Stoner leads Bradl, Bautista and Crutchlow around the infield section.

Top right: Aegerter (77) grabs a short-lived lead from Iannone (29) and Espargaro (40). Marquez (93) looms on the right, with Redding (45) at his shoulder.

Above right: Another crash that mattered. Vinales dropped it in the last corner set while fighting for Moto3 victory, a major blow to his title chances.

Above far right: If no-one was watching, would Salom still have won? He was inches ahead of Cortese in front of the empty grandstands.

Below right: A welcome return to the front for injury-stricken Julian Simon in Moto2.

Photos: Gold & Goose

The remaining quartet were still almost as close at half-distance, but with Stoner now heading the pack it would start to stretch, only Dovizioso able to stay with the injured champion. It was about now, however, that "the painkillers gradually wore off at the halfway point. As I was compensating for the injury with the other side of my body, I had no energy left." Dovizioso could see how awkwardly he was riding ("His style was completely different.") and drafted past at the start of lap 22. Casey stayed close for a while, but crossed the line 2.5 seconds adrift, after a heroic ride. "Only Casey could make that race," said a respectful Dovi. Bautista hung on behind, another two seconds down; but Bradl had dropped away steadily, blaming difficulty in putting the power down in the slow corners.

Rossi had a doleful afternoon, admitting afterwards – perhaps for the first time in racing – that "I gave up". He'd been behind Crutchlow on the first lap and watched the whole gang disappear in front of him at a second a lap, until by the eighth he was ten seconds adrift and cruising home alone. At least he had the pace to outdistance the CRT gang.

Their numbers had been depleted early on. Pasini crashed on the first lap, Petrucci pitted his sick Aprilia at the end of it; Pirro his Honda one lap later.

There were still three hard at it in the early stages: Espargaro, the increasingly noticeable and always spectacular Hernandez, and de Puniet. The Frenchman ran into engine problems and had dropped back by the time he pitted after eight laps.

The other two stayed engaged, Hernandez leading again as Abraham turned up on a late surge. The Ducati was a couple of seconds clear at the end; Hernandez was three ahead of Espargaro.

The remainder straggled home dutifully. Elias had taken over Barbera's bike and had a lonely afternoon, Silva a long way behind.

The rest were a lap down, Edwards also lonely after disappointment at having to ride the Suter BMW again. Ellison was next on track, but was deprived of the final point in favour of Rapp, having cut the course after running wide. Yates was miles behind.

MOTO2 RACE – 26 laps

Espargaro was on pole, but Marquez was close and then Iannone. The title leader had spent part of a break, which for the smaller classes had been five weeks long, testing the latest Suter chassis. Simon led the second row from Aegerter and Redding. Luthi was ninth, on the far end of row three.

This time, they all made it through the tight early corners unscathed, and by the end of lap one Espargaro was leading. But Dominique Aegerter, often fast in the first few laps, had the bit between his teeth, taking over up front for the next two laps and even gaining a gap of a full second.

It wouldn't last, and Marquez was ahead on the fourth, followed two laps later by Iannone. By then, the leader had set a pair of record-speed laps and was pulling away steadily. By half-distance, the gap was approaching five seconds; it was better than seven as he started the last lap, able to cruise home for his fifth win of the year, further boosting his title lead. He had broken the record again for the last time on lap 12.

At this point, Aegerter had a moment, dropping to seventh in a close gang. Now Espargaro was third and chewing at Iannone's heels, closely followed by Simon, Kallio and Luthi.

One lap later, Iannone would have the first of a series of slides that would see him slip down to an eventual ninth.

Espargaro later complained of chatter. "I realised I couldn't catch Marc; I was never comfortable." Simon dropped back a bit, then closed again to harry him. From lap 20, however, he fell away, finishing some three seconds adrift, but on the rostrum for the first time since his ruinous crash at Catalunya in 2011. It was by far his best result of the year so far, and a long awaited return of some good fortune instead of bad.

With eight laps left, Luthi and Kallio had escaped from the next group, now led by Corsi from Aegerter and Redding. There was still some sorting out to be done.

Ahead, the Swiss and the Finn were all over each other, Kallio gaining the upper hand with four laps to go and hanging on by the skin of his teeth.

On lap 20, Redding took seventh off Aegerter and set about Corsi, passing him also on the exit of Turn Two next

time around. Five seconds behind them, Aegerter did the same to Corsi as they crossed the line for the last time, almost side by side.

A short way behind, Iannone managed to stay half a second clear of the battling Corti, Rabat and Zarco, whose 2011 125 rival Terol was three seconds behind.

Rosell crashed out on lap eight, followed by Andreozzi, and then Simeon and de Angelis, down together. Class rookie Schrotter, recently departed from Mahindra's Moto3 time, was a debut 23rd.

MOTO3 RACE – 23 laps

It was a race of several crashes, including one that really mattered. Pre-season favourite Vinales, going for the win in the last corners, instead crashed out for zero points, while first-time winner Salom took advantage of the confusion.

Cortese was on pole from thrusting team-mate Kent; Vinales was alongside, with Salom heading row two from Khairuddin and Rins.

Kent led away from Salom, the Spaniard taking over at Turn Two on the second lap. But it was Khairuddin in front by the end of that lap and the next. Rins took over for two more,

then the Malaysian was back up front again until Vinales took over on lap ten.

At this stage, there were still nine riders within two seconds, Folger at the back; Cortese working his way through.

Vazquez crashed out of the chase group as Vinales tried to escape, gaining nine-tenths over two laps. But now Cortese moved to second, and he and Salom closed up again.

With four laps to go, Vinales, Cortese and Salom were together; Fenati, Oliveira and Folger disputing fourth.

Cortese drafted past Vinales as they started the last lap. The Spaniard fought back at once, but Cortese held the line. Vinales' next try at the end of the back straight instead handed a chance to Salom, who took the lead. As he sped to victory, Vinales slipped off in the last corner set, unable to restart.

Folger narrowly held third from Oliveira and Fenati; Khairuddin was another four seconds away, fending off Rins over the line.

A temper flair-up in the same class put Niklas Ajo in the dog-box. He had been knocked off on the first lap by Adrian Martin, along with Iwema and Antonelli. He got to his feet and took a swing at his assailant, was excluded from the race and banned from the next one as well.

FIM WORLD CHAMPIONSHIP

ROUND 11

17–19 AUGUST, 2012

motoGP | TISSOT SWISS WATCHES SINCE 1853

OFFICIAL TIMEKEEPER

RED BULL
INDIANAPOLIS GRAND PRIX

INDIANAPOLIS MOTOR SPEEDWAY

28 laps
Length: 4.216 km / 2.620 miles
Width: 16m

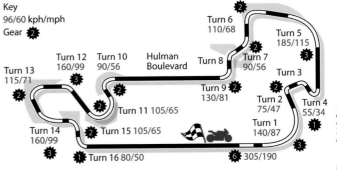

Key
96/60 kph/mph
Gear

Turn 6 110/68
Turn 5 185/115
Turn 12 160/99
Turn 10 90/56
Hulman Boulevard
Turn 8
Turn 7 90/56
Turn 13 115/71
Turn 3
Turn 9 130/81
Turn 2 75/47
Turn 4 55/34
Turn 11 105/65
Turn 1 140/87
Turn 14 160/99
Turn 15 105/65
Turn 16 80/50
305/190

Photos: Gold & Goose

MotoGP | RACE DISTANCE: 28 laps, 73.352 miles/118.048km · RACE WEATHER: Dry (air 25°C, humidity 36%, track 39°C)

Pos.	Rider	Nat.	No.	Entrant	Machine	Tyres	Race tyre choice	Laps	Time & speed
1	**Dani Pedrosa**	SPA	26	Repsol Honda Team	Honda RC213V	B	F: Ex-Hard/R: Hard	28	46m 39.631s 94.322mph/ 151.796km/h
2	Jorge Lorenzo	SPA	99	Yamaha Factory Racing	Yamaha YZR-M1	B	F: Ex-Hard/R: Medium	28	46m 50.454s
3	Andrea Dovizioso	ITA	4	Monster Yamaha Tech 3	Yamaha YZR-M1	B	F: Ex-Hard/R: Hard	28	46m 56.941s
4	Casey Stoner	AUS	1	Repsol Honda Team	Honda RC213V	B	F: Ex-Hard/R: Hard	28	46m 59.434s
5	Alvaro Bautista	SPA	19	San Carlo Honda Gresini	Honda RC213V	B	F: Ex-Hard/R: Hard	28	47m 02.187s
6	Stefan Bradl	GER	6	LCR Honda MotoGP	Honda RC213V	B	F: Ex-Hard/R: Hard	28	47m 09.703s
7	Valentino Rossi	ITA	46	Ducati Team	Ducati Desmosedici GP12	B	F: Ex-Hard/R: Hard	28	47m 37.245s
8	Karel Abraham	CZE	17	Cardion AB Motoracing	Ducati Desmosedici GP12	B	F: Ex-Hard/R: Hard	28	47m 48.073s
9	Yonny Hernandez	COL	68	Avintia Blusens	BQR FTR Kawasaki	B	F: Ex-Hard/R: Medium	28	47m 50.737s
10	Aleix Espargaro	SPA	41	Power Electronics Aspar	ART Aprilia RSV4	B	F: Ex-Hard/R: Medium	28	47m 53.710s
11	Toni Elias	SPA	24	Pramac Racing Team	Ducati Desmosedici GP12	B	F: Ex-Hard/R: Medium	28	48m 05.936s
12	Ivan Silva	SPA	22	Avintia Blusens	BQR FTR Kawasaki	B	F: Ex-Hard/R: Medium	28	48m 19.905s
13	Colin Edwards	USA	5	NGM Mobile Forward Racing	Suter BMW S1000RR	B	F: Ex-Hard/R: Hard	27	46m 46.893s
14	Steve Rapp	USA	15	Attack Performance	APR Kawasaki	B	F: Ex-Hard/R: Hard	27	47m 00.909s
15	James Ellison*	GBR	77	Paul Bird Motorsport	ART Aprilia RSV4	B	F: Ex-Hard/R: Medium	27	46m 55.629s
16	Aaron Yates	USA	20	GPTech	BCL Suzuki	B	F: Ex-Hard/R: Hard	27	47m 54.994s
	Cal Crutchlow	GBR	35	Monster Yamaha Tech 3	Yamaha YZR-M1	B	F: Ex-Hard/R: Hard	9	DNF
	Randy de Puniet	FRA	14	Power Electronics Aspar	ART Aprilia RSV4	B	F: Ex-Hard/R: Medium	8	DNF
	Ben Spies	USA	11	Yamaha Factory Racing	Yamaha YZR-M1	B	F: Ex-Hard/R: Hard	6	DNF
	Michele Pirro	ITA	51	San Carlo Honda Gresini	FTR Honda CBR1000RR	B	F: Ex-Hard/R: Medium	1	DNF
	Mattia Pasini	ITA	54	Speed Master	ART Aprilia RSV4	B	F: Ex-Hard/R: Medium	0	DNF
	Danilo Petrucci	ITA	9	Came IodaRacing Project	Ioda Aprilia RSV4	B	F: Ex-Hard/R: Medium	0	DNF
	Nicky Hayden	USA	69	Ducati Team	Ducati Desmosedici GP12	B	F: /R:	0	DNS

*Ellison was demoted one position by Race Direction for shortcutting the track.
Fastest lap: Dani Pedrosa, on lap 15, 1m 39.088s, 95.177mph/153.172km/h (record).
Previous lap record: Casey Stoner, AUS (Honda), 1m 39.807s, 94.491mph/152.069km/h (2011).
Event best maximum speed: Dani Pedrosa, 208.6mph/335.7km/h (free practice 2).

Qualifying

Weather: Dry
Air Temp: 24° Humidity: 39%
Track Temp: 48°

1	Pedrosa	1m 38.813s
2	Lorenzo	1m 38.913s
3	Dovizioso	1m 39.235s
4	Spies	1m 39.279s
5	Bradl	1m 39.437s
6	Stoner	1m 39.465s
7	Crutchlow	1m 39.549s
8	Hayden	1m 39.748s
9	Bautista	1m 40.072s
10	De Puniet	1m 40.437s
11	Rossi	1m 40.763s
12	Espargaro	1m 40.803s
13	Hernandez	1m 41.197s
14	Abraham	1m 41.295s
15	Pasini	1m 41.370s
16	Pirro	1m 41.449s
17	Elias	1m 41.866s
18	Ellison	1m 41.978s
19	Petrucci	1m 42.553s
20	Edwards	1m 42.599s
21	Silva	1m 42.768s
22	Rapp	1m 43.673s
23	Yates	1m 44.312s

Fastest race laps

1	Pedrosa	1m 39.088s
2	Spies	1m 39.289s
3	Lorenzo	1m 39.452s
4	Dovizioso	1m 39.729s
5	Stoner	1m 39.785s
6	Bautista	1m 39.827s
7	Crutchlow	1m 39.966s
8	Bradl	1m 40.036s
9	Rossi	1m 40.639s
10	Ellison	1m 40.831s
11	Espargaro	1m 41.133s
12	Hernandez	1m 41.311s
13	Abraham	1m 41.339s
14	De Puniet	1m 41.411s
15	Elias	1m 42.273s
16	Silva	1m 42.506s
17	Edwards	1m 42.725s
18	Rapp	1m 43.123s
19	Yates	1m 45.104s

Championship Points

1	Lorenzo	225
2	Pedrosa	207
3	Stoner	186
4	Dovizioso	137
5	Crutchlow	106
6	Bradl	94
7	Bautista	92
8	Rossi	91
9	Hayden	84
10	Spies	66
11	Barbera	60
12	Espargaro	39
13	De Puniet	33
14	Abraham	18
15	Hernandez	17
16	Pirro	16
17	Edwards	14
18	Pasini	13
19	Ellison	13
20	Silva	11
21	Petrucci	9
22	Elias	5
23	Rapp	2

Constructor Points

1	Honda	246
2	Yamaha	241
3	Ducati	115
4	ART	54
5	BQR	20
6	FTR	16
7	Suter	14
8	Ioda	9
9	APR	2
10	BQR-FTR	2

Grid order

Grid order	1	2	3	4	5	6	7	8	9	10	11	12	13	14	15	16	17	18	19	20	21	22	23	24	25	26	27	28	
26 PEDROSA	11	11	26	26	26	26	26	26	26	26	26	26	26	26	26	26	26	26	26	26	26	26	26	26	26	26	26	26	1
99 LORENZO	26	26	11	11	11	11	99	99	99	99	99	99	99	99	99	99	99	99	99	99	99	99	99	99	99	99	99	99	2
4 DOVIZIOSO	4	99	99	99	99	99	4	4	4	1	1	1	1	1	1	1	1	1	1	4	4	4	4	4	4	4	4	4	3
11 SPIES	99	4	4	4	4	4	6	1	4	4	4	4	4	4	4	4	4	4	4	1	1	1	1	1	1	1	1	1	4
6 BRADL	6	6	6	6	6	1	1	6	1	19	19	19	19	19	19	19	19	19	19	19	19	19	19	19	19	19	19	19	5
1 STONER	19	19	19	1	1	6	19	19	19	19	6	6	6	6	6	6	6	6	6	6	6	6	6	6	6	6	6	6	6
35 CRUTCHLOW	1	1	1	19	19	19	35	35	35	46	46	46	46	46	46	46	46	46	46	46	46	46	46	46	46	46	46	46	7
19 BAUTISTA	35	35	35	35	35	35	46	46	46	68	68	41	41	41	41	68	68	68	17	17	17	17	17	17	17	17	17	17	8
14 DE PUNIET	46	46	46	46	46	46	41	41	41	41	41	68	68	68	68	41	41	17	68	68	68	68	68	68	41	68	68		9
46 ROSSI	41	41	68	68	68	41	68	68	68	17	17	17	17	17	17	17	41	41	41	41	41	41	41	68	41	41			10
41 ESPARGARO	68	68	41	41	41	68	14	14	17	24	24	24	24	24	24	24	24	24	24	24	24	24	24	24	24	24			11
68 HERNANDEZ	14	14	14	14	14	14	17	17	24	22	22	22	22	22	22	22	22	22	22	22	22	22	22	22	22	22			12
17 ABRAHAM	24	24	24	24	24	24	24	24	22	5	5	5	5	5	5	5	5	5	5	5	5	5	5	5	5				13
54 PASINI	77	17	17	17	17	17	5	22	15	15	15	15	15	15	15	15	15	15	15	15	15	15	15	77	77				14
51 PIRRO	51	77	5	5	5	22	5	5	77	77	77	77	77	77	77	77	77	77	77	77	77	77	77	15	15				15
24 ELIAS	17	5	15	15	22	22	15	15	77	20	20	20	20	20	20	20	20	20	20	20	20	20	20						
77 ELLISON	15	15	22	22	15	15	77	77	20																				
9 PETRUCCI	5	22	20	20	20	20	20	20																					
5 EDWARDS	22	20	77	77	77	77																							
22 SILVA	20																												
15 RAPP																													
20 YATES																													

20 Lapped rider

Moto2 RACE DISTANCE: 26 laps, 68.112 miles/109.616km · RACE WEATHER: Dry (air 26°C, humidity 34%, track 42°C)

Pos.	Rider	Nat.	No.	Entrant	Machine	Laps	Time & Speed
1	**Marc Marquez**	SPA	93	Team CatalunyaCaixa Repsol	Suter	26	45m 13.763s 90.355mph/ 145.413km/h
2	**Pol Espargaro**	SPA	40	Pons 40 HP Tuenti	Kalex	26	45m 19.618s
3	**Julian Simon**	SPA	60	Blusens Avintia	Suter	26	45m 23.157s
4	**Mika Kallio**	FIN	36	Marc VDS Racing Team	Kalex	26	45m 29.312s
5	**Thomas Luthi**	SWI	12	Interwetten-Paddock	Suter	26	45m 29.901s
6	**Scott Redding**	GBR	45	Marc VDS Racing Team	Kalex	26	45m 30.568s
7	**Dominique Aegerter**	SWI	77	Technomag-CIP	Suter	26	45m 35.122s
8	**Simone Corsi**	ITA	3	Came IodaRacing Project	FTR	26	45m 35.131s
9	**Andrea Iannone**	ITA	29	Speed Master	Speed Up	26	45m 39.636s
10	**Claudio Corti**	ITA	71	Italtrans Racing Team	Kalex	26	45m 40.234s
11	**Esteve Rabat**	SPA	80	Pons 40 HP Tuenti	Kalex	26	45m 40.679s
12	**Johann Zarco**	FRA	5	JIR Moto2	Motobi	26	45m 41.037s
13	**Nicolas Terol**	SPA	18	Mapfre Aspar Team Moto2	Suter	26	45m 44.885s
14	**Anthony West**	AUS	95	QMMF Racing Team	Speed Up	26	45m 49.464s
15	**Ricard Cardus**	SPA	88	Arguinano Racing Team	AJR	26	45m 49.691s
16	Bradley Smith	GBR	38	Tech 3 Racing	Tech 3	26	45m 53.003s
17	Takaaki Nakagami	JPN	30	Italtrans Racing Team	Kalex	26	45m 56.270s
18	Randy Krummenacher	SWI	4	GP Team Switzerland	Kalex	26	45m 59.392s
19	Jordi Torres	SPA	81	Mapfre Aspar Team Moto2	Suter	26	45m 59.516s
20	Gino Rea	GBR	8	Federal Oil Gresini Moto2	Suter	26	46m 05.330s
21	Max Neukirchner	GER	76	Kiefer Racing	Kalex	26	46m 05.869s
22	Axel Pons	SPA	49	Pons 40 HP Tuenti	Kalex	26	46m 09.913s
23	Marcel Schrotter	GER	23	Desguaces La Torre SAG	Bimota	26	46m 24.832s
24	Ratthapark Wilairot	THA	14	Thai Honda PTT Gresini Moto2	Suter	26	46m 25.528s
25	Mike di Meglio	FRA	63	MZ Racing	MZ-RE Honda	26	46m 33.805s
26	Eric Granado	BRA	57	JIR Moto2	Motobi	26	46m 56.687s
27	Marco Colandrea	SWI	10	SAG Team	FTR	26	46m 56.947s
28	Yuki Takahashi	JPN	72	NGM Mobile Forward Racing	FTR	23	46m 16.045s
	Roberto Rolfo	ITA	44	Technomag-CIP	Suter	20	DNF
	Xavier Simeon	BEL	19	Tech 3 Racing	Tech 3	17	DNF
	Alex de Angelis	RSM	15	NGM Mobile Forward Racing	FTR	17	DNF
	Alessandro Andreozzi	ITA	22	S/Master Speed Up	Speed Up	10	DNF
	Elena Rosell	SPA	82	QMMF Racing Team	Moriwaki	7	DNF

Fastest lap: Marc Marquez, on lap 12, 1m 43.304s, 91.292mph/146.921km/h (record).
Previous lap record: Andrea Iannone, ITA (Suter), 1m 44.329s, 90.396mph/145.478km/h (2011).
Event best maximum speed: Pol Espargaro, 178.5mph/287.2km/h (race).

Qualifying: Dry
Air: 24° Humidity: 39% Track: 49°

1	Espargaro	1m 42.602s
2	Marquez	1m 42.833s
3	Iannone	1m 43.064s
4	Simon	1m 43.363s
5	Aegerter	1m 43.468s
6	Redding	1m 43.548s
7	Corti	1m 43.607s
8	Kallio	1m 43.637s
9	Luthi	1m 43.646s
10	Terol	1m 43.684s
11	Nakagami	1m 43.698s
12	Corsi	1m 43.753s
13	Zarco	1m 43.979s
14	Smith	1m 44.061s
15	Rabat	1m 44.063s
16	De Angelis	1m 44.078s
17	Cardus	1m 44.117s
18	Simeon	1m 44.291s
19	Rea	1m 44.457s
20	Di Meglio	1m 44.531s
21	Takahashi	1m 44.543s
22	Rolfo	1m 44.555s
23	Torres	1m 44.656s
24	West	1m 44.686s
25	Wilairot	1m 45.002s
26	Krummenacher	1m 45.139s
27	Pons	1m 45.217s
28	Neukirchner	1m 45.222s
29	Schrotter	1m 45.935s
30	Andreozzi	1m 46.238s
31	Granado	1m 46.521s
32	Colandrea	1m 46.721s
33	Rosell	1m 47.869s

Fastest race laps

1	Marquez	1m 43.304s
2	Redding	1m 43.706s
3	Corsi	1m 43.711s
4	Espargaro	1m 43.775s
5	Luthi	1m 43.883s
6	Simon	1m 43.903s
7	Aegerter	1m 44.022s
8	Rabat	1m 44.076s
9	Kallio	1m 44.095s
10	Zarco	1m 44.120s
11	Corti	1m 44.157s
12	Cardus	1m 44.176s
13	Nakagami	1m 44.197s
14	Iannone	1m 44.214s
15	West	1m 44.244s
16	Terol	1m 44.268s
17	Simeon	1m 44.428s
18	De Angelis	1m 44.488s
19	Smith	1m 44.538s
20	Wilairot	1m 44.651s
21	Krummenacher	1m 44.859s
22	Rea	1m 44.896s
23	Torres	1m 44.963s
24	Pons	1m 45.057s
25	Neukirchner	1m 45.130s
26	Di Meglio	1m 45.411s
27	Schrotter	1m 45.705s
28	Rolfo	1m 45.797s
29	Takahashi	1m 45.971s
30	Andreozzi	1m 46.016s
31	Colandrea	1m 47.115s
32	Granado	1m 47.141s
33	Rosell	1m 48.250s

Championship Points

1	Marquez	188
2	Espargaro	149
3	Iannone	136
4	Luthi	134
5	Redding	106
6	Kallio	90
7	Smith	69
8	Corti	65
9	Aegerter	61
10	Rabat	56
11	Zarco	51
12	De Angelis	48
13	Corsi	48
14	Nakagami	36
15	Elias	34
16	Simon	33
17	Krummenacher	24
18	Simeon	17
19	West	11
20	Terol	11
21	Di Meglio	10
22	Neukirchner	8
23	Wilairot	8
24	Cardus	6
25	Rea	1

Constructor Points

1	Suter	222
2	Kalex	195
3	Speed Up	136
4	Tech 3	69
5	FTR	65
6	Motobi	51
7	Moriwaki	10
8	AJR	6

Moto3 RACE DISTANCE: 23 laps, 60.253 miles/96.968km · RACE WEATHER: Dry (air 25°C, humidity 41%, track 33°C)

Pos.	Rider	Nat.	No.	Entrant	Machine	Laps	Time & Speed
1	**Luis Salom**	SPA	39	RW Racing GP	Kalex KTM	23	42m 14.300s 85.590mph/ 137.744km/h
2	**Sandro Cortese**	GER	11	Red Bull KTM Ajo	KTM	23	42m 14.356s
3	**Jonas Folger**	GER	94	Mapfre Aspar Team Moto3	Kalex KTM	23	42m 17.240s
4	**Miguel Oliveira**	POR	44	Estrella Galicia 0,0	Suter Honda	23	42m 17.367s
5	**Romano Fenati**	ITA	5	Team Italia FMI	FTR Honda	23	42m 17.964s
6	**Zulfahmi Khairuddin**	MAL	63	AirAsia-Sic-Ajo	KTM	23	42m 21.963s
7	**Alex Rins**	SPA	42	Estrella Galicia 0,0	Suter Honda	23	42m 21.997s
8	**Jakub Kornfeil**	CZE	84	Redox-Ongetta-Centro Seta	FTR Honda	23	42m 25.503s
9	**Alberto Moncayo**	SPA	23	Andalucia JHK Laglisse	FTR Honda	23	42m 25.542s
10	**Alexis Masbou**	FRA	10	Caretta Technology	Honda	23	42m 27.463s
11	**Arthur Sissis**	AUS	61	Red Bull KTM Ajo	KTM	23	42m 37.662s
12	**Danny Kent**	GBR	52	Red Bull KTM Ajo	KTM	23	42m 38.664s
13	**Louis Rossi**	FRA	96	Racing Team Germany	FTR Honda	23	42m 39.301s
14	**Isaac Vinales**	SPA	32	Ongetta-Centro Seta	FTR Honda	23	42m 45.511s
15	**Alessandro Tonucci**	ITA	19	Team Italia FMI	FTR Honda	23	42m 48.479s
16	Toni Finsterbusch	GER	9	MZ Racing	Honda	23	43m 27.245s
17	Giulian Pedone	SWI	30	Ambrogio Next Racing	Suter Honda	23	43m 28.728s
18	Kenta Fujii	JPN	51	Technomag-CIP-TSR	TSR Honda	23	43m 29.009s
19	Armando Pontone	ITA	80	IodaRacing Project	Ioda	23	43m 29.626s
20	Riccardo Moretti	ITA	20	Mahindra Racing	Mahindra	22	42m 25.646s
	Maverick Vinales	SPA	25	Blusens Avintia	FTR Honda	22	DNF
	Alan Techer	FRA	89	Technomag-CIP-TSR	TSR Honda	15	DNF
	Efren Vazquez	SPA	7	JHK t-shirt Laglisse	FTR Honda	11	DNF
	Luigi Morciano	ITA	3	Ioda Team Italia	Ioda	10	DNF
	Alex Marquez	SPA	12	Ambrogio Next Racing	Suter Honda	6	DNF
	Brad Binder	RSA	41	RW Racing GP	Kalex KTM	3	DNF
	Adrian Martin	SPA	26	JHK t-shirt Laglisse	FTR Honda	0	DNF
	Jasper Iwema	NED	53	Moto FGR	FGR Honda	0	DNF
	Niccolo Antonelli	ITA	27	San Carlo Gresini Moto3	FTR Honda	0	DNF
	Niklas Ajo	FIN	31	TT Motion Events Racing	KTM		DSQ

Fastest lap: Romano Fenati, on lap 4, 1m 48.648s, 86.802mph/139.695km/h (record).
Previous lap record: New category.
Event best maximum speed: Sandro Cortese, 144.2mph/232.1km/h (race).

Qualifying: Dry
Air: 24° Humidity: 39% Track: 43°

1	Cortese	1m 48.545s
2	Kent	1m 48.628s
3	M. Vinales	1m 48.643s
4	Salom	1m 48.990s
5	Khairuddin	1m 49.024s
6	Rins	1m 49.045s
7	Vazquez	1m 49.074s
8	Fenati	1m 49.324s
9	Moncayo	1m 49.332s
10	Kornfeil	1m 49.334s
11	Oliveira	1m 49.397s
12	Masbou	1m 49.492s
13	Tonucci	1m 49.605s
14	Rossi	1m 49.610s
15	Folger	1m 49.656s
16	I. Vinales	1m 49.797s
17	Binder	1m 49.986s
18	Miller	1m 50.056s
19	Techer	1m 50.066s
20	Marquez	1m 50.184s
21	Martin	1m 50.249s
22	Iwema	1m 50.336s
23	Sissis	1m 50.412s
24	Ajo	1m 50.443s
25	Antonelli	1m 50.483s
26	Morciano	1m 50.936s
27	Webb	1m 50.990s
28	Pedone	1m 51.073s
29	Faubel	1m 51.407s
30	Finsterbusch	1m 51.908s
31	Pontone	1m 52.070s
32	Fujii	1m 52.576s
33	Moretti	1m 52.791s

Fastest race laps

1	Fenati	1m 48.648s
2	Cortese	1m 48.746s
3	Folger	1m 48.876s
4	Oliveira	1m 48.893s
5	Salom	1m 48.988s
6	Rins	1m 48.991s
7	Vazquez	1m 49.064s
8	Marquez	1m 49.084s
9	M. Vinales	1m 49.218s
10	Khairuddin	1m 49.273s
11	Moncayo	1m 49.395s
12	Masbou	1m 49.494s
13	Sissis	1m 49.498s
14	Kent	1m 49.573s
15	Rossi	1m 49.607s
16	Kornfeil	1m 49.627s
17	Tonucci	1m 50.069s
18	Techer	1m 50.158s
19	I. Vinales	1m 50.221s
20	Morciano	1m 50.385s
21	Binder	1m 50.657s
22	Pedone	1m 51.705s
23	Finsterbusch	1m 51.789s
24	Pontone	1m 51.827s
25	Fujii	1m 51.858s
26	Ajo	1m 52.484s
27	Moretti	1m 53.161s

Championship Points

1	Cortese	184
2	M. Vinales	155
3	Salom	129
4	Fenati	96
5	Masbou	81
6	Khairuddin	76
7	Rins	72
8	Rossi	59
9	Kent	57
10	Antonelli	55
11	Oliveira	52
12	Vazquez	50
13	Faubel	44
14	Moncayo	43
15	Sissis	43
16	Kornfeil	42
17	Folger	21
18	Techer	21
19	Ajo	21
20	Marquez	15
21	Miller	14
22	Moreno	10
23	Iwema	9
24	Gruenwald	8
25	Tonucci	8
26	Pedone	7
27	Finsterbusch	7
28	Binder	5
29	Schrotter	4
30	Martin	3
31	Hanus	3
32	I. Vinales	2
33	Calia	2
34	Rinaldi	1
35	Grotzkyj	1

Constructor Points

1	FTR Honda	217
2	KTM	185
3	Kalex KTM	158
4	Suter Honda	104
5	Honda	84
6	TSR Honda	21
7	FGR Honda	9
8	Ioda	5
9	Mahindra	4
10	Oral	1

CZECH REPUBLIC
GRAND PRIX

BRNO CIRCUIT

Main photo: The moment the race, and potentially the season, turned. Lorenzo runs wide on the penultimate corner as Pedrosa lines up his race-winning pass.

Inset, left: Cal Crutchlow – first Briton on the podium since Jeremy McWilliams in 2000.

Photos: Gold & Goose

Above: Where's Casey? A depleted field sets off under its own image on the giant screen.

Top right: There was no relief yet for Rossi's blues.

Top far right: Crutchlow brought humour to the pre-race press conference. Even Jorge joined in the banter.

Above right: Bradl and Bautista battled over fifth. In the end, the German rider (6) escaped.

Right: Casey was already at Brno when the call came from Australia: don't ride.

Photos: Gold & Goose

HOW will racing be without Stoner? The answer at Brno was highly satisfactory, if only belatedly in a breathtaking last lap after 40 minutes in which tension substituted for excitement. It also vindicated Pedrosa, and his long-suspected reluctance for close combat. He took on Jorge with vigour and commitment, and beat him.

For a second race in 2012, Stoner dropped a bomb before the weekend got under way – at lunchtime on Thursday his most trusted Australian doctor, now in possession of scans and X-rays from the USA, had repeated his earlier advice in far stronger terms: do not ride. Any further damage could be permanent; immediate surgery was required. He withdrew from the race, cancelled all appointments and hours later left the track for Australia. "It's the way racing goes, but it's a big hit to the heart," he said.

Hayden was already absent, injuries to his right hand having ruled him out; likewise Barbera, after his bruising premature return only a week before. Indy had a lot to answer for. There were a number of crashes also at Brno – 55 all told, 13 in MotoGP, with Lorenzo, Pedrosa and Crutchlow all on the list, Spies and Hernandez appearing twice. But the consistent and predictable surface, and wide, long corners meant most were low-side down after losing the front, and there were few injuries, all in the smaller classes.

This fine, long circuit also brought out the best in the 1000s, offering them a chance to stretch their legs. In the end, the race came down to more or less just such a leg-stretching exercise, Honda and Yamaha head to head. As so often, Honda horsepower prevailed.

Pedrosa's second successive victory was won as much by skill and daring as by top-end speed, however, and added a very welcome new tension to the title battle, closing the points gap from 18 to a tantalising 13. With Stoner absent for an indeterminate time and nobody else likely to take points away, this made possible a sustained head-to-head battle between the Spaniards.

In the aftermath of the previous week's Rossi move, Ducati had signed Dovizioso for two years. Since the same path had led to something of a graveyard for predecessors such as Melandri and Gibernau, and now Rossi, images of a lamb to slaughter came to mind; but aside from the sweetener of an undisclosed, yet substantial fee plus the promise of imminent intervention by Audi, it was also a last resort. Dovi had now been sidelined by Yamaha and Honda. There wasn't much else left, except another year in the satellite Tech 3 squad, "and to make again the results of this year is not my target." He hadn't spoken to any of his predecessors. "There is no reason. Everybody knows the results of Ducati. You can speak to other riders, but I prefer to wait and see for myself. When I was at Honda, I thought many things about the Yamaha … and they were wrong."

This triggered another significant move during the weekend: on Friday Crutchlow signed the only significant option left for him, to stay put. With Bradley Smith already contracted for 2013, this meant an all-English line-up for the French Tech 3 squad. Crutchlow celebrated by becoming the first Briton on a premier-class rostrum since Jeremy McWilliams on the 500 Aprilia, at a wet Donington Park in 2000. Funnily enough, that was the day Rossi won his first 500 race.

National interest in MotoGP, on hold for so long, was given another fillip by the news of Stoner's replacement, for the next two races and possibly longer: Jonathan Rea flew hot-

foot from the Superbike race at Moscow to join the Brno tests on Monday, switching from the Ten Kate Fireblade on Pirellis to the top-level Honda RC211V on Bridgestones. At least he knew the circuit.

Yamaha called a press conference, combining a sort of explanation of Spies's US suspension and then engine failures with the contrastingly upbeat news of the return of Valentino.

On the first topic, MotoGP group leader Kouichi Tsuji admitted that a quality control failure had caused the collapse at Laguna. "It was probably the shock mounting," he said. "We checked the part that failed, and the quality was not as good as we expected." The engine would arrive in Japan only the following day, but the smoky blow-up had been at "the top of the engine … maybe a valve or something."

On Rossi, racing MD Lin Jarvis explained how the original approach had come from the Italian earlier in the year and insisted that Dorna had played no role, a suspicion mooted when Ezpeleta told an interviewer that the leading star of his series "will be on a competitive bike next year". Said Jarvis: "Carmelo had no influence whatsoever in the entire process. I have never discussed Valentino's return to Yamaha with him, to this day."

He declined to reveal the contract fee, but said, "Honda made maximum effort to secure Lorenzo, and he has been taken care of very well … so for Valentino there is not a huge budget remaining." The balance of the team would be very different from when Rossi had walked away two years before. "We consider Jorge the most capable to win the world championship," said Jarvis, while Tsuji added, "In development, Lorenzo will decide the direction for the bike … he will lead, but Valentino will assist."

The arrival of Crutchlow at the top table after both qualifying and the race (and perhaps the absence of Stoner) introduced some scampish English humour that had even the austere Lorenzo taking part. Crutchlow first removed Lorenzo's pole-setter's Tissot watch from the presentation, replacing it with a modest ladies' watch, then brandished the large and showy chronometer on his own wrist, saying, "I wanted to be on pole." Then followed a bargaining session that concerned potential race position, with Pedrosa leaning across behind Lorenzo to make a higher offer.

Mahindra announced their abandonment of the disappointing Oral engine for what some thought an equally risky venture: a Suter-built engine and chassis for the 2013 season. Some consolation came when teenage Czech novice Miroslav Popov (in place of injured Danny Webb, another Indy victim) took their current bike to an unprecedented third in the early laps. The other independent Moto3 entrant, Ioda, now had both riders starting from the pit lane, having exceeded the engine allowance.

MOTOGP RACE – 22 laps

Lorenzo secured pole, only his fourth of the year, with a fastest-ever lap of Brno. In free practice, Pedrosa had dominated, but he had slipped off early in qualifying, forcing a switch to his spare bike, which, in spite of identical settings, suffered severe front chatter. He moved into third only at the last gasp; Crutchlow was between them in a personal best. It was his fourth front row of the year.

Pedrosa knocked Spies back to head row two, with Dovizioso alongside. Rossi was next, his first time on row

Above: Above: Crutchlow blasts past on a lonely ride to his first rostrum.

Top right: Points lead in jeopardy, the defeated Lorenzo congratulates his old rival.

Above right: Marquez pulls the train, from Luthi and Espargaro, Iannone trailing. Marquez went on to take his sixth Moto2 win.

Right: Jonas Folger, flanked by Salom and Cortese, simply ran away in the Moto3 race.

Below right: Folger's team switch from Ioda to Aspar's KTM power brought third and first in just two races.

Photos: Gold & Goose

two in 2012, and only the third time on a Ducati, thanks to finding "a better balance". He looked more comfortable and more like his old self.

Everyone got away cleanly, though it didn't last past first gear for Spies, in trouble from the first corner and losing place after place as he tried to stay out of the way. The problem this time was a cooked clutch "As soon as I shifted to second, it hit the limiter"; the solution was to nurse it cool for a couple more laps.

For once, Lorenzo outdragged Pedrosa into the first sweeping corner. Crutchlow was third, heading Dovi; then came Rossi, briefly Spies, from Bradl and Bautista.

Before the first lap was done, Rossi's red Ducati had already sent forth an ominous plume of blue smoke, which would come and go for the rest of the race. An oil leak, they said; confirmed by Rossi's tale of his feet slipping on the pegs and foot levers as the race wore on.

The two leaders soon began pulling away, more than a second ahead of Crutchlow after four laps, a gap that would grow in fits and starts. Crutchlow noticed that "one lap I couldn't see them, then there they were again".

Bautista passed Bradl on the first lap, and they lost more than a second on Rossi until the German got ahead again on lap five; the pair was on Rossi's tail by one third distance.

Spies started regaining places from lap two, and by the sixth he was past top CRT rider de Puniet, with some five seconds to Bautista. Two laps later, the American's race was over. He'd tried that little bit too hard and slipped off.

Next time around, Bradl was past Rossi, and one lap later Bautista also. The order was now established, and it seemed as though it would be a processional race. Even when Pedrosa outbraked Lorenzo into the first corner, it didn't actually change much.

Then came a breathtaking battle on the final lap.

Lorenzo attacked on the first of the pair of left-handers in the stadium section, a hard inside move so close that "I felt his fairing on my face," said Pedrosa.

Dani pushed and probed down the hill, and up it again. The last throw of the dice came at the end of the steep climb, and the final left-right combination, scene of much last-lap drama over the 26 years at the circuit.

Lorenzo said later, "I was thinking of winning." But he underestimated the speed and forcefulness of his opponent. Suddenly Dani was alongside as they braked. Jorge eased off to pull ahead again, but he was too fast and ran wide. Pedrosa was tight and had the better line for the right. He won by less than two-tenths.

Crutchlow watched the battle on the big screen as he circulated alone behind, even wondering if they might take one another out. "I was thinking, 'I might get a win here.'" His first rostrum was "a monkey off my back".

Dovizioso chased, but couldn't match his team-mate's pace. "He gained some time in corner entry and he had more corner speed, but he lost on the exit – but he was gaining more than he lost." He was six seconds down, but comfortably clear of Bradl, who in turn had left Bautista. Rossi was another five seconds down, troubled by oily feet and increasing rear tyre slides, an endemic problem on the bike even when oil-tight.

De Puniet was alone and best CRT, clear of a good battle that lasted much of the race between Espargaro, Abraham and Elias. Abraham escaped only in the final laps; Espargaro pounced on Elias on the last lap to consign him to 11th. Hernandez had a lonely race to 12th; Edwards moved forward to 13th, ahead of Pirro; Ellison and Pasini battled to the finish, the English rider claiming the last point by just over half a second. Petrucci was a lap adrift in 17th; Silva had a mechanical failure in the early stages.

MOTO2 RACE – 20 laps

Espargaro claimed his third pole in a row, fourth of the year; rival Marquez was off the front row for only the second time all year, and four-tenths adrift. With Luthi and Redding ahead, Marquez headed row two from Corsi and Iannone, whose crash early in the session brought out red flags, giving more time for his bike to be returned and patched up so he could go out again.

Zarco was tenth, Smith 15th and de Angelis 18th after a spectacular late-session crash.

Luthi led away, from Espargaro, Marquez and Iannone, with Corsi nosing into third briefly, then falling back to head

Brno 2012

the next gang. The leading quartet had eked out a gap better than a second after six laps.

Marquez had moved to second on lap two, then Iannone consigned Espargaro to fourth. But they were still close, and they played follow my leader until lap seven, when Iannone managed to get ahead of Marquez at his second attempt. Again, it was only for a lap. It was the usual suspects, playing the usual games.

Front-row starter Redding was not among them, however, having crashed out on the first lap.

It was close and tense, with occasional changes of position. Espargaro went to second at the first corner at the start of lap 16, but he had earlier passed Iannone under a yellow flag and was penalised by one place – so he was fourth again on lap 17.

Nobody was giving an inch, and it stayed close all the way, but there was a sense of inevitability as Marquez pushed into the lead with three laps to go, and stayed there in spite of persistent efforts by Luthi on every corner. He won his sixth race of the season by six-hundredths of a second.

Less than half a second behind, Espargaro held on to third, Iannone close behind.

Not many surprises, and more tension than action. The next gang, eight-strong, made up for it – six riders crossing the line within just over a second, and the next two still within another second.

The battle had been shaping up in the closing stages, with Smith, Simon and Rabat closing up on a tight quintet, where de Angelis had just taken over the lead from Kallio, who had displaced Terol. Zarco was in the thick of it.

It got rough on the last lap, and it was tough guy Corsi first over the line, a few hundredths ahead of de Angelis, Zarco, Smith, Kallio and Rabat. Simon and Terol were right behind.

Jordi Torres, replacement at the Aspar team for Elias, was next, a couple of seconds clear of the fading Aegerter. Pons took the last point, less than a tenth behind, and a similar distance ahead of di Meglio and Nakagami.

Colandrea, Rea, Simeon and Corti joined the crash list.

It was another step for Marquez, now leading Espargaro by 48 points, the latter also coming under serious threat from Luthi and Iannone.

MOTO3 RACE – 19 laps

Vinales took his fourth pole of the year by just over three-hundredths from Cortese. Khairuddin completed the front row; rookie Antonelli led the second from Salom and Faubel.

Wet warm-up had been a warning, but the track had a mainly dry racing line by the start, and only one notable gambled on wet tyres: Vazquez. After two laps, he led Khairuddin by better than two seconds.

By now the charging Folger was second; he took the lead at the end of lap four and gained two full seconds on the next lap. Vazquez would drop to 25th by race end, but when Kornfeil took over, Folger was almost ten seconds clear and quite impregnable.

Other rookies enjoyed rewards for high risks, including injured Mahindra sub Popov, a 17-year-old Czech in only his fourth GP and his first four-stroke race. He was up to third until almost half-distance. Another was Scottish wild-card McPhee, engaged with Khairuddin for fourth.

The main contenders were in a pack a long way behind, Cortese ahead of Rins, Oliveira, Salom and Vinales. After half-distance, they closed rapidly and caught Kornfeil with one lap to go.

A frantic brawl, it was Salom, Cortese, Vinales, Rins and Kornfeil in just over half a second; Kent a couple behind, then Fenati half a second ahead of Oliveira.

Tonucci narrowly led the next gang of five; McPhee was three seconds adrift for the last point.

Popov, battling to stay with the regulars, crashed out with five laps to go after clashing with Masbou; Khairuddin and Rinaldi also crashed.

FIM WORLD CHAMPIONSHIP

ROUND 12

24–26 AUGUST, 2012

bwin
GRAND PRIX CESKE REPUBLIKY

motoGP

TISSOT SWISS WATCHES SINCE 1853

OFFICIAL TIMEKEEPER

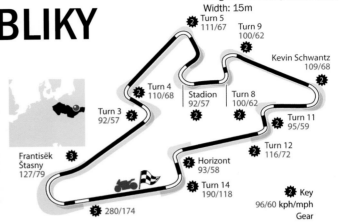

AUTODROM BRNO
22 laps
Length: 5.403 km / 3.357 miles
Width: 15m

Turn 5 111/67
Turn 9 100/62
Kevin Schwantz 109/68
Turn 4 110/68
Stadion 92/57
Turn 8 100/62
Turn 11 95/59
Turn 3 92/57
Turn 12 116/72
František Štasny 127/79
Horizont 93/58
Turn 14 190/118
Key 96/60 kph/mph Gear
280/174

Photos: Gold & Goose

MotoGP

RACE DISTANCE: 22 laps, 73.860 miles/118.866km · **RACE WEATHER:** Dry (air 18°C, humidity 79%, track 23°C)

Pos.	Rider	Nat.	No.	Entrant	Machine	Tyres	Race tyre choice	Laps	Time & speed
1	**Dani Pedrosa**	SPA	26	Repsol Honda Team	Honda RC213V	B	F: Ex-Hard/R: Medium	22	42m 51.570s 103.398mph/ 166.403km/h
2	**Jorge Lorenzo**	SPA	99	Yamaha Factory Racing	Yamaha YZR-M1	B	F: Ex-Hard/R: Medium	22	42m 51.748s
3	**Cal Crutchlow**	GBR	35	Monster Yamaha Tech 3	Yamaha YZR-M1	B	F: Ex-Hard/R: Medium	22	43m 03.913s
4	**Andrea Dovizioso**	ITA	4	Monster Yamaha Tech 3	Yamaha YZR-M1	B	F: Ex-Hard/R: Medium	22	43m 10.161s
5	**Stefan Bradl**	GER	6	LCR Honda MotoGP	Honda RC213V	B	F: Ex-Hard/R: Medium	22	43m 17.152s
6	**Alvaro Bautista**	SPA	19	San Carlo Honda Gresini	Honda RC213V	B	F: Ex-Hard/R: Medium	22	43m 21.021s
7	**Valentino Rossi**	ITA	46	Ducati Team	Ducati Desmosedici GP12	B	F: Ex-Hard/R: Medium	22	43m 26.084s
8	**Randy de Puniet**	FRA	14	Power Electronics Aspar	ART Aprilia RSV4	B	F: Ex-Hard/R: Medium	22	43m 55.855s
9	**Karel Abraham**	CZE	17	Cardion AB Motoracing	Ducati Desmosedici GP12	B	F: Ex-Hard/R: Medium	22	43m 59.848s
10	**Aleix Espargaro**	SPA	41	Power Electronics Aspar	ART Aprilia RSV4	B	F: Ex-Hard/R: Medium	22	44m 01.542s
11	**Toni Elias**	SPA	24	Pramac Racing Team	Ducati Desmosedici GP12	B	F: Ex-Hard/R: Medium	22	44m 01.573s
12	**Yonny Hernandez**	COL	68	Avintia Blusens	BQR FTR Kawasaki	B	F: Ex-Hard/R: Medium	22	44m 15.610s
13	**Colin Edwards**	USA	5	NGM Mobile Forward Racing	Suter BMW S1000RR	B	F: Ex-Hard/R: Medium	22	44m 19.468s
14	**Michele Pirro**	ITA	51	San Carlo Honda Gresini	FTR Honda CBR1000RR	B	F: Ex-Hard/R: Medium	22	44m 27.735s
15	**James Ellison**	GBR	77	Paul Bird Motorsport	ART Aprilia RSV4	B	F: Ex-Hard/R: Medium	22	44m 32.135s
16	Mattia Pasini	ITA	54	Speed Master	ART Aprilia RSV4	B	F: Ex-Hard/R: Medium	22	44m 32.796s
17	Danilo Petrucci	ITA	9	Came IodaRacing Project	Ioda Aprilia RSV4	B	F: Ex-Hard/R: Medium	21	42m 59.186s
	Ivan Silva	SPA	22	Avintia Blusens	BQR FTR Kawasaki	B	F: Ex-Hard/R: Medium	9	DNF
	Ben Spies	USA	11	Yamaha Factory Racing	Yamaha YZR-M1	B	F: Ex-Hard/R: Medium	8	DNF

Fastest lap: Jorge Lorenzo, on lap 8, 1m 56.274s, 103.945mph/167.284km/h (record).

Previous lap record: Jorge Lorenzo, SPA (Yamaha), 1m 56.670s, 103.593mph/166.716km/h (2009).

Event best maximum speed: Dani Pedrosa, 192.6mph/309.9km/h (qualifying practice).

Qualifying

Weather: Dry
Air Temp: 22° Humidity: 71%
Track Temp: 26°

1	Lorenzo	1m 55.799s
2	Crutchlow	1m 55.995s
3	Pedrosa	1m 56.327s
4	Spies	1m 56.331s
5	Dovizioso	1m 56.559s
6	Rossi	1m 56.735s
7	Bradl	1m 56.827s
8	Bautista	1m 57.068s
9	Abraham	1m 57.773s
10	De Puniet	1m 57.844s
11	Espargaro	1m 58.153s
12	Hernandez	1m 59.087s
13	Elias	1m 59.120s
14	Pirro	1m 59.387s
15	Edwards	1m 59.863s
16	Pasini	1m 59.865s
17	Ellison	2m 00.316s
18	Silva	2m 00.329s
19	Petrucci	2m 00.854s

Fastest race laps

1	Lorenzo	1m 56.274s
2	Pedrosa	1m 56.346s
3	Crutchlow	1m 56.807s
4	Dovizioso	1m 56.883s
5	Spies	1m 57.133s
6	Bradl	1m 57.305s
7	Rossi	1m 57.363s
8	Bautista	1m 57.429s
9	De Puniet	1m 58.781s
10	Espargaro	1m 59.032s
11	Abraham	1m 59.231s
12	Elias	1m 59.359s
13	Edwards	1m 59.633s
14	Hernandez	1m 59.980s
15	Pirro	2m 00.017s
16	Ellison	2m 00.556s
17	Silva	2m 00.583s
18	Pasini	2m 00.624s
19	Petrucci	2m 01.801s

Championship Points

1	Lorenzo	245
2	Pedrosa	232
3	Stoner	186
4	Dovizioso	150
5	Crutchlow	122
6	Bradl	105
7	Bautista	102
8	Rossi	100
9	Hayden	84
10	Spies	66
11	Barbera	60
12	Espargaro	45
13	De Puniet	41
14	Abraham	25
15	Hernandez	21
16	Pirro	18
17	Edwards	17
18	Ellison	14
19	Pasini	13
20	Silva	11
21	Elias	10
22	Petrucci	9
23	Rapp	2

Constructor Points

1	Honda	271
2	Yamaha	261
3	Ducati	124
4	ART	62
5	BQR	24
6	FTR	18
7	Suter	17
8	Ioda	9
9	APR	2
10	BQR-FTR	2

Grid order	1	2	3	4	5	6	7	8	9	10	11	12	13	14	15	16	17	18	19	20	21	22	
99 LORENZO	99	99	99	99	99	99	99	99	99	99	99	26	26	26	26	26	26	26	26	26	26	26	1
35 CRUTCHLOW	26	26	26	26	26	26	26	26	26	26	26	99	99	99	99	99	99	99	99	99	99	99	2
26 PEDROSA	35	35	35	35	35	35	35	35	35	35	35	35	35	35	35	35	35	35	35	35	35	35	3
11 SPIES	4	4	4	4	4	4	4	4	4	4	4	4	4	4	4	4	4	4	4	4	4	4	4
4 DOVIZIOSO	46	46	46	46	46	46	46	46	6	6	6	6	6	6	6	6	6	6	6	6	6	6	5
46 ROSSI	19	19	19	19	6	6	6	6	19	19	19	19	19	19	19	19	19	19	19	19	19	19	6
6 BRADL	6	6	6	6	19	19	19	19	46	46	46	46	46	46	46	46	46	46	46	46	46	46	7
19 BAUTISTA	14	14	14	14	14	11	11	11	14	14	14	14	14	14	14	14	14	14	14	14	14	14	8
17 ABRAHAM	41	41	41	41	11	14	14	14	41	41	17	17	17	17	17	17	17	17	17	17	17		9
14 DE PUNIET	68	68	24	11	41	41	41	41	24	17	24	24	24	24	24	24	24	24	24	24	41		10
41 ESPARGARO	24	24	11	24	24	24	24	24	17	24	41	41	41	41	41	41	41	41	41	41	24		11
68 HERNANDEZ	17	17	17	17	17	17	17	17	68	68	68	68	68	68	68	68	68	68	68	68	68		12
24 ELIAS	51	11	68	68	68	68	68	68	51	51	51	51	51	5	5	5	5	5	5	5	5		13
51 PIRRO	11	51	51	51	51	51	51	51	5	5	5	5	51	51	51	51	51	51	51	51	51		14
5 EDWARDS	22	22	22	22	22	5	5	5	54	54	77	77	77	77	77	77	77	77	77	77	77		15
54 PASINI	5	5	5	5	5	22	22	22	77	77	54	54	54	54	54	54	54	54	54	54	54		
77 ELLISON	77	77	77	77	54	54	54	54	22	9	9	9	9	9	9	9	9	9					
22 SILVA	54	54	54	54	77	77	77	77	9														
9 PETRUCCI	9	9	9	9	9	9	9	9															

9 Lapped rider

Moto2

RACE DISTANCE: 20 laps, 67.145 miles/108.060km · **RACE WEATHER:** Dry (air 19°C, humidity 81%, track 21°C)

Pos.	Rider	Nat.	No.	Entrant	Machine	Laps	Time & Speed
1	**Marc Marquez**	SPA	93	Team CatalunyaCaixa Repsol	Suter	20	41m 19.178s 97.501mph/ 156.913km/h
2	**Thomas Luthi**	SWI	12	Interwetten-Paddock	Suter	20	41m 19.239s
3	**Pol Espargaro**	SPA	40	Pons 40 HP Tuenti	Kalex	20	41m 19.618s
4	**Andrea Iannone**	ITA	29	Speed Master	Speed Up	20	41m 19.688s
5	**Simone Corsi**	ITA	3	Came IodaRacing Project	FTR	20	41m 29.497s
6	**Alex de Angelis**	RSM	15	NGM Mobile Forward Racing	FTR	20	41m 29.821s
7	**Johann Zarco**	FRA	5	JIR Moto2	Motobi	20	41m 29.895s
8	**Bradley Smith**	GBR	38	Tech 3 Racing	Tech 3	20	41m 30.051s
9	**Mika Kallio**	FIN	36	Marc VDS Racing Team	Kalex	20	41m 30.225s
10	**Esteve Rabat**	SPA	80	Pons 40 HP Tuenti	Kalex	20	41m 30.695s
11	**Julian Simon**	SPA	60	Blusens Avintia	Suter	20	41m 31.566s
12	**Nicolas Terol**	SPA	18	Mapfre Aspar Team Moto2	Suter	20	41m 31.781s
13	**Jordi Torres**	SPA	81	Mapfre Aspar Team Moto2	Suter	20	41m 34.074s
14	**Dominique Aegerter**	SWI	77	Technomag-CIP	Suter	20	41m 36.950s
15	**Axel Pons**	SPA	49	Pons 40 HP Tuenti	Kalex	20	41m 37.026s
16	Mike di Meglio	FRA	63	MZ Racing	MZ-RE Honda	20	41m 37.084s
17	Takaaki Nakagami	JPN	30	Italtrans Racing Team	Kalex	20	41m 37.673s
18	Yuki Takahashi	JPN	72	NGM Mobile Forward Racing	FTR	20	41m 49.808s
19	Anthony West	AUS	95	QMMF Racing Team	Speed Up	20	41m 53.812s
20	Roberto Rolfo	ITA	44	Technomag-CIP	Suter	20	41m 53.943s
21	Ratthapark Wilairot	THA	14	Thai Honda PTT Gresini Moto2	Suter	20	41m 54.070s
22	Randy Krummenacher	SWI	4	GP Team Switzerland	Kalex	20	41m 56.159s
23	Marcel Schrotter	GER	23	Desguaces La Torre SAG	Bimota	20	42m 13.855s
24	Gino Rea	GBR	8	Federal Oil Gresini Moto2	Suter	20	42m 38.761s
25	Alessandro Andreozzi	ITA	22	S/Master Speed Up	Speed Up	20	42m 42.394s
26	Eric Granado	BRA	57	JIR Moto2	Motobi	20	42m 44.322s
27	Elena Rosell	SPA	82	QMMF Racing Team	Speed Up	20	42m 51.386s
	Claudio Corti	ITA	71	Italtrans Racing Team	Kalex	18	DNF
	Xavier Simeon	BEL	19	Tech 3 Racing	Tech 3	11	DNF
	Marco Colandrea	SWI	10	SAG Team	FTR	11	DNF
	Scott Redding	GBR	45	Marc VDS Racing Team	Kalex	0	DNF

Fastest lap: Pol Espargaro, on lap 18, 2m 03.061s, 98.213mph/158.058km/h.

Lap record: Andrea Iannone, ITA (Suter), 2m 02.640s, 98.549mph/158.600km/h (2011).

Event best maximum speed: Pol Espargaro, 163.5mph/263.2km/h (free practice 3).

Qualifying: Dry

Air: 22° **Humidity:** 70% **Track:** 28°

1	Espargaro	2m 01.953s
2	Luthi	2m 02.235s
3	Redding	2m 02.239s
4	Marquez	2m 02.342s
5	Corsi	2m 02.838s
6	Iannone	2m 02.914s
7	Nakagami	2m 02.981s
8	Terol	2m 03.128s
9	Aegerter	2m 03.130s
10	Zarco	2m 03.142s
11	Pons	2m 03.159s
12	Kallio	2m 03.206s
13	Torres	2m 03.249s
14	Di Meglio	2m 03.279s
15	Smith	2m 03.303s
16	Rabat	2m 03.307s
17	Simon	2m 03.360s
18	De Angelis	2m 03.384s
19	Corti	2m 03.470s
20	Wilairot	2m 03.479s
21	Simeon	2m 03.594s
22	Takahashi	2m 03.636s
23	Krummenacher	2m 04.003s
24	Schrotter	2m 04.077s
25	West	2m 04.272s
26	Rea	2m 04.399s
27	Rolfo	2m 04.630s
28	Andreozzi	2m 05.233s
29	Colandrea	2m 05.428s
30	Granado	2m 06.417s
31	Rosell	2m 07.425s

Outside 107%

Neukirchner	No time
Cardus	No time

Fastest race laps

1	Espargaro	2m 03.061s
2	Iannone	2m 03.072s
3	Luthi	2m 03.211s
4	Marquez	2m 03.272s
5	Smith	2m 03.356s
6	Simon	2m 03.535s
7	De Angelis	2m 03.609s
8	Zarco	2m 03.617s
9	Kallio	2m 03.641s
10	Torres	2m 03.653s
11	Aegerter	2m 03.664s
12	Rabat	2m 03.703s
13	Pons	2m 03.705s
14	Corsi	2m 03.720s
15	Terol	2m 03.735s
16	Corti	2m 03.771s
17	Simeon	2m 03.834s
18	Nakagami	2m 03.876s
19	Di Meglio	2m 04.067s
20	Rea	2m 04.085s
21	Takahashi	2m 04.427s
22	Rolfo	2m 04.558s
23	Wilairot	2m 04.566s
24	West	2m 04.631s
25	Krummenacher	2m 04.949s
26	Schrotter	2m 05.539s
27	Colandrea	2m 06.178s
28	Andreozzi	2m 06.276s
29	Granado	2m 06.998s
30	Rosell	2m 07.480s

Championship Points

1	Marquez	213
2	Espargaro	165
3	Luthi	154
4	Iannone	149
5	Redding	106
6	Kallio	97
7	Smith	77
8	Corti	65
9	Aegerter	63
10	Rabat	62
11	Zarco	60
12	Corsi	59
13	De Angelis	58
14	Simon	38
15	Nakagami	36
16	Elias	34
17	Krummenacher	24
18	Simeon	17
19	Terol	15
20	West	11
21	Di Meglio	10
22	Neukirchner	8
23	Wilairot	8
24	Cardus	6
25	Torres	3
26	Pons	1
27	Rea	1

Constructor Points

1	Suter	247
2	Kalex	211
3	Speed Up	149
4	Tech 3	77
5	FTR	76
6	Motobi	60
7	Moriwaki	10
8	AJR	6

Moto3

RACE DISTANCE: 19 laps, 63.788 miles/102.657km · **RACE WEATHER:** Wet (air 17°C, humidity 97%, track 21°C)

Pos.	Rider	Nat.	No.	Entrant	Machine	Laps	Time & Speed
1	**Jonas Folger**	GER	94	Mapfre Aspar Team Moto3	Kalex KTM	19	43m 03.089s 88.900mph/ 143.071km/h
2	**Luis Salom**	SPA	39	RW Racing GP	Kalex KTM	19	43m 09.007s
3	**Sandro Cortese**	GER	11	Red Bull KTM Ajo	KTM	19	43m 09.052s
4	**Maverick Vinales**	SPA	25	Blusens Avintia	FTR Honda	19	43m 09.180s
5	**Alex Rins**	SPA	42	Estrella Galicia 0,0	Suter Honda	19	43m 09.579s
6	**Jakub Kornfeil**	CZE	84	Redox-Ongetta-Centro Seta	FTR Honda	19	43m 09.661s
7	**Danny Kent**	GBR	52	Red Bull KTM Ajo	KTM	19	43m 11.510s
8	**Romano Fenati**	ITA	5	Team Italia FMI	FTR Honda	19	43m 16.471s
9	**Miguel Oliveira**	POR	44	Estrella Galicia 0,0	Suter Honda	19	43m 16.998s
10	**Alessandro Tonucci**	ITA	19	Team Italia FMI	FTR Honda	19	43m 25.555s
11	**Hector Faubel**	SPA	55	Mapfre Aspar Team Moto3	Kalex KTM	19	43m 29.063s
12	**Alberto Moncayo**	SPA	23	Andalucia JHK t-shirt Laglisse	FTR Honda	19	43m 29.102s
13	**Adrian Martin**	SPA	26	JHK t-shirt Laglisse	FTR Honda	19	43m 29.638s
14	**Arthur Sissis**	AUS	61	Red Bull KTM Ajo	KTM	19	43m 29.797s
15	**John McPhee**	GBR	17	Racing Steps Foundation KRP	KRP Honda	19	43m 32.842s
16	Alexis Masbou	FRA	10	Caretta Technology	Honda	19	43m 36.038s
17	Louis Rossi	FRA	96	Racing Team Germany	FTR Honda	19	43m 38.958s
18	Joan Olive	SPA	6	TT Motion Events Racing	KTM	19	43m 43.522s
19	Luca Gruenwald	GER	43	Freudenberg Racing Team	Honda	19	43m 44.040s
20	Brad Binder	RSA	41	RW Racing GP	Kalex KTM	19	43m 44.214s
21	Alex Marquez	SPA	12	Ambrogio Next Racing	Suter Honda	19	43m 44.360s
22	Giulian Pedone	SWI	30	Ambrogio Next Racing	Suter Honda	19	43m 48.903s
23	Niccolo Antonelli	ITA	27	San Carlo Gresini Moto3	FTR Honda	19	43m 58.506s
24	Jasper Iwema	NED	53	Moto FGR	FGR Honda	19	44m 28.890s
25	Efren Vazquez	SPA	7	JHK t-shirt Laglisse	FTR Honda	19	44m 42.648s
26	Kenta Fujii	JPN	51	Technomag-CIP-TSR	TSR Honda	19	44m 47.709s
27	Luigi Morciano	ITA	3	Ioda Team Italia	Ioda	19	45m 21.017s
28	Armando Pontone	ITA	80	IodaRacing Project	Ioda	18	44m 45.641s
	Zulfahmi Khairuddin	MAL	63	AirAsia-Sic-Ajo	KTM	14	DNF
	Miroslav Popov	CZE	95	Mahindra Racing	Mahindra	14	DNF
	Michael Ruben Rinaldi	ITA	71	Caretta Technology	Honda	11	DNF
	Toni Finsterbusch	GER	9	MZ Racing	Honda	10	DNF

Fastest lap: Luis Salom, on lap 17, 2m 09.659s, 93.215mph/150.015km/h (record).

Previous lap record: New category.

Event best maximum speed: Zulfahmi Khairuddin, 134.8mph/216.9km/h (qualifying practice).

Qualifying: Dry

Air: 21° **Humidity:** 72% **Track:** 26°

1	M. Vinales	2m 08.075s
2	Cortese	2m 08.108s
3	Khairuddin	2m 08.504s
4	Antonelli	2m 08.660s
5	Salom	2m 08.719s
6	Faubel	2m 08.880s
7	Kornfeil	2m 09.019s
8	Rins	2m 09.221s
9	Kent	2m 09.307s
10	Folger	2m 09.382s
11	Vazquez	2m 09.434s
12	Tonucci	2m 09.498s
13	Fenati	2m 09.532s
14	Moncayo	2m 09.635s
15	Martin	2m 09.641s
16	Rossi	2m 09.682s
17	Masbou	2m 09.737s
18	Marquez	2m 09.821s
19	McPhee	2m 09.848s
20	Sissis	2m 09.875s
21	Oliveira	2m 10.182s
22	Finsterbusch	2m 10.511s
23	Binder	2m 10.617s
24	Olive	2m 10.682s
25	Rinaldi	2m 11.108s
26	Gruenwald	2m 11.259s
27	Iwema	2m 11.289s
28	Morciano	2m 11.349s
29	Popov	2m 11.969s
30	Fujii	2m 11.981s
31	Pontone	2m 13.726s
32	Pedone	2m 14.142s

Outside 107%

Moretti	No Time
I. Vinales	No Time
Techer	No Time

Fastest race laps

1	Salom	2m 09.659s
2	Rins	2m 09.798s
3	Kent	2m 09.862s
4	Cortese	2m 09.882s
5	M. Vinales	2m 09.897s
6	Fenati	2m 10.124s
7	Khairuddin	2m 10.235s
8	Oliveira	2m 10.460s
9	Kornfeil	2m 11.001s
10	Tonucci	2m 11.063s
11	Moncayo	2m 11.121s
12	Sissis	2m 11.217s
13	Rossi	2m 11.289s
14	Faubel	2m 11.407s
15	Binder	2m 11.642s
16	Antonelli	2m 11.707s
17	Martin	2m 11.712s
18	Masbou	2m 11.782s
19	Folger	2m 11.992s
20	Marquez	2m 12.059s
21	Gruenwald	2m 12.089s
22	Pedone	2m 12.301s
23	McPhee	2m 12.310s
24	Olive	2m 12.438s
25	Popov	2m 14.204s
26	Fujii	2m 14.267s
27	Morciano	2m 14.370s
28	Iwema	2m 15.157s
29	Rinaldi	2m 16.942s
30	Vazquez	2m 19.595s
31	Finsterbusch	2m 23.432s
32	Pontone	2m 24.406s

Championship Points

1	Cortese	200
2	M. Vinales	168
3	Salom	149
4	Fenati	104
5	Rins	83
6	Masbou	81
7	Khairuddin	76
8	Kent	66
9	Rossi	59
10	Oliveira	59
11	Antonelli	55
12	Kornfeil	52
13	Vazquez	50
14	Faubel	49
15	Moncayo	47
16	Folger	46
17	Sissis	45
18	Techer	21
19	Ajo	21
20	Marquez	15
21	Miller	14
22	Tonucci	14
23	Moreno	10
24	Iwema	9
25	Gruenwald	8
26	Pedone	7
27	Finsterbusch	7
28	Martin	6
29	Binder	5
30	Schrotter	4
31	Hanus	3
32	I. Vinales	2
33	Calia	2
34	McPhee	1
35	Rinaldi	1
36	Grotzkyj	1

Constructor Points

1	FTR Honda	230
2	KTM	201
3	Kalex KTM	183
4	Suter Honda	115
5	Honda	84
6	TSR Honda	21
7	FGR Honda	9
8	Ioda	5
9	Mahindra	4
10	KRP Honda	1
11	Oral	1

SAN MARINO GRAND PRIX

MISANO CIRCUIT

Airborne rivals. Lorenzo (*inset, left*) jumps for joy after an untroubled win reversed his championship decline; Pedrosa (*main photo*) was thrown along with his hopes on the first lap while among the CRT gang; de Puniet is forced wide to avoid him.

Photos: Gold & Goose

M ISANO would be remembered as a comedy of errors, if it had been funnier. Instead it took the heat right out of an increasingly absorbing title battle.

It sort of wasn't anybody's fault ... unless you are going to finger Barbera. But he only made a fairly typical racing mistake, in his first race lap in nine weeks. The real culprit was an extraordinary chain of coincidences, some yet to be fully explained.

It unfolded over the course of nine minutes, but had begun the previous evening, when Karel Abraham's AB Cardion mechanics replaced a leaking hydraulic clutch seal. As it would turn out, the new seal also leaked.

This revealed itself at the worst possible time: after the sighting lap, during which the level of the master cylinder had dropped below the critical level. The bike stalled on the line, but he got away on a push-start and the warm-up lap was okay. On the grid, as the start lights illuminated, Abraham selected first and it stalled again. He put his hand up, yellow flags waved – abort start.

Now the confusion began. Per regulation, instead of the lights going out as expected, amber lights on each side started flashing. Trouble was, few riders (or, as it transpired, even their teams) had read that regulation.

Some riders started, in a rather half-hearted fashion. Others stayed put. Luckily there were no mishaps, but puzzled faces as bikes were wheeled back to position, and the engines stopped. Riders started taking off their helmets, people trickled, then flooded on to the grid: photographers, TV reporters, brolly girls, more and more mechanics...

Eventually the throngs were cleared, but as the one-minute board was shown, it became clear that pole qualifier Pedrosa had a problem as mechanics fussed around the bike. The front brake had seized on and the tyre warmer was trapped. A quick bleed to relieve hydraulic pressure didn't help. With the bike still on its front- and rear-wheel stands, it was removed from the grid into the adjacent pit lane. This inevitably condemned Pedrosa to start from the back of the grid, but then something strange happened.

As the bike was dropped off the stand, the front wheel freed itself. Afterwards nobody was quite sure whether a brake line had been trapped (unlikely, given the routing, although Honda does use Teflon rather than the usual braided steel hoses); more likely there'd been a micro-weld between disc and pad, freed by the jolt off the stand. No clear explanation ever did emerge. At the time, there was only one concern: to get back on the grid, where the others were revving up for the warm-up lap.

Dani made it, but his troubles weren't over: during the shemozzle, his pit-lane speed limiter had been knocked on. As the others left, he was pop-banging along, gesticulating at his crew. After some more of this, he realised the problem and was able to get back past the safety car, only to be met by a red flag and held at the back of the grid.

He made it unscathed through Misano's troublesome tight first corners and was rapidly working his way to the front of the CRT bikes on the first fast run down to the Quercia left-hander – Turn Eight, and not even halfway around. As he heeled it in, Barbera behind him was squeezed, went for the gap, and hit the back of the Honda.

Both went down: Barbera slumped in mortification at what he had done. He'd ruined his countryman's championship.

And, as it happened, denied a crowd of 45,104 a potentially exciting and certainly important race, leaving Lorenzo to lead from start to finish at unimpressive pace. Even he admitted that he was unsure he could have matched Dani on the day; but then with a shrinking points lead suddenly boosted to 38, he could afford to be gracious.

There was a compensation for the fans – local superhero Rossi came second. With a new chassis responding well, perhaps at last the breakthrough had come... There was a background story. Practice and qualifying had been bedevilled by bad weather, leaving no time to perfect bike settings.

Vale, on the other hand, had spent two full glorious dry days at Misano after Brno, and he, his bike and his tyres were fully dialled in and ready to go.

Preziosi was on hand to enjoy the moment, after giving a series of interviews to rebut Rossi's suggestions of a lack of development. "We are the company that has done the most," he said, pointing out the chassis changes from steel tube to carbon fibre to aluminium, among other things. There was other important Ducati news: Ben Spies had signed to join the 'junior' team, alongside Iannone. Turning aside from any frying-pan/fire allusions, he opined, "Next year is going to be a big adventure and a big change."

Compatriot Colin Edwards had also signed on for another year with the NGM Forward team, during which he will reach the age of 39. However, not only had his frequently articulated demands to dispose of the "piece-of-sh*t" Suter BMW fallen on deaf ears, but also there was now a second Suter: Petrucci's Ioda squad had mothballed their slow home-brewed Aprilia CRT in favour of the hitherto ill-considered Swiss-German machine.

Nicky Hayden was back, his hand injuries troublesome under braking; Jonathan Rea was a new face on the grid, airlifted in after Brno to ride Stoner's Repsol Honda. He made a careful and considered debut, and would impress still further at the next race in two weeks, all while pursuing his SBK duties on the intervening weekends.

Yamaha caused mild amusement by describing their new blue and graphite livery (matching the latest street-bike colour scheme) as reviving memories of the early 1980s – no such livery existed then, though much later the Gauloises bikes would be slightly similar. There were wry grins also at Bridgestone's celebration of their forthcoming 100th GP win

– guaranteed, barring race cancellation, in the same way as all but 35 of the other 99.

Riders from Motos 2 and 3 were summoned on Thursday for a talking-to by the race director, who announced a new system of penalties for those doing slow laps in practice – to obviate or at least reduce the dangerous practice of gathering in slow gangs awaiting a fast rider to follow.

Naturally, the renamed circuit was rich in memories of that other local hero, Marco Simoncelli, and it coincided with the launch of an official family biography, as well as an impressive feat of cycling from a 13-strong team led over the Alps through shocking weather by Kevin Schwantz, raising money and awareness for the charity in the late rider's name.

Rossi had the last word, after his welcome rostrum finish, smiling warmly at the memory of his close friend: "I dedicate this result to him. I wanted to give him a win, but maybe he would have to wait too long."

MOTOGP RACE – 27 laps (shortened)

Persistent drizzle on Friday meant that only a handful of riders, mainly CRT, went out for the first two free practices: of the factory guys, only Spies went out morning and afternoon, although not for long; he was joined by returnee Hayden in the morning, his first ride since his Indy crash. Saturday morning was also wet; this time, everybody went out, to get some wet track time.

It put huge pressure on the hour of qualifying, which was dry and warm. Everything had to be tested and the track's intricacies re-learned, in addition to the dash for a lap time. A flurry at the end saw Crutchlow first, displaced by Lorenzo, only for Pedrosa to shade him by a scanty 0.018.

Above: Rossi revival? Second place was a reward for the rider and his adoring fans.

Top left: Ducati designer Preziosi looks over the Hondas.

Above left: Rosella and Paolo Simoncelli launched the official biography of son Marco.

Left: Jonathan Rea, substituting for the injured Stoner, acquitted himself well in his first GP.

Photos: Gold & Goose

Above: Alvaro Bautista managed to hold off a persistent Dovizioso for his first rostrum in the class.

Above right: Friends at last: Bautista was finally coming to terms with his uniquely Showa-suspended Honda.

Right: Marquez leads Iannone, Espargaro and the gang in the first attempt at Moto2. In the restart, he led the only lap that mattered.

Below right: Cortese leads Salom, Vinales and Rins as they start the last lap of a titanic Moto3 struggle.

Photos: Gold & Goose

They were shuffled behind, but significantly Rossi was on the second row for a second successive race, behind Bradl and Bautista; Dovi headed the third from Spies and Rea.

When the race finally got going, the order of the first two was established at the first corner – Lorenzo and Rossi. The Spaniard had a lead of better than a second after one lap; it dropped to one second on the fourth after he almost crashed at the start of it. From then on, it stretched and stretched, and he had a lonely afternoon. "I was lucky today," he said. "My race pace was not so good, and I almost crashed when I lost the front in the first corner on the third lap." At first, he hadn't seen the pit signal that Pedrosa was out and feared his imminent arrival.

Rossi was under pressure from the start, from Bradl, Dovizioso and Crutchlow, though the Englishman lasted only until lap five before sliding to earth – his second crash in three races.

The three stayed close as Spies gradually dropped back, succumbing to Bautista on lap six. The Spaniard was on the move, if gradually, and by half-distance had closed up on Dovizioso, now a little way behind Bradl, who in turn was losing touch with Rossi.

The battle for third became closer as the laps counted down. Bradl had been losing pace and places bit by bit, while Spies had speeded up to close a gap of a couple of seconds. With three laps to go, they were still all close: Bautista at the front from Dovi and Spies, with Bradl dropping from fourth to sixth the lap before as he ran into front-end grip problems.

At the end, it was between Bautista and Dovi, and the Italian attacked strongly at every opportunity on the last lap, finally pulling almost alongside out of the final corner.

Spies was close, but not close enough, Bradl fading fast, though the next man, Hayden, was almost half a minute behind, obliged to keep pushing in spite of the pain because of the ever closer attention of Rea. "I knew if he got closer, he'd definitely have been able to pass me on the brakes," said the American, his hand painfully swollen. The rookie was watching with interest and learning plenty, he said, "until he dropped me. I was just concentrating on my riding. I've got a bit more to give."

There'd been a good four-way CRT battle during the early laps, with Hernandez, Espargaro, Pirro and de Puniet all closely engaged.

By the time de Puniet got to the front on lap 16, he and Espargaro had escaped. They stayed close until Espargaro crashed out on lap 24. Pirro was less than five seconds adrift; Hernandez had dropped back into the clutches of Edwards, who had been moving forward throughout the latter half of the race, passing Ellison on lap 13 and Hernandez on the 23rd, a couple of seconds ahead at the end.

Petrucci, in his first ride on the Suter BMW, had outqualified Edwards, but was a lap down on the leader at the end, with newcomer David Salom 15th. Salom, cousin of Moto3 rider Luis, had been recruited to the Avintia Blusens Kawasaki team in place of Silva, who had been made test rider.

Pasini also crashed out.

Abraham, the cause of the start-line problems, had an awful afternoon. He'd switched to his spare bike for a pit-lane start, only for that to suffer a similar hydraulic failure of the rear brake slave cylinder, which deposited fluid on the tyre, precipitating a first-lap crash that finally ended his misery.

Lorenzo's points advantage stretched from 13 to 38; Dovi gained ground on the absent Stoner, now 23 adrift; no-score Crutchlow was now just two points clear of Rossi.

MOTO2 RACE – 14 laps (shortened)

There's no time for slacking in Moto2, whatever the weather, which for them dried up on Saturday morning. Qualifying was shaping up between Espargaro and Marquez when the former fell with five minutes left. Marquez's seventh pole of the year (first in four races) was unchallenged, the margin a scant four-hundredths.

Redding snitched the last front-row spot from Iannone, who then was consigned to fifth as Nakagami put in a flyer. Luthi completed row two.

The planned 20-lap race got under way with Iannone galloping away from Rabat and Espargaro. Then Gino Rea had a huge and smoky engine blow-up in the middle of the pack, spewing oil on a chunk of track. Red flags came out before any disasters; the race was restarted after 35 minutes of frenzied scrubbing for a two-thirds-distance sprint.

Rea and early crasher Odendaal missed the restart, and it played badly for Redding, who had been fourth. This time, he got away badly, eighth into the first corner.

Marquez's seventh win of the season was masterly. He took the lead for the first time only halfway through the last lap, but though rival Espargaro put up a spirited defence – the pair changing places three times on that lap – it was to no avail.

Iannone had led away, and even took a lead of 1.3 seconds as Rabat headed the pursuit. But Espargaro displaced him on lap three and gradually whittled away at the lead. On lap 11, he was on Iannone and straight past, with Marquez instantly consigning the Italian to third. The trio drew away, Iannone losing touch as Espargaro set a blistering pace; Marquez appeared to be working hard to stay in touch.

In fact, in trademark style, he was just biding his time. He set a final new record on the penultimate lap and pounced at Quercia curve. Espargaro pushed inside to block at the next right; Marquez was not to be blocked. Again the Kalex rider pushed through on the final decreasing-speed rights; Marquez pushed straight back ahead into the last one, staying just out of reach to the line.

The battle for fourth devolved to three riders, Kallio passing Rabat on lap eight and managing to stay there. Luthi was with them until two-thirds distance, by which point they'd been caught by a gang led by Redding, from Zarco, Aegerter, Smith, Nakagami and Simon.

By the finish, Kallio, Rabat and Aegerter were covered by half a second. Redding was next, a second down, bitterly frustrated by problems imposed by his size and weight: at 74kg, he was heaviest in the class. "Sometimes I come in and think I don't know why I even race in Moto2. I got stuck behind Kallio and Rabat. And I couldn't pass them in braking because on every straight they'd pass me again. It was so much hard work and killing the tyres to finish seventh."

Smith, Luthi, Zarco and Nakagami were still close. Simon had lost touch in 12th.

The crash list was swelled by Elena Rosell, Simeon, Corsi and Yuki Takahashi.

MOTO3 RACE – 23 laps

The only race to run full distance was another vindication of the quality of the new class: a gang of ten until after half-distance and still seven-strong at the end, over the line in 1.3 seconds.

Cortese took pole back from local hero Fenati, with fellow local rookie Antonelli third, marking a welcome Italian renaissance in the smallest class.

Cortese led the first two laps, then Fenati, with the German ahead now and then until the 19th lap. Vinales, qualified 11th and 15th on lap one, was moving through steadily.

Rins was prominent in the group, with Salom, Vazquez and Folger, Oliveira and Antonelli also, Vinales joining at half-distance, when 1.6 seconds covered the top nine; rookie Sissis in tenth only now began to lose touch.

Fenati tried to break away with seven laps to go, but Cortese and the rest had closed up again by lap 19, and now it became serious. When they started the last lap, Fenati had been consigned to fifth, but he wasn't for giving up.

Vinales was third as they started the final lap, and second halfway around. But his attack on Cortese went wrong, letting the German escape and giving the chance to the pursuers. Salom grabbed second and Fenati pushed into third. Rins was a close fourth, ahead of Vinales, from Folger and Vazquez. Phew.

Antonelli and Oliveira were a couple of seconds away; Sissis was alone, but clear of the next trio, where Khairuddin narrowly held off Kent and Faubel.

There were a number of fallers, four on the first corner, where Danny Webb was bumped and skittled three other back-of-the-grid unfortunates; the second Mahindra was ridden again by Popov, to a respectable 19th.

ROUND 13

GP APEROL DI SAN MARINO E RIVIERA DI RIMINI

14–16 SEPTEMBER, 2012

motoGP

TISSOT — SWISS WATCHES SINCE 1853

OFFICIAL TIMEKEEPER

MISANO WORLD CIRCUIT

28 laps
Length: 4.226 km / 2.626 miles
Width: 12m

Key
96/60 kph/mph
Gear

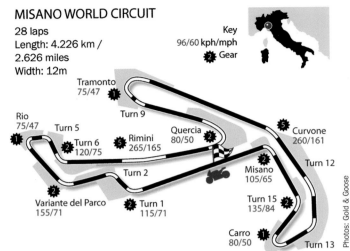

Tramonto 75/47
Rio 75/47
Turn 5
Turn 6 120/75
Rimini 265/165
Quercia 80/50
Turn 9
Curvone 260/161
Turn 12
Turn 2
Misano 105/65
Variante del Parco 155/71
Turn 1 115/71
Turn 15 135/84
Carro 80/50
Turn 13

Photos: Gold & Goose

MotoGP | RACE DISTANCE: 27 laps, 70.900 miles/114.102km · RACE WEATHER: Dry (air 23°C, humidity 56%, track 36°C)

Pos.	Rider	Nat.	No.	Entrant	Machine	Tyres	Race tyre choice	Laps	Time & speed
1	Jorge Lorenzo	SPA	99	Yamaha Factory Racing	Yamaha YZR-M1	B	F: Hard/R: Medium	27	42m 49.836s / 99.321mph/ 159.841km/h
2	Valentino Rossi	ITA	46	Ducati Team	Ducati Desmosedici GP12	B	F: Hard/R: Medium	27	42m 54.234s
3	Alvaro Bautista	SPA	19	San Carlo Honda Gresini	Honda RC213V	B	F: Hard/R: Medium	27	42m 55.891s
4	Andrea Dovizioso	ITA	4	Monster Yamaha Tech 3	Yamaha YZR-M1	B	F: Hard/R: Medium	27	42m 55.894s
5	Ben Spies	USA	11	Yamaha Factory Racing	Yamaha YZR-M1	B	F: Hard/R: Medium	27	42m 57.379s
6	Stefan Bradl	GER	6	LCR Honda MotoGP	Honda RC213V	B	F: Hard/R: Medium	27	43m 03.108s
7	Nicky Hayden	USA	69	Ducati Team	Ducati Desmosedici GP12	B	F: Hard/R: Medium	27	43m 30.743s
8	Jonathan Rea	GBR	56	Repsol Honda Team	Honda RC213V	B	F: Hard/R: Medium	27	43m 32.998s
9	Randy de Puniet	FRA	14	Power Electronics Aspar	ART Aprilia RSV4	B	F: Hard/R: Medium	27	43m 59.463s
10	Michele Pirro	ITA	51	San Carlo Honda Gresini	FTR Honda CBR1000RR	B	F: Hard/R: Medium	27	44m 03.441s
11	Colin Edwards	USA	5	NGM Mobile Forward Racing	Suter BMW S1000RR	B	F: Hard/R: Medium	27	44m 06.531s
12	Yonny Hernandez	COL	68	Avintia Blusens	BQR FTR Kawasaki ZX-10R	B	F: Hard/R: Medium	27	44m 08.909s
13	James Ellison	GBR	77	Paul Bird Motorsport	ART Aprilia RSV4	B	F: Hard/R: Medium	27	44m 09.244s
14	Danilo Petrucci	ITA	9	Came IodaRacing Project	Ioda Suter BMW S1000RR	B	F: Hard/R: Medium	26	43m 22.121s
15	David Salom	SPA	44	Avintia Blusens	BQR FTR Kawasaki ZX-10R	B	F: Hard/R: Medium	26	43m 43.915s
	Aleix Espargaro	SPA	41	Power Electronics Aspar	ART Aprilia RSV4	B	F: Hard/R: Medium	23	DNF-mechanical
	Cal Crutchlow	GBR	35	Monster Yamaha Tech 3	Yamaha YZR-M1	B	F: Hard/R: Medium	4	DNF-crash
	Mattia Pasini	ITA	54	Speed Master	ART Aprilia RSV4	B	F: Hard/R: Medium	1	DNF-crash
	Hector Barbera	SPA	8	Pramac Racing Team	Ducati Desmosedici GP12	B	F: Hard/R: Medium	0	DNF-crash
	Dani Pedrosa	SPA	26	Repsol Honda Team	Honda RC213V	B	F: Hard/R: Medium	0	DNF-crash
	Karel Abraham	CZE	17	Cardion AB Motoracing	Ducati Desmosedici GP12	B	F: Hard/R: Medium	0	DNF-crash

Fastest lap: Jorge Lorenzo, on lap 3, 1m 34.398s, 100.143mph/161.164km/h.

Lap record: Jorge Lorenzo, SPA (Yamaha), 1m 33.906s, 100.667mph/162.008km/h (2011).

Event best maximum speed: Dani Pedrosa, 179.8mph/289.4km/h (qualifying practice).

Qualifying

Weather: Dry
Air Temp: 21°   Humidity: 67%
Track Temp: 30°

1	Pedrosa	1m 33.857s
2	Lorenzo	1m 33.875s
3	Crutchlow	1m 34.001s
4	Bradl	1m 34.221s
5	Bautista	1m 34.299s
6	Rossi	1m 34.619s
7	Dovizioso	1m 34.916s
8	Spies	1m 34.988s
9	Rea	1m 35.358s
10	Hayden	1m 35.401s
11	Abraham	1m 35.648s
12	De Puniet	1m 35.756s
13	Barbera	1m 36.048s
14	Espargaro	1m 36.284s
15	Pirro	1m 36.340s
16	Ellison	1m 37.124s
17	Pasini	1m 37.162s
18	Hernandez	1m 37.316s
19	Petrucci	1m 37.751s
20	Edwards	1m 38.068s
21	Salom	1m 40.075s

Fastest race laps

1	Lorenzo	1m 34.398s
2	Bautista	1m 34.699s
3	Bradl	1m 34.707s
4	Spies	1m 34.719s
5	Dovizioso	1m 34.748s
6	Crutchlow	1m 34.785s
7	Rossi	1m 34.851s
8	Hayden	1m 35.863s
9	Rea	1m 36.201s
10	De Puniet	1m 36.621s
11	Espargaro	1m 36.918s
12	Pirro	1m 36.931s
13	Edwards	1m 37.101s
14	Ellison	1m 37.273s
15	Hernandez	1m 37.349s
16	Petrucci	1m 38.467s
17	Salom	1m 39.023s

Championship Points

1	Lorenzo	270
2	Pedrosa	232
3	Stoner	186
4	Dovizioso	163
5	Crutchlow	122
6	Rossi	120
7	Bautista	118
8	Bradl	115
9	Hayden	93
10	Spies	77
11	Barbera	60
12	De Puniet	48
13	Espargaro	45
14	Abraham	25
15	Hernandez	25
16	Pirro	24
17	Edwards	22
18	Ellison	17
19	Pasini	13
20	Petrucci	11
21	Silva	11
22	Elias	10
23	Rea	8
24	Rapp	2
25	Salom	1

Constructor Points

1	Honda	287
2	Yamaha	286
3	Ducati	144
4	ART	69
5	BQR	28
6	FTR	24
7	Suter	22
8	Ioda	9
9	Ioda-Suter	2
10	APR	2
11	BQR-FTR	2

Grid order	1	2	3	4	5	6	7	8	9	10	11	12	13	14	15	16	17	18	19	20	21	22	23	24	25	26	27	
26 PEDROSA	99	99	99	99	99	99	99	99	99	99	99	99	99	99	99	99	99	99	99	99	99	99	99	99	99	99	99	1
99 LORENZO	46	46	46	46	46	46	46	46	46	46	46	46	46	46	46	46	46	46	46	46	46	46	46	46	46	46	46	2
35 CRUTCHLOW	6	6	6	6	6	6	6	6	6	6	6	6	6	6	6	6	6	6	19	19	19	19	19	19	19	19	19	3
6 BRADL	4	4	4	4	4	4	4	4	4	4	4	4	4	4	4	19	GR	19	6	6	6	6	6	4	4	4	4	4
19 BAUTISTA	35	35	35	35	11	19	19	19	19	19	19	19	19	19	19	4	4	4	4	4	4	4	4	11	11	11	11	5
46 ROSSI	11	11	11	11	19	11	11	11	11	11	11	11	11	11	11	11	11	11	11	11	11	6	6	6	6			6
4 DOVIZIOSO	19	19	19	19	69	69	69	69	69	69	69	69	69	69	69	69	69	69	69	69	69	69	69	69	69	69	69	7
11 SPIES	69	69	69	69	56	56	56	56	56	56	56	56	56	56	56	56	56	56	56	56	56	56	56	56	56	56	56	8
56 REA	56	56	56	56	41	41	41	41	41	41	41	41	41	41	41	14	14	14	14	14	14	14	14	14	14	14	14	9
69 HAYDEN	54	68	68	41	68	14	14	14	14	14	14	14	14	14	14	41	41	41	41	41	41	41	41	51	51	51	51	10
17 ABRAHAM	68	41	41	68	14	68	68	68	68	68	68	68	68	68	68	51	51	51	51	51	51	51	5	5	5	5	5	11
14 DE PUNIET	41	51	51	51	51	51	51	51	51	51	51	51	51	51	51	68	68	68	68	68	68	68	68	68	68	68		12
8 BARBERA	51	14	14	14	77	77	77	77	77	77	77	77	5	5	5	5	5	5	5	5	5	5	68	77	77	77	77	13
41 ESPARGARO	9	9	77	77	9	5	5	5	5	5	5	77	77	77	77	77	77	77	77	77	77	77	9	9	9			14
51 PIRRO	14	77	9	9	5	9	9	9	9	9	9	9	9	9	9	9	9	9	9	9	9	44	44	44				15
77 ELLISON	77	5	5	44	44	44	44	44	44	44	44	44	44	44	44	44	44	44	44	44	44							
54 PASINI	5	44	44	44																								
68 HERNANDEZ	44																											
9 PETRUCCI																												
5 EDWARDS																												
44 SALOM																												
26 PEDROSA*																												

9 Lapped rider

* Pedrosa demoted from pole position to last place on the grid due to technical problems. Pole position left empty for the race start.

Moto2

RACE DISTANCE: 14 laps, 36.763 miles/59.164km · RACE WEATHER: Dry (air 22°C, humidity 61%, track 30°C)

Pos.	Rider	Nat.	No.	Entrant	Machine	Laps	Time & Speed
1	**Marc Marquez**	SPA	93	Team CatalunyaCaixa Repsol	Suter	14	23m 11.278s 95.125mph/ 153.089km/h
2	**Pol Espargaro**	SPA	40	Pons 40 HP Tuenti	Kalex	14	23m 11.637s
3	**Andrea Iannone**	ITA	29	Speed Master	Speed Up	14	23m 12.912s
4	**Mika Kallio**	FIN	36	Marc VDS Racing Team	Kalex	14	23m 16.356s
5	**Esteve Rabat**	SPA	80	Pons 40 HP Tuenti	Kalex	14	23m 16.524s
6	**Dominique Aegerter**	SWI	77	Technomag-CIP	Suter	14	23m 16.848s
7	**Scott Redding**	GBR	45	Marc VDS Racing Team	Kalex	14	23m 17.642s
8	**Bradley Smith**	GBR	38	Tech 3 Racing	Tech 3	14	23m 18.131s
9	**Thomas Luthi**	SWI	12	Interwetten-Paddock	Suter	14	23m 18.758s
10	**Johann Zarco**	FRA	5	JIR Moto2	Motobi	14	23m 19.267s
11	**Takaaki Nakagami**	JPN	30	Italtrans Racing Team	Kalex	14	23m 19.838s
12	**Julian Simon**	SPA	60	Blusens Avintia	Suter	14	23m 22.787s
13	**Alex de Angelis**	RSM	15	NGM Mobile Forward Racing	FTR	14	23m 29.607s
14	**Claudio Corti**	ITA	71	Italtrans Racing Team	Kalex	14	23m 29.620s
15	**Nicolas Terol**	SPA	18	Mapfre Aspar Team Moto2	Suter	14	23m 29.846s
16	Jordi Torres	SPA	81	Mapfre Aspar Team Moto2	Suter	14	23m 29.965s
17	Axel Pons	SPA	49	Pons 40 HP Tuenti	Kalex	14	23m 30.140s
18	Mike di Meglio	FRA	63	Kiefer Racing	Kalex	14	23m 36.923s
19	Ratthapark Wilairot	THA	14	Thai Honda PTT Gresini Moto2	Suter	14	23m 41.281s
20	Anthony West	AUS	95	QMMF Racing Team	Speed Up	14	23m 43.717s
21	Tomoyoshi Koyama	JPN	75	Technomag-CIP	Suter	14	23m 44.399s
22	Marcel Schrotter	GER	23	Desguaces La Torre SAG	Bimota	14	23m 44.536s
23	Alessandro Andreozzi	ITA	22	S/Master Speed Up	Speed Up	14	23m 44.810s
24	Marco Colandrea	SWI	10	SAG Team	FTR	14	23m 58.581s
	Yuki Takahashi	JPN	72	NGM Mobile Forward Racing	FTR	8	DNF
	Simone Corsi	ITA	3	Came IodaRacing Project	FTR	8	DNF
	Xavier Simeon	BEL	19	Tech 3 Racing	Tech 3	6	DNF
	Elena Rosell	SPA	82	QMMF Racing Team	Speed Up	1	DNF
	Gino Rea	GBR	8	Federal Oil Gresini Moto2	Suter	0	DNS
	Steven Odendaal	RSA	84	Arguinano Racing Team	AJR	0	DNS

Fastest lap: Marc Marquez, on lap 13, 1m 38.453s, 96.018mph/154.526km/h (record).
Previous lap record: Andrea Iannone, ITA (Suter), 1m 38.609s, 95.866mph/154.282km/h (2011).
Event best maximum speed: Esteve Rabat, 151.8mph/244.3km/h (free practice 3).

Qualifying: Dry
Air: 23° Humidity: 57% Track: 36°

1	Marquez	1m 38.242s
2	Espargaro	1m 38.286s
3	Redding	1m 38.339s
4	Nakagami	1m 38.369s
5	Iannone	1m 38.503s
6	Luthi	1m 38.617s
7	Rabat	1m 38.699s
8	Wilairot	1m 38.793s
9	Kallio	1m 38.794s
10	Smith	1m 38.849s
11	Takahashi	1m 38.866s
12	Simon	1m 38.919s
13	Corsi	1m 39.043s
14	Simeon	1m 39.074s
15	Zarco	1m 39.114s
16	Corti	1m 39.122s
17	Aegerter	1m 39.253s
18	Torres	1m 39.277s
19	Krummenacher	1m 39.417s
20	Di Meglio	1m 39.420s
21	De Angelis	1m 39.470s
22	Pons	1m 39.486s
23	Rea	1m 39.603s
24	Terol	1m 39.804s
25	West	1m 40.125s
26	Koyama	1m 40.130s
27	Andreozzi	1m 40.471s
28	Odendaal	1m 41.156s
29	Schrotter	1m 41.222s
30	Colandrea	1m 41.951s
31	Rosell	1m 42.102s

Fastest race laps

1	Marquez	1m 38.453s
2	Iannone	1m 38.493s
3	Espargaro	1m 38.527s
4	Luthi	1m 38.588s
5	Redding	1m 38.677s
6	Kallio	1m 38.700s
7	Rabat	1m 38.724s
8	Nakagami	1m 38.810s
9	Simon	1m 38.839s
10	Aegerter	1m 38.863s
11	Smith	1m 38.873s
12	Zarco	1m 38.875s
13	Corti	1m 39.051s
14	Torres	1m 39.097s
15	Corsi	1m 39.138s
16	Terol	1m 39.161s
17	Takahashi	1m 39.247s
18	De Angelis	1m 39.283s
19	Pons	1m 39.352s
20	Simeon	1m 39.368s
21	Di Meglio	1m 39.755s
22	West	1m 39.829s
23	Wilairot	1m 40.356s
24	Koyama	1m 40.458s
25	Andreozzi	1m 40.569s
26	Schrotter	1m 40.574s
27	Colandrea	1m 41.540s

Championship Points

1	Marquez	238
2	Espargaro	185
3	Iannone	165
4	Luthi	161
5	Redding	115
6	Kallio	110
7	Smith	85
8	Rabat	73
9	Aegerter	73
10	Corti	67
11	Zarco	66
12	De Angelis	61
13	Corsi	59
14	Simon	42
15	Nakagami	41
16	Elias	34
17	Krummenacher	24
18	Simeon	17
19	Terol	16
20	West	11
21	Di Meglio	10
22	Neukirchner	8
23	Wilairot	8
24	Cardus	6
25	Torres	3
26	Pons	1
27	Rea	1

Constructor Points

1	Suter	272
2	Kalex	231
3	Speed Up	165
4	Tech 3	85
5	FTR	79
6	Motobi	66
7	Moriwaki	10
8	AJR	6

Moto3

RACE DISTANCE: 23 laps, 60.396 miles/97.198km · RACE WEATHER: Dry (air 20°C, humidity 70%, track 16°C)

Pos.	Rider	Nat.	No.	Entrant	Machine	Laps	Time & Speed
1	**Sandro Cortese**	GER	11	Red Bull KTM Ajo	KTM	23	40m 22.100s 89.767mph/ 144.466km/h
2	**Luis Salom**	SPA	39	RW Racing GP	Kalex KTM	23	40m 22.567s
3	**Romano Fenati**	ITA	5	Team Italia FMI	FTR Honda	23	40m 23.037s
4	**Alex Rins**	SPA	42	Estrella Galicia 0,0	Suter Honda	23	40m 23.074s
5	**Maverick Vinales**	SPA	25	Blusens Avintia	FTR Honda	23	40m 23.245s
6	**Jonas Folger**	GER	94	Mapfre Aspar Team Moto3	Kalex KTM	23	40m 23.280s
7	**Efren Vazquez**	SPA	7	JHK t-shirt Laglisse	FTR Honda	23	40m 23.415s
8	**Niccolo Antonelli**	ITA	27	San Carlo Gresini Moto3	FTR Honda	23	40m 26.083s
9	**Miguel Oliveira**	POR	44	Estrella Galicia 0,0	Suter Honda	23	40m 26.476s
10	**Arthur Sissis**	AUS	61	Red Bull KTM Ajo	KTM	23	40m 32.972s
11	**Zulfahmi Khairuddin**	MAL	63	AirAsia-Sic-Ajo	KTM	23	40m 36.599s
12	**Danny Kent**	GBR	52	Red Bull KTM Ajo	KTM	23	40m 36.704s
13	**Hector Faubel**	SPA	55	Mapfre Aspar Team Moto3	Kalex KTM	23	40m 36.980s
14	**Alberto Moncayo**	SPA	23	Andalucia JHK t-shirt Laglisse	FTR Honda	23	40m 43.111s
15	**Jakub Kornfeil**	CZE	84	Redox-Ongetta-Centro Seta	FTR Honda	23	40m 43.162s
16	Brad Binder	RSA	41	RW Racing GP	Kalex KTM	23	40m 43.877s
17	Alessandro Tonucci	ITA	19	Team Italia FMI	FTR Honda	23	40m 46.593s
18	Toni Finsterbusch	GER	9	Racing Team Germany	Honda	23	41m 21.483s
19	Miroslav Popov	CZE	95	Mahindra Racing	Mahindra	23	41m 21.785s
20	Michael Ruben Rinaldi	ITA	71	Caretta Technology	Honda	23	41m 21.941s
21	Luigi Morciano	ITA	3	Ioda Team Italia	Ioda	23	41m 42.073s
22	Kenta Fujii	JPN	51	Technomag-CIP-TSR	TSR Honda	23	41m 45.061s
23	Josep Rodriguez	SPA	28	Ongetta-Centro Seta	FTR Honda	23	41m 45.180s
24	Stefano Valtulini	ITA	33	Team Imperiali Moto3	Honda	23	40m 53.858s
	Niklas Ajo	FIN	31	TT Motion Events Racing	KTM	21	DNF
	Alex Marquez	SPA	12	Ambrogio Next Racing	Suter Honda	4	DNF
	Louis Rossi	FRA	96	Racing Team Germany	FTR Honda	3	DNF
	Armando Pontone	ITA	80	IodaRacing Project	Ioda	3	DNF
	Giulian Pedone	SWI	30	Ambrogio Next Racing	Suter Honda	3	DNF
	Jack Miller	AUS	8	Caretta Technology	Honda	2	DNF
	Jasper Iwema	NED	53	Moto FGR	FGR Honda	1	DNF
	Kevin Calia	ITA	74	Elle 2-Ciatti	Honda	0	DNF
	Alan Techer	FRA	89	Technomag-CIP-TSR	TSR Honda	0	DNF
	Danny Webb	GBR	99	Mahindra Racing	Mahindra	0	DNF

Fastest lap: Alex Rins, on lap 8, 1m 44.043s, 90.859mph/146.224km/h (record).
Previous lap record: New category.
Event best maximum speed: Zulfahmi Khairuddin, 128.7mph/207.1km/h (race).

Qualifying: Dry
Air: 21° Humidity: 69% Track: 33°

1	Cortese	1m 44.201s
2	Fenati	1m 44.571s
3	Antonelli	1m 44.590s
4	Kent	1m 44.843s
5	Salom	1m 44.857s
6	Folger	1m 44.877s
7	Tonucci	1m 44.909s
8	Khairuddin	1m 45.078s
9	Oliveira	1m 45.116s
10	Sissis	1m 45.142s
11	M. Vinales	1m 45.230s
12	Rossi	1m 45.259s
13	Faubel	1m 45.260s
14	Binder	1m 45.289s
15	Vazquez	1m 45.332s
16	Moncayo	1m 45.332s
17	Rins	1m 45.333s
18	Kornfeil	1m 45.926s
19	Calia	1m 46.437s
20	Techer	1m 46.518s
21	Miller	1m 46.524s
22	Iwema	1m 46.589s
23	Pedone	1m 46.675s
24	Ajo	1m 46.678s
25	Marquez	1m 46.801s
26	Webb	1m 47.143s
27	Morciano	1m 47.735s
28	Rodriguez	1m 47.995s
29	Valtulini	1m 48.109s
30	Pontone	1m 48.146s
31	Rinaldi	1m 48.184s
32	Finsterbusch	1m 48.312s
33	Popov	1m 48.347s
34	Fujii	1m 48.672s
Outside 107%		
	Martin	No Time

Fastest race laps

1	Rins	1m 44.043s
2	Vazquez	1m 44.214s
3	Cortese	1m 44.305s
4	Oliveira	1m 44.311s
5	Salom	1m 44.369s
6	M. Vinales	1m 44.431s
7	Folger	1m 44.466s
8	Antonelli	1m 44.487s
9	Fenati	1m 44.554s
10	Khairuddin	1m 44.602s
11	Sissis	1m 44.644s
12	Kent	1m 44.690s
13	Faubel	1m 45.048s
14	Binder	1m 45.134s
15	Moncayo	1m 45.219s
16	Kornfeil	1m 45.327s
17	Tonucci	1m 45.403s
18	Marquez	1m 45.626s
19	Ajo	1m 46.107s
20	Morciano	1m 46.424s
21	Finsterbusch	1m 46.468s
22	Popov	1m 46.496s
23	Rinaldi	1m 46.565s
24	Rossi	1m 46.927s
25	Miller	1m 47.304s
26	Fujii	1m 47.679s
27	Rodriguez	1m 47.840s
28	Pontone	1m 48.123s
29	Valtulini	1m 48.469s
30	Pedone	1m 50.202s

Championship Points

1	Cortese	225
2	M. Vinales	179
3	Salom	169
4	Fenati	120
5	Rins	96
6	Masbou	81
7	Khairuddin	81
8	Kent	70
9	Oliveira	66
10	Antonelli	63
11	Rossi	59
12	Vazquez	59
13	Folger	56
14	Kornfeil	53
15	Faubel	52
16	Sissis	51
17	Moncayo	49
18	Techer	21
19	Ajo	21
20	Marquez	15
21	Miller	14
22	Tonucci	14
23	Moreno	10
24	Iwema	9
25	Gruenwald	8
26	Pedone	7
27	Finsterbusch	7
28	Martin	6
29	Binder	5
30	Schrotter	4
31	Hanus	3
32	I. Vinales	2
33	Calia	2
34	McPhee	1
35	Rinaldi	1
36	Grotzkyj	1

Constructor Points

1	FTR Honda	246
2	KTM	226
3	Kalex KTM	203
4	Suter Honda	128
5	Honda	84
6	TSR Honda	21
7	FGR Honda	9
8	Ioda	5
9	Mahindra	4
10	KRP Honda	1
11	Oral	1

ARAGÓN GRAND PRIX

ARAGÓN CIRCUIT

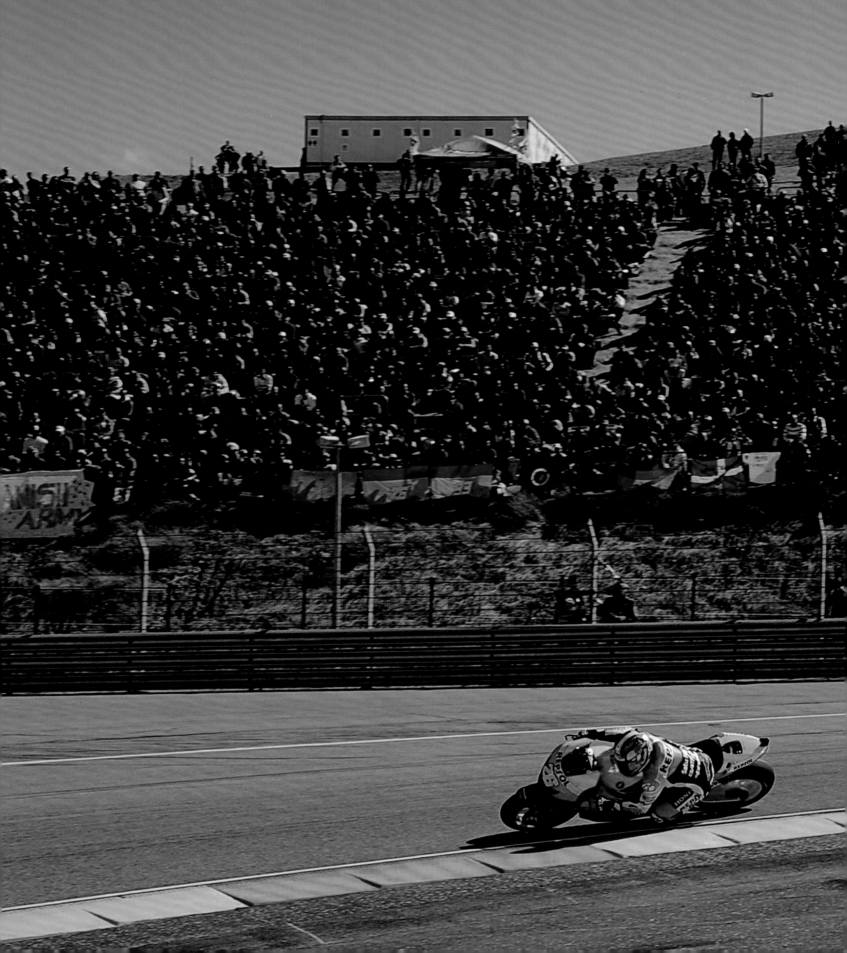

Blue skies at last, and Pedrosa out on his own. He was embarking on an unprecedented (for him) series of victories.
Photo: Gold & Goose

Above: Lorenzo's improving starts saw him off the line ahead of jack-rabbit Pedrosa once again. They lead Spies, Crutchlow, Bradl, Rea and Ducatis out of the first corners.

Top right: Misano disaster forgotten, Pedrosa kept the embers of his title hopes glowing with an emphatic win.

Above right: Team owner Jorge Martinez and Aleix Espargaro, who beat team-mate de Puniet in their private CRT contest.

Right: Dovi and Cal were at it again: the Italian beat his team-mate by this much for the rostrum.

Photos: Gold & Goose

IF the bad weather at Misano had been unkind for a sea-side resort, surely things would be better in Aragon, where the arid landscape and pale far horizons attest to a dearth of rainfall. Yet again, in a year of bad weather it turned out otherwise. Friday and Saturday morning were cold and damp, but it dried for qualifying and the race.

Yet again, the track was all but empty for first practice, prompting mutterings that perhaps it should be compulsory to go out in the interests of TV. Hayden was one to run, getting his first taste of the latest Ducati chassis; Barbera was also dialling himself back in. Rossi took a run and Abraham essayed two laps – the only prototypes amid a handful of CRT bikes, among them Salom getting some mileage.

One cure, opined the riders, would be to increase the allocation of wet tyres from four per weekend: half-and-half conditions chew them up, and at least one set must be kept for race day. On the other hand, it meant saving miles, with Lorenzo – potentially short of engines – happily admitting, "I've saved 300km in the last two races."

With only a dry hour, it was just like Misano: not enough time to find the perfect set-up. In Italy, this had played in favour of Rossi. This time, the advantage lay with the Honda and Yamaha factory teams, who had stopped off after Brno for a couple of days. The results proved the point: now it was Rossi on the back foot, and hopes of a Ducati renaissance were put back on hold.

One consequence of the lack of dry practice was that nobody had really tested the extra-hard front tyre, yet all but Petrucci, Ellison and Pasini chose it for the race. Nicky paid the price early on when he lost the front going into the 100mph corner at the end of the back straight. It was a close copy of a misadventure he'd had in practice. That time, he'd saved the bike in the gravel trap, toppling off at low speed. This time, it happened earlier and he was going faster, heading towards an unprotected barrier at speed, in the gravel and unable to slow down. Rather than jump off and risk the bike following him into the barrier, he rode it out. "I decided to let the bike take the impact, and let go at the last moment." The crash sent him looping right over the barrier, to land close to, but luckily not on top of a parked scooter. It was bad enough, though, and he sustained a new fracture in his right forearm. It could have been much worse, and that evening discussions began about how to protect against what had been an unexpected set of circumstances. The consensus was either an air-fence, or paving the gravel trap, which would have allowed him to brake. Why not both?

Pedrosa resumed what now looked like a hopeless title battle with another copybook victory. Once again, Lorenzo had no answer, his comfort zone shrinking. One non-finish could jeopardise everything.

With the European season coming to an end, there was much talk about the increasing urgency of new technical rules for 2014, the threat of the control ECU looming ever closer. The riders, rather surprisingly, were cautiously in favour, given a shared reservation that safety should not be compromised. It would be fairer for all, thought Lorenzo, especially "for those who do not have the best electronics now". Rossi opined that there might be "more fun and more fighting". Pedrosa had the last word, citing the example of F1: "It seems it works there; the drivers don't complain much. But it's a car, not a bike. Everything is unknown."

Also unknown was the outcome of the Honda-led confron-

tation between the manufacturers and Dorna over the same issue, with HRC threatening to walk out to World Superbikes; scheduled meetings between the factories and Dorna at Motegi were expected to be stormy. Among all this, Ezpeleta gave a calm and reassuring interview to a Spanish paper, saying that he thought they would "achieve finality" at Motegi. Up his sleeve, he had the knowledge that by then the Dorna takeover of Superbikes would have become public.

Back with the nuts and bolts, after extensive tests in Japan there was still no explanation of Pedrosa's so costly brake malfunction at Misano. Every possibility had been dismissed, including melting tyre-warmer straps and a hydraulic lock; it had been impossible to replicate any micro-welding condition. "It was not a Honda problem," said a brusque Nakamoto. And for brake firm boss Eugenio Gandolfi, "It was not a Brembo problem."

Once again, in the all-four-stroke new world there was a big oil spill and, given that the track was also damp, it triggered an extraordinary ten crashes. They occurred in the first Moto3 session, and the bad apple was Danny Webb's Mahindra. Webb was the last victim; by then, the trail he'd left behind in Turns Seven, Eight and Nine had accounted for wild-cards Guevara and Navarro, plus Folger, Kent, Vazquez, Martin, Tonucci, Rins and Oliveira, fortunately without any injury. During the weekend, Ioda announced that they were to abandon their own troublesome engine and would switch to Honda power for 2013, leaving Mahindra struggling alone with an independent engine. The 2012 Oral had been troublesome at best; for 2013, they would try again with an all-new Suter-built unit – up against Honda and KTM, this was not an easy option.

More Moto3 news came from thwarted pre-season favourite Vinales, who announced with proper honeyed words that he had signed for two more years with his Avintia Blusens team – one more in Moto3, then Moto2. The written statement, in pure PR-speak, quoted the 17-year-old as saying, "I think we made the right decision. I'm very young, I have a lot of opportunities to achieve the objectives I have set for myself in Moto3, and I think I have plenty of time to move up to Moto2." A very different truth would emerge in three weeks, after total disaster on race day finally scuppered his dwindling title hopes.

MOTOGP RACE – 23 laps

It finally dried – at least on the racing line – for qualifying, but the track was cold and treacherous. Demonstrated early on by Dani Pedrosa, who crashed at the end of the straight on his second flying lap: "Maybe I touched the white line or hit a bump; maybe the tyre was not warm enough." Rossi fell soon after, and Hayden at the far end of the session.

Times improved as rubber was laid down; those who had pre-tested here had a big advantage. After a slow start, Lorenzo took his fifth pole of the year. The returned Pedrosa failed to displace him by less than a tenth, then Crutchlow a similar time behind him for his sixth front row and third in succession.

Spies, fast in the wet, led row two from Bradl and Dovi. Rea impressed in his last ride on Stoner's bike, heading row three from Rossi and Hayden.

Bautista had new Showa suspension, but no time to set it up, and was 12th behind top CRT rider Espargaro.

A clean start this time, and Lorenzo led into the first left-right combination, from Pedrosa, Spies, Crutchlow, Bradl and Dovi. Crucially, Rea was ahead of the Ducatis of Hayden and Rossi, who had swapped around by the time they reached the end of the back straight, where Rossi all but hit Rea. "He braked early and took the line, and I was in the wrong place. Can happen on the first lap," said Rossi. He ran off, to finish the first lap in last place.

The two leaders drew away from Spies, by 2.5 seconds on lap three. Pedrosa matched Lorenzo's every move and slipped past on lap seven. Two laps later, Lorenzo had a mas-

Above: Chasing Corsi. Eventual winner Espargaro leads Iannone, Corti, Zarco and Rabat early in the Moto2 race.

Top right: Like father, like son? 1987 champion Wayne and Remy Gardner in the Honda garage.

Above centre right: A second win and a fourth successive podium for Luis Salom in Moto3.

Above right: Maverick Vinales with team director Ricard Jove: problems were about to erupt.

Right: Team-mates Kent (52) and Cortese dispute the lead with Vazquez (7), winner Salom half hidden behind. Rins (42) heads Folger and Rossi in pursuit.

Photos: Gold & Goose

sive slide and tank-slapper, and lost touch by more than 1.5 seconds. The gap would continue to grow from then on, each rider alone in his own world.

Hayden was chasing Dovizioso when he went flying off on lap two – a shocking sight.

Dovi in turn was closing on Crutchlow. Bradl had already blown by the Englishman "like we were standing still" on the straight on lap three, and next time around he took Spies as well, only to slip off on the first corner combination as he started the next lap.

That left the three Yamahas together, Spies holding off the satellite bikes as Crutchlow ran wide out of the last corner on lap 11, giving Dovizioso the chance he'd been waiting for.

The trio remained close, the next change coming on lap 15 when Dovizioso passed Spies. Two laps later, Crutchlow did the same, and Spies lost touch slowly, but inexorably as the team-mates resumed the battle they had been having for most of the year.

It lasted all the way, but Dovi was confident that his late braking would allow him to hold the position, for his sixth rostrum of the year. Crutchlow did his best to prove him wrong, attacking twice on the last two laps at the same slow corner and getting ahead, only to lose the position again under acceleration on the way out.

Life was fairly dull for the rest of the factory bikes: Bautista pressing on unmolested a couple of seconds adrift, and then Rea.

There was a lively battle behind, with de Puniet holding the cards until Abraham finally got by with nine laps to go. The Frenchman and Espargaro stayed close, swapping positions on the final lap.

Barbera had been involved in the early laps, but dropped back at about the same time as Rossi turned up from behind, surging past all of them by lap nine, but too far from Bautista to catch up.

A way back, Ellison was fending off the persistent Hernandez. The Colombian finally managed to get by with two laps to go, and they finished half a second apart.

Pirro had been with them for the first quarter of the race,

but lost touch while Edwards closed up, getting ahead on lap 15, only to run into a strange problem and drop away to last by the finish, 18th and a lap down. His gear-shifter had broken off and he limped home, stuck in fifth. Petrucci had a lonely ride on the Came Suter BMW to 17th.

Salom pitted to retire after three laps, and found out in the following days that his brief stint was over, as Silva was returned to favour.

Four races left, three of them on the fly, and Lorenzo's lead was shrinking again. Pedrosa was re-starting a run of domination in Stoner's absence … but was it all too late?

MOTO2 RACE – 21 laps

Corsi took his first class pole after a session of many crashes, Marquez very narrowly avoiding adding his name to the list. Corsi promptly ran off as he started his cool-down lap. He'd displaced Espargaro by almost two-tenths; Iannone completed the front row; Corti led the second from Torres and Terol.

Only then came Marquez, with Britons Smith and Redding alongside. Zarco had been fastest in the wet, with West third; they ended up tenth and 20th.

Corsi led away from Corti, Espargaro and Iannone, then Smith heading Marquez. Espargaro was up to second by the end of the lap; Smith would drop back, with both Zarco and Rabat following Marquez past. The last named was moving forward and took over from Corsi on lap five. The Italian was still third behind Marquez and the shadowing Espargaro, but would lose places as the lead gang became bigger and closer. At this point, Iannone was pressing hard; Zarco headed the next gang from Corti, Rabat, Smith, Redding and briefly di Meglio.

It was whisker close and riveting, impossible to log all the passes and changes of position. It's enough to say that Iannone took over the lead from laps 15 to 17, with Espargaro, Marquez and Redding right with him, and the rest less than a second behind.

Espargaro took to the front for the first time on lap 18,

and made the most of a clear track as the rest pushed and shoved, getting in one another's way. Positions changed corner by corner; nobody could gain an advantage that lasted longer than a few bends, and the action was furious. It was astonishing that nobody crashed.

Espargaro set fastest lap on the 18th, not a record. What helped him more in his eventual escape by 1.4 seconds was the ferocity with which Iannone and Marquez traded blows, with Redding closely involved, over the last three laps.

Marquez had a clear and significant speed advantage on the straight, renewing the debate over the need for a minimum rider-and-bike weight regulation. But it wasn't enough to let him get away.

On the last lap, Redding managed to get between them, and it was resolved only over the line: Marquez second, Redding third, Iannone fourth. The trio was covered by less than four-tenths.

Outpaced, Redding's fighting rostrum was all the more remarkable: eight days earlier, he'd had arm-pump surgery, and with eight laps to go the scar opened up.

Smith was only three-tenths from Iannone, and inches ahead of Zarco. Then, another 1.4 seconds away, came Corsi and Torres, who had been hovering at the back of the group for the latter half of the race.

Corti was half a second behind, and a tenth ahead of West, who had closed after half-distance, escaping at the end from an off-form Luthi. Rabat was still close, then came Terol, a small breathing space ahead of di Meglio. Aegerter headed the next group for the last point.

There were only three crashers. Nakagami took de Angelis down on the first lap, the Japanese rejoining to finish 30th. Xavier Simeon crashed out alone two laps later.

MOTO3 RACE – 20 laps

Championship disaster began on the warm-up lap, when Vinales's bike died following an electronics failure. Even with several marshals helping, he couldn't get it going again. Finally he dropped it, kicked it to smash the screen and stomped off.

Folger was still flying high on his new Aspar bike, taking a career-first pole by less than two-tenths from Salom. Cortese was alongside; Fenati led row two from Kent and the now absent Maverick.

He missed a great race, even closer than Moto2, the first eight finishing inside less than two seconds.

Cortese would have no leisure to appreciate his absence. Folger led away from Salom, Khairuddin and Vazquez, Cortese fifth ahead of Fenati, who retired with 11 laps to go.

Khairuddin led laps three to five, but crashed out while still a close fifth on lap 12.

The remainder kept going, a huge gang still eight-strong at the finish.

By then, Cortese had led from laps six to 12, and again on the 16th; while Rins and Kent each took a turn.

Salom led for the first time on lap 19 and immediately opened a little gap. It had shrunk again by the time they got to the end, however, with Cortese and Folger right behind; a gap of eight-tenths, then came Kent, Vazquez, Rins, Rossi and Oliveira.

Sissis had been hanging on at the back of the gang throughout, only half a second behind Oliveira over the line and a tenth ahead of the next group – Antonelli, Kornfeil, Tonucci and Moncayo. Ten seconds away, Ajo and Marquez Junior took the final points.

FIM WORLD CHAMPIONSHIP

ROUND

14

28–30 SEPTEMBER, 2012

GRAN PREMIO
IVECO
DE ARAGÓN

motogp
TISSOT SWISS WATCHES SINCE 1853

OFFICIAL TIMEKEEPER

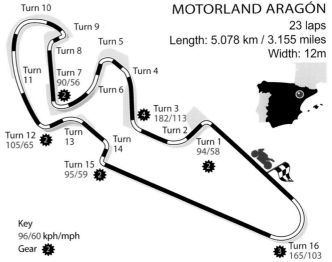

MOTORLAND ARAGÓN
23 laps
Length: 5.078 km / 3.155 miles
Width: 12m

Turn 10
Turn 9
Turn 5
Turn 8
Turn 7 90/56
Turn 11
Turn 4
Turn 6
Turn 3 182/113
Turn 2
Turn 12 105/65
Turn 13
Turn 14
Turn 1 94/58
Turn 15 95/59
Turn 16 165/103

Key
96/60 kph/mph
Gear

Photos: Gold & Goose

MotoGP RACE DISTANCE: 23 laps, 72.572 miles/116.794km · RACE WEATHER: Dry (air 18°C, humidity 51%, track 23°C)

Pos.	Rider	Nat.	No.	Entrant	Machine	Tyres	Race tyre choice	Laps	Time & speed
1	**Dani Pedrosa**	SPA	26	Repsol Honda Team	Honda RC213V	B	F: Ex. Hard/R: Medium	23	42m 10.444s 103.246mph/ 166.159km/h
2	**Jorge Lorenzo**	SPA	99	Yamaha Factory Racing	Yamaha YZR-M1	B	F: Ex. Hard/R: Medium	23	42m 16.916s
3	**Andrea Dovizioso**	ITA	4	Monster Yamaha Tech 3	Yamaha YZR-M1	B	F: Ex. Hard/R: Medium	23	42m 21.491s
4	**Cal Crutchlow**	GBR	35	Monster Yamaha Tech 3	Yamaha YZR-M1	B	F: Ex. Hard/R: Medium	23	42m 21.628s
5	**Ben Spies**	USA	11	Yamaha Factory Racing	Yamaha YZR-M1	B	F: Ex. Hard/R: Medium	23	42m 24.230s
6	**Alvaro Bautista**	SPA	19	San Carlo Honda Gresini	Honda RC213V	B	F: Ex. Hard/R: Medium	23	42m 38.610s
7	**Jonathan Rea**	GBR	56	Repsol Honda Team	Honda RC213V	B	F: Ex. Hard/R: Medium	23	42m 42.734s
8	**Valentino Rossi**	ITA	46	Ducati Team	Ducati Desmosedici GP12	B	F: Ex. Hard/R: Medium	23	42m 54.876s
9	**Karel Abraham**	CZE	17	Cardion AB Motoracing	Ducati Desmosedici GP12	B	F: Ex. Hard/R: Medium	23	43m 07.861s
10	**Aleix Espargaro**	SPA	41	Power Electronics Aspar	ART Aprilia RSV4	B	F: Ex. Hard/R: Medium	23	43m 08.969s
11	**Randy de Puniet**	FRA	14	Power Electronics Aspar	ART Aprilia RSV4	B	F: Ex. Hard/R: Medium	23	43m 10.307s
12	**Hector Barbera**	SPA	8	Pramac Racing Team	Ducati Desmosedici GP12	B	F: Ex. Hard/R: Medium	23	43m 25.005s
13	**Yonny Hernandez**	COL	68	Avintia Blusens	BQR FTR Kawasaki ZX-10R	B	F: Medium/R: Medium	23	43m 26.603s
14	**James Ellison**	GBR	77	Paul Bird Motorsport	ART Aprilia RSV4	B	F: Medium/R: Medium	23	43m 27.024s
15	**Michele Pirro**	ITA	51	San Carlo Honda Gresini	FTR Honda CBR1000RR	B	F: Medium/R: Medium	23	43m 36.259s
16	Mattia Pasini	ITA	54	Speed Master	ART Aprilia RSV4	B	F: Medium/R: Medium	23	43m 42.245s
17	Danilo Petrucci	ITA	9	Came IodaRacing Project	Ioda Suter BMW S1000RR	B	F: Ex. Hard/R: Medium	23	43m 52.744s
18	Colin Edwards	USA	5	NGM Mobile Forward Racing	Suter BMW S1000RR	B	F: Ex. Hard/R: Medium	22	42m 52.997s
	Stefan Bradl	GER	6	LCR Honda MotoGP	Honda RC213V	B	F: Ex. Hard/R: Medium	4	DNF-crash
	David Salom	SPA	44	Avintia Blusens	BQR FTR Kawasaki ZX-10R	B	F: Ex. Hard/R: Medium	3	DNF-mechanical
	Nicky Hayden	USA	69	Ducati Team	Ducati Desmosedici GP12	B	F: Ex. Hard/R: Medium	1	DNF-crash

Fastest lap: Dani Pedrosa, on lap 3, 1m 49.109s, 104.108mph/167.546km/h.
Lap record: Casey Stoner, AUS (Honda), 1m 49.046s, 104.169mph/167.643km/h (2011).
Event best maximum speed: Stefan Bradl, 211.8mph/340.8km/h (warm up).

Qualifying

Weather: Dry
Air Temp: 16° Humidity: 89%
Track Temp: 16°

1	Lorenzo	1m 49.404s
2	Pedrosa	1m 49.492s
3	Crutchlow	1m 49.576s
4	Spies	1m 49.748s
5	Bradl	1m 50.034s
6	Dovizioso	1m 50.241s
7	Rea	1m 50.410s
8	Rossi	1m 50.949s
9	Hayden	1m 51.013s
10	Barbera	1m 51.072s
11	Espargaro	1m 51.082s
12	Bautista	1m 51.155s
13	De Puniet	1m 51.459s
14	Abraham	1m 51.521s
15	Pirro	1m 52.606s
16	Pasini	1m 52.638s
17	Edwards	1m 52.853s
18	Petrucci	1m 53.140s
19	Hernandez	1m 53.233s
20	Ellison	1m 53.719s
21	Salom	1m 55.290s

Fastest race laps

1	Pedrosa	1m 49.109s
2	Lorenzo	1m 49.134s
3	Bradl	1m 49.936s
4	Spies	1m 49.952s
5	Crutchlow	1m 49.957s
6	Dovizioso	1m 50.008s
7	Bautista	1m 50.633s
8	Rossi	1m 50.718s
9	Rea	1m 50.857s
10	De Puniet	1m 51.187s
11	Espargaro	1m 51.500s
12	Abraham	1m 51.524s
13	Barbera	1m 51.856s
14	Ellison	1m 52.243s
15	Hernandez	1m 52.396s
16	Pasini	1m 52.611s
17	Edwards	1m 52.688s
18	Pirro	1m 52.832s
19	Petrucci	1m 53.660s
20	Salom	1m 56.953s

Championship Points

1	Lorenzo	290
2	Pedrosa	257
3	Stoner	186
4	Dovizioso	179
5	Crutchlow	135
6	Rossi	128
7	Bautista	128
8	Bradl	115
9	Hayden	93
10	Spies	88
11	Barbera	64
12	De Puniet	53
13	Espargaro	51
14	Abraham	32
15	Hernandez	28
16	Pirro	25
17	Edwards	22
18	Ellison	19
19	Rea	17
20	Pasini	13
21	Petrucci	11
22	Silva	11
23	Elias	10
24	Rapp	2
25	Salom	1

Constructor Points

1	Honda	312
2	Yamaha	306
3	Ducati	152
4	ART	75
5	BQR	31
6	FTR	25
7	Suter	22
8	Ioda	9
9	Ioda-Suter	2
10	APR	2
11	BQR-FTR	2

Grid order	1	2	3	4	5	6	7	8	9	10	11	12	13	14	15	16	17	18	19	20	21	22	23	
99 LORENZO	99	99	99	99	99	99	26	26	26	26	26	26	26	26	26	26	26	26	26	26	26	26	26	1
26 PEDROSA	26	26	26	26	26	26	99	99	99	99	99	99	99	99	99	99	99	99	99	99	99	99	99	2
35 CRUTCHLOW	11	11	11	6	11	11	11	11	11	11	11	11	11	11	4	4	4	4	4	4	4	4	4	3
11 SPIES	35	35	6	11	35	35	35	35	35	4	4	4	4	11	11	11	35	35	35	35	35	35	35	4
6 BRADL	6	6	35	35	4	4	4	4	4	35	35	35	35	35	35	35	11	11	11	11	11	11	11	5
4 DOVIZIOSO	4	4	4	4	19	19	19	19	19	19	19	19	19	19	19	19	19	19	19	19	19	19	19	6
56 REA	69	19	19	19	56	56	56	56	56	56	56	56	56	56	56	56	56	56	56	56	56	56	56	7
46 ROSSI	56	56	56	56	14	14	41	41	46	46	46	46	46	46	46	46	46	46	46	46	46	46	46	8
69 HAYDEN	19	14	14	14	41	41	17	17	17	14	14	14	14	17	17	17	17	17	17	17	17	17	17	9
8 BARBERA	41	41	41	41	17	17	14	14	41	14	41	41	17	14	14	14	14	14	14	14	14	14	41	10
41 ESPARGARO	8	17	17	17	8	8	8	46	14	41	17	17	41	41	41	41	41	41	41	41	41	41	14	11
19 BAUTISTA	14	8	8	8	46	46	46	8	8	8	8	8	8	8	8	8	8	8	8	8	8	8	8	12
14 DE PUNIET	17	51	51	77	77	77	77	77	77	77	77	77	77	77	77	77	77	77	77	68	68			13
17 ABRAHAM	51	54	54	68	68	68	68	68	68	68	68	68	68	68	68	68	68	68	68	77	77			14
51 PIRRO	54	77	77	51	51	51	51	51	51	51	51	51	51	5	5	5	51	51	51	51	51			15
54 PASINI	5	68	68	46	9	9	9	9	9	54	54	54	54	51	51	51	5	54	54	54				
5 EDWARDS	77	5	5	5	5	5	5	54	54	54	9	9	9	54	54	54	54	9	9	9				
9 PETRUCCI	68	9	46	9	54	54	54	5	5	9	5	5	5	9	9	9	9	5	5					
68 HERNANDEZ	9	46	9	54																				
77 ELLISON	44	44	44																					
44 SALOM	46																							

44 Pit stop   5 Lapped rider

Moto2

RACE DISTANCE: 21 laps, 66.262 miles/106.638km · RACE WEATHER: Dry (air 17°C, humidity 54%, track 22°C)

Pos.	Rider	Nat.	No.	Entrant	Machine	Laps	Time & Speed
1	**Pol Espargaro**	SPA	40	Pons 40 HP Tuenti	Kalex	21	40m 25.260s 98.357mph/ 158.290km/h
2	**Marc Marquez**	SPA	93	Team CatalunyaCaixa Repsol	Suter	21	40m 26.707s
3	**Scott Redding**	GBR	45	Marc VDS Racing Team	Kalex	21	40m 27.003s
4	**Andrea Iannone**	ITA	29	Speed Master	Speed Up	21	40m 27.085s
5	**Bradley Smith**	GBR	38	Tech 3 Racing	Tech 3	21	40m 27.453s
6	**Johann Zarco**	FRA	5	JIR Moto2	Motobi	21	40m 28.259s
7	**Simone Corsi**	ITA	3	Came IodaRacing Project	FTR	21	40m 29.577s
8	**Jordi Torres**	SPA	81	Mapfre Aspar Team Moto2	Suter	21	40m 30.375s
9	**Claudio Corti**	ITA	71	Italtrans Racing Team	Kalex	21	40m 30.779s
10	**Anthony West**	AUS	95	QMMF Racing Team	Speed Up	21	40m 30.891s
11	**Thomas Luthi**	SWI	12	Interwetten-Paddock	Suter	21	40m 31.111s
12	**Esteve Rabat**	SPA	80	Pons 40 HP Tuenti	Kalex	21	40m 31.808s
13	**Nicolas Terol**	SPA	18	Mapfre Aspar Team Moto2	Suter	21	40m 32.809s
14	**Mike di Meglio**	FRA	63	Kiefer Racing	Kalex	21	40m 39.335s
15	**Dominique Aegerter**	SWI	77	Technomag-CIP	Suter	21	40m 42.582s
16	Mika Kallio	FIN	36	Marc VDS Racing Team	Kalex	21	40m 42.650s
17	Axel Pons	SPA	49	Pons 40 HP Tuenti	Kalex	21	40m 42.752s
18	Julian Simon	SPA	60	Blusens Avintia	Suter	21	40m 43.097s
19	Alex Marinelarena	SPA	92	Targo Bank CNS Motorsport	Suter	21	40m 55.839s
20	Marcel Schrotter	GER	23	Desguaces La Torre SAG	Bimota	21	40m 58.008s
21	Steven Odendaal	RSA	84	Arguinano Racing Team	AJR	21	40m 58.139s
22	Gino Rea	GBR	8	Federal Oil Gresini Moto2	Suter	21	40m 58.531s
23	Yuki Takahashi	JPN	72	NGM Mobile Forward Racing	FTR	21	40m 59.571s
24	Tomoyoshi Koyama	JPN	75	Technomag-CIP	Suter	21	41m 01.823s
25	Ratthapark Wilairot	THA	14	Thai Honda PTT Gresini Moto2	Suter	21	41m 03.521s
26	Eric Granado	BRA	57	JIR Moto2	Motobi	21	41m 21.280s
27	Elena Rosell	SPA	82	QMMF Racing Team	Speed Up	21	41m 42.462s
28	Jesko Raffin	SWI	20	GP Team Switzerland	Kalex	21	41m 42.930s
29	Marco Colandrea	SWI	10	SAG Team	FTR	21	41m 43.623s
30	Takaaki Nakagami	JPN	30	Italtrans Racing Team	Kalex	21	41m 49.504s
31	Alessandro Andreozzi	ITA	22	S/Master Speed Up	Speed Up	21	41m 50.413s
	Xavier Simeon	BEL	19	Tech 3 Racing	Tech 3	3	DNF
	Alex de Angelis	RSM	15	NGM Mobile Forward Racing	FTR	1	DNF

Fastest lap: Pol Espargaro, on lap 18, 1m 54.511s, 99.197mph/159.642km/h.

Lap record: Marc Marquez, SPA (Suter), 1m 53.956s, 99.680mph/160.419km/h (2011).

Event best maximum speed: Takaaki Nakagami, 177.7mph/286.0km/h (qualifying practice).

Qualifying: Dry

Air: 16° Humidity: 86% Track: 16°

1	Corsi	1m 54.343s
2	Espargaro	1m 54.534s
3	Iannone	1m 54.618s
4	Corti	1m 54.712s
5	Torres	1m 54.787s
6	Terol	1m 54.828s
7	Marquez	1m 54.877s
8	Smith	1m 54.899s
9	Redding	1m 54.925s
10	Zarco	1m 54.993s
11	Rabat	1m 55.074s
12	Kallio	1m 55.224s
13	Nakagami	1m 55.235s
14	Pons	1m 55.275s
15	Simeon	1m 55.445s
16	Takahashi	1m 55.445s
17	Di Meglio	1m 55.473s
18	De Angelis	1m 55.510s
19	Luthi	1m 55.617s
20	West	1m 55.875s
21	Simon	1m 55.951s
22	Rea	1m 56.112s
23	Aegerter	1m 56.129s
24	Mariñelarena	1m 56.661s
25	Schrotter	1m 56.695s
26	Wilairot	1m 57.158s
27	Odendaal	1m 57.299s
28	Koyama	1m 57.370s
29	Granado	1m 57.462s
30	Andreozzi	1m 57.925s
31	Rosell	1m 58.367s
32	Raffin	1m 59.177s
33	Colandrea	1m 59.477s

Fastest race laps

1	Espargaro	1m 54.511s
2	Iannone	1m 54.582s
3	Corsi	1m 54.647s
4	Luthi	1m 54.707s
5	Marquez	1m 54.798s
6	Redding	1m 54.806s
7	Torres	1m 54.833s
8	Smith	1m 54.911s
9	Zarco	1m 54.915s
10	West	1m 54.981s
11	Corti	1m 55.009s
12	Rabat	1m 55.058s
13	Terol	1m 55.069s
14	Nakagami	1m 55.070s
15	Di Meglio	1m 55.259s
16	Aegerter	1m 55.356s
17	Pons	1m 55.463s
18	Kallio	1m 55.482s
19	Simon	1m 55.515s
20	Rea	1m 55.854s
21	Schrotter	1m 55.975s
22	Odendaal	1m 56.064s
23	Mariñelarena	1m 56.124s
24	Simeon	1m 56.264s
25	Takahashi	1m 56.390s
26	Koyama	1m 56.436s
27	Wilairot	1m 56.591s
28	Granado	1m 57.180s
29	Raffin	1m 57.478s
30	Rosell	1m 57.844s
31	Andreozzi	1m 57.871s
32	Colandrea	1m 58.015s

Championship Points

1	Marquez	258
2	Espargaro	210
3	Iannone	178
4	Luthi	166
5	Redding	131
6	Kallio	110
7	Smith	96
8	Rabat	77
9	Zarco	76
10	Corti	74
11	Aegerter	74
12	Corsi	68
13	De Angelis	61
14	Simon	42
15	Nakagami	41
16	Elias	34
17	Krummenacher	24
18	Terol	19
19	West	17
20	Simeon	17
21	Di Meglio	12
22	Torres	11
23	Neukirchner	8
24	Wilairot	8
25	Cardus	6
26	Pons	1
27	Rea	1

Constructor Points

1	Suter	292
2	Kalex	256
3	Speed Up	178
4	Tech 3	96
5	FTR	88
6	Motobi	76
7	Moriwaki	10
8	AJR	6

Moto3

RACE DISTANCE: 20 laps, 63.106 miles/101.560km · RACE WEATHER: Dry (air 15°C, humidity 67%, track 16°C)

Pos.	Rider	Nat.	No.	Entrant	Machine	Laps	Time & Speed
1	**Luis Salom**	SPA	39	RW Racing GP	Kalex KTM	20	40m 56.391s 92.486mph/ 148.842km/h
2	**Sandro Cortese**	GER	11	Red Bull KTM Ajo	KTM	20	40m 56.546s
3	**Jonas Folger**	GER	94	Mapfre Aspar Team Moto3	Kalex KTM	20	40m 56.753s
4	**Danny Kent**	GBR	52	Red Bull KTM Ajo	KTM	20	40m 57.506s
5	**Efren Vazquez**	SPA	7	JHK t-shirt Laglisse	FTR Honda	20	40m 57.551s
6	**Alex Rins**	SPA	42	Estrella Galicia 0,0	Suter Honda	20	40m 58.156s
7	**Louis Rossi**	FRA	96	Racing Team Germany	FTR Honda	20	40m 58.230s
8	**Miguel Oliveira**	POR	44	Estrella Galicia 0,0	Suter Honda	20	40m 58.363s
9	**Arthur Sissis**	AUS	61	Red Bull KTM Ajo	KTM	20	40m 58.806s
10	**Niccolo Antonelli**	ITA	27	San Carlo Gresini Moto3	FTR Honda	20	40m 58.978s
11	**Jakub Kornfeil**	CZE	84	Redox-Ongetta-Centro Seta	FTR Honda	20	40m 59.236s
12	**Alessandro Tonucci**	ITA	19	Team Italia FMI	FTR Honda	20	40m 59.458s
13	**Alberto Moncayo**	SPA	23	Andalucia JHK t-shirt Laglisse	FTR Honda	20	41m 00.154s
14	**Niklas Ajo**	FIN	31	TT Motion Events Racing	KTM	20	41m 11.290s
15	**Alex Marquez**	SPA	12	Ambrogio Next Racing	Suter Honda	20	41m 11.432s
16	Brad Binder	RSA	41	RW Racing GP	Kalex KTM	20	41m 32.861s
17	Isaac Vinales	SPA	32	Ongetta-Centro Seta	FTR Honda	20	41m 33.813s
18	Toni Finsterbusch	GER	9	Racing Team Germany	Honda	20	41m 33.848s
19	Jack Miller	AUS	8	Caretta Technology	Honda	20	41m 34.703s
20	Luca Amato	GER	29	Mapfre Aspar Team Moto3	Kalex KTM	20	41m 37.222s
21	Alan Techer	FRA	89	Technomag-CIP-TSR	TSR Honda	20	41m 37.240s
22	John McPhee	GBR	17	Caretta Technology	KRP Honda	20	41m 38.270s
23	Giulian Pedone	SWI	30	Ambrogio Next Racing	Suter Honda	20	41m 38.435s
24	Juan Francisco Guevara	SPA	58	Wild Wolf BST	FTR Honda	20	41m 52.287s
25	Danny Webb	GBR	99	Mahindra Racing	Mahindra	20	41m 59.078s
26	Kenta Fujii	JPN	51	Technomag-CIP-TSR	TSR Honda	20	42m 14.446s
27	Armando Pontone	ITA	80	IodaRacing Project	Ioda	20	42m 14.765s
	Adrian Martin	SPA	26	JHK t-shirt Laglisse	FTR Honda	17	DNF
	Miroslav Popov	CZE	95	Mahindra Racing	Mahindra	16	DNF
	Zulfahmi Khairuddin	MAL	63	AirAsia-Sic-Ajo	KTM	14	DNF
	Romano Fenati	ITA	5	Team Italia FMI	FTR Honda	9	DNF
	Jorge Navarro	SPA	49	Bradol Larresport	Honda	1	DNF
	Jasper Iwema	NED	53	Moto FGR	FGR Honda	1	DNF
	Maverick Vinales	SPA	25	Blusens Avintia	FTR Honda	0	DNS

Fastest lap: Danny Kent, on lap 3, 2m 1.351s, 93.605mph/150.643km/h (record).

Previous lap record: New category.

Event best maximum speed: Zulfahmi Khairuddin, 148.9mph/239.7km/h (race).

Qualifying: Dry

Air: 16° Humidity: 93% Track: 16°

1	Folger	2m 01.715s
2	Salom	2m 01.867s
3	Cortese	2m 02.041s
4	Fenati	2m 02.202s
5	Kent	2m 02.236s
6	M. Vinales	2m 02.362s
7	Khairuddin	2m 02.387s
8	Vazquez	2m 02.461s
9	Oliveira	2m 02.571s
10	Rins	2m 02.763s
11	Antonelli	2m 02.976s
12	Moncayo	2m 03.012s
13	Rossi	2m 03.081s
14	Tonucci	2m 03.290s
15	Guevara	2m 03.412s
16	Sissis	2m 03.414s
17	Kornfeil	2m 03.588s
18	Marquez	2m 03.635s
19	Martin	2m 03.753s
20	Ajo	2m 03.888s
21	Pedone	2m 03.981s
22	Amato	2m 04.030s
23	Miller	2m 04.405s
24	Iwema	2m 04.820s
25	Finsterbusch	2m 05.211s
26	Navarro	2m 05.323s
27	McPhee	2m 05.441s
28	Webb	2m 05.547s
29	I. Vinales	2m 05.830s
30	Techer	2m 05.926s
31	Pontone	2m 06.259s
32	Binder	2m 06.882s
33	Fujii	2m 07.380s
34	Popov	2m 08.406s
Outside 107%		
	Morciano	No Time

Fastest race laps

1	Kent	2m 01.351s
2	Sissis	2m 01.384s
3	Cortese	2m 01.412s
4	Vazquez	2m 01.439s
5	Fenati	2m 01.459s
6	Antonelli	2m 01.483s
7	Moncayo	2m 01.540s
8	Oliveira	2m 01.543s
9	Tonucci	2m 01.578s
10	Rossi	2m 01.603s
11	Rins	2m 01.621s
12	Khairuddin	2m 01.653s
13	Folger	2m 01.733s
14	Kornfeil	2m 01.791s
15	Ajo	2m 01.804s
16	Salom	2m 01.930s
17	Marquez	2m 01.982s
18	Finsterbusch	2m 02.625s
19	Martin	2m 02.841s
20	I. Vinales	2m 02.875s
21	Binder	2m 02.926s
22	Miller	2m 03.221s
23	Pedone	2m 03.328s
24	McPhee	2m 03.739s
25	Techer	2m 03.837s
26	Amato	2m 03.980s
27	Guevara	2m 04.014s
28	Webb	2m 04.122s
29	Pontone	2m 04.737s
30	Popov	2m 05.175s
31	Fujii	2m 05.431s

Championship Points

1	Cortese	245
2	Salom	194
3	M. Vinales	179
4	Fenati	120
5	Rins	106
6	Kent	83
7	Masbou	81
8	Khairuddin	81
9	Oliveira	74
10	Folger	72
11	Vazquez	70
12	Antonelli	69
13	Rossi	68
14	Sissis	58
15	Kornfeil	58
16	Moncayo	52
17	Faubel	52
18	Ajo	23
19	Techer	21
20	Tonucci	18
21	Marquez	16
22	Miller	14
23	Moreno	10
24	Iwema	9
25	Gruenwald	8
26	Pedone	7
27	Finsterbusch	7
28	Martin	6
29	Binder	5
30	Schrotter	4
31	Hanus	3
32	I. Vinales	2
33	Calia	2
34	McPhee	1
35	Rinaldi	1
36	Grotzkyj	1

Constructor Points

1	FTR Honda	257
2	KTM	246
3	Kalex KTM	228
4	Suter Honda	138
5	Honda	84
6	TSR Honda	21
7	FGR Honda	9
8	Ioda	5
9	Mahindra	4
10	KRP Honda	1
11	Oral	1

Main photo: Manga-style welcome at the entrance to Honda's home track.

Inset, top right: Stoner fans said hello and goodbye to their hero.

Insets, above: Motegi marketplace: souvenirs both official and wacky.

Inset, right: Rossi signs for his fans.

Inset, far right: Austere and intriguing: Pedrosa leads in another singular battle with Lorenzo.

Photos: Gold & Goose

JAPANESE GRAND PRIX

MOTEGI CIRCUIT

AT Motegi, the combination of jet lag, the inscrutable scrutiny of the factory big bosses and the regimented jollity of the fans always makes for an air of unreality. In 2012, the first of a gruelling schedule of three fly-aways on the trot took place in an even more complicated atmosphere than usual, as major off-track events overshadowed even the increasingly absorbing battle between Lorenzo and the blazingly on-form Pedrosa.

The previous week news had broken of Bridgepoint's internal re-arrangement, bringing World Superbikes under the control of Dorna and appointing Carmelo Ezpeleta as racing's new Grand Poobah, Supreme Commander of all he surveys. This put a very different complexion on his meetings with the local industry chiefs, where fierce resistance to his rev-limit plans had been expected; and also the meeting of the GP Commission.

Ezpeleta gave a press conference where he was unable to stop himself from looking like the cat that got the canary. He confirmed Dorna's complete control of SBK, turning aside questions about the fate of the current Flammini Group management and adopting a conciliatory tone when asked about whether he could now bring the factories to heel. Over at Magny-Cours, the Superbike paddock was absorbing the news, and in a state of some shock.

There was also a race meeting to be conducted, for once in dry weather, and on a very special sort of track. Honda's creation is not admired by many; it lacks rhythm and comprises too many stop-and-go sections interrupted by second- or third-gear corners. It puts a premium on acceleration. And, of course, braking.

Here was the rub. Regulations unchanged from the year before dictated maximum brake disc diameter – 320mm. But 2012's 1000s were not only 7kg heavier than 2011's

machines, they were also faster. The combination took the brakes to, and in some cases beyond, their capabilities, in spite of the fact that Brembo had brought special thicker carbon discs to cope.

A number of riders complained of running out of stopping power, and many took to the run-off at the end of the downhill back straight, the most punishing corner of all, where (by Brembo's figures) speed is cut by 195km/h in less than 250m, with a maximum force of 1.6g. The first corner is only slightly less punishing (dropping 180km/h), and of the seven major braking zones, five are to corners taken below 100km/h, all but one approached at 240km/h or a lot more.

No one suffered as much as Spies, singled out once again for further mechanical misfortune. "I think it's the way I brake," he said later, explaining how his first application is unusually hard. He had trouble in practice, with the discs reaching 950 degrees C, right at their limit, which led to very rapid wear, and crew chief Tom Houseworth warned him he was in danger of going "metal to carbon" before the end of the race. He didn't have to wait that long – lying third on only the second lap, going into Turn One, he ran out of stopping power ("the data showed we had only 30 per cent"), ran off the track, and ultimately hit the barrier and fell, by then at a sufficiently low speed to avoid injury. Brake failure joined a list that already included a cracked sub-frame, a blown engine and a rear suspension collapse.

Should the rules allow bigger discs? Motegi was the first track that showed this problem. Should the riders be allowed more fuel? Running out of the mere 21 litres allowed hadn't happened for a while because engineers had improved mechanical and electronic strategies, but again Motegi pushed the limits, because of the hard acceleration.

The most prominent victim was Cal Crutchlow, fighting

with Bautista for another rostrum only to sputter to a stop on the final lap, a cruel blow. And, like the brakes, more proof of how close racing equipment is to the edge. "We knew it would be critical," he said. "I was very fast and for almost the whole race I was on my own with no slipstream, so I used more fuel."

Stoner was back, warning that it was a bit soon, according to medical advice, but he wanted to be up to speed for his home GP in three weeks. He still had limited movement and strength, and the track's fierce and frequent acceleration was causing trouble, because, unable to brace himself with his feet, "I have to pull my weight forward with my arms, and that's causing some issues," he said.

Hayden was back with double jeopardy, his right-hand Indy fractures now joined by a forearm fracture from Aragon. For him, it was the braking zones that were most difficult.

Moto2 was up to its usual tricks, the main one in 2012 being to showcase the remarkable talent of Marc Marquez. He had missed pole, but was on the front row. Then he missed his gear selection, and as the lights went he found himself in neutral. There were heart-stopping moments as the rest of the pack whistled past on either side, those from the back of the grid by now travelling at a good speed. Thankfully, they all missed him as he stamped the pedal down and took off.

His lap was captured in a remarkable on-board video. Through the first corners, he scythes through the ducking and weaving field. He went from 32nd place to ninth in that lap, passing 22 riders in the first two corners. It seems almost superfluous to add that he won.

Moto3 brought a landmark first win for Danny Kent after a turbulent last lap, during which three top men had crashed. One was points leader Cortese, set to win and tie up the title with four races to spare. He blamed Kent and spent most of

the cool-down lap barging into his team-mate, gesticulating wildly, blind with rage. Later he viewed the video footage to see that Kent had done nothing wrong, and apologised handsomely to all.

MOTOGP RACE – 24 laps

Lorenzo was on pole again with a record lap, and Pedrosa alongside, the gap between them three-tenths, but Lorenzo not especially confident at a track where Honda acceleration was a strong suit. Alongside them, Crutchlow, in his fourth front-row slot on the trot and seventh of the season.

Spies led row two from Bautista and Dovizioso; Stoner was seventh, heading row three and the best part of a second off pole; Rossi was at the far end of that row.

Roberto Rolfo was back in the top class, having taken over Pasini's Speed Master seat: there had been dissension and financial issues for some time. He qualified second-last, ahead of Silva, who had returned to duty on the Blusens Kawasaki.

Lorenzo took a flying start to lead Pedrosa and Spies into the first corner. Crutchlow, Stoner, Bautista, Dovizioso and Rossi were in a pack behind, and they finished the first lap in the same order.

Spies would not get much further, his brake problem striking at the end of the pit straight. He stomped off in high dudgeon, another promising race ruined.

The leading pair was together, Dani shadowing Jorge once more, and more than two seconds ahead of Crutchlow after three laps. The gap would slowly and steadily grow as their austere, but intriguing battle continued.

Dani had to win; Jorge needed only to come second. Each was fully aware, and Pedrosa's intent fully clear as he stalked

Above: Yamaha tester Nakasuga gave Hayden a run for his money, finishing a tenth adrift. Barbera (8) would soon lose touch.

Top far left: Ready for action? Brakes were a very hot topic at Motegi.

Top left: Robby Rolfo, a 250 and Moto2 GP winner, took over Pasini's Speed Master ART CRT bike.

Above left: Lorenzo heads Pedrosa into the first underpass. Both are close to the limit.

Left: Ben Spies was again singled out for mechanical problems that ruined another promising race.

Photos: Gold & Goose

Above: More kisses as Bautista celebrates a second consecutive podium.

Top right: Esteve Rabat, here heading
winner Marquez, took his first rostrum
of the year.

Above right: Beneficiaries of last-lap
mayhem: Vinales, Kent and Tonucci on
the podium.

Right: Kent's maiden win came from
his first ever pole start.
Photos: Gold & Goose

patiently. On lap 12, he pounced with a clean outbraking
move before the underpass, and that was the end of that.
Each rider continued to do his duty, and Dani won by better
than four seconds, having also set a new lap record while
in pursuit.

Pedrosa described his race with words that would also
have served for Lorenzo: "We did what we needed to do,"
he said, adding, "It's just a pity there is no one else who can
stay with us, because every race I win, he's been second."

Action came from Crutchlow, and the group immediately
behind. Bautista had displaced Stoner on lap three, and
thereupon lost ground steadily on the third-placed Yamaha,
more than 1.5 seconds on lap ten. Behind him, Bradl had
pushed past Dovi on the same lap, by which point, they were
more than a second adrift of the slowly fading Stoner.

Now Bautista started to close again, on Crutchlow's tail
with ten laps to go, pushing hard and finally seizing his
chance on lap 20. They battled almost all the way, changing
places several times as the Englishman responded in kind
to every attack, promising himself success in the inevitable
closing skirmish. Instead he ended up coasting to a stop on
the last lap, out of fuel. The third rostrum place went to the
Honda, a bright spot that underlined Bautista's recent contract renewal to stay with the San Carlo team.

Stoner had no defence when Dovi closed and outbraked
him into the first corner with seven laps left, and he was five
seconds down, though still four ahead of Bradl. The German
was stricken with arm-pump, a new complaint for him, triggered by the hard braking. "It started from lap ten … it was
really hard to steer the bike," he said.

Rossi was closing on the German at the end, not fast
enough to threaten, but enough for him to comment favour-
ably on progress, though still hampered by wheelspin out of
the corners. "It was a good weekend for us," he said, adding

with a laugh, "The only problem is the other guys are faster
than us."

Injury-hampered Hayden was well down, engaged all race
long with (and once even behind) wild-card Katsuyuki Nakasuga, Yamaha factory tester. In the end, he beat him by
less than a tenth.

Barbera was a lone tenth; Abraham was next after outpac-
ing Espargaro, top CRT bike. His team-mate, de Puniet, had
crashed out on the first lap, but remounted to battle on in
last place for 14 laps before finally calling it a day.

Edwards was barely two seconds adrift, his Suter BMW
progress at last achieving some direction; Ellison in turn saw
off Pirro for 14th, the pair taking the final points. Rolfo was a
long way adrift; Petrucci and Silva both retired.

Lorenzo's damage control shrank his lead, but improved
his position: from now on, third in the remaining three races
would be enough, if Pedrosa were to win all three.

MOTO2 RACE – 23 laps

Eight riders within the first second was not especially close
for Moto2, and some fancied names were not among the
front guys, notably Corsi in 12th and Iannone – for whom
Motegi is something of a bogey circuit – down in 18th.

Espargaro took pole, his fifth of the year compared with
seven for Marquez, by less than two-tenths from his rival;
Rabat was alongside. His first time up front made it an all-
Spanish quorum.

Redding led the second from Luthi and Zarco; Smith the
third. Krummenacher was out for a second race after his
Misano injury, being replaced by Swiss rider Jesko Raffin;
and Colandrea's usual seat went to Kohta Nozane, the only
local rider, with no wild-cards. More significantly, the Italtrans
team had unaccountably dropped Claudio Corti, and maiden

Moto2 champion Toni Elias was in his place on the Kalex, and seemingly at last finding some pace again; he qualified in tenth.

Marquez's start-line snafu might have unsettled a lesser rider. His eighth win proved he is the coolest customer, fiercest competitor and fastest rider.

His first lap was an education in aggressive brinkmanship, and he was still in fast-forward mode at the end of it, gaining two more places as he passed Nakagami and Smith, who had run wide ahead; the Englishman rejoined a couple of places back.

Redding led lap one, but Rabat took over for the next eight. By then, Marquez was in the slightly spaced lead group and had just passed Espargaro for second.

He led for the first time on lap ten and, as he pulled clear, only Espargaro could go with him, Rabat steadily losing touch to finish almost ten seconds adrift.

The Spanish rivals fought closely and with increasing ferocity as the laps ticked down. They changed places more than once, but Marquez always seemed to have the upper hand, and so it proved – by less than half a second as he fought off every last-lap lunge.

Redding had lost touch with Rabat and dropped back to a lively scrap with Luthi and the revitalised Elias, until the Spaniard fell on lap 20. Redding narrowly kept Luthi at bay for fourth; behind, Corsi did the same to Nakagami for sixth.

Eighth to 13th was covered by 1.6 seconds after a fine sustained battle. Class rookie Zarco took control in the last two laps, from Pons, Aegerter, Simon, West and Torres.

Marquez left Japan needing one more race to be certain of the title. Circumstances, however, would compel him to wait a little longer.

MOTO3 RACE – 20 laps

Kent took a first ever pole by an impressive two-tenths, heading Vinales and Cortese; Khairuddin led the second row from improving rookie Tonucci – his team-mate Fenati down in tenth – and Salom, times very close now and Folger heading row three.

The first Moto3 race at Honda's track clearly favoured the faster KTMs, with four in a leading pack of six. Then three of them were eliminated in two last-lap accidents.

Kent headed the first lap, then he and Folger disputed the lead back and forth until half-distance, when the German took over. At that point, there were five more in close pursuit: Salom, Tonucci, Khairuddin and the canny Cortese, with Vinales hanging on grimly at the back.

Khairuddin would drop away to come under pressure from the pursuing Rins, but there were still six as they started the final lap.

Leader Folger swung in towards the apex of Turn One; at the same time, Salom arrived inside him at unfeasible speed, and so unlikely to be able to make the corner that Race Direction subsequently hit him with a five-position grid penalty for the next race. He did crash, into Folger, and both went down and out. The German was incandescent, and only the Spaniard's fervent apologies defused a potential gravel-trap brawl.

Now Cortese led, but Kent drafted him down the back straight and outbraked him into the notorious bottom bend before the second underpass, fishtailing to the apex. Cortese was pushed wide and Tonucci took the chance to slip past.

On the corner exit, the Italian moved over to the right just as Cortese arrived on his faster exit line. They collided and Cortese went down. Tonucci all but ran over him as Vinales slipped past inside for a lucky second.

Rins passed Khairuddin on the last lap for what was now fourth; the hastily remounted Cortese was ten seconds down in sixth. The next six were over the line in less than a second: Oliveira, Rossi, Vazquez, Fenati, Sissis and Antonelli. Ajo and Alex Marquez narrowly headed the following group for the final points.

FIM WORLD CHAMPIONSHIP

15

ROUND

12–14 OCTOBER, 2012

AIRASIA
GRAND PRIX
OF JAPAN

Photos: Gold & Goose

motoGP

T+ TISSOT
SWISS WATCHES SINCE 1853

OFFICIAL TIMEKEEPER

TWIN RING MOTEGI

24 laps
Length: 4.801 km / 2.983 miles
Width: 13m

Key
96/60 kph/mph
Gear

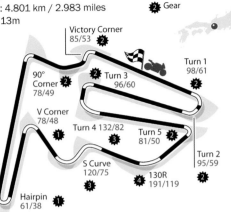

Victory Corner 85/53
90° Corner 78/49
Turn 3 96/60
Turn 1 98/61
V Corner 78/48
Turn 4 132/82
Turn 5 81/50
Turn 2 95/59
S Curve 120/75
130R 191/119
Hairpin 61/38

MotoGP · RACE DISTANCE: 24 laps, 71.597 miles/115.224km · RACE WEATHER: Dry (air 20°C, humidity 55%, track 23°C)

Pos.	Rider	Nat.	No.	Entrant	Machine	Tyres	Race tyre choice	Laps	Time & speed
1	**Dani Pedrosa**	SPA	26	Repsol Honda Team	Honda RC213V	B	F: Hard/R: Soft	24	42m 31.569s 101.016mph/ 162.569km/h
2	Jorge Lorenzo	SPA	99	Yamaha Factory Racing	Yamaha YZR-M1	B	F: Hard/R: Soft	24	42m 35.844s
3	Alvaro Bautista	SPA	19	San Carlo Honda Gresini	Honda RC213V	B	F: Hard/R: Soft	24	42m 38.321s
4	Andrea Dovizioso	ITA	4	Monster Yamaha Tech 3	Yamaha YZR-M1	B	F: Hard/R: Soft	24	42m 47.966s
5	Casey Stoner	AUS	1	Repsol Honda Team	Honda RC213V	B	F: Hard/R: Soft	24	42m 52.135s
6	Stefan Bradl	GER	6	LCR Honda MotoGP	Honda RC213V	B	F: Hard/R: Soft	24	42m 56.136s
7	Valentino Rossi	ITA	46	Ducati Team	Ducati Desmosedici GP12	B	F: Hard/R: Soft	24	42m 57.641s
8	Nicky Hayden	USA	69	Ducati Team	Ducati Desmosedici GP12	B	F: Hard/R: Soft	24	43m 08.293s
9	Katsuyuki Nakasuga	JPN	21	Yamaha YSP Racing Team	Yamaha YZR-M1	B	F: Hard/R: Soft	24	43m 08.363s
10	Hector Barbera	SPA	8	Pramac Racing Team	Ducati Desmosedici GP12	B	F: Hard/R: Soft	24	43m 42.298s
11	Karel Abraham	CZE	17	Cardion AB Motoracing	Ducati Desmosedici GP12	B	F: Hard/R: Soft	24	43m 47.227s
12	Aleix Espargaro	SPA	41	Power Electronics Aspar	ART Aprilia RSV4	B	F: Hard/R: Soft	24	43m 54.338s
13	Colin Edwards	USA	5	NGM Mobile Forward Racing	Suter BMW S1000RR	B	F: Hard/R: Soft	24	43m 56.537s
14	James Ellison	GBR	77	Paul Bird Motorsport	ART Aprilia RSV4	B	F: Hard/R: Soft	24	44m 00.957s
15	Michele Pirro	ITA	51	San Carlo Honda Gresini	FTR Honda CBR1000RR	B	F: Hard/R: Soft	24	44m 06.181s
16	Roberto Rolfo	ITA	84	Speed Master	ART Aprilia RSV4	B	F: Hard/R: Soft	24	44m 22.422s
	Cal Crutchlow	GBR	35	Monster Yamaha Tech 3	Yamaha YZR-M1	B	F: Hard/R: Soft	23	DNF-mechanical
	Danilo Petrucci	ITA	9	Came IodaRacing Project	Ioda Suter BMW S1000RR	B	F: Hard/R: Soft	23	DNF-mechanical
	Ivan Silva	SPA	22	Avintia Blusens	BQR FTR Kawasaki ZX-10R	B	F: Hard/R: Soft	14	DNF-mechanical
	Randy de Puniet	FRA	14	Power Electronics Aspar	ART Aprilia RSV4	B	F: Hard/R: Soft	14	DNF-crash
	Ben Spies	USA	11	Yamaha Factory Racing	Yamaha YZR-M1	B	F: Hard/R: Soft	1	DNF-crash
	Yonny Hernandez	COL	68	Avintia Blusens	BQR FTR Kawasaki ZX-10R	B	F: Hard/R: Soft	1	DNF-crash

Fastest lap: Dani Pedrosa, on lap 4, 1m 45.589s, 101.710mph/163.687km/h (record).
Previous lap record: Dani Pedrosa, SPA (Honda), 1m 46.090s, 101.230mph/162.914km/h (2011).
Event best maximum speed: Stefan Bradl, 192.1mph/309.1km/h (qualifying practice).

Qualifying
Weather: Dry
Air Temp: 22° Humidity: 42%
Track Temp: 22°

1	Lorenzo	1m 44.969s
2	Pedrosa	1m 45.215s
3	Crutchlow	1m 45.257s
4	Spies	1m 45.336s
5	Bautista	1m 45.481s
6	Dovizioso	1m 45.612s
7	Stoner	1m 45.745s
8	Bradl	1m 45.848s
9	Rossi	1m 45.976s
10	Hayden	1m 46.461s
11	Nakasuga	1m 46.780s
12	Barbera	1m 46.881s
13	Espargaro	1m 47.383s
14	De Puniet	1m 47.581s
15	Abraham	1m 47.791s
16	Edwards	1m 48.125s
17	Hernandez	1m 48.513s
18	Pirro	1m 48.653s
19	Petrucci	1m 48.831s
20	Ellison	1m 49.023s
21	Rolfo	1m 49.183s
22	Silva	1m 49.831s

Fastest race laps

1	Pedrosa	1m 45.589s
2	Lorenzo	1m 45.727s
3	Crutchlow	1m 45.907s
4	Bautista	1m 46.033s
5	Dovizioso	1m 46.196s
6	Bradl	1m 46.223s
7	Stoner	1m 46.240s
8	Rossi	1m 46.739s
9	Hayden	1m 47.071s
10	Nakasuga	1m 47.220s
11	Barbera	1m 47.771s
12	Abraham	1m 48.560s
13	Edwards	1m 48.820s
14	Espargaro	1m 48.842s
15	Ellison	1m 49.158s
16	Pirro	1m 49.344s
17	Petrucci	1m 49.635s
18	Silva	1m 49.636s
19	De Puniet	1m 49.642s
20	Rolfo	1m 50.023s

Championship Points

1	Lorenzo	310
2	Pedrosa	282
3	Stoner	197
4	Dovizioso	192
5	Bautista	144
6	Rossi	137
7	Crutchlow	135
8	Bradl	125
9	Hayden	101
10	Spies	88
11	Barbera	70
12	Espargaro	55
13	De Puniet	53
14	Abraham	37
15	Hernandez	28
16	Pirro	26
17	Edwards	25
18	Ellison	21
19	Rea	17
20	Pasini	13
21	Petrucci	11
22	Silva	11
23	Elias	10
24	Nakasuga	7
25	Rapp	2
26	Salom	1

Constructor Points

1	Honda	337
2	Yamaha	326
3	Ducati	161
4	ART	79
5	BQR	31
6	FTR	26
7	Suter	25
8	Ioda	9
9	Ioda-Suter	2
10	APR	2
11	BQR-FTR	2

Grid order	1	2	3	4	5	6	7	8	9	10	11	12	13	14	15	16	17	18	19	20	21	22	23	24	
99 LORENZO	99	99	99	99	99	99	99	99	99	99	99	26	26	26	26	26	26	26	26	26	26	26	26	26	1
26 PEDROSA	26	26	26	26	26	26	26	26	26	26	26	99	99	99	99	99	99	99	99	99	99	99	99	99	2
35 CRUTCHLOW	11	35	35	35	35	35	35	35	35	35	35	35	35	35	35	35	35	35	35	19	19	19	19	19	3
11 SPIES	35	1	19	19	19	19	19	19	19	19	19	19	19	19	19	19	19	19	19	35	35	35	35	4	4
19 BAUTISTA	1	19	1	1	1	1	1	1	1	1	1	1	1	1	1	1	1	4	4	4	4	4	4	1	5
4 DOVIZIOSO	19	6	6	6	6	6	4	4	4	4	4	6	6	6	6	6	6	1	1	1	1	1	1	6	6
1 STONER	4	4	4	4	4	4	6	6	6	6	6	4	4	4	4	4	4	6	6	6	6	6	6	46	7
6 BRADL	6	46	46	46	46	46	46	46	46	46	46	46	46	46	46	46	46	46	46	46	46	46	46	69	8
46 ROSSI	46	69	69	69	69	69	69	69	69	69	69	69	69	69	69	69	69	69	69	69	69	69	69	21	9
69 HAYDEN	21	21	21	21	21	21	21	21	21	21	21	21	21	21	21	21	21	21	21	21	21	21	21	8	10
21 NAKASUGA	69	8	8	8	8	8	8	8	8	8	8	8	8	8	8	8	8	8	8	8	8	8	8	17	11
8 BARBERA	8	41	41	41	17	17	17	17	17	17	17	17	17	17	17	17	17	17	17	17	17	17	17	41	12
41 ESPARGARO	41	5	17	17	17	41	41	41	41	41	41	41	41	41	41	41	41	41	41	41	41	41	41	5	13
14 DE PUNIET	68	17	5	5	5	5	5	5	5	5	5	5	5	5	5	5	5	5	5	5	5	5	5	77	14
17 ABRAHAM	17	51	51	51	51	51	77	77	77	77	77	77	77	77	77	77	77	77	77	77	77	77	77	51	15
5 EDWARDS	5	84	77	77	77	77	51	51	51	51	51	51	51	51	51	51	51	51	51	51	51	51	51	84	
68 HERNANDEZ	51	77	84	84	9	9	9	9	9	9	9	9	9	9	9	9	9	9	9	9	9	9	9		
51 PIRRO	84	9	9	9	84	84	84	84	84	84	84	84	84	84	84	84	84	84	84	84	84	84			
9 PETRUCCI	9	22	22	22	22	22	22	22	22	22	22	22	22	22											
77 ELLISON	77	14	14	14	14	14	14	14	14	14	14	14	14	14											
84 ROLFO	22																								
22 SILVA	14																								

22 Pit stop

Moto2

RACE DISTANCE: 23 laps, 68.614 miles/110.423km · RACE WEATHER: Dry (air 21°C, humidity 51%, track 23°C)

Pos.	Rider	Nat.	No.	Entrant	Machine	Laps	Time & Speed
1	**Marc Marquez**	SPA	93	Team Catalunya Caixa Repsol	Suter	23	42m 56.171s 95.882mph/ 154.307km/h
2	**Pol Espargaro**	SPA	40	Tuenti Movil HP 40	Kalex	23	42m 56.586s
3	**Esteve Rabat**	SPA	80	Tuenti Movil HP 40	Kalex	23	43m 05.755s
4	**Scott Redding**	GBR	45	Marc VDS Racing Team	Kalex	23	43m 07.240s
5	**Thomas Luthi**	SWI	12	Interwetten-Paddock	Suter	23	43m 07.766s
6	**Simone Corsi**	ITA	3	Came IodaRacing Project	FTR	23	43m 14.554s
7	**Takaaki Nakagami**	JPN	30	Italtrans Racing Team	Kalex	23	43m 14.843s
8	**Johann Zarco**	FRA	5	JIR Moto2	Motobi	23	43m 24.397s
9	**Axel Pons**	SPA	49	Tuenti Movil HP 40	Kalex	23	43m 24.622s
10	**Dominique Aegerter**	SWI	77	Technomag-CIP	Suter	23	43m 24.770s
11	**Julian Simon**	SPA	60	Blusens Avintia	Suter	23	43m 25.142s
12	**Anthony West**	AUS	95	QMMF Racing Team	Speed Up	23	43m 25.780s
13	**Jordi Torres**	SPA	81	Mapfre Aspar Team Moto2	Suter	23	43m 25.986s
14	**Xavier Simeon**	BEL	19	Tech 3 Racing	Tech 3	23	43m 35.954s
15	**Mike di Meglio**	FRA	63	Kiefer Racing	Kalex	23	43m 36.039s
16	Yuki Takahashi	JPN	72	NGM Mobile Forward Racing	FTR	23	43m 36.141s
17	Mika Kallio	FIN	36	Marc VDS Racing Team	Kalex	23	43m 36.934s
18	Andrea Iannone	ITA	29	Speed Master	Speed Up	23	43m 37.071s
19	Nicolas Terol	SPA	18	Mapfre Aspar Team Moto2	Suter	23	43m 40.550s
20	Alex de Angelis	RSM	15	NGM Mobile Forward Racing	FTR	23	43m 42.678s
21	Ratthapark Wilairot	THA	14	Thai Honda PTT Gresini Moto2	Suter	23	43m 51.732s
22	Ricard Cardus	SPA	88	Arguinano Racing Team	AJR	23	43m 51.986s
23	Tomoyoshi Koyama	JPN	75	Technomag-CIP	Suter	23	43m 52.222s
24	Marcel Schrotter	GER	23	Desguaces La Torre SAG	Bimota	23	43m 52.663s
25	Gino Rea	GBR	8	Federal Oil Gresini Moto2	Suter	23	43m 54.588s
26	Alessandro Andreozzi	ITA	22	S/Master Speed Up	Speed Up	23	44m 08.569s
27	Elena Rosell	SPA	82	QMMF Racing Team	Speed Up	23	44m 36.012s
28	Eric Granado	BRA	57	JIR Moto2	Motobi	23	44m 36.958s
29	Jesko Raffin	SWI	20	GP Team Switzerland	Kalex	22	42m 59.839s
	Toni Elias	SPA	24	Italtrans Racing Team	Kalex	19	DNF
	Bradley Smith	GBR	38	Tech 3 Racing	Tech 3	3	DNF
	Kohta Nozane	JPN	31	SAG Team	FTR		DSQ

Fastest lap: Pol Espargaro, on lap 23, 1m 51.100s, 96.665mph/155.567km/h (record).
Previous lap record: Andrea Iannone, ITA (Suter), 1m 52.307s, 95.627mph/153.896km/h (2011).
Event best maximum speed: Pol Espargaro, 164.8mph/265.2km/h (free practice 1).

Qualifying: Dry
Air: 22° Humidity: 38% Track: 22°

1	Espargaro	1m 50.886s
2	Marquez	1m 51.023s
3	Rabat	1m 51.156s
4	Redding	1m 51.273s
5	Luthi	1m 51.481s
6	Zarco	1m 51.640s
7	Smith	1m 51.736s
8	Simon	1m 51.740s
9	Terol	1m 51.977s
10	Elias	1m 51.980s
11	Nakagami	1m 52.038s
12	Corsi	1m 52.052s
13	Pons	1m 52.061s
14	Takahashi	1m 52.098s
15	Kallio	1m 52.223s
16	Torres	1m 52.239s
17	De Angelis	1m 52.309s
18	Iannone	1m 52.353s
19	Aegerter	1m 52.536s
20	West	1m 52.686s
21	Cardus	1m 52.781s
22	Simeon	1m 52.921s
23	Di Meglio	1m 53.180s
24	Schrotter	1m 53.182s
25	Wilairot	1m 53.206s
26	Andreozzi	1m 53.256s
27	Koyama	1m 53.299s
28	Rea	1m 53.413s
29	Nozane	1m 53.505s
30	Raffin	1m 54.352s
31	Rosell	1m 54.674s
32	Granado	1m 55.057s

Fastest race laps

1	Espargaro	1m 51.100s
2	Marquez	1m 51.180s
3	Rabat	1m 51.604s
4	Redding	1m 51.725s
5	Luthi	1m 51.801s
6	Elias	1m 51.814s
7	Corsi	1m 51.981s
8	Simon	1m 51.989s
9	Torres	1m 52.130s
10	Nakagami	1m 52.207s
11	Pons	1m 52.224s
12	Aegerter	1m 52.244s
13	Kallio	1m 52.265s
14	Zarco	1m 52.342s
15	Terol	1m 52.365s
16	West	1m 52.475s
17	Smith	1m 52.492s
18	Iannone	1m 52.596s
19	Simeon	1m 52.815s
20	Takahashi	1m 52.854s
21	Di Meglio	1m 52.884s
22	De Angelis	1m 52.957s
23	Cardus	1m 53.125s
24	Schrotter	1m 53.263s
25	Wilairot	1m 53.364s
26	Rea	1m 53.496s
27	Koyama	1m 53.559s
28	Andreozzi	1m 53.951s
29	Nozane	1m 54.432s
30	Granado	1m 54.900s
31	Rosell	1m 55.026s
32	Raffin	1m 55.543s

Championship Points

1	Marquez	283
2	Espargaro	230
3	Iannone	178
4	Luthi	177
5	Redding	144
6	Kallio	110
7	Smith	96
8	Rabat	93
9	Zarco	84
10	Aegerter	80
11	Corsi	78
12	Corti	74
13	De Angelis	61
14	Nakagami	50
15	Simon	47
16	Elias	34
17	Krummenacher	24
18	West	21
19	Simeon	19
20	Terol	19
21	Torres	14
22	Di Meglio	13
23	Neukirchner	8
24	Pons	8
25	Wilairot	8
26	Cardus	6
27	Rea	1

Constructor Points

1	Suter	317
2	Kalex	276
3	Speed Up	182
4	FTR	98
5	Tech 3	98
6	Motobi	84
7	Moriwaki	10
8	AJR	6

Moto3

RACE DISTANCE: 20 laps, 59.664 miles/96.020km · RACE WEATHER: Dry (air 22°C, humidity 42%, track 25°C)

Pos.	Rider	Nat.	No.	Entrant	Machine	Laps	Time & Speed
1	**Danny Kent**	GBR	52	Red Bull KTM Ajo	KTM	20	40m 02.775s 89.392mph/ 143.863km/h
2	**Maverick Vinales**	SPA	25	Blusens Avintia	FTR Honda	20	40m 03.035s
3	**Alessandro Tonucci**	ITA	19	Team Italia FMI	FTR Honda	20	40m 05.127s
4	**Alex Rins**	SPA	42	Estrella Galicia 0,0	Suter Honda	20	40m 06.179s
5	**Zulfahmi Khairuddin**	MAL	63	AirAsia-Sic-Ajo	KTM	20	40m 06.420s
6	**Sandro Cortese**	GER	11	Red Bull KTM Ajo	KTM	20	40m 16.169s
7	**Miguel Oliveira**	POR	44	Estrella Galicia 0,0	Suter Honda	20	40m 18.298s
8	**Louis Rossi**	FRA	96	Racing Team Germany	FTR Honda	20	40m 18.514s
9	**Efren Vazquez**	SPA	7	JHK t-shirt Laglisse	FTR Honda	20	40m 18.721s
10	**Romano Fenati**	ITA	5	Team Italia FMI	FTR Honda	20	40m 18.904s
11	**Arthur Sissis**	AUS	61	Red Bull KTM Ajo	KTM	20	40m 18.998s
12	**Niccolo Antonelli**	ITA	27	San Carlo Gresini Moto3	FTR Honda	20	40m 19.146s
13	**Niklas Ajo**	FIN	31	TT Motion Events Racing	KTM	20	40m 31.143s
14	**Alex Marquez**	SPA	12	Ambrogio Next Racing	Suter Honda	20	40m 31.150s
15	**Jakub Kornfeil**	CZE	84	Redox-Ongetta-Centro Seta	FTR Honda	20	40m 31.284s
16	Hyuga Watanabe	JPN	81	Project U 7C Harc	Honda	20	40m 33.846s
17	Adrian Martin	SPA	26	JHK t-shirt Laglisse	FTR Honda	20	40m 43.067s
18	Kenta Fujii	JPN	51	Technomag-CIP-TSR	TSR Honda	20	40m 45.597s
19	Jack Miller	AUS	8	Caretta Technology	Honda	20	40m 45.671s
20	Alan Techer	FRA	89	Technomag-CIP-TSR	TSR Honda	20	40m 50.226s
21	John McPhee	GBR	17	Caretta Technology	KRP Honda	20	40m 51.020s
22	Luca Amato	GER	29	Mapfre Aspar Team Moto3	Kalex KTM	20	40m 51.134s
23	Isaac Vinales	SPA	32	Ongetta-Centro Seta	FTR Honda	20	40m 51.214s
24	Josep Rodriguez	SPA	28	Moto FGR	FGR Honda	20	41m 06.537s
25	Giulian Pedone	SWI	30	Ambrogio Next Racing	Suter Honda	20	41m 13.065s
26	Danny Webb	GBR	99	Mahindra Racing	Mahindra	20	41m 13.259s
27	Yuudai Kamei	JPN	82	18 Garage Racing Team	Honda	19	40m 35.455s
	Jonas Folger	GER	94	Mapfre Aspar Team Moto3	Kalex KTM	19	DNF
	Luis Salom	SPA	39	RW Racing GP	Kalex KTM	19	DNF
	Alberto Moncayo	SPA	23	Andalucia JHK t-shirt Laglisse	FTR Honda	19	DNF
	Brad Binder	RSA	41	RW Racing GP	Kalex KTM	14	DNF
	Toni Finsterbusch	GER	9	Racing Team Germany	Honda	4	DNF
	Armando Pontone	ITA	80	IodaRacing Project	Ioda	0	DNS
	Riccardo Moretti	ITA	20	Mahindra Racing	Mahindra	0	DNS

Fastest lap: Alessandro Tonucci, on lap 11, 1m 59.111s, 90.163mph/145.104km/h (record).
Previous lap record: New category.
Event best maximum speed: Zulfahmi Khairuddin, 137.0mph/220.5km/h (free practice 2).

Qualifying: Dry
Air: 22° Humidity: 40% Track: 22°

1	Kent	1m 58.371s
2	M. Vinales	1m 58.574s
3	Cortese	1m 58.669s
4	Khairuddin	1m 58.951s
5	Tonucci	1m 59.072s
6	Salom	1m 59.097s
7	Folger	1m 59.125s
8	Rossi	1m 59.213s
9	Vazquez	1m 59.287s
10	Fenati	1m 59.359s
11	Oliveira	1m 59.494s
12	Antonelli	1m 59.652s
13	Rins	1m 59.653s
14	Sissis	1m 59.686s
15	Moncayo	1m 59.904s
16	Martin	1m 59.945s
17	Marquez	1m 59.949s
18	Binder	1m 59.974s
19	Kornfeil	1m 59.998s
20	Techer	2m 00.021s
21	Watanabe	2m 00.044s
22	Miller	2m 00.177s
23	Ajo	2m 00.386s
24	Finsterbusch	2m 00.460s
25	I. Vinales	2m 00.526s
26	McPhee	2m 00.755s
27	Kamei	2m 00.940s
28	Pedone	2m 00.987s
29	Fujii	2m 01.233s
30	Rodriguez	2m 01.256s
31	Amato	2m 01.500s
32	Webb	2m 02.362s
33	Pontone	2m 03.819s
34	Moretti	2m 05.450s

Fastest race laps

1	Tonucci	1m 59.111s
2	Kent	1m 59.131s
3	Folger	1m 59.141s
4	Rins	1m 59.148s
5	Cortese	1m 59.155s
6	Salom	1m 59.177s
7	M. Vinales	1m 59.210s
8	Khairuddin	1m 59.328s
9	Rossi	1m 59.567s
10	Fenati	1m 59.686s
11	Sissis	1m 59.835s
12	Vazquez	1m 59.919s
13	Oliveira	1m 59.956s
14	Ajo	1m 59.973s
15	Antonelli	1m 59.992s
16	Binder	2m 00.052s
17	Kornfeil	2m 00.172s
18	Marquez	2m 00.252s
19	Martin	2m 00.292s
20	Techer	2m 00.434s
21	Moncayo	2m 00.484s
22	Kamei	2m 00.602s
23	I. Vinales	2m 00.638s
24	Watanabe	2m 00.707s
25	McPhee	2m 00.935s
26	Finsterbusch	2m 01.069s
27	Miller	2m 01.130s
28	Fujii	2m 01.359s
29	Amato	2m 01.641s
30	Rodriguez	2m 01.844s
31	Pedone	2m 01.965s
32	Webb	2m 02.393s

Championship Points

1	Cortese	255
2	M. Vinales	199
3	Salom	194
4	Fenati	126
5	Rins	119
6	Kent	108
7	Khairuddin	92
8	Oliveira	83
9	Masbou	81
10	Vazquez	77
11	Rossi	76
12	Antonelli	73
13	Folger	72
14	Sissis	63
15	Kornfeil	59
16	Moncayo	52
17	Faubel	52
18	Tonucci	34
19	Ajo	26
20	Techer	21
21	Marquez	18
22	Miller	14
23	Moreno	10
24	Iwema	9
25	Gruenwald	8
26	Pedone	7
27	Finsterbusch	7
28	Martin	6
29	Binder	5
30	Schrotter	4
31	Hanus	3
32	I. Vinales	2
33	Calia	2
34	McPhee	1
35	Rinaldi	1
36	Grotzkyj	1

Constructor Points

1	FTR Honda	277
2	KTM	271
3	Kalex KTM	228
4	Suter Honda	151
5	Honda	84
6	TSR Honda	21
7	FGR Honda	9
8	Ioda	5
9	Mahindra	4
10	KRP Honda	1
11	Oral	1

FIM WORLD CHAMPIONSHIP · ROUND 16

MALAYSIAN GRAND PRIX

SEPANG CIRCUIT

Winning in the rain: Pedrosa is dwarfed by his brolly after the race was stopped. It was his first ever wet win, and his third in a row.
Photo: Gold & Goose

THE geography books tell us that Malaysia has two monsoons each year. That from the north-east brings more rain. It usually starts in November, but not in 2012. It was already getting under way when the circus came to town from Japan, and arrived in earnest on race day, minutes after the chequered flag for Moto3, first race of the day.

Both MotoGP and Moto2 races were cut short, and a number of people paid the price, hitting standing water left by sudden stair-rod rain. One was Marquez, who thereby had to wait another week to win the title; another (in the opposite way) was Stoner. After all the crashes in Moto2, and fearful that "if I tweaked my ankle, it would be game over for the season", he'd thought of pulling out of the race. Now he felt that had the race continued, he would have had every chance of improving on third place. "Heavy rain is my playground," he said.

And, for a second year running, the crowd was somewhat short-changed: 2011's MotoGP race had been cancelled after Simoncelli's fatal crash; in 2012, the race was abbreviated, and a planned re-run delayed as the rain kept rolling in, until it became too dark.

By then, however, a record home crowd had plenty to be happy about. Spurred by local talent, 77,178 – 11,000 up on 2011's record – had turned out to watch Zulfahmi Khairuddin in Moto3 and wild-carder Hafizh Syahrin in Moto2. They were fully rewarded. Each threatened to win the race, and Khairuddin (having claimed his first pole on his 21st birthday) lasted all the way to his first rostrum.

The biggest shake-up among the regulars was also in Moto3: an extraordinary walk-out by Vinales. The 17-year-old and his father had rowed with his Avintia Blusens team the night before, and as the others went out for first free practice, Vinales's bike stood idle. He did arrive in the paddock, wearing civvies, only to pass highly critical comments about his "second-division" team and the lack of development to his FTR Honda before boarding a flight home. Everyone was flabbergasted, since he had a strong chance of second overall; but many riders rallied to his support, complaining of shoddy treatment by sundry teams, and in at least one case the same team.

Bad weather was ever present, showers hitting here and there, drying quickly, only to appear again elsewhere on the long lap. In the dry spells, MotoGP riders found that either the track had deteriorated somewhat since their tests here earlier in the year or that the new-generation soft-construction front Bridgestone didn't like it. For once, it wasn't only Honda riders complaining of chatter, but all of them. Pedrosa and Stoner still led the chorus. "It's even chattering when the bike is upright on the straight," said Pedrosa; while Stoner affirmed, "If they say they have problems, ours are ten times worse." The factory Ducati pair and even the Yamahas were having similar difficulties. "It's worn out," opined Rossi. "It needs to be resurfaced."

Spies was doing more than mulling over his misfortune at Motegi, and his Yamaha was fitted with air scoops to cool the front brakes – too late, for while Sepang does have one hard braking zone before the final hairpin, it is nothing like as punishing as the Japanese track.

Stoner was steadily improving in the build-up to Phillip Island, at least in the result sheets – but not medically, with persistent pain and stiffness in his ankle and a continued fear of further derangement should he fall. "It's more week by week than day by day," he said, sounding a note of caution about his prospects at home in one week's time. Well, we would soon see about that.

Confirmation came from Yamaha at last that, once again, Rossi's full pit crew would accompany the rider in his latest switch. There had never been much doubt that Burgess would remain with him. The other five – Alex Briggs, Bernard Ansiau, Gary Coleman, Brent Stephens and Matteo Flamigni – would also stay with the rider, with Ducati releasing them from their contracts the day after Valencia so they could join Vale's first tests back on the Yamaha. Most of them have been with Rossi since his earliest MotoGP days with Honda in 2000.

Confirmation also came that Scott Redding's MotoGP hopes, tickled by his test for Ducati earlier in the year, were on hold for another year: he and team-mate Mika Kallio signed up to stay in Moto2 with the same Marc VDS team. He will be joined in the class by compatriot Danny Kent:

at Motegi, it was announced that he would replace Bradley Smith in the increasingly Anglophone French Tech 3 team's Moto2 squad alongside Louis Rossi. Smith moves up to join Crutchlow in the same team's MotoGP satellite Yamaha pit.

Meanwhile, third Englishman Gino Rea bolstered his chances of staying on in Moto2 with a superb wet-weather race; he had just taken the lead when the red flags came out, but was still a worthy third.

In Moto3, Mahindra joined perennial pit-lane-starters Ioda when Danny Webb's eighth engine failed, exceeding the allocation. A week later, his ninth also died, but this time the hard-pressed team had no spare and he was out of the race altogether. For commercial reasons (not to mention pride), Mahindra is not able to buy a Honda or a KTM; their experience with the Oral had been trying in the extreme.

Naturally, and once again, the spirit of Simoncelli was strongly present, although many in the paddock did at last feel a sense of closure after a subdued ceremony on race eve. Riders, mechanics, cooks, cleaners, journalists and hangers-on followed his San Carlos team from the pit on foot to the corner where he had fallen, where team owner Fausto Gresini affixed a permanent plaque in his memory.

MOTOGP RACE – 13 laps (shortened)

Rain for second free practice meant another empty track, none of the top six even going out, leaving them without wet testing time. Qualifying was dry, with a good battle for pole. Pedrosa snatched it from Dovizioso with two minutes to go, then Lorenzo came over the line for his third pole in a row.

Stoner led row two, battling to find a set-up to cure the chatter. "Everything we do seems to make it worse," he said. Crutchlow was alongside, then Spies; Barbera was top Ducati in seventh, heading row three from Bradl and Hayden; Rossi was next to Bautista on row four.

The start was delayed 15 minutes by earlier rain, but the full 20 laps were scheduled. The track was wet, but the rain now half-hearted; and while all started on full wet tyres, mechanics were warming up slick-shod bikes in anticipation of imminent sunshine. How wrong they turned out to be. Only the four Yamahas had gone for the softer rear, hoping for an early-laps advantage prior to a possible bike change. It would prove costly.

It was business as usual up front: Pedrosa started well, Lorenzo even better to lead through the first tight corners. The order was the same at the end of the first lap, with the pair already better than two seconds clear of Stoner. He had a gang behind him: Bradl, Rossi, Dovi, Bautista, Hayden, Spies and then catch-up Crutchlow, who'd been forced wide on the first corner.

The gap had stretched to seven seconds after seven laps, Stoner still third. Nobody could find a way past, but there was plenty of shuffling. Dovi had displaced Rossi on lap two and the pair pushed Stoner hard as Bradl lost a second behind them. At the same time, Crutchlow was moving steadily through even as Spies was losing ground behind. He would drop to the back of the factory gang, tenth when he became the first to fall, suffering season-ending shoulder injury.

By lap ten, Crutchlow was up to fifth behind Hayden, both having gained places when first Dovizioso fell chasing Stoner; and then Rossi – unsighted by a fogged visor – almost ran off, dropping from fifth to eighth behind Bradl. The German was struggling with an electronic puzzle, adjusting maps to try to cure excessive engine braking.

Left: The MotoGP fraternity make the walk in memory of Marco.

Below left: Maverick Vinales, here at a pre-race event, would shock everyone by walking out before turning a wheel.

Bottom left: Jerry Burgess contemplates yet another change of team pyjamas when he and his gang follow Rossi back to Yamaha.

Below: More 'roaming in the gloaming' than 'singing in the rain': Bradl, Hayden, Bautista and Crutchlow in treacherous conditions.

Photos: Gold & Goose

Up front, it was much like the previous few races. Pedrosa stalked until lap 11, passed Lorenzo cleanly at the last hairpin and pulled clear at a second or more each lap. All the while, the rain became heavier and more persistent, and Stoner was gaining rapidly. But now, standing water was starting to form, especially at the end of the final straight, where riders brake for the last hairpin.

Crutchlow would not finish lap 11, the front wheel tucking at high speed at that point as he touched the brakes. Luckily he was unhurt, but had to run to escape the tumbling ART of de Puniet, who suffered a copy-cat crash. Bradl and Silva also fell on the same lap.

Bradl's departure freed Rossi to close up on and ride straight past Bautista. Hayden was a long way up the road by then and out of reach.

Lorenzo was the first to wave distress signals to officials on lap 13. By then, they were poised to stop the race even before he proved the danger, with a genuinely miraculous save when he lost the front under brakes – a well-timed dab saved him from following Crutchlow and de Puniet into the gravel. This put Stoner on his back wheel and ready to pass, but the red flags came out, and that was that.

So they finished: Pedrosa imperiously ahead, Lorenzo under pressure from Stoner, then Hayden, Rossi, and Bautista.

De Puniet had been leading the CRT pack when he fell; he left team-mate Espargaro narrowly in charge from Barbera. The pair swapped on lap 13, securing a distant seventh for Barbera. Ellison had been with them in the early laps, but dropped away to fend off Abraham for a well-earned ninth. Five seconds away, Petrucci held off a late attack from Pirro.

Dovi remounted for 14th, almost half a minute behind; Edwards retired.

Rules dictate that in such circumstances, a new race must be run over a minimum of five laps, previous results dictating only grid positions. After 30 minutes of waiting in continuing rain and growing gloom, that was cancelled; and because more than two-thirds had been completed, the result stood, with full points awarded. Which meant Jorge now led Dani by less than a full race.

MOTO2 RACE – 15 laps (shortened)

Espargaro was uncatchable in qualifying, four-tenths ahead of Redding (equalling his best yet) and six ahead of Marquez, who completed the front row. Nakagami led the second from

Zarco and Smith, the Englishman battling pain from two broken toes in an earlier crash. Rabat led row three.

A 30-minute delay and a one-lap cut – to a proposed 18 laps – were announced as everyone waited for the heavy rain to pass. It was still wet and spitting, with no question of slick tyres.

Crashes started directly when Nakagami made a daring swoop to lead into the first corner, promptly falling. A little further around, fancied wet runner Zarco and Simeon crashed out together. Conditions were bad, and would become worse.

Up front, there was a mad scramble, with several first-lap leaders, including Espargaro, Redding and Smith. By the end of the lap, Simon was in front.

Top: Moto2 wild-card 'Sideways' Syahrin sensationally leads de Angelis (15) and West.

Above: A belated rostrum return for Anthony West.

Above left: Joy for Gino – only a red flag prevented a possible win for Rea.

Above far left: Last week's blind rage gave way to ecstasy for maiden Moto3 champion Sandro Cortese.

Left: Cortese snatched the lead back from Khairuddin at the last corner; Folger was a close spectator.

Top left: Pedrosa was imperious. He could do nothing more to keep his title hopes alive.

Far left: Gino Rea was leading when the race was stopped, but slipped to third on count-back.

Left: Khairuddin wowed a record home crowd with pole and a brilliant second.

Photos: Gold & Goose

In the spray behind, conditions were making unaccustomed heroes, as unsung wet-weather specialists made the most of it. Foremost among them was Gino Rea, who had leapt from 22nd to fifth in the first lap alone. West had tagged on behind. Both would be temporarily eclipsed by teenage Malaysian wild-card Syahrin in his first GP. Fastest in wet free practice, he'd been 27th in the dry – and now he was slicing through not just the mid-pack but also fancied runners: Marquez was just one to suffer the indignity of seeing the rank rookie ride right around the outside of him.

De Angelis was with Simon from the start, and took over up front on lap four. The flying Rea followed him by; West had now got past Luthi and would be third next time around as Simon dropped away into the next gang. This included Marquez and Iannone, but only briefly the flying Syahrin, also heading for the front. Briefly, too, Espargaro, who dropped back rapidly to 12th.

By lap eight, Syahrin was in the mix, with four circulating with maximum daring on a very treacherous surface as the rain became heavier. Then he was in the lead, from laps nine to eleven, before gradually losing ground to the more experienced riders.

Luthi was speeding up again, dropping off Simon as he closed on the leaders on lap 14, only to fall on the 15th.

Rea took the lead at the end of lap 16, but the red flags were about to come out – it was one lap too late for a classic first win for the Londoner: the lap before, he'd been third, behind de Angelis and West.

The crash list was long; one was important. Marquez, the title within his reach, was riding carefully while engaged with Iannone. Then he crashed under braking, to his amazement, "while I was still in a straight line". That was on lap 12. He was followed by Torres, Terol, di Meglio and finally Luthi; Wilairot had preceded him.

Simon was fifth, Iannone sixth; Kallio, Smith, Aegerter and Rabat completed the top ten. Rabat had consigned teammate Espargaro to 11th only on the last lap. Redding was five seconds down in 12th, a little way ahead of a big battle for the last points, won by Elias, from Pons and Cardus.

MOTO3 RACE – 18 laps

The only race to run full distance only just made it: the monsoon broke as the riders went to the rostrum.

On the day before, Khairuddin had made certain of his historic maiden pole by three-tenths, with second-placed Folger in the pits and unable to fight back. Cortese joined them on the front row; Rossi led the second row from Salom and Oliveira.

Khairuddin repaid his home crowd amply, even if he didn't quite win. He led away, but Folger took over to lead for the first ten laps. By then, only Khairuddin and Cortese were still with him.

Salom was dropping back into the hands of Kent, Oliveira and Rins, who by now had outpaced Vazquez.

The front battle was nail-biting to the last. Folger led again on lap 12, then it was Khairuddin, who had a small speed advantage on the straight.

Cortese finally attacked halfway around the last lap, but Khairuddin eased past him again on the straight, though he was a little wide into the last hairpin. It was just enough room for Cortese to slip through to secure the first Moto3 title with a win. Folger was a close spectator,

Salom regained fourth from Oliveira on the last lap; Kent had lost touch, with Rins even further behind, then the lone Vazquez in eighth.

Rossi had been with the leaders, until he crashed out with 13 laps to go, the only faller in the race.

A gang of nine battled behind, Sissis leading several times. In the end, Ajo was ninth, from Martin, Sissis, Binder, Miller on the top standard Honda, Marquez and Antonelli for the last point; Kornfeil, Tonucci and Moncayo just missed out. Ninth to 18th was covered by 1.43 seconds.

FIM WORLD CHAMPIONSHIP

ROUND 16

MALAYSIAN MOTORCYCLE GRAND PRIX

19–21 OCTOBER, 2012

motoGP

TISSOT SWISS WATCHES SINCE 1853

OFFICIAL TIMEKEEPER

SEPANG INTERNATIONAL CIRCUIT

13 laps
Length: 5.548 km / 3.447 miles
Width: 25m

Key
96/60 kph/mph
Gear ✦

- Langkawi curve 83/52
- Genting Curve 140/87
- Turn 5 152/94
- Turn 3 179/112
- Pangkor Laut Chicane 70/43
- Hairpin 75/47
- Turn 7 124/77
- KLIA Curve 130/81
- Berjaya Tioman Corner 63/39
- Sunway Lagoon Corner 87/54
- Turn 12 154/96
- Kenyir Lake 104/65

Photos: Gold & Goose

MotoGP

RACE DISTANCE: 13 laps, 44.816 miles/72.124km · **RACE WEATHER:** Wet (air 25°C, humidity 96%, track 31°C)

Pos.	Rider	Nat.	No.	Entrant	Machine	Tyres	Race tyre choice	Laps	Time & speed
1	**Dani Pedrosa**	SPA	26	Repsol Honda Team	Honda RC213V	B	F: Hard/R: Hard	13	29m 29.049s 91.199mph/ 146.771km/h
2	**Jorge Lorenzo**	SPA	99	Yamaha Factory Racing	Yamaha YZR-M1	B	F: Hard/R: Soft	13	29m 32.823s
3	**Casey Stoner**	AUS	1	Repsol Honda Team	Honda RC213V	B	F: Hard/R: Hard	13	29m 36.193s
4	**Nicky Hayden**	USA	69	Ducati Team	Ducati Desmosedici GP12	B	F: Hard/R: Hard	13	29m 39.567s
5	**Valentino Rossi**	ITA	46	Ducati Team	Ducati Desmosedici GP12	B	F: Hard/R: Hard	13	29m 45.808s
6	**Alvaro Bautista**	SPA	19	San Carlo Honda Gresini	Honda RC213V	B	F: Hard/R: Hard	13	29m 46.325s
7	**Hector Barbera**	SPA	8	Pramac Racing Team	Ducati Desmosedici GP12	B	F: Hard/R: Soft	13	30m 19.331s
8	**Aleix Espargaro**	SPA	41	Power Electronics Aspar	ART Aprilia RSV4	B	F: Hard/R: Hard	13	30m 20.634s
9	**James Ellison**	GBR	77	Paul Bird Motorsport	ART Aprilia RSV4	B	F: Hard/R: Soft	13	30m 25.725s
10	**Karel Abraham**	CZE	17	Cardion AB Motoracing	Ducati Desmosedici GP12	B	F: Hard/R: Soft	13	30m 26.671s
11	**Danilo Petrucci**	ITA	9	Came IodaRacing Project	Ioda Suter BMW S1000RR	B	F: Hard/R: Soft	13	30m 31.854s
12	**Michele Pirro**	ITA	51	San Carlo Honda Gresini	FTR Honda CBR1000RR	B	F: Hard/R: Hard	13	30m 31.940s
13	**Andrea Dovizioso**	ITA	4	Monster Yamaha Tech 3	Yamaha YZR-M1	B	F: Hard/R: Hard	13	30m 58.038s
	Stefan Bradl	GER	6	LCR Honda MotoGP	Honda RC213V	B	F: Hard/R: Hard	11	DNF-crash
	Cal Crutchlow	GBR	35	Monster Yamaha Tech 3	Yamaha YZR-M1	B	F: Hard/R: Soft	10	DNF-crash
	Randy de Puniet	FRA	14	Power Electronics Aspar	ART Aprilia RSV4	B	F: Hard/R: Hard	10	DNF-crash
	Ivan Silva	SPA	22	Avintia Blusens	BQR FTR Kawasaki ZX-10R	B	F: Hard/R: Soft	10	DNF-crash
	Colin Edwards	USA	5	NGM Mobile Forward Racing	Suter BMW S1000RR	B	F: Hard/R: Hard	10	DNF-mechanical
	Ben Spies	USA	11	Yamaha Factory Racing	Yamaha YZR-M1	B	F: Hard/R: Soft	8	DNF-crash
	Roberto Rolfo	ITA	84	Speed Master	ART Aprilia RSV4	B	F: Hard/R: Soft	–	DSQ

Fastest lap: Dani Pedrosa, on lap 7, 2m 14.670s, 92.155mph/148.309km/h.
Lap record: Casey Stoner, AUS (Ducati), 2m 2.108s, 101.640mph/163.566km/h (2007).
Event best maximum speed: Dani Pedrosa, 202.5mph/325.9km/h (qualifying practice).

Qualifying

Weather: Dry
Air Temp: 31° Humidity: 68%
Track Temp: 39°

1	Lorenzo	2m 00.334s
2	Pedrosa	2m 00.528s
3	Dovizioso	2m 00.567s
4	Stoner	2m 00.811s
5	Crutchlow	2m 01.178s
6	Spies	2m 01.185s
7	Barbera	2m 01.294s
8	Bradl	2m 01.491s
9	Hayden	2m 01.526s
10	Bautista	2m 01.640s
11	Rossi	2m 01.783s
12	Espargaro	2m 02.842s
13	De Puniet	2m 03.389s
14	Abraham	2m 03.774s
15	Pirro	2m 04.152s
16	Ellison	2m 04.515s
17	Petrucci	2m 04.726s
18	Edwards	2m 04.941s
19	Rolfo	2m 05.100s
20	Silva	2m 05.921s
	Hernandez	no time

Fastest race laps

1	Pedrosa	2m 14.670s
2	Lorenzo	2m 14.703s
3	Spies	2m 14.893s
4	Stoner	2m 14.954s
5	Dovizioso	2m 14.997s
6	Bradl	2m 15.076s
7	Crutchlow	2m 15.097s
8	Rossi	2m 15.181s
9	Bautista	2m 15.221s
10	Hayden	2m 15.324s
11	Barbera	2m 17.466s
12	Espargaro	2m 17.649s
13	De Puniet	2m 17.736s
14	Abraham	2m 18.006s
15	Petrucci	2m 18.391s
16	Edwards	2m 18.652s
17	Ellison	2m 18.687s
18	Pirro	2m 19.125s
19	Silva	2m 19.740s
20	Rolfo	2m 20.561s

Championship Points

1	Lorenzo	330
2	Pedrosa	307
3	Stoner	213
4	Dovizioso	195
5	Bautista	154
6	Rossi	148
7	Crutchlow	135
8	Bradl	125
9	Hayden	114
10	Spies	88
11	Barbera	79
12	Espargaro	63
13	De Puniet	53
14	Abraham	43
15	Pirro	30
16	Ellison	28
17	Hernandez	28
18	Edwards	25
19	Rea	17
20	Petrucci	16
21	Pasini	13
22	Silva	11
23	Elias	10
24	Nakasuga	7
25	Rapp	2
26	Salom	1

Constructor Points

1	Honda	362
2	Yamaha	346
3	Ducati	174
4	ART	87
5	BQR	31
6	FTR	30
7	Suter	25
8	Ioda	9
9	Ioda-Suter	7
10	APR	2
11	BQR-FTR	2

Grid order	1	2	3	4	5	6	7	8	9	10	11	12	13	
99 LORENZO	99	99	99	99	99	99	99	99	99	26	26	26	26	1
26 PEDROSA	26	26	26	26	26	26	26	26	26	99	99	99	99	2
4 DOVIZIOSO	1	1	1	1	1	1	1	1	1	1	1	1	1	3
1 STONER	6	4	4	4	4	4	4	4	4	69	69	69	69	4
35 CRUTCHLOW	46	46	46	46	46	46	46	46	69	35	19	19	46	5
11 SPIES	4	6	6	6	6	6	6	6	6	19	6	46	19	6
8 BARBERA	19	19	19	69	69	69	69	69	35	6	46	41	8	7
6 BRADL	69	69	69	19	19	35	35	35	19	46	41	8	41	8
69 HAYDEN	11	11	35	35	35	19	19	19	46	41	8	77	77	9
19 BAUTISTA	35	35	11	11	11	11	11	11	41	8	77	17	17	10
46 ROSSI	41	14	14	14	14	14	14	14	14	17	9	9	9	11
41 ESPARGARO	14	41	41	41	41	41	41	41	8	77	9	51	51	12
14 DE PUNIET	8	8	8	8	8	8	8	77	17	51	84	84	dsq	
17 ABRAHAM	51	5	77	77	77	77	77	17	9	84	4	4	13	
51 PIRRO	5	77	5	5	5	5	5	9	51	4				
77 ELLISON	77	51	51	51	17	17	17	51	22					
9 PETRUCCI	17	17	17	17	51	51	9	5	4					
5 EDWARDS	22	22	9	9	9	9	51	51	22	84				
84 ROLFO	9	9	22	22	22	22	22	22	84	5				
22 SILVA	84	84	84	84	84	84	84	84						

5 Pit stop

Moto2

RACE DISTANCE: 15 laps, 51.711 miles/83.220km · RACE WEATHER: Wet (air 26°C, humidity 99%, track 31°C)

Pos.	Rider	Nat.	No.	Entrant	Machine	Laps	Time & Speed
1	**Alex de Angelis**	RSM	15	NGM Mobile Forward Racing	FTR	15	36m 57.793s 83.938mph/ 135.085km/h
2	**Anthony West**	AUS	95	QMMF Racing Team	Speed Up	15	36m 58.503s
3	**Gino Rea**	GBR	8	Federal Oil Gresini Moto2	Suter	15	36m 59.156s
4	**Hafizh Syahrin**	MAL	86	Petronas Raceline Malaysia	FTR	15	37m 00.734s
5	**Julian Simon**	SPA	60	Blusens Avintia	Suter	15	37m 05.376s
6	**Andrea Iannone**	ITA	29	Speed Master	Speed Up	15	37m 07.855s
7	**Mika Kallio**	FIN	36	Marc VDS Racing Team	Kalex	15	37m 20.871s
8	**Bradley Smith**	GBR	38	Tech 3 Racing	Tech 3	15	37m 24.750s
9	**Dominique Aegerter**	SWI	77	Technomag-CIP	Suter	15	37m 27.856s
10	**Esteve Rabat**	SPA	80	Tuenti Movil HP 40	Kalex	15	37m 29.307s
11	**Pol Espargaro**	SPA	40	Tuenti Movil HP 40	Kalex	15	37m 29.539s
12	**Scott Redding**	GBR	45	Marc VDS Racing Team	Kalex	15	37m 34.901s
13	**Toni Elias**	SPA	24	Italtrans Racing Team	Kalex	15	37m 36.420s
14	**Axel Pons**	SPA	49	Tuenti Movil HP 40	Kalex	15	37m 36.888s
15	**Ricard Cardus**	SPA	88	Arguinano Racing Team	AJR	15	37m 38.479s
16	Yuki Takahashi	JPN	72	NGM Mobile Forward Racing	FTR	15	37m 38.550s
17	Tomoyoshi Koyama	JPN	75	Technomag-CIP	Suter	15	37m 39.652s
18	Marcel Schrotter	GER	23	Desguaces La Torre SAG	Bimota	15	37m 44.553s
19	Jesko Raffin	SWI	20	GP Team Switzerland	Kalex	15	38m 08.505s
20	Elena Rosell	SPA	82	QMMF Racing Team	Speed Up	15	38m 15.600s
21	Marco Colandrea	SWI	10	SAG Team	FTR	15	38m 17.113s
22	Ratthapark Wilairot	THA	14	Thai Honda PTT Gresini Moto2	Suter	15	38m 25.074s
23	Simone Corsi	ITA	3	Came IodaRacing Project	FTR	15	38m 39.658s
	Thomas Luthi	SWI	12	Interwetten-Paddock	Suter	14	DNF
	Mike di Meglio	FRA	63	Kiefer Racing	Kalex	14	DNF
	Marc Marquez	SPA	93	Team Catalunya Caixa Repsol	Suter	12	DNF
	Nicolas Terol	SPA	18	Mapfre Aspar Team Moto2	Suter	12	DNF
	Jordi Torres	SPA	81	Mapfre Aspar Team Moto2	Suter	12	DNF
	Eric Granado	BRA	57	JIR Moto2	Motobi	6	DNF
	Takaaki Nakagami	JPN	30	Italtrans Racing Team	Kalex	2	DNF
	Johann Zarco	FRA	5	JIR Moto2	Motobi	0	DNF
	Xavier Simeon	BEL	19	Tech 3 Racing	Tech 3	0	DNF
	Alessandro Andreozzi	ITA	22	S/Master Speed Up	Speed Up		DSQ

Fastest lap: Hafizh Syahrin, on lap 10, 2m 23.707s, 86.359mph/138.982km/h.

Lap record: Stefan Bradl, GER (Kalex), 2m 8.220s, 96.790mph/155.769km/h (2011).

Event best maximum speed: Marc Marquez, 169.8mph/273.3km/h (warm up).

Qualifying: Dry

Air: 31° Humidity: 65% Track: 40°

1	Espargaro	2m 06.962s
2	Redding	2m 07.399s
3	Marquez	2m 07.566s
4	Nakagami	2m 07.617s
5	Zarco	2m 07.672s
6	Smith	2m 07.721s
7	Rabat	2m 07.774s
8	Luthi	2m 07.832s
9	De Angelis	2m 07.849s
10	Aegerter	2m 07.872s
11	Iannone	2m 08.021s
12	Corsi	2m 08.225s
13	Simon	2m 08.327s
14	Di Meglio	2m 08.417s
15	Kallio	2m 08.599s
16	Wilairot	2m 08.675s
17	Pons	2m 08.703s
18	Torres	2m 08.705s
19	West	2m 08.739s
20	Terol	2m 08.798s
21	Koyama	2m 08.906s
22	Rea	2m 09.021s
23	Takahashi	2m 09.053s
24	Simeon	2m 09.154s
25	Schrotter	2m 09.484s
26	Cardus	2m 09.490s
27	Syahrin	2m 09.515s
28	Elias	2m 09.606s
29	Andreozzi	2m 10.151s
30	Raffin	2m 11.227s
31	Rosell	2m 11.669s
32	Colandrea	2m 11.751s
33	Granado	2m 13.144s

Fastest race laps

1	Syahrin	2m 23.707s
2	De Angelis	2m 24.107s
3	West	2m 24.366s
4	Rea	2m 24.472s
5	Simon	2m 25.035s
6	Luthi	2m 25.289s
7	Iannone	2m 25.535s
8	Smith	2m 25.730s
9	Marquez	2m 25.769s
10	Kallio	2m 25.995s
11	Di Meglio	2m 26.399s
12	Aegerter	2m 26.630s
13	Elias	2m 26.766s
14	Espargaro	2m 26.796s
15	Koyama	2m 27.129s
16	Rabat	2m 27.129s
17	Cardus	2m 27.164s
18	Pons	2m 27.194s
19	Terol	2m 27.407s
20	Redding	2m 27.412s
21	Torres	2m 27.550s
22	Takahashi	2m 27.644s
23	Schrotter	2m 28.021s
24	Andreozzi	2m 28.924s
25	Wilairot	2m 29.011s
26	Rosell	2m 29.081s
27	Corsi	2m 29.122s
28	Colandrea	2m 29.179s
29	Raffin	2m 29.620s
30	Nakagami	2m 32.051s
31	Granado	2m 41.074s

Championship Points

1	Marquez	283
2	Espargaro	235
3	Iannone	188
4	Luthi	177
5	Redding	148
6	Kallio	119
7	Smith	104
8	Rabat	99
9	Aegerter	87
10	De Angelis	86
11	Zarco	84
12	Corsi	78
13	Corti	74
14	Simon	58
15	Nakagami	50
16	West	41
17	Elias	37
18	Krummenacher	24
19	Simeon	19
20	Terol	19
21	Rea	17
22	Torres	14
23	Syahrin	13
24	Di Meglio	13
25	Pons	10
26	Neukirchner	8
27	Wilairot	8
28	Cardus	7

Constructor Points

1	Suter	333
2	Kalex	285
3	Speed Up	202
4	FTR	123
5	Tech 3	106
6	Motobi	84
7	Moriwaki	10
8	AJR	7

Moto3

RACE DISTANCE: 18 laps, 62.053 miles/99.864km · RACE WEATHER: Dry (air 32°C, humidity 60%, track 48°C)

Pos.	Rider	Nat.	No.	Entrant	Machine	Laps	Time & Speed
1	**Sandro Cortese**	GER	11	Red Bull KTM Ajo	KTM	18	40m 54.123s 91.026mph/ 146.492km/h
2	**Zulfahmi Khairuddin**	MAL	63	AirAsia-Sic-Ajo	KTM	18	40m 54.151s
3	**Jonas Folger**	GER	94	Mapfre Aspar Team Moto3	Kalex KTM	18	40m 54.370s
4	**Luis Salom**	SPA	39	RW Racing GP	Kalex KTM	18	41m 02.626s
5	**Miguel Oliveira**	POR	44	Estrella Galicia 0,0	Suter Honda	18	41m 02.797s
6	**Danny Kent**	GBR	52	Red Bull KTM Ajo	KTM	18	41m 03.458s
7	**Alex Rins**	SPA	42	Estrella Galicia 0,0	Suter Honda	18	41m 13.096s
8	**Efren Vazquez**	SPA	7	JHK t-shirt Laglisse	FTR Honda	18	41m 19.542s
9	**Niklas Ajo**	FIN	31	TT Motion Events Racing	KTM	18	41m 24.837s
10	**Adrian Martin**	SPA	26	JHK t-shirt Laglisse	FTR Honda	18	41m 24.886s
11	**Arthur Sissis**	AUS	61	Red Bull KTM Ajo	KTM	18	41m 25.009s
12	**Brad Binder**	RSA	41	RW Racing GP	Kalex KTM	18	41m 25.142s
13	**Jack Miller**	AUS	8	Caretta Technology	Honda	18	41m 25.348s
14	**Alex Marquez**	SPA	12	Ambrogio Next Racing	Suter Honda	18	41m 25.436s
15	**Niccolo Antonelli**	ITA	27	San Carlo Gresini Moto3	FTR Honda	18	41m 25.772s
16	Jakub Kornfeil	CZE	84	Redox-Ongetta-Centro Seta	FTR Honda	18	41m 25.838s
17	Alessandro Tonucci	ITA	19	Team Italia FMI	FTR Honda	18	41m 25.913s
18	Alberto Moncayo	SPA	23	Andalucia JHK t-shirt Laglisse	FTR Honda	18	41m 26.270s
19	Isaac Vinales	SPA	32	Ongetta-Centro Seta	FTR Honda	18	41m 33.487s
20	Romano Fenati	ITA	5	Team Italia FMI	FTR Honda	18	41m 39.947s
21	Alan Techer	FRA	89	Technomag-CIP-TSR	TSR Honda	18	41m 40.745s
22	John McPhee	GBR	17	Caretta Technology	KRP Honda	18	41m 40.795s
23	Toni Finsterbusch	GER	9	Racing Team Germany	Honda	18	41m 40.913s
24	Luca Amato	GER	29	Mapfre Aspar Team Moto3	Kalex KTM	18	42m 03.209s
25	Josep Rodriguez	SPA	28	Moto FGR	FGR Honda	18	42m 09.857s
26	Giulian Pedone	SWI	30	Ambrogio Next Racing	Suter Honda	18	42m 27.840s
27	Kenta Fujii	JPN	51	Technomag-CIP-TSR	TSR Honda	18	42m 27.934s
28	Armando Pontone	ITA	80	Ioda Team Italia	Ioda	18	42m 48.237s
	Danny Webb	GBR	99	Mahindra Racing	Mahindra	8	DNF
	Louis Rossi	FRA	96	Racing Team Germany	FTR Honda	5	DNF
	Riccardo Moretti	ITA	20	Mahindra Racing	Mahindra	1	DNF

Fastest lap: Zulfahmi Khairuddin, on lap 2, 2m 15.142s, 91.833mph/147.791km/h (record).

Previous lap record: New category.

Event best maximum speed: Zulfahmi Khairuddin, 139.0mph/223.7km/h (warm up).

Qualifying: Dry

Air: 31° Humidity: 82% Track: 38°

1	Khairuddin	2m 13.885s
2	Folger	2m 14.151s
3	Cortese	2m 14.599s
4	Rossi	2m 14.681s
5	Salom	2m 14.817s
6	Oliveira	2m 15.316s
7	Vazquez	2m 15.366s
8	Binder	2m 15.469s
9	Rins	2m 15.814s
10	Martin	2m 15.858s
11	Kent	2m 15.897s
12	Antonelli	2m 15.913s
13	Tonucci	2m 15.915s
14	Kornfeil	2m 16.087s
15	Moncayo	2m 16.108s
16	Ajo	2m 16.142s
17	Fenati	2m 16.229s
18	I. Vinales	2m 16.394s
19	Miller	2m 16.404s
20	Techer	2m 16.633s
21	Sissis	2m 16.650s
22	Finsterbusch	2m 16.828s
23	Rodriguez	2m 16.877s
24	Marquez	2m 16.979s
25	Webb	2m 17.545s
26	McPhee	2m 17.558s
27	Pedone	2m 17.732s
28	Fujii	2m 17.926s
29	Pontone	2m 18.817s
30	Amato	2m 18.975s
31	Moretti	2m 21.960s
	M. Vinales	no time

Fastest race laps

1	Khairuddin	2m 15.142s
2	Cortese	2m 15.174s
3	Rins	2m 15.187s
4	Rossi	2m 15.267s
5	Salom	2m 15.276s
6	Kent	2m 15.325s
7	Oliveira	2m 15.409s
8	Folger	2m 15.482s
9	Vazquez	2m 15.581s
10	Martin	2m 16.093s
11	Tonucci	2m 16.172s
12	Moncayo	2m 16.220s
13	Sissis	2m 16.348s
14	Kornfeil	2m 16.409s
15	Miller	2m 16.478s
16	Fenati	2m 16.583s
17	Binder	2m 16.598s
18	Finsterbusch	2m 16.634s
19	Antonelli	2m 16.654s
20	Marquez	2m 16.681s
21	Ajo	2m 16.681s
22	I. Vinales	2m 16.815s
23	McPhee	2m 16.830s
24	Techer	2m 16.944s
25	Amato	2m 17.725s
26	Rodriguez	2m 17.859s
27	Pedone	2m 18.392s
28	Fujii	2m 18.956s
29	Pontone	2m 19.524s
30	Webb	2m 19.838s

Championship Points

1	Cortese	280
2	Salom	207
3	M. Vinales	199
4	Rins	128
5	Fenati	126
6	Kent	118
7	Khairuddin	112
8	Oliveira	94
9	Folger	88
10	Vazquez	85
11	Masbou	81
12	Rossi	76
13	Antonelli	74
14	Sissis	68
15	Kornfeil	59
16	Moncayo	52
17	Faubel	52
18	Tonucci	34
19	Ajo	33
20	Techer	21
21	Marquez	20
22	Miller	17
23	Martin	12
24	Moreno	10
25	Iwema	9
26	Binder	9
27	Gruenwald	8
28	Pedone	7
29	Finsterbusch	7
30	Schrotter	4
31	Hanus	3
32	I. Vinales	2
33	Calia	2
34	McPhee	1
35	Rinaldi	1
36	Grotzkyj	1

Constructor Points

1	KTM	296
2	FTR Honda	285
3	Kalex KTM	244
4	Suter Honda	162
5	Honda	87
6	TSR Honda	21
7	FGR Honda	9
8	Ioda	5
9	Mahindra	4
10	KRP Honda	1
11	Oral	1

Main photo: "Casey, make us proud."
The crowds flocked in for Stoner's
masterful sixth home win in succession.
He was majestic, in line with his new
home-country nickname, 'King Casey'.

Inset: Retiring at the peak: Stoner's
trophy reflects an adoring track invasion
to rival Rossi's at Mugello.

Photos: Gold & Goose

FIM WORLD CHAMPIONSHIP · ROUND 17

AUSTRALIAN GRAND PRIX

PHILLIP ISLAND CIRCUIT

Above, from left: Mick Doohan tried out Stoner's Honda; wild-card Kris McLaren was in at the deep end; another tough weekend for Rossi at a favourite track.

Top: At least he was leading… Pedrosa's Honda slips away, and his slender title hopes with it.

Top far right: The Power Electronics pair at war over final CRT honours. They finished like this: Espargaro just in front of de Puniet.

Centre far right: Bradl, Dovizioso and Bautista had a lively scrap for fourth. Dovi took it by inches.

Far right: Crutchlow overcame illness for a fine, if lonely ride to a second podium finish.

Photos: Gold & Goose

THE previous two titles had been settled at Phillip Island, on sunny race days in front of record crowds. The fans didn't care that much, however. They'd come to see Stoner, to say goodbye, and to see if he could add a classic sixth successive home win to his groaning trophy cabinet.

Casey did it, superbly well, stamping his authority on the track and the weekend. On Thursday, his favourite corner was renamed in his honour: it used to be called Turn Three, a dazzlingly fast left-hand kink taken flat out in fifth, at 260km/h or so. Stoner Corner joins the Gardner Straight and Doohan Corner (Turn One). It was the corner, as it happens, that ended Carl Fogarty's career.

It was also the perfect showcase for Stoner's unique style: front wheel over the inside kerb, body weight well over the line, rear drifting under power. He had, he said, "a secret there – but we're not finished yet. Maybe I'll take it to the grave." Rossi was one to offer a respectful explanation: Stoner entered fast, "but especially he's able to open the throttle 20 or 30 metres before all the other guys. He puts the bike in over-steer. And he is able to gain for all the next 200 metres before the braking."

Only one landmark remained unconquered. Rather surprisingly, he didn't break Nicky Hayden's lap record from 2008, or his own pole time from the same year. He didn't have to; he wasn't pushed hard enough. Second-placed Lorenzo had a title to win, and he wasn't going to risk it, with Pedrosa down and out.

Pedrosa left the party on only the second lap, after making his first mistake of the year. He was leading, but ran a

little wide at Honda Hairpin as the front started chattering. It put him on some bumps and worn tarmac, and he fell. No regrets: he was doing what he had to do, as at the previous races. He was sad, he said later, for his team and his supporters, but not disappointed. "I'm proud of what we have done this season."

It is Lorenzo's misfortune – somewhat inconsequential, admittedly, given the degree of his success – that each time he has been crowned something happens in the crucial race to overshadow his achievement. In Malaysia, two years before, it had been Rossi's symbolic 46th win for Yamaha, greeted with the last of his then-and-again team-mate's overblown pantomimes (it had been Rossi's last win). In Australia, it was the man the Australians were now calling King Casey. Jorge should worry: he ran an immaculate season, with six strong wins, and never finished lower than second. More to the point, he's coming back to do it again. Casey not.

Equally, the race was a new low for Rossi and Ducati, as his haunted tenure of the iconic red bike drew to a merciful close. The record of five Phillip Island wins that Stoner had broken belonged to him: the track is a major favourite and the scene of one of his greatest races (overcoming a ten-second penalty in 2008 to win by five seconds). Now the bumpy track and the intractable Ducati measured progress during the year most cruelly, by Rossi's own chosen yardstick. He finished almost 40 seconds behind the winner, in a very average seventh. It was a bigger margin that at the opening round at Qatar, by more than five seconds.

Ben Spies was missing, after shoulder injuries at Sepang

turned out far worse than originally thought. As well as being dislocated, his collarbone had separated, and he had gone home for reconstructive surgery expected to keep his arm in a sling for ten weeks or more. A bitter blow to end a bitter season: he would miss not only the last two races, but also tests on his 2013 Ducati at Valencia, private tests later in November and potentially the opening tests of 2013.

Bumps were a problem for all, but with a Aus$13-million refit confirmed before the race, there wasn't much complaining, though Casey offered his services as a consultant, anxious that the track's relatively low grip level and resultant 'big balls' character be maintained.

Phillip Island conformed to its own reputation, and to the year's persistently disruptive weather, with its own specially icy and windy refinements, courtesy of the adjacent and very cold Bass Strait. Race day was relatively balmy, and more importantly dry. A mercy for the 53,100 fans who'd journeyed south for this last hurrah. Who would be the next Australian hero? The resurgent Anthony West claimed a second successive rostrum after a fine Moto2 ride, but at 31 he's at the wrong end of his career. Moto3 gave at least one alternative answer: rookie Sissis's first rostrum came after a blazing ride, during which he took control of a high-level group. Compatriot Miller's chances were wrecked, however, when he was one of five riders given ride-through penalties after a chain-reaction jumped start. Top riders Folger and Salom were in the same boat.

Fresh from victory at Sepang, and winner in Australia for the previous two years, Alex de Angelis suffered a nasty injury to his fourth finger when his left hand was trapped under the handlebar in a crash during qualifying.

Vinales was back, tail between his legs and a lawyer by his side. He read a prepared statement to the Spanish press, apologising to everybody from team and fans to Honda, FTR and Dorna, along with a long list of dutifully named sponsors. "I'm here to … ask for forgiveness and take responsibility for my mistakes," he said. That mistake had not been withdrawing at Sepang, but departure. "Although I was not mentally prepared to ride the bike, I should not have left the Sepang circuit or made such statements," he said. Sometimes, added his 'sports advisor' Paco Sanches, "a 17-year-old, who was ill-advised or misguided, can make bad decisions."

Mick Doohan was on hand, and essayed Saturday and Sunday demo rides at a respectable pace on a Repsol RC213V, fitted with a thumb brake. At the other end of the scale, Australian CEV racer Kris McLaren – riding injured Hernandez's CRT Kawasaki – crashed in qualifying, failed to make the cut and failed again when given another chance in morning warm-up.

MOTOGP RACE – 27 laps

Stoner completely dominated free practice and qualifying, undaunted by a crash 20 minutes into the final session. It was caused, he explained, by an engine-braking problem at low speed, which locked the rear, and he got away without further injury. The only rider below 1m 30s in every session, he was home, and with a vengeance.

Lorenzo and Pedrosa joined him on the front row; Crutchlow (fighting bronchitis and a fever) led the next from Bradl and Dovi. Rossi eventually pulled himself up to eighth, behind Bautista, but at least ahead of de Puniet's rapid CRT bike, unlike tenth-placed team-mate Hayden. He had had a fast, but luckily not injurious crash in morning warm-up.

Once again against the usual tide, Lorenzo managed to out-drag Pedrosa into the first corner, and he led him, Stoner, Crutchlow and Dovizioso around the Southern Loop.

Pedrosa's task was simple: he had to beat his fellow Spaniard. Accordingly, he dived up the inside first time into the hairpin and led away for the first lap, the Yamaha in hot pursuit. Then Stoner lined up the blue bike through the fast lefts on to the front straight, and was ahead as they crossed the line for the first time.

That gave him a grandstand seat for the end of Dani's slender hopes. Wide into the hairpin, he slid down and out. Game over.

This redefined Lorenzo's requirements. All he needed to do to be sure was finish 13th. He is, of course, made of sterner stuff, but now was not the time to be foolhardy. By lap four, the gap to Stoner was more than a second, and four seconds at half-distance.

A similar distance behind, Crutchlow found himself at the head of a gang of four: Dovi, Bautista and Bradl right up close. By lap eight, though, the Englishman had opened a gap of a second, and that too would keep on growing. "I felt good in the race," he said, opining that he might have had a go at Lorenzo, "but there was a good gap behind." A second rostrum would suffice.

Stoner's last lap saw the crowd urge him on with a standing ovation. "I was pretty nervous before," he admitted. "But conditions were fantastic for a Phillip Island race. I was focused on Jorge, but when there were only a couple of laps and I had a big lead, I saw the whole crowd waving me on. I'm not very emotional, but it was a fantastic feeling."

Not much less admiration for Lorenzo, whooping with glee at his second title. Sharing credit with his crew, he said, "We did a perfect season, always the best possible. And the bike never gave any problem all year."

Thus the rostrum, and the title, was settled. Fourth remained in dispute to the flag. All had a turn at the front – Bautista on laps 12 and 13, Bradl for a long spell thereafter. He alone had chosen the harder rear tyre, and it looked as though it might be paying off.

Not so, and when Dovi took over again on the 23rd lap, Bautista promptly took Bradl out of the hairpin; the Spaniard was in front again as they started the penultimate lap, only for Dovi to sweep past into Turn One and hold on to the flag. Fine racing from all three, across the line within two-tenths.

Fading behind from the start was a group of three, led for the first three laps by Hayden. Then Rossi took over, and a couple of laps later Abraham also got past the American. They circulated together until half-distance, when Hayden got back ahead of the satellite bike. He remained close to Rossi to the end; Abraham immediately fell back, quite safe in ninth.

Next up, the top CRT pair of de Puniet and Espargaro were

together from the start, both passing Barbera on the fifth lap and eventually dropping him away as de Puniet took over from his team-mate. They too battled to the end, changing places several times. De Puniet led on to the last lap, but it was an ecstatic Espargaro ahead over the line, if only by inches, giving him another point to lead by 11 in their private battle for the unofficial CRT crown.

Petrucci was the last rider still on the same lap, with Pirro and Silva behind, and points for all 15 finishers. Ellison had crashed out; Edwards and Rolfo retired.

The top four title places were now settled: Pedrosa second, then Stoner and Dovizioso. Fifth was still wide open, with just 14 points covering Bautista, Rossi and Crutchlow.

MOTO2 RACE – 25 laps

Pol Espargaro's fourth win of the year was a remarkable feat. There have been runaway winners in the production-powered class before, but never on this scale – 16.8 seconds, more than double any previous margin. The Spaniard found a way to break the rules that mean Phillip Island is a close, slipstreaming track. But that wasn't enough to stop Marquez finally winning the title he had come so close to in 2011.

The underdog took pole a full half-second ahead of Redding, who had led free practice. "I felt at one with the bike and I love this track," Espargaro glowed. Marquez was third after missing the first free practice altogether with an electrical problem.

A sunny start and, as in MotoGP, the duties of the two main protagonists were clear: Espargaro had to win, Marquez needed to score only two points.

Marquez led away into the first corner, but for a second race Nakagami was fired up, and this time he stayed on as he swept around the outside at the Southern Loop to lead the first lap. Only until the end of the straight, however: Marquez went cleanly past and into the lead.

Luthi finished the first lap in third, ahead of Espargaro, but would drop out of the top ten by lap four as the lead pack sorted itself out. Nakagami was also dropping back, and fast-starter Zarco. Redding was moving forward, likewise West and Iannone. But the Italian's race was short: he was up to fifth on lap five when his engine died.

Espargaro had moved to second on lap two, and as they

Left: Espargaro's Moto2 winning margin was more than double any previous: he just ran away.

Below left: Espargaro took the trophy, but new Moto2 champion Marquez the crown. Pol had kept him honest to the end.

Below: Moto2's battle for second on the last lap. West leads Redding; Marquez is preparing to pounce.

Photos: Gold & Goose

started the third he forcefully pushed past Marquez at the first corner. And simply took off. Sliding and shaking, it was a demonstration of brinkmanship that netted him a ten-second lead soon after half-distance, and he kept on stretching to the end.

Behind him, Redding closed on Marquez and was ahead on lap seven; the next group was led by West, who had displaced Aegerter – and the Australian was closing.

With six laps to go, he was with the pair, and now began a fascinating battle, with Marquez showing no willingness to settle for a safe fourth.

Redding was still in front as they started the last lap, then came West with a lunge into the hairpin. Redding tried and failed to get back, but worse was to come. He took a wide entry to the last corner, aiming for a run to the line, only for Marquez to fire his orange bike through the gap with a flying exit. He might have passed West as well but for a slide; he came almost alongside over the line.

"People always say to me: wait for the wet. It feels really good to do it in the dry," said West.

The brawl for fifth was resolved in favour of Aegerter, with Rabat aced on the last lap by him as well as Zarco and Corsi. Krummenacher and Nakagami were right behind, fifth to tenth within six-tenths.

Torres led Smith, Elias and Simeon over the line for 11th; di Meglio took the final point.

Kallio crashed out of sixth with two laps to go; Luthi also fell and remounted.

MOTO3 RACE – 23 laps

New champion Cortese was on pole, from Folger and Vazquez, a downbeat Vinales on row three. Cortese would win with ease, thanks to four major rivals receiving ride-through penalties after jump-starts. Then Vinales crashed out.

Folger triggered the jump-start, moving early. This set off Salom (shaking his head as he departed), Rossi and Moncayo, as well as Miller further back.

Khairuddin led away and for the first six laps before dropping to the back of the front group, eventually slowing with engine trouble before falling when his KTM seized.

Cortese took over and, with Oliveira in his tracks, soon broke free. Oliveira stayed close until Cortese let him past for

a couple of laps, then on the 20th he moved ahead again and stretched away for the win.

The battle for third was furious, dropping to six bikes as first Ajo ran wide, rejoining to crash twice, the second time terminally; Vinales fell on lap 15, just after getting to the front; and then Khairuddin fell away.

Sissis was inspired as the fight intensified. He led on to the last lap, regained the lead from Kent at Honda Hairpin and hung on grimly. Rins was fourth, then Kent, Fenati, Tonucci and Vazquez , all within nine-tenths. It took a video to confirm that Kent had beaten Fenati by two-thousandths.

Alex Marquez passed Isaac Vinales on the last lap for ninth; Folger served his ride-through and charged back, gaining three more places on the last lap for 11th; Salom was 15th; Rossi crashed, remounted to serve his penalty and finished 20th.

Danny Webb was out after the first free practice, his Mahindra in need of parts; team-mate Moretti retired after the first lap.

The battle for second overall would go to Valencia: Salom nine points up on no-score Vinales.

17

FIM WORLD CHAMPIONSHIP

AIRASIA
AUSTRALIAN GRAND PRIX

26-28 OCTOBER, 2012

PHILLIP ISLAND
27 laps
Length: 4.448 km / 2.764 miles
Width: 13m

Key
96/60 kph/mph
2 Gear

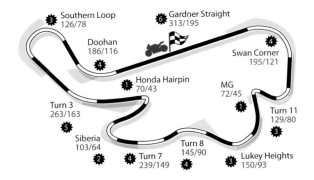

Southern Loop 126/78
Gardner Straight 313/195
Doohan 186/116
Swan Corner 195/121
Honda Hairpin 70/43
MG 72/45
Turn 3 263/163
Turn 11 129/80
Siberia 103/64
Turn 8 145/90
Turn 7 239/149
Lukey Heights 150/93

Photos: Gold & Goose

MotoGP · RACE DISTANCE: 27 laps, 74.624 miles/120.096km · RACE WEATHER: Dry (air 15°C, humidity 58%, track 26°C)

Pos.	Rider	Nat.	No.	Entrant	Machine	Tyres	Race tyre choice	Laps	Time & speed
1	Casey Stoner	AUS	1	Repsol Honda Team	Honda RC213V	B	F: Soft/R: Medium	27	41m 01.324s 109.147mph/ 175.655km/h
2	Jorge Lorenzo	SPA	99	Yamaha Factory Racing	Yamaha YZR-M1	B	F: Soft/R: Medium	27	41m 10.547s
3	Cal Crutchlow	GBR	35	Monster Yamaha Tech 3	Yamaha YZR-M1	B	F: Soft/R: Medium	27	41m 15.894s
4	Andrea Dovizioso	ITA	4	Monster Yamaha Tech 3	Yamaha YZR-M1	B	F: Soft/R: Medium	27	41m 24.627s
5	Alvaro Bautista	SPA	19	San Carlo Honda Gresini	Honda RC213V	B	F: Soft/R: Medium	27	41m 24.756s
6	Stefan Bradl	GER	6	LCR Honda MotoGP	Honda RC213V	B	F: Soft/R: Hard	27	41m 24.791s
7	Valentino Rossi	ITA	46	Ducati Team	Ducati Desmosedici GP12	B	F: Soft/R: Medium	27	41m 38.437s
8	Nicky Hayden	USA	69	Ducati Team	Ducati Desmosedici GP12	B	F: Soft/R: Medium	27	41m 39.711s
9	Karel Abraham	CZE	17	Cardion AB Motoracing	Ducati Desmosedici GP12	B	F: Soft/R: Medium	27	41m 53.937s
10	Aleix Espargaro	SPA	41	Power Electronics Aspar	ART Aprilia RSV4	B	F: Soft/R: Medium	27	42m 01.623s
11	Randy de Puniet	FRA	14	Power Electronics Aspar	ART Aprilia RSV4	B	F: Soft/R: Medium	27	42m 01.666s
12	Hector Barbera	SPA	8	Pramac Racing Team	Ducati Desmosedici GP12	B	F: Soft/R: Medium	27	42m 23.275s
13	Danilo Petrucci	ITA	9	Came IodaRacing Project	Ioda Suter BMW S1000RR	B	F: Soft/R: Medium	27	42m 29.181s
14	Michele Pirro	ITA	51	San Carlo Honda Gresini	FTR Honda CBR1000RR	B	F: Soft/R: Medium	26	41m 13.539s
15	Ivan Silva	SPA	22	Avintia Blusens	BQR FTR Kawasaki ZX-10R	B	F: Soft/R: Medium	26	41m 35.733s
	Roberto Rolfo	ITA	84	Speed Master	ART Aprilia RSV4	B	F: Soft/R: Medium	18	DNF-mechanical
	Colin Edwards	USA	5	NGM Mobile Forward Racing	Suter BMW S1000RR	B	F: Soft/R: Medium	6	DNF-mechanical
	James Ellison	GBR	77	Paul Bird Motorsport	ART Aprilia RSV4	B	F: Soft/R: Medium	5	DNF-crash
	Dani Pedrosa	SPA	26	Repsol Honda Team	Honda RC213V	B	F: Soft/R: Medium	1	DNF-crash

Fastest lap: Casey Stoner, on lap 3, 1m 30.191s, 110.320mph/177.543km/h.
Lap record: Nicky Hayden, USA (Honda), 1m 30.059s, 110.482mph/177.803km/h (2008).
Event best maximum speed: Karel Abraham, 211.0mph/339.6km/h (qualifying practice).

Qualifying
Weather: Dry
Air Temp: 12° **Humidity:** 72%
Track Temp: 26°

1	Stoner	1m 29.623s
2	Lorenzo	1m 30.140s
3	Pedrosa	1m 30.575s
4	Crutchlow	1m 30.763s
5	Bradl	1m 30.798s
6	Dovizioso	1m 31.200s
7	Bautista	1m 31.490s
8	Rossi	1m 31.661s
9	De Puniet	1m 31.667s
10	Hayden	1m 31.681s
11	Abraham	1m 31.910s
12	Espargaro	1m 31.990s
13	Barbera	1m 32.231s
14	Pirro	1m 33.050s
15	Petrucci	1m 33.069s
16	Edwards	1m 33.450s
17	Ellison	1m 33.489s
18	Rolfo	1m 33.577s
19	Silva	1m 34.156s

Outside 107%
	McLaren	1m 36.324s

Fastest race laps
1	Stoner	1m 30.191s
2	Lorenzo	1m 30.703s
3	Crutchlow	1m 30.947s
4	Bradl	1m 30.976s
5	Bautista	1m 30.986s
6	Dovizioso	1m 31.214s
7	Abraham	1m 31.646s
8	Rossi	1m 31.662s
9	Hayden	1m 31.713s
10	Espargaro	1m 32.305s
11	Barbera	1m 32.355s
12	De Puniet	1m 32.379s
13	Pirro	1m 33.013s
14	Petrucci	1m 33.096s
15	Ellison	1m 33.590s
16	Rolfo	1m 33.867s
17	Silva	1m 33.892s
18	Edwards	1m 34.131s

Championship Points
1	Lorenzo	350
2	Pedrosa	307
3	Stoner	238
4	Dovizioso	208
5	Bautista	165
6	Rossi	157
7	Crutchlow	151
8	Bradl	135
9	Hayden	122
10	Spies	88
11	Barbera	83
12	Espargaro	69
13	De Puniet	58
14	Abraham	50
15	Pirro	32
16	Ellison	28
17	Hernandez	28
18	Edwards	25
19	Petrucci	19
20	Rea	17
21	Pasini	13
22	Silva	12
23	Elias	10
24	Nakasuga	7
25	Rapp	2
26	Salom	1

Grid order	1	2	3	4	5	6	7	8	9	10	11	12	13	14	15	16	17	18	19	20	21	22	23	24	25	26	27	
1 STONER	26	1	1	1	1	1	1	1	1	1	1	1	1	1	1	1	1	1	1	1	1	1	1	1	1	1	1	1
99 LORENZO	1	99	99	99	99	99	99	99	99	99	99	99	99	99	99	99	99	99	99	99	99	99	99	99	99	99	99	2
26 PEDROSA	99	35	35	35	35	35	35	35	35	35	35	35	35	35	35	35	35	35	35	35	35	35	35	35	35	35		3
35 CRUTCHLOW	35	4	4	4	4	4	4	4	4	4	4	19	19	6	6	6	6	6	6	6	6	4	4	4	19	4		4
6 BRADL	4	19	19	19	19	19	19	19	19	19	19	4	4	4	4	4	4	4	19	4	19	19	6	19	6	19		5
4 DOVIZIOSO	6	6	6	6	6	6	6	6	6	6	6	6	6	19	19	19	19	19	4	19	19	6	4	6	4	6		6
19 BAUTISTA	19	69	69	46	46	46	46	46	46	46	46	46	46	46	46	46	46	46	46	46	46	46	46	46	46	46		7
46 ROSSI	69	46	46	69	69	17	17	17	17	17	17	17	69	69	69	69	69	69	69	69	69	69	69	69	69	69		8
14 DE PUNIET	46	17	17	17	17	69	69	69	69	69	69	69	17	17	17	17	17	17	17	17	17	17	17	17	17	17		9
69 HAYDEN	17	8	8	8	41	14	14	14	14	14	14	14	14	14	41	41	41	41	41	14	14	14	14	41	14	41		10
17 ABRAHAM	41	41	41	41	14	41	41	41	41	41	41	41	41	41	14	14	14	14	14	41	41	41	41	14	41	14		11
41 ESPARGARO	8	14	14	14	8	8	8	8	8	8	8	8	8	8	8	8	8	8	8	8	8	8	8	8	8	8		12
8 BARBERA	14	51	51	51	51	51	51	51	9	9	9	9	9	9	9	9	9	9	9	9	9	9	9	9	9	9		13
51 PIRRO	51	9	9	9	9	9	9	9	51	51	51	51	51	51	51	51	51	51	51	51	51	51	51	51	51	51		14
9 PETRUCCI	9	84	77	77	77	84	84	84	84	84	84	84	84	84	22	84	84	84	22	22	22	22	22	22	22	22		15
5 EDWARDS	77	77	84	84	84	22	22	22	22	22	22	22	22	84	22	22	22											
77 ELLISON	84	5	5	22	22	5																						
84 ROLFO	5	22	22	5	5																							
22 SILVA	22																											

26 Pit stop   51 Lapped rider

Constructor Points
1	Honda	387
2	Yamaha	366
3	Ducati	183
4	ART	93
5	FTR	32
6	BQR	32
7	Suter	25
8	Ioda-Suter	10
9	Ioda	9
10	APR	2
11	BQR-FTR	2

Moto2

RACE DISTANCE: 25 laps, 69.096 miles/111.200km · RACE WEATHER: Dry (air 15°C, humidity 59%, track 26°C)

Pos.	Rider	Nat.	No.	Entrant	Machine	Laps	Time & Speed
1	**Pol Espargaro**	SPA	40	Tuenti Movil HP 40	Kalex	25	39m 26.486s 105.112mph/ 169.162km/h
2	**Anthony West**	AUS	95	QMMF Racing Team	Speed Up	25	39m 43.297s
3	**Marc Marquez**	SPA	93	Team Catalunya Caixa Repsol	Suter	25	39m 43.323s
4	**Scott Redding**	GBR	45	Marc VDS Racing Team	Kalex	25	39m 43.443s
5	**Dominique Aegerter**	SWI	77	Technomag-CIP	Suter	25	39m 52.504s
6	**Johann Zarco**	FRA	5	JIR Moto2	Motobi	25	39m 52.514s
7	**Simone Corsi**	ITA	3	Came IodaRacing Project	FTR	25	39m 52.577s
8	**Esteve Rabat**	SPA	80	Tuenti Movil HP 40	Kalex	25	39m 52.858s
9	**Randy Krummenacher**	SWI	4	GP Team Switzerland	Kalex	25	39m 52.960s
10	**Takaaki Nakagami**	JPN	30	Italtrans Racing Team	Kalex	25	39m 53.066s
11	**Jordi Torres**	SPA	81	Mapfre Aspar Team Moto2	Suter	25	40m 03.006s
12	**Bradley Smith**	GBR	38	Tech 3 Racing	Tech 3	25	40m 03.051s
13	**Toni Elias**	SPA	24	Italtrans Racing Team	Kalex	25	40m 03.356s
14	**Xavier Simeon**	BEL	19	Tech 3 Racing	Tech 3	25	40m 04.706s
15	**Mike di Meglio**	FRA	63	Kiefer Racing	Kalex	25	40m 10.836s
16	Yuki Takahashi	JPN	72	NGM Mobile Forward Racing	FTR	25	40m 15.072s
17	Ricard Cardus	SPA	88	Arguinano Racing Team	AJR	25	40m 15.249s
18	Nicolas Terol	SPA	18	Mapfre Aspar Team Moto2	Suter	25	40m 15.254s
19	Ratthapark Wilairot	THA	14	Thai Honda PTT Gresini Moto2	Suter	25	40m 18.973s
20	Marcel Schrotter	GER	23	Desguaces La Torre SAG	Bimota	25	40m 19.055s
21	Gino Rea	GBR	8	Federal Oil Gresini Moto2	Suter	25	40m 19.193s
22	Tomoyoshi Koyama	JPN	75	Technomag-CIP	Suter	25	40m 38.573s
23	Alessandro Andreozzi	ITA	22	S/Master Speed Up	Speed Up	25	40m 47.941s
24	Elena Rosell	SPA	82	QMMF Racing Team	Speed Up	24	39m 33.846s
25	Marco Colandrea	SWI	10	SAG Team	FTR	24	39m 33.855s
	Mika Kallio	FIN	36	Marc VDS Racing Team	Kalex	23	DNF
	Axel Pons	SPA	49	Tuenti Movil HP 40	Kalex	23	DNF
	Julian Simon	SPA	60	Blusens Avintia	Suter	23	DNF
	Eric Granado	BRA	57	JIR Moto2	Motobi	23	DNF
	Thomas Luthi	SWI	12	Interwetten-Paddock	Suter	17	DNF
	Andrea Iannone	ITA	29	Speed Master	Speed Up	4	DNF

Fastest lap: Pol Espargaro, on lap 7, 1m 33.729s, 106.156mph/170.841km/h (record)
Previous lap record: Alex de Angelis, RSM (Motobi), 1m 34.549s, 105.235mph/169.359km/h (2011).
Event best maximum speed: Mika Kallio, 182.9mph/294.3km/h (race).

Qualifying: Dry
Air: 12° Humidity: 84% Track: 26°

1	Espargaro	1m 33.705s
2	Redding	1m 34.264s
3	Marquez	1m 34.408s
4	Luthi	1m 34.513s
5	Nakagami	1m 34.541s
6	Krummenacher	1m 34.596s
7	Zarco	1m 34.696s
8	Iannone	1m 34.714s
9	West	1m 34.765s
10	Rabat	1m 34.900s
11	Corsi	1m 34.973s
12	Aegerter	1m 35.020s
13	Pons	1m 35.052s
14	Kallio	1m 35.071s
15	Smith	1m 35.169s
16	Simeon	1m 35.310s
17	Simon	1m 35.466s
18	Elias	1m 35.546s
19	Di Meglio	1m 35.589s
20	Torres	1m 35.609s
21	Cardus	1m 35.864s
22	De Angelis	1m 35.906s
23	Wilairot	1m 36.026s
24	Rea	1m 36.163s
25	Schrotter	1m 36.242s
26	Terol	1m 36.550s
27	Andreozzi	1m 37.293s
28	Takahashi	1m 37.436s
29	Koyama	1m 37.524s
30	Rosell	1m 37.829s
31	Colandrea	1m 38.266s
32	Granado	1m 40.119s

Fastest race laps

1	Espargaro	1m 33.729s
2	Marquez	1m 34.496s
3	Krummenacher	1m 34.565s
4	Redding	1m 34.568s
5	Nakagami	1m 34.664s
6	Corsi	1m 34.666s
7	Iannone	1m 34.681s
8	West	1m 34.688s
9	Aegerter	1m 34.766s
10	Zarco	1m 34.811s
11	Kallio	1m 34.812s
12	Rabat	1m 34.854s
13	Luthi	1m 34.869s
14	Torres	1m 34.968s
15	Pons	1m 34.987s
16	Elias	1m 35.168s
17	Simon	1m 35.206s
18	Smith	1m 35.251s
19	Terol	1m 35.350s
20	Simeon	1m 35.363s
21	Wilairot	1m 35.461s
22	Cardus	1m 35.465s
23	Di Meglio	1m 35.519s
24	Rea	1m 35.775s
25	Takahashi	1m 35.837s
26	Schrotter	1m 35.858s
27	Koyama	1m 35.931s
28	Andreozzi	1m 36.538s
29	Rosell	1m 37.728s
30	Colandrea	1m 38.010s
31	Granado	1m 39.005s

Championship Points

1	Marquez	299
2	Espargaro	260
3	Iannone	188
4	Luthi	177
5	Redding	161
6	Kallio	119
7	Smith	108
8	Rabat	107
9	Aegerter	98
10	Zarco	94
11	Corsi	87
12	De Angelis	86
13	Corti	74
14	West	61
15	Simon	58
16	Nakagami	56
17	Elias	40
18	Krummenacher	31
19	Simeon	21
20	Torres	19
21	Terol	19
22	Rea	17
23	Di Meglio	14
24	Syahrin	13
25	Pons	10
26	Neukirchner	8
27	Wilairot	8
28	Cardus	7

Constructor Points

1	Suter	349
2	Kalex	310
3	Speed Up	222
4	FTR	132
5	Tech 3	110
6	Motobi	94
7	Moriwaki	10
8	AJR	7

Moto3

RACE DISTANCE: 23 laps, 63.569 miles/102.304km · RACE WEATHER: Dry (air 14°C, humidity 63%, track 22°C)

Pos.	Rider	Nat.	No.	Entrant	Machine	Laps	Time & Speed
1	**Sandro Cortese**	GER	11	Red Bull KTM Ajo	KTM	23	38m 20.014s 99.498mph/ 160.127km/h
2	**Miguel Oliveira**	POR	44	Estrella Galicia 0,0	Suter Honda	23	38m 22.122s
3	**Arthur Sissis**	AUS	61	Red Bull KTM Ajo	KTM	23	38m 25.045s
4	**Alex Rins**	SPA	42	Estrella Galicia 0,0	Suter Honda	23	38m 25.098s
5	**Danny Kent**	GBR	52	Red Bull KTM Ajo	KTM	23	38m 25.121s
6	**Romano Fenati**	ITA	5	Team Italia FMI	FTR Honda	23	38m 25.123s
7	**Alessandro Tonucci**	ITA	19	Team Italia FMI	FTR Honda	23	38m 25.388s
8	**Efren Vazquez**	SPA	7	JHK t-shirt Laglisse	FTR Honda	23	38m 25.908s
9	**Alex Marquez**	SPA	12	Ambrogio Next Racing	Suter Honda	23	38m 50.797s
10	**Isaac Vinales**	SPA	32	Ongetta-Centro Seta	FTR Honda	23	38m 50.925s
11	**Jonas Folger**	GER	94	Mapfre Aspar Team Moto3	Kalex KTM	23	38m 52.817s
12	**Adrian Martin**	SPA	26	JHK t-shirt Laglisse	FTR Honda	23	38m 53.316s
13	**Jakub Kornfeil**	CZE	84	Redox-Ongetta-Centro Seta	FTR Honda	23	38m 53.493s
14	**Brad Binder**	RSA	41	RW Racing GP	Kalex KTM	23	38m 54.116s
15	**Luis Salom**	SPA	39	RW Racing GP	Kalex KTM	23	39m 03.763s
16	Alan Techer	FRA	89	Technomag-CIP-TSR	TSR Honda	23	39m 03.841s
17	Alberto Moncayo	SPA	23	Andalucia JHK t-shirt Laglisse	FTR Honda	23	39m 09.408s
18	Armando Pontone	ITA	80	Ioda Team Italia	Ioda	23	39m 26.565s
19	John McPhee	GBR	17	Caretta Technology	KRP Honda	23	39m 26.602s
20	Louis Rossi	FRA	96	Racing Team Germany	FTR Honda	23	39m 28.815s
21	Jack Miller	AUS	8	Caretta Technology	Honda	23	39m 28.922s
22	Kenta Fujii	JPN	51	Technomag-CIP-TSR	TSR Honda	23	39m 30.044s
23	Giulian Pedone	SWI	30	Ambrogio Next Racing	Suter Honda	23	39m 30.425s
24	Lincoln Gilding	AUS	75	K1 Racing	Honda	23	39m 53.524s
25	Sam Clarke	AUS	36	Fastline GP Racing	Honda	22	39m 44.906s
	Zulfahmi Khairuddin	MAL	63	AirAsia-Sic-Ajo	KTM	19	DNF
	Toni Finsterbusch	GER	9	Racing Team Germany	Honda	16	DNF
	Maverick Vinales	SPA	25	Blusens Avintia	FTR Honda	14	DNF
	Niklas Ajo	FIN	31	TT Motion Events Racing	KTM	11	DNF
	Luca Amato	GER	29	Mapfre Aspar Team Moto3	Kalex KTM	8	DNF
	Riccardo Moretti	ITA	20	Mahindra Racing	Mahindra	1	DNF
	Niccolo Antonelli	ITA	27	San Carlo Gresini Moto3	FTR Honda	0	DNS
	Danny Webb	GBR	99	Mahindra Racing	Mahindra	0	DNS

Fastest lap: Alessandro Tonucci, on lap 2, 1m 38.447s, 101.069mph/162.654km/h (record).
Previous lap record: New category.
Event best maximum speed: Zulfahmi Khairuddin, 148.1mph/238.4km/h (qualifying practice).

Qualifying: Dry
Air: 12° Humidity: 71% Track: 26°

1	Cortese	1m 38.334s
2	Folger	1m 38.727s
3	Vazquez	1m 39.179s
4	Kent	1m 39.222s
5	Khairuddin	1m 39.229s
6	Oliveira	1m 39.262s
7	Sissis	1m 39.337s
8	M. Vinales	1m 39.387s
9	Salom	1m 39.430s
10	Tonucci	1m 39.451s
11	Moncayo	1m 39.514s
12	Rossi	1m 39.536s
13	Kornfeil	1m 39.572s
14	Fenati	1m 39.595s
15	Ajo	1m 39.631s
16	Rins	1m 39.649s
17	Martin	1m 39.750s
18	I. Vinales	1m 40.167s
19	Marquez	1m 40.336s
20	Binder	1m 40.372s
21	Pontone	1m 40.854s
22	McPhee	1m 40.984s
23	Miller	1m 41.177s
24	Techer	1m 41.198s
25	Rodriguez	1m 41.555s
26	Pedone	1m 42.027s
27	Fujii	1m 42.475s
28	Amato	1m 43.029s
29	Gilding	1m 43.045s
30	Moretti	1m 44.393s
31	Finsterbusch	1m 44.809s
Outside 107%		
	Clarke	1m 46.873s
	Antonelli	no time
	Webb	no time

Fastest race laps

1	Tonucci	1m 38.447s
2	Rins	1m 38.507s
3	Cortese	1m 38.638s
4	Oliveira	1m 38.657s
5	Sissis	1m 38.686s
6	Rossi	1m 38.748s
7	M. Vinales	1m 38.772s
8	Vazquez	1m 38.805s
9	Salom	1m 38.812s
10	Fenati	1m 38.852s
11	Folger	1m 38.885s
12	Ajo	1m 39.009s
13	Kent	1m 39.025s
14	Khairuddin	1m 39.059s
15	Martin	1m 39.112s
16	Moncayo	1m 39.254s
17	Binder	1m 39.397s
18	I. Vinales	1m 39.483s
19	Marquez	1m 39.537s
20	Kornfeil	1m 40.369s
21	McPhee	1m 40.469s
22	Amato	1m 40.504s
23	Techer	1m 40.527s
24	Miller	1m 40.797s
25	Pedone	1m 40.938s
26	Pontone	1m 41.181s
27	Gilding	1m 41.216s
28	Fujii	1m 41.735s
29	Finsterbusch	1m 41.772s
30	Clarke	1m 46.870s

Championship Points

1	Cortese	305
2	Salom	208
3	M. Vinales	199
4	Rins	141
5	Fenati	136
6	Kent	129
7	Oliveira	114
8	Khairuddin	112
9	Folger	93
10	Vazquez	93
11	Sissis	84
12	Masbou	81
13	Rossi	76
14	Antonelli	74
15	Kornfeil	62
16	Moncayo	52
17	Faubel	52
18	Tonucci	43
19	Ajo	33
20	Marquez	27
21	Techer	21
22	Miller	17
23	Martin	16
24	Binder	11
25	Moreno	10
26	Iwema	9
27	Gruenwald	8
28	I. Vinales	8
29	Pedone	7
30	Finsterbusch	7
31	Schrotter	4
32	Hanus	3
33	Calia	2
34	McPhee	1
35	Rinaldi	1
36	Grotzkyj	1

Constructor Points

1	KTM	321
2	FTR Honda	295
3	Kalex KTM	249
4	Suter Honda	182
5	Honda	87
6	TSR Honda	21
7	FGR Honda	9
8	Ioda	5
9	Mahindra	4
10	KRP Honda	1
11	Oral	1

FIM WORLD CHAMPIONSHIP · ROUND 18

VALENCIA GRAND PRIX

VALENCIA CIRCUIT

Inset, top: Back-to-front hero: Pedrosa was out on his own, to take one more win than the new champion.

Main photo: Lorenzo's only mistake of the year was spectacular. Blameless Ellison sticks to the dry line.
Photos: Gold & Goose

Above: Pedrosa leads fellow pit-lane starters Bautista (19) and Crutchlow (half-hidden) through the CRT bikes, Silva (22), de Puniet (14) and Petrucci (9).

Top right: Dani beams after closing off his best ever season.

Above centre right: Old paddock buddies Casey Stoner and Chaz Davies.

Above right: Former 250 champion Hiro Aoyama was back for a run on a CRT bike.

Right: With Stoner on the charge, Bautista had to accept fourth. It was good enough.

Far right: Team-mate Pirro was only one place down, the best CRT finish all year.

Below right: Midfield mayhem as Dovizioso, Stoner, Rossi, Abraham and Barbera squabble over the dry line.

Photos: Gold & Goose

ALL championships settled, no need to save engines, nothing on the table but pride. The last GP was always going to be climactic. Doubly so, under the combined effects of climate and a tricky new surface, which looked wet even when it wasn't, and which held water so much that it usually was anyway. Circumstances in which the unexpected can always happen, and where gambling and genius can shine in equal measure.

The outcome was somewhat historic – it is only seldom that a race is won from the back of the grid (though that is effectively what Marquez did at Motegi). It happened twice at Valencia, and it is hard to know which was the more inspiring – Marquez again or Pedrosa. Marquez was on the back because of yet another over-aggressive move, having knocked Corsi off on Friday afternoon in free practice. Dani was voluntarily worse off – one of four starting from the pit lane, ten seconds after the get-go.

His ride through the field was extraordinary, though he did gain nine places on laps four and five, when riders pitted to change from wet bikes to dry. Dani had taken that decision on the last corner of the warm-up lap, after noting a dry line appearing and that Lorenzo (cannily already on slicks) was already fast.

He caught Jorge after one-third distance, hit neutral and dropped away again. But now it was Lorenzo's turn for slow traffic, and the knowledge that Dani would soon be back forced him into his first mistake of the year. An ill-judged overtake on Ellison's ART set the Yamaha wobbling and took him on to a real wet patch. He was very lucky to escape unhurt from the subsequent acrobatic high-side.

There were two other heroes on the rostrum with a jubilant Dani, whose seventh win put him one up on Jorge (more poignantly, if he'd stayed on and finished second in Australia, he would have been champion). One was tearful Yamaha factory test rider Katsuyuki Nakasuga, substituting for Spies. Also on slicks, he was steadfast throughout for a fine second. His second child had been born in Japan on race eve; a whimsical father might think of naming her Valencia.

The third was Casey Stoner, saying goodbye in style. He'd cautiously chosen wets ("Going for the easy way out is not usually my choice.") and was riding cautiously also after pitting for slicks. As he gained confidence, he also gained speed, and by the end charged down Bautista to claim third with a couple of laps to spare. He'd been more than 30 seconds behind after nine laps.

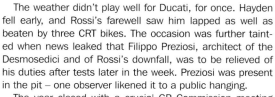
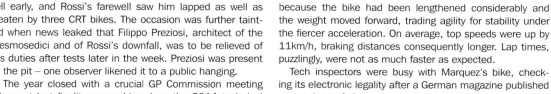

The weather didn't play well for Ducati, for once. Hayden fell early, and Rossi's farewell saw him lapped as well as beaten by three CRT bikes. The occasion was further tainted when news leaked that Filippo Preziosi, architect of the Desmosedici and of Rossi's downfall, was to be relieved of his duties after tests later in the week. Preziosi was present in the pit – one observer likened it to a public hanging.

The year closed with a crucial GP Commission meeting where at last finality was achieved on the 2014 technical rules – albeit provisional, depending on the factories committing to provide competitive production racers to replace the despised CRT bikes. Honda and cohorts achieved the goal of keeping free electronics: software only, since a control ECU will be supplied, at the cost of another litre of fuel and one of the current six engines. Those accepting control software will get an extra three litres and 12 engines.

There was relief for Moto2 bruisers like Scott Redding, with a combined bike-rider minimum weight for the class in 2013 – 215kg, as against 140 for the machine alone.

Yamaha's annual technical briefing was more guarded than usual – no numbers were given, graphs were vague; deliberately so, according to Kouichi Tsuji, MotoGP group leader. In the past, they had given away too much: the competitors were getting closer. Analysis of comparative 800/1000cc power curves and lap traces was interesting nonetheless. The former showed smoother outlines peaking at lower revs;

the latter revealed that corner speeds were lower. This was because the bike had been lengthened considerably and the weight moved forward, trading agility for stability under the fiercer acceleration. On average, top speeds were up by 11km/h, braking distances consequently longer. Lap times, puzzlingly, were not as much faster as expected.

Tech inspectors were busy with Marquez's bike, checking its electronic legality after a German magazine published suggestions of sharp practice involving interaction between the quick-shifter and the control ECU. Race director Mike Webb was assured by his own men, as well as HRC and Geo Technology, that nothing was out of order. As he had expected: the bike had been regularly checked as a matter of course, and the Alzamora-led team had been scrupulous, indeed "even paranoid, in making sure that everything they have done to the bike, they have checked with us first."

The track had been fully resurfaced, and most riders came off their first runs on it praising the smoothness, and confident that low grip levels would improve. Only one, Stoner, was firm in his condemnation (his dissenting voice will be much missed in 2013). "The new surface sucks," he said. "In general, I don't feel the bumps have gone. Some of the big ones, but there's a consistency of smaller bumps, the surface joins are bad and it holds water." By the end of the weekend, he had been proved largely right, especially his last point; while all the fast guys complained of tyres going off after five or six laps, with wear a worry should the race be fully dry. As if.

The new season started on Monday, with testing for Moto2 and MotoGP over the next three days. Among other things, Marquez was to make his MotoGP debut, Rossi and Dovizioso would be testing their swapped Yamaha and Ducati chances, and Bradley Smith getting his first MotoGP gallop. The weather didn't co-operate; the absent Ben Spies would not miss much as the 2013 season started under dark clouds.

Mahindra caused a small stir by announcing its new riders for 2013's all-new Suter-built Moto3 effort: fast rookie Miguel Oliveira and the doughty Efren Vazquez. Also in Moto3 came news that Vinales was planning a switch from Honda to KTM power – but he would have to buy himself out of his Blusens Avintia contract first.

MOTOGP RACE – 30 laps

Free practice was hit by the weather, leaving just the qualifying hour to prepare for the race. Pedrosa's fifth pole was by 0.351 second, the only rider (and finally) to break Rossi's fastest lap of 2006, on a 990. His late dash put Stoner second and Lorenzo third. Crutchlow led row two from Bradl and Dovi. Hayden had been fastest in one wet session and was top Ducati, leading row three from Bautista and Barbera; Rossi was 11th, outqualified by Espargaro's CRT bike, de Puniet's similar ART alongside. Nakasuga was 16th.

Confusion reigned on the grid and for the first few laps. It had stopped raining, but the track was still dark. When Dani dived into the pits, he was followed by Bautista, Crutchlow and Hayden, and they all lined up at the pit-lane exit, where it was still really wet – they slithered away dramatically as Espargaro took a flier to enjoy a lead that lasted two laps. Dovizioso took over at the end of lap three, but pulled in – along with Stoner, Abraham and Aoyama (substituting for Hernandez) – at the end of the fourth to change bikes. Two laps later, Rossi, Espargaro, Rolfo and Ellison did the same.

Lorenzo had inherited the lead from Dovi, but Pedrosa was charging through, significantly the fastest, and had taken second off Nakasuga on lap six, now less than three seconds adrift.

Jorge pushed, but Dani pushed harder and at the end of lap 12 was on his tail – only to hit neutral and take to the paved run-off, losing four seconds.

Lorenzo knew relief would be only temporary, but now he

was lapping slower riders – among them Abraham, behind whom he lost a lot of time, and Rossi, "the only one to move out of the way". Next up was Ellison, and impatiently Jorge went for the pass on the left-right Turns Nine and Ten. It failed spectacularly, and later he blamed Ellison, saying he'd looked behind and seen him, but stayed on line. Ellison protested. That was no place to look around, and in any case the dry line was so narrow that if he had moved out, he would have been the one to crash.

That was on lap 14. By then, Crutchlow had caught and passed Nakasuga, and was pulling clear, his lap times matching those of Pedrosa, more than 20 seconds ahead. He was comfortable in a career-best second when he was suddenly flicked off as he braked into the last corner. "I hit a wet patch that data showed was only five inches long. It locked up, then gripped, but I was still on the brakes … and I went over the handlebars," he said, nursing a bandaged left hand.

That promoted the Japanese back to a second he would hold to the end, in an unobtrusively excellent ride.

With factory riders to and fro with pit stops, all mixed up with CRT riders who had either started on slicks or pitted early to change, the lower orders were changing almost lap by lap.

By half-distance, it was becoming clearer – Bautista fourth, well clear of Pirro; Petrucci circulating steadily three seconds back, then Stoner a similar distance behind, before a big gap to Dovizioso, who in turn had got away from Abraham and Rossi.

Stoner was the one on the move, past both CRT bikes on lap 19, and on his successful mission to catch and pass Bautista for what was now the last rostrum spot. At one point, he'd been more than 30 seconds behind, but now he passed Petrucci and Pirro and was barely 12 seconds adrift. Then ten seconds. Then eight. With three laps to go, as the Spaniard's pit hung out a board reading "P4 OK", he powered past for the final rostrum spot.

Pirro held on to a good fifth, top CRT bike and four seconds ahead of Dovi, who had gone from first on lap four to last-but-one on the fifth, after his slow bike change. He and Abraham had got the better of Petrucci, now a lap down and nine seconds clear of Ellison.

Rossi was four seconds away, having ignominiously succumbed to the English CRT rider on lap 17, unable (he explained) to get enough heat into his slicks to make them work. He was miles ahead of Espargaro, in turn well clear

of team-mate de Puniet, who had started on slicks, but lost his advantage when he ran off. He was two laps down at the end, likewise Aoyama; Edwards was 14th, another lap away.

Bradl, on slicks, had just passed Nakasuga for third when he crashed on lap ten. Claudio Corti, wild-carding on the carbon-framed Blusens Inmotec Kawasaki, also crashed out, likewise Barbera, Rolfo and Silva.

Fourth was indeed good enough for Bautista to win the battle for fifth overall, from Rossi and Crutchlow. Non-scorers Bradl and Hayden took the next championship positions.

MOTO2 RACE – 27 laps

Pol Espargaro took his eighth pole by four-tenths ahead of new champion Marquez – but it was a tense wait in the pits after he fell with less than ten minutes to go. Marquez had also fallen earlier in the session, but was back out again and on the charge, only to slip off for a second time. In any case, he was condemned to a back-of-the-grid start.

That elevated third-fastest Luthi to second and moved Nakagami to the front row. Terol led the second, at a track where a corner had been named after him as final 125 champion, from team-mate Torres and Aegerter. Redding led row three; Iannone was tenth.

It was wet and tricky. With Marquez at the back, Terol took a flier to lead the early laps from Espargaro, by far his best performance in his rookie season. He stayed there as Simon took over second on lap three, while Espargaro dropped back to fourth behind Corsi in an increasingly distant group. They were all trading blows when Espargaro slithered off on lap eight, rapidly remounting in 19th to fight his way back to the points.

Simon had been closing steadily on runaway Terol and took the lead on lap eight, immediately pulling clear; Simeon took over the pursuit group, only to fall on lap 11, handing control to Aegerter. Now wet specialist Rea had come through to start attacking him – more significantly, Marquez was about to latch on and start his assault. He'd gained 22 places on the first lap to finish 11th, and had been moving forward ever since.

The three battled for a bit, then Marquez almost hit Aegerter as he outbraked him into the first corner. He turned to wave an apology; Aegerter acknowledged it, which gave Rea the chance to slip past, only for the Englishman to fall after one more lap; he remounted hurriedly.

Marquez was now third and more than five seconds adrift

Left: Petrucci took his Suter-BMW to a best-yet eighth – the reward for a year of effort against the odds.

Below left: Terol in unusual form – leading a Moto2 race. The 125 champion had not been a fast learner.

Far left: Katsuyuki Nakasuga rode unobtrusively to a sensational second.

Below: Yamaha joy: team boss Lin Jarvis joins the delighted factory staff with Nakasuga.

Photos: Gold & Goose

of Terol, with 12 laps to go. Plenty of time to catch up, blow past, then set about clawing at a gap of five seconds to Simon. He'd caught up with three laps to go and went directly past down the straight to claim a classic ninth win of his championship season.

Simon had stayed close, but was 1.25 seconds away over the line; Terol another ten.

Luthi took fourth off Aegerter with two laps to go, his Swiss countryman less than a second behind over the line. Torres was a lone sixth, then Kallio. Next was Espargaro, a second ahead of a big gang, ninth to 16th covered by just over a second: Elias, Rabat, Iannone, Rea, Rivas, Takahashi, Cardus and Smith, the Englishman out of the points by seven-tenths. Corsi was some way back; Redding 22nd.

Zarco crashed out after ten laps, having moved steadily forward from 16th to sixth; Rosell also fell; Nakagami retired.

Iannone's 11th was enough to save third, three points clear of Luthi. Non-scorer Redding had done enough for fifth.

MOTO3 RACE – 24 laps

Jonas Folger took his second career pole; Oliveira second by less than half a tenth, Salom alongside. Cortese led row two from Vinales and Vazquez; Kent headed the third.

Folger's misfortunes started when his bike stopped on the sighting lap. They managed to get it back and (eventually) running again for a pit-lane start, but his chance of a back-to-front victory was soon scuppered when it stopped for good after seven laps.

Salom led the first three laps from Oliveira and Alex Marquez, and they quickly opened up two seconds on Rossi, heading the pursuit.

As Oliveira took the lead on lap five, Marquez crashed out, and now the pack closed up. By half-distance, Cortese led. Miller had battled through to join the group and was near the front when he slipped off with five laps to go.

By then, erstwhile leader Oliveira and Vazquez had gone after the latter ran inside and fell, taking the rookie with him.

That gave Cortese a breathing space, Rossi now leading the chase until he shifted down one gear too many at the first corner on lap 19, running wide. Kent took over, and by the end he had dragged Binder and Khairuddin back up to Cortese's back wheel. Faubel was with them, but ran wide on the last lap, leaving just four.

Cortese led into the last corner, but was wide on the entry, leaving the space for Kent to slip past and win by just over half a tenth.

Inches behind, Khairuddin did exactly the same to take third off Binder.

Faubel was four seconds adrift in fifth; then came Rossi. Kornfeil outpaced Vinales for seventh. Early leader Salom was a close tenth – good enough to save second overall.

Above left: The last goodbye. Casey said it from the rostrum.

Left: Starting from the back of the grid, finishing at the front of the field. Marquez took win number nine.

Right: Moto3 by inches: Danny Kent's clenched fist signals victory over champion Cortese. Khairuddin was a similar distance ahead of Binder, just off camera.

Photos: Gold & Goose

18

GP GENERALI DE LA
COMUNITAT VALENCIANA

9–11 NOVEMBER, 2012

MotoGP · TISSOT SWISS WATCHES SINCE 1853

OFFICIAL TIMEKEEPER

CIRCUITO DE LA COMUNITAT VALENCIANA

30 laps
Length: 4.005 km / 2.489 miles
Width: 12m

Key
96/60 kph/mph
⚙ Gear

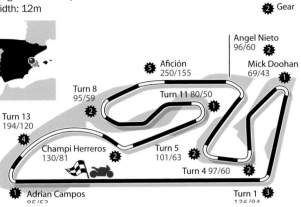

Photos: Gold & Goose

Angel Nieto 96/60
Mick Doohan 69/43
Afición 250/155
Turn 8 95/59
Turn 11 80/50
Turn 13 194/120
Champi Herreros 130/81
Turn 5 101/63
Turn 4 97/60
Adrian Campos 95/59
Turn 1 126/84

MotoGP | RACE DISTANCE: 30 laps, 74.658 miles/120.150km · RACE WEATHER: Wet (air 13°C, humidity 81%, track 15°C)

Pos.	Rider	Nat.	No.	Entrant	Machine	Tyres	Race tyre choice	Laps	Time & speed
1	**Dani Pedrosa**	SPA	26	Repsol Honda Team	Honda RC213V	B	F: Soft Slk/R: Medium Slk	30	48m 23.819s 92.556mph/ 148.955km/h
2	**Katsuyuki Nakasuga**	JPN	21	Yamaha Factory Racing	Yamaha YZR-M1	B	F: Soft Slk/R: Medium Slk	30	49m 01.480s
3	**Casey Stoner**	AUS	1	Repsol Honda Team	Honda RC213V	B	F: Hard Wt/R: Soft Wt	30	49m 24.452s
4	**Alvaro Bautista**	SPA	19	San Carlo Honda Gresini	Honda RC213V	B	F: Soft Slk/R: Medium Slk	30	49m 26.630s
5	**Michele Pirro**	ITA	51	San Carlo Honda Gresini	FTR Honda CBR1000RR	B	F: Soft Slk/R: Medium Slk	30	49m 50.427s
6	**Andrea Dovizioso**	ITA	4	Monster Yamaha Tech 3	Yamaha YZR-M1	B	F: Hard Wt/R: Hard Wt	30	49m 54.242s
7	**Karel Abraham**	CZE	17	Cardion AB Motoracing	Ducati Desmosedici GP12	B	F: Hard Wt/R: Hard Wt	30	49m 55.608s
8	**Danilo Petrucci**	ITA	9	Came IodaRacing Project	Ioda Suter BMW S1000RR	B	F: Soft Slk/R: Medium Slk	29	48m 32.847s
9	**James Ellison**	GBR	77	Paul Bird Motorsport	ART Aprilia RSV4	B	F: Soft Wt/R: Soft Wt	29	48m 41.030s
10	**Valentino Rossi**	ITA	46	Ducati Team	Ducati Desmosedici GP12	B	F: Hard Wt/R: Hard Wt	29	48m 45.740s
11	**Aleix Espargaro**	SPA	41	Power Electronics Aspar	ART Aprilia RSV4	B	F: Soft Wt/R: Soft Wt	29	49m 23.359s
12	**Randy de Puniet**	FRA	14	Power Electronics Aspar	ART Aprilia RSV4	B	F: Soft Slk/R: Medium Slk	28	48m 38.162s
13	**Hiroshi Aoyama**	JPN	73	Avintia Blusens	BQR FTR Kawasaki ZX-10R	B	F: Hard Wt/R: Hard Wt	28	49m 13.795s
14	**Colin Edwards**	USA	5	NGM Mobile Forward Racing	Suter BMW S1000RR	B	F: Soft Wt/R: Soft Wt	27	48m 55.662s
	Cal Crutchlow	GBR	35	Monster Yamaha Tech 3	Yamaha YZR-M1	B	F: Soft Slk/R: Medium Slk	22	DNF-crash
	Claudio Corti	ITA	71	Avintia Blusens	Inmotec Kawasaki ZX-10R	B	F: Soft Wt/R: Soft Wt	17	DNF-crash
	Hector Barbera	SPA	8	Pramac Racing Team	Ducati Desmosedici GP12	B	F: Hard Wt/R: Hard Wt	16	DNF-crash
	Jorge Lorenzo	SPA	99	Yamaha Factory Racing	Yamaha YZR-M1	B	F: Soft Slk/R: Medium Slk	13	DNF-crash
	Stefan Bradl	GER	6	LCR Honda MotoGP	Honda RC213V	B	F: Soft Slk/R: Medium Slk	9	DNF-crash
	Roberto Rolfo	ITA	84	Speed Master	ART Aprilia RSV4	B	F: Soft Wt/R: Soft Wt	6	DNF-crash
	Ivan Silva	SPA	22	Avintia Blusens	BQR FTR Kawasaki ZX-10R	B	F: Soft Slk/R: Medium Slk	2	DNF-crash
	Nicky Hayden	USA	69	Ducati Team	Ducati Desmosedici GP12	B	F: Soft Slk/R: Medium Slk	2	DNF-crash

* Tyre choice given for start of race. Slk = Slick, Wt = Wet

Fastest lap: Dani Pedrosa, on lap 12, 1m 33.119s, 96.209mph/154.834km/h.
Lap record: Casey Stoner, AUS (Ducati), 1m 32.582s, 96.767mph/155.732km/h (2008).
Event best maximum speed: Hector Barbera, 203.2mph/327.0km/h (qualifying practice).

Qualifying
Weather: Dry
Air Temp: 20° Humidity: 49%
Track Temp: 15°

1	Pedrosa	1m 30.844s
2	Lorenzo	1m 31.195s
3	Stoner	1m 31.428s
4	Crutchlow	1m 31.512s
5	Bradl	1m 31.757s
6	Dovizioso	1m 31.795s
7	Hayden	1m 32.503s
8	Bautista	1m 32.585s
9	Barbera	1m 32.605s
10	Espargaro	1m 32.834s
11	Rossi	1m 32.877s
12	De Puniet	1m 33.346s
13	Abraham	1m 33.442s
14	Edwards	1m 33.453s
15	Pirro	1m 33.971s
16	Nakasuga	1m 33.979s
17	Petrucci	1m 33.980s
18	Silva	1m 34.407s
19	Rolfo	1m 34.866s
20	Ellison	1m 34.918s
21	Aoyama	1m 35.363s
22	Corti	1m 36.531s

Fastest race laps

1	Pedrosa	1m 33.119s
2	Lorenzo	1m 33.296s
3	Stoner	1m 33.836s
4	Dovizioso	1m 33.909s
5	Crutchlow	1m 34.704s
6	Abraham	1m 35.000s
7	Bautista	1m 35.338s
8	Nakasuga	1m 35.529s
9	Ellison	1m 35.555s
10	Rossi	1m 35.996s
11	Bradl	1m 36.089s
12	Espargaro	1m 36.339s
13	Pirro	1m 36.597s
14	Petrucci	1m 37.789s
15	De Puniet	1m 39.482s
16	Aoyama	1m 39.603s
17	Edwards	1m 39.964s
18	Barbera	1m 41.339s
19	Corti	1m 42.579s
20	Rolfo	1m 44.398s
21	Hayden	1m 46.510s
22	Silva	1m 48.774s

Championship Points

1	Lorenzo	350
2	Pedrosa	332
3	Stoner	254
4	Dovizioso	218
5	Bautista	178
6	Rossi	163
7	Crutchlow	151
8	Bradl	135
9	Hayden	122
10	Spies	88
11	Barbera	83
12	Espargaro	74
13	De Puniet	62
14	Abraham	59
15	Pirro	43
16	Ellison	35
17	Hernandez	28
18	Nakasuga	27
19	Petrucci	27
20	Edwards	27
21	Rea	17
22	Pasini	13
23	Silva	12
24	Elias	10
25	Aoyama	3
26	Rapp	2
27	Salom	2

Constructor Points

1	Honda	412
2	Yamaha	386
3	Ducati	192
4	ART	100
5	FTR	43
6	BQR	35
7	Suter	27
8	Ioda-Suter	18
9	Ioda	9
10	APR	2
11	BQR-FTR	2

Grid order / Lap chart

Grid order	1	2	3	4	5	6	7	8	9	10	11	12	13	14	15	16	17	18	19	20	21	22	23	24	25	26	27	28	29	30	
26 PEDROSA	41	41	4	99	99	99	99	99	99	99	99	99	99	26	26	26	26	26	26	26	26	26	26	26	26	26	26	26	26	26	1
99 LORENZO	4	4	41	41	21	26	26	26	26	26	26	26	26	35	35	35	35	35	35	35	35	21	21	21	21	21	21	21	21	21	2
1 STONER	1	1	1	46	26	21	21	21	6	21	21	21	35	21	21	21	21	21	21	21	21	19	19	19	19	19	19	1	1	1	3
35 CRUTCHLOW	46	46	46	21	6	6	6	6	21	35	35	35	21	19	19	19	19	19	19	19	19	1	1	1	1	1	19	19			4
6 BRADL	8	8	99	6	35	35	35	35	19	19	19	19	19	51	51	51	51	51	1	1	1	51	51	51	51	51	51	51			5
4 DOVIZIOSO	17	17	6	26	46	19	19	19	9	51	51	51	51	9	9	9	1	1	51	51	51	4	4	4	4	17	17	4	4		6
69 HAYDEN	77	99	21	4	41	9	51	51	51	9	9	9	9	1	1	1	9	9	9	9	9	17	17	4	4	17	17				7
19 BAUTISTA	99	77	77	1	19	51	9	9	9	1	1	1	1	4	4	4	4	4	4	9	4	17	17	9	9	9	9	9			8
8 BARBERA	84	84	84	77	9	14	1	1	1	4	4	4	4	17	17	17	17	17	17	17	17	77	77	77	77	77	77	77			9
41 ESPARGARO	6	6	17	84	51	71	14	14	14	46	17	17	17	46	46	46	77	77	77	77	77	46	46	46	46	46	46	46			10
46 ROSSI	21	21	26	35	84	41	41	46	46	17	46	46	46	77	77	77	46	46	46	46	46	41	41	41	41	41	41	41			11
14 DE PUNIET	5	73	8	19	77	46	46	4	4	14	14	14	77	41	41	41	41	41	41	41	41	14	14	14	14	14					12
17 ABRAHAM	73	51	35	17	14	1	4	17	41	41	41	77	41	14	14	14	14	14	14	14	73	73	73	73	73						13
5 EDWARDS	51	5	73	9	71	5	71	17	41	77	77	41	14	8	8	8	73	73	73	73	5	5	5	5	5						14
51 PIRRO	71	26	19	51	5	84	17	77	77	8	8	8	8	73	73	73	71	5	5	5	5										
21 NAKASUGA	9	71	9	14	1	77	77	8	8	73	73	73	73	71	71	71	5														
9 PETRUCCI	14	14	51	71	17	17	8	71	73	71	71	71	71	5	5	5															
22 SILVA	22	9	71	73	8	4	5	5	71	5	5	5	5																		
84 ROLFO	19	19	14	5	4	8	73	73	5																						
77 ELLISON	26	35	5	8	73	73																									
73 AOYAMA	35	22																													
71 CORTI	69	69																													

8 Pit stop   17 Lapped rider

Moto2

RACE DISTANCE: 27 laps, 67.192 miles/108.135km · RACE WEATHER: Wet (air 13°C, humidity 76%, track 15°C)

Pos.	Rider	Nat.	No.	Entrant	Machine	Laps	Time & Speed
1	**Marc Marquez**	SPA	93	Team Catalunya Caixa Repsol	Suter	27	48m 50.706s 82.537mph/ 132.830km/h
2	**Julian Simon**	SPA	60	Blusens Avintia	Suter	27	48m 51.962s
3	**Nicolas Terol**	SPA	18	Mapfre Aspar Team Moto2	Suter	27	49m 02.078s
4	**Thomas Luthi**	SWI	12	Interwetten-Paddock	Suter	27	49m 03.712s
5	**Dominique Aegerter**	SWI	77	Technomag-CIP	Suter	27	49m 04.531s
6	**Jordi Torres**	SPA	81	Mapfre Aspar Team Moto2	Suter	27	49m 18.617s
7	**Mika Kallio**	FIN	36	Marc VDS Racing Team	Kalex	27	49m 27.044s
8	**Pol Espargaro**	SPA	40	Tuenti Movil HP 40	Kalex	27	49m 29.041s
9	**Toni Elias**	SPA	24	Italtrans Racing Team	Kalex	27	49m 30.125s
10	**Esteve Rabat**	SPA	80	Tuenti Movil HP 40	Kalex	27	49m 30.182s
11	**Andrea Iannone**	ITA	29	Speed Master	Speed Up	27	49m 30.913s
12	**Gino Rea**	GBR	8	Federal Oil Gresini Moto2	Suter	27	49m 31.903s
13	**Dani Rivas**	SPA	17	TSR Galicia School	Kalex	27	49m 32.474s
14	**Yuki Takahashi**	JPN	72	NGM Mobile Forward Racing	FTR	27	49m 32.649s
15	**Ricard Cardus**	SPA	88	Arguinano Racing Team	AJR	27	49m 33.009s
16	Bradley Smith	GBR	38	Tech 3 Racing	Tech 3	27	49m 33.770s
17	Simone Corsi	ITA	3	Came IodaRacing Project	FTR	27	49m 40.676s
18	Tomoyoshi Koyama	JPN	75	Technomag-CIP	Suter	27	49m 42.345s
19	Randy Krummenacher	SWI	4	GP Team Switzerland	Kalex	27	49m 43.904s
20	Axel Pons	SPA	49	Tuenti Movil HP 40	Kalex	27	49m 45.338s
21	Marcel Schrotter	GER	23	Desguaces La Torre SAG	Bimota	27	49m 47.107s
22	Scott Redding	GBR	45	Marc VDS Racing Team	Kalex	27	49m 47.680s
23	Alessandro Andreozzi	ITA	22	S/Master Speed Up	Speed Up	27	49m 50.385s
24	Ratthapark Wilairot	THA	14	Thai Honda PTT Gresini Moto2	Suter	27	50m 06.907s
25	Mattia Pasini	ITA	54	NGM Mobile Forward Racing	FTR	27	50m 07.058s
26	Roman Ramos	SPA	28	SAG Team	FTR	27	50m 09.060s
27	Xavier Simeon	BEL	19	Tech 3 Racing	Tech 3	27	50m 16.940s
28	Mike di Meglio	FRA	63	Kiefer Racing	Kalex	27	50m 20.236s
29	Eric Granado	BRA	57	JIR Moto2	Motobi	26	49m 43.555s
30	Rafid Topan Sucipto	INA	97	QMMF Racing Team	Speed Up	25	49m 58.806s
	Elena Rosell	SPA	82	QMMF Racing Team	Speed Up	17	DNF
	Takaaki Nakagami	JPN	30	Italtrans Racing Team	Kalex	14	DNF
	Johann Zarco	FRA	5	JIR Moto2	Motobi	10	DNF

Fastest lap: Marc Marquez, on lap 23, 1m 46.440s, 84.168mph/135.456km/h.
Lap record: Karel Abraham, CZE (FTR), 1m 36.611s, 92.732mph/149.237km/h (2010).
Event best maximum speed: Pol Espargaro, 173.7mph/279.6km/h (free practice 2).

Qualifying: Dry
Air: 19° Humidity: 45% Track: 18°

1	Espargaro	1m 35.191s
2	Marquez**	1m 35.597s
3	Luthi	1m 35.756s
4	Nakagami	1m 35.801s
5	Terol	1m 35.858s
6	Torres	1m 35.915s
7	Aegerter	1m 35.949s
8	Redding	1m 35.966s
9	Corsi	1m 35.983s
10	Iannone	1m 36.016s
11	Zarco	1m 36.108s
12	Simon	1m 36.129s
13	Simeon	1m 36.236s
14	Rabat	1m 36.278s
15	Elias	1m 36.483s
16	Kallio	1m 36.489s
17	Di Meglio	1m 36.511s
18	Takahashi	1m 36.583s
19	Krummenacher	1m 36.629s
20	Rea	1m 36.687s
21	Ramos	1m 36.701s
22	Smith	1m 36.771s
23	Pasini	1m 36.868s
24	Wilairot	1m 36.873s
25	Schrotter	1m 36.990s
26	Pons	1m 37.096s
27	Rivas	1m 37.228s
28	Koyama	1m 37.357s
29	Cardus	1m 37.384s
30	Andreozzi	1m 37.463s
31	Sucipto	1m 38.982s
32	Granado	1m 39.602s
33	Rosell	1m 40.063s

Fastest race laps

1	Marquez	1m 46.440s
2	Luthi	1m 47.039s
3	Simon	1m 47.327s
4	Aegerter	1m 47.394s
5	Elias	1m 47.478s
6	Espargaro	1m 47.669s
7	Rea	1m 47.817s
8	Torres	1m 47.906s
9	Terol	1m 47.955s
10	Cardus	1m 48.002s
11	Smith	1m 48.108s
12	Simeon	1m 48.189s
13	Zarco	1m 48.271s
14	Iannone	1m 48.353s
15	Krummenacher	1m 48.366s
16	Pons	1m 48.376s
17	Takahashi	1m 48.392s
18	Kallio	1m 48.484s
19	Rivas	1m 48.488s
20	Koyama	1m 48.491s
21	Schrotter	1m 48.500s
22	Rabat	1m 48.578s
23	Andreozzi	1m 48.757s
24	Ramos	1m 48.779s
25	Pasini	1m 48.829s
26	Wilairot	1m 48.985s
27	Granado	1m 48.997s
28	Sucipto	1m 49.024s
29	Corsi	1m 49.036s
30	Redding	1m 49.228s
31	Rosell	1m 49.258s
32	Di Meglio	1m 50.329s
33	Nakagami	1m 52.701s

Championship Points

1	Marquez	324
2	Espargaro	268
3	Iannone	193
4	Luthi	190
5	Redding	161
6	Kallio	128
7	Rabat	114
8	Aegerter	110
9	Smith	109
10	Zarco	94
11	Corsi	87
12	De Angelis	86
13	Simon	79
14	Corti	74
15	Nakagami	56
16	West*	52
17	Elias	48
18	Terol	36
19	Krummenacher	31
20	Torres	29
21	Rea	21
22	Simeon	21
23	Di Meglio	14
24	Syahrin	13
25	Pons	10
26	Neukirchner	9
27	Wilairot	9
28	Cardus	8
29	Rivas	3
30	Takahashi	2
31	Rolfo	1

Constructor Points

1	Suter	374
2	Kalex	319
3	Speed Up	227
4	FTR	134
5	Tech 3	111
6	Motobi	94
7	AJR	8
8	Moriwaki*	1

** Marquez penalised and given last place on the grid due to a collision with Corsi in practice.
* On 29 October, the FIM disqualified West from his seventh-place finish (9 points) at Le Mans and banned him from Valencia for failing an anti-doping test at the French round. *Moriwaki also lost the 9 points scored by West at Le Mans.

Moto3

RACE DISTANCE: 24 laps, 59.726 miles/96.120km · RACE WEATHER: Wet (air 12°C, humidity 84%, track 12°C)

Pos.	Rider	Nat.	No.	Entrant	Machine	Laps	Time & Speed
1	**Danny Kent**	GBR	52	Red Bull KTM Ajo	KTM	24	45m 05.891s 79.461mph/ 127.880km/h
2	**Sandro Cortese**	GER	11	Red Bull KTM Ajo	KTM	24	45m 05.947s
3	**Zulfahmi Khairuddin**	MAL	63	AirAsia-Sic-Ajo	KTM	24	45m 06.005s
4	**Brad Binder**	RSA	41	RW Racing GP	Kalex KTM	24	45m 06.322s
5	**Hector Faubel**	SPA	55	Andalucia JHK t-shirt Laglisse	FTR Honda	24	45m 10.262s
6	**Louis Rossi**	FRA	96	Racing Team Germany	FTR Honda	24	45m 13.496s
7	**Jakub Kornfeil**	CZE	84	Redox-Ongetta-Centro Seta	FTR Honda	24	45m 20.822s
8	**Maverick Vinales**	SPA	25	Blusens Avintia	FTR Honda	24	45m 24.386s
9	**Niklas Ajo**	FIN	31	TT Motion Events Racing	KTM	24	45m 29.071s
10	**Luis Salom**	SPA	39	RW Racing GP	Kalex KTM	24	45m 29.136s
11	**Philipp Oettl**	GER	65	HP Moto Kalex	Kalex KTM	24	45m 33.423s
12	**Juan Francisco Guevara**	SPA	58	Wild Wolf BST	FTR Honda	24	45m 36.222s
13	**Niccolo Antonelli**	ITA	27	San Carlo Gresini Moto3	FTR Honda	24	45m 37.146s
14	**Alessandro Tonucci**	ITA	19	Team Italia FMI	FTR Honda	24	45m 40.551s
15	**Josep Rodriguez**	SPA	28	Moto FGR	FGR Honda	24	45m 56.413s
16	Alex Rins	SPA	42	Estrella Galicia 0,0	Suter Honda	24	45m 56.445s
17	Giulian Pedone	SWI	30	Ambrogio Next Racing	Suter Honda	24	45m 57.616s
18	Romano Fenati	ITA	5	Team Italia FMI	FTR Honda	24	45m 57.717s
19	Arthur Sissis	AUS	61	Red Bull KTM Ajo	KTM	24	45m 58.861s
20	Isaac Vinales	SPA	32	Ongetta-Centro Seta	FTR Honda	24	46m 03.821s
21	Alan Techer	FRA	89	Technomag-CIP-TSR	TSR Honda	24	46m 06.649s
22	Luca Amato	GER	29	Mapfre Aspar Team Moto3	Kalex KTM	24	46m 53.685s
23	Kenta Fujii	JPN	51	Technomag-CIP-TSR	TSR Honda	24	46m 53.868s
24	Armando Pontone	ITA	80	IodaRacing Project	Ioda	23	45m 15.003s
	Jack Miller	AUS	8	Caretta Technology	Honda	19	DNF
	Toni Finsterbusch	GER	9	Racing Team Germany	Honda	19	DNF
	Danny Webb	GBR	99	Mahindra Racing	Mahindra	18	DNF
	Miguel Oliveira	POR	44	Estrella Galicia 0,0	Suter Honda	15	DNF
	Efren Vazquez	SPA	7	JHK t-shirt Laglisse	FTR Honda	15	DNF
	Miroslav Popov	CZE	95	Mahindra Racing	Mahindra	9	DNF
	John McPhee	GBR	17	Caretta Technology	KRP Honda	9	DNF
	Jonas Folger	GER	94	Mapfre Aspar Team Moto3	Kalex KTM	7	DNF
	Adrian Martin	SPA	26	JHK t-shirt Laglisse	FTR Honda	7	DNF
	Luigi Morciano	ITA	3	Ioda Team Italia	Ioda	4	DNF
	Alex Marquez	SPA	12	Ambrogio Next Racing	Suter Honda	3	DNF

Fastest lap: Zulfahmi Khairuddin, on lap 24, 1m 49.622s, 81.725mph/131.524km/h (record).
Previous lap record: New category.
Event best maximum speed: Arthur Sissis, 140.5mph/226.1km/h (qualifying practice).

Qualifying: Dry
Air: 18° Humidity: 55% Track: 15°

1	Folger	1m 41.263s
2	Oliveira	1m 41.316s
3	Salom	1m 41.441s
4	Cortese	1m 41.506s
5	M. Vinales	1m 41.774s
6	Vazquez	1m 41.828s
7	Kent	1m 41.952s
8	Antonelli	1m 42.045s
9	Rossi	1m 42.078s
10	Tonucci	1m 42.194s
11	Fenati	1m 42.241s
12	Marquez	1m 42.380s
13	Martin	1m 42.461s
14	Kornfeil	1m 42.476s
15	Binder	1m 42.497s
16	Faubel	1m 42.560s
17	Khairuddin	1m 42.698s
18	Rins	1m 42.799s
19	Sissis	1m 42.804s
20	Amato	1m 42.974s
21	Guevar	1m 43.003s
22	Ajo	1m 43.011s
23	I. Vinales	1m 43.175s
24	Techer	1m 43.419s
25	Miller	1m 43.430s
26	Oettl	1m 43.692s
27	Finsterbusch	1m 43.722s
28	Pedone	1m 43.971s
29	McPhee	1m 44.478s
30	Rodriguez	1m 44.502s
31	Pontone	1m 44.693s
32	Morciano	1m 44.778s
33	Fujii	1m 44.893s
34	Webb	1m 44.933s
35	Popov	1m 45.082s

Fastest race laps

1	Khairuddin	1m 49.622s
2	Faubel	1m 50.069s
3	Kent	1m 50.189s
4	Binder	1m 50.284s
5	Cortese	1m 50.362s
6	Kornfeil	1m 50.534s
7	M. Vinales	1m 50.755s
8	Rossi	1m 50.873s
9	Miller	1m 50.999s
10	Ajo	1m 51.120s
11	Antonelli	1m 51.261s
12	Salom	1m 51.298s
13	Guevara	1m 51.340s
14	I. Vinales	1m 51.436s
15	Rodriguez	1m 51.560s
16	Finsterbusch	1m 51.744s
17	Vazquez	1m 51.746s
18	Oliveira	1m 51.772s
19	Tonucci	1m 51.864s
20	Oettl	1m 51.882s
21	Pedone	1m 51.885s
22	Sissis	1m 51.943s
23	Rins	1m 52.077s
24	Webb	1m 52.208s
25	Fenati	1m 52.486s
26	Techer	1m 52.582s
27	Martin	1m 52.799s
28	Folger	1m 53.214s
29	Pontone	1m 53.343s
30	McPhee	1m 53.360s
31	Marquez	1m 53.760s
32	Popov	1m 54.521s
33	Fujii	1m 54.549s
34	Amato	1m 55.021s
35	Morciano	1m 57.936s

Championship Points

1	Cortese	325
2	Salom	214
3	M. Vinales	207
4	Kent	154
5	Rins	141
6	Fenati	136
7	Khairuddin	128
8	Oliveira	114
9	Folger	93
10	Vazquez	93
11	Rossi	86
12	Sissis	84
13	Masbou	81
14	Antonelli	77
15	Kornfeil	71
16	Faubel	63
17	Moncayo	52
18	Tonucci	45
19	Ajo	40
20	Marquez	27
21	Binder	24
22	Techer	21
23	Miller	17
24	Martin	16
25	Moreno	10
26	Iwema	9
27	Gruenwald	8
28	I. Vinales	8
29	Pedone	7
30	Finsterbusch	7
31	Oettl	5
32	Guevara	4
33	Schrotter	4
34	Hanus	3
35	Calia	2
36	Rodriguez	1
37	McPhee	1
38	Rinaldi	1
39	Grotzkyj	1

Constructor Points

1	KTM	346
2	FTR Honda	306
3	Kalex KTM	262
4	Suter Honda	182
5	Honda	87
6	TSR Honda	21
7	FGR Honda	10
8	Ioda	5
9	Mahindra	4
10	KRP Honda	1
11	Oral	1

WORLD CHAMPIONSHIP POINTS 2012
Compiled by PETER McLAREN

Photo: Gold & Goose

MotoGP – Riders

Position	Rider	Nationality	Machine	Qatar	Spain	Portugal	France	Catalunya	Great Britain	Netherlands	Germany	Italy	United States	Indianapolis	Czech Republic	San Marino	Aragón	Japan	Malaysia	Australia	Valencia	Points total
1	Jorge Lorenzo	SPA	Yamaha	25	20	20	25	25	25	–	20	25	20	20	20	25	20	20	20	20	–	350
2	Dani Pedrosa	SPA	Honda	20	16	16	13	20	16	20	25	20	16	25	25	–	25	25	25	–	25	332
3	Casey Stoner	AUS	Honda	16	25	25	16	13	20	25	–	8	25	13	–	–	11	16	25	16		254
4	Andrea Dovizioso	ITA	Yamaha	11	11	13	9	16	–	16	16	16	13	16	13	13	16	13	13	13	10	218
5	Alvaro Bautista	SPA	Honda	9	10	10	6	10	13	–	9	6	8	11	10	16	10	16	10	11	13	178
6	Valentino Rossi	ITA	Ducati	6	7	9	20	9	7	3	10	11	–	9	9	20	8	9	11	9	6	163
7	Cal Crutchlow	GBR	Yamaha	13	13	11	8	11	10	11	8	10	11	–	16	–	13	–	–	16	–	151
8	Stefan Bradl	GER	Honda	8	9	7	11	8	8	–	11	13	9	10	11	10	–	10	–	10	–	135
9	Nicky Hayden	USA	Ducati	10	8	5	10	7	9	10	6	9	10	–	–	9	–	8	13	8	–	122
10	Ben Spies	USA	Yamaha	5	5	8	–	6	11	13	13	5	–	–	11	11	–	–	–	–	–	88
11	Hector Barbera	SPA	Ducati	7	6	6	7	5	6	9	7	7	–	–	–	–	4	6	9	4	–	83
12	Aleix Espargaro	SPA	ART	1	4	4	3	3	5	–	3	3	7	6	6	–	6	4	8	6	5	74
13	Randy de Puniet	FRA	ART	3	–	3	–	1	4	8	5	4	5	–	8	7	5	–	–	5	4	62
14	Karel Abraham	CZE	Ducati	–	–	–	–	4	–	–	–	–	6	8	7	–	7	5	6	7	9	59
15	Michele Pirro	ITA	FTR	–	–	2	2	2	3	7	–	–	–	–	2	6	1	1	4	2	11	43
16	James Ellison	GBR	ART	–	–	–	5	–	2	2	1	2	–	1	1	3	2	2	7	–	7	35
17	Yonny Hernandez	COL	BQR	2	–	–	1	–	1	–	2	–	4	7	4	4	3	–	–	–	–	28
18	Katsuyuki Nakasuga	JPN	Yamaha	–	–	–	–	–	–	–	–	–	–	–	–	–	–	7	–	–	20	27
19	Danilo Petrucci	ITA	Ioda/Ioda-Suter	–	3	1	–	–	–	5	–	–	–	–	–	2	–	5	3	8		27
20	Colin Edwards	USA	Suter	4	–	–	–	–	–	–	4	–	3	3	3	5	–	3	–	–	2	27
21	Jonathan Rea	GBR	Honda	–	–	–	–	–	–	–	–	–	–	–	–	–	8	9	–	–		17
22	Mattia Pasini	ITA	ART	–	2	–	4	–	–	6	–	1	–	–	–	–	–	–	–	–		13
23	Ivan Silva	SPA	BQR	–	1	–	–	–	–	4	–	–	2	4	–	–	–	–	1	–		12
24	Toni Elias	SPA	Ducati	–	–	–	–	–	–	–	–	–	–	5	5	–	–	–	–	–		10
25	Hiroshi Aoyama	JPN	BQR	–	–	–	–	–	–	–	–	–	–	–	–	–	–	–	–	3		3
26	Steve Rapp	USA	APR	–	–	–	–	–	–	–	–	–	–	2	–	–	–	–	–	–		2
27	David Salom	SPA	BQR	–	–	–	–	–	–	–	–	–	–	–	–	–	1	–	–	–		1

MotoGP - Teams

Position	Team	Qatar	Spain	Portugal	France	Catalunya	Great Britain	Netherlands	Germany	Italy	United States	Indianapolis	Czech Republic	San Marino	Aragón	Japan	Malaysia	Australia	Valencia	Points total
1	Repsol Honda Team	36	41	41	29	33	36	45	25	28	41	38	25	8	34	36	41	25	41	603
2	Yamaha Factory Racing	30	25	28	25	31	36	13	33	30	20	20	20	36	31	20	20	20	20	458
3	Monster Yamaha Tech 3	24	24	24	17	27	10	27	24	26	24	16	29	13	29	13	3	29	10	369
4	Ducati Team	16	15	14	30	16	16	13	16	20	10	9	9	29	8	17	24	17	6	285
5	San Carlo Honda Gresini	9	10	12	8	12	16	7	9	6	8	11	12	22	11	17	14	13	24	221
6	Power Electronics Aspar	4	4	7	3	4	9	8	8	7	12	6	14	7	11	4	8	11	9	136
7	LCR Honda MotoGP	8	9	7	11	8	8	–	11	13	9	10	11	10	–	10	–	10	–	135
8	Pramac Racing Team	7	6	6	7	5	6	9	7	7	–	–	5	5	–	4	6	4	–	93
9	Cardion AB Motoracing	–	–	–	–	4	–	–	–	–	6	8	7	–	7	5	6	7	9	59
10	Avintia Blusens	2	1	–	1	–	1	4	2	–	6	11	4	5	3	–	–	1	–	44
11	Paul Bird Motorsport	–	–	–	5	–	2	2	1	2	–	1	1	3	2	2	7	–	7	35
12	Came IodaRacing Project	–	3	1	–	–	–	5	–	–	–	–	–	2	–	5	3	8		27
13	NGM Mobile Forward Racing	4	–	–	–	–	–	–	4	–	3	3	3	5	–	–	–	2		27
14	Speed Master	–	2	–	4	–	–	6	–	1	–	–	–	–	–	–	–	–		13

Moto2

Position	Rider	Nationality	Machine	Qatar	Spain	Portugal	France	Catalunya	Great Britain	Netherlands	Germany	Italy	Indianapolis	Czech Republic	San Marino	Aragón	Japan	Malaysia	Australia	Valencia	Points total
1	Marc Marquez	SPA	Suter	25	20	25	–	16	16	25	25	11	25	25	25	20	25	–	16	25	324
2	Pol Espargaro	SPA	Kalex	16	25	20	10	–	25	–	13	20	20	16	20	25	20	5	25	8	268
3	Andrea Iannone	ITA	Speed Up	20	2	11	13	25	13	20	–	25	7	13	16	13	–	10	–	5	193
4	Thomas Luthi	SWI	Suter	11	16	16	25	20	8	–	11	16	11	20	7	5	11	–	–	13	190
5	Scott Redding	GBR	Kalex	10	13	5	16	6	20	16	–	10	10	–	9	16	13	4	13	–	161
6	Mika Kallio	FIN	Kalex	6	9	7	11	7	6	6	20	5	13	7	13	–	–	9	–	9	128
7	Esteve Rabat	SPA	Kalex	13	–	–	6	13	3	13	4	–	5	6	11	4	16	6	8	6	114
8	Dominique Aegerter	SWI	Suter	–	8	4	2	9	7	9	6	8	9	2	10	1	6	7	11	11	110
9	Bradley Smith	GBR	Tech 3	7	5	6	7	4	9	10	9	13	–	8	8	11	–	8	4	–	109
10	Johann Zarco	FRA	Motobi	4	6	13	–	5	–	8	–	10	6	10	8	–	10	–	10	–	94
11	Simone Corsi	ITA	FTR	8	–	–	–	11	11	–	10	–	8	11	–	9	10	–	9	–	87
12	Alex de Angelis	RSM	Suter/FTR	–	4	10	–	2	5	11	16	–	10	3	–	–	25	–	–	–	86
13	Julian Simon	SPA	FTR/Suter	1	–	8	4	–	2	1	2	16	5	4	–	5	11	–	20	–	79
14	Claudio Corti	ITA	Kalex	–	10	2	20	3	10	–	7	7	6	–	2	7	–	–	–	–	74
15	Takaaki Nakagami	JPN	Kalex	2	11	–	–	10	–	–	4	–	9	–	5	–	9	–	6	–	56
16	Anthony West	AUS	Moriwaki/Speed Up	–	–	–	–	–	–	–	–	2	–	–	6	4	20	20	–	–	52
17	Toni Elias	SPA	Suter/Kalex	3	7	9	5	–	4	7	–	–	–	–	–	–	3	3	7	–	48
18	Nicolas Terol	SPA	Suter	–	–	–	3	1	–	–	2	3	3	4	1	3	–	–	–	16	36
19	Randy Krummenacher	SWI	Kalex	5	–	–	–	–	8	2	5	–	4	–	–	–	–	7	–	–	31
20	Jordi Torres	SPA	Suter	–	–	–	–	–	–	–	–	–	–	–	3	3	–	5	10	–	29
21	Gino Rea	GBR	Moriwaki/Suter	–	1	–	–	–	–	–	–	–	–	–	–	–	16	–	4	–	21
22	Xavier Simeon	BEL	Tech 3	–	3	3	–	–	3	8	–	–	–	–	2	–	2	–	–	–	21
23	Mike di Meglio	FRA	Speed Up/MZ/Kalex	9	–	–	–	–	–	1	–	–	–	2	1	–	1	–	–	–	14
24	Hafizh Syahrin	MAL	FTR	–	–	–	–	–	–	–	–	–	–	–	–	–	13	–	–	–	13
25	Axel Pons	SPA	Kalex	–	–	–	–	–	–	–	–	–	1	–	–	7	2	–	–	–	10
26	Max Neukirchner	GER	Kalex	–	–	9	–	–	–	–	–	–	–	–	–	–	–	–	–	–	9
27	Ratthapark Wilairot	THA	Moriwaki/Suter	–	–	8	1	–	–	–	–	–	–	–	–	–	–	–	–	–	9
28	Ricard Cardus	SPA	AJR	–	–	1	–	–	–	3	1	1	–	–	–	–	1	–	1	–	8
29	Dani Rivas	SPA	Kalex	–	–	–	–	–	–	–	–	–	–	–	–	–	–	–	3	–	3
30	Yuki Takahashi	JPN	Suter/FTR	–	–	–	–	–	–	–	–	–	–	–	–	–	–	–	2	–	2
31	Roberto Rolfo	ITA	Suter	–	–	1	–	–	–	–	–	–	–	–	–	–	–	–	–	–	1

Moto3

Position	Rider	Nationality	Machine	Qatar	Spain	Portugal	France	Catalunya	Great Britain	Netherlands	Germany	Italy	Indianapolis	Czech Republic	San Marino	Aragón	Japan	Malaysia	Australia	Valencia	Points total
1	Sandro Cortese	GER	KTM	16	16	25	10	20	16	20	25	16	20	16	25	20	10	25	25	20	325
2	Luis Salom	SPA	Kalex KTM	13	16	16	–	6	20	13	16	–	25	20	20	25	–	13	1	6	214
3	Maverick Vinales	SPA	FTR Honda	25	10	20	–	25	25	25	–	25	–	13	11	–	20	–	–	8	207
4	Danny Kent	GBR	KTM	8	–	8	–	–	10	16	–	11	4	9	4	13	25	10	11	25	154
5	Alex Rins	SPA	Suter Honda	6	13	9	16	–	–	10	–	9	9	11	13	10	13	9	13	–	141
6	Romano Fenati	ITA	FTR Honda	20	25	–	–	7	9	4	–	20	11	8	16	–	6	–	10	–	136
7	Zulfahmi Khairuddin	MAL	KTM	10	6	13	–	8	7	5	10	7	10	–	5	–	11	20	–	16	128
8	Miguel Oliveira	POR	Suter Honda	11	–	–	–	16	6	6	–	–	13	7	7	8	9	11	20	–	114
9	Jonas Folger	GER	Ioda/Kalex KTM	–	–	–	5	–	–	–	–	–	16	25	10	16	–	16	5	–	93
10	Efren Vazquez	SPA	Honda/FTR Honda	–	–	11	–	–	11	7	11	10	–	9	11	7	8	4	–	–	93
11	Louis Rossi	FRA	FTR Honda	7	–	–	25	13	–	11	–	–	3	–	–	–	–	–	–	10	86
12	Arthur Sissis	AUS	KTM	9	–	3	11	–	4	–	2	6	2	6	7	5	16	–	–	–	84
13	Alexis Masbou	FRA	Honda	–	11	7	–	11	13	9	20	4	6	–	–	–	–	–	–	–	81
14	Niccolo Antonelli	ITA	Honda/FTR Honda	–	8	10	13	4	3	–	4	13	–	8	6	4	1	–	–	3	77
15	Jakub Kornfeil	CZE	FTR Honda	1	–	6	–	5	5	3	6	8	8	10	1	5	1	–	3	9	71
16	Hector Faubel	SPA	Kalex KTM/FTR Honda	4	7	–	–	9	4	1	9	6	–	5	3	–	–	–	–	11	63
17	Alberto Moncayo	SPA	Kalex KTM/FTR Honda	2	9	2	20	2	1	–	–	–	7	4	2	4	–	–	–	–	52
18	Alessandro Tonucci	ITA	FTR Honda	–	5	–	2	–	–	–	–	–	1	6	–	4	16	–	9	2	45
19	Niklas Ajo	FIN	KTM	3	–	–	1	–	2	8	2	5	–	–	–	2	3	7	–	7	40
20	Alex Marquez	SPA	Suter Honda	–	4	1	–	10	–	–	–	–	–	–	–	1	2	2	7	–	27
21	Brad Binder	RSA	Kalex KTM	–	–	5	–	–	–	–	–	–	–	–	–	–	4	2	13	–	24
22	Alan Techer	FRA	TSR Honda	5	2	–	8	3	–	–	3	–	–	–	–	–	–	–	–	–	21
23	Jack Miller	AUS	Honda	–	–	–	–	1	–	13	–	–	–	–	–	–	3	–	–	–	17
24	Adrian Martin	SPA	Honda/FTR Honda	–	–	–	–	–	–	–	3	–	3	–	–	–	6	4	–	–	16
25	Ivan Moreno	SPA	FTR Honda	–	3	–	7	–	–	–	–	–	–	–	–	–	–	–	–	–	10
26	Jasper Iwema	NED	FGR Honda	–	–	–	9	–	–	–	–	–	–	–	–	–	–	–	–	–	9
27	Luca Gruenwald	GER	Honda	–	–	–	–	–	–	–	8	–	–	–	–	–	–	–	–	–	8
28	Isaac Vinales	SPA	FTR Honda	–	–	–	–	–	–	–	–	2	–	–	–	–	–	6	–	–	8
29	Giulian Pedone	SWI	Oral/Suter Honda	–	1	–	6	–	–	–	–	–	–	–	–	–	–	–	–	–	7
30	Toni Finsterbusch	GER	MZ–RE Honda/Honda	–	–	–	–	–	2	5	–	–	–	–	–	–	–	–	–	–	7
31	Philipp Oettl	GER	Kalex KTM	–	–	–	–	–	–	–	–	–	–	–	–	–	–	–	5	–	5
32	Juan Francisco Guevara	SPA	FTR Honda	–	–	–	–	–	–	–	–	–	–	–	–	–	–	–	4	–	4
33	Marcel Schrotter	GER	Mahindra	–	–	–	4	–	–	–	–	–	–	–	–	–	–	–	–	–	4
34	Kevin Hanus	GER	Honda	–	–	–	3	–	–	–	–	–	–	–	–	–	–	–	–	–	3
35	Kevin Calia	ITA	Honda	–	–	–	–	–	–	–	–	2	–	–	–	–	–	–	–	–	2
36	Josep Rodriguez	SPA	FGR Honda	–	–	–	–	–	–	–	–	–	–	–	–	–	–	–	1	–	1
37	John McPhee	GBR	KRP Honda	–	–	–	–	–	–	–	–	–	–	–	1	–	–	–	–	–	1
38	Michael Ruben Rinaldi	ITA	Honda	–	–	–	–	–	–	–	–	1	–	–	–	–	–	–	–	–	1
39	Simone Grotzkyj	ITA	Oral/Suter Honda	–	–	–	–	–	–	1	–	–	–	–	–	–	–	–	–	–	1

SUPERBIKE WORLD CHAMPIONSHIP
REVIEW OF 2012

By GORDON RITCHIE

Results and statistics
By PETER McLAREN

Photo: Gold & Goose

THE PERFECT RACER

By GORDON RITCHIE

MAYBE we should simply repeat what we said about Max Biaggi in 2010, and merely adjust the facts and figures one last time.

After all, not much appears to have changed in two years. And that is what is so remarkable about the little Roman, possibly the perfect racer. He's 41, as fit as ever, and still has that magic of being fast always, and more consistent than virtually anyone.

He capped it all, announcing his final well-earned retirement in November.

Although probably no one's pick as one of the top ten riders of all time, Max has certainly been one of the top five of his time in terms of visibility, controversy and newsworthiness. And results. Let us not forget that he has won a world championship in six of the 20 odd years he's been a GP/SBK racer – one every three years or so. Not a bad record at all.

Biaggi was in danger of being overshadowed, both on and off the track, when Marco Melandri turned up at full pace in 2011. In fact, only a few races before Max won his second SBK title by half a point from Tom Sykes, Melandri had been well on his way to eclipsing his waning star.

But, as has happened so often in the past, no matter the competitors, Biaggi won out eventually, coming back even stronger.

Not having won a 500cc or MotoGP championship will make for a large missing chapter from the final version of Biaggi's biography, but his second title put him firmly among the greats of SBK racing.

In 154 SBK races, Max has scored 21 race wins (five in 2012), 70 podiums and two titles. Like many of the best riders before him, his pole-position, fastest-lap and outright stats percentages are nowhere near as notable as some, but long ago he realised that championships matter most. Fast all the time, at every track, every year. That's how you do it.

Every point counts, and that approach proved so vital in 2012's impossibly close final showdown with surprise package Tom Sykes and Kawasaki, which Biaggi won by a mere half a point. And he had the class to say that 0.5 was really nothing at all. Because it was so close and nerve shredding right to the very last corner, winning by such a small margin was also sweeter because it underlined how hard the season had been.

And it was super-tough, with five race-winning manufacturers and ten separate race-winning riders.

Biaggi spent six years in SBK, having ridden for Suzuki in 2007, then as a privateer Ducatisti in 2008, before finding his perfect partner in Aprilia Racing and the sharply focused Aprilia RSV4 in 2009.

The Aprilia is not so much his bike as Aprilia racing chief Gigi Dall'Igna's bike, but the men in black certainly know how to tailor it to Max's needs. His exacting and highly particular nature may have contributed to him requiring a whole new crew for 2011, but Aprilia's management chose so well that the team won the title first time out together.

At one stage later in the year, it seemed possible that Max could lose the plot, but experience and a cool head prevailed in the final race, after he had suffered a crash under braking in the wet in the first race of the finale in Magny-Cours.

He admitted that the three hours or so after that race fall had been difficult to deal with, but deal with them he did, going on to finish in just the right position to win the title.

Let's not forget that the 2012 season was the wettest and most disturbed by weather that anyone can remember – and Max and the RSV4 are no particular fans of the wet. That, as much as any other good reason, proves that Biaggi and Aprilia really deserved SBK title number two.

TISSOT
SWISS WATCHES SINCE 1853
INNOVATORS BY TRADITION

OFFICIAL TIMEKEEPER
SBK SUPERBIKE
FIM WORLD CHAMPIONSHIP

TISSOT T-RACE
A watch inspired by the world of racing with a 316L stainless steel case. Scratch-resistant sapphire crystal, quartz chronograph and water resistance up to 10 bar (100m / 330ft).

IN TOUCH WITH YOUR TIME

Get in touch at www.tissot.ch

MAX BIAGGI

CARLOS CHECA

TOM SYKES

HIROSHI AOYAMA

JOHN HOPKINS

JAKUB SMRZ

LORIS BAZ

CHAZ DAVIES

LEON HASLAM

LEON CAMIER

SUPERBIKE WORLD CHAMPIONSHIP

2012 TEAMS AND RIDERS

By GORDON RITCHIE

APRILIA

Aprilia Racing Team

Max Biaggi (41) remained with the Aprilia team, despite the loss of previous title sponsorship, and was joined for 2012 by Irish talent Eugene Laverty (26). Luigi Dall'Igna was at the helm once more, but Biaggi had an all-new Aprilia crew. Laverty brought Markus Eschenbacher from Yamaha and his old crew chief from PTR Honda WSS days, Phil Marron. It took a while for him to win a race, but he ended his first RSV4 season well. Biaggi, against lots of odds, was champion again.

ParkinGO MTC Racing

Chaz Davies (25) moved on up to SBK racing with his 2011 WSS title-winning team, also rookies in the biggest class. With Alberto 'Moro' Colombo as tech chief and Lucio Nicastro in day-to-day charge, team principal Giuliano Rovelli's squad had two Aprilia techs in the garage and a largely factory bike at their disposal. Davies made the most of it when the tricky setting options worked well, winning in Portimao.

BMW

BMW Motorrad Motorsport

Marco Melandri (30) jumped from the scuttled Yamaha SBK ship to the BMW man-o-war, taking most of his crew with him. True BMW man Bernhard Gobmeier was in overall charge; Andrea Dosoli was the tech and rider manager; Silvano Galbusera looked after Melandri's bike; and Giacomo Guidotti continued to work with Leon Haslam (29). In the year they made the leap to potential champion status, they did employ a lot of Latin talent. The transition of the whole team southward was completed by the end of the season.

BMW Motorrad Italia GoldBet SBK Team

Italian from top to bottom, the other top BMW team had fast, but insufficiently consistent riders to make the most of factory engines and their own strong line-up of staff under team manager Serafino Foti and overall boss Andrea Buzzoni. Michel Fabrizio (28) and Ayrton Badovini (26) would get on the podium, but there was too much desperation mixed with the determination to produce consistently good results.

Grillini Progea Superbike Team

Strong prospect from 2011 Mark Aitchison (28) started the season in a returning SBK team, but slow private bikes and a blame game that began early on meant that he was unfairly dropped. Jacob Holden (29) raced for the team at MMP in the USA, Federico Sandi (23) was next up, then Norino Brignola (39) saw out a disappointing season.

Rossair AEP Racing

With an almost stock bike, round-one wild-cards Rossair put local man David Johnson (30) on their S1000RR and had a fast play at PI. Wild-cards are rarely seen these days, so they were welcomed.

DUCATI

Althea Racing Ducati

The 2011 champions returned, with some Ducati money, a lot of old-style tech on their bikes and Carlos Checa (39) teamed with 2011 Superstock 1000 FIM Cup champion Davide Giugliano (22). Genesio Bevilacqua's squad had a good year, but almost inevitably not a championship-winning one. An official entry in many ways, but not all, they were good representatives in the 1098R's final year.

JONATHAN REA

EUGENE LAVERTY

MARCO MELANDRI

LORENZO ZANETTI

MAXIME BERGER

MICHEL FABRIZIO

BRETT McCORMICK

AYRTON BADOVINI

DAVIDE GIUGLIANO

SYLVAIN GUINTOLI

Team Effenbert-Liberty Racing/
Liberty Racing-Team Effenbert

Sylvain Guintoli (30) started the season in the first of these identical, but differently named teams and won for them at Assen. He was inexplicably sacked on the eve of the Brno race as things started on a downward spiral that would see them fail to finish the year, despite starting out with four good riders. Maxime Berger (23) was teamed with Guintoli until he was fired before Portimao. Canadian champion and SBK rookie Brett McCormick (21) showed well when fit, but an Assen crash broke his neck and fractured his learning season into two distinct – and short – halves. Czech star and focus of the team's initial arrival Jakub Smrz (29) was fired after the Silverstone race. The team missed the Moscow race, then Lorenzo Lanzi (20) turned up to ride a few races. The team was absent from the final round altogether. A bizarre story that nobody really understood.

PATA Racing Team Ducati

Lorenzo Zanetti (25) started the season in Daniele Carli's team and was fast on occasion. The snack food-sponsored outfit (DFX behind the Pata paint) snapped up Sylvain Guintoli and he duly won two races for them, showing Effenbert-Liberty what they were missing. A good if modestly proportioned team, they battled to the end, with Guintoli winning again at Magny-Cours.

Boulder Motor Sports

Shane Turpin (44) rode as a wild-card on a Ducati at Miller Motorsports Park.

Red Devils Roma

Niccolo Canepa (24) was their lone runner until injury intervened, then Alessandro Polita (28), Matteo Baiocco (28) and finally Maxime Berger (23) rode for Andrea Petricca's team. It featured many old and some new SBK faces in the background.

Barni Racing Team Italia

Matteo Baiocco was a wild-card and respectably fast in a Ducati team that worked well in the CIV series.

HONDA

Honda World Superbike Team

Jonathan Rea (25) was back yet again, and a winner yet again, but ultimately not a challenger yet again. His bike spec was very much of the old school. His desire for a competitive team-mate could have been realised in the form of proven 250GP champion Hiroshi Aoyama (30), but the diminutive Japanese struggled all year, in spite of a very professional approach.

Team Pro Ride Motorsports/
Real Game Honda

Finance issues made the season a very short one for Raffaele de Rosa (25) and then Lorenzo Alfonsi (31) in Marco Nicotari's squad.

Prop-tech Ltd Honda

Viktor Kispataki (26) from Hungary made a wild-card appearance at Brno on a Honda, another rare visitor to increase numbers.

KAWASAKI

Kawasaki Racing Team

Tom Sykes (27) was back again with Joan Lascorz (27), but the horror of Joan's early-season testing accident ended his career cruelly. Sergio Gadea (27) arrived to ride at Monza, but it was an unfair venue for any rider to have their first SBK experience. Loris Baz (19) exceeded everybody's expectations when promoted from Stock 1000, with a win and podiums. Not bad for a teenage rookie who had joined half-way through the toughest season for years.

Team Pedercini Kawasaki

Spaniard David Salom (27) and Argentinian Leandro Mercado (20) started the season together, but injury and financial reality saw the semi-supported ZX-10Rs fitted with turnstile seat units. Gary Mason (33) rode in the UK; ZA rider David McFadden (22) had an end-of-season cameo; Stock 1000 regular Bryan Staring (25) had a top ten at home in Australia; Alexander Lundh (25) brought money and decent pace from Sweden; and David Johnson (30) showed at Donington, but did not race. Claudio Corti (25) completed the long list of Pedercini pilots and was the best of the one-off riders, at the Magny-Cours finale.

SUZUKI

FIXI Crescent Suzuki

Leon Camier (26) joined a British-based team in 2012, the FIXI Crescent Suzuki squad that had left BSB for SBK. The combo was good on paper, but the engine performance of the machine held Camier back for too long to make an impact until near the end of the year. The luckless, but determined John Hopkins (29) could have been a top rider had he not suffered almost continuous injury; he never found his previous pace. Joshua Brookes (29) replaced Hopkins at the very last minute in Australia, and then Peter Hickman (25) from the UK raced at Donington. The team was a welcome addition to the class and worthy, once they had sufficiently fast engines from partners Yoshimura.

Photos: Gold & Goose

THE SUPERBIKES OF 2012

By GORDON RITCHIE

Above: Biaggi's Aprilia RSV4R Factory – familiar, but a winner.

Above right: Checa's 1198 Ducati was old-school and in its final year.

Right: Sykes's Kawasaki Ninja, power control by electronics.

Photos: Gold & Goose

Above: Melandri's BMW S1000RR: small, but important improvements.

Right: Rea's Honda was much improved with ride-by-wire.

Photos: Gold & Goose

Photos: Gold & Goose

APRILIA RSV4 FACTORY

The specs of the Aprilia are still impressive after all these years, and for 2012 the latest Factory derivation did not disappoint. The incorporation of a full starter-motor system, weighing 3.5kg, was counteracted by some weight saving in other areas, the bike finally tipping the scales just 0.5kg over the 165kg lower limit. A new rear tank design and battery location behind the fuel cell addressed an early mass centralisation issue.

A new rear swing-arm arrived, but although it solved some chatter problems it introduced others, and it remained a work in progress. New fork settings came about because of the new swing-arm, although the units were the same as those used in 2011, Öhlins TRSP 42mm.

Brembo brakes were employed, with the T-type floating discs, but although Laverty and satellite rider Davies were given the most modern and sculpted Evo calipers, Biaggi preferred the feel of the older alloy versions.

A new engine spec was introduced at Monza and was kept for the remainder of the year, even though engine life was shortened for the Monza races – from 1,000–1,200km to maybe half that for safety. Aprilia gave up making their own clutches in 2012, opting instead for an STM unit.

Revs were up by 500 from 2011, to a high of 15,500rpm, with around 230bhp the result. Variable-length inlet trumpets, exhaust power-valves and the usual Aprilia Racing electronics package controlled the engine characteristics. Anti-wheelie was the main element to be developed in the in-house electronics array.

BMW S1000RR

There was a revised BMW road bike on which to base the racer, with some small, but important alterations to the seat unit for aerodynamic reasons, and changes to the engine and swing-arm mounts.

Engine performance was up by around five per cent, but it was how the engine produced power that really made it a winner. Even so, the crankshaft was lightened, albeit not to the regulation 15 per cent less than standard employed by some others.

The 80mm cylinder bore of the BMW makes it throw out peak power of 225bhp at a giddy 14,500rpm. Despite the revvy nature of the engine, it was good for up to 2,000km between refreshes.

The starter motor added some weight, but reductions elsewhere took the bike to just over 165kg.

An all-BMW RSM5 ECU still provided the centre of the electronics suite, but the biggest changes were to the software – all aimed at making the engine more controllable and amenable in real-world racing.

A six-axis inclinometer/accelerometer unit and a GPS unit were located in the waist of the machine.

Fuel tank shape was changed for ergonomic reasons, and an underslung swing-arm finally superseded the stock unit. Brembo Evo calipers were employed by both riders, with 320 or 328mm discs and T-type rotor mountings. Marchesini wheels were new for 2012.

Gilles Tooling supplied many of the levers and pedals, but BMW fabricated some, too. Solid, but relatively narrow-width fork yokes were also made by BMW.

DUCATI 1198 RS12

Regulations required that the big twin be force fed, to bulk up an extra 6kg. The 171kg bike found 4kg from its new starter-motor assembly, while steel exhausts and fasteners added enough to ensure it tipped the scales legally.

Inside the engine, Ducati can change the piston (to an Omega item), camshaft and valves, but the materials for these cannot change. The Desmo valve actuators are also stock, as are the cam belts.

In normal use, the top ends are refreshed every 800km, the bottom end after 1,600km. For Monza, a uniquely brutal test of any engine, these distances are halved. Peak revs are limited by the 50mm regulatory air-intake restrictor plate, but Ducati found a few more in 2012. A hydraulic dry clutch drives the bike forward.

Ride-by-wire is controlled by an old-tech Marelli system, but the software is the clever bit, as always. No GPS is used, just an accelerometer. Three different maps are rider selectable on the move. Individual gears also have individual maps.

The otherwise stock swing-arm is cut and welded to make it longer, to improve traction. Factory Öhlins forks and shocks are used, but not the most advanced forks. Custom yokes aid front-end rigidity with a very large contact area on the fork and three fasteners per side.

OZ wheels marry to Brembo brakes, but again, the old-tech Ducati eschews T-type caliper bobbins for round ones, and only 320mm floating Brembo discs are used.

HONDA CBR1000RR

The Honda engine is not the most pokey of the group, and performance does drop as the 1,500km refresh life is neared.

Electronics are handled by Cosworth hardware and software, the Ten Kate Team relaying rider requests, which Cosworth turn into code between races and tweak at races.

A gear position sensor was new for 2012, along with the elimination of the need to use the clutch on up-shifts. The ride-by-wire system (with the throttle actuator motor under the left-hand fairing panel) probably helps the old-tech Honda more than any rival bike.

With less power to work with than most, Honda visited the wind tunnel in a bid to improve airflow with their new-for-2012 bodywork. The latest swing-arm is narrowed in width at one point, so the rider can tuck his boots in, aided by new Gilles Tooling handlebars, levers, brackets, etc. Looking huge, the swing-arm is adjustable for torsional and lateral stiffness, but it employs the same linkage system as the previous version.

Extra electronics meant additional weight for the Honda, perhaps 3kg more than the 165kg lower limit even at season's end. A new aluminium tank, rear sub-frame and front fairing bracket were required to reach that level. Gilles Tooling supplied the fluted triple clamps at top and bottom.

Uniquely, the official Honda entry employs Nissin calipers, with Rea running large 330mm Yutaka discs for stronger braking. Pads are either Nissin or SBS, and PVM wheels are fitted.

KAWASAKI NINJA ZX-10R

A 15 per cent lighter crankshaft contributed to the performance improvement of the near-championship-winning Ninja ZX-10R, but the ride-by-wire system and exhaust valve (which arrived mid-season) were other major contributing factors to controlling one of the more powerful four-cylinder engines.

Kawasaki's MotoGP experience provided the philosophy behind a machine laden with sensors for the Marelli MHT ECU.

A smoother and more linear ramp on the back-torque-limiting clutch set-up was also new for 2012. Maximum revs are 15,500rpm, the motor screaming out over 220bhp just below that.

After winter testing, basically one swing-arm was employed all year, unlike 2011, when several went through the workshops.

Chassis bracing under the centre section of the frame spars improved torsional rigidity. This feature also made it stronger in the longitudinal plane, improving braking stability and overall feedback to the rider, all of which allow the riders to accelerate

harder, earlier and with more confidence from right on the edge of the tyre.

Sole KRT official team suspension supplier Showa provided new front fork internals for 2012, but the tubes and rear shock remained the same as in 2011. Kawasaki's own regular aluminium race kit fork yokes proved the best option, despite much experimentation with alternative designs.

Brembo calipers were the Lithium/Aluminium version, which Sykes preferred to the newer Evo type, but all other parts of the brake cocktail were the latest available, including the larger option 328mm discs. The Kawasaki is claimed to be right on the 165kg limit.

SUZUKI GSX-R1000K12

The oldest and maybe most traditional design in the paddock was still capable of podiums, and in no small part this was due to a neat Motec electronics suite and the best of available chassis add-ons.

A Motec ADL dashboard stored the acquired data, while a trick gyroscope unit worked as a six-axis sensor, measuring lean angles and also acceleration in three planes. A GPS unit allowed corner-by-corner mapping.

A ride-by-wire throttle system was adopted and a blipper arrangement was used for gear changes.

Yoshimura encountered trouble in increasing the engine power sufficiently early on, but various cam profiles were tried until improved acceleration was achieved, even if top speed and power were still works in progress.

A Suzuki factory gearbox was part of the power train, and a self-built Crescent slipper clutch was employed in 2012. A curvaceous 4-into-1 Yoshimura exhaust was custom made.

Hopkins used Yoshimura yokes, but MotoGP-style slotted Suzuki yokes were run by Camier. The swing-arm was a Suzuki factory item.

For improved rigidity and turning, there was gusseting around the swing-arm pivot area. Two-pad Evo calipers from Brembo gave a strong gyroscopic effect. Round-bobbin Brembo 320mm discs were the main braking options, but Sunstar discs were also tried.

Full factory contracted Öhlins 42mm TRSP25 forks and RSP40 rear shocks were employed, like most of the teams during the 2012 season. Hopkins sometimes used a TTX36 rear shock. The Suzuki was 1kg over the 165kg limit, but only because the IMS on-board camera kit weighed that much.

Left: Checa leads Rea and Sykes over Lukey Heights.

Below far left: Guintoli leads Melandri in race one.

Below centre: First time out on the works BMW, Melandri scored a second-place podium that must have felt like a win. Particularly from a fourth-row starting spot.

Below: Fabrizio looks over at Rea as he snatches sixth place in race one.

Bottom far left: Haslam tends to his injured ankle.

Bottom centre: Biaggi and Sykes give no quarter.

Bottom: Local boys Brookes and Staring at play.

Bottom right: Checa and Sykes embrace the outback headgear. Rea and Biaggi stick strictly to team attire.

Photos: Gold & Goose

O NCE more a SBK season kicked off far from the usual base of European racing, in Australia. Happy Birthday SBK; it began its 25th year a long way from the first venue in 1988, Donington Park.

In 2012, Carlos Checa and his Ducati fellows had six extra kilograms to lug about, but initially it hardly showed. He was on a fighting-fit front row, with Sykes on pole, Biaggi, and Smrz straddling Checa, and Guintoli in fifth – three of the five on Ducatis. The paddock was in subdued mood, however, after the death of teenage local Superstock 600 rider Oscar McIntyre. Superpole had been cancelled as a result, with Sykes on Sunday pole on combined qualifying results.

Kawasaki plainly had made a jump in winter testing, but so had BMW, even if 13th on the grid for Melandri was a vexing fourth-row hex.

In the first race, Checa boomed away into the lead ahead of Biaggi, looking cool and calm in his role of defending champion. That was ended by a 180km/h crash on the exit of the awesome Turn 12 sweep, his subsequent flight a combination of long jump and high jump, with not even any sand to land in.

That left Biaggi clear to win, his season starting perfectly after he had led for 17 of the 22 laps. Behind, another Italian with a big ex-GP reputation overcame his grid position to take a second place, ahead of a sparkling Guintoli. Melandri's podium first time out brought forth the sound of people eating their hats.

For Guintoli, it was a sweet result considering how previous seasons had started brightly, but fallen away at the first Aussie hurdles.

Sykes, in a preview of issues that would affect the second half of his races, was 12 seconds back in fourth, while Smrz backed up Guintoli in the notion that even at five seasons old, the 1098R was the best antique in the privateer's shop. He was fifth, 16 seconds from the win. Twenty of the 24 riders finished. Bryan Staring was the top Aussie in a one-off Team Pedercini Kawasaki Superbike ride, his own season not having started yet.

Bear with us when we say that a second place in race two was a far superior ride from Biaggi than his first-race win. It was actually one of the best races he had ever ridden, in any class, after contact with Tom Sykes early on and what Max himself described so charmingly as "some sightseeing through the green garden".

Biaggi stayed upright, got back on track and screamed through from the back to second, overtaking final podium man Sykes, but running out of laps to catch Checa.

In a very few hours, Checa had regained his peerless composure to convince himself that the old season really was finally over. A strong critic of the single-bike rule for 2012, his team nonetheless provided him with a heavily repaired and very usable twin for the second run, and he raised himself from race-one pain and despair to one of his best wins – even if Biaggi was more the star.

Sykes left Australia third overall and worthy of it after overhauling the perennially tough Jonathan Rea on the final corners after the Honda man's tyres had been used up. Rea had led on his Honda for two laps and would finish a gritty fourth, while guts and skill would take Leon Haslam and his multiple ankle fractures to fifth, one place and much less than a second ahead of Melandri. Haslam had crashed in testing and endured an 11th-hour operation. When it mattered, however, he overcame the setback in a gritty style.

A tragic, uplifting, unpredictable and thrilling opener.

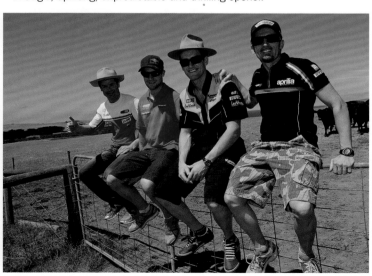

Far left: Carlos Checa was unbeatable on his Ducati.

Left: Tom Sykes seemed happy with his afternoon's work. His run of astounding pole success was also well under way.

Below left: Zanetti went well in race one. A privateer on a good Ducati was still an occasional potent force in SBK racing.

Below: Lascorz leads Camier. It would be the last event for the Spaniard, who suffered serious injuries during post-race testing.

Bottom: A perennial struggle for Hopkins in World Superbikes.

Bottom right: Haslam and Biaggi battle in race one.

Photos: Gold & Goose

THE two Superbike races at Imola entered the category of the uncommon. Double wins, where one rider takes both races on the same day, are not so rare, but identical podiums? And not only that, identical top-four finishes? It was a strange race day, but none should be surprised that Carlos Checa won both races on a Ducati.

Imola is a place where chicane- and corner-exit oomph counts, where the fastest parts are downhill, and there are lots of places to pass. Ideal Checa country when he's happy with the front end of his bike.

He rode similar races both times, and the extra 6kg on the bike seemed to add to the stability of the neo-works machine.

Podium man Sykes had taken his second Superpole of 2012, with fresh memories of good rides in 2011 at this Italian track. Undulating, blind, intense, tree-lined, this quintessentially Italian parkland circuit is a bit like the British circuits where Sykes learned to ride fast (Oulton, Brands, Cadwell Park), all the while ignoring trackside barriers and bridge supports. Maybe that's why he goes well at Imola, although he also loves leading races. Each race in 2012 was like 2011 all over again, however – he led to half-distance and then Checa passed to win.

The British riders were on form at Imola, Haslam gratefully scoring two third places, glad of the five-week break between the ankle agony of Australia and the soothing balm of podiums in Italy. He still managed to bash his ankle on a couple of kerbs, but he took the pain for the gain in his points total and BMW's first double podium.

Biaggi was fourth each time, 6.5 and then 3.9 seconds behind. The relatively low temperatures, in the mid teens, did not help his Aprilia, but at a circuit where he thought he might struggle, a brace of fourths were more than acceptable.

In race two, five of the six manufacturers put a bike into the top five places.

Behind the top four, the rest appeared to be just that, with fifth-placed Laverty 24 seconds away – more than a second a lap, and then Rea 18 seconds off in fifth in race two. He had survived a gigantic high-side in practice, so he was simply glad to be able to race.

Second-place qualifier Guintoli never scored at this race, crashing on lap two of the opener and then placing only 11th on his rebuilt bike in the second. Not easy in privateer-land of course, but a V-twin was still a good idea. Lorenzo Zanetti (PATA Racing Team Ducati) was a more-than-sound eighth in race one, but the bright start of former 250 GP champion Hiro Aoyama in Australia dimmed at his first unseen circuit. Eighteenth followed by retirement for technical reasons meant no points.

Marco Melandri's race-one sixth was respectable, tenth in race two not in the script. Like most of his peers, he tested at Imola thanks to the initiative of post-race money-saving sessions. Melandri looked like saving his season after this test. He appeared shocked when describing a list of reasons why his bike was not working anything like as well as some of the other fours, and particularly his team-mate's double-podium bike. His issues would be resolved eventually.

Kawasaki's Joan Lascorz crashed heavily, and the test day ended under a cloud as the seriousness of his injury filtered through.

Above: Rea goes down in race one.

Left: Redemption in race two as the Irishman celebrates his win with team boss Roland Ten Kate.

Far left: Sylvain Guintoli mastered the wet conditions to win race one.

Below left: Badovini looks like a maths teacher, rides like a tearaway. His podium hopes floated, then sank in the trackside swamp.

Below centre left: Riders displayed stickers supporting Joan Lascorz, who had been gravely injured in a testing accident at Imola.

Bottom left: The hardy crowd endured the wet conditions.

Below far left: Rea took his Honda to a win in race two.

Below: Giugliano leads Laverty. Biaggi and the rest in the shortened nine-lap race one.

Photos: Gold & Goose

ASSEN is a remarkable stopover on the SBK trail, a place with a vast MotoGP/TT history, but still with a love for Superbikes. The event is always something of a festival of two-wheel sport, but in 2012 the weather refused to co-operate at particularly inopportune moments.

It was already making itself felt at the start of race one, which was red-flagged as the rain became heavier. As it had been declared a dry race, a restart was called, over only nine laps, but with full points.

After almost an hour of delays, this was run in the cold and wet, but it was competitive enough, even if eventual winner Guintoli ended up 2.6 seconds out in front – the first win at this level for both rider and Liberty Racing Team Effenbert.

Haslam led before falling, then Checa took over, until Guintoli got by him for the only two laps that mattered, the final two.

Superstock champion in 2011, Davide Giugliano took his first podium in SBK racing at the expense of Checa. The sage Spaniard understood a youthful rider's need to make a name, however, and was not too upset by his own third-place finish. Team-owner Genesio Bevilaqua's choice of Giugliano had come good early.

On full wets, Guintoli was always going to be a threat, but other rain-dancers fell: Badovini, Haslam, Rea, Hopkins, Camier, Zanetti all out after slips in the heavy rain.

Only 21 had lined up for the restart; only 15 finished.

Race two was also called wet, but really was only damp in patches. The disappointment of Rea's race-one fall was transposed into one of his most charging wins, by almost three seconds from Guintoli. It was the kind of floating, fearless ride that makes people wonder why it is not possible for him (or more likely his bike set-up) to be that good every week. At his Ten Kate crew's home-round, his victory was a gift.

In second place, Guintoli underlined why his earlier win was no wet-weather fluke. His team-mate, Smrz, was looking for a top finish of his own before going off line to pass a back-marker, hitting paint and crashing fast.

New Liberty Racing Team Effenbert rider Brett McCormick suffered a fast and ultimately injurious crash, breaking bones in his neck, but suffering no neurological damage.

The battle for third was just that, Laverty, Melandri and Haslam slugging it out and crossing the line as one vehicle; the Aprilia just pinched a gap on the flying BMWs.

Sykes, once more on pole, was only sixth, but that was a lot better than his failure to re-start race one after a technical problem.

Checa and crew had gambled on full wets, but the clouds passed and he had to come in for dry tyres. Then he won the Pirelli award for fastest lap, which was nice in its own way, but also no good at all because he finished 17th and last, a lap down.

Badovini went from medical centre following race one to seventh in race two, ahead of Biaggi. Smrz, Guintoli and Rea all took turns to lead the full 22-lap race.

There was a lot of rain about on race day in the Netherlands, but that will teach them to run a race in late April. The promise of sunshine beckoned as the pack headed to Monza for round four. Fat chance.

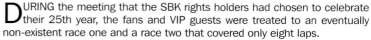

DURING the meeting that the SBK rights holders had chosen to celebrate their 25th year, the fans and VIP guests were treated to an eventually non-existent race one and a race two that covered only eight laps.

The background story is so immense, however, that we have no room to cover it all. Suffice to say that the main points range from the Machiavellian to the Shakespearean.

The aborted race one went for two laps before it was called, for rain and a crash that claimed Salom, Hopkins and stand-in KRT rider Sergio Gadea. Melandri had also crashed, on his own, at the Parabolica.

Biaggi, who had been having bike problems, was pushed back to the pit lane by old GP mate Checa, to rousing ovation/derision from the crowd.

The pit lane opened again at 12.25, but when the riders re-formed more rain spots began to appear, while there were reports of heavier showers on the other side of the track. This left one section that the riders considered to be too wet when other parts had already dried. Not all the riders, though, as pole man Guintoli (with around 30bhp less than the best fours) was ready to race. A safety-car inspection of the track showed how wet it was away from the bulk of fans on the pit-lane side of the circuit, and then the rains hit properly in the pit lane, too. Race cancelled.

Normally the riders would have gone to a wet set-up, but after some wild scenes in practice, with smoke coming from the rear tyres of the Superbikes when running full wets down the main straight, that was a gamble too far. The problem was that the fastest half of the circuit was too dry to use wets, while the newly surfaced other half (Ascari, etc) was holding surface water for what seemed like ten times longer than the old tarmac at Monza. Poor drainage under new tarmac – the blame game started early and lasted long.

Verbal jousting began, but the simple fact is that no wet tyre of any make or design can handle the uniquely flat-out straight at Monza unless it is actually fully wet. Thanks to Pirelli's frequently criticised steel belts, a roadbike design feature blamed for some of the squishiness of their tyres' sidewalls, there were no blowouts. That was just as well, as Tom Sykes set a new SBK record top speed of 339.5km/h (near 210.9mph), his rear smoking heavily. Monza proved unraceable in such conditions.

Race two was supposed to start at 15.30 as usual and run for all 18 planned laps, but rain intervened once more and, after two warm-up laps and a drop in the lap count to 17, there was another start-line delay; then another lap was taken off.

At 15.55, the race got under way – sans pole man and race-one rebel Guintoli after his bike broke down.

Sykes put his faith in himself out front by setting laps that were four seconds off the lap record on a patchily damp track, but still two seconds a lap faster then the rest.

A great fight for second was ended when the rain returned. As riders raised their hands, Sykes was declared a clear winner by nearly ten seconds, although he and the top 15 received only half points.

Podium men Haslam and Laverty, plus Melandri, Biaggi, Rea and Checa, all ripped across the line with just a second separating them. It would have been a great full race…

Above: High-level discussion between riders and officials led to the cancellation of race one.

Left: Giugliano brings a halt to race two.

Far left: Laverty was involved in an entertaining scrap with Melandri and Biaggi before proceedings were halted.

Below, centre row, left to right: Sergio Gadea was a KRT substitute; Pirelli rear wets, like this one on Chaz Davies' Aprilia, melted on the uniquely long and fast Monza straights. On many occasions during race weekend, there was no suitable tyre choice for a whole lap; SBK's 25th Anniversary was marked with a display of top bikes from all eras; Fabrizio and Laverty had a frank post-race discussion.

Bottom left: Confusion reigns on the grid as the race-two start is halted due to water on parts of the track.

Below: Sunshine on an all-British podium after the day's only race.

Photos: Gold & Goose

DONINGTON

ROUND 5 · GREAT BRITAIN

Left: A BMW layer cake for Melandri and Haslam as Rea (65) nips past to snatch victory.

Centre row, far left: French youngster Baz made a very good impression on the Kawasaki.

Centre row, second left: Toseland and Burnett after receiving their SBK Hall of Fame gongs.
Photos: Gold & Goose

Centre row, second right: Gary Mason was a wild-card on the Team Pedercini Kawasaki.
Photo: Clive Challinor Motorsport Photography

Centre row, right: Injured John Hopkins with his substitute, Peter Hickman.

Bottom left: Haslam and Melandri in charge of race two – before their last-corner faux pas.

Bottom: Checa was an early casualty after a collision with Smrz on the opening lap of race two.

Bottom right: Rea and Biaggi can't believe their good fortune after race two.
Photos: Gold & Goose

AFTER the controversy and contention of Monza, it was good to get back to where it all began for SBK, 25 years before, in the hope of seeing the series return to its usual role of competitive championship, hard but fair.

Nice idea, but the gloves and all bets were off on race day.

It was a momentous day in the history of SBK racing all right: BMW became the eighth manufacturer to record a win in 24-and-a-bit years. Melandri and Haslam even made it a 1-2 as well.

Haslam, Sykes and Melandri made the early break in the opener and were joined by Biaggi, with Rea just behind near the end.

Melandri's pace took him to a clear lead after he had despatched Sykes, and as the final laps counted down he was all set to win BMW's first ever SBK victory.

Both Haslam and Biaggi would run wide, the former trying to get by Melandri, but failing by only 0.7 second. Sykes just held off Rea for third after Biaggi's run-on let the Honda man through. Max was fifth, Checa a lonely sixth.

A brilliant second race was full of incident. At the first corner, Laverty was forced to slow and Checa had nowhere to go, with Giugliano and Smrz joining him in the gravel. The Italian would get going again, unlike Checa and Smrz.

Laverty fell at high speed at Craner on lap 11, his bike destructing on the way to the bottom.

Sykes led laps 1–16, Haslam 17–22, but on lap 23 Rea was a winner for the second time after a final-corner skittles session that topped off a brilliant race that will live long in the memory.

Mid-race, Haslam, Biaggi, Melandri and Rea had traded places, before passing Sykes. Then it was Rea's turn to do the same, lining up and overtaking Biaggi and Melandri, but then the latter got him back to launch an attack on Haslam.

Now it was Haslam's race to win, then a straight fight, or so it seemed, between Melandri, Rea, Biaggi and the tailing Sykes.

On the very last corner, Melandri went for an ambitious pass on Haslam, missed the chance and ran past the English rider, eventually recovering his place and poise to head back towards the final straight.

His move had pushed Haslam wide and, as he turned back into the corner, Rea, having seen all the commotion, went for the small gap on the inside line. He and Haslam clashed, the latter cannoning into Melandri, who went down, too.

Another seemingly certain BMW 1-2 suddenly became a no-score for Melandri and a push home for Haslam, with one point for 15th.

Ex-motocrosser Rea was ecstatic to win and Biaggi amazed to be second, while Sykes felt justified with third: he had only slid backwards when his rear traction had let him down.

Who was to blame for the final-corner melee remains uncertain, but it drove a wedge between the BMW team-mates on a day when they should have been celebrating all the way to America for the next round.

The thus far relatively subdued FIXI Crescent Suzuki team and their lead rider, Leon Camier, got in on the act, finishing fourth and only 4.2 seconds from the win. Still using not-fast-enough Yoshimura engines in their GSX-Rs, this made less difference at Donington than most places.

In a tight second race, only 15 finished again. There were two stand-in riders: Peter Hickman for Hopkins on the second Suzuki, and Gary Mason in the Pedercini Kawasaki team.

Loris Baz acquitted himself well in his first replacement ride for Lascorz, his eighth in race two a particular highlight.

Above: Race two winner Melandri leads the pack away against the dramatic high-desert backdrop.

Right: Rain even plagued practice. Jonathan Rea takes shelter under his brolly.

Centre right: Race two was aborted after Aoyama's Honda dumped oil on the track, necessitating a long clean-up operation.

Below right: Race one winner Checa crashed out of the re-started race two.

Photos: Gold & Goose

Above: Americans Scott Russell and Ben Bostrom were the latest recipients of SBK Hall of Fame medals.

Top: Jake Holden was a wild-card rider on the Grillini Progea BMW.

Below left: Shane Turpin was another US wild-card on a Ducati.

Bottom left: Wayne Rainey was in attendance to support longstanding buddy Carlos Checa.

Below: Chaz Davies rode well in both races. The Herefordshire rider leads Sykes, Rea, Giugliano, Biaggi and Laverty in race-two action.

Photos: Gold & Goose

THERE was a special guest in the Althea Racing Ducati pit box at Miller Motorsports Park: Wayne Rainey. Good mates with Carlos Checa for years, he finally made it to a full Superbike race day in support of his Spanish friend.

Rainey brought good fortune, because pole man Smrz was not the Ducati rider who won the first race on Memorial Day Holiday Monday, it was Checa.

Locked in a fight with Rea for a time, then Melandri, Checa finally put the screws on when it mattered and won by 2.3 seconds. Melandri had been trying to get back to him almost right to the end, but when he realised it was a bust he slowed to make sure of second place.

Biaggi and Rea scrapped it out for the final place on the podium, the former taking it after a pass inside the Honda, which was noticeably slower than the Aprilia on the long MMP straight.

A 12-second gap back to a toiling Laverty in fifth place, with Smrz a second behind, was a small surprise, but seeing front-row man Sykes in eighth mystified for a while. It was simply a less-than-perfect set-up and tyre choice on a track that Sykes loves, but which does not love his Kawasaki in return.

Having won at Miller on both Honda and Ducati, such was his sense of ease and smoothness in race one that surely Checa would double up again.

Not a bit of it, as he fell and retired in the real second race after losing the front end.

Checa had led an aborted first running of race two, which was stopped after Aoyama fell and his bike emptied its sump on to the track at the Attitude corners. The extensive oil spill required exhaustive cleaning, and the second race was restarted at a much-delayed 16.58.

It lasted 18 laps and was a winning outing for Melandri, by only 0.195 second from the tenacious Rea. The Northern Irish rider had experienced a couple of nightmare Miller weekends in the past, but on this occasion he led for seven laps and was only beaten by a rider who was stamping his authority on things after the Donington debacle.

Team-mate Haslam was 13th on the grid, then tenth and eighth in the races. Melandri was ninth in Superpole, but he and his crew found a sweet spot on race day.

Biaggi was third in race two, losing ground to new second-place man Melandri, but gaining a bigger points gap overall.

This event was something of a minor coming-of-age for ex-AMA rider Chaz Davies, as he rode in the front group in race two for a while before finishing fourth, only four seconds behind Melandri. Sykes was in the early fight once more, but dropped back to fifth, putting him third overall on points.

What may be the last MMP round for World Superbike delivered strongly in terms of action and drama – a bit too much with yet another heavy delay – but still not enough people came to a race that even in American terms is pretty far from anywhere but Salt Lake City. Americans get few holiday weekends, so they have to make them count, and sadly MMP is just in the wrong place.

There was also another spell of poor weather in practice, in a year plagued with rain and accident delays.

Another milestone in its quarter-centenary as SBK clicked up a 600th individual race at Miller.

Above: Giugliano scored a podium in race one.

Top: Biaggi shaded Checa in race one.

Above right: Leon Camier rode the wheels off his Suzuki for little reward.

Above far right: Local wild-card Baiocco was impressive on his Ducati, scoring points in both races.

Right: In front of almost empty grandstands, Sykes leads Rea, Haslam, Laverty and Co. in race two.

Photos: Gold & Goose

Below: Badovini on his BMW.

Bottom: A double-header win for Biaggi.

Below right: Rea and Haslam contest second place in race two.

Photos: Gold & Goose

SEVEN rounds in, and the last of three in Italy, the Santamonica circuit near the Adriatic coast hosted the San Marino round, at the newly renamed Misano World Circuit Marco Simoncelli.

An Italian rider from a different independent European nation state proved unbeatable, as Monaco resident Biaggi recovered from tenth on the grid – after another two-part wet Superpole – to win both races.

The first was a close contest with Checa, the second a more comfortable finish, five seconds ahead of Rea and Haslam.

It was Melandri's turn to endure a less than sparkling weekend. Down in 13th on the grid, he was forced to retire in race one; then he finished one place off the podium in race two.

Checa was a strong second in the first outing, with team-mate Giugliano behind him, the Roman lad getting even more of a taste for the podium champers. At the closest thing to a truly home race, he was aggressive and determined, and right on the edge. He had even led for five laps.

He crashed twice in race two, though, eventually posting a DNF. A few others did the same, notably Checa, who had a crash forced on him, rejoined, but then retired.

Rea had led 17 laps of the 24 in race one, but dropped back to finish fifth, fighting off Davies and Laverty.

Race two had Sykes in the lead for three laps, having scored a Superpole win yet again, but he would slither to seventh, having been fourth in race one.

Four BMWs filled the places from third to sixth in race two, ridden by Haslam, Melandri, Badovini and Fabrizio.

If Kawasaki had a dull day with Sykes, new permanent signing Baz was coming on brightly: eighth in race two despite a technical retirement in the opener.

For a hangdog expression, however, you had to look no further than the FIXI Crescent Suzuki garage. Camier had ridden out of his skin for tenth in race one, with Hopkins 17th. In race two, Camier was 15th, Hopkins 14th.

Race two was costly for riders and teams, with only 17 crossing the line; Salom was in the medical centre with yet another arm and shoulder injury.

Melandri was placed under investigation for knockings-off, first of Guintoli and then of Checa. Nothing came of it, except more disapprobation aimed at the Italian. He was becoming very unpopular with his rivals, as he had been at the centre of several incidents in 2012 already, usually by block passing or lifting other riders late in the corner. At Misano, this tactic became an art form all round, with Checa doing it to Melandri in race one, Biaggi doing the same to Rea, and many others making desperate passes in unlikely spots.

Local wild-card rider Matteo Baiocco deserves special mention. He took his Barni Racing Team Italia Ducati to 15th, then tenth, just over a second a lap slower than Biaggi in race two. Wild-cards appear a lot less in SBK racing now, partly because of a disparity in rules in most domestic series in 2012, so when one shows well it makes the fans come over all nostalgic.

Biaggi left Misano with a 38.5-point championship lead, a vast gap in this year of ups and downs. He was the last top rider with a perfect score of race finishes, and that as much as anything kept him out front. But his brilliance at Misano, shortly before his 41st birthday, proved he was still much more than just a consistent rider.

FIM WORLD CHAMPIONSHIP

Above: Laverty (58) leads Sykes, Checa and Badovini in race one.

Above left: Chaz Davies found his feet at Aragon with two strong races and a podium appearance.

Right: David Salom highlights his support for Spain in the final of the European football championship.

Top: Carlos Checa unveils a sculpture in his honour.

Left: A no-holds-barred battle between Biaggi and Melandri ended in favour of the Aprilia rider in race one.

Far left: Race two podium: Melandri is flanked by Laverty (*left*) and Davies.

Below left: Rea and Smrz were the victims of this race one collision. Fabrizio (84) took avoiding action to finish sixth.

Right: The sparse crowd was rewarded with some fine racing. Haslam (91) leads Sykes (66), Rea and Checa in a battle for the race two minor placings.

Photos: Gold & Goose

THERE wasn't a cat's chance in hell of any official attendance figure being forthcoming from Motorland. There were too few to count.

It was a shame because on the same day that Spain beat Italy in the Euro 2012 soccer final, a far more entertaining pair of spectacles, particularly race two, took place at the superbly designed and executed circuit in this sparsely populated region of Aragón.

The first featured a superb fight between the championship's leading duo, with Biaggi finally heading Melandri over the line by 0.278 second. There was still no love lost between the two, but there was mutual respect, and they stopped short of taking each other out, even though each had a few chances. It was close and compelling, but it was not the best race of the day.

Behind, Checa was lucky to get a home podium, particularly at a track with a remarkably long straight to punish his air-restricted V-twin.

Ahead of him, near the end, the fight for third was a foregone conclusion for Sykes, who had made a small defendable gap to the fast, but increasingly frantic Badovini. For a reason only known to the Italian rider, he attempted to get back under the long shadow of Sykes on the inside at one of the fast corners, Turn Four, but only succeeded in losing the front, his bike wiping out Sykes as it slid from under him. Thus Checa cashed in, nearly ten seconds back from the win, but far enough ahead of Davies.

Race two was one of those classics you get in Superbike sometimes, with the leading riders' numbers painted on the faces of dice, and every corner a new throw to see who would come out ahead.

Melandri won the only throw that mattered, confessing on the podium that until he crossed the line, just 0.042 second up on Laverty, he did not know who would win. Strategy and tactics had been used up long before the end; it was just a case of get past the other guy somehow.

Davies, strong in race one, looked like he had been competing at the top level of Superbikes all his life as he held off Biaggi for third by a sliver, with the top four separated by only 0.484 second at the flag. After 20 intense laps, it was exhausting simply to be an observer.

An unseen protagonist was at work at Aragón, particularly in race two: a strong wind that pushed riders around and occasionally too close to one another. The new lap record was set in race one, by Melandri, with the force of the afternoon gusts holding back the pace.

Suzuki man Camier could be justifiably proud of his effort in race one, finishing ninth; and Hopkins also of even scoring a point, given his pain from recent crashes. In race two, neither Suzuki rider finished, each being plagued with technical issues.

Sykes and Badovini were at it again in race two, but this time the former just held him off for a disappointed eighth, the BMW rider ninth. In this meeting, Sykes went from overall third to fifth, despite setting a new best lap in qualifying trim and winning Superpole. Again.

Even though Biaggi had extended his championship lead to 48 points, and previous second-place rider Rea was taken out in race one after a collision involving Smrz and Baz, the sense after Aragón was that Biaggi's luck had to change some time, and Melandri was now the most viable challenger.

Above: Baz strengthened his growing reputation with a podium in race one.

Right: Not a good day for Rea, who crashed out of race one and hitched a ride back to the pits.

Photos: Gold & Goose

Left: Melandri leads Rea, Checa and Giugliano at the start of race one.

Below left: BMW's Bernhard Gobmeier celebrates the first part of his team's double-header with Melandri and the Kawasaki pair of Sykes (*left*) and Baz.

Below centre: Melandri's pit board proclaims the Italian's five SBK wins of the 2012 season so far.

Bottom: Melandri edged out Sykes as they battled for victory in race two.

Photos: Gold & Goose

ARGUABLY the best new-build track design of the late 20th century, Brno is a classic in so many ways, but mostly in that it affords almost boundless overtaking opportunities. Many of these are made entering chicanes so wide you could neatly park all the top riders' motor homes between the rumble strips and still have room to spare for their scooters and barbecues.

The result of this expansive tarmac is usually close racing and outbreaks of last-lap fever into the final chicane.

Thankfully for Melandri in race one, eventual second-place rider – and pole man yet again (in wet Superpole yet again) – Sykes was just too far back to go for that last-lap overtaking effort.

That may have been because he and Rea had clashed over the same piece of tarmac on the penultimate lap, as Rea attempted to pass and stay with Melandri as he headed off into the lead. When Sykes and Rea arrived at the apex of Turn Ten, trying to squeeze too many molecules through the same point in space, the result was a spectacular, if undesirable, outcome for Rea – a DNF.

It had been a bizarre 42 minutes for Sykes. At the beginning, he'd realised that the outside metre or so of track surface was dry, while the racing line was damp. So he made a few laps almost on the outside white line as other riders took much more conventional, if slipperier, trajectories.

Melandri had been sixth on lap one in the opener, but eighth on lap two, making his win a worthy effort, given the many high-calibre riders and the tricky surface. He was beginning to exude confidence and exuberance.

The French young bloods, Baz and Berger, mixed it up early in race one, but Baz had the set-up, tyre choice, factory bike and sang-froid to stick with it for third place.

Checa was half a second back in fourth in the opener, Laverty fifth, and all top five riders were covered by just 3.8 seconds. Biaggi was sixth, having qualified third.

It was the same eventual fight between Melandri and Sykes in race two, but it was much closer this time. Sykes harried and pushed, and looked for a gap that would never quite show itself. He stopped himself from doing anything too extreme and thus Melandri won again, this time by only 0.140 second, with Checa in third, six seconds back.

With Melandri proving unbeatable and two 20-pointers hard-earned, Sykes was happy enough after the disappointments of no podiums since Donington. Significantly, his team had found a setting that threatened to cure the Kawasaki's one glaring weakness – the inability of the rear tyre to last as well as the other top fours.

The celebrations in the BMW pit were understandably boundless, however. Not only had Melandri significantly narrowed Biaggi's lead, but also he had scored BMW's first SBK double. It was Melandri's first double, too, something he could not do even on a factory Yamaha in 2011.

And all this after a high-speed crash at Turn Five in second qualifying on Saturday that had sent his lone bike vaulting the catch fence, breaking important frame brackets and key footrest/gear-change mounts. It was quickly welded, bashed and bolted back into shape to enter free practice a short time later, then take fifth in Superpole.

The history kept coming at Brno, as Baz had scored his first career podium in race one. He was less than two seconds down at the flag, in a race that had started out damp and had lasted a minute and 40 seconds longer than the second one as a result. Baz the teenager had the decency to be surprised as well as elated.

SUPERBIKE WORLD CHAMPIONSHIP
SILVERSTONE
ROUND 10 · GREAT BRITAIN

Above: A return to the podium for Fabrizio in race one.
Photo: Gold & Goose

Above right: Wet-weather ace Guintoli kept his bike in shape to win race two for the Pata team.
Photo: Clive Challinor Motorsport Photography

Right: BMW Italia team-mate Badovini joined Fabrizio in the top three.

Centre right: A first-time win for Baz.
Photos: Gold & Goose

Left: Race-one winner Baz trades fairings with Checa while Camier (2), Haslam (91), Biaggi (3), Laverty and Berger jostle for position

Photo: Clive Challinor Motorsport Photography

Below: Revenge was sweet for race-two victor Guintoli. Former Liberty Racing team-mate Smrz had to be content with third.

Bottom: The field comes to a halt as race two is red-flagged.

Photos: Gold & Goose

Below right: Joy for Mrs Guintoli at her husband's win.

Photo: Clive Challinor Motorsport Photography

WITH the London 2012 Olympics in full stride some 60 miles south of Silverstone, it was a mildly odd weekend before it had even started.

After bad weather had played its malevolent part for the countless time in the season, eventually both races were declared wet. One of them was negated and restarted; the other was started and then stopped, in controversial circumstances.

Having won a wet Superpole, Smrz shared a front-row spot with his former team-mate, Guintoli. Sylvain had been fired by/walked away from/had a near fist fight with his previous Effenbert team at Brno. Their press release cited his bad results as one of the reasons for the split. Guintoli was offended irretrievably, and thus a little mini-drama of hate was acted out behind the main stage.

The Pata Racing Team had picked up Guintoli after Brno, to run alongside regular rider Lorenzo Zanetti. This set up an edgy Ducati privateer battle on race day. Round one went to Effenbert thanks to Smrz's pole. Both Guintoli and Smrz would finish a lap down, however.

Up front, young French rider Baz joined the Superbike winning elite for Kawasaki, carrying on a game of risk and skill to the very last corner and across the line.

Held in changing conditions, the final laps of race one were on a damp, but drying track and with four riders in with a real chance Baz emerged from the final corner to win, by 0.3 second from a rejuvenated Michel Fabrizio; Badovini and Rea followed on, the top four separated by only 0.539 second. Then as Badovini crossed the line, his rear unhooked and he slid off. Rea, riding immediately behind and at full throttle, had no time to react and hit the bike square on. It happened so close to the finish line that we had to look again to check the result. No worries, top four as it was. At least Rea had some points despite the crash, unlike at Brno.

Checa was fifth, but the other real big guns were in trouble.

Melandri was seventh, Sykes eighth and Biaggi a faller on the last lap after hitting a white line.

In race two, another French rider, Guintoli, splashed through some real rain to record his second 2012 win, his first for Pata. Revenge was a dish served cold and soggy. And late.

Like many in the second race, eventual second-place rider Baz was lucky to be classified, as arguments raged after the red flag was waved on lap ten.

Many riders felt the race should have been flagged earlier, despite having been declared wet, because of unseen spilt petrol and oil on the track. Both Sykes and Checa were fallers, and both incandescent with rage at Race Direction. Sykes had been told that he would be one of the riders whom Race Control would look to for signs that conditions had become too bad. He signalled, but there was no response until he fell. The tardy decisions continued.

As the count-back rules were read and re-read, the clock ticked on, and the riders and teams expected a restart over the remaining laps. But how many had been completed?

In the end, the restart never happened and the final results were declared after lap eight. Half-points were awarded. So officially Guintoli won, from Baz, from a recovered and still confident Smrz, with Laverty, Berger and Checa next up.

Melandri was fined later for taking too long to clear his grid, but he finished eighth on a day when just finishing was a good job all round. Biaggi was 11th, Sykes 12th, both seething with anger at officialdom.

SUPERBIKE WORLD CHAMPIONSHIP
MOSCOW
ROUND 11 · RUSSIA

Left: From Russia With Love...

Far left: The field stream away in front of the impressive pit lane facilities and highly vocal crowd.

Below left: South African McFadden joined the ever-changing roster of Pedercini riders for a one-off appearance.

Below: Checa shaves the grass on his Ducati. The Spaniard's title hopes took a dive with only a fourth place from the Moscow meeting, at another circuit with a vast main straight.

Bottom right: Healthy race day crowd was the highlight of the meeting. New track had issues but allowed for brilliant racing.

Photos: Gold & Goose

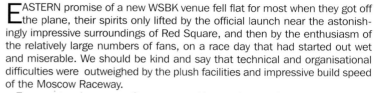

EASTERN promise of a new WSBK venue fell flat for most when they got off the plane, their spirits only lifted by the official launch near the astonishingly impressive surroundings of Red Square, and then by the enthusiasm of the relatively large numbers of fans, on a race day that had started out wet and miserable. We should be kind and say that technical and organisational difficulties were outweighed by the plush facilities and impressive build speed of the Moscow Raceway.

Two spectacular races, afternoon sunshine, a change of championship lead for the first time, and the championship top three becoming ever more closely bunched – it provided a good end to a tough first Russian WSBK experience. The first ever short-haul/long-haul race in Eastern Europe had even involved a ferry ride from Germany to Latvia, and then an escorted road trip for the team trucks and the occasional rider's motor home.

The circuit itself was judged a little tight and a little weird, and with a long uphill straight before the final corner, it clearly suited the best four-cylinder pilots only.

We were treated to fights. The tricky little layout and ever changing grip levels played a part, but manners were in short supply when the races took place before a thrilled 32,500 crowd, seated in well-positioned grandstands. Although few turned up on Friday and Saturday, they showed up full of enthusiasm on Sunday.

Sykes did his favourite kind of disappearing act in race one, 8.8 seconds beyond the reach of a chasing Melandri, with Biaggi a curious third. 'Curious' as in hollow, given that team-mate Laverty had been given orders from the pit wall to let him pass, to minimise the championship leader's points damage.

The final numbers were thinned out in race one because a bunch of top riders never finished. Checa went out after being put off by Rea; Guintoli was early into the gravel; then Rea crashed out himself; Giugliano fell; and after a coming-together with Haslam, Davies also crashed.

Fabrizio took his satellite BMW to fifth, fully half a minute behind the winner in a very untypical, strung-out WSBK leg. The twenty-five laps had seemed like more during 41 minutes of intense action. The race had been declared wet to start, but only faller Guintoli and gambler Camier opted for any Pirelli solution other than slicks. Only 16 finished, giving Camier a point, despite finishing two laps behind.

A race-two win for Melandri and a crash for Biaggi (under braking into the final corner on lap ten) saw the championship dynamic move up a gear. Biaggi's fall had taken out Haslam, Max drifting on to the green tarmac and not being able to stop in time. Canepa, Fabrizio and Aoyama also fell, but the most frantic crash was yet to come.

Behind the short one-second advantage enjoyed by a determined Melandri, Sykes was pushing to get back to the lead while trying to keep squabbling Laverty and Rea behind. Laverty was desperate to get his own podium this time after race one's enforced demotion; Rea needed the points just as badly after his fall. The result was a self-defeating pass and re-pass routine, which ended in a splintering of bodywork as Laverty high-sided spectacularly.

Rea had nowhere to go behind a crashing rival on the final lap, for the second weekend in a row, but he got back on to score seventh. The following Checa had to run off the track to avoid the melee and take fourth, leaving Davies to pounce and score his second podium of the year.

It was breathless stuff, a spectacular and invigorating end to the most draining and disorientating weekend of 2012.

Above left: Sykes, Melandri and Davies hopped up to podium status in the second race as Biaggi lost a bunch of points.

Above centre left: Biaggi took a controversial third in race one, courtesy of team orders issued to Laverty.

Left: Chaz Davies made up for a race-one off with a third place in race two.

Far left: St. Basil's provided a colourful backdrop for Haslam to conduct his PR duties in style.

Photos: Gold & Goose

Above: Checa fell in race one but remounted to finish 12th and garner some points.

Right: Laverty, winner Davies and Camier silenced the biggest 2012 guns for a time.

Far right: Leon Camier shone on a circuit that was more suited to his Suzuki. He leads Laverty and Rea on his way to third place in race two, after some brilliant overtaking.

Photos: Gold & Goose

Left: A rare Superpole for Biaggi.

Far left: Good mates Eugene Laverty and Chaz Davies engaged in vigorous wheel-to-wheel Aprilia action.

Below left: Mrs Max endured the highs and lows of her man's weekend, as the title fight got increasingly surreal and compacted.

Below: Max bites the dust in race two as Melandri and Davies stay on course.

Photos: Gold & Goose

WARM sunshine each day is not normally part of the September experience during a visit to the Eifel Mountains, but it was very welcome, the Nurburgring becoming one of the few races in 2012 where weather played a consistently benevolent part in proceedings.

The cream rose to the top very quickly, Biaggi, Sykes and Melandri leading the rest after Superpole. It was only Biaggi's fifth career Superpole win; evidently he had sharpened his focus since Russia.

Max scored his 21st career win in race one and, better still for his overall campaign, Melandri crashed out, falling from third while chasing the leader.

Sykes had made his usual early attack, but blamed an eventual drop to fourth on a tyre issue, despite trying the same soft rear in two successful race simulations.

That left Biaggi free and clear to win by 3.027 seconds from team-mate Laverty, who had got the better of satellite Aprilia rider Davies. Good mates off the track, Laverty and Davies gave not an inch under throttle-open conditions. Three Aprilias in the top three positions was uncharted, but lush territory for the Noale factory.

A remarkable ride from Camier, who had started from the back row because of a technical issue on the sighting lap, put him fifth.

Once again, lots of top riders never made it to the finish. Baz, Giugliano, Rea, Fabrizio and, of course, Melandri all fell and stopped. Even Checa, who usually is only involved in dramas of other riders' making, fell on his own while braking into the bizarre first downhill turn. He got back on to finish 12th.

Race two was another train wreck for the aspirations of many riders, with returnee McCormick eventually out in the pit lane, Haslam a faller again, Lundh a retiree, Fabrizio a technical victim and, most dramatically of all, Melandri a sinful binner (again), and in strange straight-line circumstances. He had recently taken the lead from Sykes, but took no points for the day.

For Biaggi, race two was also a disappointment, and more of a salvage operation, albeit with modest returns. He had fallen on lap one while entering the bumpy NGK chicane, when Sykes and Laverty had touched, forcing the latter to run wide suddenly, Biaggi lost the front and slid into the gravel beds uninjured. He got back into contention to record a lowly 13th place, but those three little points were potentially gold-plated.

With the top two out of the way, the first five home were all either British or Irish. The score was Celts two, Home Counties one in the final analysis, as Welshman Chaz Davies capitalised on his unusually good start to power to a clear first WSBK race victory for himself and his ParkinGO MTC team. Not bad for a combo that had won the WSS crown in 2011 and were rookies in WSBK.

Laverty was second, only just holding off Camier, who had delivered an impressive and somewhat miraculous ride. His run to third brought him and his team their first WSBK podium of the year. It would have been second had Laverty not re-passed him at the end.

Race two was a confidence booster for a FIXI Crescent Suzuki team who had had everything well worked out long before, but who had simply lacked competitive power from their Yoshimura engines. At the Nurburgring, with no massive straight and lots of corner varieties, Camier had been able to overcome that handicap in impressive style. Rea posted fourth, five seconds off the lead, while Sykes resisted Checa's breathless Ducati for fifth.

Above: Portimao flooding was biblical on Sabbath morning, in the worst season ever for weather intrusions.

Right: Marshals took cover wherever they could until the deluge abated.

Centre right: Eugene Laverty took his first win for Aprilia, the third of his career.

Top left: Genuine title threat Sykes took a win from Checa and Guintoli in race one.

Photos: Gold & Goose

Left: Rea took a second in race two for Honda's official team.

Below: Lorenzo Lanzi had an unexpected outing for the Effenbert squad.

Bottom right: In tricky conditions Canadian Brett McCormick entered the Portuguese version of dancing with the stars and took a truly fine fifth in race one.

Photos: Gold & Goose

ONCE again, the WSBK riders got to run on the biggest rollercoaster in the world, near the holiday playground of the Algarve – but only just. The circuit's financial problems were mollified by the intervention of the local government, ensuring that the planned 14 rounds in 2012 became a reality.

Stunning autumnal weather in practice and qualifying gave way to astonishingly harsh and sustained rain on race morning, some areas of track being submerged completely. It was yet another weather disaster to deal with in this year of interrupted sessions and races.

Once things finally got under way, the first attempt to run the WSBK race was ended when the Grillini BMW of Norino Brignola crashed, and then Melandri and Biaggi suffered a bizarre collision after six laps. Biaggi remained upright, but Melandri fell off and Chaz Davies unavoidably hit him amidships. The Italian ended up with broken ribs and a bruised kidney; he was hospitalised as the race was restarted, over only 16 laps, not 22, but also a whole hour late, after extensive track cleaning.

Sykes, who had to defend and keep up the pace at the same time, eventually won the opener, still held in tricky wet and changeable conditions. Checa had looked for a way around the Kawasaki, but couldn't find one and finished 0.3 second down. During winter tests, he had said that Sykes was likely to be one of the top men in 2012 and had been the first to take the Yorkshireman that seriously.

A rain specialist on another Ducati, Guintoli, slid into third place, one ahead of Biaggi. He'd had to work to keep the fully recovered and determined Brett McCormick and his Effenbert Liberty Racing Ducati behind him. McCormick showed what we had been missing for most of his rookie year, the wet conditions still a great leveller even in these days of electronics and ride-by-wire. Rea was sixth, the last rider in a group of three fighting for fourth place.

Baz, a wet winner at Silverstone, was disappointed at being 28 seconds down on Sykes, but happy to be in the top seven again.

In race two, a great fight between Northern Irish riders Laverty and Rea played out in warm and dry conditions that were a pleasant contrast to the previous race. They had been left to conduct the most recent of their on-track showdowns by the early oil bath suffered by Sykes' engine. It failed early on, and although it took Sykes some time to notice the problem – long enough to let three Aprilias escape to the lead – he then pulled in promptly with three laps gone. Despair for Kawasaki, redemption for Biaggi and Aprilia.

Davies fell, on lap five, leaving Laverty to complete the 22 laps only 0.162 second faster than Rea. The upshot was that Laverty joined Rea as one of the nine riders who would win a WSBK race in 2012, a remarkable total that was only beaten in the early days, when fierce wild-cards regularly topped the bill in America, Australia and Japan.

Behind the leading two in race two, Biaggi was a safe third, seven seconds ahead of Guintoli, with Checa fifth and 20 seconds down on Laverty.

Only 15 finished, in a race where lots of bikes never made it to the end under their own power. Davies was a faller again, but Haslam, Giugliano, Baiocco, Aoyama and Camier all pitted to depart the contest.

Portimao? It was something of a points suicide mission for Biaggi's closest challengers, despite a fine race-one win by Sykes.

Biaggi had an advantage of 30.5 points over Sykes entering the final round. Cruelly, the half-point would be the more important figure.

Above: Melandri's fortunes got worse in race one and he ended up in hospital, with painful but temporary injuries.

Above centre: SBK's Paolo Flammini with FIM president Vito Ippolito. Who knew what was about to happen?

Photos: Gold & Goose

MAGNY-COURS

From chump to champ. Biaggi fell in a wet race one *(above left)*, but bounced back to claim the title by the narrowest of margins.

Left: Roman Emperor Max the Second offers a victory proclamation to the Magny-Cours crowd.

Far left: Biaggi did just enough in race two to claim his second title in three years.

Bottom left: Tom Sykes (66), gave everything he could in his attempt to be champion. The Kawasaki rider battled with Jonathan Rea in race one before the Honda rider crashed out, but Sykes could only manage third. Even a crushing win in race two was not enough to deny Biaggi.

Photos: Gold & Goose

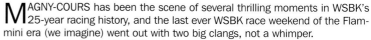

MAGNY-COURS has been the scene of several thrilling moments in WSBK's 25-year racing history, and the last ever WSBK race weekend of the Flammini era (we imagine) went out with two big clangs, not a whimper.

All that is good about WSBK racing culminated in France in October and won the hearts of the fairly large crowd, which was not put off by the appearance of – you guessed it – wet weather on race day.

Tom Sykes' ninth pole for Kawasaki, a remarkable feat in such a closely contested season, put him first away on the grid. A resurgent, but still injured Melandri was also on the front row, while Biaggi, showing as many jitters as he had done when he had won the title at Imola in 2010, was only on row three after a poor Superpole.

Any of the three could have won the championship still, and with the relative starting positions as they were, and a damp/wet/changeable track for race one, hope still sprung eternal for the official Kawasaki and BMW entries.

When Biaggi fell early on in race one, while still bolt upright on the brakes, the mood must have jumped in Sykes' and Melandri's hospitality units.

Sykes had his usual front-running go at winning race one, but with only a short warm-up to prepare wet settings, remarkable rain-master Guintoli found better ones and, significantly, Melandri showed his MotoGP winning experience and class to consign the Yorkshireman to third.

A one-off ride for regular WSBK entrant Maxime Berger at home on the Red Devils Roma Ducati team saw him fourth. Race one was Guintoli's third privateer Ducati win of 2012, all on a cooking 1098RS. The rules can't be that bad then, can they?

Haslam, broken right index finger and all, was fifth.

With the gap down to 14.5 points over Sykes and 18.5 over Melandri, Biaggi certainly was in fresh trouble – for a while.

Gathering all his experience and motivation, he made an okay launch in race two, but found himself seventh after the race had settled down. With Sykes in the lead, which he would maintain to the end, despite the determined efforts of Rea and Guintoli at various times, Biaggi had to move on up.

So did Melandri, but his hopes and his already battered body moved violently skywards, then suddenly earthwards when he suffered a fast and heavy high-side on lap six. He was out, of the race and the title challenge.

Down to two then.

Sykes, wearing a helmet painted with the number 17 badge of his paralysed former team-mate, Joan Lascorz, was doing all that he could out front. Biaggi, in passing Giugliano and the particularly determined Checa, did all he could further back in fifth place and had a half-point advantage.

Max ran off track slowly once, then regained the asphalt. Sykes had a big slide, but corrected, and all the while the laps counted down.

It was impossibly, wonderfully tense.

Sykes blasted across the line to win; Rea was over a second back and Guintoli took third, only 2.3 seconds adrift of Sykes.

Laverty, having slowed to let team-mate Biaggi past if he had to (he had been told to give way long before, but had worked out that it was not necessary), finished fourth, just ahead of Max. No matter, in finishing fifth, the Roman rider had achieved his championship goal.

It was his second WSBK title, by only half a point from Sykes. Half a point. Not even a complete integer. The maths were merciless.

The closest ever WSBK title finish was a fitting end to the closest and most even-handed season perhaps there had ever been.

Above: Frenchman Sylvain Guintoli may not be the most consistent rider in SBK, but when he is peaking even privateer status cannot stop him winning.

Left: Tom Sykes ran in a special tribute helmet to Joan Lascorz, which was later auctioned to raise funds for the paralysed Spanish rider.

Right: Brave Melandri (33) rode through the pain barrier and the quality field to take second place in race one. Cross-channel invader Leon Haslam (81) and plucky local privateer Maxime Berger (121) battle for position ahead.

Photos: Gold & Goose

2012 WORLD SUPERBIKE CHAMPIONSHIP RESULTS

Compiled by Peter McLaren

Round 1 · **PHILLIP ISLAND, Australia** · 26 February, 2012 · 2.762-mile/4.445km circuit · WEATHER: Race 1 · Dry · Track 42°C · Air 31°C; Race 2 · Dry · Track 54°C · Air 34°C

Race 1: 22 laps, 60.764 miles/97.790km
Time of race: 34m 13.963s · Average speed: 106.501mph/171.397km/h

Pos.	Rider	Nat.	No.	Entrant	Machine	Tyres	Time & Gap	Laps
1	**Max Biaggi**	ITA	3	Aprilia Racing Team	Aprilia RSV4 Factory	P		22
2	**Marco Melandri**	ITA	33	BMW Motorrad Motorsport	BMW S1000 RR	P	7.104s	22
3	**Sylvain Guintoli**	FRA	50	Team Effenbert Liberty Racing	Ducati 1098R	P	7.378s	22
4	**Tom Sykes**	GBR	66	Kawasaki Racing Team	Kawasaki ZX-10R	P	12.189s	22
5	**Jakub Smrz**	CZE	96	Liberty Racing Team Effenbert	Ducati 1098R	P	16.424s	22
6	**Michel Fabrizio**	ITA	84	BMW Motorrad Italia GoldBet	BMW S1000 RR	P	20.200s	22
7	**Jonathan Rea**	GBR	65	Honda World Superbike Team	Honda CBR1000RR	P	20.223s	22
8	**Hiroshi Aoyama**	JPN	4	Honda World Superbike Team	Honda CBR1000RR	P	24.108s	22
9	**Davide Giugliano**	ITA	34	Althea Racing	Ducati 1098R	P	28.072s	22
10	**Bryan Staring**	AUS	67	Team Pedercini	Kawasaki ZX-10R	P	34.232s	22
11	**Lorenzo Zanetti**	ITA	87	PATA Racing Team	Ducati 1098R	P	34.450s	22
12	**Leon Haslam**	GBR	91	BMW Motorrad Motorsport	BMW S1000 RR	P	35.648s	22
13	**Maxime Berger**	FRA	121	Team Effenbert Liberty Racing	Ducati 1098R	P	36.392s	22
14	**David Salom**	ESP	44	Team Pedercini	Kawasaki ZX-10R	P	41.500s	22
15	**Joan Lascorz**	ESP	17	Kawasaki Racing Team	Kawasaki ZX-10R	P	42.086s	22
16	Joshua Brookes	AUS	25	Crescent Fixi Suzuki	Suzuki GSX-R1000	P	42.605s	22
17	Leon Camier	GBR	2	Crescent Fixi Suzuki	Suzuki GSX-R1000	P	43.366s	22
18	Mark Aitchison	AUS	18	Grillini Progea Superbike Team	BMW S1000 RR	P	45.225s	22
19	David Johnson	AUS	20	Rossair AEP Racing	BMW S1000 RR	P	1m 08.782s	22
20	Niccolo Canepa	ITA	59	Red Devils Roma	Ducati 1098R	P	1m 10.440s	22
	Eugene Laverty	IRL	58	Aprilia Racing Team	Aprilia RSV4 Factory	P	DNF	19
	Ayrton Badovini	ITA	86	BMW Motorrad Italia GoldBet	BMW S1000 RR	P	DNF	14
	Carlos Checa	ESP	7	Althea Racing	Ducati 1098R	P	DNF	5
	Raffaele de Rosa	ITA	35	Team Pro Ride Real Game Honda	Honda CBR1000RR	P	DNS	0

Fastest race lap: Max Biaggi on lap 4, 1m 31.785s, 108.331mph/174.342km/h (record).

Race 2: 22 laps, 60.764 miles/97.790km
Time of race: 34m 26.728s · Average speed: 105.844mph/170.339km/h

Pos.	Rider	Time & Gap	Laps
1	**Carlos Checa**		22
2	**Max Biaggi**	5.707s	22
3	**Tom Sykes**	12.521s	22
4	**Jonathan Rea**	12.655s	22
5	**Leon Haslam**	18.179s	22
6	**Marco Melandri**	18.831s	22
7	**Maxime Berger**	18.939s	22
8	**Eugene Laverty**	19.478s	22
9	**Hiroshi Aoyama**	19.554s	22
10	**Niccolo Canepa**	26.289s	22
11	**Jakub Smrz**	26.479s	22
12	**Leon Camier**	29.145s	22
13	**Davide Giugliano**	36.482s	22
14	**Lorenzo Zanetti**	38.113s	22
15	**Joshua Brookes**	43.234s	22
16	Bryan Staring	43.526s	22
17	Raffaele de Rosa	53.929s	22
	Ayrton Badovini	DNF	11
	Joan Lascorz	DNF	10
	Sylvain Guintoli	DNF	9
	David Salom	DNF	8
	Michel Fabrizio	DNF	4
	David Johnson	DNF	4
	Mark Aitchison	DNF	1

Fastest race lap: Carlos Checa on lap 6, 1m 32.846s, 107.093mph/172.350km/h.
Previous lap record: Troy Corser, AUS (Yamaha), 1m 31.826s, 108.280mph/174.260km/h (2007).

Qualifying Times*

1	Sykes	1m 31.323s
2	Biaggi	1m 31.477s
3	Checa	1m 31.621s
4	Smrz	1m 31.783s
5	Guintoli	1m 31.832s
6	Camier	1m 31.904s
7	Canepa	1m 31.953s
8	Rea	1m 31.959s
9	Berger	1m 31.966s
10	Fabrizio	1m 32.068s
11	Laverty	1m 32.069s
12	Haslam	1m 32.082s
13	Melandri	1m 32.123s
14	Giugliano	1m 32.198s
15	Davies	1m 32.338s
16	Lascorz	1m 32.411s
17	Aoyama	1m 32.576s
18	Staring	1m 32.613s
19	Salom	1m 32.640s
20	Badovini	1m 32.703s
21	Zanetti	1m 32.782s
22	Brookes	1m 33.384s
23	Aitchison	1m 33.396s
24	De Rosa	1m 33.401s
25	Johnson	1m 33.816s

* After Q1 & Q2; Superpole cancelled.

Points

1	Biaggi	45
2	Melandri	30
3	Sykes	29
4	Checa	25
5	Rea	22
6	Guintoli	16
7	Smrz	16
8	Haslam	15
9	Aoyama	15
10	Berger	12
11	Fabrizio	10
12	Giugliano	10
13	Laverty	8
14	Zanetti	7
15	Canepa	6
16	Staring	6
17	Camier	4
18	Salom	2
19	Brookes	1
20	Lascorz	1

Round 2 · **IMOLA, Italy** · 1 April, 2012 · 3.067-mile/4.936km circuit · WEATHER: Race 1 · Dry · Track 11°C · Air 13°C; Race 2 · Dry · Track 18°C · Air 15°C

Race 1: 21 laps, 64.409 miles/103.656km
Time of race: 38m 6.264s · Average speed: 101.420mph/163.219km/h

Pos.	Rider	Nat.	No.	Entrant	Machine	Tyres	Time & Gap	Laps
1	**Carlos Checa**	ESP	7	Althea Racing	Ducati 1098R	P		21
2	**Tom Sykes**	GBR	66	Kawasaki Racing Team	Kawasaki ZX-10R	P	3.206s	21
3	**Leon Haslam**	GBR	91	BMW Motorrad Motorsport	BMW S1000 RR	P	5.593s	21
4	**Max Biaggi**	ITA	3	Aprilia Racing Team	Aprilia RSV4 Factory	P	6.519s	21
5	**Eugene Laverty**	IRL	58	Aprilia Racing Team	Aprilia RSV4 Factory	P	24.662s	21
6	**Marco Melandri**	ITA	33	BMW Motorrad Motorsport	BMW S1000 RR	P	27.261s	21
7	**Joan Lascorz**	ESP	17	Kawasaki Racing Team	Kawasaki ZX-10R	P	27.384s	21
8	**Lorenzo Zanetti**	ITA	87	PATA Racing Team	Ducati 1098R	P	28.299s	21
9	**Jonathan Rea**	GBR	65	Honda World Superbike Team	Honda CBR1000RR	P	34.067s	21
10	**Niccolo Canepa**	ITA	59	Red Devils Roma	Ducati 1098R	P	35.724s	21
11	**Jakub Smrz**	CZE	96	Liberty Racing Team Effenbert	Ducati 1098R	P	36.738s	21
12	**Maxime Berger**	FRA	121	Team Effenbert Liberty Racing	Ducati 1098R	P	37.257s	21
13	**John Hopkins**	USA	21	Crescent Fixi Suzuki	Suzuki GSX-R1000	P	50.418s	21
14	**Leandro Mercado**	ARG	36	Team Pedercini	Kawasaki ZX-10R	P	53.623s	21
15	**Ayrton Badovini**	ITA	86	BMW Motorrad Italia GoldBet	BMW S1000 RR	P	53.942s	21
16	Brett McCormick	CAN	68	Liberty Racing Team Effenbert	Ducati 1098R	P	54.139s	21
17	Mark Aitchison	AUS	18	Grillini Progea Superbike Team	BMW S1000 RR	P	57.944s	21
18	Hiroshi Aoyama	JPN	4	Honda World Superbike Team	Honda CBR1000RR	P	1m 06.233s	21
19	David Salom	ESP	44	Team Pedercini	Kawasaki ZX-10R	P	5 laps	16
	Michel Fabrizio	ITA	84	BMW Motorrad Italia GoldBet	BMW S1000 RR	P	DNF	8
	Davide Giugliano	ITA	34	Althea Racing	Ducati 1098R	P	DNF	8
	Sylvain Guintoli	FRA	50	Team Effenbert Liberty Racing	Ducati 1098R	P	DNF	1
	Chaz Davies	GBR	19	ParkinGO MTC Racing	Aprilia RSV4 Factory	P	DNF	1
	Leon Camier	GBR	2	Crescent Fixi Suzuki	Suzuki GSX-R1000	P	DNF	0
	Lorenzo Alfonsi	ITA	15	Team Pro Ride Real Game Honda	Honda CBR1000RR	P	DNF	0

Fastest race lap: Carlos Checa on lap 13, 1m 47.877s, 102.353mph/164.721km/h.

Race 2: 21 laps, 64.409 miles/103.656km
Time of race: 37m 57.571s · Average speed: 101.807mph/163.842km/h

Pos.	Rider	Time & Gap	Laps
1	**Carlos Checa**		21
2	**Tom Sykes**	1.935s	21
3	**Leon Haslam**	2.969s	21
4	**Max Biaggi**	3.346s	21
5	**Jonathan Rea**	18.925s	21
6	**Eugene Laverty**	21.180s	21
7	**Jakub Smrz**	21.392s	21
8	**Leon Camier**	23.797s	21
9	**Joan Lascorz**	24.219s	21
10	**Marco Melandri**	25.599s	21
11	**Sylvain Guintoli**	25.776s	21
12	**Maxime Berger**	26.004s	21
13	**Lorenzo Zanetti**	31.172s	21
14	**Chaz Davies**	33.837s	21
15	**Ayrton Badovini**	45.541s	21
16	Brett McCormick	50.807s	21
17	David Salom	51.083s	21
18	Mark Aitchison	57.833s	21
	Davide Giugliano	DNF	20
	Niccolo Canepa	DNF	17
	Leandro Mercado	DNF	14
	Hiroshi Aoyama	DNF	12
	Lorenzo Alfonsi	DNF	8
	John Hopkins	DNF	4
	Michel Fabrizio	DNF	0

Fastest race lap: Tom Sykes on lap 7, 1m 47.552s, 102.662mph/165.219km/h (record).
Previous lap record: Carlos Checa, SPA (Ducati) 1m 47.934s, 102.296mph/164.630km/h (2011).

Superpole

1	Sykes	1m 46.748s
2	Guintoli	1m 47.221s
3	Checa	1m 47.423s
4	Haslam	1m 47.458s
5	Biaggi	1m 47.611s
6	Melandri	1m 47.642s
7	Rea	1m 47.643s
8	Lascorz	1m 47.740s
9	Zanetti	1m 48.108s
10	Smrz	1m 48.137s
11	Laverty	1m 48.299s
12	Giugliano	
13	Berger	1m 48.267s
14	Canepa	1m 48.382s
15	Camier	1m 48.415s
16	Badovini	1m 48.631s

Points

1	Checa	75
2	Biaggi	71
3	Sykes	69
4	Haslam	47
5	Melandri	46
6	Rea	40
7	Smrz	30
8	Laverty	29
9	Guintoli	21
10	Berger	20
11	Zanetti	18
12	Lascorz	17
13	Aoyama	15
14	Camier	12
15	Canepa	12
16	Fabrizio	10
17	Giugliano	10
18	Staring	6
19	Hopkins	3
20	Davies	2
21	Mercado	2
22	Salom	2
23	Badovini	2
24	Brookes	1

SBK · OFFICIAL TIMEKEEPER · TISSOT

Round 3 · ASSEN, Holland · 22 April, 2012 · 2.822-mile/4.542km circuit · WEATHER: Race 1 · Wet · Track 7°C · Air 9°C; Race 2 · Wet · Track 12°C · Air 14°C

Race 1: 9 laps, 25.400 miles/40.878km

Time of race: 18m 38.395s · Average speed: 81.761mph/131.582km/h

Pos.	Rider	Nat.	No.	Entrant	Machine	Tyres	Time & Gap	Laps
1	Sylvain Guintoli	FRA	50	Team Effenbert Liberty Racing	Ducati 1098R	P		9
2	Davide Giugliano	ITA	34	Althea Racing	Ducati 1098R	P	2.633s	9
3	Carlos Checa	ESP	7	Althea Racing	Ducati 1098R	P	3.031s	9
4	Max Biaggi	ITA	3	Aprilia Racing Team	Aprilia RSV4 Factory	P	3.927s	9
5	Eugene Laverty	IRL	58	Aprilia Racing Team	Aprilia RSV4 Factory	P	4.374s	9
6	Michel Fabrizio	ITA	84	BMW Motorrad Italia GoldBet	BMW S1000 RR	P	11.359s	9
7	Jakub Smrz	CZE	96	Liberty Racing Team Effenbert	Ducati 1098R	P	26.412s	9
8	Niccolo Canepa	ITA	59	Red Devils Roma	Ducati 1098R	P	37.562s	9
9	Marco Melandri	ITA	33	BMW Motorrad Motorsport	BMW S1000 RR	P	49.896s	9
10	Leandro Mercado	ARG	36	Team Pedercini	Kawasaki ZX-10R	P	1m 08.847s	9
11	Maxime Berger	FRA	121	Team Effenbert Liberty Racing	Ducati 1098R	P	1m 11.760s	9
12	Hiroshi Aoyama	JPN	4	Honda World Superbike Team	Honda CBR1000RR	P	1m 13.988s	9
13	David Salom	ESP	44	Team Pedercini	Kawasaki ZX-10R	P	1m 27.019s	9
14	Lorenzo Zanetti	ITA	87	PATA Racing Team	Ducati 1098R	P	1 lap	8
15	Mark Aitchison	AUS	18	Grillini Progea Superbike Team	BMW S1000 RR	P	3 laps	6
	Ayrton Badovini	ITA	86	BMW Motorrad Italia GoldBet	BMW S1000 RR	P	DNF	6
	Chaz Davies	GBR	19	ParkinGO MTC Racing	Aprilia RSV4 Factory	P	DNF	3
	Leon Haslam	GBR	91	BMW Motorrad Motorsport	BMW S1000 RR	P	DNF	2
	John Hopkins	USA	21	Crescent Fixi Suzuki	Suzuki GSX-R1000	P	DNF	1
	Leon Camier	GBR	2	Crescent Fixi Suzuki	Suzuki GSX-R1000	P	DNF	0
	Jonathan Rea	GBR	65	Honda World Superbike Team	Honda CBR1000RR	P	DNF	0

Fastest race lap: Sylvain Guintoli on lap 9, 1m 57.793s, 86.254mph/138.813km/h.

Race 2: 22 laps, 62.090 miles/99.924km

Time of race: 36m 45.936s · Average speed: 101.328mph/163.072km/h

Pos.	Rider	Time & Gap	Laps
1	Jonathan Rea		22
2	Sylvain Guintoli	2.819s	22
3	Eugene Laverty	12.638s	22
4	Marco Melandri	12.762s	22
5	Leon Haslam	12.764s	22
6	Tom Sykes	20.393s	22
7	Ayrton Badovini	36.317s	22
8	Max Biaggi	37.747s	22
9	Davide Giugliano	41.350s	22
10	Michel Fabrizio	43.930s	22
11	John Hopkins	57.515s	22
12	David Salom	1m 32.593s	22
13	Hiroshi Aoyama	1m 33.576s	22
14	Leon Camier	1 lap	21
15	Leandro Mercado	1 lap	21
16	Mark Aitchison	1 lap	21
17	Carlos Checa	1 lap	21
	Lorenzo Zanetti	DNF	20
	Jakub Smrz	DNF	18
	Chaz Davies	DNF	11
	Maxime Berger	DNF	11
	Brett McCormick	DNF	9
	Niccolo Canepa	DNF	7

Superpole (declared Wet)

1	Sykes	1m 35.399s
2	Rea	1m 36.432s
3	Smrz	1m 36.566s
4	Guintoli	1m 36.875s
5	Checa	1m 37.156s
6	Fabrizio	1m 37.311s
7	Haslam	1m 37.592s
8	Hopkins	1m 37.913s
9	Melandri	1m 40.516s
10	Salom	1m 40.523s
11	Davies	1m 40.627s
12	Camier	1m 40.681s
13	McCormick	1m 41.962s
14	Laverty	1m 43.947s
15	Berger	1m 44.022s
16	Badovini	1m 44.500s

Points

1	Biaggi	92
2	Checa	91
3	Sykes	79
4	Guintoli	66
5	Melandri	66
6	Rea	65
7	Haslam	58
8	Laverty	56
9	Smrz	39
10	Giugliano	37
11	Fabrizio	26
12	Berger	25
13	Aoyama	22
14	Canepa	20
15	Zanetti	20
16	Lascorz	17
17	Camier	14
18	Badovini	11
19	Mercado	9
20	Salom	9
21	Hopkins	8
22	Staring	6
23	Davies	2
24	Aitchison	1
25	Brookes	1

Fastest race lap: Carlos Checa on lap 16, 1m 38.092s, 103.578mph/166.692km/h.
Lap record: Jonathan Rea, GBR (Honda), 1m 36.312s, 105.492mph/169.770km/h (2010).

Round 4 · MONZA, Italy · 6 May, 2012 · 3.590-mile/5.777km circuit · WEATHER: Race 2 · Dry · Track 25°C · Air 20°C · (Race 1 cancelled)

Race 2: 8 laps, 28.717m/46.216km

Time of race: 14m 8.800s · Average speed: 121.798mph/196.015km/h

Pos.	Rider	Nat.	No.	Entrant	Machine	Tyres	Time & Gap	Laps
1	Tom Sykes	GBR	66	Kawasaki Racing Team	Kawasaki ZX-10R	P		8
2	Leon Haslam	GBR	91	BMW Motorrad Motorsport	BMW S1000 RR	P	9.709s	8
3	Eugene Laverty	IRL	58	Aprilia Racing Team	Aprilia RSV4 Factory	P	10.119s	8
4	Marco Melandri	ITA	33	BMW Motorrad Motorsport	BMW S1000 RR	P	10.294s	8
5	Max Biaggi	ITA	3	Aprilia Racing Team	Aprilia RSV4 Factory	P	10.527s	8
6	Jonathan Rea	GBR	65	Honda World Superbike Team	Honda CBR1000RR	P	10.638s	8
7	Carlos Checa	ESP	7	Althea Racing	Ducati 1098R	P	10.899s	8
8	Davide Giugliano	ITA	34	Althea Racing	Ducati 1098R	P	12.195s	8
9	Jakub Smrz	CZE	96	Liberty Racing Team Effenbert	Ducati 1098R	P	13.199s	8
10	Ayrton Badovini	ITA	86	BMW Motorrad Italia GoldBet	BMW S1000 RR	P	19.372s	8
11	Hiroshi Aoyama	JPN	4	Honda World Superbike Team	Honda CBR1000RR	P	24.551s	8
12	Chaz Davies	GBR	19	ParkinGO MTC Racing	Aprilia RSV4 Factory	P	24.655s	8
13	Maxime Berger	FRA	121	Team Effenbert Liberty Racing	Ducati 1098R	P	24.662s	8
14	Lorenzo Zanetti	ITA	87	PATA Racing Team	Ducati 1098R	P	24.668s	8
15	Leon Camier	GBR	2	Crescent Fixi Suzuki	Suzuki GSX-R1000	P	24.810s	8
16	Leandro Mercado	ARG	36	Team Pedercini	Kawasaki ZX-10R	P	24.935s	8
17	Niccolo Canepa	ITA	59	Red Devils Roma	Ducati 1098R	P	25.278s	8
	Michel Fabrizio	ITA	84	BMW Motorrad Italia GoldBet	BMW S1000 RR	P	DNS	0
	Sylvain Guintoli	FRA	50	Team Effenbert Liberty Racing	Ducati 1098R	P	DNS	0
	Sergio Gadea	ESP	199	Kawasaki Racing Team	Kawasaki ZX-10R	P	DNS	0
	Mark Aitchison	AUS	18	Grillini Progea Superbike Team	BMW S1000 RR	P	DNS	0

Superpole (declared Wet)

1	Guintoli	1m 54.276s
2	Sykes	1m 54.990s
3	Melandri	1m 55.971s
4	Checa	1m 56.793s
5	Rea	1m 57.630s
6	Biaggi	1m 58.666s
7	Smrz	1m 59.718s
8	Giugliano	2m 00.645s
9	Hopkins	1m 59.489s
10	Laverty	1m 59.680s
11	Fabrizio	1m 59.681s
12	Camier	1m 59.845s
13	Badovini	1m 59.978s
14	Haslam	2m 00.093s
15	Salom	2m 00.602s
16	Davies	2m 01.772s

Points

1	Biaggi	97.5
2	Checa	95.5
3	Sykes	91.5
4	Melandri	72.5
5	Rea	70
6	Haslam	68
7	Guintoli	66
8	Laverty	64
9	Smrz	42.5
10	Giugliano	41
11	Berger	26.5
12	Fabrizio	26
13	Aoyama	24.5
14	Zanetti	21
15	Canepa	20
16	Lascorz	17
17	Camier	14.5
18	Badovini	14
19	Mercado	9
20	Salom	9
21	Hopkins	8
22	Staring	6
23	Davies	4
24	Aitchison	1
25	Brookes	1

Fastest race lap: Tom Sykes on lap 7, 1m 44.707s, 123.419mph/198.623km/h.
Lap record: Cal Crutchlow, GBR (Yamaha), 1m 42.937s, 125.542mph/202.040km/h (2010).

Round 5 · DONINGTON PARK, Great Britain · 13 May, 2012 · 2.500-mile/4.023km circuit · WEATHER: Race 1 · Dry · Track 31°C · Air 17°C; Race 2 · Dry · Track 31°C · Air 18°C

Race 1: 23 laps, 57.495 miles/92.529km
Time of race: 34m 26.736s · Average speed: 100.149mph/161.174km/h

Pos.	Rider	Nat.	No.	Entrant	Machine	Tyres	Time & Gap	Laps
1	Marco Melandri	ITA	33	BMW Motorrad Motorsport	BMW S1000 RR	P		23
2	Leon Haslam	GBR	91	BMW Motorrad Motorsport	BMW S1000 RR	P	0.728s	23
3	Tom Sykes	GBR	66	Kawasaki Racing Team	Kawasaki ZX-10R	P	1.609s	23
4	Jonathan Rea	GBR	65	Honda World Superbike Team	Honda CBR1000RR	P	1.819s	23
5	Max Biaggi	ITA	3	Aprilia Racing Team	Aprilia RSV4 Factory	P	2.102s	23
6	Carlos Checa	ESP	7	Althea Racing	Ducati 1098R	P	4.820s	23
7	Davide Giugliano	ITA	34	Althea Racing	Ducati 1098R	P	7.520s	23
8	Sylvain Guintoli	FRA	50	Team Effenbert Liberty Racing	Ducati 1098R	P	7.927s	23
9	Leon Camier	GBR	2	FIXI Crescent Suzuki	Suzuki GSX-R1000	P	15.144s	23
10	Michel Fabrizio	ITA	84	BMW Motorrad Italia GoldBet	BMW S1000 RR	P	16.065s	23
11	Ayrton Badovini	ITA	86	BMW Motorrad Italia GoldBet	BMW S1000 RR	P	19.805s	23
12	Chaz Davies	GBR	19	ParkinGO MTC Racing	Aprilia RSV4 Factory	P	20.170s	23
13	Maxime Berger	FRA	121	Team Effenbert Liberty Racing	Ducati 1098R	P	21.274s	23
14	Jakub Smrz	CZE	96	Liberty Racing Team Effenbert	Ducati 1098R	P	21.517s	23
15	Eugene Laverty	IRL	58	Aprilia Racing Team	Aprilia RSV4 Factory	P	26.920s	23
16	Loris Baz	FRA	76	Kawasaki Racing Team	Kawasaki ZX-10R	P	35.025s	23
17	Hiroshi Aoyama	JPN	4	Honda World Superbike Team	Honda CBR1000RR	P	39.193s	23
18	Lorenzo Zanetti	ITA	87	PATA Racing Team	Ducati 1098R	P	42.334s	23
19	Niccolo Canepa	ITA	59	Red Devils Roma	Ducati 1098R	P	43.554s	23
	Mark Aitchison	AUS	18	Grillini Progea Superbike Team	BMW S1000 RR	P	NC	21
	Peter Hickman	GBR	60	FIXI Crescent Suzuki	Suzuki GSX-R1000	P	NC	15
	Gary Mason	GBR	101	Team Pedercini	Kawasaki ZX-10R	P	DNF	14
	Leandro Mercado	ARG	36	Team Pedercini	Kawasaki ZX-10R	P	DNF	0

Fastest race lap: Max Biaggi on lap 6, 1m 28.992s, 101.124mph/162.743km/h.

Race 2: 23 laps, 57.495 miles/92.529km
Time of race: 34m 31.847s · Average speed: 99.902mph/160.777km/h

Pos.	Rider	Time & Gap	Laps
1	Jonathan Rea		23
2	Max Biaggi	0.508s	23
3	Tom Sykes	2.029s	23
4	Leon Camier	4.245s	23
5	Sylvain Guintoli	6.595s	23
6	Ayrton Badovini	17.469s	23
7	Chaz Davies	17.788s	23
8	Loris Baz	21.093s	23
9	Peter Hickman	21.866s	23
10	Hiroshi Aoyama	22.620s	23
11	Niccolo Canepa	26.764s	23
12	Lorenzo Zanetti	27.043s	23
13	Michel Fabrizio	28.390s	23
14	Mark Aitchison	56.618s	23
15	Leon Haslam	1m 20.196s	23
	Marco Melandri	DNF	22
	Leandro Mercado	DNF	19
	Gary Mason	DNF	14
	Maxime Berger	DNF	12
	Davide Giugliano	DNF	11
	Eugene Laverty	DNF	10
	Carlos Checa	DNF	0
	Jakub Smrz	DNF	0

Fastest race lap: Max Biaggi on lap 4, 1m 28.995s, 101.120mph/162.737km/h.
Lap record: Carlos Checa, SPA (Ducati) 1m 28.988s, 101.128mph/162.750km/h (2011).

Superpole

1	Sykes	1m 27.716s
2	Haslam	1m 27.864s
3	Melandri	1m 28.177s
4	Biaggi	1m 28.340s
5	Guintoli	1m 28.420s
6	Rea	1m 28.546s
7	Camier	1m 28.551s
8	Smrz	1m 28.785s
9	Checa	1m 28.497s
10	Badovini	1m 28.614s
11	Fabrizio	1m 28.683s
12	Laverty	1m 29.032s
13	Giugliano	1m 29.236s
14	Canepa	1m 29.319s
15	Berger	1m 29.371s
16	Davies	1m 29.493s

Points

1	Biaggi	128.5
2	Sykes	123.5
3	Rea	108
4	Checa	105.5
5	Melandri	97.5
6	Haslam	89
7	Guintoli	85
8	Laverty	65
9	Giugliano	50
10	Smrz	44.5
11	Fabrizio	35
12	Camier	34.5
13	Aoyama	30.5
14	Berger	29.5
15	Badovini	29
16	Canepa	25
17	Zanetti	25
18	Lascorz	17
19	Davies	17
20	Mercado	9
21	Salom	9
22	Baz	8
23	Hopkins	8
24	Hickman	7
25	Staring	6
26	Aitchison	3
27	Brookes	1

Round 6 · MILLER, USA · 28 May, 2012 · 3.049-mile/4.907km circuit · WEATHER: Race 1 · Dry · Track 32°C · Air 23°C; Race 2 · Dry · Track 42°C · Air 20°C

Race 1: 21 laps, 64.030 miles/103.047km
Time of race: 38m 21.283s · Average speed: 100.166mph/161.201km/h

Pos.	Rider	Nat.	No.	Entrant	Machine	Tyres	Time & Gap	Laps
1	Carlos Checa	ESP	7	Althea Racing	Ducati 1098R	P		21
2	Marco Melandri	ITA	33	BMW Motorrad Motorsport	BMW S1000 RR	P	2.313s	21
3	Max Biaggi	ITA	3	Aprilia Racing Team	Aprilia RSV4 Factory	P	5.338s	21
4	Jonathan Rea	GBR	65	Honda World Superbike Team	Honda CBR1000RR	P	5.517s	21
5	Eugene Laverty	IRL	58	Aprilia Racing Team	Aprilia RSV4 Factory	P	12.201s	21
6	Jakub Smrz	CZE	96	Liberty Racing Team Effenbert	Ducati 1098R	P	13.262s	21
7	Chaz Davies	GBR	19	ParkinGO MTC Racing	Aprilia RSV4 Factory	P	19.662s	21
8	Tom Sykes	GBR	66	Kawasaki Racing Team	Kawasaki ZX-10R	P	21.292s	21
9	Michel Fabrizio	ITA	84	BMW Motorrad Italia GoldBet	BMW S1000 RR	P	21.450s	21
10	Leon Haslam	GBR	91	BMW Motorrad Motorsport	BMW S1000 RR	P	23.433s	21
11	Davide Giugliano	ITA	34	Althea Racing	Ducati 1098R	P	23.696s	21
12	Sylvain Guintoli	FRA	50	Team Effenbert Liberty Racing	Ducati 1098R	P	24.752s	21
13	Leon Camier	GBR	2	FIXI Crescent Suzuki	Suzuki GSX-R1000	P	29.400s	21
14	Ayrton Badovini	ITA	86	BMW Motorrad Italia GoldBet	BMW S1000 RR	P	31.222s	21
15	Loris Baz	FRA	76	Kawasaki Racing Team	Kawasaki ZX-10R	P	32.966s	21
16	Maxime Berger	FRA	121	Team Effenbert Liberty Racing	Ducati 1098R	P	35.409s	21
17	Hiroshi Aoyama	JPN	4	Honda World Superbike Team	Honda CBR1000RR	P	52.153s	21
18	Shane Turpin	USA	14	Boulder Motor Sports	Ducati 1098R	P	1 lap	20
19	Jake Holden	USA	16	Grillini Progea Superbike Team	BMW S1000 RR	P	1 lap	20
	Leandro Mercado	ARG	36	Team Pedercini	Kawasaki ZX-10R	P	DNF	13
	Lorenzo Zanetti	ITA	87	PATA Racing Team	Ducati 1098R	P	DNF	11
	John Hopkins	USA	21	FIXI Crescent Suzuki	Suzuki GSX-R1000	P	DNF	7
	David Salom	ESP	44	Team Pedercini	Kawasaki ZX-10R	P	DNF	7
	Niccolo Canepa	ITA	59	Red Devils Roma	Ducati 1098R	P	DNF	6

Fastest race lap: Marco Melandri on lap 18, 1m 48.867s, 100.826mph/162.264km/h.

Race 2: 18 laps, 54.883 miles/88.326km
Time of race: 32m 56.257s · Average speed: 99.977mph/160.897km/h

Pos.	Rider	Time & Gap	Laps
1	Marco Melandri		18
2	Jonathan Rea	0.195s	18
3	Max Biaggi	2.137s	18
4	Chaz Davies	4.245s	18
5	Tom Sykes	9.534s	18
6	Eugene Laverty	9.798s	18
7	Davide Giugliano	11.891s	18
8	Leon Haslam	12.715s	18
9	Jakub Smrz	13.017s	18
10	Sylvain Guintoli	13.703s	18
11	Leon Camier	15.687s	18
12	Michel Fabrizio	21.923s	18
13	Ayrton Badovini	23.940s	18
14	Loris Baz	24.051s	18
15	Maxime Berger	33.897s	18
16	John Hopkins	38.692s	18
17	Leandro Mercado	47.703s	18
18	Jake Holden	1m 07.223s	18
19	Shane Turpin	1m 41.714s	18
	David Salom	DNF	13
	Carlos Checa	DNF	11
	Niccolo Canepa	DNF	9
	Lorenzo Zanetti	DNF	5
	Hiroshi Aoyama	DNS	0

Fastest race lap: Carlos Checa on lap 2, 1m 48.820s, 100.870mph/162.334km/h.
Lap record: Carlos Checa, SPA (Ducati) 1m 48.045s, 101.594mph/163.500km/h (2010).

Superpole

1	Smrz	1m 47.626s
2	Checa	1m 47.810s
3	Sykes	1m 48.062s
4	Giugliano	1m 48.220s
5	Rea	1m 48.563s
6	Guintoli	1m 48.568s
7	Biaggi	1m 48.794s
8	Laverty	No time
9	Melandri	1m 48.422s
10	Fabrizio	1m 48.566s
11	Davies	1m 48.669s
12	Zanetti	1m 49.929s
13	Haslam	1m 49.552s
14	Berger	1m 49.750s
15	Canepa	1m 49.818s
16	Hopkins	1m 49.966s

Points

1	Biaggi	160.5
2	Melandri	142.5
3	Sykes	142.5
4	Rea	141
5	Checa	130.5
6	Haslam	103
7	Guintoli	95
8	Laverty	86
9	Giugliano	64
10	Smrz	61.5
11	Fabrizio	46
12	Camier	42.5
13	Davies	39
14	Badovini	34
15	Berger	30.5
16	Aoyama	30.5
17	Canepa	25
18	Zanetti	25
19	Lascorz	17
20	Baz	11
21	Mercado	9
22	Salom	9
23	Hopkins	8
24	Hickman	7
25	Staring	6
26	Aitchison	3
27	Brookes	1

SBK **TISSOT**
OFFICIAL TIMEKEEPER

Round 7 · MISANO, Italy · 10 June, 2012 · 2.626-mile/4.226km circuit · WEATHER: Race 1 · Dry · Track 28°C · Air 25°C; Race 2 · Dry · Track 41°C · Air 27°C

Race 1: 24 laps, 63.022 miles/101.424km
Time of race: 38m 58.471s · Average speed: 97.020mph/156.139km/h

Pos.	Rider	Nat.	No.	Entrant	Machine	Tyres	Time & Gap	Laps
1	**Max Biaggi**	ITA	3	Aprilia Racing Team	Aprilia RSV4 Factory	P		24
2	**Carlos Checa**	ESP	7	Althea Racing	Ducati 1098R	P	0.305s	24
3	**Davide Giugliano**	ITA	34	Althea Racing	Ducati 1098R	P	4.503s	24
4	**Tom Sykes**	GBR	66	Kawasaki Racing Team	Kawasaki ZX-10R	P	8.858s	24
5	**Jonathan Rea**	GBR	65	Honda World Superbike Team	Honda CBR1000RR	P	11.627s	24
6	**Chaz Davies**	GBR	19	ParkinGO MTC Racing	Aprilia RSV4 Factory	P	12.258s	24
7	**Eugene Laverty**	IRL	58	Aprilia Racing Team	Aprilia RSV4 Factory	P	12.551s	24
8	**Sylvain Guintoli**	FRA	50	Team Effenbert Liberty Racing	Ducati 1098R	P	13.561s	24
9	**Jakub Smrz**	CZE	96	Liberty Racing Team Effenbert	Ducati 1098R	P	17.014s	24
10	**Leon Camier**	GBR	2	FIXI Crescent Suzuki	Suzuki GSX-R1000	P	18.361s	24
11	**Ayrton Badovini**	ITA	86	BMW Motorrad Italia GoldBet	BMW S1000 RR	P	20.029s	24
12	**Leon Haslam**	GBR	91	BMW Motorrad Motorsport	BMW S1000 RR	P	22.082s	24
13	**Maxime Berger**	FRA	121	Team Effenbert Liberty Racing	Ducati 1098R	P	22.966s	24
14	**Michel Fabrizio**	ITA	84	BMW Motorrad Italia GoldBet	BMW S1000 RR	P	27.014s	24
15	**Matteo Baiocco**	ITA	151	Barni Racing Team Italia	Ducati 1098R	P	31.133s	24
16	Hiroshi Aoyama	JPN	4	Honda World Superbike Team	Honda CBR1000RR	P	31.719s	24
17	John Hopkins	USA	21	FIXI Crescent Suzuki	Suzuki GSX-R1000	P	31.902s	24
18	Niccolo Canepa	ITA	59	Red Devils Roma	Ducati 1098R	P	43.770s	24
19	Leandro Mercado	ARG	36	Team Pedercini	Kawasaki ZX-10R	P	55.071s	24
20	Federico Sandi	ITA	23	Grillini Progea Superbike Team	BMW S1000 RR	P	6 laps	18
	Marco Melandri	ITA	33	BMW Motorrad Motorsport	BMW S1000 RR	P	DNF	21
	Loris Baz	FRA	76	Kawasaki Racing Team	Kawasaki ZX-10R	P	DNF	13
	David Salom	ESP	44	Team Pedercini	Kawasaki ZX-10R	P	DNF	12
	Lorenzo Zanetti	ITA	87	PATA Racing Team	Ducati 1098R	P	DNF	6

Fastest race lap: Carlos Checa on lap 8, 1m 36.080s, 98.390mph/158.343km/h (record).

Race 2: 24 laps, 63.022 miles/101.424km
Time of race: 39m 1.869s · Average speed: 96.879mph/155.912km/h

Pos.	Rider	Time & Gap	Laps
1	**Max Biaggi**		24
2	**Jonathan Rea**	5.355s	24
3	**Leon Haslam**	5.731s	24
4	**Marco Melandri**	7.004s	24
5	**Ayrton Badovini**	7.921s	24
6	**Michel Fabrizio**	17.291s	24
7	**Tom Sykes**	17.351s	24
8	**Loris Baz**	17.630s	24
9	**Jakub Smrz**	18.211s	24
10	**Matteo Baiocco**	28.131s	24
11	**Maxime Berger**	28.407s	24
12	**Hiroshi Aoyama**	38.060s	24
13	**Niccolo Canepa**	49.003s	24
14	**John Hopkins**	51.881s	24
15	**Leon Camier**	55.502s	24
16	Leandro Mercado	1m 06.361s	24
17	Federico Sandi	1m 29.918s	24
	Eugene Laverty	DNF	19
	Chaz Davies	DNF	15
	David Salom	DNF	7
	Davide Giugliano	DNF	5
	Carlos Checa	DNF	3
	Lorenzo Zanetti	DNF	2
	Sylvain Guintoli	DNF	1

Superpole (declared Wet)		
1	Sykes	1m 35.375s
2	Rea	1m 35.991s
3	Badovini	1m 36.083s
4	Giugliano	1m 36.147s
5	Smrz	1m 36.183s
6	Haslam	1m 36.283s
7	Laverty	1m 36.365s
8	Guintoli	1m 36.559s
9	Baiocco	1m 37.509s
10	Biaggi	1m 37.686s
11	Baz	1m 37.704s
12	Fabrizio	1m 37.796s
13	Melandri	1m 37.806s
14	Camier	1m 37.985s
15	Zanetti	1m 38.078s
16	Checa	1m 38.977s

Points		
1	Biaggi	210.5
2	Rea	172
3	Sykes	164.5
4	Melandri	155.5
5	Checa	150.5
6	Haslam	123
7	Guintoli	103
8	Laverty	95
9	Giugliano	80
10	Smrz	75.5
11	Fabrizio	58
12	Badovini	50
13	Camier	49.5
14	Davies	49
15	Berger	38.5
16	Aoyama	34.5
17	Canepa	28
18	Zanetti	25
19	Baz	19
20	Lascorz	17
21	Hopkins	10
22	Mercado	9
23	Salom	9
24	Hickman	7
25	Baiocco	7
26	Staring	6
27	Aitchison	3
28	Brookes	1

Fastest race lap: Max Biaggi on lap 3, 1m 36.557s, 97.904mph/157.561km/h.

Previous lap record: Max Biaggi, ITA (Aprilia), 1m 36.344s, 98.120mph/157.909km/h (2011).

Round 8 · ARAGON, Spain · 1 July, 2012 · 3.321-mile/5.344km circuit · WEATHER: Race 1 · Dry · Track 32°C · Air 22°C; Race 2 · Dry · Track 41°C · Air 25°C

Race 1: 20 laps, 66.412 miles/106.880km
Time of race: 39m 51.188s · Average speed: 99.985mph/160.911km/h

Pos.	Rider	Nat.	No.	Entrant	Machine	Tyres	Time & Gap	Laps
1	**Max Biaggi**	ITA	3	Aprilia Racing Team	Aprilia RSV4 Factory	P		20
2	**Marco Melandri**	ITA	33	BMW Motorrad Motorsport	BMW S1000 RR	P	0.278s	20
3	**Carlos Checa**	ESP	7	Althea Racing	Ducati 1098R	P	9.462s	20
4	**Chaz Davies**	GBR	19	ParkinGO MTC Racing	Aprilia RSV4 Factory	P	10.827s	20
5	**Eugene Laverty**	IRL	58	Aprilia Racing Team	Aprilia RSV4 Factory	P	15.708s	20
6	**Michel Fabrizio**	ITA	84	BMW Motorrad Italia GoldBet	BMW S1000 RR	P	27.597s	20
7	**Leon Haslam**	GBR	91	BMW Motorrad Motorsport	BMW S1000 RR	P	29.032s	20
8	**Davide Giugliano**	ITA	34	Althea Racing	Ducati 1098R	P	39.374s	20
9	**Leon Camier**	GBR	2	FIXI Crescent Suzuki	Suzuki GSX-R1000	P	40.887s	20
10	**Maxime Berger**	FRA	121	Team Effenbert Liberty Racing	Ducati 1098R	P	41.440s	20
11	**Niccolo Canepa**	ITA	59	Red Devils Roma	Ducati 1098R	P	42.056s	20
12	**Sylvain Guintoli**	FRA	50	Team Effenbert Liberty Racing	Ducati 1098R	P	42.369s	20
13	**Lorenzo Zanetti**	ITA	87	PATA Racing Team	Ducati 1098R	P	42.669s	20
14	**Hiroshi Aoyama**	JPN	4	Honda World Superbike Team	Honda CBR1000RR	P	48.010s	20
15	**John Hopkins**	USA	21	FIXI Crescent Suzuki	Suzuki GSX-R1000	P	49.752s	20
16	Jonathan Rea	GBR	65	Honda World Superbike Team	Honda CBR1000RR	P	54.590s	20
17	Norino Brignola	ITA	64	Grillini Progea Superbike Team	BMW S1000 RR	P	1m 59.653s	20
	Tom Sykes	GBR	66	Kawasaki Racing Team	Kawasaki ZX-10R	P	DNF	19
	Ayrton Badovini	ITA	86	BMW Motorrad Italia GoldBet	BMW S1000 RR	P	DNF	19
	David Salom	ESP	44	Team Pedercini	Kawasaki ZX-10R	P	DNF	12
	Leandro Mercado	ARG	36	Team Pedercini	Kawasaki ZX-10R	P	DNF	10
	Loris Baz	FRA	76	Kawasaki Racing Team	Kawasaki ZX-10R	P	DNF	8
	Jakub Smrz	CZE	96	Liberty Racing Team Effenbert	Ducati 1098R	P	DNF	0

Fastest race lap: Marco Melandri on lap 6, 1m 58.251s, 101.092mph/162.691km/h (record)

Race 2: 20 laps, 66.412 miles/106.880km
Time of race: 39m 59.200s · Average speed: 99.651mph/160.373km/h

Pos.	Rider	Time & Gap	Laps
1	**Marco Melandri**		20
2	**Eugene Laverty**	0.042s	20
3	**Chaz Davies**	0.446s	20
4	**Max Biaggi**	0.484s	20
5	**Jonathan Rea**	6.611s	20
6	**Leon Haslam**	7.491s	20
7	**Carlos Checa**	9.325s	20
8	**Tom Sykes**	10.444s	20
9	**Ayrton Badovini**	10.828s	20
10	**Davide Giugliano**	10.925s	20
11	**Michel Fabrizio**	21.955s	20
12	**Maxime Berger**	22.046s	20
13	**Sylvain Guintoli**	22.486s	20
14	**Lorenzo Zanetti**	42.801s	20
15	**Hiroshi Aoyama**	49.144s	20
16	David Salom	50.961s	20
17	Niccolo Canepa	1m 00.863s	20
18	Leandro Mercado	1m 14.149s	20
19	Norino Brignola	1m 53.388s	20
20	Loris Baz	1 lap	19
	Leon Camier	DNF	17
	John Hopkins	DNF	3

Superpole		
1	Sykes	1m 56.552s
2	Biaggi	1m 57.260s
3	Laverty	1m 57.592s
4	Haslam	1m 57.710s
5	Melandri	1m 57.784s
6	Rea	1m 58.033s
7	Checa	1m 58.243s
8	Davies	1m 58.485s
9	Guintoli	1m 58.073s
10	Badovini	1m 58.249s
11	Giugliano	1m 58.264s
12	Smrz	1m 59.160s
13	Fabrizio	1m 58.534s
14	Camier	1m 58.660s
15	Baz	1m 59.302s
16	Zanetti	1m 59.549s

Points		
1	Biaggi	248.5
2	Melandri	200.5
3	Rea	183
4	Checa	175.5
5	Sykes	172.5
6	Haslam	142
7	Laverty	126
8	Guintoli	110
9	Giugliano	94
10	Davies	78
11	Smrz	75.5
12	Fabrizio	73
13	Badovini	57
14	Camier	56.5
15	Berger	48.5
16	Aoyama	37.5
17	Canepa	33
18	Zanetti	30
19	Baz	19
20	Lascorz	17
21	Hopkins	11
22	Mercado	9
23	Salom	9
24	Hickman	7
25	Baiocco	7
26	Staring	6
27	Aitchison	3
28	Brookes	1

Fastest race lap: Marco Melandri on lap 3, 1m 58.950s, 100.497mph/161.735km/h.

Previous lap record: Carlos Checa, SPA (Ducati), 1m 58.862s, 100.572mph/161.850km/h (2011).

2012 WORLD SUPERBIKE CHAMPIONSHIP RESULTS

Round 9 — BRNO, Czech Republic · 22 July, 2012 · 3.357-mile/5.403km circuit · WEATHER: Race 1 · Wet · Track 24°C · Air 17°C; Race 2 · Dry · Track 26°C · Air 19°C

Race 1: 20 laps, 67.145 miles/108.060km

Time of race: 41m 59.808s · Average speed: 95.929mph/154.383km/h

Pos.	Rider	Nat.	No.	Entrant	Machine	Tyres	Time & Gap	Laps
1	**Marco Melandri**	ITA	33	BMW Motorrad Motorsport	BMW S1000 RR	P		20
2	**Tom Sykes**	GBR	66	Kawasaki Racing Team	Kawasaki ZX-10R	P	1.360s	20
3	**Loris Baz**	FRA	76	Kawasaki Racing Team	Kawasaki ZX-10R	P	1.948s	20
4	**Carlos Checa**	ESP	7	Althea Racing	Ducati 1098R	P	2.494s	20
5	**Eugene Laverty**	IRL	58	Aprilia Racing Team	Aprilia RSV4 Factory	P	3.832s	20
6	**Max Biaggi**	ITA	3	Aprilia Racing Team	Aprilia RSV4 Factory	P	7.139s	20
7	**Leon Haslam**	GBR	91	BMW Motorrad Motorsport	BMW S1000 RR	P	11.293s	20
8	**Michel Fabrizio**	ITA	84	BMW Motorrad Italia GoldBet	BMW S1000 RR	P	11.945s	20
9	**Maxime Berger**	FRA	121	Team Effenbert Liberty Racing	Ducati 1098R	P	18.988s	20
10	**Jakub Smrz**	CZE	96	Liberty Racing Team Effenbert	Ducati 1098R	P	19.117s	20
11	**Chaz Davies**	GBR	19	ParkinGO MTC Racing	Aprilia RSV4 Factory	P	22.938s	20
12	**Alessandro Polita**	ITA	53	Red Devils Roma	Ducati 1098R	P	1m 05.646s	20
13	**Norino Brignola**	ITA	64	Grillini Progea Superbike Team	BMW S1000 RR	P	1m 05.733s	20
14	**Leon Camier**	GBR	2	FIXI Crescent Suzuki	Suzuki GSX-R1000	P	1m 08.248s	20
15	**John Hopkins**	USA	21	FIXI Crescent Suzuki	Suzuki GSX-R1000	P	1m 12.120s	20
16	Lorenzo Zanetti	ITA	87	PATA Racing Team	Ducati 1098R	P	1m 13.057s	20
17	Viktor Kispataki	HUN	13	Prop-tech ltd	Honda CBR1000RR	P	3 laps	17
18	David Salom	ESP	44	Team Pedercini	Kawasaki ZX-10R	P	3 laps	17
	Jonathan Rea	GBR	65	Honda World Superbike Team	Honda CBR1000RR	P	DNF	18
	Leandro Mercado	ARG	36	Team Pedercini	Kawasaki ZX-10R	P	DNF	10
	Hiroshi Aoyama	JPN	4	Honda World Superbike Team	Honda CBR1000RR	P	DNF	10
	Davide Giugliano	ITA	34	Althea Racing	Ducati 1098R	P	DNF	4
	Ayrton Badovini	ITA	86	BMW Motorrad Italia GoldBet	BMW S1000 RR	P	DNF	0

Fastest race lap: Carlos Checa on lap 20, 2m 0.741s, 100.100mph/161.095km/h.

Race 2: 20 laps, 67.145 miles/108.060km

Time of race: 40m 12.837s · Average speed: 100.182mph/161.228km/h

Pos.	Rider	Time & Gap	Laps
1	**Marco Melandri**		20
2	**Tom Sykes**	0.140s	20
3	**Carlos Checa**	6.801s	20
4	**Max Biaggi**	9.840s	20
5	**Eugene Laverty**	11.775s	20
6	**Chaz Davies**	11.950s	20
7	**Leon Haslam**	12.547s	20
8	**Loris Baz**	13.088s	20
9	**Leon Camier**	18.141s	20
10	**Michel Fabrizio**	25.332s	20
11	**Davide Giugliano**	28.458s	20
12	**Jonathan Rea**	29.254s	20
13	**Jakub Smrz**	29.513s	20
14	**John Hopkins**	34.875s	20
15	**Maxime Berger**	41.861s	20
16	Lorenzo Zanetti	42.139s	20
17	Norino Brignola	1m 15.743s	20
18	Viktor Kispataki	1m 41.325s	20
	Alessandro Polita	DNF	10
	Ayrton Badovini	DNF	9
	David Salom	DNF	7
	Hiroshi Aoyama	DNF	4

Superpole (Superpole 2 declared Wet)

1	Sykes	1m 58.010s
2	Checa	1m 58.470s
3	Laverty	1m 58.741s
4	Giugliano	1m 58.789s
5	Melandri	1m 58.885s
6	Rea	1m 59.560s
7	Haslam	1m 59.583s
8	Fabrizio	1m 59.621s
9	Davies	1m 59.748s
10	Smrz	1m 59.871s
11	Salom	No Time
12	Badovini	No Time
13	Camier	1m 59.439s
14	Biaggi	1m 59.453s
15	Baz	1m 59.627s
16	Hopkins	1m 59.973s

Points

1	Biaggi	271.5
2	Melandri	250.5
3	Sykes	212.5
4	Checa	204.5
5	Rea	187
6	Haslam	160
7	Laverty	148
8	Guintoli	110
9	Giugliano	99
10	Davies	93
11	Fabrizio	87
12	Smrz	84.5
13	Camier	65.5
14	Badovini	57
15	Berger	56.5
16	Baz	43
17	Aoyama	37.5
18	Canepa	33
19	Zanetti	30
20	Lascorz	17
21	Hopkins	14
22	Mercado	9
23	Salom	9
24	Hickman	7
25	Baiocco	7
26	Staring	6
27	Polita	4
28	Brignola	3
29	Aitchison	3
30	Brookes	1

Fastest race lap: Tom Sykes on lap 2, 1m 59.728s, 100.947mph/162.458km/h.

Lap record: Cal Crutchlow, GBR (Yamaha) 1m 59.291s, 101.316mph/163.053km/h (2010).

Round 10 — SILVERSTONE, Great Britain · 5 August, 2012 · 3.667-mile/5.902km circuit · WEATHER: Race 1 · Wet · Track 27°C · Air 17°C; Race 2 · Wet · Track 34°C · Air 19°C

Race 1: 18 laps, 66.012 miles/106.236km

Time of race: 40m 46.128s · Average speed: 97.151mph/156.349km/h

Pos.	Rider	Nat.	No.	Entrant	Machine	Tyres	Time & Gap	Laps
1	**Loris Baz**	FRA	76	Kawasaki Racing Team	Kawasaki ZX-10R	P		18
2	**Michel Fabrizio**	ITA	84	BMW Motorrad Italia GoldBet	BMW S1000 RR	P	0.383s	18
3	**Ayrton Badovini**	ITA	86	BMW Motorrad Italia GoldBet	BMW S1000 RR	P	0.459s	18
4	**Jonathan Rea**	GBR	65	Honda World Superbike Team	Honda CBR1000RR	P	0.539s	18
5	**Carlos Checa**	ESP	7	Althea Racing	Ducati 1098R	P	1.012s	18
6	**Leon Haslam**	GBR	91	BMW Motorrad Motorsport	BMW S1000 RR	P	2.619s	18
7	**Marco Melandri**	ITA	33	BMW Motorrad Motorsport	BMW S1000 RR	P	6.123s	18
8	**Tom Sykes**	GBR	66	Kawasaki Racing Team	Kawasaki ZX-10R	P	9.170s	18
9	**Davide Giugliano**	ITA	34	Althea Racing	Ducati 1098R	P	19.022s	18
10	**Eugene Laverty**	IRL	58	Aprilia Racing Team	Aprilia RSV4 Factory	P	19.087s	18
11	**Maxime Berger**	FRA	121	Team Effenbert Liberty Racing	Ducati 1098R	P	29.840s	18
12	**Lorenzo Zanetti**	ITA	87	PATA Racing Team	Ducati 1098R	P	30.158s	18
13	**Hiroshi Aoyama**	JPN	4	Honda World Superbike Team	Honda CBR1000RR	P	44.222s	18
14	**Chaz Davies**	GBR	19	ParkinGO MTC Racing	Aprilia RSV4 Factory	P	1m 20.387s	18
15	**David Salom**	ESP	44	Team Pedercini	Kawasaki ZX-10R	P	1m 42.698s	18
16	Sylvain Guintoli	FRA	50	PATA Racing Team	Ducati 1098R	P	1 lap	17
17	Jakub Smrz	CZE	96	Liberty Racing Team Effenbert	Ducati 1098R	P	1 lap	17
	Max Biaggi	ITA	3	Aprilia Racing Team	Aprilia RSV4 Factory	P	DNF	17
	Leon Camier	GBR	2	FIXI Crescent Suzuki	Suzuki GSX-R1000	P	DNF	14
	Niccolo Canepa	ITA	59	Red Devils Roma	Ducati 1098R	P	DNF	14
	John Hopkins	USA	21	FIXI Crescent Suzuki	Suzuki GSX-R1000	P	DNF	10
	Norino Brignola	ITA	64	Grillini Progea Superbike Team	BMW S1000 RR	P	DNS	0
	David Johnson	AUS	20	Team Pedercini	Kawasaki ZX-10R	P	DNS	0

Fastest race lap: Ayrton Badovini on lap 6, 2m 6.764s, 104.149mph/167.612km/h.

Race 2: 8 laps, 29.339 miles/47.216km

Time of race: 19m 42.051s · Average speed: 89.353mph/143.799km/h

Pos.	Rider	Time & Gap	Laps
1	**Sylvain Guintoli**		8
2	**Loris Baz**	0.881s	8
3	**Jakub Smrz**	1.671s	8
4	**Eugene Laverty**	19.045s	8
5	**Maxime Berger**	22.116s	8
6	**Carlos Checa**	23.736s	8
7	**Chaz Davies**	24.690s	8
8	**Marco Melandri**	26.197s	8
9	**Jonathan Rea**	26.861s	8
10	**John Hopkins**	27.194s	8
11	**Max Biaggi**	29.243s	8
12	**Tom Sykes**	30.328s	8
13	**Michel Fabrizio**	32.746s	8
14	**Hiroshi Aoyama**	34.905s	8
15	**Niccolo Canepa**	35.849s	8
16	Lorenzo Zanetti	40.091s	8
17	Leon Haslam	58.530s	8
	Ayrton Badovini	DNF	7
	Davide Giugliano	DNF	6
	Leon Camier	DNF	4
	David Salom	DNF	1

Superpole (declared Wet)

1	Smrz	2m 20.810s
2	Camier	2m 20.846s
3	Guintoli	2m 21.385s
4	Haslam	2m 21.613s
5	Giugliano	2m 21.951s
6	Melandri	2m 21.960s
7	Checa	2m 23.356s
8	Sykes	2m 24.025s
9	Baz	2m 23.777s
10	Rea	2m 23.889s
11	Biaggi	2m 24.176s
12	Hopkins	2m 24.274s
13	Berger	2m 24.294s
14	Laverty	2m 25.260s
15	Fabrizio	2m 26.137s
16	Davies	2m 26.360s

Points

1	Biaggi	274
2	Melandri	263.5
3	Sykes	222.5
4	Checa	220.5
5	Rea	203.5
6	Haslam	170
7	Laverty	160.5
8	Guintoli	122.5
9	Fabrizio	108.5
10	Giugliano	106
11	Davies	99.5
12	Smrz	92.5
13	Baz	78
14	Badovini	73
15	Berger	67
16	Camier	65.5
17	Aoyama	41.5
18	Zanetti	34
19	Canepa	33.5
20	Lascorz	17
21	Hopkins	17
22	Salom	10
23	Mercado	9
24	Hickman	7
25	Baiocco	7
26	Staring	6
27	Polita	4
28	Brignola	3
29	Aitchison	3
30	Brookes	1

Fastest race lap: Loris Baz on lap 6, 2m 24.324s, 91.478mph/147.219km/h.

Lap record: Cal Crutchlow, GBR (Yamaha) 2m 05.259s, 105.401mph/169.626km/h (2010).

SBK **TISSOT**
OFFICIAL TIMEKEEPER

Round 11 **MOSCOW, Russia** · 26 August, 2012 · 2.442-mile/3.931km circuit · WEATHER: Race 1 · Wet · Track 18°C · Air 18°C; Race 2 · Dry · Track 37°C · Air 21°C

Race 1: 25 laps, 61.065 miles/98.275km
Time of race: 41m 7.852s · Average speed: 89.079mph/143.359km/h

Pos.	Rider	Nat.	No.	Entrant	Machine	Tyres	Time & Gap	Laps
1	**Tom Sykes**	GBR	66	Kawasaki Racing Team	Kawasaki ZX-10R	P		25
2	**Marco Melandri**	ITA	33	BMW Motorrad Motorsport	BMW S1000 RR	P	8.878s	25
3	**Max Biaggi**	ITA	3	Aprilia Racing Team	Aprilia RSV4 Factory	P	12.603s	25
4	**Eugene Laverty**	IRL	58	Aprilia Racing Team	Aprilia RSV4 Factory	P	13.027s	25
5	**Michel Fabrizio**	ITA	84	BMW Motorrad Italia GoldBet	BMW S1000 RR	P	29.582s	25
6	**Leon Haslam**	GBR	91	BMW Motorrad Motorsport	BMW S1000 RR	P	30.587s	25
7	**Niccolo Canepa**	ITA	59	Red Devils Roma	Ducati 1098R	P	32.170s	25
8	**Lorenzo Zanetti**	ITA	87	PATA Racing Team	Ducati 1098R	P	34.704s	25
9	**John Hopkins**	USA	21	FIXI Crescent Suzuki	Suzuki GSX-R1000	P	40.366s	25
10	**David Salom**	ESP	44	Team Pedercini	Kawasaki ZX-10R	P	41.143s	25
11	**Loris Baz**	FRA	76	Kawasaki Racing Team	Kawasaki ZX-10R	P	44.363s	25
12	**Ayrton Badovini**	ITA	86	BMW Motorrad Italia GoldBet	BMW S1000 RR	P	47.813s	25
13	**Hiroshi Aoyama**	JPN	4	Honda World Superbike Team	Honda CBR1000RR	P	52.650s	25
14	**Alexander Lundh**	SWE	5	Team Pedercini	Kawasaki ZX-10R	P	1m 20.273s	25
15	**Leon Camier**	GBR	2	FIXI Crescent Suzuki	Suzuki GSX-R1000	P	2 laps	23
16	David McFadden	RSA	69	Team Pedercini	Kawasaki ZX-10R	P	3 laps	22
	Chaz Davies	GBR	19	ParkinGO MTC Racing	Aprilia RSV4 Factory	P	DNF	23
	Davide Giugliano	ITA	34	Althea Racing	Ducati 1098R	P	DNF	13
	Jonathan Rea	GBR	65	Honda World Superbike Team	Honda CBR1000RR	P	DNF	10
	Carlos Checa	ESP	7	Althea Racing	Ducati 1098R	P	DNF	2
	Sylvain Guintoli	FRA	50	PATA Racing Team	Ducati 1098R	P	DNF	2

Race 2: 25 laps, 61.065 miles/98.275km
Time of race: 40m 14.677s · Average speed: 91.041mph/146.516km/h

Pos.	Rider	Time & Gap	Laps
1	**Marco Melandri**		25
2	**Tom Sykes**	0.976s	25
3	**Chaz Davies**	4.213s	25
4	**Carlos Checa**	5.954s	25
5	**Leon Camier**	13.568s	25
6	**Davide Giugliano**	15.173s	25
7	**Jonathan Rea**	23.125s	25
8	**Ayrton Badovini**	23.696s	25
9	**Loris Baz**	23.884s	25
10	**Lorenzo Zanetti**	24.096s	25
11	**Sylvain Guintoli**	24.881s	25
12	**John Hopkins**	39.643s	25
13	**David Salom**	1m 01.449s	25
14	**Alexander Lundh**	1m 36.596s	25
	Eugene Laverty	DNF	24
	Leon Haslam	DNF	9
	Max Biaggi	DNF	9
	Niccolo Canepa	DNF	1
	Michel Fabrizio	DNF	0
	David McFadden	DNF	0
	Hiroshi Aoyama	DNF	0

Superpole		
1	Checa	1m 34.193s
2	Sykes	1m 34.549s
3	Laverty	1m 34.562s
4	Haslam	1m 35.170s
5	Melandri	1m 35.224s
6	Rea	1m 35.237s
7	Biaggi	1m 35.253s
8	Giugliano	no time
9	Baz	1m 35.224s
10	Canepa	1m 35.255s
11	Hopkins	1m 35.678s
12	Aoyama	1m 35.834s
13	Davies	1m 35.629s
14	Zanetti	1m 35.678s
15	Guintoli	1m 35.689s
16	Salom	1m 35.798s

Points		
1	Melandri	308.5
2	Biaggi	290
3	Sykes	267.5
4	Checa	233.5
5	Rea	212.5
6	Haslam	180
7	Laverty	173.5
8	Guintoli	127.5
9	Fabrizio	119.5
10	Giugliano	116
11	Davies	115.5
12	Smrz	92.5
13	Baz	90
14	Badovini	85
15	Camier	77.5
16	Berger	67
17	Zanetti	48
18	Aoyama	44.5
19	Canepa	42.5
20	Hopkins	28
21	Salom	19
22	Lascorz	17
23	Mercado	9
24	Hickman	7
25	Baiocco	7
26	Staring	6
27	Polita	4
28	Lundh	4
29	Brignola	3
30	Aitchison	3
31	Brookes	1

Fastest race lap: Leon Haslam on lap 13, 1m 36.729s, 90.908mph/146.302km/h.

Fastest race lap: Marco Melandri on lap 10, 1m 35.794s, 91.795mph/147.730km/h (record).
Previous lap record: New circuit.

Round 12 **NURBURGRING, Germany** · 9 September, 2012 · 3.192-mile/5.137km circuit · WEATHER: Race 1 · Dry · Track 35°C · Air 24°C; Race 2 · Dry · Track 47°C · Air 25°C

Race 1: 20 laps, 63.840 miles/102.740km
Time of race: 38m 52.751s · Average speed: 98.520mph/158.553km/h

Pos.	Rider	Nat.	No.	Entrant	Machine	Tyres	Time & Gap	Laps
1	**Max Biaggi**	ITA	3	Aprilia Racing Team	Aprilia RSV4 Factory	P		20
2	**Eugene Laverty**	IRL	58	Aprilia Racing Team	Aprilia RSV4 Factory	P	3.027s	20
3	**Chaz Davies**	GBR	19	ParkinGO MTC Racing	Aprilia RSV4 Factory	P	3.127s	20
4	**Tom Sykes**	GBR	66	Kawasaki Racing Team	Kawasaki ZX-10R	P	12.306s	20
5	**Leon Camier**	GBR	2	FIXI Crescent Suzuki	Suzuki GSX-R1000	P	14.131s	20
6	**Sylvain Guintoli**	FRA	50	PATA Racing Team	Ducati 1098R	P	19.523s	20
7	**Leon Haslam**	GBR	91	BMW Motorrad Motorsport	BMW S1000 RR	P	27.017s	20
8	**Lorenzo Zanetti**	ITA	87	PATA Racing Team	Ducati 1098R	P	33.116s	20
9	**Ayrton Badovini**	ITA	84	BMW Motorrad Italia GoldBet	BMW S1000 RR	P	34.937s	20
10	**Hiroshi Aoyama**	JPN	4	Honda World Superbike Team	Honda CBR1000RR	P	39.132s	20
11	**Maxime Berger**	FRA	121	Team Effenbert Liberty Racing	Ducati 1098R	P	41.000s	20
12	**Carlos Checa**	ESP	7	Althea Racing	Ducati 1098R	P	41.125s	20
13	**John Hopkins**	USA	21	FIXI Crescent Suzuki	Suzuki GSX-R1000	P	46.925s	20
14	**Lorenzo Lanzi**	ITA	57	Liberty Racing Team Effenbert	Ducati 1098R	P	54.659s	20
15	**Brett McCormick**	CAN	68	Team Effenbert Liberty Racing	Ducati 1098R	P	56.342s	20
16	Alexander Lundh	SWE	5	Team Pedercini	Kawasaki ZX-10R	P	1m 09.730s	20
17	Norino Brignola	ITA	64	Grillini Progea Superbike Team	BMW S1000 RR	P	1m 43.679s	20
	Loris Baz	FRA	76	Kawasaki Racing Team	Kawasaki ZX-10R	P	DNF	17
	Marco Melandri	ITA	33	BMW Motorrad Motorsport	BMW S1000 RR	P	DNF	5
	Davide Giugliano	ITA	34	Althea Racing	Ducati 1098R	P	DNF	3
	Jonathan Rea	GBR	65	Honda World Superbike Team	Honda CBR1000RR	P	DNF	2
	Michel Fabrizio	ITA	84	BMW Motorrad Italia GoldBet	BMW S1000 RR	P	DNF	0
	David Salom	ESP	44	Team Pedercini	Kawasaki ZX-10R	P	DNS	0
	Niccolo Canepa	ITA	59	Red Devils Roma	Ducati 1098R	P	DNS	0

Race 2: 20 laps, 63.840 miles/102.740km
Time of race: 39m 0.327s · Average speed: 98.201mph/158.039km/h

Pos.	Rider	Time & Gap	Laps
1	**Chaz Davies**		20
2	**Eugene Laverty**	3.022s	20
3	**Leon Camier**	3.222s	20
4	**Jonathan Rea**	5.705s	20
5	**Tom Sykes**	7.304s	20
6	**Carlos Checa**	7.541s	20
7	**Davide Giugliano**	14.709s	20
8	**Loris Baz**	19.782s	20
9	**Ayrton Badovini**	19.925s	20
10	**Sylvain Guintoli**	20.028s	20
11	**Lorenzo Zanetti**	25.653s	20
12	**John Hopkins**	29.142s	20
13	**Max Biaggi**	29.579s	20
14	**Maxime Berger**	36.090s	20
15	**Hiroshi Aoyama**	40.912s	20
16	Lorenzo Lanzi	50.401s	20
17	Norino Brignola	3 Laps	17
	Brett McCormick	DNF	15
	Leon Haslam	DNF	9
	Marco Melandri	DNF	8
	Michel Fabrizio	DNF	8
	Alexander Lundh	DNF	6
	David Salom	DNS	0
	Niccolo Canepa	DNS	0

Superpole		
1	Biaggi	1m 53.855s
2	Sykes	1m 53.904s
3	Melandri	1m 53.912s
4	Laverty	1m 54.148s
5	Rea	1m 54.300s
6	Checa	1m 54.322s
7	Camier	1m 55.165s
8	Baz	1m 55.734s
9	Giugliano	1m 54.540s
10	Davies	1m 54.800s
11	Zanetti	1m 55.671s
12	Haslam	
13	Fabrizio	1m 56.290s
14	Hopkins	1m 56.530s
15	Canepa	no time
16	Salom	no time

Points		
1	Biaggi	318
2	Melandri	308.5
3	Sykes	291.5
4	Checa	247.5
5	Rea	225.5
6	Laverty	213.5
7	Haslam	189
8	Davies	156.5
9	Guintoli	143.5
10	Giugliano	125
11	Fabrizio	119.5
12	Camier	104.5
13	Badovini	99
14	Baz	98
15	Smrz	92.5
16	Berger	74
17	Zanetti	61
18	Aoyama	51.5
19	Canepa	42.5
20	Hopkins	35
21	Salom	19
22	Lascorz	17
23	Mercado	9
24	Hickman	7
25	Baiocco	7
26	Staring	6
27	Polita	4
28	Lundh	4
29	Brignola	3
30	Aitchison	3
31	Lanzi	2
32	McCormick	1
33	Brookes	1

Fastest race lap: Max Biaggi on lap 3, 1m 55.267s, 99.692mph/160.438km/h (record).

Fastest race lap: Carlos Checa on lap 4, 1m 56.148s, 98.935mph/159.221km/h.
Previous lap record: Jonathan Rea, GBR (Honda) 1m 55.392s, 99.583mph/160.260km/h (2010).

SBK OFFICIAL TIMEKEEPER

Round 13 PORTIMAO, Portugal · 23 September, 2012 · 2.853-mile/4.592km circuit · WEATHER: Race 1 · Wet · Track 22°C · Air 21°C; Race 2 · Dry · Track 32°C · Air 25°C

Race 1: 16 laps, 45.653 miles/73.472km

Time of race: 31m 42.011s · Average speed: 86.410mph/139.063km/h

Pos.	Rider	Nat.	No.	Entrant	Machine	Tyres	Time & Gap	Laps
1	**Tom Sykes**	GBR	66	Kawasaki Racing Team	Kawasaki ZX-10R	P		16
2	**Carlos Checa**	ESP	7	Althea Racing	Ducati 1098R	P	0.300s	16
3	**Sylvain Guintoli**	FRA	50	PATA Racing Team	Ducati 1098R	P	2.732s	16
4	**Max Biaggi**	ITA	3	Aprilia Racing Team	Aprilia RSV4 Factory	P	11.564s	16
5	**Brett McCormick**	CAN	68	Team Effenbert Liberty Racing	Ducati 1098R	P	11.771s	16
6	**Jonathan Rea**	GBR	65	Honda World Superbike Team	Honda CBR1000RR	P	11.792s	16
7	**Loris Baz**	FRA	76	Kawasaki Racing Team	Kawasaki ZX-10R	P	28.693s	16
8	**Hiroshi Aoyama**	JPN	4	Honda World Superbike Team	Honda CBR1000RR	P	29.581s	16
9	**Ayrton Badovini**	ITA	86	BMW Motorrad Italia GoldBet	BMW S1000 RR	P	31.507s	16
10	**Michel Fabrizio**	ITA	84	BMW Motorrad Italia GoldBet	BMW S1000 RR	P	31.587s	16
11	**Leon Camier**	GBR	2	FIXI Crescent Suzuki	Suzuki GSX-R1000	P	31.710s	16
12	**John Hopkins**	USA	21	FIXI Crescent Suzuki	Suzuki GSX-R1000	P	33.167s	16
13	**Eugene Laverty**	IRL	58	Aprilia Racing Team	Aprilia RSV4 Factory	P	37.843s	16
14	**Alexander Lundh**	SWE	5	Team Pedercini	Kawasaki ZX-10R	P	37.993s	16
15	**Matteo Baiocco**	ITA	151	Red Devils Roma	Ducati 1098R	P	39.397s	16
16	Lorenzo Zanetti	ITA	87	PATA Racing Team	Ducati 1098R	P	39.666s	16
17	Norino Brignola	ITA	64	Grillini Progea Superbike Team	BMW S1000 RR	P	42.434s	16
18	Lorenzo Lanzi	ITA	57	Liberty Racing Team Effenbert	Ducati 1098R	P	1m 00.356s	16
19	Leon Haslam	GBR	91	BMW Motorrad Motorsport	BMW S1000 RR	P	1 lap	15
	David Salom	ESP	44	Team Pedercini	Kawasaki ZX-10R	P	DNF	10
	Davide Giugliano	ITA	34	Althea Racing	Ducati 1098R	P	DNS	0
	Chaz Davies	GBR	19	ParkinGO MTC Racing	Aprilia RSV4 Factory	P	DNS	0
	Marco Melandri	ITA	33	BMW Motorrad Motorsport	BMW S1000 RR	P	DNS	0

Race 2: 22 laps, 62.773 miles/101.024km

Time of race: 38m 35.105s · Average speed: 97.613mph/157.0893km/h

Pos.	Rider	Time & Gap	Laps
1	**Eugene Laverty**		22
2	**Jonathan Rea**	0.162s	22
3	**Max Biaggi**	3.766s	22
4	**Sylvain Guintoli**	10.440s	22
5	**Carlos Checa**	20.153s	22
6	**Ayrton Badovini**	23.152s	22
7	**Loris Baz**	27.314s	22
8	**Michel Fabrizio**	35.682s	22
9	**Brett McCormick**	35.766s	22
10	**Lorenzo Lanzi**	38.311s	22
11	**John Hopkins**	47.814s	22
12	**Lorenzo Zanetti**	57.359s	22
13	**David Salom**	1m 11.035s	22
14	**Alexander Lundh**	1m 28.197s	22
15	**Norino Brignola**	1m 42.589s	22
	Davide Giugliano	NC	10
	Leon Camier	DNF	21
	Hiroshi Aoyama	DNF	9
	Matteo Baiocco	DNF	8
	Chaz Davies	DNF	4
	Tom Sykes	DNF	3
	Leon Haslam	DNF	2
	Marco Melandri	DNS	0

Superpole

1	Sykes	1m 41.415s
2	Checa	1m 41.780s
3	Laverty	1m 41.789s
4	Melandri	1m 42.015s
5	Biaggi	1m 42.140s
6	Haslam	1m 42.271s
7	Rea	1m 42.717s
8	Davies	1m 43.459s
9	Camier	1m 42.767s
10	Giugliano	1m 42.799s
11	Guintoli	1m 42.995s
12	Baz	1m 43.199s
13	McCormick	1m 43.410s
14	Badovini	1m 43.483s
15	Fabrizio	1m 43.863s
16	Salom	1m 44.479s

Points

1	Biaggi	347
2	Sykes	316.5
3	Melandri	308.5
4	Checa	278.5
5	Rea	255.5
6	Laverty	241.5
7	Haslam	189
8	Guintoli	172.5
9	Davies	156.5
10	Fabrizio	133.5
11	Giugliano	125
12	Baz	116
13	Badovini	116
14	Camier	109.5
15	Smrz	92.5
16	Berger	74
17	Zanetti	65
18	Aoyama	59.5
19	Hopkins	44
20	Canepa	42.5
21	Salom	22
22	McCormick	19
23	Lascorz	17
24	Mercado	9
25	Lanzi	8
26	Baiocco	8
27	Lundh	8
28	Hickman	7
29	Staring	6
30	Polita	4
31	Brignola	4
32	Aitchison	3
33	Brookes	1

Fastest race lap: Carlos Checa on lap 16, 1m 56.477s, 88.189mph/141.927km/h.

Fastest race lap: Eugene Laverty on lap 5, 1m 44.578s, 98.223mph/158.075km/h.
Lap record: Max Biaggi, ITA (Aprilia) 1m 42.774s, 99.948mph/160.850km/h (2010).

Round 14 MAGNY-COURS, France · 7 October, 2012 · 2.741-mile/4.411km circuit · WEATHER: Race 1 · Wet · Track 17°C · Air 17°C; Race 2 · Wet · Track 24°C · Air 20°C

Race 1: 23 laps, 63.040 miles/101.453km

Time of race: 44m 6.299s · Average speed: 85.759mph/138.016km/h

Pos.	Rider	Nat.	No.	Entrant	Machine	Tyres	Time & Gap	Laps
1	**Sylvain Guintoli**	FRA	50	PATA Racing Team	Ducati 1098R	P		23
2	**Marco Melandri**	ITA	33	BMW Motorrad Motorsport	BMW S1000 RR	P	6.127s	23
3	**Tom Sykes**	GBR	66	Kawasaki Racing Team	Kawasaki ZX-10R	P	16.595s	23
4	**Maxime Berger**	FRA	121	Red Devils Roma	Ducati 1098R	P	21.857s	23
5	**Leon Haslam**	GBR	91	BMW Motorrad Motorsport	BMW S1000 RR	P	25.149s	23
6	**Ayrton Badovini**	ITA	86	BMW Motorrad Italia GoldBet	BMW S1000 RR	P	32.778s	23
7	**Eugene Laverty**	IRL	58	Aprilia Racing Team	Aprilia RSV4 Factory	P	34.311s	23
8	**Davide Giugliano**	ITA	34	Althea Racing	Ducati 1098R	P	47.269s	23
9	**Claudio Corti**	ITA	71	Team Pedercini	Kawasaki ZX-10R	P	49.720s	23
10	**Loris Baz**	FRA	76	Kawasaki Racing Team	Kawasaki ZX-10R	P	50.192s	23
11	**Norino Brignola**	ITA	64	Grillini Progea Superbike Team	BMW S1000 RR	P	1 lap	22
12	**Michel Fabrizio**	ITA	84	BMW Motorrad Italia GoldBet	BMW S1000 RR	P	2 laps	21
13	**Jonathan Rea**	GBR	65	Honda World Superbike Team	Honda CBR1000RR	P	5 laps	18
	Leon Camier	GBR	2	FIXI Crescent Suzuki	Suzuki GSX-R1000	P	DNF	9
	Carlos Checa	ESP	7	Althea Racing	Ducati 1098R	P	DNF	7
	Hiroshi Aoyama	JPN	4	Honda World Superbike Team	Honda CBR1000RR	P	DNF	7
	Lorenzo Zanetti	ITA	87	PATA Racing Team	Ducati 1098R	P	DNF	5
	Max Biaggi	ITA	3	Aprilia Racing Team	Aprilia RSV4 Factory	P	DNF	2
	Chaz Davies	GBR	19	ParkinGO MTC Racing	Aprilia RSV4 Factory	P	DNF	

Race 2: 23 laps, 66.040 miles/101.453km

Time of race: 38m 15.725s · Average speed: 98.855mph/159.092km/h

Pos.	Rider	Time & Gap	Laps
1	**Tom Sykes**		23
2	**Jonathan Rea**	1.354s	23
3	**Sylvain Guintoli**	2.393s	23
4	**Eugene Laverty**	13.122s	23
5	**Max Biaggi**	13.955s	23
6	**Davide Giugliano**	18.229s	23
7	**Carlos Checa**	18.430s	23
8	**Chaz Davies**	26.648s	23
9	**Ayrton Badovini**	33.809s	23
10	**Leon Camier**	37.217s	23
11	**Maxime Berger**	38.871s	23
12	**Claudio Corti**	55.714s	23
13	**Lorenzo Zanetti**	57.621s	23
14	**Hiroshi Aoyama**	1m 05.487s	23
15	**Norino Brignola**	1 lap	22
	Leon Haslam	DNF	15
	Michel Fabrizio	DNF	8
	Marco Melandri	DNF	5
	Loris Baz	DNF	5

Superpole (declared Wet)

1	Sykes	1m 36.950s
2	Checa	1m 37.422s
3	Laverty	1m 37.516s
4	Melandri	1m 37.658s
5	Guintoli	1m 37.901s
6	Rea	1m 38.252s
7	Haslam	1m 38.280s
8	Davies	1m 38.425s
9	Camier	1m 38.072s
10	Biaggi	1m 38.095s
11	Fabrizio	1m 38.318s
12	Corti	1m 38.516s
13	Baz	1m 38.548s
14	Berger	1m 38.727s
15	Giugliano	1m 38.807s
16	Zanetti	1m 39.354s

Points

1	Biaggi	358
2	Sykes	357.5
3	Melandri	328.5
4	Checa	287.5
5	Rea	278.5
6	Laverty	263.5
7	Guintoli	213.5
8	Haslam	200
9	Davies	164.5
10	Giugliano	143
11	Fabrizio	137.5
12	Badovini	133
13	Baz	122
14	Camier	115.5
15	Smrz	92.5
16	Berger	92
17	Zanetti	68
18	Aoyama	61.5
19	Hopkins	44
20	Canepa	42.5
21	Salom	22
22	McCormick	19
23	Lascorz	17
24	Corti	11
25	Brignola	10
26	Mercado	9
27	Lanzi	8
28	Baiocco	8
29	Lundh	8
30	Hickman	7
31	Staring	6
32	Polita	4
33	Aitchison	3
34	Brookes	1

Fastest race lap: Sylvain Guintoli on lap 17, 1m 53.143s, 87.209mph/140.350km/h.

Fastest race lap: Davide Giugliano on lap 5, 1m 39.237s, 99.430mph/160.017km/h.
Lap record: Noriyuki Haga, JPN (Ducati), 1m 38.619s, 100.053mph/161.020km/h (2009).

Photo: Gold & Goose

2012 POINTS TABLE

Position	Rider	Nationality	Machine	Phillip Island/1	Phillip Island/2	Imola/1	Imola/2	Assen/1	Assen/2	Monza/1	Monza/2	Donington/1	Donington/2	Miller/1	Miller/2	Misano/1	Misano/2	Aragon/1	Aragon/2	Brno/1	Brno/2	Silverstone/1	Silverstone/2	Moscow/1	Moscow/2	Nürburgring/1	Nürburgring/2	Portimao/1	Portimao/2	Magny-Cours/1	Magny-Cours/2	Total Points
1	Max Biaggi	ITA	Aprilia	25	20	13	13	13	8	–	5.5	11	20	16	16	25	25	25	13	10	13	–	2.5	16	–	25	3	13	16	–	11	358
2	Tom Sykes	GBR	Kawasaki	13	16	20	20	–	10	–	12.5	16	16	8	11	13	9	–	8	20	20	8	2	25	20	13	11	25	–	16	25	357.5
3	Marco Melandri	ITA	BMW	20	10	10	6	7	13	–	6.5	25	–	20	25	–	13	20	25	25	25	9	4	20	25	–	–	–	–	20	–	328.5
4	Carlos Checa	ESP	Ducati	–	25	25	25	16	–	–	4.5	10	–	25	–	20	–	16	9	13	16	11	5	–	13	4	10	20	11	–	9	287.5
5	Jonathan Rea	GBR	Honda	9	13	7	11	–	25	–	5	13	25	13	20	11	20	–	11	–	4	13	3.5	–	9	–	13	10	20	3	20	278.5
6	Eugene Laverty	IRL	Aprilia	–	8	11	10	11	16	–	8	1	–	11	10	9	–	11	20	11	11	6	6.5	13	–	20	20	3	25	9	13	263.5
7	Sylvain Guintoli	FRA	Ducati	16	–	–	5	25	20	–	–	8	11	4	6	8	–	4	3	–	–	12.5	–	–	5	10	6	16	13	25	16	213.5
8	Leon Haslam	GBR	BMW	4	11	16	16	–	11	–	10	20	1	6	8	4	16	9	10	9	9	10	–	10	–	9	–	–	–	11	–	200
9	Chaz Davies	GBR	Aprilia	–	–	–	2	–	–	–	2	4	9	9	13	10	–	13	16	5	10	2	4.5	–	16	16	25	–	–	–	8	164.5
10	Davide Giugliano	ITA	Ducati	7	3	–	–	20	7	–	4	9	–	5	9	16	–	8	6	–	5	7	–	–	10	–	9	–	–	8	10	143
11	Michel Fabrizio	ITA	BMW	10	–	–	–	10	6	–	6	3	7	4	2	10	10	5	8	6	20	1.5	11	–	–	6	8	4	–	–	–	137.5
12	Ayrton Badovini	ITA	BMW	–	–	1	1	–	9	–	3	5	10	2	3	5	11	–	7	–	–	16	–	4	8	7	7	7	10	10	7	133
13	Loris Baz	FRA	Kawasaki	–	–	–	–	–	–	–	–	8	1	2	–	8	–	–	–	16	8	25	10	5	7	–	8	9	9	6	–	122
14	Leon Camier	GBR	Suzuki	–	4	–	8	–	2	–	0.5	7	13	3	5	6	1	7	–	2	7	–	–	1	11	11	16	5	–	–	6	115.5
15	Jakub Smrz	CZE	Ducati	11	5	5	9	9	–	–	3.5	2	–	10	7	7	7	–	–	6	3	–	8	–	–	–	–	–	–	–	–	92.5
16	Maxime Berger	FRA	Ducati	3	9	4	4	5	–	–	1.5	3	–	–	1	3	5	6	4	7	1	5	5.5	–	–	5	2	–	–	13	5	92
17	Lorenzo Zanetti	ITA	Ducati	5	2	8	3	2	–	–	1	–	4	–	–	3	2	–	–	4	–	–	–	8	6	8	5	–	4	–	3	68
18	Hiroshi Aoyama	JPN	Honda	8	7	–	–	4	3	–	2.5	–	6	–	–	4	2	1	–	–	3	1	3	–	–	6	1	8	–	–	2	61.5
19	John Hopkins	USA	Suzuki	–	–	3	–	–	5	–	–	–	–	–	–	2	1	–	–	1	2	–	3	7	4	3	4	4	5	–	–	44
20	Niccolo Canepa	ITA	Ducati	–	6	6	–	8	–	–	–	5	–	–	–	3	5	–	–	–	–	0.5	9	–	–	–	–	–	–	–	–	42.5
21	David Salom	ESP	Kawasaki	2	–	–	–	3	4	–	–	–	–	–	–	–	–	–	–	–	–	1	–	6	3	–	–	–	3	–	–	22
22	Brett McCormick	CAN	Ducati	–	–	–	–	–	–	–	–	–	–	–	–	–	–	–	–	–	–	–	–	–	–	1	–	11	7	–	–	19
23	Joan Lascorz	ESP	Kawasaki	1	–	9	7	–	–	–	–	–	–	–	–	–	–	–	–	–	–	–	–	–	–	–	–	–	–	–	–	17
24	Claudio Corti	ITA	Kawasaki	–	–	–	–	–	–	–	–	–	–	–	–	–	–	–	–	–	–	–	–	–	–	–	–	–	–	7	4	11
25	Norino Brignola	ITA	BMW	–	–	–	–	–	–	–	–	–	–	–	–	–	–	–	–	3	–	–	–	–	–	–	–	–	1	5	1	10
26	Leandro Mercado	ARG	Kawasaki	–	–	–	2	6	1	–	–	–	–	–	–	–	–	–	–	–	–	–	–	–	–	–	–	–	–	–	–	9
27	Lorenzo Lanzi	ITA	Ducati	–	–	–	–	–	–	–	–	–	–	–	–	–	–	–	–	–	–	–	–	–	–	–	–	2	–	6	–	8
28	Matteo Baiocco	ITA	Ducati	–	–	–	–	–	–	–	–	–	–	–	–	1	6	–	–	–	–	–	–	–	–	–	–	1	–	–	–	8
29	Alexander Lundh	SWE	Kawasaki	–	–	–	–	–	–	–	–	–	–	–	–	–	–	–	–	–	–	–	–	2	2	–	–	2	2	–	–	8
30	Peter Hickman	GBR	Suzuki	–	–	–	–	–	–	–	–	7	–	–	–	–	–	–	–	–	–	–	–	–	–	–	–	–	–	–	–	7
31	Bryan Staring	AUS	Kawasaki	6	–	–	–	–	–	–	–	–	–	–	–	–	–	–	–	–	–	–	–	–	–	–	–	–	–	–	–	6
32	Alessandro Polita	ITA	Ducati	–	–	–	–	–	–	–	–	–	–	–	–	–	–	–	–	4	–	–	–	–	–	–	–	–	–	–	–	4
33	Mark Aitchison	AUS	BMW	–	–	–	–	1	–	–	–	2	–	–	–	–	–	–	–	–	–	–	–	–	–	–	–	–	–	–	–	3
34	Joshua Brookes	AUS	Suzuki	–	1	–	–	–	–	–	–	–	–	–	–	–	–	–	–	–	–	–	–	–	–	–	–	–	–	–	–	1

TURKISH DELIGHT

By GORDON RITCHIE

Above: Kenan Sofuoglu returned for a third title, this time on a Kawasaki.

Top far right: Veteran Fabien Foret was a sometimes challenging team-mate.

Above far right: Podium at Portimao. Newly-crowned champion Sofuoglu (*left*) joins winner Jacques Cluzel and third-placed Foret.

Right: South African Supersport champion Ronan Quarmby on his Honda at Monza.

Photos: Gold & Goose

THERE were two special Ks in 2012, one man, one machine: Kenan Sofuoglu and his Kawasaki Ninja ZX-6R. Sofuoglu was not only the most successful Supersport world champion ever, after his third championship win, but also so dominant that the only rider capable of beating him looked to be himself. More of that later.

The ZX-6R received a certain amount of official support in a team that finished the season as the plain old Kawasaki Lorenzini team, after losing their early title sponsor at the mid-point of the season.

At one point, Lorenzini's funding situation appeared so dire that it seemed they would not see out the year. However, a combination of Sofuoglu foregoing his team salary and Kawasaki finding money from nowhere brought the championship back to life for the leading Kawasaki squad.

There was no shortage of competition for the Turkish rider, who had returned after a hard season in Moto2. There was a dire shortage of consistent competition, however, at least until nearer the end of the year, by which time it was too late. Among that competition was Fabien Foret (Kawasaki Intermoto Step Racing), in the Czech team that had run Gino Rea on Hondas the year before, while at PTR Honda, rookie WSS rider Jules Cluzel (from France via Moto2) proved a top addition. He was teamed with an outside bet for a top-six place, Ronan Quarmby.

More of an expected points prospect than either of those Honda men was Bogdanka PTR Honda rider Sam Lowes,

still looking for a full race win, but a potential champion if all went well.

Then, in a last-minute deal that kept Ten Kate in the WSS business they used to simply own, Broc Parkes gained a Ten Kate Racing Products Honda in a shoestring team with a peerless pedigree.

The only truly strong Yamahas were resting once more in the workshops of Yamaha Europe, so the ambitious Yakhnich team from Russia used their own R6s. There were no regular Suzukis, just a couple of good wild-cards.

There were decent Triumphs, but these were the Power Team by Suriano regular versions rather than the Daytona 675 R – long in the denture department, but still good enough for consistent top tens, and more.

Add in a smattering of other decent Honda and some Yamaha privateers, a limit of eight engines per season, and it looked a close thing to start. A big regular field of over 30 was heartening for the health of the class, even if all struggled for cash.

The long trip to Australia proved a worthwhile effort for Sofuoglu, who won first time out on his return, from the closely following Foret. Third was Parkes, two seconds back, with Cluzel not only a good fourth in his first ever Supersport race, but also third in qualifying, on a front row that was headed by Parkes.

The usual PI tyre controversy arose, some riders once again blistering tyres badly in race simulations, others not.

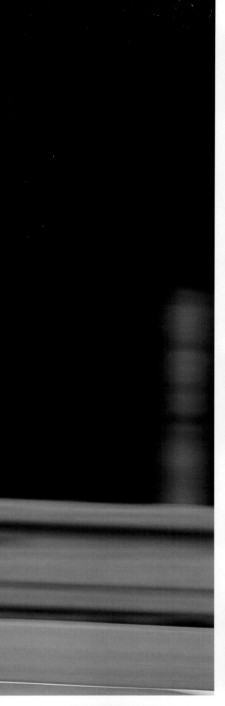

The race distance was cut to 15 laps, which made those who had tuned and tweaked to avoid overheating their tyres on the uniquely left-handed circuit utterly livid. In general terms, the top Kawasaki riders had been happy to go full distance. As ZX-6Rs were 1-2 in the shortened race, they saw justice being done, in their eyes at least.

Pleas for fair play, controversy and not a little regulatory interference were features of round two.

Sofuoglu was excluded at Imola, for ignoring ride-through signals after cutting a chicane and rejoining not in accordance with the regulations. He had crashed heavily and damaged his knee in recent tests, a problem that would never be fully resolved all year, and in the race he was on strong painkillers. He felt ill and tired as a result. He went from potential winner to no-scorer in this first, and by no means last, brush with officialdom.

The man who picked up the pieces was Foret – two wins from two for the Kawasaki guys, one for each of the main teams. Honda riders were second and third at Imola in the shapes of Lowes and Quarmby. Sheridan Morais (Kawasaki Lorenzini) and Cluzel had crashed from good positions in this race. Two rounds in, five different podium placers; it was shaping up well for the neutrals.

Round three added two completely new names to the podium list. Assen was wet, wet and wetter, and a surprise rain master emerged, in bizarre circumstances.

Ex-Superbike works Ducati rider and race winner Lorenzo Lanzi replaced PRORACE Honda rider Lukas Pesek for this weekend only. (Fresh out of retirement, Gabor Talmacsi would finally inherit the ride from Misano onwards.) A lowly 21st in dry qualifying suggested a tough return for Lanzi – until he swept all before him in the full wet and scored his first WSS win.

Second was Sofuoglu, but Vladimir Leonov (Yakhnich Yamaha) was good value for his first ever podium in this class, in third place, dancing through the rain and cold.

The first regular Honda rider win came one round later, and again in wet conditions. The slick track claimed Sofuoglu early on, but he got going again to rally to a remarkable third. Up front, Cluzel would stave off PTR team-mate Lowes to win his first ever WSS race, at only his fourth attempt.

Lowes finally took his own first win, on home tarmac, at Donington. He headed off Sofuoglu by 0.678 second in a dry race, with Cluzel third and Parkes eight seconds back. British-based Aussie Glen Richards took his Smiths Triumph Daytona to fifth in a good wild-card showing. There was better to come for the three-cylinder model, which had been born just down the road in Hinckley.

With no Supersport race in America, the next round was at Misano.

Sofuoglu was now naming Cluzel as his main title threat, and the Frenchman duly gave him most trouble as the Turkish star headed for victory in the warm and dry Adriatic air. Cluzel was only 1.228 seconds back.

Above: Sam Lowes (11) leads from the start at Misano.

Right: Stand-in rider Lorenzo Lanzi took a surprise wet win at Assen.

Far right: Alex Baldolini was the leading Triumph runner.

Opposite page, top: Frenchman Jules Cluzel, also fresh from Moto2, took the championship fight to Sofuoglu.

Opposite page, above: Broc Parkes headed the Ten Kate Honda team, but could do no better than fifth overall.

Opposite page, centre: The Superstock 600 European championship went to Michael van der Mark after a fierce fight with Riccardo Russo.

Opposite page, bottom: Sylvain Barrier (BMW) took victory in the Superstock 1000 FIM Cup.

Photos: Gold & Goose

A local scrap between WSS regulars Alex Baldolini (Power Team by Suriano Triumph) and Roberto Tamburini (Lorini Honda) was taken by the Daytona 675 rider. A full house of regular competing manufacturers now had a top-three to crow about, but the real battle was still between Kawasaki and Honda.

The Aragon race had far-reaching effects on the rest of the season. With Foret disturbing what Sofuoglu saw as his right to get to the front of the pack and win unhindered, the points leader made an astoundingly bad error of judgement at the end of the extra-long straight (SBK riders use the longer straight and tighter hairpin than MotoGP). In high winds that were already pushing riders around and sometimes into each other's paths, Sofuoglu gesticulated to Foret at top speed as he drew alongside. His wild head movement made his bike veer towards Foret in a dangerous manner that looked more reckless and risky every time it was replayed. Race Direction took a dim view and penalised him four positions, making him fifth at the end.

Lowes was confident that Sofuoglu would be penalised, so let him cross the line first. The Turk took his bike into the winners' circle, but was shooed out by officials. His rage and sense of injustice lasted all year, but nobody else really saw his point.

Foret was publicly vague about it all, but secretly infuriated. Maybe second place, 1.4 seconds from Lowes, assuaged his anger somewhat. The main benefactor of

Sofuoglu's penalty was actually his own team-mate, Morais, who took his only podium of his rookie year in third.

At Brno, a great three-way fight between Foret, Sofuoglu and Parkes saw them finish in that order, with only 0.434 second covering the trio. It was a sponsor pleasing home win for Foret's Czech team, and the joy was unbounded.

Normality (i.e., rain) returned at Silverstone.

Four Honda riders headed three Kawasakis on a damp track. Cluzel, Lowes and Parkes were covered by a tiny margin of 0.591 second, with Quarmby only two seconds away in fourth. Sofuoglu, Foret and Morais followed on.

The Russian race was held in basically dry conditions following morning rains. Back to form, Sofuoglu took the biggest Russian doll of all back to Turkey. Cluzel was five seconds down after a great attempt at sticking with him, but the large and enthusiastic crowd went into ecstasy when Leonov posted a strong third place, his second of the year. Foret was sixth.

Cluzel made an even better job of chasing Sofuoglu in a sun-kissed German round, but his defeat by 0.541 second may as well have been by a minute, as Sofuoglu put it all together in readiness for a coronation at the next round in Portugal. Foret was third, Parkes fourth and Lowes a crasher, restarting for 13th.

At Portimao, an early multi-rider fight was won by Cluzel, but by taking second place Sofuoglu was champion one round early. Foret was third in the race, Parkes fourth, the

Kenan Sofuoglu

Jules Cluzel

Sam Lowes

Fabien Foret

Broc Parkes

Sheridan Morais

Alex Baldolini

Ronan Quarmby

Vittorio Iannuzzo

Andrea Antonelli

Vladimir Leonov

Roberto Tamburini

top four covered by only 1.035 seconds after 20 laps of the intense track.

The title being decided brought liberation for all at the final round in Magny-Cours. Or more points peril for Sofuoglu, who T-boned another Kawasaki rider, MSD R-N Racing Team India man Dan Linfoot, under braking into the hairpin near the end. Linfoot got back on for fourth place, which was upgraded to a remarkable third after Sofuoglu was given a 25-second penalty – just enough to place him fourth. His sense of injustice was higher than ever, but again few could see his point.

Up front, Cluzel won his fourth race of the year, and at home, with Lowes making small errors that stopped him from getting any closer than 1.591 seconds in second.

It was a controversial end to a controversial 13-round season, but overall the best rider won, on a bike that was made good enough every weekend by a team that only just made it to the end.

Cluzel was second overall, Lowes third, Foret fourth and Parkes fifth. Sofuoglu is now the only rider in WSS history to have taken three crowns, two of them with Honda and now one with Kawasaki.

In the Superstock 1000 FIM Cup class, there were five different race winners, but Sylvain Barrier (BMW Motorrad Italia GoldBet) won the title on the last (wet!) day of the season. Eddi La Marra was second on his Barni Racing Team Italia Ducati 1199 Panigale, Jeremy Guarnoni third on his MRS Kawasaki and Bryan Staring (Team Pedercini Kawasaki) fourth by a sliver. Barrier won four races, Staring three; Guarnoni, La Marra and Lorenzo Savadori (Barni Racing Team Italia Ducati 1199 Panigale) all won a single contest apiece.

The Superstock 600 European Championship ended with a man-to-man fight – in all possible forms except off-track fisticuffs – between eventual champion Michael van der Mark (EAB Ten Kate Junior Team Honda) and Riccardo Russo (Team Italia FMI Yamaha). Russo tried to slow van der Mark and the action was often tactile, but van der Mark overcame the pressure to win both race and championship alike. He had won six races, and Russo the remaining four.

The eight-round KTM single-make European Junior Cup was won by Austrian rider Lukas Wimmer (MSC Schalchen KTM Duke 690).

Photos: Gold & Goose

ISLE OF MAN TT
MOUNTAIN MAN
By GARY PINCHIN

Above: A class apart. John McGuinness, on the gas at Glen Vine, opened his week with a Superbike win on the Padgetts Honda.

Photo: David Collister/photocycles.com

Right: Superbike top-three: Cameron Donald (*left*), John McGuinness and Bruce Anstey.

Photo: Gavan Caldwell

THE rain gods robbed John McGuinness of the chance of winning another Senior TT trophy in 2012 when bad weather caused the race, postponed from Friday to Saturday, to be cancelled for the first time since the event began in 1907.

McGuinness had already won the Superbike and Superstock races, and was looking to notch up TT victory number 20 to edge ever closer to Joey Dunlop's all-time record of 26 TT wins.

On the superbike, McGuinness was a class apart once again, but to listen to the talk before the meeting began, you might have thought his crown was in jeopardy.

That was before events contrived to stymie the efforts of some of his rivals, the strong top end of the TT favourites list taking a few knocks before practice week had even started on the famed 37.73-mile Mountain course.

There was the usual hype surrounding Guy Martin, poised to take his first ever TT victory, but he was still far from hundred per cent in body or mind after his monumental NW200 crash. Tyco TAS Suzuki team-mate Conor Cummins was in a worse physical state, with a badly smashed hand, also from the North West.

Michael Dunlop had hit an all-time psychological low at the big Irish race, too. With so little staff, he was struggling to cope with the workload of not just maintaining all the bikes, but also getting them all to work on the track, especially the supersport-spec Suzuki, which, despite having a Stephen Fleming-built engine (the same tuning guru who works for TAS Suzuki and who built Alastair Seeley's NW200-winning GSX-R600), simply was not on the pace.

At the TT, help arrived. Dunlop's former sparring partner and sponsor, Gary Ryan, was back in the awning. The long-term allies had split during the winter (some said acrimoniously), but Ryan was now on hand to help. As Dunlop quipped, "It's what real friends do."

Ryan brought with him a brand-new Yamaha R6 that the pair had started building back home, but he had been left to complete the machine while the rider travelled to the Island to start practice week.

William Dunlop was still nursing an ankle injury, a reminder of his crash at the North West, but the consensus was that while the Wilson Craig Honda rider was a potential threat on a 600 (as ever), even if fit he still lacked the track time on a superbike to pose a real threat.

Bruce Anstey, though, was a rider no one could overlook, and even McGuinness acknowledged that the 43-year-old Kiwi remained a potential winner, particularly since joining Padgetts a year earlier, a move that, some would say, has rejuvenated his career.

Gary Johnson was also racing in Padgetts colours in the Superbike class, but had the superstocker he had ridden in the National championship for Samsung Honda (albeit in

Honda TT Legends colours) and his own 600 backed by Call-Mac Scaffolding/Lincs Lifting. Following his first ever TT win in 2011's second Supersport, and his tight link with Honda and Padgetts, the feeling was that 2012 could have been the year for him to really assert himself on the Mountain course.

The other major player was Cameron Donald, the Aussie adopting a different approach to what he had suggested could be his last TT. Normally outgoing, Donald kept to himself throughout practice week, turning up at the Wilson Craig awning at the last minute each evening of practice to ride the Honda.

He had finished on the podium in two of the NW200 races and had been close in the others, but with talk of retirement from the TT in the air, there was a feeling that he was back to his very best, with a good chance of taking the races to McGuinness. Adding credence to the theory, the Wilson Craig team had been revamped and now benefited from having Mark 'Brains' Woodage overseeing technical development, while Chris Mehew continued to build the team's engines.

Practice week opened with a bang in the Superbike class: McGuinness fastest at 128.267mph. First night out, this was a stunning start, creating a real buzz on the Island, which normally only occurs later in the week when the lap times really begin to tumble.

Donald was second at 126.379; Anstey was third at 125.306; and then came Simon Andrews, in his second TT and now part of the Honda TT Legends team. He showed no signs that he was still recovering from his monster crash at Snetterton the previous year (when surgeons had considered amputating his leg). Another big off during tyre testing at Castle Combe had re-broken the leg, but somehow he had been passed fit to race at the North West and now was gung-ho for a good run on the Island.

Through practice week, McGuinness continued to hold the upper hand. He was the only rider to clock 130mph, actually 130.079mph on Wednesday. Anstey wound up second fastest at 129.566, Donald third (129.075), Martin fourth (128.866), Rutter fifth on the Bathams MSS Kawasaki (128.072), and the impressive James Hiller sixth (127.811), riding a Bournemouth Kawasaki.

Michael Dunlop had struggled to get his Honda to handle and occupied seventh place on the time sheets, while Andrews had dropped to ninth behind perennial privateer Dan Stewart on a Wilcox Honda.

Johnson was tenth, far from happy on the Dunlop-shod Padgetts Honda, while the top 12 were rounded out by

William Dunlop and Ian Hutchinson, the latter's best of 126.760mph suggesting that he was still far from fit (which he wasn't); in reality, he was far from happy with the set-up of the Swan Yamaha R1.

Rutter topped the Superstock time sheets with a lap of 128.072 on Thursday aboard his NW200-winning ZX-10R. William Dunlop was a surprise second at 126.913 from Anstey, McGuinness, Johnson and Ryan Farquhar.

Donald was tenth, Andrews 13th and Michael Dunlop a lowly 17th, unhappy with the speed and handling of his Ard Na Mara/McAdoo Kawasaki.

In Supersport, however, the Dunlop brothers reigned supreme throughout practice week, William topping the time sheets after a 126.184mph run on Wednesday, while Michael clocked a 124.656 on his new Yamaha.

Donald underlined the competitive nature of the Wilson Craig Honda CBR600RRs by backing up his team-mate with the third fastest time. Anstey, Johnson (who seemed beset by handling problems), Dan Kneen, Martin, McGuinness, veteran Ian Lougher and Farquhar completed the top ten.

Hillier was the surprise of the new Lightweight class (for 650cc production-based twins on treaded tyres), posting fastest time with his Bournemouth Kawasaki at 114.770mph from William Dunlop and Ian Lougher. Ben Wylie was first Suzuki and fourth fastest, followed by Kawasaki-mounted Russ Mountford, Ryan Farquhar, Adrian Archibald, TT rookie Jamie Hamilton and Rutter – the last two on KMR Kawasakis built by Farquhar.

SUPERBIKE

The Superbike TT sets the trend for the week, and McGuiness was on a charge from the start. He led Donald by 1.31 seconds at Glen Helen, with Martin another 0.6 second adrift; Hiller, Rutter and Anstey filled the top six.

Donald, though, pegged back McGuiness on the run to Ballaugh and had taken a tenuous 0.13-second lead by the time they reached the Bungalow.

Crossing the line at the end of the first lap, it was still Donald by 0.21 second (130.258mph lap from a standing start) from McGuinness (130.232mph); Martin was in the mix, too, with a 130.135mph first lap, just 0.98 second down on the leaders. Gary Johnson was fourth, but now 10.19 seconds off the leader's pace, from Anstey and Hillier.

News came that Andrews was off at Graham's and had suffered a shoulder injury, but was conscious.

Michael Rutter retired to the pits, his machine suffering from a broken gearbox – the legacy of not having the bike in gear on the start line when he had the revs ready to launch, and then stomping it into gear. Farquhar was another early retirement.

Michael Dunlop was down in 11th at the end of the lap. His Honda had blown a head gasket when the team warmed it up, so he was faced with no option but to ride his super-stock Kawasaki.

By the time the leaders reached Glen Helen on lap two, McGuinness was back in the lead from Donald by 0.2 second, while Martin had dropped off the pace and was 2.6 seconds behind the second Honda.

Donald kept McGuinness honest until the end of the second lap, when the latter pulled out 2.16 seconds on the run over the Mountain to lap at 130.382mph (Donald recorded 130.087mph).

McGuinness's Honda TT Legends crew performed another of their legendary slick pit stops to give him a six-second cushion over the Wilson Craig Honda rider. Martin was third, four seconds further back. Donald pegged the Honda TT Legends star back again, and by Glen Helen it was 3.88 seconds, but at the Bungalow it was back up to 6.35 seconds, McGuinness now firmly in control.

By the next round of pit stops at the end of the fourth lap, McGuinness enjoyed a 9.88-second lead going into the pits and 13 seconds coming out; then it was a case of defending his lead.

McGuinness crossed the line for his 18th TT victory with 14.86 seconds in hand over Donald. "That was pretty special," he said. "I set off number one and it's just me versus the track and riding to my [pit] boards. I hit all the apexes and felt strong everywhere. We had two fantastic pit stops: the boys, the same crew I've had since 2006, seem to wave a magic wand in there.

"I got an okay start, but there were lots of leaves down, foliage everywhere. I had a bit of a go on lap two, plus laps three and five when we had a full fuel load. Once you get a buffer, it's hard [for your rival] to come back.

"I'm 40, married and I should be slowing down. I'm a bit of a fattie, but I'm still enjoying my racing. The job's ace. Big

thanks to all the spectators out there. I came into the Creg and Hillberry and got real emotional. So many people were cheering."

No racer is happy to finish second, but Donald was magnanimous in defeat. "It's a shame I couldn't push him to the end, but it was a great race. I figured John had it all worked out from the pit stops.

"In the middle of the race, he put a buffer on us, so I knew I had no chance to close that. I just rode safe and learned some. It's the first time we've run six laps with the bike, so we know what changes we can make for the Senior. There were so many Australian flags out there, so that made it really special for me."

Anstey became faster as the race progressed and, despite a glitch in the pit stop when his Honda refused initially to fire, he took third – a 23rd TT podium, having got the better of Martin on the fifth lap on the run from Ramsey to the Bungalow. With a 130.234mph final lap, he finished almost ten seconds up on the Suzuki rider, who later complained of no consistency in grip from his Pirellis all race. He had to run the final four laps of the race on the same rear anyway, after the thread on his rear axle had been damaged by grit during the first pit stop.

But Anstey didn't get a clear ride either. "My bike wouldn't fire up in the pits and my visor wasn't on properly," he said. "I slowed at Quarter Bridge to make sure it was okay.

"The first couple of laps were horrible and I struggled to find a rhythm. It was really gusty out there, but we had a good race and battled away. I lost sixth gear on the last lap, so I just had to bring it home. We've never had much luck on the superbike at the TT, so third is good for me."

SUPERSPORT – Race One

As he prepared for the first Supersport TT of the week, pre-race favourite William Dunlop told Manx Radio, "It's going to be hard work here. There's four or five lads who can win. It's handy to have the speed, which we have. I know I can do one quick lap, but I'm not sure I can do four. My ankle is still sore. We're going into unknown territory."

Dunlop started fast, but brother Michael started faster and

was running away with the race at the end of lap one, 10.06 seconds ahead of Donald, with William third, just tenths off his team-mate. Gary Johnson was fourth from Anstey; Kneen completed the top six. Guy Martin was an early retirement, his Tyco Suzuki not revving out.

Lap two, and Michael Dunlop smashed the lap record at 126.948mph. He was 21.42 seconds clear of Johnson, while William was still third, Anstey fourth and Donald fifth.

But by Glen Helen on lap three, Johnson was leading by 3.49 seconds from Donald, Anstey and William Dunlop; Michael's R6 had blown up at Ballig Bridge.

Towards the end of the third lap, slow-starting Anstey was up to second and eating into Johnson's lead, down to 2.06 seconds at the end of the lap. He'd halved that by Glen Helen, but Johnson countered and was 2.09 seconds in front at Ballaugh. But Anstey wasn't done. He closed the gap again, with the charging Donald 0.22 second behind the Padgetts Honda in third.

At the Bungalow, Anstey led – by 0.93 second from Donald, while Johnson had dropped a couple of seconds to third.

Anstey posted a 126.634mph final lap to take the win by a scant 0.77 from Donald, but Johnson had to push in, his bike out of fuel. He was credited with 28th. At least he crossed the line. Farquhar also ran out of fuel at the Creg after going through the Bungalow in fourth.

Anstey was also lucky to finish to claim his ninth career TT victory. He said, "That's my toughest TT victory so far. I ran out of fuel at Governors. I didn't think I was going to make it to the line. I can't believe it [winning]. I wasn't going fast enough early on. I got P5 and P6 boards and thought, 'I have to pull my finger out.' I started to push and could see the gap

coming down and down. I tried as hard as I could, but my pit boards just kept saying plus zero, plus zero."

Donald found it hard to accept that he had lost the race by such a small margin, but said, "We ride thousands of corners and have to do a pit stop, yet it comes down to seven-tenths of a second. But I'm proud to have finished second to Bruce. It's the closest TT finish I've ever had. I could tell by my boards and the people waving like crazy that it was going to be close. I gave it absolutely everything."

William Dunlop took third – his first Mountain course podium – from McGuinness and admitted afterwards, "I'm not using it as an excuse, but I got tired at the end there. I was glad to see Gary [Johnson] pushing his bike home at the end there."

SUPERSPORT – Race Two

After the first race blow-up and myriad engine problems in practice, Michael Dunlop went to the line for the second Supersport race praying that his engine would hold together. It had been rebuilt by Swan Yamaha's chief engineer, Pete Jennings, using bits from two blown motors (Dunlop's plus one of Ian Hutchinson's, a victim of over-revving) and some new engine parts.

Jennings said, "The big-end shells we had weren't ideal. They were to Yamaha's spec, but not to the tighter oil clearances that I prefer. I used Michael's cases and crank, and a cylinder head of ours. Michael wrote off his R6 head when a valve broke and jammed up, also wrecking a piston. The cam chain tensioner was also wrecked, so it was impossible to say what really caused the blow-up."

Above: Michael Dunlop speeds past 'the Creg' on his way to Supersport race-two victory on his hastily assembled Yamaha.

Photo: Gavan Caldwell

Left: Bruce Anstey won the first Supersport race by 0.77 second – his ninth TT win was his luckiest.

Photo: David Collister/photocycles.com

Above: Win number 19 for McGuinness in Superstock: only Joey Dunlop (26) has more. Here he scythes his Honda past the Mitre Hotel in Kirkmichael in a classic TT scene.

Photo: Gavan Caldwell

Jennings also replaced Dunlop's worn-out clutch with one from Sigma, a component he had not even tested before. But it hung together perfectly as Michael dominated the race. William led him at Glen Helen by 2.62 seconds, but broke down at Kirkmichael with an electronics problem, and from that point on, Michael was in control of the race, winning by 13.26 seconds.

After his third TT victory, he said, "I can't believe it after all the trouble we've been through this week. I can't thank the lads enough for all the hard work they've done, or Gary, who bought me another engine. Pete [Jennings] built a great engine, and winning the race was the only way I could think of repaying them for all their hard work. It's a pity Winston [McAdoo, title sponsor of the team] could not be here to see this.

"When I got P1 plus five on my board, I thought, 'Let's really show you boys how I operate.' Then I got P1 plus 12

and decided to chill out over the Mountain. I wasn't wanting to blow her up again!"

Donald said, "I gave it my all to finish second again! But hey, three seconds so far, I'm proud of that and I'm enjoying my week. Sun's out over the Mountain. Big crowd. It's a magnificent TT.

"I passed Ryan near the end, but he jumped on the back of me and he came back by me, and I thought, 'He's on it, it must be close.'"

Farquhar claimed third by 0.01 second from Anstey, who had lost 13 seconds on the third lap thanks to a misfire, which then cleared itself for the rest of the race.

Farquhar knew it would be a close finish: "Last lap, I got P3 plus one, so I rode as hard as I could. I had to use the speed of Cam's bike to tow me along and then I passed him at Signpost. I wasn't really expecting a podium. It doesn't get any tighter."

SUPERSTOCK
• •

Time was when TT leaderboard gaps were measured in seconds and even minutes. These days, the races are fought out over tenths of a second, and the first Superstock lap was just such an event.

McGuinness held a tiny 0.53-second lead on the Padgetts Honda over Hillier at Glen Helen. But Farquhar, 1.42 down on the leader and in fourth place, fought back to second at Ballaugh 1.02 seconds adrift, and was leading at Ramsey – by 0.09 second.

At the Bungalow, it was 0.17 second; by the Grandstand, McGuinness held the advantage, but it was virtually nothing –0.17 second from Farquhar.

Martin was third, but 5.66 down on the leader, and then came Anstey, Rutter, Hillier, Johnson and Michael Dunlop.

During the second lap, though, McGuinness asserted his authority and, coming into the pits for the fuel stop, was 3.99 seconds in front of Farquhar. Anstey was just under ten seconds further back in third, with Dunlop now up to fourth, from Martin, Rutter and Hillier.

Although he gained nothing in the pit stop on this occasion, McGuinness was charging again with a full fuel load and had 5.89 seconds over Farquhar by the time they reached Glen Helen.

It was virtually game over. McGuinness won the race by 7.80 seconds – his first Superstock win on the Mountain course and his 19th career TT victory. After the race, however, he revealed how close he had come to a dnf.

"That was tough," he admitted. "I concentrated really hard, but the bike was stronger this year and I really wanted it. I pushed and pushed, but on lap two I was running out of gas. I rolled into corners, never blipped the throttle and rode like a district nurse over the Mountain.

"It was so hard to win. I was P1 plus zero, but I was up for the fight. I've won all sorts here, but never one on the big road bike. I'm well pleased."

Behind McGuinness, the race was very much on for second, with Dunlop closing the gap to Farquhar in every sector, to the point where he took second on the run from Ramsey to the Bungalow and crossed the finish line with almost five seconds on his fellow Irishman, whose ZX-10R had sprung an oil leak.

Dunlop said, "It's not what I wanted [coming second], but I've no one to blame but myself. I just didn't ride hard enough in the first two laps.

"I'd like to thank Jeb [MSS Kawasaki engine builder]. My motor he built was hundred per cent on the money today. I knew I was catching Ryan, but I wasn't sure how far he was behind John. I just kept trying to plug away. The Mountain's not my strongest point, but I rode as hard as I could. I got beat, but I'll be back."

SENIOR

There was no Senior TT for the first time in the event's 105-year history after it succumbed to bad weather. The only previous Senior stoppage had been when the TT itself had been cancelled by two world wars, and the 2001 foot-and-mouth crisis.

The race was postponed from Friday, and then time ran out on Saturday, with the roads still soaking wet and big puddles around much of the course.

LIGHTWEIGHT

The all-new 650 twin Lightweight class had Ryan Farquhar's name written all over it, but nothing can be taken for granted at the TT. The 36-year-old from Dungannon showed signs of real pressure before the start of the three-lap race – especially as conditions were far from ideal following the squally showers and fog that had brought about the cancellation of the Senior.

Although it was too risky to set the 200bhp superbikes loose, the new Lightweights, on treaded tyres, saved the day for the thousands of fans who braved the elements.

Farquhar led from the start, 2.48 seconds up on Hillier at Glen Helen and 14.11 at the end of the first lap, and in front, when he dived in for fuel while Hillier pressed on, his own stop being planned for lap two.

For one lap, the time sheets didn't reflect the true picture, as Farquhar turned a 25-second deficit at Glen Helen to 6.76 seconds at the end of the lap and Hillier pulled in. The former kept stretching to win the race by 28.71 seconds.

Hillier was second on a bike that used Farquhar-produced parts, while Rutter was third and rookie Hamilton was tenth, both on KMR Kawasakis.

"I've worked so hard for this," said Farquhar. "The last four years I've spent promoting the class by building bikes and putting top riders on them. I even helped prep James's bike, so I'll take the credit of a 1-2-3.

"I rode really cautiously on the first lap because of the wet. James passed me at Ramsey on the second lap and I thought, 'Oh no, I don't want to get into a dogfight here,' but then he had to pit.

"We did 115mph today, but I reckon 117 would be no problem in better conditions. And hopefully, now we've proved how competitive the class is, we might get two TT races for Supertwins next year."

TT ZERO

TT Zero exists largely to promote the Island's 'green' policies, and once again it lacked any depth of entry – only six bikes qualified for the one-lap race. But at least there was the tantalising prospect of the all-new Mugen Shinden from Japan. Ridden by McGuinness, it took on the American-built Moto

Czysz pairing of Michael Rutter and Mark Miller.

Rutter topped practice at 102.508mph, compared to McGuinness's 96.953mph, but many thought the Japanese were merely playing safe on battery life and would unleash the beast come race day.

They certainly gave McGuinness more power, but not enough, as Rutter won with a lap of 104.056mph, compared to McGuinness's 102.215.

Rutter took the £10,000 prize (which he shared with team-mate Miller) for being the first man to lap the TT course at over 100mph in a zero-emissions TT race.

Miller finished third at 101.065mph, with Rob Barber – on a tardy 78mph lap – the fourth and final rider home.

SIDECAR – Race One

After a year out, Dave Molyneux made a stunning return to the TT, winning both Sure Sidecar three-lappers. The double success took his career total to 16 victories, putting him third in the all-time TT winners list, with only Joey Dunlop and John McGuinness ahead.

The 48-year-old Manxman had developed his own Kawasaki-powered DMR outfit for 2012. It marked a unique achievement for the rider, who has won Sidecar TTs with Honda, Yamaha, Suzuki and now Kawasaki, machinery.

With Pat Farrance in the chair, Moly won the first race by over 20 seconds from the Birchall brothers, Ben and Tom. It was Farrance's first ever TT victory.

The Birchalls, on their Cofain Racing by Klaffi LCR Honda, showed no adverse effects from their Monday evening practice crash, taking the challenge to Moly early in the race and going on to their first ever TT podium.

Conrad Harrison and Mike Aylott finished third on a Shelbourne Honda, 14 seconds down.

SIDECAR – Race Two

After breaking down in the opening Sidecar race (following a practice week full of problems), Tim Reeves and Dan Sayle set the pace in the second outing on their NCR Haith Racing LCR Honda and led Molyneux by 4.5 seconds at the end of the first lap. But Molyneux was charging and closed the gap to 0.8 second on lap two, then took the lead on the final lap before going on to win by over 16 seconds.

Reeves's second place marked his best Sidecar TT result yet, while the Birchalls were on the podium again in third.

Above: Lightweight TT winner Ryan Farquhar aviates his Kawasaki in practice for the all-new class, run to Supertwins 650cc rules. The machines' treaded tyres meant they could save the day after the Senior was cancelled.

Left: Michael Rutter won the race – and scooped the £10,000 prize for a 100mph lap – in the TT Zero class.

Far left: A double victory in the Side-cars for veteran Dave Molyneux and passenger Pat Farrance brought the Manx pilot's total to 16.

Photos: David Collister/photocycles.com

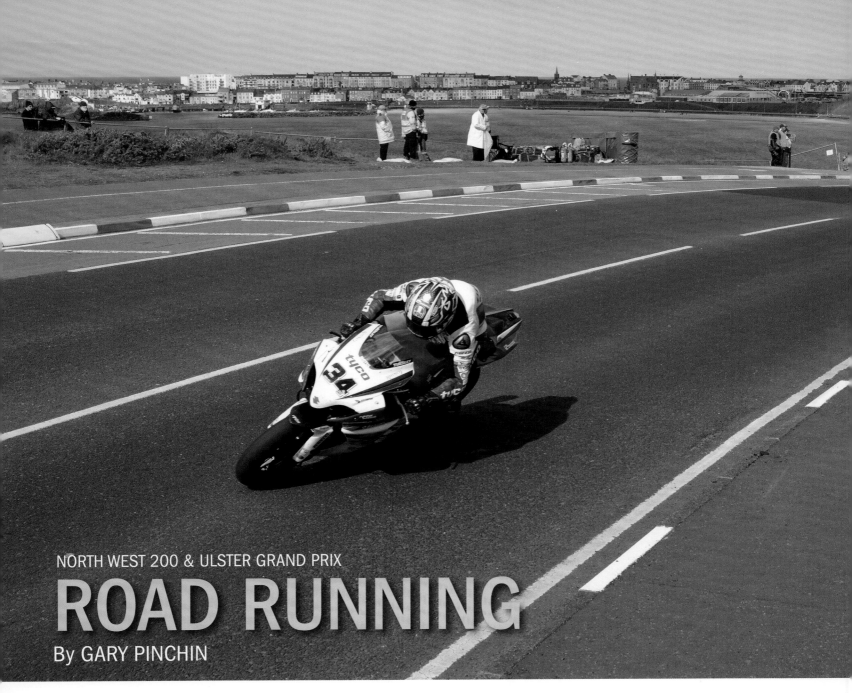

NORTH WEST 200 & ULSTER GRAND PRIX

ROAD RUNNING

By GARY PINCHIN

Above: Alastair Seeley departs Portrush at speed on the final run to the second Superbike chequered flag.

Above right: Class evangelist Ryan Farquhar won the new Supertwins race. Track first-timer Jeremy McWilliams was delighted with second place.

Right: Fast and furious. Ian Hutchison (9), Bruce Anstey (5), Cameron Donald and Ryan Farquhar (77), wheel to wheel over the North West's infamous Black Hill.

Photos: Gavan Caldwell

THERE was a lot of pressure on Alastair Seeley going into the North West 200. After all, this was *his* race.

Tyco TAS Suzuki team manager Philip Neill had signed the 2011 British Supersport champion to race in BSB – a thank-you for a hard-won title. But Neill also knew that Seeley was a banker for North West success, a combination of his aggressive short-circuit skills and good circuit knowledge making him the stand-out pre-race favourite.

Seeley had been a must-have for the 2011 race, when the team had been backed by Relentless, also the event sponsor. A year on, he was even more important, Neill needing to create a favourable early winning impression with new backers Tyco.

People were happily talking of Seeley winning all six solo races (in the process equalling Phillip McCallen's record of five in a day, the maximum allowed) – and even the self-styled 'Wee Wizard' let his confidence spill over to go along with the hype.

It didn't quite go all the way, but three wins and three seconds marked out the 32-year-old from Carrickfergus, County Antrim as the man of the meet for a second year running on the 8.97-mile triangle of public roads linking the towns of Portstewart, Coleraine and Portrush on the Causeway Coast of his home county.

The 2012 programme was a major departure, featuring two races on Thursday, designed to provide some spare time on Saturday to cater for unexpected delays because of weather, crashes or the myriad incidents that happen off track at a race on public roads.

TT Legend John McGuinness grabbed the hole-shot on a Padgetts Honda in Thursday afternoon's Superstock opener, but Seeley dominated as the sun came out three laps into what had started as a wet race.

Philip Neill admitted, "That's taken a wee bit of weight off my mind. The North West is a big event for us, being the local team."

Seeley crossed the line a whopping 22.511 seconds clear of second-place surprise Lee Johnston on a Millsport Ducati Panigale, while Cameron Donald came home third for Wilson Craig Honda, albeit briefly having to share the podium with Stefan Bonnetti.

Initially officials had posted the Italian as third thanks to a computer glitch mid-race. To be fair, Bonnetti had ridden an impressive race on the Speed Motor Kawasaki, and only after the TV coverage had been studied was Donald finally confirmed third. He had sneaked ahead of Ryan Farquhar in one of the chicanes on the last lap; Bonnetti was finally accredited with fifth, three-tenths down.

Also on Thursday was the inaugural Vauxhall-backed Supertwins race, won by Farquhar from NW200 rookie Jeremy McWilliams and Michael Rutter. All three were riding Farquhar-built KMR Kawasakis – as was sixth-placed Jamie Hamilton, another first-timer.

With the demise of the two-strokes, Supertwins – a class of racing championed by Farquhar – seemed a perfect replacement. Based on either the ER6 Kawasaki or SV650 Suzuki road bikes, the 650 twins offered a reasonably-priced entry-level class, with user-friendly performance, but also

provided seriously competitive racing in the hands of the professionals, as Thursday's racing showed.

Rutter said, "I was terrified in the drizzle. It was horrible. I wish it had been a sunny day because it would have been a mega race."

McWilliams didn't seem to care. The former MotoGP man was over the moon with just racing on the North West course and said, "It's a dream come true for me, and I'm sure it's a dream come true for Ryan. I'm so glad I've finally done the North West. I'm a convert."

For Farquhar, it was his fourth NW200 race win. "It's unreal. It's taken a lot of work and effort preparing the bikes, helping develop and promote the class, but it's all been worth it. To get four bikes to finish, and finish in the top six, is an achievement, but to have Jezza and Michael up on the podium with me is a dream come true," he said.

Seeley didn't have a bike for the Supertwins, but his chances of a clean sweep of six wins quickly disappeared in Saturday's first race, which had to be red-flagged when Guy Martin crashed in the high-speed right-hander at Black Hill.

With the results being counted back one lap, Honda rider William Dunlop took the race by 2.66 seconds from Seeley, but there was a touch of irony, since the latter had been

closing in on the Wilson Craig Honda and had looked poised to make a bid for the lead when his Tyco TAS team-mate caused the stoppage.

It was William Dunlop's first four-stroke win at the North West, and the first to congratulate him was his younger brother, Michael. It was also Craig's first international road race victory as a team owner. Dunlop said, "It's great to get that off my back. Alastair only caught me after I'd run on to the grass at Juniper."

John McGuinness finished a strong third, but Donald and Gary Johnson were over nine seconds adrift of the winner. Sixth-placed Michael Dunlop was 16.8 seconds away on his Ard Na Mara/McAdoo Racing Suzuki – a tardy slug of a bike that a very frustrated Dunlop couldn't wait to park up.

Things didn't get any better for Seeley in the first Superbike race when he overshot at Church Corner under intense pressure from McGuinness on lap two.

Seeley set the fastest lap on lap four of six in his charge back from 11th, but McGuinness was riding to his pit board and crossed the line with 4.2 seconds in hand.

It was his sixth NW200 victory: "Any win is fantastic, but this is special because the superbike is always the hardest and fastest. I gave Alastair a run for his money. It looked like he'd checked out, but I put him under pressure and he made the mistake."

After the Superstock race, everyone began asking whether Seeley was ever going to add to his solitary Thursday victory. In a six-lap slipstreaming fest that typifies NW200 racing, he crossed the finish line ahead of James Hillier, Farquhar and McGuinness. However, Michael Rutter, after being caught out by the changing weather conditions in practice, had to start from the second wave. It worked in his favour, though, because it gave him clear track. On corrected time, he took the win by 6.9 seconds from Seeley after smashing the lap record on the final lap with the first ever 120mph Superstock lap (120.153mph, beating the previous record of 119.588).

Rutter's victory, on an MSS Kawasaki, was gained on what he thought was a brand-new ZX-10R, but in fact it was actually a tired press hack that had over 7,500 miles on it. MSS team owner Nick Morgan said, "Jeb, our engine guy, stripped the motor, degree'd the cams and threw on a skinny head gasket. The thing was proper fast and Rutter rode brilliantly."

The rider was aghast when he discovered the truth, but it did not spoil his enjoyment of the win: "I kept getting pit boards saying P1, and I was thinking, 'No way.' But it was nice to have clear track."

It was Rutter's 13th NW200 race win, putting him equal with Joey Dunlop and two behind all-time wins record holder Robert Dunlop.

Three successive second places didn't sap Seeley's confidence, and he came out in the second Supersport race with guns blazing in a cracking scrap with William Dunlop to win by 1.351 seconds – Dunlop was smarting from an ankle injury, having crashed his superbike earlier in the afternoon. He was smarting even more after Seeley passed him at Church on the final lap, in what some viewed as an overly harsh move.

"It was hard work because our 600 is down on speed," said Seeley. "I just tried to stay in the slipstream and then made my pass at Church, like I did to Stuart Easton in 2010. William and I never touched."

Dunlop countered, "Seeley tried to put me up the slip road. But he would have won it anyway. Because of my ankle, I couldn't steer how I wanted. I was going to sit in the van, but then I thought about the money and decided to come out and give it a go."

Neill retorted, "William's not happy [about Seeley's move]? If he was Ben Wilson, how would he have felt if he had that treatment every corner? Welcome to British Supersport." Neill was referring to the sensational 2011 season that had seen Seeley and Wilson bashing fairings and trading paint all year.

To wrap up Seeley's day, he saw off a stiff challenge from McGuinness and Rutter in the final Superbike race to claim his third win.

Seeley said, "We worked hard for that one. I knew from the first Superbike race that we had the pace. I was determined to hit every apex. It's been a frustrating day at times, but the Superbike race is *the* one to win."

The flip side to Seeley's win for the Tyco TAS team was team-mate Conor Cummins being taken out by Gary Johnson at Mathers. Cummins sustained a serious wrist injury that would ruin his TT. It was the team's second big crash of the day.

Team boss Neill added, "This is the feature race, the one everyone wants to win and Alastair rode so well. But we've had a topsy-turvy weekend. Conor was off in the final Superbike race. Guy is okay after what was a really nasty tumble. His helmet is scrap; that underlines how bad it was. He was passed fit to race on, but after a bang like that, no way was I going to allow him to continue."

McGuinness's Honda TT Legends team-mate, Simon Andrews, produced a brilliant ride from the second wave to finish fourth on corrected time ahead of Michael Dunlop and James Hillier. Ian Hutchinson, who was still far from fit after the 2010 Silverstone crash that had smashed his left leg, was seventh on the Swan Yamaha – his best result of a difficult day.

Finally, the 2012 North West belonged to Alastair Seeley. While he celebrated his win and looked forward to a season of BSB (one that ultimately would drain all his confidence), the road racing regulars were heading to the Isle of Man TT.

ULSTER GRAND PRIX

Michael Dunlop hit a rich vein of form going into the 90th-anniversary Ulster Grand Prix – the last big international road race of the season and an event that has been revamped to live up to its prestigious history from the 1960s and early 1970s at the super-fast road circuit.

Dunlop was fresh from five wins from five starts at the Southern 100, the superb meeting on the scary 4.25-mile Billown course near Castletown being the first chance for the Irish national racing regulars to cross swords with the English stars following the TT.

Then, in the Armoy national back home, the 23-year-old Ballymoney hero had won the three big races, but had slipped a couple of discs in his back just before that weekend. Between then and the Ulster, he'd had physiotherapy to ease them back into place, and he arrived at the Dundrod paddock in good spirits, despite having been advised not to ride.

Disaster struck first time out on his Kawasaki Supertwin during Wednesday practice. The discs popped out and Dunlop spent the rest of the weekend in sheer agony. The sight of him shuffling around the paddock, hunched over, eyes screwed up in pain, was pitiful. It took extensive physio and painkilling injections to see him through the weekend, but once on his bikes, out on the 7.4-mile Dundrod course, he still commanded the utmost respect.

He lapped at 132mph in Thursday morning practice on his Kawasaki superstocker. The marker had been laid down.

The week-long Ulster Grand Prix festival actually supports two meetings. On Thursday afternoon, it's the Dundrod 150 national, the six-lap superbike race acting as a taster for Saturday's UGP meeting. Dunlop won it, his third lap of 133.379mph not quite beating Bruce Anstey's outright lap record of 133.977 set in the second Ulster GP Superbike race of 2010.

Saturday opened for Dunlop with four painkilling injections one hour before the Superstock opener. Then it was time to race. Guy Martin led a four-rider slipstreaming scrap that included Ian Lougher, Bruce Anstey and Dunlop. But with a

130.927mph fourth lap, followed by 131.530mph the next time around, Dunlop cut loose from the pack on the Ard Na Mara/McAdoo Kawasaki to win by over four seconds from Lougher, Martin and Anstey.

Conor Cummins, back to something like his old form with the Tyco TAS Suzuki, nipped by Lee Johnston's Millsport Panigale on the last lap for fifth.

"I didn't want to ride too hard in that one. I need to save myself for later in the day. I'm sore enough, but on the bike it's not too bad. We'll be alright," said Dunlop, almost trying to convince himself.

The Ulster, like the North West, is a whirlwind of races, with riders getting very little down time during the day. Supersport was next up.

It was William Dunlop's turn to soak up some glory. He'd been in the wars after a nasty 140mph crash at the Skerries that had left the 26-year-old with a dislocated shoulder. There was talk that he wouldn't be fit enough to ride at the Ulster, but with another display of Dunlop grit he was just holding off Anstey at the end of the fourth lap when the red flags came out after Michael Pearson crashed at Tornagrough. The result was declared at three laps.

Johnston, having leased Gary Johnson's Honda for the weekend, was third from Cummins. Michael Dunlop was sixth on his Yamaha R6, behind Tyco's Guy Martin.

The premature finish threw Anstey's game plan. He said, "I was just sitting there behind William. I knew where he was slow and had everything planned to nab him on the final lap."

But Dunlop disagreed and said, "I think I could have held

Left: Superbike winner Michael Dunlop overcame near-crippling back pain and an earlier crash in Ulster to take his first international win.

Below left: Popular showman Guy Martin took a clear win in the first Superbike race after Dunlop's spill.

Photos: Gavan Caldwell

him off. The bike is really good. It's been fast all year and I'm just glad I was able to win one for Wilson [Craig, the team owner]. I'm not so bad on the 600, but the injury is a bit of a bigger issue on a superbike."

The Ulster is the only major road race continuing to support the 250 two-strokes, but with only nine entries the 2012 race was run concurrently with the Supertwins. Predictably, Ryan Farquhar won the red-flagged Twins, to complete a hat trick of international road race wins on the ER6 and his ninth UGP race victory. He also celebrated a KMR Kawasaki 1-2 with team-mate Jamie Hamilton, who crossed the line a distant 13.2 seconds back.

Forty-one-year-old Davey Morgan, one of road racing's great characters, won the 250 race – his first UGP victory. "I hope this is not the end of the 250s, but it's getting worse year on year trying to keep these things going. There's no bits," he said.

Guy Martin won the first Superbike race. He took the lead from the Padgetts Honda of Gary Johnson during the second lap, but then faced terrific pressure from Michael Dunlop until the man with the bad back lost the front while braking for the Hairpin.

The crash held up the pursuing pack for long enough to give Martin a comfortable 5.49-second margin over Johnson at the end of the race. Cummins was third from Anstey.

It was Martin's first big win of the year. At the Southern, the Tyco TAS Suzuki rider had bemoaned the lack of Pirelli tyre development (team-mate Cummins, however, voiced no complaints). At the Ulster, Pirelli offered the same-construction 17-inch tyres developed for 2013 WSBK racing, but with an anti-chunking, high-durability centre tread to cope with Dundrod's sustained high speeds.

With that, plus a DOT Supercorsa treaded front tyre, which he claimed gave him better feel, Martin was a lot happier and said, "That was the one to win! Thank you Pirelli. I was riding my own race then Michael came by me, but I got him at Wheeler's [a super-fast, sweeping corner]. Then he came off at the Hairpin. I heard the scratching and banging. I knew it was never going to be an easy race after the ding-dongs we had at the Southern."

The second Supersport race was Anstey's, but it came

down to the last lap, and Anstey said, "I knew it would. I saw back-markers and William tried to squeeze two or three of them, but I passed him at the Hairpin. He tried to come back, but I just got him into the next fast right-hander."

Cummins was third, with Johnson holding off Johnston and Michael Dunlop for fourth.

The final Superbike race saw Martin grab the hole-shot and lead for the first three laps. Martin's third lap was 133.181mph, but second-placed Michael Dunlop clocked 133.433, and Johnson in third, 132.735, with 1.2 seconds covering them on the road.

The charging Dunlop took the lead between Jordan's Cross and Wheelers. A lap later, Martin was in front at Joey's Windmill, but Dunlop fought back. Johnson by now was almost nine seconds back in third.

At Joey's on the final lap, Dunlop was trying so hard to maintain the lead that he kicked up a rooster-tail of dirt, but it was just enough to give him a 0.347-second advantage as the two bikes flashed across the line.

Bad back or not, Dunlop forced himself out of the saddle as he went past the Joey Dunlop start-line grandstand, punching the air after his first ever international superbike road race victory. The partisan crowd went mad.

Dunlop said, "That's pay-back for the first race! On my own, I was okay on the bike, but when I was scrapping with Guy, I was struggling going from left to right. But I knew I could win this one. I done him in a move into the Hairpin, which I didn't think was my strong point after my crash there this morning. I'm delighted with my first international superbike win … I think I've been the strongest rider all year [in Ireland] and I've proved I can win races at international level."

Dunlop was right. From a difficult start to the season trying to get all his bikes built and missing any kind of pre-season testing, he'd finished up as the man to beat.

John McGuinness might have something to say about that at the TT in 2013, but as the shutters came down on the 2012 road racing season, the feeling was that if Dunlop was prepared to accept the restrictions of being part of a big, professional road racing team, to allow him to focus just on racing, then he really would have an opportunity to exploit his boundless talent.

The North West 200 meeting was much saddened by the death of **Mark Buckley**. The 35-year-old from Loch Lomond died in hospital following an accident near Millbank Avenue on the first lap of Saturday's Superstock race. No other competitor was involved.

Mark was an experienced competitor on the roads. He had joined the Splitlath Redmond Aprilia team a month earlier and had been planning to race the superstock RSV-4 and a Kawasaki 600 at the TT.

The Ulster Grand Prix was marred by the death of **Lee Vernon**. The 24-year-old from Stoke-on-Trent had been competing in the Dundrod 150 superbike race on Thursday when he crashed his BMW at Rock Bends. He passed away in Belfast Royal Victoria Hospital the following day.

Lee had first raced at the Ulster as an 18-year-old novice. He finished fifth in the 2011 UGP 250 race, and was fifth in 2012's Supertwins race earlier in the day before his tragic accident. He ran his second TT, and at the Southern 100 posted the 11th-fastest lap of all time on the Billown course. He had also finished on the podium at Armoy only weeks before the Ulster GP.

BYRNE'S MIGHT

By OLLIE BARSTOW

Above: Champion again, Shane Byrne leads Brookes, Laverty and Westmoreland at the Brands finale. Shakey sealed it with a win.

Photo: Gavan Caldwell

Right: Australian rider Josh Brookes put up a flaming title challenge on the Tyco Suzuki.

Photo: Clive Challinor Motorsport Photography

ARMED with a sizeable 23-point advantage over Josh Brookes, Shane Byrne could afford to favour caution going into the final race of the 2012 MCE British Superbike Championship season. In fact, 'Shakey' could have trundled around in 14th place and still have had enough in hand to hold the champion's trophy aloft at the end of the day.

Not only did Byrne throw that caution to the wind, but also he concluded his title-winning campaign in peerless fashion with a trio of conclusive victories at the season-ending Brands Hatch round.

What better way to celebrate a third career BSB title than from the very top of the podium?

Although BSB 2012 didn't need a photo-finish to decide its outcome – unlike 2011 – the latest iteration of the ultra-competitive series still offered its fair share of heart-stopping moments and high-quality racing courtesy of an entry list that, more than ever, blended home-grown talent with a sprinkling of motorcycling stardust from overseas.

Having pioneered the Title Showdown format in 2010, British Superbikes continued to blaze its own trail in 2012 with the adoption of a spec ECU, a move intended to level the playing field, lower costs, and promote rider skill by banning launch control and traction control.

Furthermore, with the EVO sub-category abolished to make way for a full 32-strong grid of 'championship-class' machines, BSB 2012 was a tantalising prospect even before the entry list began to take shape.

Notably, the prestigious No.1 plate would be seen in 2012, reigning champion Tommy Hill having opted to stay on at Swan Yamaha and defend the crown he had won from John Hopkins in 2011. Though his sparring partner would not be present, having followed Crescent Suzuki to World Superbikes, the Hopkins-effect was credited with enticing Noriyuki Haga to the series.

Joining Hill at Swan Yamaha, 43-time SBK race winner Haga arguably became the highest-profile coup for British Superbikes since its inception, although some would question the wisdom of his decision come season's end…

Heading out of Swan Yamaha, Michael Laverty switched to the factory Honda team – resplendent in new Samsung colours – to lead their challenge alongside Jon Kirkham, while WFR (Alex Lowes, James Westmoreland and Graeme Gowland) and series returnees Padgetts (Ian Lowry and Luca Scassa) ensured that the CBR1000RR was well represented yet again.

Despite the defection of Crescent, TAS Racing continued to head Suzuki's challenge with their new Tyco-backed GSXR-1000s, Brookes and reigning British Supersport champion Alastair Seeley forming a familiar line-up.

Putting a concerted effort into winning their first British Superbike title in two decades, Kawasaki's ranks were bolstered by having four team representatives, including returning ex-champions Paul Bird Motorsport (under the Rapid Solicitors banner), who lured back 2003 champion Byrne and Stuart Easton.

Elsewhere, BMW's invigorated campaign was headed up by Buildbase and Italian newcomers Supersonic Racing; Ducati's much vaunted 1199 Panigale was given its international racing debut courtesy of Moto Rapido Racing and

– initially at least – Jentin Doodson; and Splitlath Redmond Racing retained their Aprilia RSV4 machinery.

As ever, the opening round of the season at Brands Hatch coincided with the Easter bank holiday weekend, though Mother Nature marked her presence with a typical sprinkling of rain, wind and grey skies.

If the weather was dismal, the racing was entertaining, even if it gave very little hint of the eventual outcome, Samsung Honda's Kirkham claiming victory over Tyco Suzuki's Seeley, the latter's wobble out of the final bend allowing his rival to snatch the win on the line. Traditional wet-weather specialist Michael Rutter on the MSS Bathams Kawasaki was in third, but it is telling that not one of these riders was seen on the podium for the remainder of the season.

By contrast, the anticipated title challengers endured a torrid start to their campaigns: Byrne faded to seventh, Brookes – who had started on pole – finished tenth, while Hill paid for an error in qualifying with a crash-induced DNF.

For their benefit, it was perhaps just as well that there was no further Superbike action for the remainder of the day, an earlier crash in the Supersport race having caused fluid to contaminate the already damp surface. Despite a determined clean-up operation, the second BSB race was abandoned on safety grounds.

After the tight, tricky bends of Brands Hatch came the fast, open sweeps of Thruxton, the notorious Hampshire circuit playing host to an exciting – and uninterrupted – second round, with yet more surprises in store as BSB welcomed a new member to the winners' circle in Ian Lowry.

Having struggled to find a full-time ride since his break-out rookie campaign in 2009, Lowry's switch to Clive Padgett's team – returning to the Superbike stage after years of success in other categories – swiftly bore fruit as he saw off the challenge of Hill and Brookes to claim a popular win.

After a run to fifth place in race two and with his fourth place at the Brands Hatch opener, Lowry left Thruxton with a wholly unexpected lead in the overall standings.

Even so, the second Thruxton race offered a more precise hint of things to come as Brookes's charging ride through the order saw him take victory, ahead of Hill and Byrne. From that point on, at least two of those riders would stand on the podium for 21 of the next 23 races.

The first British rider to defend the BSB title since Niall Mackenzie in 1998, Hill stumbled out of the blocks during the opening two rounds, but was back to full speed come round three at Oulton Park, designated a triple-header to accommodate the abandoned Brands Hatch race. He notched up his first win of the season and with it the series lead. He had started the first encounter of the weekend from 19th on the grid, but was already up to third place when it was red-flagged due to a high-speed crash involving Kirkham, who had slid off spectacularly at Water Tower.

Taking advantage of his vastly improved starting position, Hill would eventually get the better of Haga – up from 17th on the grid – to lead his decorated team-mate home for a popular Swan Yamaha 1-2.

With fourth in race two and second in race three, Hill left Oulton Park having gained a slender advantage over the opposition. His swift return to prominence was certainly helped by the fact that no other rider had assumed control of the standings: the opening six races yielded six different winners.

In fact, Oulton Park was one for the BSB historians as a misty-eyed Chris Walker capitalised on the damp conditions of race two to claim a hugely unexpected win for Pr1mo Bournemouth Kawasaki – his first BSB victory in 12 years – while Byrne returned former champions Paul Bird Motorsport to the top of the podium in race three to officially kick-start his run at the title.

While there was something familiar about the top three of Hill, Brookes and Byrne heading to round four at Snetterton, there was one notable absentee from the upper echelon of the standings in the form of Laverty, one of the pre-season favourites. Struggling initially to make the transition from Yamaha to Honda machinery, he languished in 11th prior to the Norfolk round, but in just four races he would propel himself back into contention.

He began with a run to second in the opening race at Snetterton, followed by a win in race two, which was enough for him to break clear and lift himself into the critical top six at the round's end, behind the front-running trio.

That said, Snetterton would bring mixed success for those three riders. Hill followed a win in the first race (making him the first double winner of the season) with a mechanical retirement in race two, while technical gremlins also kept Byrne

Above: Tommy Hill at Cadwell Park. His title defence was patchy.

Top right: Ian Lowry took a surprise win at Thruxton on the Padgett's Honda.

Above right: Snetterton top three: Byrne (*left*) and Josh Brookes flank race winner Michael Laverty.

Photos: Clive Challinor Motorsport Photography

Right: Alex Lowes keeps it neat ahead of Brookes at Cadwell Park.

Photo: Gavan Caldwell

off the race-two podium. Thus, despite climbing no higher than the third step on the podium all weekend, Brookes went to the top overall.

If Snetterton merely pointed to a four-strong hierarchy at the top of the standings, the annual jaunt across the Scottish border to Knockhill confirmed it: Brookes, Hill, Byrne and Laverty locked out the top four in each race.

Byrne and Laverty picked up wins in race one and two respectively, while podiums for Hill and a pair of fourth places for Brookes mirrored their positions in the classification.

Back ahead in the overall standings, despite failing to win at Knockhill, Hill struck a psychological blow on the return to Oulton Park for the second triple-header of the season, the reigning champion reeling off a trio of dominant wins. Though Byrne and Brookes worked hard to keep their rival honest by joining him on the podium on each occasion, Hill's maximum haul of 75 points put him 28 clear in the standings and secured nine potentially precious 'podium credits'.

Indeed, with Hill, Byrne, Brookes and Laverty clear of the chasing pack three rounds before the Title Showdown, attention was beginning to turn to acquiring the podium credits that potentially would give them the edge in the much anticipated three-round shoot-out.

With this in mind, it was Byrne's turn to fight back during round seven at Brands Hatch, this time around the longer Grand Prix configuration, the Kawasaki rider preluding his title triumph at the same venue later in the year by winning both races at a relative canter, each time from Brookes in second and Hill in third.

With the Showdown looming, the fearsome Cadwell Park, scene of many pivotal championship moments in the past, duly lived up to its reputation for drama by throwing Byrne a curve ball in the form of a shoulder injury, sustained when he crashed heavily in free practice.

Ruled out at Cadwell and from the following Donington Park round, at least Byrne could rely on the Title Showdown to keep him in the championship hunt while he focused on

getting fully fit for the shoot-out. Without it, his title hopes would have been dashed.

With Byrne out of the equation, Hill and Brookes took full advantage, the former picking up both wins at Cadwell Park, while Brookes secured his first victories since Thruxton with a dominant double at Donington.

Each had comfortably earned his place in the Showdown. Byrne was also safe – despite his absence – while four consecutive podiums at Cadwell and Donington saw Laverty back in the mix for the third season in succession.

With this foursome something of a foregone conclusion for some events, attention was turned to those who would be joining them as the fifth and sixth championship challengers. This battle raged all season: the likes of Lowry, Haga and Easton all enjoyed top-six stints at some stage, while fellow podium winners Kirkham, Seeley and Walker were never far from the reckoning.

Ironically, however, silverware proved no substitute for consistency, since Tommy Bridewell emerged as the man to beat, despite not once cracking the top three. Bridewell had only joined Supersonic Racing – which had made the ambitious switch from SBK to BSB over the winter – on the eve of the opening round in place of Moto2-bound Anthony West. Nonetheless, the youngster shrugged off a lack of pre-season testing on the little-fancied BMW S1000RR to become a regular presence near the front of the field from the very first round.

Often a better racer than qualifier, although Bridewell never found himself on the podium during the opening nine events, he was rarely far from it, so much so that he held down an overall top-five spot all the way to Donington Park, earning himself an unexpected, but fully deserved place in the Title Showdown.

The sixth and final spot was tougher to call, with Haga and Lowry initially emerging as the most likely candidates. However, as Lowry struggled to replicate the pace that had put him atop the podium earlier in the year, Haga looked

set to get the nod, despite having managed only a single rostrum finish.

Then the Japanese rider's hopes received a blow with an accident at Cadwell Park, which ruled him out for the remainder of the event. Though he battled through the pain at Donington Park, fortune didn't favour the brave and 'Nitro Nori's' dip in results coincided with a peak of form from the revitalised Alex Lowes.

Back on the WFR Honda in 2012 after a tumultuous previous season, which had seen him descend from grace almost as quickly as he had ascended, Lowes maintained a fairly low profile during the first half of the year, with consistency the highlight of an otherwise average score sheet. However, the youngster would hit his stride in convincing fashion from Cadwell Park with an impressive pole position and first BSB podium. Holding his nerve at Donington Park to see off the battered Haga – not to mention five other riders mathematically capable of reaching the Showdown – Lowes left the round having transformed himself from mid-fielder to title contender in less than two events.

With just three rounds and seven races to decide the outcome of the 2012 MCE British Superbike Championship, once the points had been equalised and the podium credits added, Hill held the initial advantage with 535 points, ahead of Brookes on 525, Byrne on 523, Laverty on 514, Lowes on 502 and Bridewell on 500.

To ramp up the tension, BSB had a treat in store for both riders and fans with a visit to the iconic Assen TT circuit in the Netherlands for the opening Showdown round. It was the first time BSB had left Britain since it visited Ireland's Mondello Park in 2007, and the legendary 'Cathedral' threatened to level the playing field further for the six contenders.

Assen would turn the title battle on its head before the lights had even gone out, Hill suffering a bizarre incident on the sighting lap. The championship leader fell while attempt-

ing to avoid a mechanic from a rival team as he lined up on the grid. Having damaged the Yamaha just moments before the start, he didn't make it out on time – a costly no-score.

Buoyed by his recent spike in form, Lowes started from pole, ahead of Laverty and Jakub Smrz, the SBK exile making headlines on his BSB debut by unexpectedly putting the Splitlath Redmond Aprilia on the front row. But nobody could prevent Byrne from pushing to the front and securing victory on his return from injury.

He seemed on the cusp of repeating the victory in race two, but he came up against Brookes for honours, the two rivals building to a thrilling last-lap crescendo typical of the circuit's reputation, which culminated in the Australian squeezing past into the final Geert Timmer chicane to claim the win.

With Hill only fourth behind Lowes – who secured a brace of third-place finishes – Brookes and Byrne found themselves at the head of the standings, the Tyco Suzuki man in front by two points, while Hill was now 22 points adrift.

When the series returned to the more familiar surroundings of Silverstone for the potentially critical penultimate round, all eyes were on Hill: could he recover the ground to Brookes and Byrne, and swell the title battle into a three-way dice?

As it happens, a third name was thrown back into the title mix, but it wasn't Hill's. Instead, it was an on-form Lowes who catapulted himself into contention with a stunning double victory, a first for both himself and WFR Honda. He did it in style, too, rebuffing the attentions of his rivals in race one to cruise home comfortably ahead, before prevailing in a boisterous battle with Brookes and Byrne in race two, the 22-year-old getting the better of the latter with a perfectly executed last-corner pass.

Perhaps more significantly, Byrne's brace of seconds, compared to Brookes's fourth and third, were enough to push him to the top of the standings heading into the season finale, a slim nine points clear of his main rival.

Lowes, meanwhile, was only 24 points off the lead, while Hill's hopes of recovering ground were scuppered by an unusually poor weekend that yielded just two sevenths. With only one round remaining, the reigning champion was all but out of contention just two weeks after beginning the Title Showdown as the hot favourite.

With Brands Hatch once again setting the scene for the three races that would decide the outcome of the series, Byrne arrived as hot favourite, despite his relatively slender advantage over Brookes. Indeed, based on prior form at Brands, Byrne was the man to beat, the Rapid Solicitors Kawasaki rider having won five of the previous seven races held around the GP configuration.

Thus few were surprised when he snatched the initiative from the opening bend of the first race and barely looked back for the remainder of the day. Even when nature added its own challenge with rain in the closing stages, Byrne didn't miss a beat.

The rain forced a red flag three laps from the end, but the stoppage came moments too late for Lowes. He had crashed out of second, abruptly halting his title momentum. Byrne was declared the winner, ahead of Hill and Brookes, extending his margin to 18 points.

That meant Byrne was in a position to wrap up the title with one race in hand, so long as he repeated his victory and Brookes finished lower than second.

To his credit, Byrne did his utmost to put the championship out of Brookes's reach by leading from start to finish,

Above: High profile, poor results. Big name Noriyuki Haga had a disappointing year on the Swan Yamaha.

Top left: Jon Kirkham scored an early win for Samsung Honda in the wet at Brands Hatch.

Top centre: Rolling back the years. Chris Walker took an emotional win at Oulton Park.

Top right: Consistency gave James Westmoreland the BSB Riders Cup as best of the rest.

Right: Tommy Bridewell's flame-thrower BMW was a regular presence near the front. He made it to the shoot-out.

Photos: Clive Challinor Motorsport Photography

only for the determined Australian to keep his dwindling hopes alive by following home in second.

Even so, with 23 points in hand – and only 25 available – Byrne's name was being etched into the winners' trophy even before the final race had started.

Not that he was content with cruising to the finish line. He held station behind Brookes for almost the whole race before unexpectedly diving by on the penultimate lap. In a performance befitting a champion, Byrne crossed the line for his third win of the weekend, his eighth win of the season and yet another BSB title.

Following his successes with MonsterMob Ducati in 2003 and Airwaves Ducati in 2008, Byrne's title win signalled a return to glory for Paul Bird Motorsport (who had masterminded his MonsterMob win) after a few dry years at World Superbike level. It was also a significant day for Kawasaki, who celebrated their first BSB glory since 1992.

For the second time in three years, Brookes had to settle for the runner-up spot, though at least he had the distinction of scoring the highest number of points overall, reaching the chequered flag of each race and finishing inside the top four on all but two occasions.

Capitalising on a triple DNF for Lowes during the final round, outgoing champion Hill recovered to third overall, though it was a somewhat disappointing return for a rider who had appeared to be in control prior to the Showdown.

Reviving his reputation as a potential star, Lowes got the better of fellow Honda rider Laverty for fourth overall, while Bridewell was certainly no disgrace by finishing sixth of six, having out-scored Laverty and Hill in the final three events.

Outside the top six, Westmoreland picked up the BSB Riders' Cup as best of the non-title challengers, the WFR Honda rider mirroring Bridewell by achieving his feat with consistency, but no podiums.

Unable to follow the path laid by Hopkins, Haga's first attempt in BSB didn't live up to the pre-season hype and he tailed off in eighth with only a single podium, just ahead of Walker, whose win at Oulton Park was more than enough for his 2012 campaign to be labelled a big success.

Rounding out the top ten, niggling injury problems ham-pered Easton's return, though the Scot did fare better than many had expected given the severity of his North West 200 crash just months earlier.

After another exciting year, though home-grown talent ultimately came out on top in 2012, with the likes of Haga, Smrz, Scassa, Robbin Harms and Mark Aitchison – all internationally renowned riders – joining the fray with varying degrees of success, there was certainly an impression that British Superbikes had begun to command respect on the global stage.

This can only propel BSB further into the limelight, not least when you consider that there were eight race winners, twelve podium winners, large grids and five different manufacturers inside the overall top six in 2012.

To say that British Superbikes is in rude health would be quite the understatement…

British Supersport Championship

With the British Superbike Championship channelling its emphasis towards the much-hyped three-round Title Showdown during the final throes of the season, the 2012 Motorpoint British Supersport Championship protected by Datatag needed no such tinkering to produce yet another thrilling season-long battle and final face-off.

Though the British Supersport Championship may be seen as a 'support' to the main BSB event, there were more than a few occasions in 2012 when the 600s (or in Triumph's case, 675s) produced action befitting a headline act.

A glance at the pre-season entry list would have hinted at what was to come, a roll call of accomplished names lining up to succeed BSB-bound Alastair Seeley as champion, not least Ben Wilson, the Gearlink Kawasaki rider returning for another crack at the title he had lost by just a single point in 2011.

Other notable stand-outs included 2009 champion Glen Richards, returning to Triumph machinery for a shot at a second BSS crown. The reigning BSB EVO Cup champion was joined in the Smiths Gloucester team by countryman Billy McConnell and Luke Mossey.

Above: Supersport was super-close: Glen Richards (Triumph) leads team-mate Billy McConnell and the pack. He went on to take the title.

Photo: Gavan Caldwell

Heading up the Yamaha charge was Jack Kennedy, the Irishman having established himself as a pre-season title tip following his race-winning comeback from injury in 2011 and a move to the well-backed Mar-Train Racing team; YZF-R6 counterpart Sam Warren stayed with Seton Interceptor.

Unlike the 2011 season, which had seen Seeley and Wilson engaged in a fierce two-horse race for the title, the 2012 British Supersport Championship proved a rather more competitive affair, with seven different race winners emerging over 26 races.

Four of those winners would be established in the opening four races: Warren, Kennedy, Richards and McConnell marked their impression on the winner's trophy early on by taking a victory apiece at the Brands Hatch and Thruxton double-headers.

Even so, though the top five (including the consistent Wilson) remained fairly evenly matched during the first half of the season, two names began to emerge from the chasing pack as the year progressed: Kennedy and Richards.

Kennedy became the first two-time winner of the season during round three at Oulton Park, while a double success at the following Snetterton round put the 25-year-old clear of his main rivals, now headed by Richards, 27.5 points adrift.

From this point, Kennedy and Richards annexed the top two positions in the overall standings for the remainder of the season, embarking on an entertaining duel that saw the pendulum of momentum swing continuously between them.

Though the intensity threatened to reach boiling point when they collided at Oulton Park, it was Richards who enjoyed the better mid-season fortune, wins at Knockhill, Oulton Park, Brands Hatch and Cadwell Park helping him to reel in Kennedy and nose ahead with four rounds remaining.

A bizarre crash for Richards at Donington Park, where the Triumph tucked on a discarded visor tear-off, handed the overall lead back to Kennedy with three rounds to go, but there remained little to choose between the two as points became increasingly precious. Indeed, with pressure on both riders growing, neither Kennedy nor Richards won again, though a costly crash for Kennedy at Assen shifted the initiative in Richards's favour at Silverstone and into the final round at Brands Hatch

With Kennedy chasing down a deficit of 12.5 points heading into the season finale, a better result during the first en-

counter of the weekend nibbled the margin down to 8.5, setting the scene for an exciting last-race dice.

Fittingly, the conclusion proved dramatic, Richards committing a rare error to crash out early on, leaving Kennedy needing a mere seventh-place finish to snatch the champion's trophy from his rival's grasp. Just as Mar-Train was preparing to celebrate, however, a final twist in the story saw Kennedy's Yamaha cry enough and grind to a halt with technical gremlins.

Kennedy's heartbreak prompted joy for Richards on the sidelines. The title marked his second in British Supersport, adding to his National Superstock 1000 and British Superbike EVO successes.

A devastated Kennedy had to settle for the runner-up spot. He had taken six wins during the season, well ahead of third-place rider McConnell, who matched him for his victory tally, but lacked the consistency to sustain a title challenge.

After a mediocre start to the season, Christian Iddon's first BSS wins at Assen and Silverstone saw the Oxford TAG Triumph rider soar up the order to secure fourth position, ahead of Wilson, the Gearlink Kawasaki rider unable to replicate the form of 2011, with just a single victory at Silverstone to his name.

Like team-mate Iddon, a strong end to the year saw reigning Superstock 1000 champion Richard Cooper make gains for sixth overall, just ahead of Mossey on the third of the Smiths Gloucester Triumphs. Elsewhere, Warren's bright start to the season had dwindled by the final third of the year, leading to a split with Seton Interceptor Yamaha, while American wild-card PJ Jacobsen was a surprise winner on a Suzuki GSX-R600 at Assen after Tyco Suzuki dusted off the 2011 title-winner for a one-off comeback outing.

In the British Supersport Cup, Glenn Irwin emerged victorious over Luke Jones, the pair impressing many with a series of giant-killing performances that regularly saw them breach the overall top ten.

National Superstock 1000 Championship

Having picked up the Metzeler National Superstock 600 title at his first attempt in 2011, Keith Farmer made the natural progression to 1000cc machinery in 2012 and promptly furthered his reputation as a rising motorcycle talent.

Having joined the Rapid Solicitors Kawasaki operation alongside Superbike contemporaries Shane Byrne and Stuart Easton, Farmer immediately stamped his mark on proceedings by taking wins in the first two rounds at Brands Hatch and Thruxton.

A combination of crashes and indifferent results in the following four events, however, turned the championship into a two-way fight between Farmer and Jason O'Halloran on the Samsung Honda, the Australian picking up wins at Donington Park and Snetterton to nose ahead in the standings at the mid-point in the season.

When Farmer struck back with a victory at Knockhill, though, he was never headed again, the Ulsterman keeping O'Halloran at a comfortable distance before wrapping up the championship during the penultimate round at Silverstone. That made for double domestic titles for the Paul Bird Motorsport-run team following Byrne's success in BSB. Farmer was tipped for a full graduation to Superbikes in 2013.

Despite skipping the final event, O'Halloran held on to the runner-up spot, ahead of the consistent Victor Cox and Jimmy Storrar on their respective ILR Kawasaki and JSR BMW machines, the pair following up in third and fourth, despite not once tasting the winner's champagne.

By contrast, Lee Costello (Halsall Kawasaki), Steve Brogan (Buildbase BMW), David Johnson (Carbontek BMW), Danny Buchan (MSS Bathams Kawasaki) and PJ Jacobsen (Tyco Suzuki) all enjoyed moments on the top of the podium in what proved to be a competitive season of racing in the SSTK 1000 class.

National Superstock 600 Championship

Lee Jackson had a flourish in the final third of the season to thank for his impressive run to the 2012 Metzeler National Superstock 600 Championship title, the 17-year-old prevailing in a three-way final-round showdown with Ben Burke and James Rose.

Indeed, at the mid-point of the season, Chris Walker Racing School Kawasaki rider Jackson hadn't finished any higher than third, but four wins in the final six races propelled him all the way to the title at the expense of Seton Tuning Yamaha's Burke, whose three mid-season victories were negated by costly DNFs in the final two races.

Keeping his title hopes alive to the final round, Rose (Moto-Breakers Yamaha) had to settle for third position in a season built on regular podiums, rather than wins, while teammate Jake Dixon and Alex Olsen (Haribo Starmix Yamaha) completed the overall top five.

Motostar British Championship

Newly rebranded for 2012 to accommodate Moto3 machinery alongside the existing 125GP package, the Motostar British Championship lived up to its reputation as a breeding ground for exciting new talent as 16-year-old Luke Hedger sealed a comfortable title win.

Bradley Ray followed him in the runner-up spot, his five wins negated by a series of no-scores, while Catherine Green grabbed headlines by finishing third overall, becoming the first woman to win a British championship motorcycling race in the process.

Ducati 848 Challenge

The Ducati 848 Challenge continued to go from strength to strength in 2012 with a calendar that blended BSB support events with fly-away rounds at Misano and Assen.

Despite a competitive field of riders, however, Robbie Brown emerged as the dominant champion with eight wins to his name, well ahead of James Folkard and Darren Fry.

Triumph Triple Challenge

With the promise of a guaranteed ride in the British Supersport Championship or National Superstock Championship, the Triumph Triple Challenge was keenly contested in 2012, but it was James Egan who picked up the coveted prize with an impressive 12 wins in 18 races as he put triple figures between himself and runner-up David Sellers.

British Sidecar Challenge

Always an entertaining fixture on the BSB support bill, the Eastern Airways British Sidecar Championship saw Roger Lovelock and Rick Lawrence pick up the 2012 title after taking four victories.

Above: Keith Farmer came back from the doldrums to win Superstock 1000 on the Rapid Solicitors Kawasaki.

Top left: Eight-times winner Robbie Brown was a convincing Ducati 848 Challenge champion.

Above left: National Superstock 600 champion Lee Jackson is joined on the podium by mentor Chris Walker.

Top: Sixteen-year-old Luke Hedger and his team after their Motostar British championship win at Silverstone.

Photos: Clive Challinor Motorsport Photography

GRAND FINALE

By JOHN McKENZIE

AFTER three titles in four seasons, it might have appeared that the highly experienced pairing of Pekka Paivarinta and the age-defying Adolf Haenni would start as favourites, but nothing can be taken for granted in sidecar racing.

With a line-up featuring three world champions – Paivarinta, Reeves and Birchall – and seven different recent race winners, including the aforementioned plus Jorg Steinhausen, Kurt Hock, Markus Schlosser and Seb Delannoy, it was a tough season, ultimately decided only at the final round.

The quality of the contenders was greatly enhanced by the return of Steinhausen, arguably the best sidecar driver never to have won the title, and now passengered by Greg Cluze. They were riding a beautifully presented BMW-powered (and HP supported) LCR outfit. Eight-time race winner Steinhausen had left the championship in 2005, and the return of his title-winning potential was a real boon.

The always-fast Ben and Tom Birchall were hoping to shed the bad luck that had dogged them over the previous couple of years and regain the title they had won in 2009.

Some observers could have been forgiven for assuming that Tim Reeves's star was on the wane after a tricky couple of seasons and eight races without a win, but only a fool would have written off the tough three-time world champion.

With ten races at seven venues, and the series seemingly settled into a recognisable pattern – blessed relief after the turmoil of the previous few years – and a new 'big four' reminiscent of the glory days of Biland, Webster, Streuer and Michel, it was going to be a great show.

Round 1 – 14 April, Magny-Cours, France

The series opened with a support slot at the Bol d'Or, and with two back-to-back titles in the previous two years, it was no surprise that reigning champion Paivarinta set the pace in practice.

From pole position, the Team Finland Suzuki shot away with Reeves close behind, Steinhausen third. Birchall threw his grid second place away with a fluffed start and became trapped in sixth in the melee of Turn One, but was up to fourth by the end of the first lap and chasing Steinhausen. By lap two, Birchall's Yamaha R1 powered LCR was third, and on the next lap past Reeves into second.

Paivarinta's fast start had paid off, however, and he was 3.5 seconds clear. With two laps to go, however, the race was red-flagged due to an oil spill and a passenger needing medical attention.

Paivarinta had a lucky high-speed escape after hitting the oil, which sent him off on to the grass, but he managed to regain the tarmac and took the chequered flag.

The results were counted from lap eight, giving Paivarinta a win by 6.2 seconds; only 2.6 seconds separated Birchall, Reeves and fourth-placed Steinhausen, whose passenger, Cluze, did a magnificent job just to stay on the bike after a water hose came loose, soaking his platform grips.

Reeves was pleased. "We were battling for second, so I'm happy with the result. It's going to be a close season" he said. At that point, no one realised quite how close.

Round 2 – 10 June, Hungaroring, Hungary

The outfits were back at the Hungaroring for the first time since May, 2005, but after just two laps the rain brought out the red flags. The restarted event was run as a 17-lapper, rather than the planned 18.

It was Birchall's first visit to the testing track, but the novelty factor didn't stop him from posting pole, edging Paivarinta out by a mere 0.016 second.

Markus Schlosser was quick off the blocks, but Paivarinta forced through into the first turn. Then the heavens opened and the race was quickly stopped.

For the restart, declared a wet race even though the track was drying, Paivarinta was first into Turn One again, with Birchall tucked in behind, but the race was soon under the control of the Finn and the ominously quick Steinhausen, leaving Birchall and Reeves to tussle for third.

With seven laps to go, Steinhausen, still some five seconds down, was on a charge and hunting down Paivarinta. With only two laps remaining, he took the lead, holding on to win by 0.312 second.

It was a momentous victory for the 41-year-old German, his first at this level since Schleiz in 2005. More notably, it was also the first win by a BMW-powered outfit since the great Klaus Enders had driven his Busch-BMW 500 to win at the Dutch TT in 1974.

The Birchall brothers had defended third until the last corner of the final lap, when Reeves managed to force a pass and snatch the last rostrum place by 0.4 second.

Paivarinta's second place consolidated his points lead with 45 to Steiny's 38.

Round 3 – 16/17 June, Rijeka, Croatia

It was on to a very hot and sunny Croatia for the first two-race weekend of the series. The Birchalls, double winners in 2009, threw down the gauntlet with a pole time of 1m 33.540s, but were beset by electrical gremlins all weekend, which held them back to fourth and fifth places. Tim Reeves and Ashley Hawes had no problems, however, and left with a full 50 points in the bag.

In Saturday's ten-lap sprint, Reeves was in the lead after two laps, with a clattering three-way battle for second behind him between Schlosser, Paivarinta and the Birchalls.

Reeves won by a comfortable ten seconds, heat-

Left: The Birchalls were one of four crews going for gold at the last race.

Far left: Hovermower. Tim Reeves takes a tight line, passenger Ashley Hawes smells the roses.

Below left: Jorg Steinhausen, partnered by Gegory Cluze, returned to the series and won BMW's first three-wheeler race in more than 30 years.

Below: Reeves and Hawes took the gold – it was the driver's fourth title, his young passenger's first.

Photos: Mark Walters

induced tyre problems holding up the rest. Old stager Schlosser held on for second; Paivarinta was third. It was Reeves's first win since the closing race of 2010 at Magny-Cours.

Sunday dawned hotter for the 18-lap second race. This time, Reeves shot away into a first-lap lead, again with Markus Schlosser/Thomas Hofer on his tail. He managed to hold them off by less than a tenth at the flag, with Steinhausen making up the rostrum.

Round 4 – 8 July, Sachsenring, Germany

With a dry time of 1m 28.312s squeezed in between squalls, it was a third pole in a row for the so far win-less Birchalls, this time in front of the damp and windswept MotoGP crowd.

Kurt Hock was first away with his LCR Suzuki, no doubt with thoughts of repeating his 2010 win here, but with the Birchalls, Paivarinta, Steinhausen and Reeves in close company, Hock dragged Birchall along with him. The 2009 champion bided his time. letting his rival do the work.

With two corners left, Birchall made his move, taking his first win of the season by 0.411 second.

Steinhausen had battled through to third in his first race at Sachsenring for six years, while points leader Reeves had had to undergo a race fitness test after getting a nasty insect bite on his gear-change foot overnight. Fourth extended his championship lead to 11 points after Paivarinta had dropped to sixth.

Round 5 – 21/22 July, Schleiz, Germany

Once again, it was Birchall on pole, but with less than a second separating the top six qualifiers, two very close races were expected.

Reeves started from the second row, scythed through and led into the first corner. He was never

headed, keeping Steinhausen at arm's length. At the flag, the gap was 1.6 seconds; it was Reeves's third win of the campaign, which gave him a 19-point lead. Birchall was third after hurriedly replacing the Yamaha R1 engine following late practice problems.

Any hope Reeves might have had of extending his lead in Sunday's 22-lapper was marred by a first-corner incident when Joseph Moser outbraked himself and torpedoed Reeves into the gravel. Passenger Hawes was catapulted from the outfit, luckily without serious injury.

Pekka Paivarinta and Adolf Haenni capitalised with a win, putting them level on points, at 120.

With the Birchalls and Steinhausen now equal in third on 114 points, only six points split the leading four crews with just three races to go.

Round 6 – 11 August, Oschersleben, Germany

Jorg Steinhausen picked up his second win of the year in Saturday's 15-lap sprint, after his first pole of the season. The BMW LCR had taken the lead by the end of the first lap and, despite huge pressure from Birchall, Reeves and Paivarinta, Steinhausen held on to win by 3.63 seconds. Paivarinta benefited from Reeves running wide to take second, with Schlosser placed fourth. However, he was disqualified later for not accepting a jury decision on sealing his engine, elevating Birchall to fourth. That also meant Schlosser would not be competing in the following day's race. Paivarinta now took the lead in the points table, on 140 to Steinhausen's 139, and Reeves dropped to third, but only on 136. It was getting closer.

Hoping to continue his success of the previous day, Steinhausen was first away in the 22-lapper, with the usual pack snapping at his heels.

By the mid-point, Paivarinta had overcome both Birchall and Steinhausen, but his efforts were un-

done when he incurred a drive-through penalty for passing under a yellow flag. He recovered to take fifth and 11 points, but it blew his title hopes wide open. Birchall's win, with Reeves second and Steinhausen third meant that just five points separated the top four going into the final race: Reeves 156, Steiny 155, Birchall 152 and Paivarinta 151.

Round 7 – 8 September, Le Mans, France

At the last round, the championship was up for grabs by the bravest. It was the best possible finale, with everyone needing to win.

Once more, Birchall was on pole, his fifth of the season, and although Reeves was first into the first turn, Birchall was right behind him. Then, hurtling into Turn Four, Birchall and Paivarinta found themselves trying to use the same piece of road. The Finn's outfit clipped the front of the Brit's machine, spinning him out. Paivarinta thought he'd got away with it, but two corners and barely seconds later Haenni fell from the outfit, ending their title hopes.

With Reeves clear, he soon opened a gap over Steinhausen, but as he slowed to conserve his tyres, the BMW LCR began to make up ground, forcing him into outbraking himself at the chicane, which handed Steinhausen the lead. With three laps to go, however, Reeves regained the lead and held it to the flag for his 33rd world championship race win and fourth world title.

"I'm absolutely over the moon," said Reeves. "This has undoubtedly been the hardest one to win. There's been nothing between the leading six outfits all year, so to come out on top is truly special."

Once again, the sidecars had proved that they could deliver high-quality cut-and-thrust racing. With four such closely matched teams and a settled calendar, the future looks healthy for the sport.

IN ANOTHER LEAGUE

By PAUL CARRUTHERS

Above: With a record 16 wins, Josh Hayes dominated on his way to a second consecutive AMA Superbike championship for Yamaha.
Photo: Gold & Goose

Above right: Job done. Hayes celebrated his race victory at Miami as well as cementing his championship.
Photo: AMA Pro Series

JOSH Hayes is quite pointed about who and what we can blame for a boring 2012 AMA Superbike Championship: Blake Young, tennis and Xbox – not necessarily in that order. Oh, and there's one more thing he'd like us to remember – don't kill the messenger. Or in this case, the dominator.

Going into the 2012 season, AMA Superbike fans were foaming at the mouth in anticipation of the series ahead. In 2011, Hayes and Young had fought to the bitter end, with the championship in doubt right up to the final lap of the final race of the season. It could only get better, right?

Wrong.

After winning the championship title by the skin of his teeth in the previous year, Hayes did a few things differently in the off-season leading up to the Daytona opener. He went back to work.

"One of the things is that I've always trained extremely hard," Hayes said as the season drew to a close. "Last year, I did a lot less of the cycling and did some other things. I played a lot of tennis and a lot of Xbox. I refuse to say I was less fit last year, but this year I've done so much more cycling and physical things."

But it wasn't just what he did; it's what the others didn't do that led to him winning a record 16 races during the season. They really didn't put up much of a fight, Hayes said.

"I've done a little bit of my own research because it's contract time. I've actually led 86 per cent of every session, every time we've gone on track, excluding tests – just race weekends. Last year, the number was just a little bit different because of the races. That was it. Not as much has changed from last year as what you actually see.

"Last year, I led most of the sessions in practice, I was on pole in all but one race the entire season, and I had the pace and was fastest in just about every race. Blake [Young] was a little different guy last year. He got up in there and he raced extremely well. The thing that Blake hasn't shown is the pace to ride away from me. I was the only guy who could get away. Otherwise the other guys hung on, stalked and followed me, and beat me in the last couple of laps. Blake was good at slowing the pace in the beginning of the race and not allowing me to do my own thing. This year with the bike has improved, but not the percentage of what people think. And I definitely went back and did my homework."

Hayes is diligent in the way he goes about his business. He's got a plan that works and he doesn't change it from race to race. In fact, he doesn't alter it from lap to lap. Start fast and end fast. And go fast in the middle as well.

"I show up feeling confident," he said. "I know how much work I did. I show up at the racetrack and act like a professional. I get up to speed quickly, and I have a good routine and a lot of experience, and I stick to it. Even on a bad weekend, when I go through my routine, things work."

For his rivals and fans looking for a closer series, it works too well. Hayes went from winning three races in 2011 to 16 in 2012. And Young, still his main rival, went from winning seven races to winning just three. Only one other rider won a race in 2012 and he was the youngest of the Hayden brothers – Roger Lee. He earned his first career Superbike win in the 17th race of the year at Homestead-Miami Raceway in south Florida.

For Hayes, it was his third successive AMA Superbike Championship, the 37-year-old continuing to blossom at a time when most in the sport are hanging up their boots for good. He won early and he continued to win. By mid-season, it was over. After a promising start, Young quickly became a defeated man, racing for second place against the likes of Hayden and Hayes's young Yamaha team-mate, Josh Herrin. Hayes was in another league.

When he didn't win, he finished second, twice. The only time he didn't stand on one of the top two spots of the podium was when he crashed. The first came at Infineon Raceway in Northern California in round six (he remounted to finish seventh); the second was at Homestead (remounted for 12th) as Hayden won. Two blemishes in a record-setting season by the factory Yamaha star. He also tied Mat Mladin when he earned pole position in the final race of the season in New Orleans – his tenth in eleven tries. Mladin had earned every pole position back in 2005.

The season started at Daytona in March with two Superbike races book-ending the Daytona 200 (run for the past several years on 600s and not full-blown superbikes).

On paper, Yamaha had the strongest team, with Hayes and Superbike rookie Herrin, the youngster having moved up from the Daytona SportBike class. Yoshimura Suzuki, meanwhile, had Young and young Chris Clark, the latter on a pay-for ride that basically kicked Tommy Hayden to the kerb.

The second Suzuki team was fielded by basketball legend

Michael Jordan. Half the team was sponsored by Jordan, that GSX-R1000 being ridden by veteran Ben Bostrom; the other side of the tent featured a National Guard-backed machine for Roger Lee Hayden.

There were two of Eric Buell's EBRs at the opener – one for non-defending Daytona SportBike champion Danny Eslick and the other for Geoff May. Buell had attracted Indian bike maker Hero as a sponsor… one with deep pockets.

Larry Pegram was the top BMW in the series in his self-owned team backed by Foremost Insurance; and KTM was on board with a factory RC8R for Chris Fillmore. With no official Honda or Kawasaki teams, the rest were privateers, led by the likes of Steve Rapp on the Attack Kawasaki ZX-10R.

So when Daytona rolled around, it was expected to be a two-man fight for the title: Hayes vs Young. And it started out in just that manner. Hayes won the season opener, but lost out to Young the following day. And we left Florida wringing our hands in anticipation of the season to come. Hayes and Young were going at it again. And Hayden was third both times out, proving that he too could offer up a championship challenge. Splendid stuff.

The two races at Road Atlanta only reinforced the notion of a thrilling season. The first of the two (all the AMA Superbike events are run as double-headers, with the exception of the Laguna Seca round run in conjunction with MotoGP and Miller Motorsports Park, with World Superbike) was the most dramatic of the season. Young and his Yoshimura Suzuki recovered from a frightening crash, which brought out a red flag, to hold off Hayes in a thrilling last-lap battle. The pair had come together on the 14th of 20 laps, going down the hill that closes out a lap. Young crashed, had the wind knocked out of him and appeared injured. He wasn't. Instead he made short work of the field in coming from the back row on the restart to beat Hayes on the final lap. Whew! This was going to be good.

The following day, Hayes took the win in what was really a preview of things to come. He was methodical in assuming the lead on the third of the 20-lap race and he was never headed. Oh-oh.

Not to worry. After four races, the top two men had won a pair each and the series headed to California full of hope.

While Hayes won on Saturday at Infineon, but crashed out on Sunday, Young was second and first. Hayes's championship lead was 14 points leaving California, and the series headed slightly east with anticipation of a battle still high.

The two races in Sonoma were also historic in that Eslick rode the Eric Buell Racing (EBR) 1190RS to its first AMA Superbike podium in race one, then team-mate May backed that up in race two, also third.

Oh, how quickly things change. Although it had started with such promise, the championship battle went south rapidly when it resumed at Miller Motorsports Park. It was there, at the World Superbike round, that Hayes started a tear that would see him reel off ten straight race wins. And not many of them would feature much of a battle. In fact, the only one that comes to mind was the Yamaha rider holding off Hayden and his Suzuki on the final lap in the second of two races at the Mid-Ohio Sports Car Course. As for the rest…

At Miller, Hayes blistered the field, winning by almost eight seconds over Herrin, the youngster starting to get the hang of this Superbike thing in his rookie season. Young was even further back in third.

Hayes beat team-mate Herrin by 5.1 seconds in the first race at Barber Motorsports Park in Alabama; in race two, he topped Young by 4.9 seconds. But surely it would get closer at Young's home track of Road America, right? Wrong. Hayes beat Young by yawning margins of 11.3 and 13.9 seconds respectively in the two races in Wisconsin.

After the first 11 races, Hayes had won eight of them.

In the first race at Mid-Ohio, Hayes romped to victory over Young after Herrin crashed out of the battle. On Sunday, he had his battle with Hayden, and it was a good one. The Suzuki rider actually led on the last lap, but it was Hayes at the finish line first – by just 0.224 second. It was an aberration.

At Mazda Raceway Laguna Seca – in front of the MotoGP contingent – Hayes was dominant again, the Mississippian winning his 28th AMA Superbike race by a tick over nine seconds. Young barely bested Herrin for second, but their battle took place miles behind Hayes.

By the time the series arrived in New Jersey for the 15th and 16th rounds, all that was left for Hayes was to amass records. On Saturday, he tied Mladin with his 11th consecutive pole position, then he went out and won his 12th race of the season, again tying a record set by the Australian. He'd also won his ninth in a row, moving him out of a tie with Ben Spies, yet another record.

Michael Jordan Motorsports' Ben Bostrom was a popular second – his best finish of the year and one he would match in the final race of the season.

On Sunday, Hayes won for a 13th time, giving him the single-season mark for victories. It also gave him a points lead of 98. The title was basically his. Herrin, meanwhile,

Above: The Yamahas of Hayes (1) and Herrin lead Ben Bostrom (23), Geoff May (99), Danny Eslick (69), Steve Rapp (15) and Blake Young (79) over the hill at Barber. Hayes would win both races.
Photo: AMA Pro Series

Far left: Yoshimura Suzuki's Blake Young was the runner-up to Hayes again, but this time by a huge margin.
Photo: Gold & Goose

Left: Roger Lee Hayden was third overall with a first win, but unsure of retaining his Suzuki ride for 2013.

Right: The ever popular Ben Bostrom was Hayden's team-mate on the Michael Jordan-backed Suzuki.
Photos: AMA Pro Series

Above: Champion Martin Cardenas was the stand-out rider in Daytona Sport-Bike – for the first half of the season at least.

Top right: Joey Pasquarella scored a surprise win in the Daytona 200.
Photos: AMA Pro Series

Above right: Cameron Beaubier's season was marred by injury, but he still offered the strongest challenge to Cardenas.
Photo: Gold & Goose

Right: Consistent Dane Westby was the SportBike runner-up.

Far right: One for the future: James Rispoli took victory in the West-side Supersport series.

Bottom right: Jake Lewis from Kentucky was the Supersport Eastern division champion.
Photos: AMA Pro Series

earned his third second-place of the season on Sunday.

The series moved to Homestead-Miami Speedway in Florida, where Hayden earned his first pole position in iffy conditions, denying Hayes another record. In Saturday's race, Hayden backed up his first pole with his first win – a win made easier when Hayes crashed out on the third lap. Still, the youngest Hayden made good with a victory over Eslick and his EBR, with Young ending up third.

The following day, normality returned to the series, with Hayes winning the title before the race. With the Homestead track deemed dangerous by some in the poor conditions, Young opted not to start, thus giving the title to Hayes. Though he didn't have to win, he knows no other way, so win he did – for a 14th time in the season. And at the end of the day, he was crowned champion for a third straight year.

Second went to veteran Steve Rapp in his best ride of the year on the Attack Kawasaki ZX-10R. Rapp beat Bostrom, and the podium was one for the aged: Hayes (37), Rapp (38) and Bostrom (38).

The series came to a close with two races at the brand-new NOLA Motorsports Park on the outskirts of New Orleans, with two more runaway wins by Hayes. Of course. The race also took place without team-mate Herrin, the youngster having suffered a shoulder injury while riding Supermoto, which ended his season prematurely. Young and Hayden were second and third respectively on Saturday, and then Hayden took them both out in a crash on Sunday, giving second to Bostrom, with Eslick third on the EBR. Fourth and fifth over the course of the weekend was Fillmore in his best rides of the season on the KTM.

Young again finished second in the title chase, but this one would be tougher to swallow. He'd lost to Hayes by 154 points. Yes, 154 points – only a year after losing out to him by just five.

Hayden, meanwhile, improved to third – the spot his older brother Tommy had earned in the previous season. And like Tommy, Roger Lee wasn't sure that he'd done enough to

earn another Superbike ride for 2012. If you recall, Tommy won three races in 2011, but still wasn't rehired by the Yoshimura Suzuki team. And he didn't attract a ride until practice at Daytona had already started, when he got the call to fill in at Yamaha for the injured Garrett Gerloff. But that was in the Daytona SportBike class.

Roger Lee left New Orleans unsure of his future, though he was hopeful of returning to the Michael Jordan fold.

DAYTONA SPORTBIKE

The Daytona SportBike Championship was like two seasons in one. The first belonged to GEICO Suzuki's Martin Cardenas, the second to Y.E.S. Graves Yamaha's Cameron Beaubier – the young man many, including Josh Hayes, believe to be the real deal and America's next hope in international road racing.

Neither won the Daytona 200. That went to young Joey Pascarella after the race of his life, the Californian only getting on the podium one other time during the season. Still, he was a Daytona 200 winner and no one can take that away from him.

Beaubier ended up third in the 200, but the week after the race the youngster was hurt in a scooter accident. He suffered a broken kneecap that required surgery and he missed both of the Road Atlanta rounds while recuperating. He came back and finished third at Infineon in the fourth race of the series, but it proved too much for him and he sat out Sunday's race to rest the knee.

With Beaubier out of action, Cardenas took full advantage. In total, the Colombian won six of the first eight races. When he recovered to full strength, Beaubier went to the forefront, winning seven of the last races. The class featured the best racing in the series, and once Beaubier had recovered, he and Cardenas fought it out at nearly every race. The final in New Orleans encapsulated the series perfectly. The pair went at it in both races, with Beaubier winning on Saturday and

Cardenas on Sunday. A fitting conclusion.

Others also won: Jason DiSalvo on a Triumph in the second race at Infineon Raceway; Dane Westby on an M4 Suzuki in race one at Mid-Ohio; and Red Bull RoadRace Factory's Jake Gagne in the rain at Homestead.

Westby had the best year of the rest and actually ended up second in the title chase behind Cardenas as a result of his consistency. He would finish ten points ahead of Beaubier and 45 points behind Cardenas.

Tommy Hayden ended the season fourth, his string of consistent rides early in the season, replacing injured Gerloff, tempered by a late-season shoulder injury. DiSalvo ended up fifth, his season in disarray with financial woes.

SUPERSPORT

The Supersport class in AMA racing is for young upstarts, and is split into East and West divisions, with points kept separately. The top kids with better-funded efforts end up racing in both series, but earn points only in the one they choose at the beginning.

The best of the 'kids' in 2012 was James Rispoli. The East champion in 2011 elected to return to the class in 2012, and promptly went out and won the West portion of the series. Rispoli is hoping to move up to the Daytona SportBike class for 2013.

The East series was won by Jake Lewis, the Kentuckian under the wing of Hayden patriarch, Earl Hayden. When he's not watching his sons, Earl is watching Lewis, and the youngster didn't disappoint in winning the title at his first attempt.

VANCE & HINES XR1200

The Vance & Hines XR1200 spec class was back for a second season and with a championship within a championship called the Showdown. The title was won by veteran Michael Barnes over Benny Carlson and Tyler O'Hara, though O'Hara won four races to Barnes's three. Kyle Wyman also won four races early on and was the man to beat prior to suffering injury in a big crash at New Jersey Motorsports Park.

The series ended in a winner-take-all finale between Barnes and O'Hara, and it went down the final lap. That's when things got weird. Coming out of the last corner, with Barnes leading, O'Hara reached out and grabbed his opponent's right arm, pulling himself past. An incensed Barnes shut the throttle and started his complaints instantly. The AMA docked O'Hara for "intentionally impeding another rider", which gave Barnes the title (and the $25,000 prize money that went with it), while for his blunder O'Hara slipped to third overall.

THE FUTURE

Other than Josh Hayes, not many were sure of their Superbike futures after the final race in Louisiana. Hayes hadn't signed his Yamaha contract yet, but he was certain to. He will be joined again by Josh Herrin, though upstart Cameron Beaubier will be nipping at Herrin's heels for that second Yamaha R1 in short order.

No one knows about the Jordan Suzuki team, though they are expected to return. Ditto for the Yoshimura Suzuki squad, but will they bring back Young? And will Clark's dad keep paying for his ride? More questions than answers.

The Buells are almost certain to return, and probably with the same two riders.

Pegram's BMWs were for sale at season's end...

As for racetracks, there still wasn't a schedule at press time, but it was known that Infineon Raceway had pulled the plug on its National.

Similarly, no one knows about the TV package. What is known is that the 2012 schedule had the races airing late on the west coast and very late on the east coast. Not quite a shambles, but plenty of room for improvement.

MAJOR RESULTS

OTHER CHAMPIONSHIP RACING SERIES WORLDWIDE

Compiled by PETER McLAREN

AMA Championship Road Race Series (Superbike)

DAYTONA INTERNATIONAL SPEEDWAY, Daytona Beach, Florida, 16–17 March, 44.300 miles/70.006km
Race 1
1 Josh Hayes (Yamaha); **2** Blake Young (Suzuki); **3** Roger Lee Hayden (Suzuki); **4** Larry Pegram (BMW); **5** Steve Rapp (Kawasaki); **6** Geoff May (EBR); **7** Jake Holden (BMW); **8** Robertino Pietri (Suzuki); **9** Chris Clark (Suzuki); **10** David Anthony (Suzuki)

Race 2
1 Blake Young (Suzuki); **2** Josh Hayes (Yamaha); **3** Roger Lee Hayden (Suzuki); **4** Josh Herrin (Yamaha); **5** Larry Pegram (BMW); **6** Steve Rapp (Kaw); **7** Chris Clark (Suzuki); **8** Jake Holden (BMW); **9** Danny Eslick (EBR); **10** Robertino Pietri (Suzuki)

ROAD ATLANTA, Braselton, Georgia, 21–22 April, 50.800 miles/81.700km
Race 1
1 Blake Young (Suzuki); **2** Josh Hayes (Yamaha); **3** Josh Herrin (Yamaha); **4** Roger Lee Hayden (Suzuki); **5** Geoff May (EBR); **6** Chris Fillmore (KTM); **7** Steve Rapp (Kawasaki); **8** Ben Bostrom (Suzuki); **9** Chris Clark (Suzuki); **10** Danny Eslick (EBR)

Race 2
1 Josh Hayes (Yamaha); **2** Blake Young (Suzuki); **3** Josh Herrin (Yamaha); **4** Roger Lee Hayden (Suzuki); **5** Larry Pegram (BMW); **6** Taylor Knapp (Suzuki); **7** Chris Fillmore (KTM); **8** Steve Rapp (Kawasaki); **9** Danny Eslick (EBR); **10** Chris Clark (Suzuki)

INFINEON RACEWAY, Sonoma, California, 5–6 May, 51.040 miles/82.141km
Race 1
1 Josh Hayes (Yamaha); **2** Blake Young (Suzuki); **3** Danny Eslick (EBR); **4** Josh Herrin (Yamaha); **5** Geoff May (EBR); **6** Steve Rapp (Kawasaki); **7** Ben Bostrom (Suzuki); **8** David Anthony (Suzuki); **9** Larry Pegram (BMW); **10** Roger Lee Hayden (Suzuki)

Race 2
1 Blake Young (Suzuki); **2** Roger Lee Hayden (Suzuki); **3** Geoff May (EBR); **4** Ben Bostrom (Suzuki); **5** Chris Fillmore (KTM); **6** Danny Eslick (EBR); **7** Josh Hayes (Yamaha); **8** David Anthony (Suzuki); **9** Robertino Pietri (Suzuki); **10** Larry Pegram (BMW).

MILLER MOTORSPORTS PARK, Tooele, Utah, 28 May, 48.780 miles/78.400km
1 Josh Hayes (Yamaha); **2** Josh Herrin (Yamaha); **3** Blake Young (Suzuki); **4** Geoff May (EBR); **5** Ben Bostrom (Suzuki); **6** Danny Eslick (EBR); **7** Larry Pegram (BMW); **8** Chris Clark (Suzuki); **9** David Anthony (Suzuki); **10** Chris Fillmore (KTM).

ROAD AMERICA, Elkhart Lake, Wisconsin, 2–3 June, 52.000 miles/83.686km
Race 1
1 Josh Hayes (Yamaha); **2** Blake Young (Suzuki); **3** Josh Herrin (Yamaha); **4** Ben Bostrom (Suzuki); **5** Larry Pegram (BMW); **6** Jason Farrell (Kawasaki); **7** Chris Clark (Suzuki); **8** Geoff May (EBR); **9** Chris Fillmore (KTM); **10** Stefan Nebel (KTM).

Race 2
1 Josh Hayes (Yamaha); **2** Blake Young (Suzuki); **3** Josh Herrin (Yamaha); **4** Ben Bostrom (Suzuki); **5** Danny Eslick (EBR); **6** Geoff May (EBR); **7** Chris Clark (Suzuki); **8** David Anthony (Suzuki); **9** Chris Fillmore (KTM); **10** Larry Pegram (BMW).

BARBER MOTORSPORTS PARK, Birmingham, Alabama, 23–24 June, 49.890 miles/80.435km
Race 1
1 Josh Hayes (Yamaha); **2** Josh Herrin (Yamaha); **3** Blake Young (Suzuki); **4** Geoff May (EBR); **5** Roger Lee Hayden (Suzuki); **6** Larry Pegram (BMW); **7** Danny Eslick (EBR); **8** Chris Clark (Suzuki); **9** Steve Rapp (Kawasaki); **10** David Anthony (Suzuki).

Race 2
1 Josh Hayes (Yamaha); **2** Blake Young (Suzuki); **3** Josh Herrin (Yamaha); **4** Geoff May (EBR); **5** Roger Lee Hayden (Suzuki); **6** Ben Bostrom (Suzuki); **7** Steve Rapp (Kawasaki); **8** Larry Pegram (BMW); **9** David Anthony (Suzuki); **10** Chris Ulrich (Suzuki).

MID-OHIO SPORTS CAR COURSE, Lexington, Ohio, 14–15 July, 50.400 miles/81.100km
Race 1
1 Josh Hayes (Yamaha); **2** Blake Young (Suzuki); **3** Roger Lee Hayden (Suzuki); **4** Steve Rapp (Kawasaki); **5** Larry Pegram (BMW); **6** Geoff May (EBR); **7** Ben Bostrom (Suzuki); **8** Taylor Knapp (Suzuki); 9. Danny Eslick (EBR); **10** Chris Ulrich (Suzuki).

Race 2
1 Josh Hayes (Yamaha); **2** Roger Lee Hayden (Suzuki); **3** Josh Herrin (Yamaha); **4** Steve Rapp (Kawasaki); **5** Geoff May (EBR); **6** Larry Pegram (BMW); **7** Danny Eslick (EBR); **8** Taylor Knapp (Suzuki); **9** Chris Clark (Suzuki); **10** Chris Ulrich (Suzuki).

MAZDA RACEWAY LAGUNA SECA, Monterey, California, 29 July, 41.400 miles/66.627km
1 Josh Hayes (Yamaha); **2** Blake Young (Suzuki); **3** Josh Herrin (Yamaha); **4** Danny Eslick (EBR); **5** Ben Bostrom (Suzuki); **6** Geoff May (EBR); **7** Taylor Knapp (Suzuki); **8** Roger Lee Hayden (Suzuki); **9** Stefan Nebel (KTM); **10** Larry Pegram (BMW).

NEW JERSEY MOTORSPORTS PARK, Millville, New Jersey, 8–9 September, 51.750 miles/82.284km
Race 1
1 Josh Hayes (Yamaha); **2** Ben Bostrom (Suzuki); **3** Blake Young (Suzuki); **4** Taylor Knapp (Suzuki); **5** Josh Herrin (Yamaha); **6** Geoff May (EBR); **7** Larry Pegram (BMW); **8** Chris Fillmore (KTM); **9** Roger Lee Hayden (Suzuki); **10** David Anthony (Suzuki).

Race 2
1 Josh Hayes (Suzuki); **2** Josh Herrin (Yamaha); **3** Roger Lee Hayden (Suzuki); **4** Blake Young (Suzuki); **5** Ben Bostrom (Suzuki); **6** Steve Rapp (Kawasaki); **7** Taylor Knapp (Suzuki); **8** Danny Eslick (EBR); **9** Larry Pegram (BMW); **10** Chris Fillmore (KTM).

HOMESTEAD-MIAMI SPEEDWAY, Homestead, Florida, 22–23 September, 52.900 miles/85.100km
Race 1
1 Roger Lee Hayden (Suzuki); **2** Danny Eslick (EBR); **3** Blake Young (Suzuki); **4** Geoff May (EBR); **5** Ben Bostrom (Suzuki); **6** Chris Ulrich (Suzuki); **7** David Anthony (Suzuki); **8** Larry Pegram (BMW); **9** Taylor Knapp (Suzuki); **10** Aaron Yates (BMW).

Race 2
1 Josh Hayes (Yamaha); **2** Steve Rapp (Kawasaki); **3** Ben Bostrom (Suzuki); **4** Josh Herrin (Yamaha); **5** Geoff May (EBR); **6** Robertino Pietri (Suzuki); **7** Bruno Silva (Kawasaki); **8** Chris Ulrich (Suzuki); **9** Sean Dwyer (Suzuki); **10** Roger Lee Hayden (Suzuki).

NOLA MOTORSPORTS PARK, New Orleans, Louisiana, 6–7 October, 49.500 miles/79.560km
Race 1
1 Josh Hayes (Yamaha); **2** Blake Young (Suzuki); **3** Roger Lee Hayden (Suzuki); **4** Chris Fillmore (KTM); **5** Robertino Pietri (Suzuki); **6** Larry Pegram (BMW); **7** Taylor Knapp (Suzuki); **8** Steve Rapp (Kawasaki); **9** David Anthony (Suzuki); **10** Aaron Yates (BMW).

Race 2
1 Josh Hayes (Yamaha); **2** Ben Bostrom (Suzuki); **3** Danny Eslick (EBR); **4** Aaron Yates (BMW); **5** Chris Fillmore (KTM); **6** Chris Ulrich (Suzuki); **7** Robertino Pietri (Suzuki); **8** David Anthony (Suzuki); **9** Steve Rapp (Kawasaki); **10** Jordan Burgess (Suzuki).

Final Championship Points

1	Josh Hayes	580
2	Blake Young	426
3	Roger Lee Hayden	314
4	Josh Herrin	307
5	Geoff May	277
6	Ben Bostrom	271

7 Larry Pegram, 260; **8** Danny Eslick 242, 157; **9** Steve Rapp, 216; **10** Chris Ulrich, 186.

Endurance World Championship

BOL D'OR 24 HEURES, Magny-Cours, France, 14–15 April
FIM Endurance World Championship Round 1, 781 laps of the 2.741-mile/4.411km circuit, 2,140.600 miles/3,445.000km
1 Team SRC Kawasaki, FRA: Da Costa/Leblanc/Four (Kawasaki), 24h 0m 23.531s, 89.168mph/143.502km/h.
2 Suzuki Endurance Racing Team, FRA: Philippe/Delhalle/Foret (Suzuki), 781 laps; **3** Monster Energy Yamaha YART, AUT: Jerman/Martin/Giabbani (Yamaha), 776 laps; **4** Yamaha France GMT 94 Michelin Yamalube, FRA: Checa/Foray/Lagrive (Yamaha), 776 laps; **5** Yamalube Folch Endurance, ESP: Ribalta/Dos Santos/Tizon (Yamaha), 765 laps; **6** 3D Endurance Moto Center, FRA: Debise/Delegue/Holub (Kawasaki), 750 laps; **7** Kraftwerk Penz13.com RT, GER: Buisson/Fastre/Vallcaneras (BMW), 749 laps; **8** MCP Starteam 67, FRA: Lucas/Hardt/Diguet (Suzuki), 748 laps; **9** Honda TT Legends, GBR: Donald/McGuinness/Andrews (Honda), 747 laps; **10** DG Sport Herock, BEL: Van Keymeulen/Cudlin/Vizziello (Yamaha), 741 laps; **11** Atomic MotoSport, FRA: Muteau/Jond (Suzuki), 737 laps; **12** Team 18 Sapeurs Pompiers, FRA: Molinier/Prulhiere/Briere (BMW), 736 laps; **13** Racing Team Sarazin, FRA: Gerouah/Kokes/Bernon (Kawasaki), 735 laps; **14** Louit Moto 33, FRA: Baz/Guamoni/Chevaux (Kawasaki), 732 laps; **15** Team Dunlop Motors Events, FRA: Charpin/Maccio/Wolf (Suzuki), 730 laps.
Fastest lap: Suzuki Endurance Racing Team, 1m 41.359s, 97.348mph/156.667km/h.
Endurance World Championship (EWC) points: 1 Team SRC Kawasaki, 40; **2** Suzuki Endurance Racing Team, 33; **3** Monster Energy Yamaha YART, 28; **4** Yamaha France GMT 94 Michelin Yamalube, 24; **5** Yamalube Folch Endurance, 21; **6** Honda TT Legends, 19.

8 HOURS OF DOHA, Losail, Qatar, 9 June
FIM Endurance World Championship, Round 2, 226 laps of the 3.343-mile/5.380km circuit, 755.500 miles/1,215.900km
1 BMW Motorrad France Team Thevent, BEL: Gimbert/Cudlin/Nigon (BMW), 8h 1m 18.847s, 94.181mph/151.570km/h.
2 Bolliger Team Switzerland, SUI: Saiger/Stamm/Tangre (Kawasaki), 223 laps; **3** Honda TT Legends, GBR: Kiyonari/Laverty/O'Halloran (Honda), 222 laps; **4** Suzuki Endurance Racing Team, FRA: Philippe/Delhalle/Kagayama (Suzuki), 222 laps; **5** Qatar Endurance Racing Team, QAT: Al Malki/West/Prinz (Suzuki), 220 laps; **6** Team Motors Events AMT Assurances, FRA: Savary/Dietrich/Moreira (Suzuki), 219 laps; **7** Penz13 Kraftwerk Herpigny Racing, GER: Vallcaneras/Fila/Fastre (BMW), 219 laps; **8** DG Sport Herock, BEL: Van Keymeulen/Cudlin/Vizziello (Yamaha), 218 laps; **9** Maco Racing Team, SVK: Pridmore/Junod/Black (Yamaha), 216 laps; **10** Atomic MotoSport, FRA: Muteau/Jond/Devoyon (Suzuki), 215 laps; **11** Yamalube Folch Endurance, ESP: Ribalta/Tizon/Martinez (Yamaha), 209 laps; **12** Team R2CL, FRA: Capela/Baratin/Chausse (Suzuki), 206 laps; **13** Ecurie Chrono Sport, FRA: Herveux/Pibolleau/Mathie (Kawasaki), 203 laps; **14** Team Flembbo Djimiant Serbia, SER: Bosio/Cersosimo/Perisic (Kawasaki), 202 laps; **15** MotoRacingParts Endurance Penz13, GER: Lehnherr/Al Marikhi/Seidel (BMW), 201 laps.
Fastest lap: BMW Motorrad France Team Thevent, 2m 1.231s, 99.271mph/159.761km/h.
Endurance World Championship (EWC) points: 1 Suzuki Endurance Racing Team, 54; **2** Honda TT Legends, 44; **3** Team SRC Kawasaki, 40; **4** Yamalube Folch Endurance, 37; **5** BMW Motorrad France Team Thevent, 35; **6** Bolliger Team Switzerland, 29.

SUZUKA 8 HOURS, Suzuka, Japan, 29 July
FIM Endurance World Championship, Round 3, 215 laps of the 3.617-mile/5.821km circuit, 777.700 miles/1,251.500km
1 FCC TSR Honda, JPN: Rea/Akiyoshi/Okada (Honda), 8h 1m 35.450s, 96.880mph/155.920km/h.
2 Toho Racing with Moriwaki, JPN: Yamaguchi/Takahashi/Teshima (Honda), 211 laps; **3** Yamaha France GMT 94 Michelin Yamalube, FRA: Checa/Foray (Yamaha), 211 laps; **4** Moto Map Supply, JPN: Konno/Tsuda/Tamitsuji (Suzuki), 210 laps; **5** Honda Suzuka Racing Team, JPN: Tokudome/Yasuda/Kitaguchi (Honda), 210 laps; **6** Honda Dream Sakurai, JPN: Stauffer/Maxwell (Honda), 209 laps; **7** Teluru & Emobile Kohara RT, JPN: Tsujimura/Noda/Watanabe (Honda), 209 laps; **8** Team Motorrad 39, JPN: Teramoto/Sakai/Yagi (BMW), 208 laps; **9** BMW Motorrad France Team Thevent, BEL: Gimbert/Cudlin/Nigon (BMW), 208 laps; **10** Honda TT Legends, GBR: Donald/McGuinness/O'Halloran (Honda), 207 laps; **11** Bolliger Team Switzerland, SWI: Saiger/Stamm/Tangre (Kawasaki), 206 laps; **12** Team Sugai Racing Japan, JPN: Sugai/Takeishi (Ducati), 206 laps; **13** RS Itoh & Asia, JPN: Higashimura/Iwazaki/Watanabe (Kawasaki), 206 laps; **14** Honda Ryokuyoukai Kumamoto, JPN: Yoshida/Kitaori/Iida (Honda), 204 laps; **15** Suzuki Endurance Racing Team, FRA: Philippe/Delhalle/Kagayama (Suzuki), 204 laps.
Fastest lap: MuSASHi RT HARC-PRO, JPN: Kiyonari/Aoyama/Takahashi (Honda), 2m 7.943s, 101.770mph/163.790km/h.
Endurance World Championship (EWC) points: 1 Suzuki Endurance Racing Team, 60; **2** Honda TT Legends, 55; **3** Yamaha France GMT 94 Michelin Yamalube, 49; **4** BMW Motorrad France Team Thevent, 47; **5** Team SRC Kawasaki, 40; **6** Bolliger Team Switzerland, 39.

OSCHERSLEBEN 8 HOURS, Oschersleben, Germany, 11 August
FIM Endurance World Championship, Round 4, 313 laps of the 2.279-mile/3.667km circuit, 713.200 miles/1,147.800km
1 Suzuki Endurance Racing Team, FRA: Philippe/Delhalle/Kagayama (Suzuki), 8h 1m 10.113s, 88.933mph/143.123km/h.
2 BMW Motorrad France Team Thevent, BEL: Gimbert/Cudlin/Nigon (BMW), 312 laps; **3** Yamaha France GMT 94 Michelin Yamalube, FRA: Checa/Foray/Giabbani (Yamaha), 312 laps; **4** Honda TT Legends, GBR: Donald/McGuinness/O'Halloran (Honda), 309 laps; **5** Team Motors Events AMT Assurances, FRA: Dietrich/Savary/Guittet (Suzuki), 306 laps; **6** 3D Endurance Moto Center, FRA: Debise/Echard/Di Carlo (Kawasaki), 306 laps; **7** Qatar Endurance Racing Team, QAT: West/Prinz/Al Malki (Suzuki), 305 laps; **8** Yamalube Folch Endurance, ESP: Ribalta/Tizon (Yamaha), 304 laps; **9** DG Sport Herock, BEL: Van Keymeulen/Cudlin/Vizziello (Yamaha), 303 laps; **10** AM Moto Racing Compétition, FRA: Loiseau/Maitre/Masson (Suzuki), 300 laps; **11** Bolliger Team Switzerland, SWI: Saiger/Stamm/Tangre (Kawasaki), 300 laps; **12** Monster Energy Yamaha YART, AUS: Jerman/Martin/Nakasuga (Yamaha), 298 laps; **13** RS Speedbikes Racing, GER: Albrecht/Hanke/Kollan (BMW), 297 laps; **14** Motobox Kremer by Shell Advance, GER: Scherrer/Paavilainen/Szalai (Suzuki), 297 laps; **15** TSV Völpke powered by Schubert, GER: Bergau/Reichmann/Stuppi (BMW), 296 laps.
Fastest lap: Monster Energy Yamaha YART, 1m 27.426s, 93.826mph/150.999km/h.
Endurance World Championship (EWC) points: 1 Suzuki Endurance Racing Team, 95; **2** BMW Motorrad France Team Thevent, 76; **3** Honda TT Legends, 76; **4** Yamaha France GMT 94 Michelin Yamalube, 74; **5** Bolliger Team Switzerland, 55; **6** Yamalube Folch Endurance, 55.

24 HEURES DU MANS, Le Mans Bugatti Circuit, France, 8–9 September
FIM Endurance World Championship, Round 5, 844 laps of the 2.600-mile/4.185km circuit, 2,194.800 miles/3,532.100km
1 Team SRC Kawasaki, FRA: Da Costa/Leblanc/Foray (Kawasaki), 24h 1m 24.808s, 91.359mph/147.028km/h.
2 Suzuki Endurance Racing Team, FRA: Philippe/

Delhalle/Tsuda (Suzuki), 844 laps; **3** BMW Motorrad France Team Thevent, BEL: Gimbert/Cudlin/Nigon (BMW), 840 laps; **4** Yamaha France GMT 94 Michelin Yamalube, FRA: Checa/Foray/Lagrive (Yamaha), 839 laps; **5** Honda TT Legends, GBR: Donald/McGuinness/Gines (Honda), 828 laps; **6** National Motos, FRA: Bocquet/Buisson/Masson (Honda), 815 laps; **7** Monster Energy Yamaha YART, AUT: Jerman/Martin/Giabbani (Yamaha), 811 laps; **8** Louit Moto 33, FRA: Perret/Salchaud/Chevaux (Kawasaki), 809 laps; **9** Penz13 Kraftwerk Herpigny Racing, GER: Vos/Vallcaneras/Pridmore (BMW), 806 laps; **10** RAC 41 Yam Avenue Ipone, FRA: Denis/Brivet/Gantner (Yamaha), 803 laps; **11** Viltaïs Racing Division, FRA: Bardet/Besnard/Berthome (Yamaha), 802 laps; **12** Team 18 Sapeurs Pompiers, FRA: Molinier/Prulhiere/Briere (BMW), 800 laps; **13** Atomic MotoSport, FRA: Bellucci/Jond/Devoyon (Suzuki), 795 laps; **14** Team R2CL, FRA: Baratin/Diguet/Capela (Suzuki), 793 laps; **15** 3D Endurance Moto Center, FRA: Egea/Di Carlo/Holub (Kawasaki), 786 laps.
Fastest lap: Yamaha France GMT 94 Michelin Yamalube, 1m 38.562s, 94.982mph/152.858km/h.

Final Endurance World Championship (EWC) points:

1	Suzuki Endurance Racing Team, FRA	128
2	BMW Motorrad ... France Thevent, BEL	104
3	Yamaha France GMT 94 ..., FRA	98
4	Honda TT Legends, GBR	97
5	Team SRC Kawasaki, FRA	80
6	Monster Energy Yamaha YART, AUT	59

7 Bolliger Team Switzerland, SUI, 55; **8** Yamalube Folch Endurance, ESP, 55; **9** Team R2CL, FRA, 49; **10** FCC TSR Honda, JPN, 35; **11** Team 18 Sapeurs Pompiers, FRA, 30; **12** Toho Racing with Moriwaki, JPN, 29; **13** Team Flembbo Dijamant Serbia, SER, 29; **14** National Motos, FRA, 29; **15** Maco Racing Team, SVK, 23.

Isle of Man Tourist Trophy Races

ISLE OF MAN TOURIST TROPHY COURSE, 2–9 June, 37.730-mile/60.720km circuit
Dainese Superbike TT (6 laps, 226.380 miles/364.320km)
1 John McGuinness (1000 Honda), 1h 46m 3.06s, 128.078mph/206.122km/h.
2 Cameron Donald (1000 Honda), 1h 46m 17.92s; **3** Bruce Anstey (1000 Honda), 1h 47m 0.22s; **4** Guy Martin (1000 Suzuki), 1h 47m 20.18s; **5** Gary Johnson (1000 Honda), 1h 47m 35.65s; **6** William Dunlop (1000 Honda), 1h 47m 53.79s; **7** James Hillier (1000 Kawasaki), 1h 49m 1.23s; **8** Ian Hutchinson (1000 Yamaha), 1h 49m 41.52s; **9** Dean Harrison (1000 BMW), 1h 50m 11.13s; **10** Michael Dunlop (1000 Honda), 1h 50m 18.92s; **11** Dan Kneen (1000 Suzuki), 1h 50m 22.17s; **12** Steve Mercer (1000 Honda), 1h 50m 46.22s; **13** Dan Stewart (1000 Honda), 1h 50m 54.36s; **14** David Johnson (1000 Kawasaki), 1h 51m 22.06s; **15** Davy Morgan (1000 Suzuki), 1h 51m 46.73s.
Fastest lap: John McGuinness (1000 Honda), 17m 20.97s, 130.483mph/209.992km/h.
Superbike TT lap record: Conor Cummins (1000cc Kawasaki), 17m 12.83s, 131.511mph/211.646km/h (2010).

Sure Sidecar TT Race 1 (3 laps, 113.190 miles/182.160km)
1 Dave Molyneux/Patrick Farrance (600 DMR), 1hr 0m 4.29s, 113.055mph/181.944km/h.
2 Ben Birchall/Tom Birchall (600 LCR Honda), 1hr 0m 26.63s; **3** Conrad Harrison/Mike Aylott (600 Shelbourne Honda), 1hr 0m 40.89s; **4** Gary Bryan/Jamie Winn (600 Baker Honda), 1hr 1m 32.79s; **5** Robert Handcock/Ken Edwards (600 Shelbourne Honda), 1hr 3m 14.92s; **6** Mike Cookson/Kris Hibberd (600 Ireson Honda), 1hr 3m 30.99s; **7** Gary Knight/Dan Knight (600 DMR Kawasaki), 1hr 3m 42.13s; **8** Frank Lelias/Charlie Richardson (600 LCR Honda), 1hr 3m 52.87s; **9** John Saunders/Shaun Parker (600 Shelbourne Honda), 1hr 4m 19.18s; **10** Tony Thirkell/Nigel Barlow (600 MR Equipe Honda), 1hr 4m 27.78s; **11** Francois Leblond/Johnathan Huet (600 Shelbourne Suzuki), 1hr 4m 55.75s; **12** Mick Donovan/Aaron Galligan (600 Honda), 1hr 5m 11.18s; **13** David Atkinson/Phil Knapton (600 LCR Suzuki), 1hr 5m 12.12s; **14** Douglas Wright/Martin Hull (600 Baker Honda), 1hr 5m 25.96s; **15** Gordon Shand/Stuart Clark (600 Shand F2 Suzuki), 1hr 5m 26.72s.
Fastest lap: Molyneux/Farrance (600 DMR), 19m 55.77s, 113.590mph/182.805km/h.
Sidecar lap record: Nick Crowe/Dan Sayle (600cc LCR Honda), 19m 24.24s, 116.667mph/187.757km/h (2007).

Monster Energy Supersport TT Race 1 (4 laps, 150.920 miles/242.880km)
1 Bruce Anstey (600 Honda), 1h 12m 55.92s, 124.160mph/199.816km/h.
2 Cameron Donald (600 Honda), 1h 12m 56.69s; **3** William Dunlop (600 Honda), 1h 13m 17.80s; **4** John McGuinness (600 Honda), 1h 13m 26.06s; **5** James Hillier (600 Kawasaki), 1h 15m 25.86s; **6** Ian Lougher (600 Kawasaki), 1h 15m 36.06s; **7** Roy Richardson (600 Yamaha), 1h 15m 36.07s; **8** Dan Stewart (600 Honda), 1h 15m 46.43s; **9** Ian Hutchinson (600 Yamaha), 1h 15m 54.82s; **10** Ivan Lintin (600 Kawasaki), 1h 16m 21.57s; **11** Daniel Cooper (675 Triumph), 1h 16m 39.52s; **12** Adrian Archibald (600 Yamaha), 1h 16m 41.23s; **13** Robert Wilson (600 Kawasaki), 1h 16m 47.01s; **14** Russ Mountford (600 Yamaha), 1h 16m 54.32s; **15** Stefano Bonetti (600 Honda), 1h 16m 54.54s.
Fastest lap: Michael Dunlop (600 Yamaha), 17m 49.95s, 126.948mph/204.303km/h.
Supersport lap record: Michael Dunlop (600cc Yamaha), 17m 42.52s, 127.836mph/205.732km/h (2010).

Royal London 360 Superstock TT (4 laps, 150.920 miles/242.880km)
1 John McGuinness (1000 Honda), 1h 11m 29.65s, 126.657mph/203.835km/h.
2 Michael Dunlop (1000 Kawasaki), 1h 11m 37.45s; **3** Ryan Farquhar (1000 Kawasaki), 1h 11m 42.41s; **4** Bruce Anstey (1000 Honda), 1h 12m 5.98s; **5** Guy Martin (1000 Suzuki), 1h 12m 6.85s; **6** James Hillier (1000 Kawasaki), 1h 12m 11.09s; **7** Michael Rutter (1000 Kawasaki), 1h 12m 18.48s; **8** Gary Johnson (1000 Honda), 1h 12m 35.48s; **9** Dan Stewart (1000 Honda), 1h 12m 40.09s; **10** Cameron Donald (1000 Honda), 1h 12m 42.25s; **11** Ian Hutchinson (1000 Yamaha), 1h 13m 33.35s; **12** Stefano Bonetti (1000 Kawasaki), 1h 13m 48.49s; **13** David Johnson (1000 Kawasaki), 1h 14m 0.95s; **14** Ian Mackman (1000 Kawasaki), 1h 14m 3.89s; **15** Adrian Archibald (1000 Kawasaki), 1h 14m 15.92s.
Fastest lap: Michael Dunlop (1000 Kawasaki), 17m 30.87s, 129.253mph/208.013km/h.
Superstock lap record: Ian Hutchinson (1000cc Honda), 17m 18.91s, 130.741mph/210.407km/h (2010).

SES TT Zero (1 lap, 37.730 miles/60.720km)
1 Michael Rutter (2012 MotoCzysz E1PC), 21m 45.33s, 104.056mph/167.462km/h (record).
2 John McGuinness (MUGEN Shinden), 22m 8.85s; **3** Mark Miller (2012 MotoCzysz E1PC), 22m 23.97s; **4** Rob Barber (Zero Emission TGM), 28m 56.45s.
Previous lap record: Michael Rutter (2011 MotoCzysz E1PC), 22m 43.68s, 99.604mph/160.297km/h (2011).

Monster Energy Supersport TT Race 2 (4 laps, 150.920 miles/242.880km)
1 Michael Dunlop (600 Yamaha), 1h 13m 17.76s, 123.543mph/198.823km/h.
2 Cameron Donald (600 Honda), 1h 13m 31.02s; **3** Ryan Farquhar (600 Kawasaki), 1h 13m 50.37s; **4** Bruce Anstey (600 Honda), 1h 13m 50.38s; **5** John McGuinness (600 Honda), 1h 14m 1.46s; **6** Ian Hutchinson (600 Yamaha), 1h 15m 6.97s; **7** James Hillier (600 Kawasaki), 1h 15m 11.20s; **8** Guy Martin (600 Suzuki), 1h 15m 17.95s; **9** Dan Stewart (600 Honda), 1h 15m 45.73s; **10** Daniel Cooper (675 Triumph), 1h 15m 52.62s; **11** Roy Richardson (600 Yamaha), 1h 15m 53.98s; **12** Ian Lougher (600 Kawasaki), 1h 16m 17.68s; **13** Dean Harrison (600 Yamaha), 1h 16m 18.97s; **14** Ivan Lintin (600 Kawasaki), 1h 16m 24.95s; **15** Ben Wylie (600 Yamaha), 1h 16m 41.01s.
Fastest lap: Michael Dunlop (600 Yamaha), 18m 1.19s, 125.629mph/202.180km/h.
Supersport lap record: Michael Dunlop (600cc Yamaha), 17m 42.52s, 127.836mph/205.732km/h (2010).

Sure Sidecar TT Race 2 (3 laps, 113.190 miles/182.160km)
1 Dave Molyneux/Patrick Farrance (600 DMR), 1hr 0m 3.80s, 113.071mph/181.970km/h.
2 Tim Reeves/Dan Sayle (600 LCR Honda), 1hr 0m 20.92s; **3** Ben Birchall/Tom Birchall (600 LCR Honda), 1hr 0m 48.94s; **4** Gary Bryan/Jamie Winn (600 Baker Honda), 1hr 2m 24.04s; **5** Douglas Wright/Martin Hull (600 Baker Honda), 1hr 2m 38.06s; **6** Gregory Lambert/Jason Crowe (600 GLR Honda), 1hr 2m 51.68s; **7** Robert Handcock/Ken Edwards (600 Shelbourne Honda), 1hr 3m 42.93s; **8** Tony Baker/Fiona Baker-Milligan (600 Baker Suzuki), 1hr 3m 58.52s; **9** Karl Bennett/Lee Cain (600 DMR Honda), 1hr 4m 5.46s; **10** Frank Lelias/Charlie Richardson (600 LCR Honda), 1hr 4m 24.25s; **11** Mike Cookson/Kris Hibberd (600 Ireson Honda), 1hr 4m 30.67s; **12** Mick Donovan/Aaron Galligan (600 Honda), 1hr 4m 40.67s; **13** Francois Leblond/Johnathan Huet (600 Shelbourne Suzuki), 1hr 5m 9.46s; **14** Wayne Lockey/Owen Clements (600 Ireson Honda), 1hr 5m 11.59s; **15** Tony Thirkell/Nigel Barlow (600 MR Equipe Honda), 1hr 5m 14.32s.
Fastest lap: Dave Molyneux/Patrick Farrance (600 DMR), 19m 46.42s, 114.486mph/184.247km/h.
Sidecar lap record: Nick Crowe/Dan Sayle (600cc LCR Honda), 19m 24.24s, 116.667mph/187.757km/h (2007).

Bikerpetition.co.uk Lightweight TT (3 laps, 113.190 miles/182.160km)
1 Ryan Farquhar (650 Kawasaki), 59m 29.57s, 114.155mph/183.715km/h.
2 James Hillier (650 Kawasaki), 59m 58.57s; **3** Michael Rutter (650 Kawasaki), 1h 0m 3.61s; **4** Cameron Donald (650 Kawasaki), 1h 0m 34.51s; **5** Russ Mountford (650 Kawasaki), 1h 0m 44.04s; **6** William Dunlop (650 Kawasaki), 1h 0m 46.25s; **7** Ivan Lintin (650 Kawasaki), 1h 0m 57.24s; **8** Ian Lougher (650 Kawasaki), 1h 1m 39.18s; **9** Olie Linsdell (650 Flitwick), 1h 1m 44.78s; **10** Jamie Hamilton (650 Kawasaki), 1h 2m 4.57s; **11** Dave Moffitt (650 Suzuki), 1h 2m 6.56s; **12** Dean Harrison (650 Kawasaki), 1h 2m 29.98s; **13** Roger Maher (650 Kawasaki), 1h 2m 30.64s; **14** John Burrows (650 Kawasaki), 1h 2m 32.96s; **15** Michael Dunlop (650 Kawasaki), 1h 2m 40.29s.
Fastest lap: Michael Rutter (650 Kawasaki), 19m 35.45s, 115.554mph/185.966km/h (record).

PokerStars Senior TT
Cancelled due to weather/track conditions.
Senior TT and Outright lap record: John McGuinness (1000cc Honda), 17m 12.30s, 131.578mph/211.754km/h (2009).

British Championships

BRANDS HATCH INDY, 9 April, 1.208-mile/1.944km circuit
MCE British Superbike Championship With Pirelli, Round 1
Race 1 (30 laps 36.240 miles/58.323km)
1 Jon Kirkham (Honda), 28m 48.680s, 75.560mph/121.600km/h.
2 Alastair Seeley (Suzuki); **3** Michael Rutter (Kawasaki); **4** Ian Lowry (Honda); **5** Gary Mason (Kawasaki); **6** Tommy Bridewell (BMW); **7** Shane Byrne (Kawasaki); **8** James Westmoreland (Honda); **9** Freddy Foray (Kawasaki); **10** Josh Brookes (Suzuki); **11** Alex Polita (Ducati); **12** Chris Walker (Kawasaki); **13** Noriyuki Haga (Yamaha); **14** Scott Smart (Ducati); **15** James Hillier (Kawasaki).
Fastest lap: Seeley, 54.233s, 80.180mph/129.040km/h.
Championship points: 1 Kirkham, 25; **2** Seeley, 20; **3** Rutter, 16; **4** Lowry, 13; **5** Mason, 11; **6** Bridewell, 10.

Race 2
Postponed until Oulton Park due to track conditions.

Motorpoint British Supersport Championship Protected By Datatag, Round 1
Race 1 (11 laps 13.288 miles/21.385km)
1 Sam Warren (Yamaha), 10m 2.911s, 79.330mph/127.670km/h.
2 Ben Wilson (Kawasaki); **3** Pauli Pekkanen (Triumph); **4** Christian Iddon (Triumph); **5** Glenn Irwin (Yamaha); **6** Jack Kennedy (Yamaha); **7** Jimmy Hill (Triumph); **8** Dean Hipwell (Yamaha); **9** Billy McConnell (Triumph); **10** Daniel Cooper (Suzuki); **11** James East (Kawasaki); **12** Richard Cooper (Triumph); **13** Kev Coghlan (Yamaha); **14** Samuel Hornsey (Suzuki); **15** Luke Stapleford (Kawasaki).
Fastest lap: Warren, 52.883s, 82.230mph/132.330km/h.

Race 2 (7 laps 8.456 miles/13.609km)
1 Jack Kennedy (Yamaha), 6m 37.678s, 76.540mph/123.180km/h.
2 Sam Warren (Yamaha); **3** Billy McConnell (Triumph); **4** Christian Iddon (Triumph); **5** Deane Brown (Yamaha); **6** Richard Cooper (Triumph); **7** Luke Jones (Triumph); **8** Glen Richards (Triumph); **9** Kev Coghlan (Yamaha); **10** James East (Kawasaki); **11** Daniel Cooper (Suzuki); **12** Dean Hipwell (Yamaha); **13** Luke Stapleford (Kawasaki); **14** Samuel Hornsey (Suzuki); **15** Jimmy Hill (Triumph).
Fastest lap: Wilson, 55.119s, 78.890mph/126.960km/h.
Championship points: 1 Warren, 35; **2** Kennedy, 22.5; **3** Wilson, 20; **4** Iddon, 19.5; **5** Pekkanen, 16; **6** McConnell, 15.

Monster Energy British Motostar Championship & Motostar Cup, Round 1
Postponed until Thruxton due to track conditions.

THRUXTON, 15 April, 2.356-mile/3.792km circuit
MCE British Superbike Championship With Pirelli, Round 2 (2 x 20 laps, 47.120 miles/75.832km)
Race 1
1 Ian Lowry (Honda), 25m 37.097s, 110.350mph/177.590km/h.
2 Tommy Hill (Yamaha); **3** Josh Brookes (Suzuki); **4** Shane Byrne (Kawasaki); **5** Stuart Easton (Kawasaki); **6** Michael Laverty (Honda); **7** Jon Kirkham (Honda); **8** Luca Scassa (Honda); **9** James Westmoreland (Honda); **10** Graeme Gowland (Honda); **11** Tommy Bridewell (BMW); **12** Dan Linfoot (BMW); **13** Gary Mason (Kawasaki); **14** Barry Burrell (BMW); **15** Alastair Seeley (Suzuki).
Fastest lap: Lowes, 1m 15.865s, 111.790mph/179.920km/h.

Race 2
1 Josh Brookes (Suzuki), 25m 36.122s, 110.420mph/177.700km/h.
2 Tommy Hill (Yamaha); **3** Shane Byrne (Kawasaki); **4** Stuart Easton (Kawasaki); **5** Ian Lowry (Honda); **6** Luca Scassa (Honda); **7** Jon Kirkham (Honda); **8** Alex Lowes (Honda); **9** James Westmoreland (Honda); **10** Noriyuki Haga (Yamaha); **11** Dan Linfoot (BMW); **12** Peter Hickman (Kawasaki); **13** Michael Laverty (Honda); **14** Graeme Gowland (Honda); **15** Chris Walker (Kawasaki).
Fastest lap: Brookes, 1m 16.034s, 111.540mph/179.520km/h.
Championship points: 1 Lowry, 49; **2** Brookes, 47; **3** Kirkham, 43; **4** Hill, 40; **5** Byrne, 38; **6** Easton, 24.

Motorpoint British Supersport Championship Protected By Datatag, Round 2
Race 1 (12 laps 28.272 miles/45.499km)
1 Glen Richards (Triumph), 15m 42.924s, 107.930mph/173.700km/h.
2 Sam Warren (Yamaha); **3** Ben Wilson (Kawasaki);4 Jack Kennedy (Yamaha); **5** Luke Mossey (Triumph); **6** Christian Iddon (Triumph); **7** Pauli Pekkanen (Triumph); **8** Richard Cooper (Triumph); **9** Kev Coghlan (Yamaha); **10** Luke Jones (Triumph); **11** Jimmy Hill (Triumph); **12** Glenn Irwin (Yamaha); **13** Dean Hipwell (Yamaha); **14** Nikki Coates (Yamaha); **15** Luke Stapleford (Kawasaki).
Fastest lap: Warren, 1m 17.188s, 109.880mph/176.830km/h.

Race 2 (18 laps 42.408 miles/68.249km)
1 Billy McConnell (Triumph), 23m 40.743s, 107.450mph/172.920km/h.
2 Jack Kennedy (Yamaha); **3** Glen Richards (Triumph); **4** Luke Mossey (Triumph); **5** Ben Wilson (Kawasaki); **6** Luke Jones (Triumph); **7** Glenn Irwin (Yamaha); **8** Pauli Pekkanen (Triumph); **9** Richard Cooper (Triumph); **10** Christian Iddon (Triumph); **11** Kev Coghlan (Yamaha); **12** Dean Hipwell (Yamaha); **13** Jimmy Hill (Triumph); **14** Adam Blacklock (Yamaha); **15** Nikki Coates (Yamaha).
Fastest lap: Kennedy, 1m 17.520s, 109.410mph/176.080km/h.
Championship points: 1 Kennedy, 55.5; **2** Warren, 55; **3** Wilson, 47; **4** Richards, 45; **5** McConnell, 40; **6** Iddon, 35.5.

Monster Energy British Motostar Championship & Motostar Cup, Rounds 1 and 2
Race 1 (10 laps 23.560 miles/37.916km)
1 Bradley Ray (Honda), 13m 49.305s, 102.27mph/164.59km/h.
2 Kyle Ryde (Aprilia); **3** Jordan Weaving (Honda); **4** Luke Hedger (Luyten Honda); **5** Joe Irving (Honda); **6** William Dunlop (Honda); **7** Joe Francis (Honda); **8** Tom Carne (RCS); **9** Harry Hartley (Honda); **10** Bradley Hughes (Honda); **11** Simon Low (Honda); **12** Callum Bey (Honda); **13** Catherine Green (Honda); **14** Tommy Philp (Honda); **15** Xavier Zayat (Honda).
Fastest lap: Ryde, 1m 21.869s, 103.590mph/166.720km/h.

Race 2 (5 laps 11.780 miles/18.958km)
1 Bradley Ray (Honda), 6m 57.666s, 101.530mph/163.400km/h.
2 Luke Hedger (Luyten Honda); **3** Jordan Weaving (Honda); **4** Ryan Watson (KR/SEEL); **5** Hafiq Azmi (KTM); **6** Joe Irving (Honda); **7** William Dunlop (Honda); **8** Joe Francis (Honda); **9** Catherine Green (Honda); **10** Tom Carne (RCS); **11** Bradley Hughes (Honda); **12** Tommy Philp (Honda); **13** Callum Bey (Honda); **14** Harry Hartley (Honda); **15** Peter Sutherland (RCS).
Fastest lap: Ray, 1m 22.258s, 103.100mph/165.930km/h.
Championship points: 1 Ray, 50; **2** Hedger, 33; **3** Weaving, 32; **4** Irving, 21; **5** Ryde, 20; **6** Dunlop, 19.

OULTON PARK, 6–7 May, 2.692-mile/4.332km circuit
MCE British Superbike Championship With Pirelli, Round 3
Race 1 (8 laps 21.536 miles/34.659km)
1 Tommy Hill (Yamaha), 12m 55.805s, 99.930mph/160.820km/h.
2 Noriyuki Haga (Yamaha); **3** Josh Brookes (Suzuki); **4** Alastair Seeley (Suzuki); **5** Tommy Bridewell (BMW); **6** Michael Laverty (Honda); **7** Chris Walker (Kawasaki); **8** Michael Rutter (Kawasaki); **9** Stuart Easton (Kawasaki); **10** James Westmoreland (Honda); **11** Shane Byrne (Kawasaki); **12** Patric Muff (BMW); **13** Luca Scassa (Honda); **14** Luke Quigley (Honda); **15** Dan Linfoot (BMW).
Fastest lap: Hill, 1m 35.842s, 101.110mph/162.730km/h.

Race 2 (18 laps 48.456 miles/77.982km)
1 Chris Walker (Kawasaki), 32m 20.110s, 89.910mph/144.700km/h.
2 Shane Byrne (Kawasaki); **3** Josh Brookes (Suzuki); **4** Tommy Hill (Yamaha); **5** Stuart Easton (Kawasaki); **6** Alastair Seeley (Suzuki); **7** Tommy Bridewell (BMW); **8** Patric Muff (BMW); **9** Dan Linfoot (BMW); **10** Alex Lowes (Honda); **11** Peter Hickman (Kawasaki); **12** Michael Laverty (Honda); **13** Noriyuki Haga (Yamaha); **14** James Westmoreland (Honda); **15** Graeme Gowland (Honda).
Fastest lap: Gowland, 1m 43.391s, 93.730mph/150.850km/h.

Race 3 (18 laps 48.456 miles/77.982km)
1 Shane Byrne (Kawasaki), 29m 8.916s, 99.740mph/160.520km/h.
2 Tommy Hill (Yamaha); **3** Stuart Easton (Kawasaki); **4** Josh Brookes (Suzuki); **5** Tommy Bridewell (BMW); **6** Noriyuki Haga (Yamaha); **7** Michael Laverty (Honda); **8** Graeme Gowland (Honda); **9** Chris Walker (Kawasaki); **10** Alex Lowes (Honda); **11** Alastair Seeley (Suzuki); **12** Dan Linfoot (BMW); **13** Ian Lowry (Honda); **14** Patric Muff (BMW); **15** Michael Rutter (Kawasaki).
Fastest lap: Byrne, 1m 36.200s, 100.740mph/162.120km/h.
Championship points: **1** Hill, 98; **2** Brookes, 92; **3** Byrne, 88; **4** Easton, 58; **5** Lowry, 52; **6** Seeley, 49.

Motorpoint British Supersport Championship Protected By Datatag, Round 3 (2 x 10 laps, 26.920 miles/43.324km)
Race 1
1 Jack Kennedy (Yamaha), 16m 33.922s, 97.500mph/156.910km/h.
2 Ben Wilson (Kawasaki); **3** Sam Warren (Yamaha); **4** Glen Richards (Triumph); **5** Billy McConnell (Triumph); **6** Christian Iddon (Triumph); **7** Richard Cooper (Triumph); **8** Luke Mossey (Triumph); **9** Pauli Pekkanen (Triumph); **10** Glenn Irwin (Yamaha); **11** Luke Jones (Triumph); **12** Jimmy Hill (Triumph); **13** Samuel Hornsey (Suzuki); **14** Kev Coghlan (Yamaha); **15** Nikki Coates (Yamaha).
Fastest lap: Wilson, 1m 38.515s, 98.370mph/158.310km/h.

Race 2
1 Glen Richards (Triumph), 16m 40.233s, 96.890mph/155.930km/h.
2 Ben Wilson (Kawasaki); **3** Jack Kennedy (Yamaha); **4** Sam Warren (Yamaha); **5** Christian Iddon (Triumph); **6** Richard Cooper (Triumph); **7** Billy McConnell (Triumph); **8** Pauli Pekkanen (Triumph); **9** Luke Mossey (Triumph); **10** Glenn Irwin (Yamaha); **11** Kev Coghlan (Yamaha); **12** Jimmy Hill (Triumph); **13** Luke Jones (Triumph); **14** Nikki Coates (Yamaha); **15** Dean Hipwell (Yamaha).
Fastest lap: Richards, 1m 38.854s, 98.030mph/157.770km/h.
Championship points: **1** Kennedy, 96.5; **2** Wilson, 87; **3** Warren, 84; **4** Richards, 83; **5** McConnell, 60; **6** Iddon, 56.5.

Monster Energy British Motostar Championship & Motostar Cup, Round 3 (12 laps, 32.304 miles/51.988km)
1 Luke Hedger (Luyten Honda), 22m 2.376s, 87.940mph/141.530km/h.
2 Ryan Watson (KR/SEEL); **3** William Dunlop (Honda); **4** Christian Elkin (Honda); **5** Harry Hartley (Honda); **6** Bradley Hughes (Honda); **7** Joe Francis (Honda); **8** Arnie Shelton (Honda); **9** Tom Carne (RCS); **10** Callum Bey (Honda); **11** Oliver Fitzpatrick (Honda); **12** Tommy Philp (Honda); **13** Simon Low (Honda); **14** Jon Vincent (JVR Honda); **15** Ian Stanford (Honda).
Fastest lap: Hedger, 1m 49.232s, 88.720mph/142.780km/h.
Championship points: **1** Hedger, 58; **2** Ray, 50; **3** Dunlop, 35; **4** Watson, 33; **5** Weaving, 32; **6** Francis, 26.

SNETTERTON 300, 27 May, 2.969-mile/4.778km circuit
MCE British Superbike Championship With Pirelli, Round 4 (2 x 16 laps, 47.504 miles/76.450km)
Race 1
1 Tommy Hill (Yamaha), 29m 22.601s, 97.020mph/156.140km/h.
2 Michael Laverty (Honda); **3** Josh Brookes (Suzuki); **4** Noriyuki Haga (Yamaha); **5** Alex Lowes (Honda); **6** Tommy Bridewell (BMW); **7** Chris Walker (Kawasaki); **8** Ian Lowry (Honda); **9** Patric Muff (BMW); **10** Barry Burrell (BMW); **11** Dan Linfoot (BMW); **12** James Westmoreland (Honda); **13** Luke Quigley (Honda); **14** Michael Rutter (Kawasaki); **15** Tristan Palmer (Honda).
Fastest lap: M. Laverty, 1m 49.343s, 97.740mph/157.310km/h.

Race 2
1 Michael Laverty (Honda), 29m 23.876s, 96.950mph/156.030km/h.
2 Shane Byrne (Kawasaki); **3** Josh Brookes (Suzuki); **4** Ian Lowry (Honda); **5** Graeme Gowland (Honda); **6** Alex Lowes (Honda); **7** Chris Walker (Kawasaki); **8** Stuart Easton (Kawasaki); **9** James Westmoreland (Honda); **10** Patric Muff (BMW); **11** Dan Linfoot (BMW); **12** Luke Quigley (Honda); **13** Michael Rutter (Kawasaki); **14** Jon Kirkham (Honda); **15** Scott Smart (Ducati).
Fastest lap: M. Laverty, 1m 49.007s, 98.040mph/157.790km/h.
Championship points: **1** Brookes, 124; **2** Hill, 123; **3** Byrne, 108; **4** M. Laverty, 81; **5** Lowry, 73; **6** Easton, 66.

Motorpoint British Supersport Championship Protected By Datatag, Round 4
Race 1 (10 laps 29.690 miles/47.781km)
1 Jack Kennedy (Yamaha), 18m 53.914s, 94.250mph/151.680km/h.
2 Glen Richards (Triumph); **3** Ben Wilson (Kawasaki); **4** Luke Mossey (Triumph); **5** Billy McConnell (Triumph); **6** Sam Warren (Yamaha); **7** Christian Iddon (Triumph); **8** Luke Jones (Triumph); **9** Glenn Irwin (Yamaha); **10** Kev Coghlan (Yamaha); **11** Jimmy Hill (Triumph); **12** Nikki Coates (Yamaha); **13** Deane Brown (Yamaha); **14** David Paton (Yamaha); **15** Dean Hipwell (Yamaha).
Fastest lap: Richards, 1m 52.367s, 95.110mph/153.070km/h.

Race 2 (15 laps 44.535 miles/71.672km)
1 Jack Kennedy (Yamaha), 29m 21.673s, 91.000mph/146.450km/h.
2 Billy McConnell (Triumph); **3** Glen Richards (Triumph); **4** Sam Warren (Yamaha); **5** Christian Iddon (Triumph); **6** Glenn Irwin (Yamaha); **7** Nikki Coates (Yamaha); **8** Pauli Pekkanen (Triumph); **9** David Paton (Yamaha); **10** Ben Field (Honda); **11** Samuel Hornsey (Suzuki); **12** Josh Caygill (Triumph); **13** Matt Layt (Triumph); **14** Craig Neve (Triumph); **15** Gary Winfield (Triumph).
Fastest lap: McConnell, 1m 52.757s, 94.780mph/152.540km/h.
Championship points: **1** Kennedy, 146.5; **2** Richards, 119; **3** Warren, 107; **4** Wilson, 103; **5** McConnell, 91; **6** Iddon, 76.5.

Monster Energy British Motostar Championship & Motostar Cup, Round 4 (12 laps 35.628 miles/57.338km)
1 Kyle Ryde (Honda), 24m 37.532s, 86.800mph/139.690km/h.
2 Jordan Weaving (Honda); **3** Luke Hedger (Luyten Honda); **4** Ryan Watson (KR/SEEL); **5** Joe Irving (Honda); **6** Catherine Green (Honda); **7** Tarran Mackenzie (KTM); **8** Philip Wakefield (Seel); **9** Tom Carne (RCS); **10** Joe Francis (Honda); **11** Harry Hartley (Honda); **12** Callum Bey (Honda); **13** Arnie Shelton (Honda); **14** Xavier Zayat (Honda); **15** Bradley Hughes (Honda).
Fastest lap: Ray, 2m 1.941s, 87.640mph/141.050km/h.
Championship points: **1** Hedger, 74; **2** Weaving, 52; **3** Ray, 50; **4** Watson, 46; **5** Ryde, 45; **6** Dunlop, 35.

KNOCKHILL, 24 June, 1.271-mile/2.046km circuit
MCE British Superbike Championship With Pirelli, Round 5 (2 x 30 laps, 38.130 miles/61.364km)
Race 1
1 Shane Byrne (Kawasaki), 24m 48.730s, 92.220mph/148.410km/h.
2 Tommy Hill (Yamaha); **3** Michael Laverty (Honda); **4** Josh Brookes (Suzuki); **5** Tommy Bridewell (BMW); **6** Noriyuki Haga (Yamaha); **7** Alastair Seeley (Suzuki); **8** Graeme Gowland (Honda); **9** Alex Lowes (Honda); **10** Michael Rutter (Kawasaki); **11** James Westmoreland (Honda); **12** Jon Kirkham (Honda); **13** Tristan Palmer (Honda); **14** Luke Quigley (Honda); **15** Patric Muff (BMW).
Fastest lap: Hill, 49.112s, 93.190mph/149.970km/h.

Race 2
1 Michael Laverty (Honda), 24m 42.773s, 92.590mph/149.010km/h.
2 Shane Byrne (Kawasaki); **3** Tommy Hill (Yamaha); **4** Josh Brookes (Suzuki); **5** James Westmoreland (Honda); **6** Tommy Bridewell (BMW); **7** Alastair Seeley (Suzuki); **8** Alex Lowes (Honda); **9** Graeme Gowland (Honda); **10** Ian Lowry (Honda); **11** Barry Burrell (BMW); **12** Tristan Palmer (Honda); **13** Peter Hickman (BMW); **14** Jon Kirkham (Honda); **15** Luke Quigley (Honda).
Fastest lap: M. Laverty, 48.861s, 93.660mph/150.740km/h.
Championship points: **1** Hill, 159; **2** Byrne, 153; **3** Brookes, 150; **4** M. Laverty, 122; **5** Lowry, 79; **6** Bridewell, 77.

Motorpoint British Supersport Championship Protected By Datatag, Round 5
Race 1 (18 laps, 22.878 miles/36.819km)
1 Glen Richards (Triumph), 15m 50.866s, 86.630mph/139.420km/h.
2 Jack Kennedy (Yamaha); **3** Sam Warren (Yamaha); **4** Billy McConnell (Triumph); **5** Richard Cooper (Triumph); **6** Luke Mossey (Triumph); **7** Christian Iddon (Triumph); **8** Pauli Pekkanen (Triumph); **9** Luke Jones (Triumph); **10** Glenn Irwin (Yamaha); **11** Ben Wilson (Kawasaki); **12** Kev Coghlan (Yamaha); **13** Deane Brown (Yamaha); **14** Nikki Coates (Yamaha); **15** James East (Kawasaki).
Fastest lap: Iddon, 50.371s, 90.860mph/146.220km/h.

Race 2 (25 laps 31.775 miles/51.137km)
1 Billy McConnell (Triumph), 21m 27.650s, 88.850mph/142.990km/h.
2 Glen Richards (Triumph); **3** Jack Kennedy (Yamaha); **4** Ben Wilson (Kawasaki); **5** Luke Mossey (Triumph); **6** Richard Cooper (Triumph); **7** Pauli Pekkanen (Triumph); **8** Luke Jones (Triumph); **9** Deane Brown (Yamaha); **10** Dan Cooper (Kawasaki); **11** Taylor Mackenzie (Yamaha); **12** Dean Hipwell (Yamaha); **13** James East (Kawasaki); **14** Jimmy Hill (Triumph); **15** David Jones (Triumph).
Fastest lap: Iddon, 50.008s, 91.520mph/147.280km/h.
Championship points: **1** Kennedy, 182.5; **2** Richards, 164; **3** McConnell, 129; **4** Warren, 123; **5** Wilson, 121; **6** Iddon, 85.5.

Monster Energy British Motostar Championship & Motostar Cup, Round 5 (17 laps 21.607 miles/34.773km)
1 Kyle Ryde (Honda), 16m 4.277s, 80.680mph/129.840km/h.
2 Tarran Mackenzie (KTM); **3** Catherine Green (Honda); **4** Philip Wakefield (Seel); **5** Tom Carne (RCS); **6** Joe Francis (Honda); **7** Callum Bey (Honda); **8** Ryan Watson (KR/SEEL); **9** Robert English (Honda); **10** Xavier Zayat (Honda); **11** Arnie Shelton (Honda); **12** Bradley Hughes (Honda); **13** Harry Hartley (Honda); **14** Peter Sutherland (RCS); **15** Tommy Philp (Honda).
Fastest lap: Ryde, 54.485s, 84.000mph/135.180km/h.
Championship points: **1** Hedger, 74; **2** Ryde, 70; **3** Watson, 54; **4** Weaving, 52; **5** Ray, 50; **6** Francis, 42.

OULTON PARK, 7–8 July, 2.692-mile/4.332km circuit
MCE British Superbike Championship With Pirelli, Round 6
Race 1 (16 laps 43.072 miles/69.318km)
1 Tommy Hill (Yamaha), 25m 57.830s, 99.530mph/160.180km/h.
2 Josh Brookes (Suzuki); **3** Shane Byrne (Kawasaki); **4** Noriyuki Haga (Yamaha); **5** James Westmoreland (Honda); **6** Tommy Bridewell (BMW); **7** Chris Walker (Kawasaki); **8** Peter Hickman (BMW); **9** Graeme Gowland (Honda); **10** Barry Burrell (BMW); **11** Patric Muff (BMW); **12** Luke Quigley (Honda); **13** Scott Smart (Ducati); **14** Michael Rutter (Kawasaki); **15** Mark Aitchison (Kawasaki).
Fastest lap: Lowes, 1m 36.481s, 100.440mph/161.650km/h.

Race 2 (18 laps 48.456 miles/77.982km)
1 Tommy Hill (Yamaha), 29m 7.975s, 99.790mph/160.600km/h.
2 Josh Brookes (Suzuki); **3** Shane Byrne (Kawasaki); **4** Michael Laverty (Honda); **5** Noriyuki Haga (Yamaha); **6** Ian Lowry (Honda); **7** Tommy Bridewell (BMW); **8** Alastair Seeley (Suzuki); **9** Alex Lowes (Honda); **10** Graeme Gowland (Honda); **11** James Westmoreland (Honda); **12** Chris Walker (Kawasaki); **13** Peter Hickman (BMW); **14** Patric Muff (BMW); **15** Scott Smart (Ducati).
Fastest lap: Brookes, 1m 36.321s, 100.610mph/161.920km/h.

Race 3 (18 laps 48.456 miles/77.982km)
1 Tommy Hill (Yamaha), 29m 5.719s, 99.920mph/160.810km/h.
2 Shane Byrne (Kawasaki); **3** Josh Brookes (Suzuki); **4** Noriyuki Haga (Yamaha); **5** Michael Laverty (Honda); **6** Alex Lowes (Honda); **7** Ian Lowry (Honda); **8** Tommy Bridewell (BMW); **9** James Westmoreland (Honda); **10** Graeme Gowland (Honda); **11** Chris Walker (Kawasaki); **12** Peter Hickman (BMW); **13** Alastair Seeley (Suzuki); **14** Jon Kirkham (Honda); **15** Scott Smart (Ducati).
Fastest lap: Hill, 1m 36.194s, 100.740mph/162.130km/h.
Championship points: **1** Hill, 234; **2** Brookes, 206; **3** Byrne, 205; **4** M. Laverty, 146; **5** Bridewell, 104; **6** Haga, 102.

Motorpoint British Supersport Championship Protected By Datatag, Round 6
Race 1 (10 laps 26.920 miles/43.324km)
1 Billy McConnell (Triumph), 16m 40.709s, 96.840mph/155.850km/h.
2 Ben Wilson (Kawasaki); **3** Luke Mossey (Triumph); **4** Pauli Pekkanen (Triumph); **5** Kev Coghlan (Yamaha); **6** Glenn Irwin (Yamaha); **7** Nikki Coates (Yamaha); **8** Deane Brown (Yamaha); **9** Samuel Hornsey (Suzuki); **10** Dan Cooper (Kawasaki); **11** Dean Hipwell (Yamaha); **12** Taylor Mackenzie (Yamaha); **13** Philip Atkinson (Triumph); **14** James East (Kawasaki); **15** Jonathan Lodge (Triumph).
Fastest lap: Richards, 1m 38.784s, 98.100mph/157.880km/h.

Race 2 (15 laps 40.380 miles/64.985km)
1 Glen Richards (Triumph), 24m 49.341s, 97.600mph/157.070km/h.
2 Billy McConnell (Triumph); **3** Jack Kennedy (Yamaha); **4** Ben Wilson (Kawasaki); **5** Luke Mossey (Triumph); **6** Richard Cooper (Triumph); **7** Pauli Pekkanen (Triumph); **8** Kev Coghlan (Yamaha); **9** Luke Jones (Triumph); **10** Glenn Irwin (Yamaha); **11** Dan Cooper (Kawasaki); **12** Deane Brown (Yamaha); **13** Nikki Coates (Yamaha); **14** Taylor Mackenzie (Yamaha); **15** Dean Hipwell (Yamaha).
Fastest lap: Richards, 1m 38.430s, 98.450mph/158.450km/h.
Championship points: **1** Kennedy, 198.5; **2** Richards, 189; **3** McConnell, 174; **4** Wilson, 154; **5** Warren, 123; **6** Mossey, 100.

Monster Energy British Motostar Championship & Motostar Cup, Round 6 (12 laps, 32.304 miles/51.988km)
1 Luke Hedger (Luyten Honda), 21m 55.816s, 88.380mph/142.230km/h.
2 Philip Wakefield (Seel); **3** Connor Behan (Honda); **4** Joe Francis (Honda); **5** Tom Carne (RCS); **6** Harry Hartley (Honda); **7** Callum Bey (Honda); **8** Martin Glossop (Aprilia); **9** Joe Irving (Honda); **10** Arnie Shelton (Honda); **11** Jon Vincent (JVR Honda); **12** Bradley Hughes (Honda); **13** Xavier Zayat (Honda); **14** Richard Ferguson (Honda); **15** Ryan Watson (KR/SEEL).
Fastest lap: Hedger, 1m 48.687s, 89.160mph/143.500km/h.
Championship points: **1** Hedger, 99; **2** Ryde, 70; **3** Watson, 55; **4** Francis, 55; **5** Weaving, 52; **6** Ray, 50.

BRANDS HATCH GP, 22 July, 2.433-mile/3.916km circuit
MCE British Superbike Championship With Pirelli, Round 7 (2 x 18 laps, 43.794 miles/70.480km)
Race 1
1 Shane Byrne (Kawasaki), 26m 13.972s, 100.170mph/161.210km/h.
2 Josh Brookes (Suzuki); **3** Tommy Hill (Yamaha); **4** Michael Laverty (Honda); **5** Tommy Bridewell (BMW); **6** Chris Walker (Kawasaki); **7** Alex Lowes (Honda); **8** Stuart Easton (Kawasaki); **9** Alastair Seeley (Suzuki); **10** Michael Rutter (Kawasaki); **11** Barry Burrell (BMW); **12** Jon Kirkham (Honda); **13** Karl Harris (Kawasaki); **14** Luca Scassa (Honda); **15** Patric Muff (BMW).
Fastest lap: Brookes, 1m 26.795s, 100.920mph/162.420km/h.

Race 2
1 Shane Byrne (Kawasaki), 26m 10.330s, 100.410mph/161.590km/h.
2 Josh Brookes (Suzuki); **3** Tommy Hill (Yamaha); **4** Michael Laverty (Honda); **5** Noriyuki Haga (Yamaha); **6** Alex Lowes (Honda); **7** Tommy Bridewell (BMW); **8** Ian Lowry (Honda); **9** Graeme Gowland (Honda); **10** James Westmoreland (Honda); **11** Alastair Seeley (Suzuki); **12** Karl Harris (Kawasaki); **13** Barry Burrell (BMW); **14** Jon Kirkham (Honda); **15** Patric Muff (BMW).
Fastest lap: Byrne, 1m 26.454s, 101.320mph/163.060km/h.
Championship points: **1** Hill, 266; **2** Byrne, 255; **3** Brookes, 246; **4** M. Laverty, 172; **5** Bridewell, 124; **6** Haga, 113.

Motorpoint British Supersport Championship Protected By Datatag, Round 7
Race 1 (10 laps 24.330 miles/39.155km)
1 Glen Richards (Triumph), 14m 51.777s, 98.220mph/158.070km/h.

2 Jack Kennedy (Yamaha); 3 Christian Iddon (Triumph); 4 Luke Jones (Triumph); 5 Luke Mossey (Triumph); 6 Ben Wilson (Kawasaki); 7 Pauli Pekkanen (Triumph); 8 Deane Brown (Yamaha); 9 Richard Cooper (Triumph); 10 Sam Warren (Yamaha); 11 Nikki Coates (Yamaha); 12 James East (Kawasaki); 13 Dean Hipwell (Yamaha); 14 Taylor Mackenzie (Yamaha); 15 David Paton (Yamaha).
Fastest lap: Kennedy, 1m 28.382s, 99.110mph/159.500km/h.

Race 2 (6 laps 14.598 miles/23.493km)
1 Jack Kennedy (Yamaha), 8m 57.700s, 97.740mph/157.300km/h.
2 Glen Richards (Triumph); 3 Billy McConnell (Triumph); 4 Christian Iddon (Triumph); 5 Ben Wilson (Kawasaki); 6 Richard Cooper (Triumph); 7 Pauli Pekkanen (Triumph); 8 Luke Mossey (Triumph); 9 James East (Yamaha); 10 Nikki Coates (Yamaha); 11 Glenn Irwin (Yamaha); 12 Dean Hipwell (Yamaha); 13 Dan Cooper (Kawasaki); 14 Taylor Mackenzie (Yamaha); 15 David Paton (Yamaha).
Fastest lap: McConnell, 1m 28.506s, 98.970mph/159.280km/h.
Championship points: 1 Kennedy, 243.5; 2 Richards, 234; 3 McConnell, 190; 4 Wilson, 175; 5 Warren, 129; 6 Mossey, 119.

Monster Energy British Motostar Championship & Motostar Cup, Round 7 (12 laps, 29.196 miles/46.986km)
1 Bradley Ray (Honda), 19m 20.203s, 90.600mph/145.810km/h.
2 Luke Hedger (Luyten Honda); 3 Tarran Mackenzie (KTM); 4 Catherine Green (Honda); 5 Joe Irving (Honda); 6 Philip Wakefield (Seel); 7 Callum Bey (Honda); 8 Joe Francis (Honda); 9 Arnie Shelton (Honda); 10 Ryan Watson (KR/SEEL); 11 Tom Carne (RCS); 12 Bradley Hughes (Honda); 13 Harry Hartley (Honda); 14 Oliver Fitzpatrick (Honda); 15 Tommy Philp (Honda).
Fastest lap: Ray, 1m 35.657s, 91.570mph/147.370km/h.
Championship points: 1 Hedger, 119; 2 Ray, 75; 3 Ryde, 70; 4 Francis, 63; 5 Watson, 61; 6 Carne, 55.

CADWELL PARK, 27 August, 2.180-mile/3.508km circuit
MCE British Superbike Championship With Pirelli, Round 8 (2 x 18 laps, 39.240 miles/63.151km)
Race 1
1 Tommy Hill (Yamaha), 26m 38.402s, 88.370mph/142.220km/h.
2 Alex Lowes (Honda); 3 Michael Laverty (Honda); 4 Danny Buchan (Kawasaki); 5 Jon Kirkham (Honda); 6 Josh Brookes (Suzuki); 7 Karl Harris (Kawasaki); 8 James Westmoreland (Honda); 9 Tommy Bridewell (BMW); 10 Peter Hickman (BMW); 11 Michael Rutter (Kawasaki); 12 Ian Lowry (Honda); 13 Chris Walker (Kawasaki); 14 Alastair Seeley (Suzuki); 15 Luca Scassa (Honda).
Fastest lap: Hill, 1m 27.986s, 89.190mph/143.540km/h.

Race 2
1 Tommy Hill (Yamaha), 26m 32.851s, 88.680mph/142.720km/h.
2 Josh Brookes (Suzuki); 3 Michael Laverty (Honda); 4 Alex Lowes (Honda); 5 Tommy Bridewell (BMW); 6 James Westmoreland (Honda); 7 Ian Lowry (Honda); 8 Peter Hickman (BMW); 9 Karl Harris (Kawasaki); 10 Michael Rutter (Kawasaki); 11 Chris Walker (Kawasaki); 12 Jon Kirkham (Honda); 13 Alastair Seeley (Suzuki); 14 Stuart Easton (Kawasaki); 15 Barry Burrell (BMW).
Fastest lap: Lowes, 1m 27.804s, 89.380mph/143.840km/h.
Championship points: 1 Hill, 316; 2 Brookes, 276; 3 Byrne, 255; 4 M. Laverty, 204; 5 Bridewell, 142; 6 Lowes, 125.

Motorpoint British Supersport Championship Protected By Datatag, Round 8
Race 1 (10 laps 21.800 miles/35.084km).
1 Billy McConnell (Triumph), 15m 2.215s, 86.980mph/139.980km/h.
2 Christian Iddon (Triumph); 3 Glen Richards (Triumph); 4 Jack Kennedy (Yamaha); 5 Luke Mossey (Triumph); 6 Richard Cooper (Triumph); 7 Sam Warren (Yamaha); 8 Pauli Pekkanen (Triumph); 9 Glenn Irwin (Yamaha); 10 Deane Brown (Yamaha); 11 James East (Kawasaki); 12 Luke Stapleford (Kawasaki); 13 Taylor Mackenzie (Yamaha); 14 Shaun Winfield (Triumph); 15 Jonathan Lodge (Triumph).
Fastest lap: Richards, 1m 29.139s, 88.040mph/141.690km/h.

Race 2 (15 laps 32.700 miles/52.626km)
1 Glen Richards (Triumph), 22m 41.322s, 86.410mph/139.160km/h.
2 Christian Iddon (Triumph); 3 Richard Cooper (Triumph); 4 Billy McConnell (Triumph); 5 Luke Mossey (Triumph); 6 Ben Wilson (Kawasaki); 7 Jack

Kennedy (Yamaha); 8 Pauli Pekkanen (Triumph); 9 Glenn Irwin (Yamaha); 10 Luke Stapleford (Kawasaki); 11 Dean Hipwell (Yamaha); 12 Nikki Coates (Yamaha); 13 Scott Hudson (Kawasaki); 14 Matt Layt (Triumph); 15 Taylor Mackenzie (Yamaha).
Fastest lap: Mossey, 1m 29.702s, 87.490mph/140.800km/h.
Championship points: 1 Richards, 275; 2 Kennedy, 265.5; 3 McConnell, 228; 4 Wilson, 185; 5 Iddon, 154.5; 6 Mossey, 141.

Monster Energy British Motostar Championship & Motostar Cup, Round 8 (7 laps, 15.260 miles/24.559km)
1 Catherine Green (Honda), 12m 30.186s, 73.230mph/117.850km/h.
2 Joe Francis (Honda); 3 Joe Irving (Honda); 4 Arnie Shelton (Honda); 5 Harry Hartley (Honda); 6 Luke Hedger (Luyten Honda); 7 Callum Bey (Honda); 8 Philip Wakefield (Seel); 9 Tommy Philp (Honda); 10 Ryan Watson (KR/SEEL); 11 Xavier Zayat (Honda); 12 Tom Carne (RCS); 13 Sam Burman (Honda); 14 Elliot Lodge (Honda); 15 Greg Greenwood (Honda).
Fastest lap: Green, 1m 45.289s, 74.530mph/119.950km/h.
Championship points: 1 Hedger, 129; 2 Francis, 83; 3 Ray, 75; 4 Green, 74; 5 Ryde, 70; 6 Watson, 67.

DONINGTON PARK, 9 September, 2.487-mile/3.508km circuit
MCE British Superbike Championship With Pirelli, Round 9
Race 1 (7 laps 17.409 miles/28.017km)
1 Josh Brookes (Suzuki), 10m 36.914s, 98.410mph/158.380km/h.
2 Tommy Hill (Yamaha); 3 Michael Laverty (Honda); 4 Stuart Easton (Kawasaki); 5 James Westmoreland (Honda); 6 Alex Lowes (Honda); 7 Jon Kirkham (Honda); 8 Chris Walker (Kawasaki); 9 Tommy Bridewell (BMW); 10 Barry Burrell (BMW); 11 Luca Scassa (Honda); 12 Patric Muff (BMW); 13 Danny Buchan (Kawasaki); 14 Luke Quigley (Honda); 15 Robbin Harms (Honda).
Fastest lap: Brookes, 1m 30.264s, 99.200mph/159.650km/h.

Race 2 (20 laps 49.740 miles/80.049km)
1 Josh Brookes (Suzuki), 30m 15.305s, 98.650mph/158.760km/h.
2 Michael Laverty (Honda); 3 Tommy Hill (Yamaha); 4 Tommy Bridewell (BMW); 5 Alex Lowes (Honda); 6 James Westmoreland (Honda); 7 Stuart Easton (Kawasaki); 8 Luca Scassa (Honda); 9 Jon Kirkham (Honda); 10 Chris Walker (Kawasaki); 11 Patric Muff (BMW); 12 Noriyuki Haga (Yamaha); 13 Barry Burrell (BMW); 14 Michael Rutter (Kawasaki); 15 Peter Hickman (BMW).
Fastest lap: Brookes, 1m 30.048s, 99.440mph/160.030km/h.
The top six BSB riders in points after Donington Park qualified for 'The Showdown', to decide the championship over the last three rounds. These six title fighters had their points equalised at 500 and then podium credits added from their main season results (3 points for each 1st place, 2 points for 2nd, 1 point for 3rd).

Championship points for start of Showdown:
1 Hill, 535; 2 Brookes, 525; 3 Byrne, 523; 4 M. Laverty, 514; 5 Lowes, 502; 6 Bridewell, 500.

Motorpoint British Supersport Championship Protected By Datatag, Round 9
Race 1 (5 laps 12.435 miles/20.012km)
1 Jack Kennedy (Yamaha), 7m 45.897s, 96.090mph/154.640km/h.
2 Billy McConnell (Triumph); 3 Christian Iddon (Triumph); 4 Glenn Irwin (Yamaha); 5 Luke Mossey (Triumph); 6 Deane Brown (Yamaha); 7 Pauli Pekkanen (Triumph); 8 Luke Jones (Triumph); 9 Taylor Mackenzie (Yamaha); 10 Samuel Hornsey (Suzuki); 11 Dean Hipwell (Yamaha); 12 Ben Field (Honda); 13 Luke Stapleford (Kawasaki); 14 Josh Caygill (Triumph); 15 Tom McHale (Honda).
Fastest lap: McConnell, 1m 31.977s, 97.350mph/156.670km/h.

Race 2 (15 laps 37.305 miles/60.037km)
1 Glen Richards (Triumph), 23m 11.796s, 96.500mph/155.300km/h.
2 Jack Kennedy (Yamaha); 3 Christian Iddon (Triumph); 4 Billy McConnell (Triumph); 5 Glenn Irwin (Yamaha); 6 Richard Cooper (Triumph); 7 Pauli Pekkanen (Triumph); 8 Luke Jones (Triumph); 9 Taylor Mackenzie (Yamaha); 10 Samuel Hornsey (Suzuki); 11 Dean Hipwell (Yamaha); 12 Nikki Coates (Yamaha); 13 Ben Field (Honda); 14 Jonathan Lodge (Triumph); 15 Luke Stapleford (Kawasaki).
Fastest lap: Richards, 1m 31.972s, 97.360mph/156.680km/h.
Championship points: 1 Kennedy, 310.5; 2 Richards, 300; 3 McConnell, 261; 4 Iddon, 186.5; 5 Wilson, 185; 6 Mossey, 152.

Monster Energy British Motostar Championship & Motostar Cup, Round 9 (10 laps, 24.870 miles/40.024km)
1 Bradley Ray (Honda), 16m 48.793s, 88.760mph/142.850km/h.
2 Catherine Green (Honda); 3 Jordan Weaving (Honda); 4 Luke Hedger (Luyten Honda); 5 Tarran Mackenzie (KTM); 6 Joe Irving (Honda); 7 Callum Bey (Honda); 8 Harry Hartley (Honda); 9 Olly Simpson (Honda); 10 Philip Wakefield (Seel); 11 Elliot Lodge (Honda); 12 Peter Sutherland (Aprilia); 13 Arnie Shelton (Honda); 14 Ryan Watson (KR/SEEL); 15 Joseph Thomas (Honda).
Fastest lap: Green, 1m 39.887s, 89.640mph/144.270km/h.
Championship points: 1 Hedger, 142; 2 Ray, 100; 3 Green, 94; 4 Francis, 83; 5 Irving, 76; 6 Ryde, 70.

ASSEN, 23 September, 2.822-mile/4.452km circuit
MCE British Superbike Championship With Pirelli, Round 10 (2 x 18 laps, 50.796 miles/81.748km)
Race 1
1 Shane Byrne (Kawasaki), 29m 45.302s, 102.430mph/164.850km/h.
2 Josh Brookes (Suzuki); 3 Alex Lowes (Honda); 4 Luca Scassa (Honda); 5 Noriyuki Haga (Yamaha); 6 Tommy Bridewell (BMW); 7 Michael Laverty (Honda); 8 James Westmoreland (Honda); 9 Stuart Easton (Kawasaki); 10 Robbin Harms (Honda); 11 Patric Muff (BMW); 12 Barry Burrell (BMW); 13 Jon Kirkham (Honda); 14 Ian Lowry (Honda); 15 Chris Walker (Kawasaki).
Fastest lap: Hill, 1m 38.008s, 103.660mph/166.830km/h.

Race 2
1 Josh Brookes (Suzuki), 29m 43.606s, 102.530mph/165.010km/h.
2 Shane Byrne (Kawasaki); 3 Alex Lowes (Honda); 4 Tommy Hill (Yamaha); 5 Tommy Bridewell (BMW); 6 Noriyuki Haga (Yamaha); 7 Michael Laverty (Honda); 8 James Westmoreland (Honda); 9 Robbin Harms (Honda); 10 Stuart Easton (Kawasaki); 11 Luca Scassa (Honda); 12 Barry Burrell (BMW); 13 Patric Muff (BMW); 14 Chris Walker (Kawasaki); 15 Jakub Smrz (Aprilia).
Fastest lap: Brookes, 1m 38.309s, 103.340mph/166.320km/h.
Championship points: 1 Brookes, 570; 2 Byrne, 568; 3 Hill, 548; 4 Lowes, 534; 5 M. Laverty, 532; 6 Bridewell, 521.

Motorpoint British Supersport Championship Protected By Datatag, Round 10
Race 1 (12 laps 33.864 miles/54.499km)
1 Christian Iddon (Triumph), 20m 26.408s, 99.410mph/159.980km/h.
2 Jack Kennedy (Yamaha); 3 Richard Cooper (Triumph); 4 Luke Mossey (Triumph); 5 Raymond Schouten (Yamaha); 6 Glen Richards (Triumph); 7 Ben Wilson (Kawasaki); 8 Glenn Irwin (Yamaha); 9 PJ Jacobsen (Yamaha); 10 Taylor Mackenzie (Yamaha); 11 Pauli Pekkanen (Triumph); 12 Billy McConnell (Triumph); 13 Luke Jones (Triumph); 14 Deane Brown (Yamaha); 15 David Paton (Yamaha).
Fastest lap: Kennedy, 1m 40.792s, 100.800mph/162.220km/h.

Race 2 (15 laps 42.330 miles/68.124km)
1 PJ Jacobsen (Suzuki), 25m 24.960s, 99.930mph/160.820km/h.
2 Christian Iddon (Triumph); 3 Glen Richards (Triumph); 4 Raymond Schouten (Yamaha); 5 Richard Cooper (Triumph); 6 Glenn Irwin (Yamaha); 7 Ben Wilson (Kawasaki); 8 Luke Jones (Triumph); 9 Luke Mossey (Triumph); 10 Billy McConnell (Triumph); 11 Brodie Waters (Suzuki); 12 David Paton (Yamaha); 13 John Simpson (Triumph); 14 Nikki Coates (Yamaha); 15 Dean Hipwell (Yamaha).
Fastest lap: Iddon, 1m 40.338s, 101.250mph/162.960km/h.
Championship points: 1 Kennedy, 330.5; 2 Richards, 326; 3 McConnell, 271; 4 Iddon, 231.5; 5 Wilson, 203; 6 Mossey, 172.

Monster Energy British Motostar Championship & Motostar Cup, Round 10 (12 laps, 33.864 miles/54.499km)
1 Bryan Schouten (Honda), 21m 39.066s, 93.850mph/151.040km/h.
2 Thomas Van Leeuwen (KTM); 3 Scott Deroue (KTM); 4 Kyle Ryde (Honda); 5 Jerry Van De Bunt (Honda); 6 Henning Flathaug (Honda); 7 Jordan Weaving (Honda); 8 Joe Irving (Honda); 9 Marcel Ter Braake (Honda); 10 Mike Brouwers (Honda); 11 Tarran Mackenzie (KTM); 12 Catherine Green (Seel Honda); 13 Luke Hedger (Luyten Honda); 14 Olly Simpson (Honda); 15 Tasia Rodink (NA).
Fastest lap: Van Leeuwen, 1m 46.912s, 95.030mph/152.940km/h.
Championship points: 1 Hedger, 152; 2

Green, 105; 3 Ray, 100; 4 Ryde, 95; 5 Irving, 92; 6 Weaving, 88.

SILVERSTONE, 30 September, 3.667-mile/5.902km circuit
MCE British Superbike Championship With Pirelli, Round 11 (2 x 14 laps, 51.338 miles/82.621km)
Race 1
1 Alex Lowes (Honda), 30m 5.589s, 102.360mph/164.730km/h.
2 Shane Byrne (Kawasaki); 3 Michael Laverty (Honda); 4 Josh Brookes (Honda); 5 Tommy Bridewell (BMW); 6 Tommy Hill (Yamaha); 7 Luca Scassa (Honda); 8 Ian Lowry (Honda); 9 Chris Walker (Kawasaki); 10 Robbin Harms (Honda); 11 Jon Kirkham (Honda); 12 Karl Harris (Kawasaki); 13 Peter Hickman (BMW); 14 Patric Muff (BMW).
Fastest lap: Bridewell, 2m 7.940s, 103.190mph/166.070km/h.

Race 2
1 Alex Lowes (Honda), 29m 59.702s, 102.700mph/165.280km/h.
2 Shane Byrne (Kawasaki); 3 Josh Brookes (Suzuki); 4 Tommy Bridewell (BMW); 5 Michael Laverty (Honda); 6 Luca Scassa (Honda); 7 Tommy Hill (Yamaha); 8 Chris Walker (Kawasaki); 9 James Westmoreland (Honda); 10 Peter Hickman (BMW); 11 Barry Burrell (BMW); 12 Jakub Smrz (Aprilia); 13 Ian Lowry (Honda); 14 Jon Kirkham (Honda); 15 Noriyuki Haga (Yamaha).
Fastest lap: Lowes, 2m 7.652s, 103.420mph/166.440km/h.
Championship points: 1 Byrne, 608; 2 Brookes, 599; 3 Lowes, 584; 4 Hill, 566; 5 M. Laverty, 559; 6 Bridewell, 544.

Motorpoint British Supersport Championship Protected By Datatag, Round 11
Race 1 (9 laps 33.003 miles/53.113km)
1 Christian Iddon (Triumph), 19m 44.113s, 100.340mph/161.480km/h.
2 Glen Richards (Triumph); 3 Richard Cooper (Triumph); 4 Billy McConnell (Triumph); 5 Ben Wilson (Kawasaki); 6 Graeme Gowland (Yamaha); 7 Glenn Irwin (Yamaha); 8 Luke Jones (Triumph); 9 Pauli Pekkanen (Triumph); 10 James East (Kawasaki); 11 Brodie Waters (Suzuki); 12 Dean Hipwell (Yamaha); 13 Samuel Hornsey (Suzuki); 14 Luke Stapleford (Kawasaki); 15 John Simpson (Triumph).
Fastest lap: Kennedy, 2m 10.396s, 101.240mph/162.940km/h.

Race 2 (12 laps, 44.004 miles/70.818km)
1 Ben Wilson (Kawasaki), 26m 25.287s, 99.930mph/160.820km/h.
2 Richard Cooper (Triumph); 3 Christian Iddon (Triumph); 4 Jack Kennedy (Yamaha); 5 Graeme Gowland (Yamaha); 6 Glen Richards (Triumph); 7 Luke Jones (Triumph); 8 Taylor Mackenzie (Yamaha); 9 Brodie Waters (Suzuki); 10 Billy McConnell (Triumph); 11 James East (Kawasaki); 12 Samuel Hornsey (Suzuki); 13 Dean Hipwell (Yamaha); 14 Nikki Coates (Yamaha); 15 Luke Stapleford (Kawasaki).
Fastest lap: Cooper, 2m 10.797s, 100.930mph/162.440km/h.
Championship points: 1 Richards, 356; 2 Kennedy, 343.5; 3 McConnell, 290; 4 Iddon, 272.5; 5 Wilson, 239; 6 Cooper, 190.

Monster Energy British Motostar Championship & Motostar Cup, Round 11 (10 laps, 36.670 miles/59.015km)
1 Harry Stafford (Aprilia), 23m 52.627s, 92.150mph/148.300km/h.
2 Tom Carne (Honda); 3 Joe Irving (Honda); 4 Luke Hedger (Luyten Honda); 5 Philip Wakefield (Seel); 6 Anthony Alonso (Honda); 7 Joe Francis (Honda); 8 Peter Sutherland (Aprilia); 9 Olly Simpson (Honda); 10 Callum Bey (Honda); 11 Arnie Shelton (Honda); 12 Asher Durham (Honda); 13 Xavier Zayat (Honda); 14 Ricky Tarren (Honda); 15 Jake Bayford (Honda).
Fastest lap: Carne, 2m 21.597s, 93.230mph/150.050km/h.
Championship points: 1 Hedger, 165; 2 Irving, 108; 3 Green, 105; 4 Ray, 100; 5 Ryde, 95; 6 Francis, 92.

BRANDS HATCH GP, 13–14 October, 2.433-mile/3.912km circuit
MCE British Superbike Championship With Pirelli, Round 12
Race 1 (15 laps 36.495 miles/58.733km)
1 Shane Byrne (Kawasaki), 21m 49.663s, 100.320mph/161.450km/h.
2 Tommy Hill (Yamaha); 3 Josh Brookes (Suzuki); 4 James Westmoreland (Kawasaki); 5 Stuart Easton (Kawasaki); 6 Barry Burrell (BMW); 7 Tommy Bridewell (BMW); 8 Noriyuki Haga (Yamaha); 9 Jon Kirkham (Honda); 10 Michael Laverty (Honda); 11 Patric Muff (BMW); 12 Karl Harris (Ka-

wasaki); **13** Michael Rutter (Kawasaki); **14** Mark Aitchison (Aprilia); **15** Jakub Smrz (Aprilia).
Fastest lap: Lowes, 1m 26.317s, 101.480mph/163.320km/h.

Race 2 (23 laps 55.959 miles/90.057km)
1 Shane Byrne (Kawasaki), 34m 27.058s, 97.470mph/156.860km/h.
2 Josh Brookes (Suzuki); **3** Michael Laverty (Honda); **4** Barry Burrell (BMW); **5** Tommy Bridewell (BMW); **6** Tommy Hill (Yamaha); **7** Stuart Easton (Kawasaki); **8** Jon Kirkham (Honda); **9** Noriyuki Haga (Yamaha); **10** Peter Hickman (BMW); **11** Jason O'Halloran (Honda); **12** Robbin Harms (Honda); **13** John Laverty (Kawasaki); **14** Jakub Smrz (Aprilia); **15** Luca Scassa (Honda).
Fastest lap: Brookes, 1m 26.555s, 101.200mph/162.870km/h.

Race 3 (20 laps 48.660 miles/78.311km)
1 Shane Byrne (Kawasaki), 28m 58.294s, 100.780mph/162.190km/h.
2 Josh Brookes (Suzuki); **3** Tommy Hill (Yamaha); **4** Tommy Bridewell (BMW); **5** Barry Burrell (BMW); **6** James Westmoreland (Honda); **7** Peter Hickman (BMW); **8** Jon Kirkham (Honda); **9** Chris Walker (Kawasaki); **10** Noriyuki Haga (Yamaha); **11** Jason O'Halloran (Honda); **12** Stuart Easton (Kawasaki); **13** Patric Muff (BMW); **14** Luca Scassa (Honda); **15** Michael Rutter (Kawasaki).
Fastest lap: Brookes, 1m 26.170s, 101.650mph/163.600km/h.

Motorpoint British Supersport Championship Protected By Datatag, Round 12
Race 1 (10 laps 24.330 miles/39.155km)
1 Billy McConnell (Triumph), 15m 37.976s, 93.390mph/150.300km/h.
2 Jack Kennedy (Yamaha); **3** Glen Richards (Triumph); **4** Christian Iddon (Triumph); **5** Richard Cooper (Triumph); **6** Luke Jones (Triumph); **7** Ben Wilson (Kawasaki); **8** Glenn Irwin (Yamaha); **9** Graeme Gowland (Yamaha); **10** Taylor Mackenzie (Yamaha); **11** James East (Kawasaki); **12** Dean Hipwell (Yamaha); **13** Brodie Waters (Suzuki); **14** Shaun Winfield (Triumph); **15** Craig Neve (Triumph).
Fastest lap: Cooper, 1m 28.553s, 98.920mph/159.190km/h.

Race 2 (18 laps 43.794 miles/70.480km)
1 Billy McConnell (Triumph), 26m 53.194s, 97.740mph/157.300km/h.
2 Richard Cooper (Triumph); **3** Luke Jones (Triumph); **4** Graeme Gowland (Yamaha); **5** Ben Wilson (Kawasaki); **6** Taylor Mackenzie (Yamaha); **7** James East (Kawasaki); **8** Deane Brown (Yamaha); **9** Brodie Waters (Suzuki); **10** Dean Hipwell (Yamaha); **11** Shaun Winfield (Triumph); **12** John Simpson (Triumph); **13** David Paton (Yamaha); **14** Jonathan Lodge (Triumph); **15** Scott Hudson (Triumph).
Fastest lap: McConnell, 1m 28.713s, 98.740mph/158.910km/h.

Monster Energy British Motostar Championship & Motostar Cup, Round 12 (14 laps, 34.062 miles/54.817km)
1 Bradley Ray (Honda), 22m 38.642s, 90.260mph/145.260km/h.
2 Luke Hedger (Luyten Honda); **3** Joe Francis (Honda); **4** Catherine Green (Seel Honda); **5** Jordan Weaving (Honda); **6** Kyle Ryde (Honda); **7** Joe Irving (Honda); **8** Tom Carne (Honda); **9** Tarran Mackenzie (KTM); **10** Oliver Fitzpatrick (Honda); **11** Callum Bey (Honda); **12** Anthony Alonso (Honda); **13** Elliot Lodge (Honda); **14** Ryan Watson (Honda); **15** Max Hunt (Honda).
Fastest lap: Ray, 1m 35.880s, 91.360mph/147.030km/h.

Final British Superbike Championship points:

1	Shane Byrne	683
2	Josh Brookes	655
3	Tommy Hill	612
4	Alex Lowes	584
5	Michael Laverty	581
6	Tommy Bridewell	577

7 James Westmoreland, 182; **8** Noriyuki Haga, 160; **9** Chris Walker, 138; **10** Stuart Easton, 135; **11** Ian Lowry, 131; **12** Jon Kirkham, 122; **13** Alastair Seeley, 95; **14** Barry Burrell, 84; **15** Luca Scassa, 76.

Final British Supersport Championship points:

1	Glen Richards	372
2	Jack Kennedy	363.5
3	Billy McConnell	340
4	Christian Iddon	285.5
5	Ben Wilson	259
6	Richard Cooper	221

7 Luke Mossey, 172; **8** Pauli Pekkanen, 159; **9** Glenn Irwin, 153; **10** Luke Jones, 141.5; **11** Sam Warren, 138; **12** Dean Hipwell, 69; **13** Deane Brown, 64.5; **14** Taylor Mackenzie, 63; **15** Nikki Coates, 56.

Final British Motostar Championship points:

1	Luke Hedger	185
2	Bradley Ray	125
3	Catherine Green	118
4	Joe Irving	117
5	Joe Francis	108
6	Kyle Ryde	105

7 Jordan Weaving, 99; **8** Tom Carne, 87; **9** Philip Wakefield, 84; **10** Tarran Mackenzie, 76; **11** Callum Bey, 73; **12** Ryan Watson, 71; **13** Harry Hartley, 60; **14** Arnie Shelton, 50; **15** Bradley Hughes, 39.

Supersport World Championship

PHILLIP ISLAND, Australia, 26 February, 2.762-mile/4.445km circuit
Supersport World Championship, Round 1 (15 laps, 41.430 miles/66.675km)
1 Kenan Sofuoglu, TUR (Kawasaki), 24m 08.130s, 102.994mph/165.752km/h.
2 Fabien Foret, FRA (Kawasaki); **3** Broc Parkes, AUS (Honda); **4** Jules Cluzel, FRA (Honda); **5** Sam Lowes, GBR (Honda); **6** Sheridan Morais, RSA (Kawasaki); **7** Ronan Quarmby, RSA (Honda); **8** Alex Baldolini, ITA (Triumph); **9** Vittorio Iannuzzo, ITA (Triumph); **10** Lucas Pesek, CZE (Honda); **11** Jed Metcher, AUS (Yamaha); **12** Joshua Day, USA (Kawasaki); **13** Luca Marconi, ITA (Yamaha); **14** Mathew Scholtz, RSA (Honda); **15** Fabio Menghi, ITA (Yamaha).
Fastest lap: Fabien Foret, FRA (Kawasaki), 1m 35.274s, 104.364mph/167.958km/h.
Championship points: 1 Sofuoglu, 25; **2** Foret, 20; **3** Parkes, 16; **4** Cluzel, 13; **5** Lowes, 11; **6** Morais, 10.

IMOLA, Italy, 1 April, 3.067-mile/4.936km circuit
Supersport World Championship, Round 2 (19 laps, 58.275 miles/93.784km)
1 Fabien Foret, FRA (Kawasaki), 35m 44.653s, 97.819mph/157.425km/h.
2 Sam Lowes, GBR (Honda); **3** Ronan Quarmby, RSA (Honda); **4** Roberto Tamburini, ITA (Honda); **5** Vittorio Iannuzzo, ITA (Triumph); **6** Vladimir Leonov, RUS (Yamaha); **7** Balazs Nemeth, HUN (Honda); **8** Andrea Antonelli, ITA (Honda); **9** Massimo Roccoli, ITA (Yamaha); **10** Sheridan Morais, RSA (Kawasaki); **11** Alex Baldolini, ITA (Triumph); **12** Joshua Day, USA (Kawasaki); **13** Romain Lanusse, FRA (Kawasaki); **14** Luca Marconi, ITA (Yamaha); **15** Jed Metcher, AUS (Yamaha).
Fastest lap: Broc Parkes, AUS (Honda), 1m 51.952s, 98.627mph/158.725km/h (record).
Championship points: 1 Foret, 45; **2** Lowes, 31; **3** Sofuoglu, 25; **4** Quarmby, 25; **5** Iannuzzo, 18; **6** Parkes, 16.

ASSEN, Holland, 22 April, 2.822-mile/4.542km circuit
Supersport World Championship, Round 3 (21 laps, 59.268 miles/95.382km)
1 Lorenzo Lanzi, ITA (Honda), 42m 56.376s, 82.815mph/133.278km/h.
2 Kenan Sofuoglu, TUR (Kawasaki); **3** Vladimir Leonov, RUS (Yamaha); **4** Broc Parkes, AUS (Honda); **5** Alex Baldolini, ITA (Triumph); **6** Jules Cluzel, FRA (Honda); **7** Andrea Antonelli, ITA (Honda); **8** Twan Van Poppel, NED (Yamaha); **9** Roberto Tamburini, ITA (Honda); **10** Stuart Voskamp, NED (Suzuki); **11** Romain Lanusse, FRA (Kawasaki); **12** Thomas Caiani, SUI (Honda); **13** Patrick Jacobsen, USA (Honda); **14** Luca Marconi, ITA (Yamaha); **15** Sheridan Morais, RSA (Kawasaki).
Fastest lap: Lorenzo Lanzi, ITA (Honda), 1m 59.828s, 84.790mph/136.456km/h.
Championship points: 1 Sofuoglu, 45; **2** Foret, 45; **3** Lowes, 31; **4** Parkes, 29; **5** Leonov, 26; **6** Lanzi, 25.

MONZA, Italy, 6 May, 3.590-mile/5.777km circuit
Supersport World Championship, Round 4 (16 laps, 57.435 miles/92.432km)
1 Jules Cluzel, FRA (Honda), 33m 8.897s, 103.959mph/167.306km/h.
2 Sam Lowes, GBR (Honda); **3** Kenan Sofuoglu, TUR (Kawasaki); **4** Imre Toth, HUN (Honda); **5** Stefano Cruciani, ITA (Kawasaki); **6** Alex Baldolini, ITA (Triumph); **7** Massimo Roccoli, ITA (Yamaha); **8** Andrea Antonelli, ITA (Honda); **9** Vittorio Iannuzzo, ITA (Triumph); **10** Raffaele De Rosa, ITA (Honda); **11** Jed Metcher, AUS (Yamaha); **12** Fabien Foret, FRA (Kawasaki); **13** Luca Marconi, ITA (Yamaha); **14** Kieran Clarke, GBR (Honda); **15** Martin Jessopp, GBR (Honda).
Fastest lap: Sam Lowes, GBR (Honda), 2m 0.653s, 107.107mph/172.372km/h.
Championship points: 1 Sofuoglu, 61; **2** Lowes, 51; **3** Foret, 49; **4** Cluzel, 48; **5** Baldolini, 34; **6** Parkes, 29.

DONINGTON PARK, Great Britain, 13 May, 2.500-mile/4.023km circuit
Supersport World Championship, Round 5 (22 laps, 54.995 miles/88.506km)
1 Sam Lowes, GBR (Honda), 33m 43.603s, 97.837mph/157.453km/h.
2 Kenan Sofuoglu, TUR (Kawasaki); **3** Jules Cluzel, FRA (Honda); **4** Broc Parkes, AUS (Honda); **5** Glen Richards, AUS (Triumph); **6** Sheridan Morais, RSA (Kawasaki); **7** Ronan Quarmby, RSA (Honda); **8** Valentine Debise, FRA (Honda); **9** Billy McConnell, AUS (Triumph); **10** Fabien Foret, FRA (Kawasaki); **11** Roberto Tamburini, ITA (Honda); **12** Alex Baldolini, ITA (Triumph); **13** Jed Metcher, AUS (Yamaha); **14** Massimo Roccoli, ITA (Yamaha); **15** Luke Mossey, GBR (Triumph).
Fastest lap: Sam Lowes, GBR (Honda), 1m 31.097s, 98.787mph/158.982km/h.
Championship points: 1 Sofuoglu, 81; **2** Lowes, 76; **3** Cluzel, 64; **4** Foret, 55; **5** Parkes, 42; **6** Baldolini, 38.

MISANO, Italy, 10 June, 2.623-mile/4.226km circuit
Supersport World Championship, Round 6 (22 laps, 57.770 miles/92.972km)
1 Kenan Sofuoglu, TUR (Kawasaki), 36m 44.023s, 94.360mph/151.858km/h.
2 Jules Cluzel, FRA (Honda); **3** Alex Baldolini, ITA (Triumph); **4** Roberto Tamburini, ITA (Honda); **5** Broc Parkes, AUS (Honda); **6** Sheridan Morais, RSA (Kawasaki); **7** Jed Metcher, AUS (Yamaha); **8** Fabien Foret, FRA (Kawasaki); **9** Vittorio Iannuzzo, ITA (Triumph); **10** Andrea Antonelli, ITA (Yamaha); **11** Raffaele De Rosa, ITA (Honda); **12** Balazs Nemeth, HUN (Honda); **13** Imre Toth, HUN (Honda); **14** Dino Lombardi, ITA (Yamaha); **15** Gabor Talmacsi, HUN (Honda).
Fastest lap: Fabien Foret, FRA (Kawasaki), 1m 39.513s, 94.996mph/152.881km/h.
Championship points: 1 Sofuoglu, 106; **2** Cluzel, 84; **3** Lowes, 76; **4** Foret, 63; **5** Baldolini, 54; **6** Parkes, 53.

ARAGON, Spain, 1 July, 3.321-mile/5.344km circuit
Supersport World Championship, Round 7 (18 laps, 59.771 miles/96.192km)
1 Sam Lowes, GBR (Honda), 37m 14.284s, 96.306mph/154.990km/h.
2 Fabien Foret, FRA (Kawasaki); **3** Sheridan Morais, RSA (Kawasaki); **4** Broc Parkes, AUS (Honda); **5** Kenan Sofuoglu*, TUR (Kawasaki); **6** Ronan Quarmby, RSA (Honda); **7** Vittorio Iannuzzo, ITA (Triumph); **8** Jed Metcher, AUS (Yamaha); **9** Gabor Talmacsi, HUN (Honda); **10** Joshua Day, USA (Kawasaki); **11** Romain Lanusse, FRA (Kawasaki); **12** Luca Marconi, ITA (Yamaha); **13** Raffaele De Rosa, ITA (Honda); **14** Fabio Menghi, ITA (Yamaha); **15** Roberto Tamburini, ITA (Honda).
** Penalised **4** positions.*
Fastest lap: Sheridan Morais, RSA (Kawasaki), 2m 3.300s, 96.952mph/156.029km/h.
Championship points: 1 Sofuoglu, 117; **2** Lowes, 101; **3** Cluzel, 84; **4** Foret, 83; **5** Parkes, 66; **6** Baldolini, 54.

BRNO, Czech Republic, 22 July, 3.357-mile/5.403km circuit
Supersport World Championship, Round 8 (13 laps, 43.644 miles/70.239km)
1 Fabien Foret, FRA (Kawasaki), 27m 2.236s, 96.854mph/155.872km/h.
2 Kenan Sofuoglu, TUR (Kawasaki); **3** Broc Parkes, AUS (Honda); **4** Sam Lowes, GBR (Honda); **5** Jules Cluzel, FRA (Honda); **6** Ronan Quarmby, RSA (Honda); **7** Sheridan Morais, RSA (Kawasaki); **8** Stefano Cruciani, ITA (Kawasaki); **9** Vittorio Iannuzzo, ITA (Triumph); **10** Vladimir Leonov, RUS (Yamaha); **11** Romain Lanusse, FRA (Kawasaki); **12** Gabor Talmacsi, HUN (Honda); **13** Florian Marino, FRA (Kawasaki); **14** Valentine Debise, FRA (Honda); **15** Luca Marconi, ITA (Yamaha).
Fastest lap: Broc Parkes, AUS (Honda), 2m 4.011s, 97.460mph/156.847km/h.
Championship points: 1 Sofuoglu, 137; **2** Lowes, 114; **3** Foret, 108; **4** Cluzel, 95; **5** Parkes, 82; **6** Morais, 62.

SILVERSTONE, Great Britain, 5 August, 3.667-mile/5.902km circuit
Supersport World Championship, Round 9 (16 laps, 58.677 miles/94.432km)
1 Jules Cluzel, FRA (Honda), 34m 48.860s, 101.126mph/162.747km/h.
2 Sam Lowes, GBR (Honda); **3** Broc Parkes, AUS (Honda); **4** Ronan Quarmby, RSA (Honda); **5** Kenan Sofuoglu, TUR (Kawasaki); **6** Fabien Foret, FRA (Kawasaki); **7** Sheridan Morais, RSA (Kawasaki); **8** Alex Baldolini, ITA (Triumph); **9** Andrea Antonelli, ITA (Yamaha); **10** Gabor Talmacsi, HUN (Honda); **11** Mathew Scholtz, RSA (Honda); **12** Roberto Tamburini, ITA (Honda); **13** Vittorio Iannuzzo, ITA (Triumph); **14** Romain Lanusse, FRA (Kawasaki); **15** Raffaele De Rosa, ITA (Honda).
Fastest lap: Jules Cluzel, FRA (Honda), 2m 9.313s, 102.096mph/164.308km/h.
Championship points: 1 Sofuoglu, 148; **2** Lowes, 134; **3** Cluzel, 120; **4** Foret, 118; **5** Parkes, 98; **6** Morais, 71.

MOSCOW, Russia, 26 August, 2.442mile/3.931km circuit
Supersport World Championship, Round 10 (22 laps, 53.737 miles/86.482km)
1 Kenan Sofuoglu, TUR (Kawasaki), 36m 13.935s, 88.988mph/143.213km/h.
2 Jules Cluzel, FRA (Honda); **3** Vladimir Leonov, RUS (Yamaha); **4** Sheridan Morais, RSA (Kawasaki); **5** Broc Parkes, AUS (Honda); **6** Fabien Foret, FRA (Kawasaki); **7** Andrea Antonelli, ITA (Yamaha); **8** Gabor Talmacsi, HUN (Honda); **9** Roberto Tamburini, ITA (Honda); **10** Mathew Scholtz, RSA (Honda); **11** Alex Baldolini, ITA (Triumph); **12** Sam Lowes, GBR (Honda); **13** Ronan Quarmby, RSA (Honda); **14** Florian Marino, FRA (Kawasaki); **15** Luca Marconi, ITA (Yamaha).
Fastest lap: Jules Cluzel, FRA (Honda), 1m 38.167s, 89.576mph/144.158km/h. (record).
Championship points: 1 Sofuoglu, 173; **2** Cluzel, 140; **3** Lowes, 138; **4** Foret, 128; **5** Parkes, 109; **6** Morais, 84.

NURBURGRING, Germany, 9 September, 3.192-mile/5.137km circuit
Supersport World Championship, Round 11 (19 laps, 60.648 miles/97.603km)
1 Kenan Sofuoglu, TUR (Kawasaki), 38m 13.709s, 95.187mph/153.189km/h.
2 Jules Cluzel, FRA (Honda); **3** Fabien Foret, FRA (Kawasaki); **4** Broc Parkes, AUS (Honda); **5** Alex Baldolini, ITA (Triumph); **6** Gabor Talmacsi, HUN (Honda); **7** Vittorio Iannuzzo, ITA (Triumph); **8** David Linortner, AUT (Yamaha); **9** Ronan Quarmby, RSA (Honda); **10** Massimo Roccoli, ITA (Yamaha); **11** Romain Lanusse, FRA (Kawasaki); **12** Florian Marino, FRA (Kawasaki); **13** Sam Lowes, GBR (Honda); **14** Andrea Antonelli, ITA (Yamaha); **15** Jed Metcher, AUS (Yamaha).
Fastest lap: Sam Lowes, GBR (Honda), 2m 0.222s, 95.582mph/153.825km/h.
Championship points: 1 Sofuoglu, 198; **2** Cluzel, 160; **3** Foret, 144; **4** Lowes, 141; **5** Parkes, 122; **6** Morais, 84.

PORTIMAO, Portugal, 23 September, 2.853-mile/4.592km circuit
Supersport World Championship, Round 12 (20 laps, 57.067 miles/91.840km)
1 Jules Cluzel, FRA (Honda), 36m 5.886s, 94.853mph/152.651km/h.
2 Kenan Sofuoglu, TUR (Kawasaki); **3** Fabien Foret, FRA (Kawasaki); **4** Broc Parkes, AUS (Honda); **5** Sam Lowes, GBR (Honda); **6** Sheridan Morais, RSA (Kawasaki); **7** Dan Linfoot, GBR (Kawasaki); **8** Alex Baldolini, ITA (Triumph); **9** Ronan Quarmby, RSA (Honda); **10** Mathew Scholtz, RSA (Honda); **11** Massimo Roccoli, ITA (Yamaha); **12** Vladimir Leonov, RUS (Yamaha); **13** Andrea Antonelli, ITA (Yamaha); **14** Jed Metcher, AUS (Yamaha); **15** Gabor Talmacsi, HUN (Honda).
Fastest lap: Jules Cluzel, FRA (Honda), 1m 47.416s, 95.628mph/153.899km/h.
Championship points: 1 Sofuoglu, 218; **2** Cluzel, 185; **3** Foret, 160; **4** Lowes, 152; **5** Parkes, 135; **6** Morais, 94.

MAGNY-COURS, France, 7 October, 2.741-mile/4.411km circuit
Supersport World Championship, Round 13 (22 laps, 60.299 miles/97.042km)
1 Jules Cluzel, FRA (Honda), 42m 20.985s, 85.430mph/137.487km/h.
2 Sam Lowes, GBR (Honda); **3** Dan Linfoot, GBR (Kawasaki); **4** Kenan Sofuoglu, TUR (Kawasaki); **5** Fabien Foret, FRA (Kawasaki); **6** Alex Baldolini, ITA (Triumph); **7** Mathew Scholtz, RSA (Honda); **8** Andrea Antonelli, ITA (Yamaha); **9** Gabor Talmacsi, HUN (Honda); **10** Jed Metcher, AUS (Yamaha); **11** Florian Marino, FRA (Kawasaki); **12** Balazs Nemeth, HUN (Honda); **13** Imre Toth, HUN (Honda); **14** Sheridan Morais, RSA (Kawasaki); **15** Massimo Roccoli, ITA (Yamaha).
Fastest lap: Kenan Sofuoglu, TUR (Kawasaki), 1m 51.861s, 88.209mph/141.958km/h.

Final World Supersport Championship points:

1	Kenan Sofuoglu, TUR,	231
2	Jules Cluzel, FRA,	210
3	Sam Lowes, GBR,	172
4	Fabien Foret, FRA,	171
5	Broc Parkes, AUS,	135
6	Sheridan Morais, RSA,	96

7 Alex Baldolini, ITA, 96; **8** Ronan Quarmby, RSA, 84; **9** Vittorio Iannuzzo, ITA, 60; **10** Andrea Antonelli, ITA, 60; **11** Vladimir Leonov, RUS, 52; **12** Roberto Tamburini, ITA, 50; **13** Gabor Talmacsi, HUN, 44; **14** Jed Metcher, AUS, 40; **15** Massimo Roccoli, ITA, 30.